HUMAN NATURE

Edited by / Herausgegeben von
Gerfried Stocker / Christine Schöpf

ARS ELECTRONICA

HATJE
CANTZ

Contents

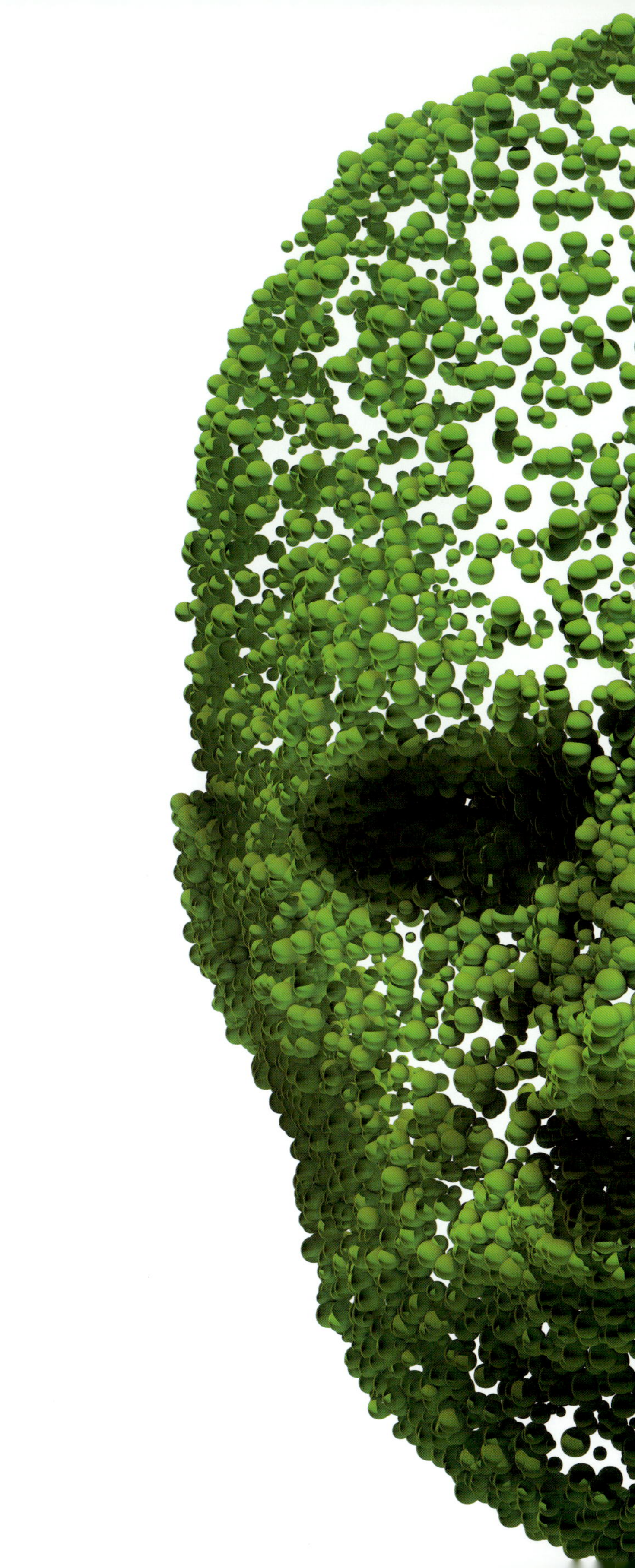

Gerfried Stocker, Christine Schöpf

Human Nature

We are entering a new age here on Earth: the Anthropocene. An age definitively characterized by humankind's massive and irreversible influences on our home planet. Population explosion, climate change, the poisoning of the environment and our venturing into outer space have been the most striking symbols of this development so far.

But to a much more enormous extent, the achievements of genetic engineering and biotechnology are the truly indicative markers of this transition to a new epoch. Now, we're not only changing our environment; we're revising the fundamentals of life itself—even our own human life.

Humankind has appropriated the mantle of Creator. Though we just barely understand how this functions, we're already modifying entire genomes, constructing new organisms, cloning, creating and inventing new life.

We're using innovative high-tech methods to observe the human brain while it thinks, so that we can now look behind the veil of our consciousness and see how our mechanisms of perception and decision-making capacities are reflected in our neurons. The long-established boundaries segregating nature and culture are breaking down, and we are once again confronted by the question of the essence of humanness and the nature of the human being.

Thirty years after its founding, this globally established festival's mission remains the same—we are steadfastly dedicated to the pursuit of the curiosity that is so deeply rooted in humankind's nature, and we continue to intrepidly peer far into the future. Our immediate objective: to once again foment a fruitful, fascinating dialog at the interface of art, technology and society.

The new Ars Electronica Center that debuted at the outset of this year plays a key role in this endeavor, in that its extraordinary exhibition concept is totally focused on the question of how scientific findings and methods are changing the way we see the world and our views of humankind.

Linz is Europe's 2009 Capital of Culture. As a major contribution to our city's big year, the festival's first project *80+1—A journey around the world*— is already being launched on June 17, the day the *80+1* Base Camp is being set up on Linz's Main Square as the point of departure of a virtual round-the-world journey that, following completion of its 81-day itinerary, returns to Linz just in time for the festival. There, *80+1* will culminate in a globally-networked symposium on cloud intelligence.

2009 also brings us to a joyous milestone: Ars Electronica's 30th anniversary! As befitting this occasion, an intense retrospective look at the dynamic development of media art will be a key component of the festival program. Led, curated and produced by artists and scientists—and inspired by their work—the festival's jam-packed lineup of fascinating events constitutes, as ever, an expedition into hybrid reality and the future of our world.

So, just what is this going to be like, this new nature that human beings are going about engendering?

Gerfried Stocker, Christine Schöpf

Human Nature

Wir sind in einem neuen Erdzeitalter angekommen, dem Anthropozän. Ein Zeitalter, das durch die massiven und irreversiblen Einflüsse des Menschen auf seinen Heimatplaneten gekennzeichnet ist. Bevölkerungsexplosion, Klimawandel, Umweltvergiftung, Aufbruch in den Weltraum, das waren die bislang markantesten Symbole für diese Entwicklung.

Doch in viel stärkerem Ausmaß sind es die Errungenschaften der Gen- und Biotechnologie, die diesen Übergang in eine neue Epoche markieren. Nicht nur mehr unsere Umwelt verändern wir, sondern die Grundlagen des Lebens selbst, auch unseres eigenen Lebens.

Der Mensch hat sich zum Schöpfer aufgeschwungen. Wir wissen zwar noch kaum, wie es überhaupt funktioniert, aber schon verändern wir ganze Genome, konstruieren neue Organismen, klonen, erschaffen, erfinden neues Leben.

Wir beobachten mit neuen technischen Methoden unser Gehirn beim Denken und sehen, wie sich hinter dem Vorhang unseres Bewusstseins die Mechanismen der Wahrnehmung und Entscheidungsfindung in unseren Neuronen spiegeln. Lange tradierte Grenzziehungen zwischen Natur und Kultur werden brüchig, und abermals steht die Frage nach dem Wesen des Menschlichen, nach der Natur des Menschen im Raum.

Auch 30 Jahre nach seiner Gründung bleibt das weltweit etablierte Festival der tief in der Natur des Menschen verwurzelten Neugierde verschrieben und kann es nicht lassen, den Blick weit nach vorne zu richten. Mit dem Ziel, einmal mehr einen spannenden Dialog zwischen Kunst, Technologie und Gesellschaft anzuzetteln.

Das zu Jahresbeginn eröffnete neue Ars Electronica Center spielt dabei eine zentrale Rolle, widmet es sich doch mit seiner außergewöhnlichen Ausstellungskonzeption ganz der Frage, wie wissenschaftliche Erkenntnisse und Methoden unsere Welt- und unser Menschenbilder verändern.

2009 ist Linz Europäische Kulturhauptstadt, und darum startet das erste Festivalprojekt – *80+1 – eine Weltreise* – auch schon am 17. Juni, dem Tag, an dem das Basislager von *80+1* am Linzer Hauptplatz aufgeschlagen wird und damit eine virtuelle Weltreise startet, die nach 81 Tagen rechtzeitig zum Festival wieder nach Linz zurückführt und in einem vernetzen Symposium über *Cloud Intelligence* münden wird.

2009 gilt es aber auch, das 30-jährige Bestehen der Ars Electronica zu feiern, und der Rückblick auf die dynamische Entwicklung der Medienkunst nimmt einen wichtigen Platz im Festivalprogramm ein. Angeführt von KünstlerInnen und WissenschaftlerInnen und inspiriert durch ihre Arbeiten begibt sich das Festival mit seinem dicht gewobenen Programm auf eine Expedition in die hybride Realität und Zukunft unserer Welt.

Wie wird diese neue Natur, die der Mensch erschaffen will, aussehen?

Human Nature Lectures
Encounter and Confrontation

The field of theory at the 2009 Ars Electronica Festival 2009 is divided into a few segments. The opening chapter is a continuation of 80+1, a series of events Ars Electronica has been producing in conjunction with Linz 2009 European Capital of Culture: the *Cloud Intelligence Symposium*. As its theme and title would suggest, this conference will be setting for a very lively and highly diverse array of brief speeches and statements (see pp 20–81). Things will then get a little more "elaborate"—and more encounter-oriented and confrontational—at the *Human Nature Lectures*. Panels of two or three speakers and a moderator will scrutinize various aspects of *Human Nature*, Ars Electronica's 2009 theme, over the course of two hours.

The first session's lineup includes Hiroshi Ishiguro, creator of the Geminoid HI-1, Ishiguro's exact robot double and a creature associated with the idea of an expanded form of telepresence, and media theorist Friedrich Kittler, a man who has made major contributions to the history of automation and telecommunications. This will be followed by a panel discussion led by Derrick de Kerckhove, himself the author of works that, in the context of "Human Nature," treat such issues as the hybridization of nature by technology.

The second lecture block brings together two Austrians who have made names for themselves in the life sciences: Eduardo Kac and Josef Penninger. Kac, this year's winner of the Golden Nica in the Hybrid Art category, assumes the role of the artist who seeks collaboration with science, while Penninger, the scientist, claims—at least rhetorically—that there is an affinity between biotechnology and art. Their discussion will be moderated by Jens Hauser, the organizer of *L'Art Biotech*, the 2003 exhibition that made him a superstar curator in the field of biotechnological art.

The third pairing brings Michael Schmidt-Salomon, author of the *Manifesto of Evolutionary Humanism* and an outspoken opponent of religiously motivated thinking such as creationism and the theory of intelligent design, face to face with anthropologist Maja Petrovic-Steger of etoy.CORPORATION, whose *MISSION ETERNITY* project has been hard at work on a sort of cemetery of the future. Derrick de Kerckhove will moderate this discussion as well.

The fourth group of speakers includes Bernhard Fink, an evolutionary psychologist doing research on attractiveness at the University of Göttingen; Shinsuke Shimojo, a cognition researcher at the California Institute of Technology; and Lawrence Malstaf, winner of the 2009 Golden Nica in Interactive Art. Andy Cameron, member of the jury in the Prix's Interactive Art category, will moderate.

(Text: Heimo Ranzenbacher, translated from German by Mel Greenwald)

Das Feld der Theorie des Ars Electronica Festivals 2009 gliedert sich in mehrere Teile. Das erste Kapitel wird in Fortsetzung der Veranstaltungsreihe *80+1* - des Ars-Electronica-Beitrages zum Programm der Europäischen Kulturhauptstadt Linz - mit dem *Cloud Intelligence Symposium* aufgeschlagen. Dessen Thema und Titel wirken auch in die Form einer möglichst lebendigen Vielzahl von Kurz-Referaten und Statements hinein (siehe Seite 20ff). Dieser Form gegenüber stehen die "elaborierten", durch Begegnung und Konfrontation charakterisierten *Human Nature Lectures*: Jeweils zwei bis drei Referenten und ein Moderator erörtern in Einheiten von zwei Stunden Aspekte des Themenkomplexes der Ars Electronica 2009, *Human Nature*.

Die erste Session wird bestritten von Hiroshi Ishiguro, Schöpfer u.a. des Geminoid HI-1, der exakten Roboter-Kopie Ishiguros, mit der die Idee einer erweiterten Form von Telepräsenz assoziiert ist, und dem Medientheoretiker Friedrich Kittler, der für maßgebliche Beiträge zur Geschichte der Automation und Telekommunikation verantwortlich zeichnet. Darauf folgt eine Gesprächsrunde, geleitet von Derrick de Kerckhove, selbst Autor von Schriften, die im Kontext von "Human Nature" etwa die Hybridisierung der Natur durch Technologie behandeln.

In der zweiten Lecture-Einheit begegnen einander der renommierte österreichische Biowissenschaftler Josef Penninger und Eduardo Kac – moderiert von Jens Hauser, der spätestens seit der von ihm 2003 organisierten Ausstellung *L'Art Biotech* als einer der profiliertesten Kuratoren im Bereich biotechnologische Kunst gilt. Eduardo Kac, Gewinner der Goldenen Nica 2009 in der Kategorie Hybrid Art, hat dabei die Position des Künstlers inne, der die Zusammenarbeit mit der Wissenschaft sucht, und Penninger vertritt als Naturwissenschafter – zumindest rhetorisch – ein Verwandtschaftsverhältnis zwischen Biotechnologie und Kunst.

An dritter Stelle trifft einer der umtriebigsten Gegenspieler, die sich die Vertreter religiös bestimmten Denkens etwa in Sachen Kreationismus und Intelligent Design eingehandelt haben, Michael Schmidt-Salomon, Autor u. a. von *Manifest des evolutionären Humanismus*, auf die Anthropologin Maja Petrovic-Steger von der Gruppe etoy.CORPORATION, die mit ihrem Projekt *MISSION ETERNITY* seit geraumer Zeit an einer Art Friedhof der Zukunft arbeitet. Diskussionsleiter ist wieder Derrick de Kerckhove.

Die vierte Einheit auf dem Podium bilden der – als Attraktivitätsforscher tätige – Evolutionspsychologe Bernhard Fink von der Georg-August-Universität Göttingen, der im Bereich der Neuropsychologie auch mit Kognitionsforschung beschäftigte Shinsuke Shimojo vom California Institute of Technology, der Gewinner der Goldenen Nica für Interaktive Kunst 2009, Lawrence Malstaf, und Andy Cameron, Mitglied der Prix-Jury für Interaktive Kunst, als Moderator.

(Text: Heimo Ranzenbacher)

Hannes Leopoldseder

Nothing Would Ever Be the Same
The 30th Anniversary of Ars Electronica

2009 is not only Linz's year to serve as European Capital of Culture. It also has very special significance in conjunction with Ars Electronica. The Internet is a direct descendant of the ARPANET that was developed 40 years ago; Ars Electronica made its debut 30 years ago; it's been 20 years since the Iron Curtain fell and Tim Berners-Lee designed the World Wide Web at CERN in Geneva. We celebrate the birth of the digital future. Nothing would ever be the same. In this timeline, Linz's most significant milestone is 1979. With the founding of Ars Electronica, a festival for art, technology and society, this city became an early adopter in a new technical epoch. This move would trigger an earth-shaking process of development and change that would proceed at unprecedented speed. For Linz, this opened up the chance to create a higher-profile image for itself between Austria's two great cultural centers, Vienna and Salzburg.

"The Future: All Aboard!" became Linz's new slogan in 1998—literally words of welcome to bus and streetcar passengers, but, in a larger sense, a mission statement for an entire city. The Ars Electronica Festival established in 1979 was organized by the Brucknerhaus and the ORF—Austrian Broadcasting Company's Upper Austria Regional Studio. Herbert W. Franke, Hubert Bognermayr, Ulli A. Rützel and I were involved in the original conception. Ars Electronica commenced on September 18 with the Linzer Klangwolke (Cloud of Sound), a classical open-air event featuring Bruckner's 8th Symphony visualized with lights and lasers. The ORF called upon locals to put their radios in their windows to let the music resound throughout the entire city. And 100,000 people came to experience the first Klangwolke live in Donaupark. The result was a reverberation heard 'round the world.

The 1980 Klangwolke was visualized by Otto Piene of MIT's Center for Advanced Visual Studies; *Blue Star Linz* featured a helium-filled sculpture. In 1982 in Linz, Piene organized the Skyart Conference, an international conclave of media artists including Charlotte Moorman, Nam June Paik, Bazon Brock, Jürgen Claus, Tom van Sant and Bernd Kracke. Several projects were produced with the express aim of creating a following for Ars Electronica among the general public in Linz—for example, Klaus Schulze's Linzer *Steel Symphony* that entailed steel workers and voest-alpine machinery in the Brucknerhaus in 1980, and Georgio Battistelli's *Steel Opera* performed before an audience of 10,000 on Hauptplatz in 1982.

Isao Tomita's *Universum* got an enthusiastic reception from a crowd of more than 60,000 in Donaupark. Its' production was made possible by a $1 million grant from Japan's Casio Corp. During these years, the scientific and artistic focus was on staging exhibitions, commissioning works of art and holding symposia on the emergence of computer culture. In 1984 in the Brucknerhaus, scholar and media artist Peter Weibel produced the multimedia opera *The Artistic Will*, a hymn to electricity ("the light bulb is the new human sun"). Over the ensuing years, Weibel, as festival consultant, together with Regina Patsch and Gottfried Hattinger, were the driving forces determining the festival's orientation. From 1991 on, responsibility for the festival was turned over to a board of directors with Karl Gerbel, myself and Peter Weibel as chairman of the artistic advisory council.

In 1987, ORF took the next step on the basis of an idea I proposed: launching the Prix Ars Electronica as an international competition in the computer arts featuring three categories:

computer animation, computer music and computer graphics. The prize's most noteworthy features: the Golden Nica statuette as its symbol, a million Austrian schillings (72,672 euros) in prize money for the artists, and a jury comprised of world-renowned experts.

From 1987 to 2003, the ORF's Christine Schöpf was in charge of the organization of the competition and the jury selection process. Her strong commitment and people skills in dealing with the artists contributed decisively to the Prix Ars Electronica's successful development. The first sponsor of the Prix Ars Electronica was Siemens AG. From 2004 on, Festival and Prix were organized jointly by the Ars Electronica Center and the ORF.

Since 1987—thus, over the last 22 years—42,245 works have been submitted and evaluated by the juries. The Prix Ars Electronica functions not only as a trendsetter in the individual categories; many of the competition's entrants, jurors and prizewinners also go on to become part of Ars Electronica's extensive international network. A fortuitous happenstance: the first Golden Nica in Computer Animation went to *Luxo Jr.* by John Lasseter, then a member of the staff of a small animation studio; today he is probably Hollywood's most successful animated filmmaker (*Toy Story*, *Find Nemo*, *Cars*, *Wall-E* and *Up*). In 2009, the Prix Ars Electronica encompasses seven categories that reflect the development of digital media.

Ars Electronica's activities in the late 1980s and '90s focused on the strategic triangle of art, technology and society in accordance with the dominant technological themes of this period.

1989 *In the Network of Systems*, in 1990 *Digital Dreams-Virtual Worlds*: participants included Marvin Minsky, William Gibson, Laron Lannier, Timothy Leary and Bruce Sterling.

1991 *Out of Control*, a critical encounter with technological development starring, among others, Jean Baudrillard, Hans Morawec and Elfriede Jelinek.

1992 *Endo & Nano*, 1993 *Genetic Art—Artificial Life*, 1994 *Intelligent Ambience*, 1995 *Information Myth*—and in this year, the Ars Electronica Award for Innovation was given to Tim Berners-Lee for the development of the World Wide Web, the birth of a new era. Nothing would ever be the same.

This was also the beginning of a new era for Ars Electronica. Mayor Franz Dobusch began considering a cultural use for a planned building adjacent to the Nibelungen Bridge in Urfahr. Many proposals were submitted; the City of Linz eventually decided on the construction of the Ars Electronica Center as a Museum of the Future. Thus, Ars Electronica was to get its own facility. Director of Cultural Affairs Siegbert Janko and I, the originators of the concept, were put in charge of project content; Edouard Bannwart (Art+Com , Berlin) conducted a feasibility study; the Ars Electronica Center opened in 1996.

Gerfried Stocker, a 31-year-old media artist was appointed artistic director; Horst Hörtner was named director of the Futurelab R&D laboratory; each still serve in his respective capacity. Financial director since July 1, 2009 is Diethard Schwarzmair; he is in charge of the business end and is also responsible for running for the Futurelab.

The AEC was set up as a corporation with a board of directors; it is wholly owned by the City of Linz. Ars Electronica thus has a solid legal and financial footing. Gerfried Stocker and Christine Schöpf share responsibility for planning the Festival program.

The Ars Electronica Center sees itself as an educational facility. The most important aspect of its mission is to raise consciousness of the digital transformation that is making an impact on all areas of our life: education, career, the economy and, above all, communications. Gerfried

Nothing Would Ever Be the Same—The 30th Anniversary of Ars Electronica

Stocker has succeeded in imparting a fresh new impetus to the Festival and to making the facility an international hub for media artists from all over the world. Ars Electronica's annual themes look to the future: 1999 *LifeScience*, 2000 *Next Sex*, 2001 *Takeover—Who's Doing the Art of Tomorrow*, 2002 *Unplugged—Art as the Scene of Global Conflicts*, 2003 *Code—The Language of Our Time*, 2004 *TimeShift*, 2006 *Simplicity*, 2007 *Goodbye Privacy*, 2008 *A New Cultural Economy* and, now, 2009 *Human Nature*.

The Futurelab has become a very innovative, high-profile and extremely successful R&D facility that not only develops infrastructure for the Museum of the Future itself, but also works on projects worldwide (USA, China, Japan, Berlin, Madrid, Lisbon, etc.) either as sole proprietor or together with partners. One of the Futurlab's chief areas of emphasis is music visualization; in this area, important commissions have come from the Brucknerhaus, Germany's WDR and the eArts Festival in Shanghai, to name just a few. Gerfried Stocker has continually expanded Ars Electronica's regional, national and, above all, international network. Numerous cultural institutions in Linz collaborate with Ars Electronica—the Brucknerhaus, the Lentos Art Museum, the OK Center for Contemporary Art, the Linz Art University, the ORF, Architekturforum, Stadtwerkstadt, Times Up et al.

The Ars Electronica Center also played a key role in the preparations for Linz's stint as European Capital of Culture. For the AEC itself, 2009 has also represented a giant step forward: the architectural expansion of the Ars Electronica Center. Treusch Architecture created the design that dovetailed nicely with the pre-existing structure. On January 2, 2009 the new Museum of the Future made its debut. The 4,000 square meters of new space brought the facility's total to 6,500. The entire ensemble is enwrapped in a glass shell—a 5,100 m² LED façade.

The AEC also got a reorientation with respect to its content. "New Views of Humankind" goes boldly forward on a path that brings artists and scientists even closer together. The BrainLab focuses primarily on the neuro-anatomy of the eye; BioLab provides visitors with glimpses into the human body and lets them experiment with DNA; the FabLab presents possibilities for the handicrafts of the future—a design is created on a computer screen, and a 3D laser printer transforms the data into a real object; and, finally, the RoboLab offers insights into the world of robotics. As an enterprise, Ars Electronica had a staff of 190 in July 2009—one-third full-time employees; two-thirds part-time.

As its major contribution to the 2009 European Capital of Culture year, the AEC is collaborating with voestalpine to produce "80+1," a virtual round-the-world journey to shed light on the most pressing issues now facing humankind.

The festival that premiered in 1979 with a budget of only 120,000 euros has developed over the course of 30 years into a globe-spanning network of artists, scientists, and technicians representing all fields having to do with digital media. Over this time span, Ars Electronica has achieved sustainable synergy as the Ars Electronica Cluster whose components include the Festival, the Prix Ars Electronica, the Ars Electronica Center, the Futurelab, the Ludwig Boltzmann Institute Media.Art.Research as well as cultural and scholarly institutions in Linz, Austria and abroad. In this configuration, Ars Electronica is nicely positioned to face the challenges of the coming decade that will bring a quantum leap in the digitization of everyday life, and in the wake of which nothing will ever be the same again.

(Translated from German by Mel Greenwald)

Hannes Leopoldseder

Alles wird anders
30 Jahre Ars Electronica

Im Jahr 2009 ist Linz nicht nur Europäische Kulturhauptstadt, sondern durch die Ars Electronica hat dieses Jahr noch eine besondere Bedeutung: Aus dem vor 40 Jahren entwickelten ARPANET entsteht das Internet, vor 30 Jahren startet die Ars Electronica, vor 20 Jahren fällt nicht nur der Eiserne Vorhang, sondern im CERN in Genf entwirft Tim Berners-Lee das World Wide Web. Es ist die Geburtsstunde der digitalen Zukunft. Alles wird anders.

In dieser Timeline setzt Linz 1979 mit der Ars Electronica, einem Festival für Kunst, Technologie und Gesellschaft, frühzeitigauf den Katalysator einer neuen technischen Epoche. Es beginnt eine weichenstellende Zukunftsentwicklung mit einer historisch einzigartigen Geschwindigkeit des Wandels. Für Linz eröffnet sich die Chance, zwischen den beiden Kulturstädten Wien und Salzburg ein eigenständiges Profil zu entwickeln.

„Zukunft. Einsteigen bitte" wird für Linz1998 zum neuen Slogan, der die Fahrgäste in Bus und Straßenbahn willkommen heißt, Zukunft wird zum Signum für die ganze Stadt. Das 1979 ins Leben gerufene Festival Ars Electronica wirdvom Brucknerhaus Linz und vom ORF Oberösterreich organisiert. An der ersten Konzeption sind Herbert W. Franke, Hubert Bognermayr, Ulli A. Rützel und Hannes Leopoldseder beteiligt. Die Ars Electronica wird am 18. September mit der „Linzer Klangwolke" eröffnet, einem klassischen Open-Air mit Bruckners 8. Symphonie, visualisiert mit Licht und Laser. Der ORF fordert die Linzer Bevölkerung auf, ihre Radios ins Fenster zu stellen, um die Musik über der Stadt erklingen zu lassen. 100.000 Menschen kommen zur ersten Klangwolke in den Donaupark, der Eröffnung der Ars Electronica. Ein weltweites Echo ist die Folge.

1980 visualisiert Otto Piene vom Center for Advanced Visual Studies am MIT mit dem *Blue Star Linz*, einer mit Helium gefüllten Luftplastik, die Klangwolke. 1982 organisiert Piene die Skyart-Conference in Linz, ein internationales Treffen von MedienkünstlerInnen wie Charlotte Moorman, Nam June Paik, Bazon Brock, Jürgen Claus, Tom van Sant, Bernd Kracke. Mehrere Projekte zielen bewusst auf ein breites Publikum, um die Ars Electronica in der Stadt zu verankern: im Brucknerhaus 1980 die *Linzer Stahlsymphonie* von Klaus Schulze, mit Stahlarbeitern und Maschinen der voestalpine, 1982 auf dem Hauptplatz die *Linzer Stahloper* von Georgio Battistelli vor 10.000 Besuchern.

Das *Universum* von Isao Tomita begeistert im Donaupark über 60.000 Menschen, es wird durch den japanischen Konzern Casio mit einer Million Dollar ermöglicht. Den jeweils wissenschaftlichen und künstlerischen Schwerpunkt dieser Jahre bilden Ausstellungen, Werkaufträge und Symposien über das Werden der Computerkultur. 1984 präsentiert der Wissenschafter und Medienkünstler Peter Weibel im Brucknerhaus die Multimedia-Oper *Der künstliche Wille*, einen Hymnus an die Elektrizität („die Glühbirne ist die neue menschliche Sonne"). In den folgenden Jahren bestimmt Weibel als Berater, zusammen mit Regina Patsch und Gottfried Hattinger, die Ausrichtung des Festivals. Von 1991 an ist ein Direktorium für das Festival verantwortlich, Karl Gerbel, Hannes Leopoldseder und Peter Weibel als Vorsitzender des künstlerischen Beirats.

1987 setzt der ORF mit einer Projektidee von Hannes Leopoldseder einen neuen Schritt: mit dem Prix Ars Electronica, einen weltweiten Wettbewerb für Computerkünste, ausgeschrieben in den Kategorien Computeranimation, Computermusik, Computergrafik. Besondere Kennzeichen des

Preises: die „Goldene Nica"-Statue als Symbol, eine Million Schilling (72.672 Euro) Preisgeld für die KünstlerInnen und eine hochkarätig zusammengesetzte internationale Jury.

Organisation und Juryauswahl liegen von 1987 bis 2003 in den Händen von Christine Schöpf, ORF. Ihr Engagement und ihr Umgang mit Künstlerinnen und Künstlern haben entscheidend zur erfolgreichen Entwicklung des Prix Ars Electronica beigetragen. Der erste Sponsor des Prix Ars Electronica ist die Siemens AG. Von 2004 an werden Festival und Prix gemeinsam vom Ars Electronica Center organisiert.

Seit 1987, also seit 22 Jahren, sind 42.245 Arbeiten eingereicht und von der Jury begutachtet worden. Der Prix Ars Electronica fungiert nicht nur als Trendsetter in den einzelnen Kategorien, sondern ließ gleichzeitig durch Juroren, PreisträgerInnen und Einreicher ein weltweites Netzwerk für die Ars Electronica entstehen. Ein Glücksfall: Der erste „Goldene Nica"-Preisträger in der Computeranimation ist John Lasseter mit *Luxo Jr.*, damals Mitarbeiter in einem kleinen Animationsteam, heute wohl der weltweit erfolgreichste Animationsfilmer in Hollywood (*Toy Story, Findet Nemo, Cars, Wall-E, Up*). 2009 umfasst der Prix Ars Electronica sieben Kategorien, die die Entwicklung der digitalen Medien widerspiegeln.

Die Ars Electronica bewegt sich in der zweiten Hälfte der 1980er Jahre und in den 1990er Jahren in der strategischen Triangel Kunst-Technologie-Gesellschaft, entsprechend der Zeitphase dominieren Technologiethemen.

1989 *Im Netzwerk der Systeme*, 1990 *Digitale Träume – Virtuelle Welten*, u. a. mit Marvin Minsky, William Gibson, Jaron Lannier, Timothy Leary, Bruce Sterling.

1991 *Out of Control*, eine kritische Auseinandersetzung mit der technologischen Entwicklung, u. a. mit Jean Baudrillard, Hans Moravec, Elfriede Jelinek.

1992 *Endo & Nano*, 1993 *Genetische Kunst – Artificial Life*, 1994 *Intelligente Ambiente*, 1995 *Mythos Information* – in diesem Jahr verleiht die Ars Electronica den „Ars Electronica Award für Innovation" an Tim Berners-Lee für die Entwicklung des World Wide Web, den Beginn einer neuen Ära.

Auch die Ars Electronica steht vor einem Neubeginn. Bürgermeister Franz Dobusch sucht nach einer kulturellen Nutzung für ein geplantes Gebäude am Brückenkopf in Urfahr. Aus mehreren Vorschlägen entscheidet sich die Stadt Linz für den Bau des Ars Electronica Centers als „Museum der Zukunft". Die Ars Electronica erhält damit ein eigenes Haus. Kulturdirektor Siegbert Janko und Hannes Leopoldseder, der die Projektidee eingebracht hat, werden als inhaltliche Projektleiter bestellt, Edouard Bannwart (Art+Com, Berlin) erstellt eine Machbarkeitsstudie, 1996 wird das Ars Electronica Center eröffnet.

Gerfried Stocker, ein 31-jähriger Medienkünstler, wird zum Künstlerischen Leiter bestellt, Horst Hörtner zum Leiter des Futurlabs als Entwicklungslabor. Beide haben diese Funktionen noch inne. Kaufmännischer Leiter ist seit 1. Juli 2009 Mag. Diethard Schwarzmair, er ist für alle kaufmännischen Agenden sowie für das Futurelab verantwortlich.

Das AEC erhält die juristische Form einer GmbH, mit einem eigenen Aufsichtsrat, Eigentümerin ist die Stadt Linz. Damit ist für die Ars Electronica ein solides Fundament gelegt. Dem Direktorium für die Programmplanung des Festivals gehören Gerfried Stocker und Christine Schöpf an. Das Ars Electronica Center versteht sich als Bildungseinrichtung, es will vor allem eines sein – ein Haus der Bewusstseinsbildung für den digitalen Wandel, der in der Zwischenzeit alle Bereiche unseres Lebens erfasst hat, Ausbildung, Beruf, Wirtschaft und vor allem Kommunikation.

Gerfried Stocker ist es gelungen, nicht nur dem Festival neue Impulse zu geben, sondern das Haus selbst zu einem internationalen Treffpunkt für MedienkünstlerInnen aus aller Welt zu machen. Die Themen der Ars Electronica greifen in die Zukunft: 1999 *LifeScience*, 2000 *Next Sex*, 2001 *Takeover – Who is doing the Art of Tomorrow*, 2002 *Unplugged – Art as the Scene of Global Conflicts*, 2003 *Code – The Language of Our Time*, 2004 *TimeShift*, 2006 *Simplicity*, 2007 *Goodbye Privacy*, 2008 *A New Cultural Economy* und schließlich 2009 *Human Nature*.

Das Futurelab ist zu einer innovativen, profilierten und erfolgreichen Forschungs- und Entwicklungseinrichtung geworden, die nicht nur Produkte für das eigene Museum, sondern auch weltweit Projekte realisiert, allein oder mit Partnern, in den USA, in China, Japan, Europa, wie in Berlin, Madrid, Lissabon u. a. Ein weiterer Schwerpunkt des Futurlab ist Musikvisualisierung – Werkaufträge des Brucknerhauses, des WDR oder des eArts Festival Shanghai. Gerfried Stocker hat kontinuierlich das regionale, nationale und vor allem das weltweite Netzwerk der Ars Electronica erfolgreich erweitert. Nach 30 Jahren sind viele Kultureinrichtungen in Linz an der Ars Electronica beteiligt – vom Brucknerhaus, dem Lentos, dem OK, der Kunstuniversität, dem ORF über das Architekturforum zur Stadtwerkstadt und Times Up. Diese Aufzählung ist freilich keineswegs vollständig.

Das Ars Electronica Center war auch wesentlich an den Vorbereitungen für das Europäische Kulturjahr Linz 09 beteiligt. Für das AEC selbst bedeutet 2009 ebenfalls wieder einen gewaltigen Schritt vorwärts: Der Gemeinderat der Stadt Linz beschließt eine bauliche Erweiterung des Ars Electronica Centers. Dem Architektenteam Treusch Architecture gelingt ein Entwurf, der nicht zwischen altem und neuem Gebäude unterscheidet, sondern seit 1. Jänner 2009 präsentiert sich das AEC als neues Museum der Zukunft. Die Erweiterungsfläche beträgt 4.000, die Gesamtfläche 6.500 Quadratmeter. Das Gebäude wird von einem gläsernen Kubus umschlossen, einer 5.100 Quadratmeter großen LED-Fassade.

Auch inhaltlich startet das AEC mit einer Neuorientierung – mit „Neuen Bildern vom Menschen" beginnt ein Weg, der Künstler und Wissenschaftler noch enger zusammenführt. Im BrainLab geht es primär um die Neuroanatomie des Auges, das BioLab lässt in den eigenen Körper blicken, aber auch mit DNA experimentieren, das FabLab präsentiert eine potentielle Möglichkeit des Handwerks der Zukunft, am Bildschirm wird ein Objekt entworfen, ein 3D-Laserprinter wandelt die Datenwelt in reale Gegenstände, und schließlich das RoboLab, das einen Einblick in die Welt der Roboter ermöglicht. Als Betrieb hat die Ars Electronica mit Juli 2009 190 MitarbeiterInnen, ein Drittel ist ganztägig beschäftigt, zwei Drittel sind Teilzeitbeschäftigte.

Als Beitrag zum Europäischen Kulturjahr 2009 realisiert das AEC in Zusammenarbeit mit voestalpine das weltweite Projekt *80+1 – eine Weltreise* rund um den Globus, um die brennenden Fragen der Menschen zu beleuchten.

Aus dem Festival von 1979, das nur über ein Budget von 120.000 Euro verfügte, ist innerhalb von 30 Jahren ein weltumspannendes Netzwerk von Künstlern, Wissenschaftern, Technikern aus dem Bereich der digitalen Medien geworden. Die Ars Electronica Linz hat in dieser Zeit ein Alleinstellungsmerkmal erreicht: ein Ars Electronica Cluster, dessen Teile in Wechselbeziehungen miteinander verbunden sind – das Festival, der Prix Ars Electronica, das Ars Electronica Center, das Futurelab, das Ludwig Boltzmann Institut für Medien.Kunst.Forschung sowie kulturelle und wissenschaftliche Institutionen in Linz sowie im In- und Ausland. Mit dieser Aufstellung ist die Ars Electronica für die Herausforderungen des kommenden Jahrzehnts gerüstet, die der Quantensprung der Digitalisierung unseres Lebens mit sich bringen und durch die alles anders sein wird.

David Sasaki, Isaac Mao

Cloud Intelligence
Explore Human Nature, Envision Human Future

The whole world is now facing a crossroads. It seems as if everything around us is either shaking or, to phrase it optimistically, re-shaping, which triggers more reflection on our own human nature.

The problems we face today come from human nature—and it is mainly egotism that is to blame. Sharing, the driving force behind our evolution, is being ignored. We are losing the ability to open up, to engage in conversation and to prevent harm from spreading around the world. What's the best way to deal with large-scale problems like global warming, financial crises, international conflicts and potential risks to all human beings? These problems all remain unsolved.

Luckily, we didn't miss the chance of grasping the Internet as the last nerve God left us. After 40 years of evolution, the Internet now gives more social meaning to human beings. Based on a foundation of openness, linking and connecting, we now see the emergence of a new Cloud epoch.

The Cloud includes Cloud Computing, Cloud Activism and Cloud Intelligence as three layers, but these layers support each other. Cloud Computing upgrades the Internet infrastructure to a new level to enable global roaming as digital nomads. Cloud Activism improves how people collaborate and take action to change the world. Then we have Cloud Intelligence from persistent connections between people and the information they generate every second. The Social Brain, with billions of social neurons and exponentially more connections, emerges as a new type of singularity.

We have experienced a whole new adventure traveling around the world, in an 80+1-day manner. However, 80+1 means more than this. In 80+1 minutes, you can publish a new article to your blog before sleeping and wake up to new comments from readers living in other time zones. In 80+1 seconds, your new meme published to a micro-blogging tool may have traveled around the world from network to network of followers. In 80+1 milliseconds, one new idea could pop up in your working memory to make you feel very excited.

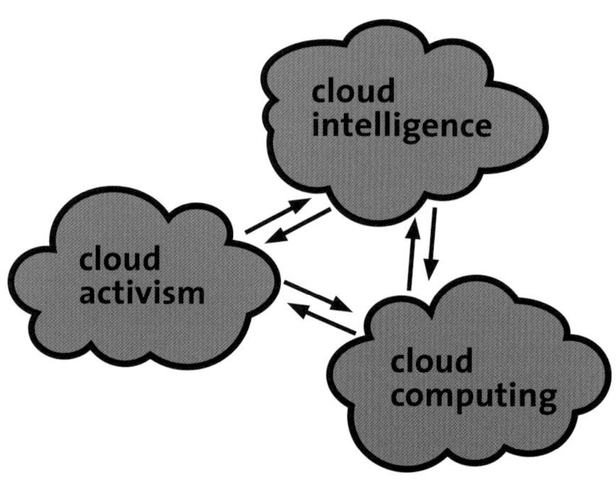

Time matters because crises spread quickly and social intelligence is required to match the speed. If technology continues its evolution along the path of Cloud Computing, we can see that almost all people have the chance to connect to a social pipeline in the coming 30 years. The boom of digital communities and social networks play an increasingly important role. Economic, political and social norms will change dramatically.
It might even take 80+1 years.

Cloud Computing: Enabling

> A little over fifty years ago, Thomas Watson from IBM said that he could foresee a need for perhaps five computers worldwide, and we now know that that figure was wrong, because he overestimated by four. *(Clay Shirky, Napster Speech 2)*

> The term cloud is used as a metaphor for the Internet, based on how the Internet is depicted in computer network diagrams and is an abstraction for the complex infrastructure it conceals. *(Wikipedia)*

Whether you speak in terms of clouds, streams, or waves (the modern internet sounds like a naturalist's dreamscape), the preview of Google Wave is indicative of a fundamental change that has transformed how we interact with the Internet and how the Internet enables us to interact with one another.

The modern web was developed in order to enable academics and scientists to share their research with one another. This was done primarily via email, but also via static (and often ugly) web pages. The second chapter began in the 1990's when, during a bubble of investment, web programmers developed new technologies that made websites more dynamic by using data-bases, and more interactive thanks to JavaScript and Flash. The investment bubble burst, but those same technologies were implemented to create the tools that make up the Internet as we know it today: wikis, blogs, RSS readers, YouTube, Flickr, MySpace, Twitter and Facebook.

We have now come to the third chapter of the Internet. The "cloud" refers to all those servers based around the world that store our personal data, but which we rarely ever think about. If you are a Gmail user, then your emails live "in the cloud", on a server at one of Google's many server farms. Our daily thoughts, in the form of Twitter messages, live in the cloud, as does our search history, our Facebook activity, all of the pictures we publish on Flickr and Picasa.

Just two years ago I stored all of my text documents on my own computer and would send them via email to anyone who showed interest. If they made edits to my documents, then I would need to update my own local copy. Today my documents are stored "in the cloud", on Google Docs, where they can be instantly accessed by trusted friends and colleagues. At any time I can access the most recent copy of any document on my computer or mobile phone. Today we don't just publish information to the Internet; we actually create it online and then download it to our computers and cell phones when we need it.

The meaning of cloud computing is not only distributing the computing power to different places, but also giving individuals the power to share information around the world. The speed of spreading that information is dramatically increased as it passed through different social media tools. New symbols (e.g. "RT" in Twitter) and processes (e.g. "Shift+S" means "share" in Google Reader) were invented to enable people to relay information through six degrees of separation to any connected corner of the world.

The Cloud is growing exponentially. Every day more and more of us spend a small percentage of our cognitive energy to add value to the Cloud. And as we do so, the cloud itself becomes more intelligent, a vast social brain in which every Internet user is a metaphorical neuron. In fact, the structure of the Internet and the processes it depends on are similar to those of the human brain.

David Sasaki, Isaac Mao

Cloud Activism: the power we need

Every morning we—all seven billion of us—wake up with a certain amount of cognitive energy, our mental fuel tank for the day to come. We use up this cognitive energy every time our brain has to process information and apply knowledge. This includes tasks as seemingly mundane as packing a school lunch for our children, and as complex as understanding the fundamentals of quantum mechanics.

On the one hand, today's competitive knowledge economy is requiring a larger percentage of the world's population to expend more cognitive energy than human beings have ever done in the past. Software programmers, for example, often spend 60 hours a week thinking about the logical rules behind the applications on our computers and cell phones. The need to make a day's worth of cognition as efficient as possible has led to a whole industry of productivity gurus, and to a market of "neuro-enhancing drugs."

On the other hand, the efficiency of the modern global economy means that many individuals in the developed world are working far fewer hours than ever before. Tim Ferriss has recruited a large following on the Internet by recommending a four-hour work week. Even those who aren't able to heed Ferriss' call to abandon the 9 to 5 office life still spend an average of two office hours per day (one-fourth of their working time) surfing the web for personal use. Salary.com estimated that those 2.09 hours of "wasted time" per 8-hour workday add up to $759 billion per year that employers in the United States spent on salaries "for which real work was expected, but not actually performed."

In terms of discussing cloud intelligence, however, corporate America's economic loss is far less interesting than what those millions of office employees are doing with their two hours of personal Internet use every day.

Cognitive Surplus and The New Socialism

> Starting with the Second World War a whole series of things happened—rising GDP per capita, rising educational attainment, rising life expectancy and, critically, a rising number of people who were working five-day weeks. For the first time, society forced onto an enormous number of its citizens the requirement to manage something they had never had to manage before—free time.
> And what did we do with that free time? Well, mostly we spent it watching TV.
> *(Clay Shirky, Gin, Television, and Social Surplus)*

In fact, Clay Shirky points out that in the United States we still spend an average of 100 million hours every single weekend *just watching advertisements*. What else can you do with 100 million hours? According to Shirky, it took roughly 100 million "thought hours" to build Wikipedia, the largest encyclopedia ever assembled and the most popular general reference work on the Internet.

It would be wrong to overstate Shirky's argument that all of human society is waking from a sitcom-watching slumber to become active producers of online content; after all, most young people today who give up their expensive cable packages for slightly less expensive Internet connections are now watching those same sitcoms on their laptops, clips from American Idol dominate YouTube, and the vast majority of the most popular daily search terms on Google are related to celebrity news. The passive consumption, which defined decades of television watching, is also a mainstay of today's connected generation.

Still, even if only an estimated ten percent of Internet users actively contribute content, they have already constructed a vast online repository of culture, knowledge and tools. And we are just at the beginning of what's to come.

Kevin Kelly calls Wikipedia, Flickr, and Twitter the "vanguard of a cultural movement", an emerging "global collectivist society." Amateur photographers, he reminds us, have published over three billion photographs on Flickr. Six billion videos are uploaded to YouTube every month. The blog search engine Technorati tracks over a million blog posts published every single day. Apple's pervasive iTunes media player serves over 125,000 podcasts, including more than 25,000 video podcasts.

The small minority of Internet users who actively contribute content sure do contribute a lot of it. They review restaurants and businesses on Yelp. They fulfill the role of editors by recommending content on Delicious, StumpleUpon, Digg and Reddit. They share their medical history on Patients Like Me and Google Health. They create high quality maps of their communities on OpenStreetMap and design 3D models of buildings, monuments, and landmarks using Google's free SketchUp software. They report news just like traditional journalists. On Flickr they help the United States' Library of Congress describe and contextualize the photographs in their collection. They translate blog posts, articles, magazines, and videos into different languages.

What is even more incredible is that they do this all for free, without receiving any economic compensation whatsoever. Hundreds of millions of Internet users are spending a small amount of their day's cognitive energy not on the work that they are paid to do, but rather on the online projects and forms of self-expression that interest them. Kevin Kelly calls it a "New Socialism", while Isaac Mao calls it Sharism, based on sharing and community, but not limited by political ideology. (The most active contributors of free content are as likely to idolize Adam Smith as Karl Marx.)

In China, we see a growing movement trying to disrupt the censorship system. The openness of the modern economy leaves more and more space for free thinking, however, the political system and ruling party still keep an old-fashioned mentality that created the national censorship system—Great Firewall(GFW) and the newly mandatory Green Dam software. Since the beginning of 2009, an online meme called "Caonima"(Grass-mud Horse) which uses the alpaca as a symbol, has been giving China's censors a headache. A cartoon mashup animation suddenly spread over the Internet, not only in China, but all around the world. Along with the previous creation of the "River Crab", which pokes fun at censorship, Xiao Qiang from the University of Berkeley, called Caonima "the most vicious crackdown in years.". He added, "Where there is river crab, there must be Caonima".

The Chinese blogosphere is not alone. In Iran, the green revolution adopted new media technologies from the Cloud to garner support from around the world. Neda Agha Soltan, the 26-year-old girl who was shot to death in Tehran, has become a symbol and 'martyr', whose death moved not only Iran, but the whole world. She died with her eyes wide open, and her last moments transcended citizen media to mainstream media, reaching millions of people.

Cloud Activism gives us hopes and spawns changes. We see it's dispersing everywhere around the world, from the United States to the Middle East, from China to the Pacific Islands, from the Earth to the International Space Station.

David Sasaki, Isaac Mao

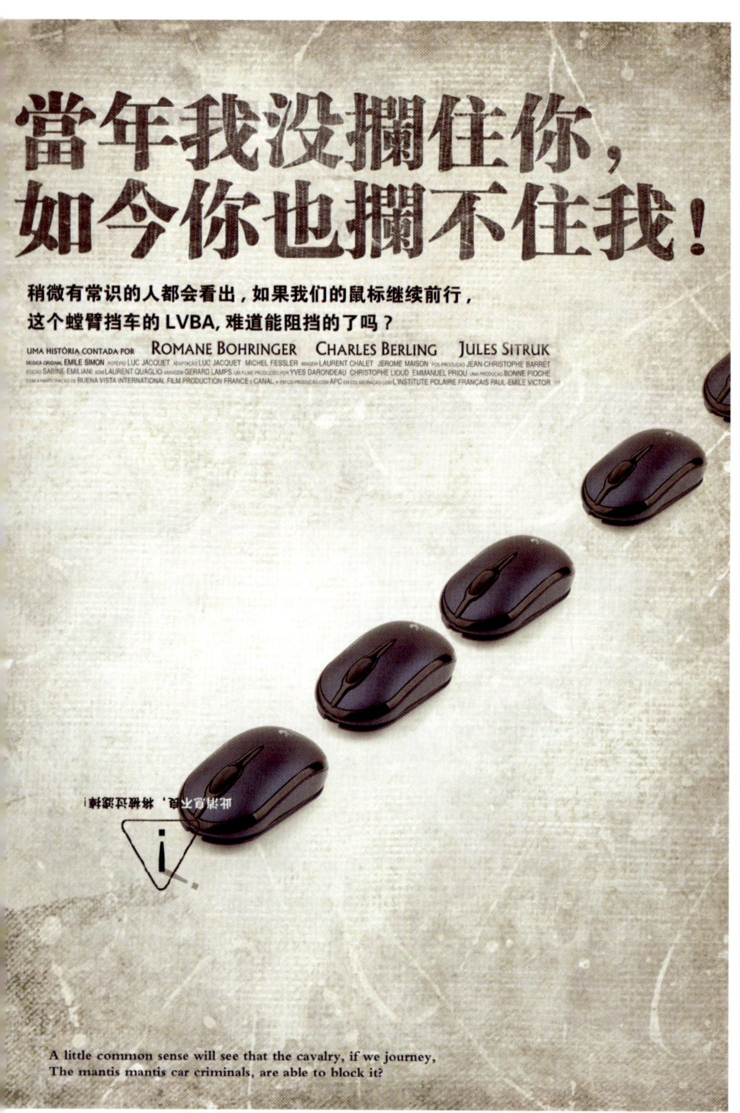

Cloud Intelligence: Envisioning the Future

The human brain is by far the most complex organ that three to four billion years of natural selection on this planet have been able to produce. It consists of roughly 100 billion neurons, each linked to 10,000 synaptic connections. Information travels across the brain via small electrical impulses that are transmitted from neuron to neuron, much in the same way that information travels across the Internet. Right now, while you're reading this, billions of small electrical impulses are firing away in your brain as you parse the information, store it in your memory, and apply your own knowledge to add context and challenge what we write.

In comparison, the Internet is a decidedly less complex and less evolved organ. Internet World Stats estimates that there are 1.6 billion Internet users, or "social neurons". According to one study, the average Facebook user is connected to 164 "friends", a far cry from the 10,000 synaptic connections between our 100 billion brain cells. In other words, while the Internet could one day become self-aware, it is still in the earliest chapters of its evolution. Yet, already there are several examples that reveal how the Internet is rapidly becoming humanity's social nervous system. Joshua-Michele Ross points to the emergency response following the Mumbai terrorist attacks, Obama's "Project Houdini", and Google's global virus forecasting as three manifestations of the networked social brain.

The human brain formed its present structure over 10,000 years ago when our ancestors encountered environments that required the type of advanced reasoning only provided by a larger brain. With a larger brain came moral reasoning, consciousness and, most importantly,

language, without which we could not transmit culture and knowledge across generations. The organ we each carry around in our skulls today, however, has evolved little in the past 10,000 years. It formed when our ancestors lived in tribes of roughly 150 people, not mega-cities filled with millions, and personal address books filled with thousands of contacts.
As the cloud continues to expand exponentially with more information, more social neurons, and more connections between them, our own humble human brains will need to adapt in order to make the most effective use of the cloud without succumbing to lifetimes of mere "continuous partial attention."
No matter how actively or passively we spend our time online, what we can all be sure of is that one day sooner or later our brain will stop functioning and our stay here on planet Earth will conclude. We will remain, of course, in the memories of our friends and family, and also in the bits and bytes of digital footprints that we leave in the cloud for the generations that follow. What they do with the information we leave behind—or, indeed, what the cloud itself does with the information—will depend on a new type of networked evolution that values sharing and community over proprietary protection.

The Intelligence We Need

We need new intelligence that requires new science to envision, new art to imagine, new spirit to participate and new technologies to implement. With more and more people affected by commercial globalization, new technologies like social networking can help people share sentiments around common challenges.
We employ the concept of "Cloud" because both problems and solutions are becoming more and more connected, as is global society. For Ars Electronica, 30 years of exploration has earned it a world reputation and it is now moving on from the existing milestones to a new era with new paradigms. The next 30 years may even be more promising than its splendid legacies to date.
"Cloud Intelligence" is more than a singularity. We have just invented a word, but you will define its meaning. From technical advancement to global actions, the long trail of information with new identities will dramatically boost the thinking speed of the entire society. It raises challenges and, at the same time, it fosters hopes for all of us. If we could really collect such intelligence, we could evolve as human beings to a new level of order. Or maybe even become the *new sacred* as Stuart Kauffman suggests.

1   *80+1—A Journey Around the World,* see pp. 82–131

David Sasaki, Isaac Mao

Cloud-Intelligence: Eine Zukunftsvision für die Menschheit

Die Welt steht heute an einer Wegscheide. Es hat den Anschein, als ob sie gerade in ihren Grundfesten erschüttert würde oder, um es optimistisch auszudrücken, in Umbildung begriffen wäre. Dies zwingt uns, neu über die menschliche Natur nachzudenken.

Die Probleme, vor denen wir heute stehen, sind nämlich auf die menschliche Natur, insbesondere den Egotismus, zurückzuführen. Der Austausch, eine treibende Kraft unserer Evolution, wird vernachlässigt. Wir verlieren die Fähigkeit, uns zu öffnen, einen Dialog zu führen und das Wohlergehen der gesamten Menschheit im Auge zu behalten. Wie können wir am besten mit den großen ungelösten Problemen wie der Erderwärmung, der Finanzkrise, internationalen Konflikten und anderen potentiellen Risiken für die gesamte Menschheit umgehen?

Zum Glück haben wir die Chance ergriffen, uns an den letzten Anker zu klammern, den Gott uns ließ: das Internet. Nach vierzig Jahren Entwicklung vermittelt das Internet den Menschen wieder einen Sinn für das Soziale. Wir stehen am Beginn einer neuen Epoche, die auf Offenheit, Verbundenheit und Vernetzung basiert und im Zeichen der Wolke – der Cloud – steht.

Diese Cloud umfasst die drei einander ergänzenden Ebenen Cloud-Computing, Cloud-Aktivismus und Cloud-Intelligence. Cloud-Computing hebt die Internet-Infrastruktur auf eine neue Ebene und ermöglicht die globale Erreichbarkeit digitaler Nomaden. Cloud-Aktivismus verbessert die Zusammenarbeit und die Möglichkeiten, die Welt zu verändern. Cloud Intelligence schließlich entsteht aus der permanenten Vernetzung von Menschen und den von ihnen im Sekundentakt aktualisierten Informationen. Das Gehirn als „soziales Organ" mit Milliarden „sozialer Neuronen" und exponentiell anwachsenden Verbindungen bildet sich als eine neue Singularität heraus.

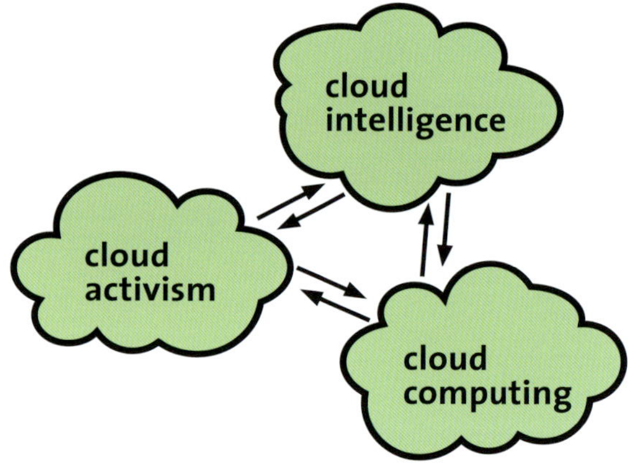

Die virtuelle Reise um die Welt in 80+1 Tagen[1] hat uns ganz neue Erfahrungen gebracht. Doch das ist nicht alles, wofür 80+1 steht.

In 80+1 Minuten kann man beispielsweise vor dem Schlafengehen rasch noch einen neuen Artikel in seinem Blog publizieren, um gleich nach dem Erwachen Kommentare von Lesern aus anderen Zeitzonen vorzufinden. In 80+1 Sekunden kann das in einem Mikro-Blogging-Dienst veröffentlichte neue Mem von einem Netzwerk zum anderen rund um die Welt gereist sein. In 80+1 Millisekunden könnte in Ihrem Blog ein Beitrag mit einer neuen Idee auftauchen, die Sie in helle Aufregung versetzt.

Zeit spielt eine große Rolle, weil sich die Krise rasch ausweitet und soziale Intelligenz vonnöten ist, um mit dieser Geschwindigkeit mitzuhalten. Wenn die Technologie den Weg des Cloud-Computing fortsetzt, werden in den nächsten dreißig Jahren fast alle Menschen die Möglichkeit bekommen, an einer sozialen Infrastruktur teilzuhaben. Die boomenden digitalen Gemeinschaften sozialer Netzwerke spielen dabei eine immer wichtigere Rolle. Wirtschaftliche, politische und soziale Normen werden sich dramatisch verändern. Dieser Prozess könnte vielleicht sogar 80+1 Jahre dauern.

Cloud-Computing: die Schaffung von Rahmenbedingungen

> Vor etwas mehr als fünfzig Jahren meinte Thomas Watson von IBM, dass er weltweit einen Bedarf von fünf Computern sehe. Wir wissen, dass er sich verschätzte und die Zahl um vier zu hoch ansetzte. *(Clay Shirky, Napster Speech)*

> Der als Metapher für das Internet verwendete Begriff Cloud geht auf die Darstellung des Internets in Computernetzwerk-Diagrammen zurück und wird als Abstraktion der sich dahinter verbergenden komplexen Infrastruktur gebraucht. *(Wikipedia)*

Ob man nun von Clouds, Streams oder Waves spricht (der moderne Internetjargon erinnert an die Traumlandschaft eines Naturforschers, die jüngste Präsentation von Google Wave ist bezeichnend für die fundamentale Veränderung, der unsere Interaktion mit dem Internet und anderen Internetnutzern unterliegt.

Das moderne World Wide Web wurde entwickelt, um Akademikern und Wissenschaftlern den Austausch ihrer Forschungsergebnisse zu ermöglichen. Dies erfolgte in erster Linie per E-Mail, aber auch über statische (und oft hässliche) Web-Seiten. Das zweite Kapitel der Internet-Geschichte begann in den 90er Jahren, als Web-Programmierer während einer Investmentblase neue Technologien entwickelten, mit deren Hilfe Websites durch die Verwendung von Datenbanken dynamischer und dank JavaScript und Flash interaktiver wurden. Die Investmentblase platzte, aber besagte Technologien wurden implementiert und ermöglichten jene Tools und Dienste, die das Internet, wie wir es heute kennen, ausmachen: Wikis, Blogs, RSS-Reader, YouTube, Flickr, MySpace, Twitter und Facebook.

Heute stehen wir am Anfang des dritten Kapitels der Internet-Geschichte. Die „Cloud" umfasst alle Server, weltweit, auf denen unsere Daten gespeichert sind, ohne dass wir Notiz davon nehmen. Wenn Sie Gmail verwenden, befinden sich Ihre E-Mails in der Cloud, auf einem Server in einem der vielen Serverzentren von Google. Die Gedanken, die uns Tag für Tag bewegen, existieren in Form von Twitter-Botschaften ebenso in der Cloud wie unser Web-Protokoll, unsere Facebook-Aktivitäten und alle Bilder, die wir auf Flickr und Picasa publizieren.

Vor zwei Jahren speicherte ich noch alle meine Textdokumente auf meinem eigenen Computer und verschickte sie per E-Mail. Wurden meine Dokumente von den Adressaten bearbeitet, musste ich meine eigene lokale Version aktualisieren. Heute sind meine Dokumente „in der Cloud" gespeichert, auf Google Docs, wo vertrauenswürdige Freunde und Kollegen jederzeit zugreifen können. Ich habe vom Computer oder Mobiltelefon aus jederzeit Zugang zur neuesten Version eines Dokuments. Heute publizieren wir nicht nur Informationen im Internet, wir kreieren sie online und laden sie auf unsere Computer und Handys, wenn wir sie brauchen.

David Sasaki, Isaac Mao

Cloud-Computing verteilt nicht nur die Rechenkapazität auf verschiedene Orte, sondern ermöglicht den einzelnen Usern auch, weltweit Informationen auszutauschen. Die Geschwindigkeit der Informationsverbreitung ist durch diverse soziale Medien massiv beschleunigt worden. Neue Sprachen (z. B. „RT" in Twitter) und Shortcuts (z. B. „Shift+S" für „share" im Google Reader) wurden erfunden, um Informationen einfacher nach dem Prinzip, demzufolge jeder jeden über sechs Ecken kennt, in jeden Winkel der Erde verbreiten zu können.

Die Cloud wächst exponentiell. Tag für Tag bringen mehr und mehr Personen einen kleinen Prozentsatz ihrer kognitiven Energie ein, um die Cloud zu erweitern. Und dadurch wird die Cloud selbst intelligenter, zu einem gigantischen *social brain*, in dem jeder Internet-Nutzer metaphorisch ein Neuron ist. Tatsächlich gleichen die Struktur des Internet und die Prozesse, auf denen es basiert, dem menschlichen Gehirn.

Cloud-Aktivismus: die Macht, die wir brauchen

Jeden Tag erwachen wir – etwa sieben Milliarden Menschen – mit einer gewissen kognitiven Energie, unserem mentalen Treibstoff für den kommenden Tag. Wir verwenden diese kognitive Energie, wann immer unser Gehirn Informationen zu verarbeiten und Wissen anzuwenden hat. Dies umfasst simple Tätigkeiten wie die Vorbereitung des Jausenpakets für die Kinder, aber auch so komplexe wie das Verständnis der Prinzipien der Quantenmechanik.

Einerseits verlangt die konkurrenzbetonte Wissensgesellschaft von heute, dass ein immer größerer Prozentsatz der Weltbevölkerung mehr kognitive Energie aufwendet als je zuvor. Software-Programmierer beispielsweise brüten oft sechzig Stunden pro Woche über den logischen Gesetzen, auf denen die Anwendungen unserer Computer und Mobiltelefone basieren. Das Bedürfnis, die tägliche kognitive Ausbeute nach Möglichkeit zu maximieren, hat Heerscharen von Produktivitätsgurus und einen Markt für Neuropillen geschaffen.

Andererseits impliziert die Effizienzorientierung der modernen globalisierten Wirtschaft, dass viele in den Industrieländern heute weniger Stunden arbeiten als je zuvor. Tim Ferriss gewann eine große Anhängerschaft im Internet, indem er die Vier-Stunden-Woche empfahl. Auch wer Ferriss' Aufruf, das 9-to-5-Job aufzugeben, nicht gelesen hat, verbringt durchschnittlich zwei Bürostunden (ein Viertel der Arbeitszeit) damit, zu seinem Vergnügen durch das Web zu surfen. Laut Salary.com fallen für diese 2,09 Stunden „verschwendeter Zeit" pro Arbeitstag in den Vereinigten Staaten 759 Milliarden Dollar an Lohnkosten an, für die der Arbeitgeber „reale Arbeit erwartet, aber nicht erhalten hat". Für unsere Diskussion über Cloud-Intelligence ist jedoch der Verlust der amerikanischen Privatwirtschaft weniger interessant als das, womit sich diese Millionen von Büroangestellten in diesen zwei Stunden eigentlich beschäftigen.

Kognitiver Mehrwert und der neue Sozialismus

> Die zweite Hälfte des 20. Jahrhunderts brachte einschneidende Veränderungen: einen Anstieg des Bruttoinlandsprodukts pro Kopf, höhere Bildung, eine höhere Lebenserwartung sowie – und das ist in diesem Zusammenhang entscheidend – eine wachsende Anzahl von Menschen, die fünf Tage pro Woche arbeiteten. Zum ersten Mal zwang die Gesellschaft den größten Teil ihrer Bürger, mit etwas zurechtzukommen, das sie nicht kannten – Freizeit. Und was haben wir mit dieser Freizeit gemacht? Nun, meistens sahen wir fern.
> (Clay Shirky, Gin, Television and Social Surplus)

Wie Clay Shirky zeigt, vergeuden wir in den Vereinigten Staaten nach wie vor jedes Wochenende durchschnittlich hundert Millionen Stunden damit, uns Werbung anzusehen. Was könnte man nicht alles in hundert Millionen Stunden tun! Shirky zufolge waren etwa hundert Millionen Stunden „Brainstorming" erforderlich, um Wikipedia zu schaffen, die größte Enzyklopädie, die je kompiliert wurde, und das populärste Referenzwerk im Internet.

Es wäre falsch, aus Shirkys Argumentation abzuleiten, dass die gesamte Menschheit sich aus der Fernsehcouch erheben sollte, um aktiv Online-Content zu produzieren – schließlich schauen sich heute die meisten jungen Leute, die ihre teuren Kabelfernsehanschlüsse für etwas günstigere Internet-Verbindungen eintauschen, ebendiese Sitcoms auf ihren Laptops an; auf YouTube dominieren Videoclips aus *American Idol*; und die populärsten täglichen Suchbegriffe auf Google stehen in Zusammenhang mit Prominententratsch. Der passive Konsum, der Jahrzehnte des Fernsehens kennzeichnete, ist auch in der heutigen vernetzten Generation angesagt.

Doch auch wenn nur geschätzte zehn Prozent der Internet-User aktiv Content beitragen, so haben sie bereits einen riesigen Online-Fundus an kulturellen Inhalten, Wissen und Tools zusammengetragen. Und wir stehen erst am Beginn.

Kevin Kelly nennt Wikipedia, Flickr und Twitter die „Avantgarde einer kulturellen Bewegung" und konstatiert die Entstehung einer „globalen kollektivistischen Gesellschaft". Amateurfotografen haben, wie er hervorhebt, mehr als drei Milliarden Fotos auf Flickr publiziert. Sechs Milliarden Videos werden jeden Monat auf YouTube gestellt. Die Blog-Suchmaschine Technorati findet mehr als eine Million Blogeinträge, die täglich publiziert werden. Für Apples omnipräsenten Media-Player iTunes werden mehr als 125.000 Podcasts angeboten, darunter mehr als 25.000 Video-Podcasts.

Die kleine Minderheit an Internet-Nutzern, die aktiv Content beisteuert, leistet dafür sicherlich einen großen Beitrag. Sie beurteilen Restaurants und Firmen auf Yelp. Sie übernehmen die Rolle von Redakteuren, indem sie Content auf Delicious, StumpleUpon, Digg und Reddit empfehlen. Sie lassen andere an ihrer Krankengeschichte auf Patients Like Me und Google Health teilhaben. Sie erstellen qualitativ hochwertige Landkarten auf OpenStreetMap und entwerfen 3D-Modelle von Gebäuden, Monumenten und Sehenswürdigkeiten mit Googles Gratis-Software SketchUp. Sie berichten über aktuelle Ereignisse wie Journalisten. Auf Flickr helfen sie der Library of Congress, die Fotografien ihrer Sammlung zu beschreiben und zu kontextualisieren. Sie übersetzen Blogbeiträge, Artikel, Magazine und Videos in verschiedene Sprachen.

Unglaublicher noch ist, dass sie all dies unentgeltlich, ohne jede Aufwandsentschädigung tun. Hunderte Millionen Internet-User wenden täglich einen kleinen Teil ihrer kognitiven Energie für Online-Projekte und Formen der Selbstdarstellung auf, die sie interessieren – nicht für die Arbeit, für die sie bezahlt werden. Kevin Kelly nennt dies einen „neuen Sozialismus", Isaac Mao bezeichnet es als *Sharism*, wobei er sich auf *Sharing* und *Community* bezieht und die politische Ideologie hier ausgeklammert lässt. (Die aktivsten Content-Ersteller könnten ebenso gut Bewunderer von Adam Smith wie von Karl Marx sein.)

In China entsteht eine immer größer werdende Bewegung, die versucht, das Zensursystem zu unterlaufen. Die Liberalisierung der modernen Wirtschaft lässt immer mehr Freiraum für freies Denken, das politische System und die Regierungspartei hält jedoch an der alten Mentalität fest, die auf dem staatlichen Zensursystem basiert – man denke nur an die unter dem Namen „Great Firewall" (GFW) bekannte Zensur-Software und die neuerdings vorgeschriebene Filter-

David Sasaki, Isaac Mao

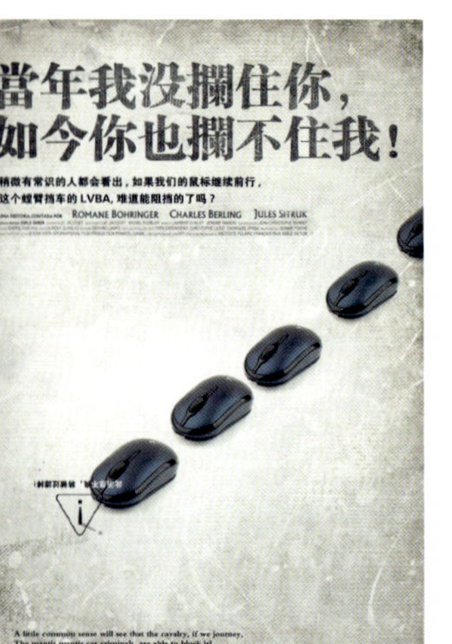

software „Green Dam". Seit Anfang 2009 verursacht ein Online-Cartoon namens *Caonima* („Pferd aus Gras und Lehm"), das ein Alpaka als Symbol verwendet, den Zensoren in China Kopfzerbrechen. Ein Cartoon-Mashup verbreitete sich in Windeseile nicht nur in China, sondern weltweit über das Internet. Xiao Qiang von der Universität Berkley bezeichnete *Caonima* als „die boshafteste Aktion seit Jahren" neben der früheren Kreation „River Crab", die sich ebenfalls über die Zensur lustig machte. Er fügte hinzu: „Wo Flusskrebse sind, sind auch Pferde aus Gras und Schlamm nicht weit." (Siehe den Text von Xiao Qiang auf S. 44)

Die chinesische Bloggerszene ist nicht alleine. Im Iran nutzte die grüne Revolution die neue Cloud-Technologie, um sich Unterstützung aus der ganzen Welt zu holen. Neda Agha-Soltan, die 26-jährige junge Frau, die in Teheran erschossen wurde, wurde zu einem Symbol und einer „Märtyrerin", deren Tod nicht nur die Iraner, sondern die ganze Welt bewegte. Als sie mit weit aufgerissenen Augen starb, wurden aus Bürgermedien Massenmedien, die Millionen Menschen erreichten. Cloud-Aktivismus weckt Hoffnung und setzt Veränderungen in Gang. Wir sehen, dass er sich auf der ganzen Welt ausbreitet, von den Vereinigten Staaten bis zum Nahen Osten, von China bis zu den Pazifischen Inseln, vom Planeten Erde bis zur Internationalen Raumstation.

Cloud-Intelligence: eine Zukunftsvision

Das menschliche Gehirn ist bei Weitem das komplexeste Organ, das in drei bis vier Milliarden Jahren natürlicher Selektion entstand. Es besteht aus etwa 100 Milliarden Neuronen, die jeweils bis zu 10.000 synaptische Verbindungen aufweisen. Informationen wandern mittels kleiner elektrischer Impulse durch das Gehirn und werden von Neuron zu Neuron übertragen – ähnlich finden auch Informationen ihren Weg durch das Internet. Während Sie dies lesen, die Informationen des Textes analysieren, in Ihrem Gedächtnis speichern und Ihr Wissen abrufen, um das Gelesene zu kontextualisieren und zu reflektieren, durchströmen Ihr Gehirn Milliarden kleiner elektrischer Impulse.

Das Internet ist im Vergleich dazu deutlich weniger komplex. *Internet Word Stats* geht davon aus, dass es 1,6 Milliarden Internet-User oder „soziale Neuronen" gibt. Der Studie zufolge steht der durchschnittliche Facebook-User mit 164 „Freunden" in Verbindung, eine Zahl, die weit entfernt ist von den 10.000 synaptischen Verbindungen zwischen unseren 100 Milliarden Gehirnzellen. Mit anderen Worten, obwohl das Internet das Potential hat, eines Tages so etwas wie Selbstreflexion zu entwickeln, steht es noch am Beginn seiner Entwicklung. Doch gibt es bereits mehrere Beispiele, die zeigen, dass das Internet sich rasch zum sozialen Nervensystem der Menschheit entwickelt. Joshua-Michele Ross erwähnt drei Manifestationen des vernetzten sozialen Gehirns: die Blog-Postings nach den Terrorangriffen in Bombay, Obamas *Project Houdini* und Googles globale Virusprognosen. Das menschliche Gehirn in seiner heutigen Ausformung bildete sich vor mehr als 10.000 Jahren, als unsere Vorfahren mit Umständen konfrontiert wurden, die jenes avancierte Denken erforderten, das nur ein größeres Gehirn leistet. Mit einem größeren Gehirn entwickelten sich moralisches Urteilsvermögen, Bewusstsein und, allem voran, die Sprache, ohne die wir Kultur und Wissen nicht über Generationen weitergeben könnten. Das Organ, das wir in unseren Schädeln herumtragen, hat sich jedoch in den letzten

10.000 Jahren kaum weiterentwickelt. Es bildete sich, als unsere Vorfahren noch in Stammesverbänden mit etwa 150 Stammesangehörigen lebten, nicht in Millionenstädten. Die Menschen hatten damals natürlich auch noch keine Adressbücher mit Tausenden Kontakten. Da die Cloud sich exponentiell zu den Informationen, sozialen Neuronen und Verbindungen zwischen ihnen weiterentwickelt, muss sich unser bescheidenes menschliches Gehirn anpassen, um die Cloud optimal zu nutzen, ohne unser Leben in einem Zustand permanenter Zerstreuung zu verbringen, um den größten Nutzen aus der Cloud zu ziehen, ohne dass wir überfordert und permanent in einem Zustand „zerstreuter, partieller Aufmerksamkeit" sind.

Ungeachtet dessen, wie aktiv oder passiv wir unsere Online-Zeit verbringen, steht fest, dass unser Gehirn früher oder später seine Tätigkeit einstellen wird und unser Aufenthalt auf Erden endlich ist. Wir leben natürlich im Gedächtnis unserer Freunde und unserer Familie weiter – und auch in den Bits und Bytes digitaler Spuren, die wir für Generationen in der Cloud hinterlassen. Was mit den Informationen geschieht, die wir hinterlassen – oder was die Cloud selbst damit macht –, wird von einer neuen vernetzten Entwicklung abhängen, die Werte wie Teilen und Gemeinschaft über den Schutz von Privateigentum stellt.

Die Intelligenz, die wir brauchen

Wir brauchen eine neue Intelligenz, die eine neue Wissenschaft, eine neue Kunst, eine neue partizipative Kultur und neue Technologien hervorbringt. In einer Zeit, in der immer mehr Menschen von der kommerziellen Globalisierung betroffen sind, können neue Technologien und Kommunikationsdienste wie soziale Netzwerke dazu beitragen, dass die Menschen gemeinsam Lösungen für anstehende Probleme suchen.

Wir verwenden das Konzept „Cloud", weil die Probleme und deren Lösungen ebenso wie die globale Gesellschaft zunehmend vernetzt sind. Die Ars Electronica genießt nach dreißig Jahren Forschungsarbeit weltweites Ansehen und bewegt sich nun von erreichten Zielen in eine neue Ära mit neuen Paradigmen weiter. Die nächsten dreißig Jahre versprechen noch spannender zu werden und das bisher Erreichte in den Schatten zu stellen.

Cloud-Intelligence ist mehr als eine Singularität. Wir haben lediglich ein Wort geprägt, seine Bedeutung aber werden Sie definieren. Vom technischen Fortschritt bis hin zu globalen Aktionen – die lange Spur der Informationen von neuen Identitäten wird die Geschwindigkeit des Denkens in der gesamten Gesellschaft massiv beschleunigen. Dies stellt uns vor neue Herausforderungen und weckt gleichzeitig große Hoffnungen. Wenn wir eine solche Intelligenz wirklich bündeln könnten, würden wir uns zu einer neuen Stufe des Menschseins weiterentwickeln. Oder vielleicht sogar das Heilige neu erfinden, wie Stuart Kauffmann meint.

(Aus dem Englischen von Martina Bauer)

1   *80+1 – Eine Weltreise*, S. 82–131

Stephen Downes

The Cloud and Collaboration

Let's take as a starting point the discussion about "cloud intelligence" on the conference website:

> In the cloud of connections, we each become social neurons, mimicking the biological human brain but on a giant scale. This collective knowledge is far beyond anything a single search engine could index and archive. Intelligence is spreading everywhere, every minute, and cloud computing can draw new links across new ideas. *(David Sasaki, 2009)*

This idea of the connected world as a global brain is not new, nor surprising. It seems clear that we can identify something like social intelligence in the community, and the analogy between humans and neurons is compelling.

As we read and hear more about the growing Internet and the emerging cloud, we are also hearing more about the way in which we, as connected members of the cloud, work together. The conference website also addresses this point:

> We think together but remain independent in our identity. If we could foster co-thinking to reach consensus about new solutions, we may be able to find a new direction for the future. Hope can emerge from new collaborative models based on a new paradigm; science and art will act gracefully to match human nature, and to shape the future of humanity. *(David Sasaki, 2009)*

This is a common refrain. It expresses the idea that the cloud enables us to work together, to collaborate and to forge a new consensus. The cloud, in other words, reinforces the ways with which we have attempted hitherto to organize ourselves. The divisiveness, the factionalism, the disputes and conflicts that have blocked our efforts in the past are effectively overcome using the new technology.

Dimitar Tchurovsky's Google Knol titled the *Global Virtual Brain and Mind Project* is a good example of this. (Tchurovsky, 2009) He cites the conflicts of interests, media manipulations, bribery and the influence industry as barriers to a genuine global consensus. The response is a "worldwide social network of self-selected people resembling human brain and mind, who will collaborate in the attempt to solve social problems."

The associating of collaboration and global conscious is natural, as collaboration is central to our concept of community, and the global mind can be seen as an extension of community. We see much the same language as that used to describe the global mind, for example, "people inspired to create healthy communities, cross-pollinate ideas, connect and exchange stories that harness our collective wisdom." (McCarthy) These examples are typical; they could be multiplied almost indefinitely.

What is collaboration, though? Is it something that neurons in a human brain actually do? Can we describe the organization of our mind in the same terms we currently use to describe the organization of society?

The characteristics identified by the National Network for Collaboration (The National Network for Collaboration, 1995) are typical:

- Accomplish shared vision and impact benchmarks
- Build interdependent system to address issues and opportunities
- Consensus used in shared decision making
- Roles, time and evaluation formalized
- Links are formal and written in work assignments
- Leadership high, trust level high, productivity high
- Ideas and decisions equally shared
- Highly developed communication

Collaboration, on this model, can be contrasted with looser forms of association such as networking, alliance-formation or cooperation.

What distinguishes collaboration from these other forms of organization is a commonality of understanding or purpose. This theme permeates writing on the subject. Schrage calls collaboration "an act of shared creation and/or shared discovery" (Schrage, 1990, p. 6) Senge talks about the creation of a shared vision. (Senge, 1994)

In learning communities as well we see commonality or shared vision as central to the creation of a learning community. The idea that learning is social in nature has been a recurring theme in education, from Dewey to Brown and Duguid. Learning communities, write Kilpatrick, Barrett, and Jones, "are operationalised through collaboration, cooperation, and/or partnerships. The shared goals are achieved through working together and potentially building or creating new knowledge." (Kilpatrick, Barrett and Jones, 2003) Or as Brown and Duguid write:

> Reciprocity is strong. People are able to affect one another and the group as a whole directly. Changes can propagate easily. Coordination is tight. Ideas and knowledge may be distributed across the group, not held individually. These groups allow for highly productive and creative work to develop collaboratively. *(Brown and Duguid, 2000, p. 143)*

Or, as they write: "Forging a single group around a shared task, overlapping knowledge, blurred boundaries and a common working identity." (Brown and Duguid, 2000, p. 127)

Do neurons collaborate like this? Though there may be a sense to be made of vocabulary such as a 'common identity' and 'shared task' for a collection of neurons, it seems highly artificial, based on a certain perspective of their activities as a whole and, most significantly, of limited utility in describing the mechanisms that neurons employ to form a mind.

If we push the language a bit, we can see how awkward this characterization becomes. Does it make sense to say of two neurons that they have a "shared understanding"? Neurons are not the sort of things that can even *have* an understanding. Do neurons unite behind a 'common vision'? Do they 'reach a consensus' and 'share in decision-making'? Does one neuron 'trust' another neuron? The language begins to stretch credibility.

Equally, the forms and mechanisms of social organization, as we understand them in contemporary society, are completely alien to the functioning of neurons. There is no 'lead neuron' that articulates a vision for all to share. Neurons don't employ a mission statement, strategies or mechanisms in order to complete organizational tasks. Neurons are not client-focused, results-driven or process-oriented. Neurons are not *managed* and there is no sense to be made of them belonging to a community in anything like the normal usage of the term.

What characterizes collaborative forms of organization is, in one sense or another, *sameness in the people*. Sometimes this sameness is a mental property—a sameness of vision, understanding or belief. Other times this sameness may be of some aptitude or capacity—a shared vocabulary, a shared skill set, shared comprehension. In other forms of community, a more basic sameness is required: sameness of residency, of nationality, of language or of religion.

By the same token, collaborative forms of organization are directed toward mental *content*. Communication consists of a transfer of information, with some process undertaken to ensure sameness of content in the receiver as was found in the sender. It is a model of learning and communication as *diffusion*. There are clear roles of knowledge production and knowledge reception. Collaboration involves all its members working on the *same content* (even if each has only a partial view of that content). There is a *semantic consistency* in their work.

Space precludes a detailed analysis of this phenomenon, however, it can be seen in a wide variety of models of learning and communication, from Moore's theory of transactional distance, to the concepts of knowledge translation or knowledge mobilization, to the power law model of online community, to "core knowledge" advocacy, to Vygotsky's concept of the zone of proximal development (of the latter Cheyne and Tarulli write, "all of this is organized around the issue of control which, through ontogenesis, becomes transformed from that of an external agent over a subordinate to one of an internal agent over self and ultimately to a principle over an instance"). (Cheyne and Tarulli, 1999)

This "sameness of entity" thesis (as we may call it) may be distinguished from an alternative representation in which diversity among entities is expected and accepted. Such an alternative model can seem quite radical. Insofar as entities are diverse, so therefore also are their mental contents, which means that when one person says: "Paris is the capital of France" he or she means something different from what another person means when uttering the same sentence.

Such approaches to communication have their grounding in "incommensurability" or "indeterminacy" theses of meaning; we see these reflected in Kuhn's theory of paradigm change and Quine's discussion of radical translation respectively. As Quine says, it's not simply that we can't say that two utterances have the same meaning, it's that there might not even be an objective meaning to be right about. (Quine, 1960, p. 73) What underlies communication, what makes community possible in such cases, is not sameness of entity or shared meaning, but rather our entering into a system of interaction with each other, into what Wittgenstein calls a "language game", the result of negotiation calls and responses, where thinking is an activity, similar to, as he says in the *Blue Book*, a movement of the hand, the presumption of meaning being an ungrounded inference, a projection, or as Quine says, an "analytic hypothesis." (Wittgenstein, 1991, p. 16)

When we are not concerned with sameness of entity, when we are not concerned with shared meaning, when we are not concerned with diffusion of content, then the mechanisms for community look very different. They do not resemble *collaboration*, as we have described it above, but rather, what we may style here as *cooperation*. For the purposes of the current discussion, "cooperation" may be thought of as the sharing by entities of a common *system of communication* or infrastructure. Community, then, would be defined by the interactions or connections among those entities, and the process of the global brain described in terms of those interactions.

From the perspective of a human brain, there is a very good reason why we would want the structure of neural interaction to proceed in this way. If the creation of a neural community—a *mind*—depended on neurons achieving a commonality of meaning, then the mind as a whole would never be capable of entertaining more meaning than a single neuron. From the perspective of a mind, meaning is not something that is passed from one neuron to the next, but rather, something that emerges from the interaction of neurons. Whether or not one neuron means the same thing as another is completely irrelevant from the point of view of the mind.

The foundation of community understood as arising from the sharing of a common system of communication is not collaboration, but is rather cooperation, as suggested above. A cooperation then is formed through the creation or formation of links or connections among its entities, a negotiation of communications among them. A cooperation among entities implies a separation or distinctness of interests between them; we see game-theoretic models of cooperation, for example, in such scenarios as the prisoner's dilemma, where individual interests create the possibility of conflict or betrayal. (Mayberry, Harsanyi, Scarf and Selten, 1992) It is a mechanism similar to what we see in market economics; there is no presumption of shared objectives or goals, only a negotiation of a means of interaction.

There is no clear statement as to the exact mechanisms through which neurons connect with each other (though the biological and chemical processes are reasonably well understood, LeDoux, 2002) but for the purposes of this paper four major models of association can be described, each of which does appear to comprise at least a part of the overall process: Hebbian associationism, association by proximity, competitive systems (also known as "back propagation") and harmony systems.

Associations are distinct from the mechanisms we described above, under the heading of "collaboration", in that there is no presumption of management or authority, no privileged nodes and no hierarchy. The idea is that each entity is *autonomous*—a model most popularized in Marvin Minsky's *The Society of Mind*, where "each mind is made of many smaller processes" that he calls "agents". (Minsky, 1985, p. 17) A (human) society of agents also sounds more like what we would want to describe as constituting a global mind, a society in which each individual is autonomous, performing his or her individual (and unique) function, forming intelligence through *interaction* with the rest of society, rather than by conforming with it.

We hear, sometimes, the emerging structure of the web described as a "new socialism". (Kelly, 2009) But there is a tendency to represent this new socialism as an economic theory, in terms of the creation and consumption of content. "They have already constructed a vast online repository of culture, knowledge and tools. And we are just at the beginning of what's to come." (David Sasaki, 2009) There is, it seems, a desire to represent this as a collaboration or type of collectivism, "Wikipedia, Flickr, and Twitter the 'vanguard of a cultural movement', an emerging 'global collectivist society.'" And concordantly there seems an inclination to weight people according to the value of their contribution (and by extension even to value people by the number of their connections). The content-based "new socialism" is the same as the authority-based power-law driven old capitalism.

In reality, the "new socialism" that ought to be understood as emerging on the Internet is not one dogged by the tired stereotypes that seem to characterize American descriptions of the term (Lawrence Lessig, for example, defining "socialism as coercion", Lessig, 2009). A more modern version of socialism may be found in the forms of 'democratic socialism' current around the world, forms of socialism as a form of personal empowerment, equality of opportunity, and association and interaction.

The concept echoes what Illich talks about as "conviviality":

> Illich's 'tools for conviviality' are appropriate and congenial alternatives to tools of domination, as convivial tools promote learning, sociality, community, "autonomous and creative intercourse among persons, and the intercourse of per sons with their environment" (Illich, 1973, p. 27). These criteria, he felt, could guide reconstruction of education to serve the needs of varied communities, to promote democracy and social justice, and to redefine learning and work to promote creativity, community, and an ecological balance between people and the earth. *(Kahn & Kellner, 2007)*

If we are to think of the Internet as a global mind, then the interpretation of the community created by such a network is characterized by cooperation rather than collaboration. So we need to reframe some of the discussion about the attributes of that network, and reform our understanding of the processes and the technologies most appropriate for the creation of such a network.

Instead of attempting to identify thought-leaders, for example, and instead of attempting to identify and understand the content created on the web, the various activities of participants in the network are acts of *interaction and communication*. The semantics and the meaning of interactions are not deducible from their contents; indeed, their contents are, from the larger perspective, irrelevant. Rather, we should treat them as content-less 'words' or 'signals' in a complex communication that is taking place among the entities. A web video created by a skateboarder: that's a word. A lolcat created in photoshop: that's a word. This article: that's a word.

We communicate with each other with these words, and the important things are, first *that we communicate*, not the particular nature or content of our communication, and second, what we *as a species* do as a consequence of that communication, not in the sense of having common ideas or doctrines or philosophies, but rather in terms of global expressions or behavior. In such a network there are no special, privileged nodes; being a consumer is as important as being a creator, and indeed (as has often been noted) the roles of creator and consumer become indistinguishable and, more importantly, so do the roles of master and servant.

David Sasaki (2009). *Day 81: Ars Electronica Symposium Examines Cloud Intelligence*. Retrieved from 80+1: *http://www.8oplus1.org/blog/day-81-ars-electronica-symposium-examines-cloud-intelligence*.
Brown, J. S., & Duguid, P. (2000). *The social life of information*. Cambridge: Harvard Business School Press.
Cheyne, J., & Tarulli, D. (1999). Dialogue, difference, and the "third voice" in the zone of proximal development. *Theory and Psychology*, 9, 5–29.
Hebb, D. O. (2002). *The Organization of Behavior: A Neuropsychological Theory*. Lawrence Erlbaum Associates.
Hofkirchner, W. (2005). *Beyond the Third Culture! Science in the Information Age*. Salzburg.
Kahn, R., & Kellner, D. (2007). Paulo Freire and Ivan Illich: "Technology, Politics and the Reconstruction of Education", *Policy Futures in Education*, 5 (4).
Kelly, K. (2009, May 22). *The New Socialism: Global Collectivist Society Is Coming Online*. Retrieved from *Wired*: *http://www.wired.com/culture/culturereviews/magazine/17-06/nep_newsocialism?currentPage=all*
Kilpatrick, S., Barrett, M., & Jones, T. (2003). Defining Learning Communities. *International Education Research Conference*. Association for Research in Education.
LeDoux, J. (2002). *Synaptic Self: How Our Brains Become Who We Are*. Viking.
Lessig, L. (2009, May 28). *Et tu, KK? (aka, No, Kevin, this is not "socialism")*. Retrieved from Lessig Blog: *http://www.lessig.org/blog/2009/05/et_tu_kk_aka_no_kevin_this_is.html*
Mayberry, J. P., Harsanyi, J. F., Scarf, H. E., & Selten, R. (1992). *Game-Theoretic Models of Cooperation and Conflict*. Westview Press.
McCarthy, M. (n.d.). *Collaboration in Community*. Retrieved from Ning: *http://www.collaborationincommunity.com/*
Minsky, M. (1985). *The Society of Mind*. New York: Simon & Shuster.
David Sasaki (El Oso) (2009, June 12). *Cloud Intelligence*. Retrieved from el-oso.net: *http://el-oso.net/blog/archives/2009/06/12/cloud-intelligence/*
Quine, W. (1960). *Word and Object*. Cambridge: MIT press.
Rumelhart, D. E., & McClelland, J. L. (1986). *Parallel Distributed Processing*, Volume 1. Cambridge: MIT Press.
Russell, P. (2008). *The Global Brain: The Awakening Earth in a New Century*. Floris Books; 3rd edition.
Schrage, M. (1990). *Shared minds: The new technologies of collaboration*. New York: Random House.
Senge, P. (1994). *The Fifth Discipline: The Art & Practice of the Learning Organization*. Doubleday Business.
Tchurovsky, D. (2009). *Global Virtual Brain and Mind Project*. Retrieved from Google Knol: *http://knol.google.com/k/dimitar-tchurovsky/global-virtual-brain-and-mind-project/mp8du5m8vcjb/4#*
The National Network for Collaboration. (1995). *Collaboration Framework - Addressing Community Capacity*. Retrieved from The National Network for Collaboration: *http://crs.uvm.edu/nnco/collab/framework.html*
Wittgenstein, L. (1991). *Preliminary studies for the 'Philosophical Investigations'*. London: Wiley-Blackwell.

Stephen Downes

Cloud und Kollaboration

Beginnen wir mit der Darstellung von „Cloud Intelligence" auf der Konferenz-Website:

> In der Wolke aus Verbindungen werden wir alle zu sozialen Neuronen, die
> das menschliche Gehirn imitieren, nur in einem gigantischen Maßstab.
> Das kollektive Wissen geht weit über alles hinaus, was eine einzelne Suchmaschine
> indizieren und archivieren könnte. Intelligenz breitet sich im Minutentakt in alle
> Richtungen aus, und mit Cloud-Computing werden neue Verbindungen zwischen
> neuen Ideen geschaffen. (*David Sasaki*, 2009)

Die Vorstellung von der vernetzten Welt als Gehirn ist weder neu noch überraschend. Selbstverständlich ist eine Art gemeinschaftlicher Intelligenz zu erkennen, und die Analogie zwischen Menschen und Neuronen ist einfach unwiderstehlich.

Je mehr vom wachsenden Internet und der damit entstehenden Wolke, der Cloud, die Rede ist, umso mehr ist auch von unserer Zusammenarbeit als vernetzte Mitglieder dieser Cloud zu hören. Auf der Konferenz-Website wird auch dieser Punkt angesprochen:

> Wir denken gemeinsam, bewahren aber eine unabhängige Identität. Wenn wir
> uns durch gemeinsames Denken auf neue Lösungen einigen, können wir vielleicht
> auch der Zukunft eine neue Richtung geben. Auf einem neuen Paradigma
> beruhende Kollaborationsmodelle geben Anlass zur Hoffnung; Wissenschaft
> und Kunst handeln dann menschengemäß und unter Berücksichtigung der
> Zukunftsfolgen. (*David Sasaki*, 2009)

Der Refrain ist bekannt. Er bringt zum Ausdruck, dass uns die Wolke in die Lage versetzt, zusammenzuarbeiten und einen neuen Konsens zu schmieden. Kurzum, sie verstärkt die Art, wie wir uns auch bisher zu organisieren versucht haben. Die Teilungen, Spaltungen, Zwistigkeiten und Zerwürfnisse, die uns früher in unseren Bemühungen behindert haben, werden mithilfe der neuen Technik überwunden.

Dimitar Tchurovskys Knol-Artikel *Global Virtual Brain and Mind Project* ist ein gutes Beispiel dafür (Tchurovsky, 2009). Er führt Interessenskonflikte, Medienmanipulation, Bestechung und industrielle Einflussnahme als Hindernisse für einen wahren globalen Konsens an. Die Antwort darauf ist ein „dem menschlichen Gehirn und Geist gleichendes, weltweites, soziales Netzwerk von Menschen, die sich selbst dazu ausersehen haben, gemeinsam an der Lösung sozialer Probleme arbeiten."

Dass wir Kollaboration mit globalem Bewusstsein verbinden, ist durchaus natürlich, denn Zusammenarbeit ist ja ein zentrales Moment unseres Gemeinschaftsbegriffs und der menschliche Geist kann als eine Erweiterung der Gemeinschaft gesehen werden. Dieses globale Bewusstsein wird immer wieder in einer ganz ähnlichen Sprache beschrieben. Noch ein Beispiel: „Menschen mit dem Bedürfnis, gesunde Gemeinschaften zu bilden, befruchten sich gegenseitig mit Ideen, verbinden sich und tauschen Geschichten aus, die unserem kollektiven Wissen zugute kommen" (McCarthy). Solche Beispiele könnte man unendlich fortführen.

Was ist aber nun Zusammenarbeit? Entspricht sie wirklich der Tätigkeit der Neuronen im menschlichen Gehirn? Können wir die Organisation unseres Geists auf die gleiche Art beschreiben wie die Organisation der Gesellschaft?

Laut dem National Network for Collaboration sind für Kollaboration folgende Dinge kennzeichnend (The National Network for Collaboration, 1995):

- gemeinsame Zielvorstellungen und Wirkungsabsichten
- der Aufbau eines interdependenten Systems zur Problemlösung und zum Ergreifen von Gelegenheiten
- konsensorientierte gemeinsame Entscheidungsfindung
- formalisierte Rollen, Zeiten und Bewertungsverfahren
- formelle, als Arbeitsaufgaben ausgedrückte Verbindungen
- hoher Führungsgrad, hoher Vertrauensgrad, hohe Produktivität
- gleichberechtigter Ideenaustausch und gemeinsame Entscheidungsfindung
- stark entwickelte Kommunikation

Kollaboration lässt sich nach diesem Modell von anderen loseren Assoziierungsformen wie Networking, Allianzen oder Kooperationen unterscheiden. Was die Kollaboration von anderen Organisationsformen unterscheidet, ist ein gemeinsames Verständnis oder Ziel. Dieser Punkt durchzieht die gesamte Literatur zu dem Thema. Schrage nennt die Kollaboration „einen Akt gemeinsamer Produktion und/oder Entdeckung" (Schrage, 1990, S. 6); Senge spricht vom Entwickeln einer gemeinsamen Vision (Senge, 1996).

Auch bei Lerngemeinschaften sieht man die gemeinsame Vision als wesentlich für deren Entstehung an. Lernen als sozialer Vorgang ist – von Dewey bis Brown & Duguid – ein zentrales Thema der Pädagogik. Lerngemeinschaften – so Kilpatrick, Barrett & Jones – „werden durch Kollaboration, Kooperation und/oder Partnerschaften operationalisiert. Die gemeinsamen Ziele werden dadurch erreicht, dass man miteinander arbeitet und potentiell neues Wissen generiert" (Kilpatrick, Barrett, & Jones, 2003).

Oder, wie Brown & Duguid schreiben:

> Es gibt starke Wechselwirkungen. Man kann direkt aufeinander oder auf die gesamte Gruppe einwirken. Veränderungen verbreiten sich schnell. Alles ist gut aufeinander abgestimmt. Ideen und Wissen können auf alle verteilt und müssen nicht individuell erbracht werden. In solchen Gruppen bringt Zusammenarbeit oft überaus produktive und kreative Ergebnisse hervor. *(Brown & Duguid, 2000, S. 143)*

Anderswo sprechen sie auch von der Bildung einer Gruppe rund um eine gemeinsame Aufgabe, mit überlappenden Wissensgebieten, fließenden Grenzen und einer gemeinsamen Arbeitsidentität (Brown & Duguid, 2000, S. 127).

Arbeiten Neuronen auf diese Art zusammen? Zwar mögen sich Begriffe wie „gemeinsame Identität" oder „gemeinsame Aufgabe" auch auf eine Ansammlung von Neuronen übertragen lassen, doch scheint mir das höchst artifiziell zu sein, nur auf einer bestimmten Sicht ihrer Gesamtaktivität beruhend, vor allem aber von beschränktem Nutzen für die Beschreibung der Mechanismen, mit denen Neuronen einen Geist bilden.

Stephen Downes

Wenn wir diese Ausdrucksweise ein wenig überdehnen, zeigt sich, wie absurd eine derartige Beschreibung ist. Kann man von zwei Neuronen sagen, sie hätten ein „gemeinsames Verständnis"? Neuronen gehören nicht zu der Sorte von Dingen, die überhaupt so etwas wie Verständnis besitzen können. Vereinen sich Neuronen hinter einer „gemeinsamen Vision"? Gelangen sie „zu einem Konsens" und „partizipieren sie an der Entscheidungsfindung"? Haben Neuronen „Vertrauen" zueinander? Hier überschreitet die Sprache die Grenzen der Glaubwürdigkeit.

Gleichermaßen haben die Formen und Mechanismen sozialer Organisation, wie wir sie aus der heutigen Gesellschaft kennen, nicht das Mindeste mit der Funktionsweise von Neuronen zu tun. Es gibt kein „Leitneuron", das allen eine gemeinsame Vision vorgäbe. Neuronen verwenden keine *Mission Statements*, Strategien oder Mechanismen, um organisatorische Aufgaben zu erfüllen. Neuronen sind nicht kunden-, ergebnis- oder prozessorientiert. Neuronen werden nicht geführt, und es ist sinnlos davon zu sprechen, dass sie in irgendeinem herkömmlichen Sinn des Worts einer Gemeinschaft angehörten.

Kollaborative Organisationsformen sind in der einen oder anderen Hinsicht stets durch eine Gleichheit der daran beteiligten Menschen gekennzeichnet. Manchmal besteht diese Gleichheit in einer Geistesverfassung – einer Gemeinsamkeit der Vision, des Verständnisses oder Glaubens –, ein andermal eher in einer Befähigung oder Begabung – einer gemeinsamen Sprache, besonderen Fertigkeit oder Auffassungsgabe. Und in wieder anderen Gemeinschaftsformen ist vielleicht eine noch grundsätzlichere Gleichheit vonnöten: gleicher Wohnort, gleiche Nationalität, Sprache oder Religion.

Genauso sind kollaborative Organisationsformen auf geistige Inhalte ausgerichtet. Bei Kommunikation geht es um Übermittlung von Information, wobei Einiges dafür getan wird, die Gleichheit des Inhalts bei Empfänger und Sender zu gewährleisten. Es handelt sich hier um ein Diffusionsmodell des Lernens und der Kommunikation. Die Rollen von Wissensproduktion und Wissensrezeption sind klar verteilt. Zusammenarbeit heißt, dass alle Mitarbeiter am gleichen Inhalt arbeiten (auch wenn sie jeweils nur eine Teilansicht dieses Inhalts kennen). Ihre Arbeit ist *semantisch konsistent*.

Für eine eingehendere Analyse diese Phänomens ist hier nicht der Raum, man begegnet ihm jedoch in vielen verschiedenen Lern- und Kommunikationsmodellen, von Moores Theorie der transaktionalen Distanz über Konzepte der „Knowledge Translation" und der Wissensmobilisierung, das Potenzgesetz der Online-Partizipation, die Förderung von „Grundwissen" bis zu Wygotskis Zone der proximalen Entwicklung (über letztere schreiben Cheyne und Tarulli: „Hinter all dem steht die Frage der Kontrolle, die sich qua Ontogenese von der einer externen Instanz über einen Untergebenen zu der einer internen Instanz über das Selbst und schließlich zu einem den Einzelfall regierenden Prinzip entwickelt", Cheyne & Tarulli, 1999).

Dieser These von der „Entitätsgleichheit" (wie wir sie nennen wollen) lässt sich ein Alternativmodell gegenüberstellen, das von einer Verschiedenheit der Entitäten ausgeht. Ein solches Alternativmodell mag radikal erscheinen. Die Verschiedenheit von Entitäten impliziert nämlich, dass auch die damit verbundenen geistigen Inhalte verschieden sind, dass also zwei Personen z. B. mit der Äußerung „Paris ist die Hauptstadt Frankreichs" jeweils etwas anderes meinen.

Solche Ansätze der Kommunikationstheorie gründen in Thesen der „Unvereinbarkeit" oder „Unbestimmtheit". Beispiele dafür finden wir etwa in Kuhns Theorie vom Paradigmenwechsel oder Quines Erörterung der Ur-Übersetzung. Laut Quine können wir nicht nur nicht sagen, dass zwei Äußerungen dasselbe bedeuten, sondern sie besitzen vielleicht nicht einmal eine objektive Bedeutung, auf die sie zutreffen könnten (Quine, 1960, S. 73). Was in diesem Fall Kommunikation und damit auch Gemeinschaft ermöglicht, ist nicht eine Gleichheit des Gegenstands oder der Bedeutung, sondern vielmehr unsere Teilnahme an einem Interaktionssystem, an dem, was Wittgenstein als „Sprachspiel" bezeichnet; das Ergebnis eines Prozesses von Rufen und Antworten, in dem Denken zu einer Tätigkeit wird, die, wie er im *Blauen Buch* sagt, der Bewegung einer Hand gleicht, eine Auffassung, der zufolge Bedeutung eine grundlose Schlussfolgerung ist, eine Projektion, oder wie Quine sagt, eine „analytische Hypothese" (Wittgenstein, 1984, S. 35).

Wenn es uns nicht um Entitätsgleichheit, nicht um eine gemeinsame Bedeutung, nicht um die Verbreitung von Inhalten geht, dann sehen die Mechanismen für Gemeinschaftsbildung ganz anders aus. Dann gleichen sie nicht der Kollaboration, sondern vielmehr dem, was wir hier als „Kooperation" bezeichnen könnten. Für unsere momentanen Zwecke können wir unter „Kooperation" die gemeinsame Nutzung des gleichen Kommunikationssystems oder der gleichen Infrastruktur durch irgendwelche Entitäten verstehen. Gemeinschaft würde dann durch die Interaktionen oder Verbindungen zwischen diesen Entitäten definiert und die Arbeit des globalen Gehirns in Form dieser Interaktionen beschrieben.

Aus der Perspektive des menschlichen Gehirns gibt es einen sehr guten Grund dafür, warum die neuronale Interaktion so vonstatten gehen sollte. Hinge die Schaffung einer neuronalen Gemeinschaft – eines Bewusstseins – davon ab, dass die Neuronen zu einer gemeinsamen Bedeutung gelangen, dann könnte das Bewusstsein als Ganzes nie mehr Bedeutung fassen als ein einzelnes Neuron. Vom Gesichtspunkt eines Bewusstseins ist Bedeutung nichts, das von einem Neuron an das nächste weitergegeben wird, sondern etwas, das der Interaktion von Neuronen entspringt. Ob ein Neuron dasselbe meint wie das andere ist aus der Sicht des Bewusstseins vollkommen unerheblich.

Versteht man Gemeinschaftsbildung als das Resultat einer gemeinsamen Nutzung des gleichen Kommunikationssystems, so ist das nicht Kollaboration, sondern, wie schon gesagt, Kooperation. Kooperation kommt also durch die Herstellung von Verbindungen zwischen den beteiligten Entitäten zustande, die Kommunikationsarbeit zwischen ihnen. Kooperation zwischen Entitäten setzt die Getrenntheit oder Eigenständigkeit ihrer jeweiligen Interessen voraus; in spieltheoretischen Kooperationsmodellen, wie etwa dem Gefangenendilemma, schaffen z. B. erst Einzelinteressen die Möglichkeit zu Konflikt oder Verrat (Mayberry, Harsanyi, Scarf, & Selten, 1992). Der Mechanismus gleicht dem der Marktwirtschaft; auch in ihr werden keine gemeinsamen Ziele vorausgesetzt, sondern lediglich Verhandlungen über ein Interaktionsmittel.

Es gibt keine eindeutige Darstellung davon, wie sich Neuronen miteinander verbinden, wiewohl die biologischen und chemischen Prozesse hinreichend bekannt sind (LeDoux, 2002). Für die Zwecke des vorliegenden Artikels lassen sich aber vier Assoziationsmodelle anführen, die jeweils zumindest einen Teil des Gesamtprozesses beschreiben: die Hebb'sche Assoziation, Assoziation durch Nähe sowie kompetitive („Backpropagation") und harmonische Systeme.

Assoziationsmechanismen unterscheiden sich von den oben unter „Kollaboration" beschriebenen insofern, als dabei keinerlei Leitung oder Führung, kein privilegierter Knoten und keine Hierarchie vorausgesetzt wird. Jede Entität ist autonom. Die bekannteste Form dieses Modells ist wohl Mavin Minskys *Mentopolis*, wo „jeder Geist aus vielen kleineren Prozessen entstanden ist", die er als „Agenten" bezeichnet (Minsky, 1990, S. 17). Eine aus Agenten bestehende (menschliche) Gesellschaft konstituiert für uns wohl auch am ehesten ein globales Bewusstsein, eine Gesellschaft, in der jedes Individuum autonom handelt, seine eigene (einmalige) Funktion ausübt und durch Interaktion (nicht Konformität) mit dem Rest der Gesellschaft Intelligenz ausbildet.

Wir finden die emergente Struktur des Netzes manchmal als „neuen Sozialismus" beschrieben (Kelly, 2009). Doch wird dieser neue Sozialismus gerne im Sinn einer ökonomischen Theorie

Stephen Downes

beschrieben, als Produktion und Konsum von Content. „Es ist bereits ein gewaltiger Online-Fundus an kulturellen Inhalten, Wissen und Tools entstanden. Und wir stehen erst am Anfang der Entwicklung." (David Sasaki, 2009). Es besteht anscheinend der Wunsch, dies als Kollaboration oder eine Art Kollektivismus darzustellen: „Wikipedia, Flickr und Twitter – die ‚Avantgarde einer kulturellen Bewegung', eine im Entstehen begriffene ‚kollektivistische Weltgesellschaft'." Entsprechend scheint es auch die Neigung zu geben, Menschen nach dem Wert ihrer Beiträge (oder gar nach der Anzahl ihrer Verbindungen) zu beurteilen. Der inhaltsgestützte „neue Sozialismus" ist nichts anderes als der autoritätsgestützte, dem Potenzgesetz gehorchende alte Kapitalismus.

Tatsächlich ist der im Internet entstehende „neue Sozialismus" nicht von den alten Stereotypen belastet, die unweigerlich mit seinen US-amerikanischen Beschreibungen einherzugehen scheinen (etwa auch Lawrence Lessigs Definition des „Sozialismus als Zwang", Lessig, 2009). Eine modernere Version des Sozialismus sind die weltweit verbreiteten Formen des „demokratischen Sozialismus", eines Sozialismus der persönlichen Ermächtigung, Chancengleichheit und gleichberechtigten Verbindungs- und Interaktionsmöglichkeiten.

Dieses Konzept ähnelt dem, was Illich „Konvivialität" nennt. Illichs „konvivialen Werkzeuge" sind angemessene, kongeniale Alternativen zu den Herrschaftsinstrumenten, denn sie fördern Lernen, Geselligkeit, Gemeinschaft, „den autonomen und kreativen Austausch zwischen Menschen und zwischen Mensch und Umwelt" (Illich, 1973, S. 27). Damit ließ sich seiner Ansicht nach die Pädagogik so erneuern, dass sie den Bedürfnissen verschiedener Gemeinschaften zu dienen vermag, Demokratie und soziale Gerechtigkeit fördert sowie Lernen und Arbeit im einem Kreativität, Gemeinschaft und ein ökologisches Gleichgewicht zwischen Mensch und Erde fördernden Sinn redefiniert. (Kahn & Kellner, 2007)

Wenn wir das Internet als globales Bewusstsein denken wollen, dann ist die Gemeinschaft, die durch ein solches Netzwerk entsteht, auch eher durch Kooperation als durch Kollaboration gekennzeichnet und wir müssen einige der Attribute dieses Netzwerks überdenken und zu einem neuen Verständnis der Prozesse und Technologien gelangen, die sich am besten für die Herausbildung eines solchen Netzwerks eignen.

Statt Vordenker ausfindig machen zu wollen oder im Netz produzierte Inhalte entdecken und verstehen zu wollen, sollten wir die verschiedenen Teilnehmeraktivitäten als *Interaktions-* und *Kommunikationsakte* begreifen. Die Semantik, die Bedeutung von Interaktionen lässt sich nicht aus ihren Inhalten erschließen, ja die Inhalte sind, aus einem größeren Blickwinkel betrachtet, sogar irrelevant. Wir sollten sie eher als inhaltsleere „Wörter" oder „Zeichen" in einem komplexen, zwischen den einzelnen Entitäten stattfindenden Kommunikationsvorgang behandeln. Ein von einem Skateboarder gemachtes Webvideo: ein Wort. Eine in Photoshop erzeugte Lolcat: ein Wort. Dieser Artikel hier: ein Wort.

Wir kommunizieren miteinander vermittels dieser Worte, und das Wichtige daran ist, erstens, *dass* wir kommunizieren und nicht *wie* oder *was* wir kommunizieren, und zweitens, was diese Kommunikation für uns als Spezies für Konsequenzen hat, und das nicht etwa im Sinn gemeinsamer Ideen, Lehren oder Philosophien, sondern globaler Ausdrucksformen und Verhaltensweisen. In einem solchen Netz gibt es keine besonderen, privilegierten Knoten; Konsumieren ist genauso wichtig wie Produzieren, ja die Rolle von Produzent und Konsument wird (wie oft bemerkt worden ist) geradezu ununterscheidbar, wie übrigens auch – und das ist wesentlich bedeutsamer – die Rolle von Herr und Knecht.

(Aus dem Englischen von Wilfried Prantner)

David Sasaki: *Day 81: Ars Electronica Symposium Examines Cloud Intelligence*, 2009, *http://www.80plus1.org/blog/day-81-ars-electronica-symposium-examines-cloud-intelligence*
Brown, John Seely & Duguid, Paul: *The social life of information*, Harvard Business School Press, Cambridge, Mass. 2000
Cheyne, J. Allan & Tarulli, Donato: „Dialogue, difference, and the ‚third voice' in the zone of proximal development", in *Theory and Psychology* 9, 1999, 5-29
Hebb, Donald O.: *The Organization of Behavior: A Neuropsychological Theory* Lawrence Erlbaum Associates, Mahwah, N.J. 2002
Hofkirchner, Wolfgang: *Beyond the Third Culture! Science in the Information Age*, 2005, *http://www.uti.at/hofkirchner.html*
Kahn, Richard & Kellner, Douglas, „Paulo Freire and Ivan Illich: technology, politics and the reconstruction of education", in *Policy Futures in Education* 5 (4), 2007
Kelly, Kevin: The New Socialism: Global Collectivist Society Is Coming Online, 2009, May 22, *http://www.wired.com/culture/culturereviews/magazine/17-06/nep_newsocialism?currentPage=all*
Kilpatrick, S., Barrett, M., & Jones, T. *Defining Learning Communities*, in *International Education Research Conference*, Association for Research in Education, 2003
LeDoux, Joseph: *Synaptic Self: How Our Brains Become Who We Are*, Viking, New York 2002
Lessig, Laurence: *Et tu, KK? (aka, No, Kevin, this is not „socialism")*, 2009, May 28, *http://www.lessig.org/blog/2009/05/et_tu_kk_aka_no_kevin_this_is.html*
Mayberry, J. P., Harsanyi, J. F., Scarf, H. E., & Selten, R.: *Game-Theoretic Models of Cooperation and Conflict*, Westview Press, 1992
McCarthy, M., *Collaboration in Community*, *http://www.collaborationincommunity.com/*
Marvin Minsky: *Mentopolis*, übers. v. Malte Heim, Klett-Cotta, Stuttgart 1990
David Sasaki (El Oso): *Cloud Intelligence*, 2009, June 12, *http://el-oso.net/blog/archives/2009/06/12/cloud-intelligence/*
Quine, Willard van Orman: *Word and Object*, MIT Press, Cambridge, Mass. 1960
(dt.: *Wort und Gegenstand*, Reclam, Stuttgart 1980)
Rumelhart, D. E., & McClelland, J. L.: *Parallel Distribuuted Processing*, vol. 1, MIT Press, Cambridge, Mass. 1986
Russell, Peter: *The Global Brain: The Awakening Earth in a New Century*, 3rd edition, Floris Books, 2008
Schrage, Michael: *Shared minds: The new technologies of collaboration*, Random House, New York 1990
Senge, Paul: *Die Fünfte Disziplin. Kunst und Praxis der lernenden Organisation*, übers. v. Maren Klostermann, Klett-Cotta, Stuttgart 1996
Tchurovsky, Dimitar: *Global Virtual Brain and Mind Project*, 2009, *http://knol.google.com/k/dimitar-tchurovsky/global-virtual-brain-and-mind-project/mp8du5m8vcjb/4#*
The National Network for Collaboration: *Collaboration Framework – Addressing Community Capacity*, 1995, *http://crs.uvm.edu/nnco/collab/framework.html*
Wittgenstein, Ludwig: *Das Blaue Buch. Eine philosophische Betrachtung (Das braune Buch)*, Werkausgabe, Bd. 5, Suhrkamp, Frankfurt a. M. 1984

Xiao Qiang

Constructing Self-Identity
in the Connected Age

While Google Wave appears to be just a new tool, there are also some great metaphors involved. The flow of bites, a cloud of calculations, a sea of information—these new technologies and their accompanying metaphors all relate to water. Melting, transforming and reorganizing, it's as if mountainous terrain was forming into swamps and wetlands. Interpersonal communiqués and collaborations bring us together in ever more revolutionary ways. Now, we all need to learn to surf on this sea of information. This means that we cannot huddle together on an island any more, nor can we just ride along like passengers on a cruise ship, allowing others to control the direction in which we head.

Clouds are tangible, but lack solid form. They precipitate to form rain, disperse back into vapor, and when they touch the ground, fog is formed. The information age has a kind of new freedom to it, but it also misleads in new ways and brings with it a new kind of danger. The world in which we live has produced new dimensions of information spaces and new organization structures are emerging. These structures form the "network". The network is constantly being reorganized, rejoined, developed and then broken up, and we are left asking, what kind of new world is this that we live in? Amidst the sea of information, every person will ask themselves, how can I get the information that I need. Our memories, languages, lines of thinking, communications and actions all mutually and inseparably influence the cloud of calculations that we have mentioned above. So then how do we define I?

It may be that, as an exile myself, I am particularly sensitive about the question of self-identity that I have created within this fluctuating environment. It may be that, as an activist, I pay particular attention to collective action performed through communication technologies. It may be that my background as a theoretical physicist draws me toward emergent phenomena with rapt attention. In the clouds of calculations and the sea of information, we all have the ability to be innovators.

But life is limited. Time is limited. People's attention spans are limited. For every person on a mission, focusing one's attention for an extended period of time is particularly crucial. As our environment becomes ever more connected and flowing, it becomes more and more important to preserve a relatively stable identity. In modern society, the power to identify is not innate, but rather acquired, changed and created. But the process of identifying is a creative one, and the relative stability that it brings with it enables the ever-changing clouds to assimilate information and gain significance for their existence. Those people who devote themselves to changing the world and who bring about innovation are the inspirational new sources of energy.

When you have discovered where your journey is leading you, when you have found your Noah's ark, part of your identity has been established.

In our cloud of information, we are connected, but we also remain individuals. At the same time we are both searching for and creating our identities. But to find a stable self or identity does not just mean to reach a state of balance in this new "cloud" and sea of information, but also to achieve maturity in life and furthermore, to broaden our horizons and create new things.

Being interconnected has taught us that we need a stable identity, otherwise we fall into chaos and generate without order. Our lives then just continue without us experiencing any kind of intensive excitement or new sources of information. The Cloud is constantly changing. This helps us to become more aware of the importance of the state of changelessness. The process of establishing self-identity is not just a lonely, inward-looking process. On the contrary: our identity can only be formed if we allow ourselves to engage in the world and to explore its processes. When we find our self or our *I* then we also find our *we*. In the clouds of calculations and the sea of information, society has reorganized and defined the relationship between *I* and *we*. Even in the most traditional nation states, this process of re-definition and disintegration is taking place.

Let us take a look at China: an up and coming nation. The revolution in information technology, including the Internet and mobile phones, is currently launching an assault on the ancient nation of tradition. Can the one-party system, which gives the economic development and nationalism as reasons for legitimacy—the Beijing model—really be a sustainable model?

The rulers will, of course, also use technology to control and suppress. But I believe that the real power of the Internet will empower the masses to freely express themselves and work in mutual cooperation. But can this potential be proactively brought into existence? This will largely depend on the ability of individuals to reconstruct their own, new, identity in the digital age. Only when we have constructed an independent, interlinked identity, will we able to become responsible citizens who have reaffirmed truth, justice and freedom, and not just be a disorganized mass that formed within the sea of information.

In the 2.0 network, the updated and increasingly powerful technologies of communication and cooperation will continuously emerge. In the age of the Internet, how will the power of new public spaces and the politics of the people grow? How can the universal values of democracy, human rights and freedom in new media and social organizations coordinate a platform to broaden their impact on China?

We are living in an age of sudden change brought about by technology. Faced with this ever-changing technology, each and every person needs to learn how to use the potential of these powerful tools so that they can grasp their own opportunities, instead of letting technology take control. Not knowing the limitations of technology is dangerous. Those who let themselves just drift along with the currents, superficial and divided, who oppose change and are unable to recognize themselves, end up being the losers. The same is true of those people who lose themselves in these new technologies and are unable to find the right balance between their bodies and minds. And organizations and systems whose purpose consists in controlling people through technology are the biggest enemies of freedom.

Whether in real life or in the Internet, creative innovation constitutes the true meaning of life, and freedom forms the basis of all respect and innovation. But without a substantial identity in life, freedom becomes meaningless. Whether we're concerned with the establishment of identity or with the protection of freedom, this is the era in which the clouds of information fill the air and encompass our entire lives—and we have the opportunity to take action at every moment.

The process of change will inevitably take place. Or perhaps we are already in the middle of this process, regardless of whether we are in China or elsewhere in the world. And there is always a price to pay for change. In the background the law of emerging complexity is at work, which does not, however, prevent individuals from taking the initiative. On the contrary, personal freedom and initiative come into their own during times of sudden change. In the Cloud, the flutter

Xiao Qiang

of a butterfly's wings is enough to stir up a thunderstorm in a tropical rainforest.
Our personal potential and the cloud of information, inside the sea of information, form a brand
new composition in which our skills and efficiency are increased. But it is precisely for this reason that we must retain our modesty and humility. We have to keep simplicity, for this is the
only option open to our souls in this world that inundates us with information.
Our reverence for this new order is unchangeable. If we preserve our identity, don't lose direction and remain humble towards the universe, we can do our best to sail as far as possible in
this sea of clouds

(Translated from Chinese by Reed Riggs)

Xiao Qiang

Identitätskonstruktion im Zeitalter der Vernetzung

„Google Wave" ist nicht nur ein neues Tool, sondern auch eine Metapher. Der Fluss der Bites, die Wolke des Digitalen, das Meer der Information – diese neuen Technologien und die sie begleitenden Metaphern scheinen alle mit „Wasser" zu tun zu haben. Alles verflüssigt, verwandelt und reorganisiert sich; es ist, als würden sich Berge in Sümpfe und Feuchtgebiete verwandeln. Neue Methoden der Kommunikation und Zusammenarbeit vernetzen uns auf immer revolutionärere Weise. Jeder Mensch muss lernen, durch dieses Meer aus Information zu navigieren. Das bedeutet, dass wir uns nicht mehr auf einer kleinen Insel einigeln können, und wir können auch nicht so tun, als wären wir als Passagiere auf einem großen Schiff unterwegs und könnten es anderen Menschen überlassen, die Richtung der Reise zu bestimmen.

Eine Wolke hat eine Gestalt, allerdings wandelt sich diese ständig. Verdichtet sie sich, fällt Regen; zerstreut sie sich, bildet sich Dunst; berührt sie die Erde, bildet sich Nebel. Das Informationszeitalter beschert uns neue Freiheiten, aber birgt gleichzeitig auch neue Verführungen und neue Gefahren. Die Welt, in der wir leben, hat neue Dimensionen von Informationsräumen hervorgebracht, und es tauchen neue emergente Organisationsstrukturen auf. Diese Strukturen bilden das „Netzwerk". Angesichts dieses Netzwerkes, das sich jederzeit neu konfiguriert, neu vernetzt, wächst und unterbrochen werden kann, stellt sich die Frage, in welch neuer Welt wir uns eigentlich bewegen. Im Ozean der Information muss sich jeder Mensch fragen: Wie finde ich die für „mich" nützliche Information? Unsere Erinnerung, Sprache, unser Denken, unsere Kommunikation, unser Verhalten – alles beeinflusst sich gegenseitig innerhalb dieser „Wolke": Wie kann da ein „Ich" definiert werden?

Es mag sein, dass ich als Exilant gegenüber dieser Frage der Identität, die wir uns in einer sich ständig ändernden Umgebung aufbauen, besonders sensibel bin. Es mag sein, dass ich mich als Aktivist besonders dafür interessiere, inwieweit diese neuen Technologien für kollektives Handeln genutzt werden können; vielleicht faszinieren mich all diese neuen, in vernetzten Systemen emergierenden Phänomene, weil ich theoretische Physik studiert habe. In der Wolke dieser Rechenoperationen und im Meer der Information haben wir alle die Chance, auf ganz andere Weise schöpferisch zu werden.

Aber das Leben ist begrenzt. Die Zeit ist begrenzt. Die Aufmerksamkeit des Menschen ist begrenzt. Für Menschen, die sich dem kreativen Schaffen verschrieben haben, ist es besonders wichtig, die Aufmerksamkeit über eine relativ lange Zeit aufrechterhalten zu können. Je vernetzter und fluider unser Umfeld wird, desto wichtiger ist es, dass wir uns eine relativ stabile Identität bewahren können. In unserer modernen Gesellschaft ist Identität nichts „Angeborenes" mehr, sondern etwas, das wir uns nach und nach aneignen, das sich ständig verändert und das wir uns immer wieder aufs Neue erschaffen. Aber der Prozess des ständigen Neuerschaffens einer Identität und damit einer relativen Stabilität ist ausschlaggebend dafür, dass wir in dieser sich unablässig verändernden, unendlichen „Wolke" die für uns relevanten Informationen finden und überleben können. Er ist auch die Inspirations- und Kraftquelle für all jene, die sich für die Verbesserung der Welt einsetzen und Neues schaffen.

Wenn du weißt, wohin deine Reise geht, wenn du deine Arche Noah gefunden hast, dann hast du deine Identität gefunden.

Xiao Qiang

In der „Cloud" sind wir sowohl vernetzte Wesen als auch Individuen. Unsere Identität realisieren wir im Prozess des Suchens, des schöpferischen Aktes. Wenn wir ein stabiles Ich finden wollen, so bedeutet das nicht nur, einen Zustand des Gleichgewichts in dieser neuen „Wolke" und im Meer der Information zu finden, es heißt auch, das Leben reifen zu lassen und zum Teil der umfassenderen, tieferen, neuen Welt zu werden.

Dieses Vernetztsein sagt uns, dass wir eine stabile Identität brauchen, denn sonst bleibt alles Chaos und regelloses Werden. Dann sind wir auch abgeschnitten von diesem tiefen Impuls des Lebens und jeder Quelle von Information.

Die „Wolke" ist im stetigen Wandel begriffen. Dadurch wird uns auch die Wichtigkeit des Nichtwandels bewusster.

Dieser Prozess der Identitätsfindung ist nicht bloß ein einsamer, nach innen gewandter Prozess, ganz im Gegenteil: Unsere Identität kann sich nur dann herausbilden, wenn wir uns auf die Welt einlassen und sie erforschen. Haben wir unser „Ich" gefunden, dann haben wir auch unser „Wir" gefunden. In der „Wolke" der Rechenoperationen und im Meer der Information wird die Gesellschaft durch die Beziehung zwischen dem neuen „Ich" und dem neuen „Wir" reorganisiert und definiert. Und sogar die nach hergebrachter Definition mächtigsten Nationalstaaten sind in diesem Prozess auf dem Rückmarsch und in Auflösung begriffen.

Wenden wir uns nun China zu, einer aufstrebenden Großmacht. Eine technologische Revolution, die vom Internet und den Handy-Netzwerken ausgeht, überrollt gerade dieses so traditionsreiche Land. Kann ein Einparteiensystem, das sich über Wirtschaftswachstum und Nationalismus rechtfertigt – das „Beijing-Modell" –, im Zeitalter der Vernetzung tatsächlich ein nachhaltiges Modell sein?

Natürlich können die Herrschenden die Technologie genauso für Kontrolle und Unterdrückung einsetzen. Aber ich bin überzeugt, dass die eigentliche Macht des Internet darin liegt, dass es die Bürger dazu ermächtigt, ihre Meinung frei zu äußern und koordiniert zu handeln. Ob dieses Potential tatsächlich genutzt werden kann, hängt in hohem Maß auch davon ab, ob die individuelle Identität im digitalen Zeitalter neu konstruiert werden kann. Erst wenn wir uns eine unabhängige, aber vernetzte Identität aufgebaut haben, werden wir in der Lage sein, als verantwortliche Bürger, die für Wahrheit, Gerechtigkeit und Freiheit eintreten, zu handeln und mehr zu sein als nur eine desorganisierte Masse im Meer der Information.

Im Web2.0 tauchen ständig neue, immer mächtigere Tools auf, die Kommunikation und Zusammenarbeit unterstützen. Wie werden sich in einem derart vernetzten Umfeld neue öffentliche Orte herausbilden und die politische Macht der Bürger formieren können? Wie können universelle Werte wie Demokratie, Menschenrechte, Freiheit über diese neuen Technologien und sozialen Netzwerke ihre Wirkung auf die Entwicklung in China ausbauen?

Wir leben in einer Zeit, in der neue Technologien regelrechte Umbrüche herbeiführen. Angesichts der Fülle mächtiger Tools muss jeder Einzelne deren Potential für sich nutzen lernen und seine Chancen selbst wahrnehmen, statt sie der Technologie zu überlassen. Die Grenzen der Technologie nicht zu erkennen ist gefährlich. Wer sich einfach treiben lässt, wer oberflächlich und gespalten ist, sich dem Wandel widersetzt und unfähig ist, sich selbst zu erkennen, wird zu den Verlierern zählen, genauso wie Menschen, die sich in diesen Technologien verlieren und unfähig sind, eine Balance zwischen Körper und Geist herzustellen. Auch sind Organisationen und Systeme, deren Sinn und Zweck darin besteht, mittels Technologie andere Menschen zu kontrollieren, die größten Feinde der Freiheit.

Egal, ob im Internet oder im echten Leben: Kreatives Schaffen ist der eigentliche Sinn des Lebens, und Freiheit ist die Grundlage für Respekt und Kreativität. Aber ohne substanzielle Identität im Leben kann von Freiheit keine Rede sein. Egal, ob es um den Aufbau einer Identität oder um den Schutz der Freiheit geht, in unserer Zeit, in der die Wolke des Digitalen unser ganzes Leben einhüllt, haben wir ständig die Möglichkeit, aktiv zu werden.

Eine abrupte Veränderung wird mit Sicherheit stattfinden. Oder vielleicht befinden wir uns ja gerade in einem derartigen Umbruch, egal, ob in China oder sonst wo auf der Welt. Veränderung hat immer ihren Preis. Das Gesetz der Emergenz von Komplexität, das im Hintergrund wirkt, bedeutet nicht, dass dem Einzelne kein Spielraum für initiatives Handeln bliebe. Im Gegenteil: Persönliche Freiheit und Initiative kommen erst in einer Zeit plötzlichen Wandels so richtig zum Tragen. In der „Cloud" kann der Flügelschlag eines Schmetterlings einen Gewittersturm im Regenwald auslösen.

Unsere persönliche Initiative und die digitale „Cloud" organisieren sich im Meer der Information auf gänzlich neue Weise, wodurch unsere Fähigkeiten und Effizienz eine Steigerung erfahren. Aber genau deswegen muss unser Geist umso demütiger bleiben. Wir müssen uns die Einfachheit wahren – das ist die einzige Wahl, die einer Seele in diesem Überfluss von Information bleibt.

Was wir nicht ändern können, ist unsere Ehrfurcht vor der neuen, fremden Ordnung. Wenn wir unser Ich wahren, die Richtung nicht verlieren und dem Universum Demut entgegenbringen, dann können wir alle unsere Kräfte bündeln, um in der Welt der Wolke am weitesten zu segeln.

(Aus dem Chinesischen von Ingrid Fischer-Schreiber)

Teddy Ruge

A Manifesto for Ages

On February 20th 1909, Filippo Tommaso Marinetti challenged Italy's status quo by laying to white paper his generation's blue print for an awakening.[1] It was a stinging criticism of all that was, a violent cry for what could be but wasn't, a generation's trumpet call for all to shake off a staid past and take on the responsibility of defining a new path. Italy had become too complacent with its rich history of accomplishments. The museums, centuries-old architecture, and dusty libraries—Marinetti was intent on destroying them all. He sent out a call for a new future defined by bold ideas, unapologetic disregard for tradition and the status quo, and a fully clenched punch into the gut of old-schoolism. F. T. Marinetti's *Futurist Manifesto* spawned a Futurist movement that left an indelible mark on every sector of European society—from art to transportation to heavy industry. It was a campaign that defined an era. A defiant movement that crossed oceans and embedded itself all the way into mid-century America's design culture. To Marinetti, Futurism celebrated industrialization, infrastructure, mechanization, militarism and the fiery beauty of machine-gunned speed.

Just a month after the *The Futurist Manifesto* was published, Theodore Roosevelt boarded a steamboat (a symbol of Marinetti's mechanical beasts of speed) in New York for a trip across the Atlantic.[2] He was heading for a safari in Africa. Ironically it was an expedition funded by the Smithsonian Institute and National Geographic Society—the very institutions that Marinetti vociferated against. Institutions that were the gatekeepers and archivists of human and global culture—full of "professors, archaeologists, tourist guides and antiquaries"—worshipers of cemeteries full of strangers.[3] Marinetti believed that prolonging these very institutions wasn't pushing humanity forward, rather, it was holding it back from an overdue, unceremonious and violent push into the future.

Because of it's ferocity and indignation however, it's easy to dismiss *The Futurist Manifesto* as the work of a disgruntled Italian socialite—a histrionic collision of pen and paper, masterfully orchestrated by the mind of an antisocial Italian. While he was Italian by nationality, Marinetti was actually born and raised in Alexandria, Egypt.[4] Marinetti was the most prominent Africa Diasporan of his time—Africa's earliest social commentator. A mastermind at attracting attention, he had the swagger and self-confidence of an accomplished gentleman and commanded respect for fiery manifestos that defined a generation. It's a pity that none of his manifestos openly denounced imperialistic *joie de vivre* and colonial umbrage in Africa.

Migration and the Modern African Diaspora

The Africa of 1909 was characterized by suffocating and imperialistic colonial rule. Natural resources and museum keepsakes, as amassed by the likes of Teddy Roosevelt, exited African shores. The movement to stop the trans-Atlantic slave trade involving millions of Africans had taken place a century earlier, in 1807.[5] 1909 marked nearly 100 years of cultural separation between the last Africans to be exported en masse off the continent. The cultural divide widened by another 50 years, to the 1950's and 1960's, when colonial rule began to disintegrate and be replaced by independent African rule. Voluntary migration patterns resumed in the subsequent decades after independence. One hundred years removed from Marinetti's manifesto, the modern-day voluntary African Diaspora population has grown to just over 3 million in the United States alone.[6]

The Connected Palm

A century after Marinetti's "indefatigable" future, as defined by violent speed, it lives on in the near-instantaneous way we communicate. It is debatable that Marinetti envisioned his "eternal, omnipresent speed" as being applied to the pace of innovation and, conversely, ever-expanding modes of connectivity. Gone are the days spent anticipating the arrival of cross-country letters from loved ones. Enter the always-on, globally-connected network where you are the mailbox and the mailman. Your mailbox is no longer relegated to the sidewalk. It has been uprooted, shrunk and firmly planted in the palm of your hand. The mailbox is digital and mobile; the mailman relegated to schlepping credit card offers and coupons. Not too long ago, it took a month for a letter that I wrote-to-reach my mother deep in the village of Masindi, Uganda. Today, she's able to text me minute by minute updates from a family gathering and I can call her while she swelters over the dinner in her wood-burning stove. We can talk at any time, and in an increasing number of ways. Today's social construct has evolved from John Doe's with physical addresses to walking online personas with witty Twitter handles and an insatiable thirst to broadcast wanton social commentary.

Web 2.0 is the term bestowed upon these various blogging, microblogging, social networking, and media sharing technologies that define today's connected experience—all engineered with a heavy emphasis on interoperability.[7] Simplified, web 2.0 is a "cloud" of multimodal, omnipresent tools that span software and devices, individuals to corporations, civil institutions to presidential elections. Your Facebook network account is connected to your Twitter micro-blog, your Twitter account also feeds content to your blog, which is also populated by your photo stream. So, perhaps it's prophetic that as I write this text, the lexicographers at the English Language Monitor chose "web 2.0" to represent the millionth "neologism" to join the English language.[8] Web 2.0 as a concept—and its encompassing technologies—while less than 10 years old, has revolutionized how the world communicates, collaborates and defines itself—and to Marinetti's probable chagrin, archives itself.[9] This amorphous cloud is quickly becoming the de facto storage locker of human intelligence—a virtual library of man's greatest contribution to destructive manifestos and ideas.

Marinetti would be enraptured, not only by the pervasive speed and disruptive nature of this cloud intelligence, but also by the way the modern day African Diaspora has swiftly adopted web 2.0 as a platform to launch its own digital revolutions and manifestos. He would also be proud of the platform that has democratized the seat of power, transferring the responsibility of archiving man's achievement from the "professors and archeologists" of his time to the global populace. Every connected human being adds his or her contribution to this ever-expanding library.

Africa's Diaspora Contributes to the Cloud

So how are Africa's far-flung children using the cloud as a platform for change? What role is the cloud playing in preserving Africa's cultural connections, knowledge transfer and community building? Is the cloud good for Africa's development, or is it detrimental to Africa's progress?

As much as Marinetti was passionate about Italy's state of development, today's Diaspora is keenly vested in the future of their homelands. Africa's Diaspora is discovering each other in social media networks—exchanging, sharing and broadcasting common bonds and groundbreaking ideas. They are creating virtual communities so far from home and location is no longer as daunting a barrier to the preservation of traditional cultural ties. The village gathering is no longer summoned by the beat of a distant drum, but by the click of a mouse and pregnant mango trees no longer need to serve as shelter for the gatherers. The cloud is the new town hall, the new mango tree. The collective intelligence of Africa's Diaspora population can, for the first time, congregate in the cloud.

For the first time, Africa is also adding its rich history and collective voice to the human archive. No longer are Africa's rich cultural heritage, development and identity championed and hijacked by those from outside and treated as a footnote to human history. Increasingly, Africa's dispersed Diaspora are amassing a collective intelligence of their own—earning and editing their own Wikipedia entries. Just recently, Zambian economist Dambisa Moyo added her voice to the decades-old aid to Africa debate with the release of her book, *Dead Aid*.[10] Until now, the 60-year discussion on the effectiveness of providing aid to Africa has been passionately debated *ad nauseam* in the halls of Western academia by middle-aged, white men. Moyo's consistently firm stance and passionate argument against government-to-government aid is laced with a Marinetti-esque rejection of the status quo. Her command of social media tools—Twitter, Facebook, and Youtube in particular—has spread her message to the masses. Love her or hate her, agree or disagree, Moyo's *Dead Aid* is Marinetti's "roaring motor car which seems to run on machine-gun fire," tearing through "cemeteries of wasted effort" in the aid regime.[11] Moyo's main stream media savvy provides an almost daily stream of recorded interviews, debates and book reviews from around the world, accessible from anywhere at anytime—a virtual pervasive library of an African voice challenging the establishment.

A recent sample survey of the Diaspora's use of technology conducted by my own organization, "Project Diaspora", revealed that Africa's Diaspora is far flung and relying more and more on the cloud to stay connected. 82.35% of respondents said that web 2.0 tools are somewhat or very much responsible for helping them find and connect with other like-minded Diasporans. From a cultural preservation angle, 47% felt web 2.0 very much contributed to their staying integrated with their home cultures. What is surprising though is that a 26.5% majority spent an average of 5 to 8 hours online. More than 17% of the respondents spent more than 10 hours online.[12]

Additionally, Africa's Internet presence, while nascent by Western standards, is also beginning to stay connected. 54.2 million Africans have regular access to the Internet.[13] Recent investments in expanding Africa's access to broadband backhaul infrastructure by Google's 03B Network, and a consortium of undersea cable initiatives on the East and Western shores of Africa will undoubtedly connect more Africans to the cloud in the next few years.[14] A connected Africa is a working Africa, a working Africa is an Africa that's one step closer to economic independence. Paul Kagame, president of Rwanda, recently wrote an op-ed piece on *The Huffington Post* in which he states: "Our economy grew by more than 11% last year, even as the world entered a recession. We have chosen high-end segments of the coffee and tea markets in which to compete, and attract the most demanding world travelers to our tourism experiences. This has enabled us to increase wages by over 20% each year over the last eight years—sustained by, among other things, investment in education, health and ICT."[15]

Conclusion

There's a cloud gathering over Africa—a storm of connected thoughts and ideas that are pushing African countries violently forward. The Diaspora is using emerging web technologies in increasing numbers, frequency, and variety to stay connected with Africa, simultaneously charting a new digital course for its economic independence on the world stage. The Diaspora is also taking on the mantle of issuing its own brand of manifesto for the future of the continent. Africa it seems, is listening. Ten decades removed from Marinetti and Roosevelt's colonial Africa, *The Futurist Manifesto* lives on in the cloud, re-interpreted and broadcast to inspire anew. A media savvy Diaspora charts a new course. What will Africa's collective contribution to the collective human intelligence look like 100 years from now? What role will history say the Diaspora played in Africa's rise? A hundred year's from now, will Marinetti's Futurist celebration of "industrialization, infrastructure, mechanization, and speed" have graced the shores and borders of African countries? Perhaps the only lens one can use to answer those questions is to meditate on this African proverb that has achieved immortality based on its easily retweetable nature: The best time to plant a tree was 20 years ago, the next best time is now.

1   *http://en.wikipedia.org/wiki/Futurist_Manifesto*
2   *http://en.wikipedia.org/wiki/1909*
3   *http://www.cscs.umich.edu/~crshalizi/T4PM/futurist-manifesto.html*
4   *http://bit.ly/BkoXh*
5   *http://en.wikipedia.org/wiki/Atlantic_slave_trade*
6   *http://www.prb.org/pdf07/62.4immigration.pdf*
7   *http://oreilly.com/web2/archive/what-is-web-20.html*
8   *http://www.slate.com/id/2139611/*
9   *http://en.wikipedia.org/wiki/Web_2.0*
10 *http://www.dambisamoyo.com/*
11 *http://www.youtube.com/watch?v=HY8kVaoqB9Q (Futurist Manifesto)*
12 *http://projectdiaspora.org/2009/05/27/survey-the-african-diaspora-and-web-20/*
13 *http://africaincorp.net/cms/wp/2009/06/07/the-10-largest-internet-markets/*
14 *http://manypossibilities.net/african-undersea-cables/*
15 *http://www.huffingtonpost.com/pres-paul-kagame/a-different-discussion-ab_b_213370.html*

Teddy Ruge

Ein Manifest für Jahrhunderte

Am 20. Februar 1909 stellte Filippo Tommaso Marinetti die herrschenden Verhältnisse in Italien infrage, indem er das Manifest seiner Generation als einen Aufruf zur radikalen Erneuerung zu Papier brachte.[1] Es war eine ätzende Kritik an allem Bestehenden, ein wütender Ruf nach allem, was sein könnte, aber nicht war, das Fanfarensignal einer Generation, das an alle appellierte, eine farblose Vergangenheit abzuwerfen und selbst die Verantwortung für einen neuen Weg zu übernehmen. Er rief auf zu einer neuen Zukunft, geprägt von kühnen Ideen, einer kompromisslosen Missachtung der Tradition und des Status quo – ein Fausthieb in das Innerste des Altschulischen und Althergebrachten. F. T. Marinettis *Futuristisches Manifest* löste eine Bewegung aus, die in jedem Bereich der europäischen Gesellschaft dauerhaft Spuren hinterließ. Es war ein Feldzug, der eine Ära prägte. Eine trotzige Bewegung, die Ozeane überquerte und die Designkultur Amerikas um 1950 beeinflusste. Marinetti zufolge besang der Futurismus Industrialisierung, Infrastruktur, Mechanisierung, Militarismus und die kühne Schönheit der Geschwindigkeit, die wie ein Maschinengewehr ratternd dahinbraust.

Nur einen Monat nach dem Erscheinen des *Futuristischen Manifests* ging Theodore Roosevelt in New York an Bord eines Dampfschiffs (ein Symbol für Marinettis „schnaufende Bestien"), um den Atlantik zu überqueren.[2] Er nahm Kurs auf Afrika, wo er an einer Safari teilnehmen wollte. Paradoxerweise wurde die Expedition vom Smithsonian Institute und der National Geographic Society finanziert, jenen Institutionen, gegen die Marinetti ins Feld zog. Institutionen, die die Hüter und Archivare der globalen Kultur waren, voller „Professoren, Archäologen, Fremdenführer und Antiquare", Anbeter von Friedhöfen voller Fremder.[3] Marinetti glaubte, dass die Fortführung dieser Institutionen die Menschheit nicht weiterbrachte, sondern sie vielmehr von einem längst überfälligen, radikalen Kurswechsel abhalten würden.

Es ist leicht, das *Futuristische Manifest* aufgrund seines Furors und seiner Destruktivität als Werk eines aufgebrachten italienischen Salonlöwen abzutun; als theatralische Kollision von Feder und Papier, die von einem gesellschaftsfeindlichen Italiener meisterhaft instrumentiert wurde. Zwar war Marinetti italienischer Staatsbürger, doch wurde er in Alexandria, Ägypten, geboren, wo er auch seine Jugendjahre verbrachte.[4] Marinetti war das prominenteste Mitglied der afrikanischen Diaspora seiner Zeit, Afrikas erster Kommentator. Es ist bedauerlich, dass er in keinem seiner Manifeste offen die imperialistische *joie de vivre* und die koloniale Vorherrschaft in Afrika angriff, die den Kontinent überschatteten.

Migration und die moderne afrikanische Diaspora

Das Afrika des Jahres 1909 war gezeichnet von der Unterdrückung durch die imperialistische Kolonialherrschaft. An den Stränden Afrikas wurden nur Bodenschätze und von Teddy Roosevelt und seinesgleichen angehäufte museale Andenken verschifft. Die Bewegung zur Abschaffung des transatlantischen Sklavenhandels, dessen Leidtragende Millionen Afrikaner waren, hatte sich ein Jahrhundert früher, im Jahr 1807, formiert.[5] 1909 waren fast 100 Jahre vergangen, seit Afrikaner in Massen verschleppt worden waren. Die kulturelle Kluft verbreitete sich nach weiteren 50 Jahren, in den 1950er und 1960er Jahren, als der Kolonialismus bereits im Niedergang begriffen war und durch unabhängige afrikanische Regierungen ersetzt wurde. Die Jahrzehnte nach der Unabhängigkeit waren durch freiwillige Migration gekennzeichnet. Hundert Jahre nach Marinettis Manifest ist die freiwillige afrikanische Diaspora alleine in den Vereinigten Staaten auf mehr als drei Millionen Menschen angewachsen.[6]

Vernetzte Handflächen

Ein Jahrhundert nach Marinettis „rastloser" Zukunft, die durch rasende Geschwindigkeit definiert war, lebt diese in unserer Echtzeitkommunikation weiter. Es ist fraglich, ob Marinetti seine „ewige, allgegenwärtige Geschwindigkeit" auf das Tempo der Innovationen und die unablässig fortschreitende Vernetzung angewendet sehen wollte. Vorbei ist die Zeit, die man in Erwartung des Briefs eines geliebten Menschen verbrachte. Wir sind in ein stets bereites, globales Netzwerk eingebunden, in dem wir Briefkasten und Postbote zugleich sind. Der Briefkasten befindet sich nicht mehr vor dem Haus. Er wurde abgenommen, geschrumpft und in unsere Handflächen implantiert. Der Briefkasten ist digital und mobil, der Postbote dazu degradiert, Kreditkartenangebote und Gutscheine zuzustellen. Vor nicht allzu langer Zeit brauchte ein Brief, den ich meiner Mutter nach Masindi, einem Dorf in Uganda, schickte, einen Monat. Heute kann sie mir im Minutentakt die Neuigkeiten von einem Familientreffen mitteilen, und ich kann sie anrufen, während sie in brütender Hitze das Nachtmahl auf ihrem mit Holz befeuerten Herd zubereitet. Wir können jederzeit miteinander reden und auf immer mehr verschiedene Arten. Otto Normalbürger mit konkreter Adresse hat sich im heutigen gesellschaftlichen Konstrukt zu einer mobilen Online-Person mit witzigem Twitter-Alias entwickelt, die darauf versessen ist, übermütige gesellschaftliche Kommentare zu verbreiten.

Verschiedene Kommunikationsformen wie Blogging, Mikro-Blogging, soziale Netzwerke und Media Sharing Technologies, die die heutige Erfahrung von Vernetzung definieren und alle auf Interoperabilität beruhen, werden unter dem Begriff Web 2.0 zusammengefasst.[7] Vereinfacht ist das Web 2.0 eine „Cloud" multimodaler, omnipräsenter Tools, die Software und Geräte umfasst, die sowohl von Einzelpersonen als auch von Konzernen, staatlichen Institutionen oder bei Präsidentschaftswahlen genutzt werden. Ihr Facebook-Profil ist mit Ihrem Twitter-Mikro-Blog verbunden; Ihr Twitter-Account versieht auch Ihren Blog mit Content, der von Ihrem Foto-Stream mit Bildern ergänzt wird. Vielleicht ist es prophetisch, dass die Lexikografen des *Global Language Monitor*, während ich diesen Text schrieb, den Neologismus Web 2.0 als das millionste Wort in die englische Sprache aufnahmen.[8] Obwohl noch keine zehn Jahre alt, hat das Web 2.0 die Kommunikation, Zusammenarbeit und Selbstdefinition der Welt verändert – und es archiviert sich darüber hinaus selbst, was Marinetti vermutlich gar nicht gefallen hätte.[9] Diese amorphe Cloud entwickelt sich rasch zum Speicher der menschlichen Intelligenz, zu einer virtuellen Bibliothek mit den umfangreichsten Beiträgen der Menschheit zu destruktiven Manifesten und Ideen.

Marinetti wäre nicht nur von der Geschwindigkeit und dem Unruhe stiftenden Potential dieser geballten *Cloud Intelligence* begeistert gewesen, sondern auch davon, wie die moderne afrikanische Diaspora sich das Web 2.0 als Plattform für ihre eigenen digitalen Revolutionen und Manifeste angeeignet hat. Er wäre auch stolz auf eine Plattform gewesen, die eine Demokratisierung von Macht ermöglichte und die Verantwortung für die Archivierung der Errungenschaften der Menschheit von den „Professoren und Archäologen" seiner Zeit auf die breite Masse übertrug. Jede vernetzte Person leistet einen Beitrag zu dieser sich unablässig erweiternden Bibliothek.

Teddy Ruge

Afrikas Diaspora leistet einen Beitrag zur Cloud

Und wie verwenden Afrikas in alle Winde verstreute Kinder die Cloud als Plattform der Veränderung? Welche Rolle spielt diese bei der Bewahrung kultureller Verbindungen, des Wissenstransfers und der Gemeinschaftsbildung in Afrika? Nützt sie der Entwicklung Afrikas oder steht sie dem Fortschritt im Weg?

So wie Marinetti sich leidenschaftlich für die Entwicklung Italiens engagierte, setzt sich die heutige Diaspora für die Zukunft ihrer Heimat ein. Die Mitglieder der afrikanischen Diaspora entdecken einander in sozialen Mediennetzwerken, wo sie ihre Verbundenheit und revolutionäre Ideen austauschen und verbreiten. Sie gründen, weit weg von ihrer Heimat, virtuelle Communitys, und der Ort, an dem man sich befindet, ist kein Hindernis mehr für die Bewahrung kultureller Bande. Die Dorfversammlung wird nicht länger durch den Schlag einer fernen Trommel einberufen, sondern per Mausklick, und die Gemeinde versammelt sich nicht mehr im Schatten fruchtbehangener Mangobäume. Die Cloud ist der neue Mangobaum. Die kollektive Intelligenz der Bevölkerung der afrikanischen Diaspora kann sich erstmals in der Cloud bündeln.

Zum ersten Mal bringt Afrika seine reiche Geschichte und kollektive kulturelle Identität in das Archiv der Menschheit ein. Das kulturelle Erbe, die Entwicklung und Identität Afrikas werden nicht länger von Eindringlingen gerühmt oder ausgebeutet und als Fußnote der Menschheitsgeschichte behandelt. Afrikas zerstreute Diaspora bündelt in Eigeninitiative ihre kollektive Intelligenz, verfasst und editiert ihre eigenen Wikipedia-Einträge. Erst kürzlich mischte sich die Ökonomin Dambisa Moyo aus Sambia mit der Veröffentlichung ihres Buches *Dead Aid* in die seit Jahrzehnten währende Entwicklungshilfedebatte ein.[10] Bis heute wurde die seit 60 Jahren geführte Diskussion über die Wirksamkeit der Hilfe für Afrika ad nauseam in den Hörsälen westlicher Hochschulen von weißen Männern mittleren Alters geführt. Moyos konsequente Stellungnahme und leidenschaftliche Argumentation gegen Entwicklungshilfe von Regierung zu Regierung ist von einer Ablehnung des Status quo im Stil Marinettis geprägt. Ihr geschickter Einsatz sozialer Medien – Twitter, Facebook und insbesondere YouTube – bewirkte, dass ihre Botschaft die Massen erreichte. Man mag sie lieben oder hassen, mit ihr übereinstimmen oder nicht, Moyos *Dead Aid* ist Marinettis „brüllendes Auto, das aus einem Maschinengewehr zu schießen scheint".[11] Moyos intelligente Nutzung der Massenmedien sorgt für eine Flut an Interviews, Diskussionen und Buchbesprechungen aus aller Welt, die täglich aktualisiert und überall und jederzeit zugänglich sind – eine virtuelle omnipräsente Bibliothek einer afrikanischen Stimme, die das Establishment herausfordert.

Eine kürzlich durchgeführte Umfrage über die Verwendung von Technologie in der Diaspora, die von meiner Organisation *Project Diaspora* durchgeführt wurde, ergab, dass Afrikas Diaspora weit verstreut ist und zunehmend über die Cloud miteinander in Verbindung tritt. 82,35 Prozent der Teilnehmer sagten aus, dass die Web-2.0-Tools ein wenig oder sehr dabei behilflich sind, gleichgesinnte Mitglieder der Diaspora zu finden und mit ihnen in Kontakt zu treten. Hinsichtlich der Bewahrung der Kultur meinten 47 Prozent, dass das Web 2.0 einen großen Betrag dazu leistet, dass sie mit ihrer Kultur in Verbindung blieben. Überraschend ist, dass eine Mehrheit von 26,5 Prozent täglich 5,8 Stunden online verbrachte. Mehr als 17 Prozent der Teilnehmer verbrachten über zehn Stunden online.[12]

Auch Afrikas Internet-Infrastruktur, die nach westlichen Standards erst im Entstehen begriffen ist, wurde verbessert. 54,2 Millionen Afrikaner haben regelmäßig Zugang zum Internet.[13] Kürzlich erfolgte Investitionen in den Ausbau von Afrikas Breitband-Internet über das in erster Linie von Google finanzierte O3B-Netzwerk und eine Reihe von Initiativen zur Unterseeverkabelung an den Ost- und Westküsten des Kontinents werden den Afrikanern zweifellos in den kommenden Jahren eine Anbindung an die Cloud ermöglichen.[14] Ein vernetztes Afrika ist ein Afrika der Arbeitsmöglichkeiten und damit der ökonomischen Unabhängigkeit einen Schritt näher. Paul Kagame, der Präsident von Ruanda, schrieb kürzlich in einem Gastkommentar in der *Huffington Post*: „Unsere Wirtschaft wuchs im letzen Jahr, in einer Zeit, in der die Welt in eine Rezession geriet, um mehr als elf Prozent. Wir haben uns auf den Kaffee- und Teemärkten für das Segment Qualitätsprodukte entschieden und unser Tourismus zieht die anspruchsvollsten Reisenden an. Dies hat uns ermöglicht, die Löhne jährlich um mehr als 20 Prozent anzuheben und zusätzlich Investitionen in Bildung, Gesundheit und Informations- und Kommunikationstechnologie zu leisten."[15]

Conclusio

Eine Wolke formiert sich über Afrika, eine Cloud von Gedanken und Ideen, die miteinander verbunden sind und die afrikanischen Länder einen großen Schritt vorwärtsbringen. Die Diaspora verwendet zunehmend und auf verschiedenste Weise neu entstehende Web-Technologien, um mit Afrika in Verbindung zu bleiben, während gleichzeitig in Bezug auf die ökonomische Unabhängigkeit ein neuer digitaler Kurs eingeschlagen wird. Die Diaspora nimmt die Zügel in die Hand, um ihr eigenes Manifest für die Zukunft des Kontinents zu verkünden. Afrika, so hat es den Anschein, hört die Botschaft. Ein Jahrhundert nach Marinetti und Roosevelts Kolonialafrika lebt das *Futuristische Manifest* in der Cloud fort, wird neu interpretiert und verbreitet, um erneut zu inspirieren. Eine medienbewusste Diaspora schlägt einen neuen Kurs ein. Was wird Afrikas kollektiver Beitrag zur kollektiven menschlichen Intelligenz hundert Jahre später sein? Welche Rolle wird die Geschichtsschreibung der Diaspora bei Afrikas Aufstieg zuschreiben? Wird Marinettis futuristische Würdigung von „Industrialisierung, Infrastruktur, Mechanisierung und Geschwindigkeit" hundert Jahre später die Strände und Grenzen der afrikanischen Länder erreichen? Vielleicht lassen sich diese Fragen nur durch das folgende afrikanische Gedicht beantworten, das aufgrund seiner Twitter-Eignung Unsterblichkeit erlangte: Der beste Zeitpunkt, einen Baum zu pflanzen, war vor zwanzig Jahren, der nächstbeste ist jetzt.

(Aus dem Englischen von Martina Bauer)

1   *http://en.wikipedia.org/wiki/Futurist_Manifesto*
2   *http://en.wikipedia.org/wiki/1909*
3   *http://www.cscs.umich.edu/~crshalizi/T4PM/futurist-manifesto.html*
4   *http://bit.ly/BkoXh*
5   *http://en.wikipedia.org/wiki/Atlantic_slave_trade*
6   *http://www.prb.org/pdf07/62.4immigration.pdf*
7   *http://oreilly.com/web2/archive/what-is-web-20.html*
8   *http://www.slate.com/id/2139611/*
9   *http://en.wikipedia.org/wiki/Web_2.0*
10 *http://www.dambisamoyo.com/*
11 *http://www.youtube.com/watch?v=HY8kVaoqB9Q (Futurist Manifesto)*
12 *http://projectdiaspora.org/2009/05/27/survey-the-african-diaspora-and-web-20/*
13 *http://africaincorp.net/cms/wp/2009/06/07/the-10-largest-internet-markets/*
14 *http://manypossibilities.net/african-undersea-cables/*
15 *http://www.huffingtonpost.com/pres-paul-kagame/a-different-discussion-ab_b_213370.html*

Andrés Monroy-Hernández

Unpacking the Cloud
Computation, Media and People

The *cloud* is one of those terms that Marvin Minsky, in his book *The Emotion Machine*, would call a "suitcase word". These words are seemingly well understood in casual conversations, but are often hard to define more formally. Minsky unpacks suitcase words such as "consciousness" and "emotions" with an Artificial Intelligence angle, trying to understand how one could infuse machines with these properties. As something neither synthetic nor human, but a symbiosis of both, what would it mean to unpack the cloud's suitcase?

Built on the idea of cloud computing, the cloud goes beyond it. Often described by its elasticity when it comes to computational capabilities, and by its large and heterogeneous storage when it comes to data and media, the cloud is also about the people it engages. Computation, media and people, all in large numbers, are the core elements that make the cloud our new platform for human expression.

From Cloud Intelligence to Cloud Creativity

The first wave of cloud applications has radically changed communications and information dissemination. Cloud-supported communication such as Twitter and Facebook connect us in real-time in persistent and open spaces. These sites not only let people talk to each other, they also allow us to leave a permanent record of our interactions, building a collective memory of ourselves. On the other hand, Google and Wikipedia have shifted the mechanisms for accessing and spreading knowledge and information. These types of applications have perhaps redefined our epistemological understanding and challenge the meaning of knowing. What does it mean to know something, is it being able to recall the appropriate keywords to retrieve the desired knowledge from a Google search? Or is it more about our capacity to share our insights through an article on Wikipedia?

The discourse around the cloud often emphasizes its capacity to enrich human communication and information dissemination, however, there is a third and perhaps more important capacity that gets less attention: the cloud's role in leveraging human creativity. Media sharing web sites like YouTube, Flickr and LiveJournal are initial explorations of this Cloud Creativity. There are, however, still a lot of limitations and unexplored opportunities for building and creating on the cloud. Broadening participation for engaging more people in creative experiences and building using the cloud's own resources, instead of simply using the cloud to share content, is still ongoing work.

Media sharing is on the path of full democratization thanks to a myriad of sites, some of them for general purposes and others devoted to such specific things like pictures of cats with funny captions. However, building using the cloud as a platform for computation, media storage and crowdsourcing is still only within the reach of expert programmers. For example, creating a new service on the cloud that involves mashing up maps, microblogging and geolocated images is relatively cheap and scalable, but the skills and tools to do it are still not accessible. From a Kurzweilian perspective, cloud creativity seems to obey the laws of accelerating returns, where creating on the cloud would only lead to even more innovation. The open questions are: how to use the technical and social infrastructure of the cloud to give people new opportunities for creative expression and, overall, how can cloud intelligence support cloud creativity?

Democratizing digital expression

In a society mediated by the cloud, the ability to create and build personally meaningful objects using the cloud's own resources seems akin to reading and writing in a society mediated by printed media. What is the meaning of literacy in the age of the cloud? Is reading and writing enough? Are we seeing the need for some kind of new cloud literacy?

Henry Jenkins and other media scholars point out the need for developing New Media Literacies that help young people engage in the participatory culture. The *Scratch* project we have developed at MIT Media Laboratory aims at democratizing digital expression by lowering the barriers to programming. *Scratch* is designed to lets kids and novices create and share their own interactive media, such as games and animations, in an on-line community where people can download each others' creations to remix and learn from them. In two years close to half a million creations have been shared at a rate of about 1,500 a day by more than a thousand people from around the world. The Scratch web site, dubbed the "YouTube of programming", receives more than 600,000 visitors a month from showing that lowering the barriers to programming can engage a wide audience.

One thing that has become evident in the creation of the Scratch online community is that programming is not only more relevant than ever before, it's also a lot more social, more expressive and more artistic. However, there seems to be a disconnect between what traditional programming enables people to do and what is relevant to people's lives on the cloud. A recent survey by the American Computer Machinery found that youth is "driven away" from Computer Science due to the lack of opportunities to "work with people in an interconnected, social and innovative way". This is surprising at first, but when we look closer at the kind of activities students learn in traditional introductory courses to programming, they are mostly about concepts like conditional loops and sort algorithms, which are important, but they are almost not at all about programming mashups using YouTube's RSS feeds or Facebook and Google Maps APIs.

Some would question the relevance of a lot of what we see now in Scratch and in the cloud in general. The content is often superfluous, e.g. remixes of videos of cute cats playing music. However, this is about people, especially young people, building capacities for a future where their participation will be mediated by these same technologies.

Inspired by the success of Scratch 1.0, one could imagine future versions of this or similar tools, to let people build more on this kind of resources. Designers of these technologies need to have a better understanding not only of the evolving cloud computing infrastructure, but also of the social infrastructure on which these tools thrive. Issues of human cooperation and collaboration become as relevant as the challenges of distributed technologies. As culture, politics, arts and sciences become more participatory and engage more amateurs, we need to better understand and develop the social and technical platforms that will support the needs for participation, collaboration and cooperation that people will expect.

Andrés Monroy-Hernández

Die Cloud

Datenverarbeitung, Medien und Menschen

Der Begriff *Cloud* zählt zu jenen Begriffen, die Marvin Minsky in seinem Buch *The Emotion Machine* als „Kofferwort" bezeichnen würde. Solche Begriffe sind im alltäglichen Sprachgebrauch durchwegs verständlich, entziehen sich jedoch oft einer formellen Definition. Packt Minsky Kofferwörter wie etwa „Bewusstsein" oder „Gefühle" aus, so tut er das aus der Perspektive der Künstlichen Intelligenz, d. h. er will herausfinden, wie sich diese Eigenschaften auf Maschinen übertragen lassen. Was würde etwa geschehen, wenn man die Cloud – die ja weder synthetisch noch menschlich, sondern eine Symbiose aus beidem ist – „auszupacken" versucht?

Die Cloud beruht auf dem Konzept des *Cloud Computing*, geht jedoch darüber hinaus. Hinsichtlich ihrer Rechenkapazitäten wird häufig ihre Skalierbarkeit hervorgehoben, im Hinblick auf Daten und Medien ihre enorme, heterogene Speicherfähigkeit – doch auch die Menschen, die sich mit ihr befassen, spielen eine wesentliche Rolle. Rechnen, Medien und Menschen – und zwar jeweils in gewaltigen Dimensionen – sind die Schlüsselelemente, die die Cloud zur neuen Plattform menschlicher Ausdrucksweise machen.

Von der *Cloud Intelligence* zur *Cloud Creativity*

Die erste Welle von Anwendungen in der Cloud hat radikale Veränderungen im Kommunikationsbereich und in der Informationsverbreitung bewirkt. Auf die Cloud gestützte Kommunikation, etwa über Twitter und Facebook, verbindet uns in Echtzeit über weite, persistente Räume hinweg. Solche Websites ermöglichen nicht nur die Kommunikation, sondern auch die dauerhafte Protokollierung der erfolgten Interaktionen – und konstruieren so eine kollektive Erinnerung an uns selbst. Google und *Wikipedia* wiederum haben zu einer Verschiebung der Zugriffs- und Verbreitungsmechanismen für Informationen und Wissen geführt. Anwendungen dieser Art haben das Potential, unser erkenntnistheoretisches Verständnis neu zu definieren und unsere Auffassung von „Wissen" zu hinterfragen. Was bedeutet es heute, etwas zu wissen? Heißt „wissen", die richtigen Stichwörter zu kennen, die bei einer Google-Suche das erwünschte Ergebnis liefern? Oder geht es eher darum, dass man weiß, wie man über einen *Wikipedia*-Artikel andere an seinen Erkenntnissen teilhaben lässt?

Im fachlichen Diskurs wird häufig betont, wie bereichernd die Cloud für die menschliche Kommunikation und die Verbreitung von Informationen ist. Doch gibt es eine dritte und vielleicht wichtigeren Funktion, die gerne übersehen wird: Die Cloud verhilft der menschlichen Kreativität zum Durchbruch. Websites wie YouTube, Flickr und LiveJournal, die auf Media-Sharing beruhen, sind erste Spielwiesen der *Cloud Creativity*. Doch unterliegt die kreative Nutzung der Cloud derzeit noch zahlreichen Einschränkungen, und viele Ausbaumöglichkeiten sind nach wie vor unerforscht. Noch gilt es in erster Linie, den Teilnehmerkreis zu erweitern, sodass mehr Menschen auf die Ressourcen in der Cloud zugreifen, kreative Erfahrungen machen und am weiteren Ausbau der Cloud mitwirken können, statt sie bloß zum (Mit)Teilen von Inhalten zu nutzen.

Dank zahlloser Websites, die entweder für allgemeine Zwecke eingerichtet wurden oder sehr spezifischen Zwecken dienen (wie etwa der Verbreitung von Katzenfotos mit lustigen Untertiteln) schreitet die Demokratisierung des Media-Sharing unaufhaltsam voran. Doch der weitere

Ausbau dieser Technologie auf Basis der Cloud als Plattform für Computation, Media-Storage und Crowdsourcing bleibt weiterhin Berufsprogrammierern vorbehalten. In der Cloud einen neuen Dienst einzurichten, der Map-Mashups, Microblogging und im Geo-Location-Verfahren erstellte Bilder umfasst, ist relativ kostengünstig und skalierbar, aber die dafür erforderlichen Kenntnisse und Werkzeuge sind nach wie vor nicht allen zugänglich. Aus einer Kurzweil'schen Perspektive scheint die Cloud Creativity den Gesetzen des sich beschleunigenden Nutzens zu unterliegen. Demzufolge würde schöpferische Tätigkeit in der Cloud zu immer weiteren Innovationen führen. Es stellt sich also die Frage, wie mittels der technischen und sozialen Infrastruktur der Cloud neue Möglichkeiten zur kreativen Entfaltung geschaffen werden können – oder ganz allgemein, wie sich Cloud Intelligence zur Unterstützung von Cloud Creativity nutzen lässt.

Die Demokratisierung der digitalen Ausdrucksmöglichkeit

In einer von der Cloud mediierten Gesellschaft ist die Fähigkeit, unter Nutzung von Cloud-Ressourcen Objekte von persönlicher Bedeutung zu erschaffen und weiterzuentwickeln, vergleichbar mit der Fähigkeit des Schreibens und Lesens in der von den Printmedien mediierten Gesellschaft. Was sind also die erforderlichen Grundkenntnisse im Zeitalter der Cloud? Reicht Schreiben und Lesen auch weiterhin aus? Oder zeichnet sich ab, dass zur Nutzung der Cloud ganz neue Grundkenntnisse erforderlich sind?

Henry Jenkins und andere Medienwissenschaftler verweisen auf die Notwendigkeit, im Bereich Neue Medien spezifische Grundkenntnisse (sogenannte New Media Literacies) zu vermitteln, die junge Menschen zur Teilnahme an dieser partizipatorischen Kultur befähigen sollen. Das am MIT Media Laboratory entwickelte Projekt *Scratch* versucht, durch Abbau programmiertechnischer Barrieren die digitale Ausdrucksform zu demokratisieren. *Scratch* ist so konzipiert, dass Kinder und Computerneulinge ihre eigenen interaktiven Medien – etwa Spiele und Animationen – schaffen und gemeinsam nutzen können. Dies erfolgt im Rahmen einer Community, deren Teilnehmer die Kreationen der anderen herunterladen, neu kombinieren und sich so neue Fertigkeiten aneignen. Innerhalb von zwei Jahren wurde so – bei einer Rate von rund 1.500 Zugriffen pro Tag – knapp eine halbe Million Werke von mehr als tausend Personen weltweit genutzt. Die *Scratch*-Website, die auch als „*YouTube* für Programmierer" bezeichnet wird, verzeichnet monatlich mehr als 600.000 Zugriffe aus der ganzen Welt – was eindeutig beweist, dass geringere Einstiegshürden beim Programmieren auf breites Interesse stoßen.

Die Entstehung der *Scratch*-Community hat außerdem gezeigt, dass Programmieren nicht nur relevanter ist als je zuvor, sondern dass es darüber hinaus viel sozialer, expressiver und künstlerischer geworden ist. Dennoch scheint die Verbindung zwischen herkömmlichen Programmierkenntnissen und den für das virtuelle Leben der Teilnehmer an der Cloud erforderlichen Fertigkeiten gekappt zu sein. Laut einer kürzlich von der American Computer Machinery durchgeführten Umfrage wenden sich junge Menschen von der Computerwissenschaft ab, da diese zu wenige Möglichkeiten bietet, „auf vernetzte, soziale und innovative Art mit Menschen zu arbeiten". Dies scheint auf den ersten Blick erstaunlich. Bei näherer Betrachtung stellt sich jedoch rasch heraus, dass die in „Programmieren für Anfänger" vermittelten Standardkenntnisse in erster Linie bedingte Schleifen oder Sortieralgorithmen umfassen – gewiss wichtige Inhalte, die einem aber so gut wie gar nicht weiterhelfen, wenn man Mashups mit RSS-Feeds von YouTube oder mit APIs von Facebook oder Google Maps programmieren will.

Vieles, was sich derzeit in *Scratch* im Besonderen und in der Cloud im Allgemeinen abspielt, lässt

Andrés Monroy-Hernández

sich kritisch hinterfragen. Oft mag es tatsächlich überflüssig sein – etwa der Remix eines Videos niedlicher, musizierender Kätzchen. Doch der springende Punkt ist, dass sich hier – insbesondere junge – Menschen Fertigkeiten für eine Zukunft aneignen, in der sie genau mit Hilfe dieser Technologien kommunizieren und interagieren werden.

Inspiriert vom Erfolg von *Scratch 1.0* wären künftige Versionen dieses oder ähnlicher Tools denkbar, die noch stärker auf den Ressourcen der Cloud aufbauen. Wer solche Technologien entwirft, muss nicht nur die sich laufend weiterentwickelnde Infrastruktur des Cloud Computing besser verstehen lernen, sondern auch die ihr zugrunde liegende soziale Infrastruktur. Fragen des menschlichen Zusammenarbeitens und Zusammenwirkens spielen dabei ebenso eine Rolle wie die Herausforderungen verteilter Technologien. Je stärker Kultur, Politik, Kunst und Wissenschaft auf dem Partizipationsprinzip aufbauen und je öfter in diesen Bereichen Amateure miteinbezogen werden, desto wichtiger werden Verständnis und Entwicklung von sozialen und technischen Plattformen, die den zu erwartenden Bedarf an Partizipation, Kooperation und Zusammenwirken unterstützen.

(Aus dem Englischen von Susanne Steinacher)

Ethan Zuckerman

The Cloud: Bringing About the Prophecy

In the distant past, when the Internet was without form and void, before the days of Twitter, web 2.0 and graphical browsers, there was Usenet. It was a vast, rowdy community of conversations, where the tens of thousands of people connected by the early Internet talked about everything from Esperanto to espresso.

One April morning, a message arrived on the network from a computer named "Kremvax". It began, "Well, today, 840401, this is at last the Socialist Union of Soviet Republics joining the Usenet network and saying hallo to everybody."

Arriving in the late days of the Cold War, the message provoked a flurry of reactions. Some welcomed the unexpected new users to the net; others expressed their hope that the Soviets wouldn't use Usenet for propaganda. A skeptical few noticed the date on the message and realized the post was an elegant April Fools' joke.

The joke was funny because it was eminently believable. Usenet users were used to conversing with people all around the world—the advice on brewing a great cup of espresso might come from Texas or from Tokyo. And, despite the fact that the Internet wasn't far from its past as a US military research project, there were no restrictions on who could connect a computer to the Internet. It was technically possible that someone had connected a phone line between a computer that was connected and a machine in Moscow.

Usenet gave users a very real experience of a larger, more connected world. It made it possible to imagine a world one step more connected, where an online space would permit encounters between cold war rivals. It made it possible to imagine a form of cosmopolitanism not yet present in the physical world.

This type of imagining can be useful, and it can also be deceptive. We need to imagine a more connected world before we work to make one possible. But we need to be careful that this imaginary cosmopolitanism doesn't fool us into thinking that we live in a world where barriers of language, culture and national identity have vanished.

Like many of the infrastructures that hold together our connected world, the Internet disguises distance. Just as airplanes allow us the useful illusion that New York and London are as close as Vienna and Innsbruck, the Internet allows us to imagine ourselves co-present with people halfway across the globe. (It is easier to maintain this illusion in a comfortable apartment with a high-speed connection than in a cybercafé in Freetown, Sierra Leone, where you are paying a dollar an hour for a painfully slow connection.)

It's a useful illusion because it enables new and productive behaviors. It turns my living room into the world's largest record store, a library filled with scholars jointly writing an encyclopedia, a coffee shop filled with friends I've known for decades and those I've never met. The danger is in embracing the analogy too thoroughly. When I forget that we're not physically in the same place and assume that my colleague in Nairobi will understand the reference I make to US politics or the local sports team, I'm reminded that the death of distance is just a useful illusion.

We're now invited to partake in an exciting and useful new illusion—the Cloud. The Cloud promises us that it no longer matters where our bits live. Instead of focusing on the complex, intricate infrastructure that makes the Internet work, we're asked to trust that our email, our photographs, our memos and love letters are somewhere out there, somewhere safe, being watched over by "machines of loving grace".

While this all sounds hauntingly familiar to those of us who remember the age of mainframe computing, it's a useful illusion because it encourages us to behave as if our bits are part of a larger whole. They're not just my vacation photos from Denmark—they're part of a global collection of photos of Copenhagen, helping the Filipino student studying Hans Christian Andersen or the Danish urban planner, mapping her city, to better understand it. With little effort, and sometimes with less intention, we find ourselves as collaborators in thousands of global projects.

This sort of sharing can feel good and rewarding, encouraging us to look beyond our local orbits for ideas, support and solidarity. Or it can feel involuntary and coerced. Every time I search, every time I place a link to a webpage on my blog, I help Google tune its search algorithms a bit more precisely. I benefit from an improving search engine, but can't help wondering if I shouldn't get a stock dividend as well.

The Cloud invites us to ignore the infrastructure that makes everyday miracles—reading my email on my phone in Accra, Ghana—possible. But before we accept this useful illusion, it's worth a close look at what we're choosing to ignore. There's a complex web of electrical lines, telecommunications cables and cellular towers that makes my email reading possible. The single, overcrowded cable that connects West Africa to the global Internet helps explain why there's not a lot of video from Accra posted on YouTube—while Ghana's 3G mobile phone system is faster and more powerful than the system I use in the US, the connection to the Internet is so tenuous that uploading videos from my phone is prohibitively expensive. Look at the map of electric connections and it becomes clear why there aren't a lot of bloggers in rural Mali—there's not a lot of electrical power to power the towers or allow bloggers to charge their phones.

Humans have a fascination with mapping infrastructure. Atlases from the 19th century are filled with intricate spiderwebs of railroad tracks and the gentle arcs of oceanic shipping routes. At the end of the twentieth century, we drew impossibly complex maps of the Internet, maps that ceased to be useful for any sort of navigation, but showed an intricacy that evoked spiderwebs, snarled yarn and connected neurons.

Mapping infrastructure tells us what's possible. We discover the road that leads to the small mountain town, the airplane service that connects the island nation to the rest of the world. But these maps can be deceptive as well. While they show us what's possible, they're not very informative about what actually happens.

Imagine the street map of a city. Those streets show you the locations where a taxi might go, picking up and dropping off passengers. Now imagine another map. This one emerges over time, and it's drawn by taxis trailing lines of light behind themselves. We'd see patterns emerge very quickly—from the train station to the business district, from the business district to the airport. We'd see patterns we might not expect, from poorer neighborhoods to hospitals, carrying patients. And we'd discover that some parts of town remain unmarked—the taxis could go there, but they don't, perhaps because no one wants a ride, or perhaps because taxi drivers don't want the passengers who live there.

The map that would emerge—a map built by artists at Stamen Design of the city of San Francisco—isn't a map of infrastructure, but a map of flow. The designers used the GPS system in taxicabs to watch the movements of taxis over the course of a day and combined their paths into a map. The resulting map shows us how taxis actually move in the city, the neighborhoods where traffic ebbs and flows, the parts of town where taxis never go. While the street map—a map of infrastructure—shows us what's possible, a map of flow shows us what actually happens.

Maps of flow aren't very common yet, but they are exceedingly useful. Knowing if the road out of the city to the weekend house is packed with traffic or empty is critical information before leaving town. Knowing how pedestrians move from the train to their workplaces is critical for the shopkeeper who wants to place his cafe in the right area. But while infrastructure stays put—making it easy to map—flow is always changing. Mapping flow is a form of surveillance.

If we map the infrastructures of communication, we discover that it's possible for people in almost every nation to connect to the Internet. We discover that the Internet connects big cities, but not many rural areas; that people in east Africa are connected by satellite dish, not by undersea cable; that farmers in Nigeria can call relatives in Lagos or in London. What these maps of cables don't tell us is what actually happens, who speaks to whom, who reads what, who shares what.

When I read the morning newspaper twenty years ago, I had two choices—the thin local newspaper, and the thick New York Times, both available at the corner store. Today, I can read the *Daily Nation* from Nairobi, the *Mail and Guardian* from South Africa, the *Manchester Guardian*, the *Times of India* or the *Shanghai Daily*. If I'm willing to stretch my language skills—or trust online translation services—my options expand further. And if I include the hundreds of millions of bloggers, twitterers, message board posters, videomakers and podcasters, my options expand exponentially.

But most days, I read the *New York Times*, my local paper, the blogs of a few friends I know well. And, in this, I'm like most people in the world. I'm connected to an infrastructure that allows me information, opinion and perspective from vast swaths of the globe. I can read bloggers from Borneo, or watch television from Bulgaria. But the media I actually encounter—the flow of my attention—is local, focused on my home community and nation and on my particular interests.

When we track attention in a connected world, we look at infrastructure and flow, as we might with airplanes. The map of infrastructure shows you that there's a series of flights that connects Linz and Lilongwe—the map of flow shows you that virtually no one ever makes that journey. Most flights take off and land in the same country. Most people read, listen and watch locally, nationally, more than globally.

It's okay. It's a fundamental human tendency. We're not used to living in this massively interconnected world. As Kwame Appiah observes, a dozen generations ago, very few of us would have encountered people of another religion or race. It's only very recently that we've all had the opportunity to become cosmopolitans, and only within the past few years that we've lived in a world where it was possible to know what someone in Samoa was thinking and feeling moment to moment. Our instinct is to pay attention to the familiar, to follow the suggestions of people we already know, to flock with those who look and think like us.

But just because the tendency to choose a smaller world is a basic human frailty doesn't mean we should accept it. The infrastructures that hold us together also bind us, inextricably. Our problems are global ones—pandemic, global warming, terrorism—and so are our solutions. If we can imagine healing and bettering the world, we are imagining connecting with people across the globe to build solutions and find different ways of living.

Ethan Zuckerman

The Cloud encourages us to imagine a world where infrastructure doesn't matter, where ideas and solutions can come from anyone and anywhere. Perhaps this is the useful illusion that frees us from old ways of thinking, lets us embrace solutions that come from halfway around that world, that we might have rejected had we known its provenance.

I fear that, if we're honest with ourselves, we'll discover that the flow of ideas through the Cloud isn't as frictionless and global as we might hope. The steep, sheer barriers of language render much of what's posted online incomprehensible to us—the Chinese blog posts and the Spanish language videos. On a polyglot Internet, there's more to read everyday, but less that each of us, individually, can understand. We've made great strides in making it possible for everyone to write online, releasing our words into the Cloud, but we've done far less work ensuring that we can read and understand what each other has to say.

In a world where many, if not everyone, can write online, we need editors, gatekeepers and filters more than ever. We're experimenting with new techniques to sift through the Cloud and discover what interests us. We build tools that let us see what pages our friends find interesting, that let groups of people vote for what should be featured on the front page. With many eyes, we can see a broader stretch of the Cloud. But ultimately, our view is as broad as that of the people we ask to help us navigate. If we flock together with like-minded fellows—as humans tend to do—we risk missing the serendipity of the critical recommendation from Nepal or Nigeria.

The Cloud tempts us into thinking that we are more global than we actually are. When we imagine a Cloud of bits from everywhere, divorced from physical reality, we can forget that infrastructure doesn't yet extend to every corner of the world and systematically excludes places that are poor, un-free, disconnected. We are tempted to forget that our attention tends to flow towards our co-linguists, our countrymen, our friends, and that we must consciously and continually challenge ourselves to break away from our flock and experience a wider world.

Shortly before the first World War, radio pioneer Marconi predicted that radio would make war impossible, because we'd be able to hear and understand the voices of people of other nations and would realize the futility of attacking and destroying them. Nine decades later, Internet enthusiast John Perry Barlow predicted a world without borders, where states no longer mattered, where humans would organize themselves in a new, egalitarian way through the Internet. Barlow and Marconi made poor predictions, but they were both excellent prophets. The prophet's job is not to tell you what will happen, but what could happen, if you work to make it happen.

The Cloud is a prophecy. It's a beautiful dream of the future where we find ways to connect every corner of the world. It asks us to overcome the challenges of language, to break out of our usual orbits and familiar flocks and discover new, global, connected solutions to new, global, connected problems. We need to imagine this future so we can build it. But we must remember what we're imagining and what's real. We must continually challenge ourselves and not merely embrace and celebrate a useful illusion.

Ethan Zuckerman

The Cloud: Der Traum von der Zukunft

In ferner Vergangenheit, als das Internet noch formlos und leer war, lang vor Twitter, Web 2.0 und grafischen Browsern, da gab es das Usenet. Es war eine riesige streitlustige Diskussionsrunde, in der sich Zehntausende, über das frühe Internet miteinander verbundene Menschen über alles Mögliche unterhielten – von Esperanto bis Espresso.

An einem Aprilmorgen traf in diesem Netzwerk eine Nachricht von einem Computer namens „Kremvax" ein, die mit den Worten begann: „Heute, am 1. 4. 84, schließt sich endlich auch die Sozialistische Union der Sowjetrepubliken dem Usenet an und grüßt allerseits."

Die in der Endphase des Kalten Krieges einlangende Nachricht versetzte alle in Aufregung. Manche hießen die unerwarteten neuen Nutzer im Netz willkommen, andere gaben der Hoffnung Ausdruck, die Sowjets möchten das Usenet nicht für Propagandazwecke missbrauchen. Ein paar Skeptikern fiel das Datum der Nachricht auf, und sie erkannten, dass es sich dabei um einen gelungenen Aprilscherz handelte.

Der Scherz war gelungen, weil er so glaubhaft war. Usenet-Nutzer waren es gewohnt, mit Leuten aus aller Welt zu kommunizieren – der Rat, wie man einen tollen Espresso macht, konnte ebenso aus Texas wie aus Tokio kommen. Und auch wenn das Internet gerade erst seinen Anfängen als US-Militärforschungsprojekt entwachsen war, so konnte doch jeder seinen Computer uneingeschränkt daran anschließen. Es war technisch durchaus möglich, dass jemand einen ans Netz angeschlossenen Computer über eine Telefonleitung mit einem Rechner in Moskau verbunden hatte.

Das Usenet vermittelte seinen Nutzern glaubhaft das Gefühl einer größeren, verbundenen Welt. In ihm konnte man sich eine Welt vorstellen, die ein Stück zusammengerückt war und in der online sogar Begegnungen zwischen den Rivalen des Kalten Kriegs denkbar waren. In ihm konnte man sich einen Kosmopolitismus vorstellen, der in der physischen Welt noch nicht existierte.

Solche Vorstellungen können nützlich sein, sie können aber auch täuschen. Wir müssen uns eine verbundene Welt vorstellen, um sie in die Tat umsetzen zu können. Wir müssen aber auch aufpassen, dass uns ein solcher imaginierter Kosmopolitismus nicht vorgaukelt, wir lebten bereits in einer Welt, in der alle sprachlichen, kulturellen und nationalen Barrieren verschwunden sind. Wie viele der Infrastrukturen, die unsere vernetzte Welt zusammenhalten, verschleiert das Internet Entfernungen. Lassen Flugzeuge die Distanz zwischen New York und London auf die zwischen Wien und Innsbruck schrumpfen, so vermittelt uns das Internet die Illusion einer Ko-Präsenz mit Menschen auf der anderen Seite des Erdballs. (In einer gemütlichen Wohnung mit Breitbandanschluss ist man klarerweise anfälliger für diese Illusion als in einem Cybercafé in Freetown, Sierra Leone, wo man einen Dollar die Stunde für eine lähmend langsame Verbindung zahlt.)

Es ist eine nützliche Illusion, weil sie neue und produktive Verhaltensweisen ermöglicht. Sie verwandelt mein Wohnzimmer in den größten Plattenladen der Welt, eine Bibliothek voller Wissenschaftler, die gemeinsam an einer Enzyklopädie schreiben, ein Café voller Freunde – solcher, die ich seit Jahren kenne, und solcher, denen ich noch nie begegnet bin. Gefährlich wird's, wenn man die Analogie zu weit treibt. Wenn ich vergesse, dass wir physisch nicht denselben Raum teilen und gegenüber meinem Kollegen in Nairobi ganz selbstverständlich auf die US-Politik oder ein lokales Sportteam Bezug nehme, dann wird mir plötzlich klar, dass der „Tod der Entfernung" lediglich eine nützliche Illusion ist.

Jetzt sollen wir uns einer neuen nützlichen Illusion hingeben – der Cloud. In der Cloud – so verspricht man uns – spielt es keine Rolle mehr, wo unsere Bits zu Hause sind. Statt uns mit der komplexen, verschlungenen Struktur des Internet herumzuschlagen, sollen wir einfach darauf vertrauen, dass unsere E-Mails, Fotos, Memos und Liebesbriefe sich irgendwo da draußen befinden, an einem sicheren Ort, „behütet von fürsorglichen Maschinen"[1].

Zwar klingt das für diejenigen von uns, die sich noch an die Zeit der Großrechner erinnern, gespenstisch vertraut, doch handelt es sich durchaus um eine neue nützliche Illusion, weil sie uns dazu ermutigt, uns so zu verhalten, als seien unsere Bits Teil eines größeren Ganzen. Es sind nicht mehr bloß meine Urlaubsfotos aus Dänemark, sie sind vielmehr Teil eines globalen Fotoalbums über Kopenhagen, das z. B. einem philippinischen Studenten beim Verständnis von Hans Christian Andersen oder einer dänischen Stadtplanerin beim Kartieren ihrer Stadt hilft. Mit geringem Aufwand und manchmal noch weniger Absicht, werden wir plötzlich zu Mitarbeitern bei Tausenden Projekten in aller Welt.

Diese Art Austausch kann als angenehm und lohnend empfunden werden, uns ermutigen, in puncto Ideen, Hilfestellung und Solidarität über den eigenen Tellerrand hinauszuschauen, kann aber auch als von außen aufgezwungen erscheinen. Bei jedem Suchvorgang, immer wenn ich meinem Blog einen Link hinzufüge, helfe ich Google seine Suchalgorithmen zu verfeinern. Ich profitiere zwar von einer verbesserten Suchmaschine, aber ich frage mich auch, ob ich dafür nicht ein paar Freiaktien kriegen sollte.

Die Cloud verleitet uns, die Infrastruktur zu ignorieren, die Alltagswunder wie das Lesen meiner E-Mails auf dem Telefon in Accra, Ghana, möglich macht. Ehe wir diese nützliche Illusion akzeptieren, ist es aber ratsam, einen näheren Blick auf das zu werfen, was wir ignorieren. Das Lesen meiner E-Mails wird mir durch ein verschlungenes Netz elektrischer Leitungen, Telefonkabel und Mobilfunkmasten ermöglicht. Aus dem überlasteten einzigen Kabelstrang, der Westafrika mit dem globalen Internet verbindet, erklärt sich, warum auf YouTube nicht gerade viele Videos aus Accra zu sehen sind. Zwar ist Ghanas 3G-Mobilfunksystem schneller und leistungsstärker als das, das ich in den USA benutze, aber die Internetverbindung ist dermaßen langsam, dass sich das Hochladen von Videos vom Telefon aus Kostengründen verbietet. Ein Blick auf die Karte der elektrischen Leitungen macht klar, warum es im ländlichen Mali nicht viele Blogger gibt – es gibt einfach zu wenig Strom, um die Funkmasten zu versorgen oder das Aufladen der Telefone zu ermöglichen.

Menschen scheinen eine Vorliebe für Infrastrukturkarten zu haben. Die Atlanten des 19. Jahrhunderts sind überzogen vom dichten Liniennetz der Eisenbahnen und den sanft geschwungenen Bögen ozeanischer Schifffahrtsrouten. Ende des 20. Jahrhunderts wurden dann unmöglich komplexe Karten des Internets angefertigt, Karten, die von keinerlei Nutzen für die Navigation mehr waren, aber in ihrer Komplexität an Spinnengewebe, Fadengewirre oder Neuronenverbindungen erinnerten.

Infrastrukturkarten zeigen uns, was möglich ist. Mit ihrer Hilfe finden wir den Weg, der in das kleine Bergdorf führt, die Fluglinie, die den Inselstaat mit dem Rest der Welt verbindet. Aber diese Karten können auch trügerisch sein. Sie zeigen uns zwar, was möglich ist, sind aber nicht sonderlich informativ in Bezug auf das, was wirklich der Fall ist. Stellen wir uns einen Stadtplan vor. Die Straßen zeigen, wo z. B. Taxis hinfahren können, um Passagiere aufzunehmen und abzusetzen. Nun stellen wir uns eine andere Karte vor, eine, die im Lauf der Zeit entsteht, indem die Taxis Lichtspuren hinterlassen. Wir würden schon bald bestimmte Muster wahrnehmen – vom Bahnhof zum Geschäftsviertel, vom Geschäftsviertel zum Flughafen. Wir würden auch weniger erwartete Muster wahrnehmen, aus ärmeren Vierteln in Spitäler: Patiententransporte. Und wir würden sehen, dass einige Stadtteile leer bleiben – dass die Taxis da zwar hinfahren könnten, aber es nicht tun, weil da niemand hin will oder weil die Fahrer etwas gegen die Passagiere haben, die da wohnen.

Die so entstehende Karte – wie sie Künstler der Firma Stamen Design für San Francisco entwickelt haben – ist dann keine Infrastrukturkarte mehr, sondern eine Karte der Ströme. Die Designer verfolgten mithilfe des in die Taxis eingebauten GPS-Systems die Fahrten, die diese im Lauf eines Tages absolvierten, und verknüpften ihre Wege zu einer Karte. Diese zeigt, wie sich die Taxis tatsächlich durch die Stadt bewegen, wie der Verkehr in bestimmten Vierteln zu- und abnimmt, und wo Taxis niemals hinkommen. Zeigt uns der Stadtplan – eine Infrastrukturkarte –, was möglich ist, so zeigt uns die Karte der Ströme, was tatsächlich gemacht wird.

Flow-Maps sind noch wenig verbreitet, aber überaus nützlich. Ob die Ausfallsstraße, die aus der Stadt zum Wochenendhaus führt, verstopft oder frei ist, ist eine entscheidende Information für den, der die Stadt verlassen will. Welchen Weg Fußgänger vom Zug zu ihrem Arbeitsplatz nehmen, ist eine entscheidende Information für jemand, der die günstigste Lage für ein Café sucht. Doch während die Infrastruktur unverändert bleibt – und damit leicht zu kartografieren ist –, sind Ströme ständig in Bewegung. Ströme aufzuzeichnen ist eine Form der Überwachung.

Auf Karten von Kommunikationsinfrastrukturen kann man erkennen, dass man in fast jedem Land der Welt Zugang zum Internet hat. Man kann erkennen, dass das Internet große Städte verbindet, aber nicht viele ländliche Regionen; dass Menschen in Ostafrika über Satellit und nicht über Seekabel angeschlossen sind; dass Bauern in Nigeria ihre Verwandten in Lagos oder London anrufen können. Diese Karten der Kabelwege zeigen uns aber nicht, wie sie wirklich verwendet werden, wer mit wem spricht, wer was liest, wer was austauscht.

Wenn ich vor zwanzig Jahren eine Morgenzeitung lesen wollte, konnte ich zwischen zwei Möglichkeiten wählen: der dünnen Lokalzeitung oder der dicken *New York Times*, die beide im Laden an der Ecke erhältlich waren. Heute kann ich auch die *Daily Nation* aus Nairobi, die *Mail & Guardian* aus Südafrika, den *Guardian* aus Manchester, die *Times of India* oder die *Shanghai Daily* wählen. Wenn ich bereit bin, meine Sprachkenntnisse zu erweitern – oder mich auf Übersetzungsdienste zu verlassen –, habe ich sogar noch mehr Auswahl. Und wenn ich die Millionen Blogger, Twitterer, Forumsposter, Videomacher und Podcaster noch dazu nehme, steigern sich meine Optionen fast ins Unendliche.

Meistens aber lese ich die *New York Times*, meine Lokalzeitung und die Blogs einiger guter Freunde – und bin darin nicht anders als meisten Menschen auf der Welt. Ich bin mit einer Infrastruktur verbunden, die mir Informationen, Meinungen und Sichtweisen aus weiten Teilen der Welt liefert – ich kann Blogs aus Borneo lesen oder mir bulgarisches Fernsehen anschauen –, doch die Medien, mit denen ich tatsächlich in Berührung komme – meine Aufmerksamkeitsströme – sind lokal, auf meine Gemeinde, mein Land, meine Interessen bezogen.

Wenn wir in einer verbundenen Welt die Verteilung von Aufmerksamkeit erfassen wollen, sehen wie uns wie beim Fliegen Infrastruktur und Ströme an. Die Infrastrukturkarte verrät uns, dass Linz über eine Reihe von Flügen mit Lilongwe verbunden ist – die Karte der Ströme zeigt uns, dass diese Strecke fast nie jemand bucht. Die meisten Flüge starten und landen im selben Land. Die meisten Menschen lesen, hören und sehen lokal und national, weniger global.

Das ist auch in Ordnung so. Es ist ein Grundzug des Menschen. Wir sind es nicht gewohnt, in einer dermaßen vernetzen Welt zu leben. Vor zwölf Generationen – so Kwame Appiah – wären die Wenigsten von uns jemals einem andersgläubigen oder andersfarbigen Menschen begegnet. Die Gelegenheit zum Weltbürgertum haben wir alle erst seit Kurzem, und seit wenigen Jahren erst leben wir in einer Welt, in der es möglich ist zu erfahren, was Tag für Tag in einem Samoaner vorgeht. Unser Instinkt gebietet uns, auf das Vertraute zu achten, den Vorschlägen derer zu folgen, die wir bereits kennen, uns an die zu halten, die ebenso aussehen und denken wie wir selbst.

Die menschliche Schwäche, dass wir von Haus aus zu einer kleineren Welt neigen, ist aber nichts, das wir akzeptieren müssen. Die Infrastrukturen, die uns verbinden, binden uns auch unentwirrbar aneinander. Unsere Probleme sind global – ob Pandemien, Erderwärmung, Terrorismus – und die Lösungen nicht minder. Wenn wir uns vorstellen können, die Welt zu retten und zu verbessern, dann als Verbindung von Menschen in aller Welt, die gemeinsam nach neuen Lösungen und Lebensweisen suchen.

Die Cloud ermutigt uns, uns eine Welt vorzustellen, in der Infrastruktur keine Rolle spielt, in der Ideen und Lösungen von jedem und überall kommen können. Vielleicht ist das die nützliche Illusion, die uns von alten Denkweisen befreit, uns Lösungen aus allen möglichen Teilen der Welt akzeptieren lässt, die wir vielleicht abgelehnt hätten, wäre uns ihre Herkunft bekannt gewesen.

Wenn wir ehrlich sind, müssen wir allerdings zugeben, dass die Ideen nicht so reibungslos und global durch die Cloud strömen, wie wir vielleicht hoffen. Schon die Sprachgrenzen machen vieles von dem, was online veröffentlicht wird, unverständlich – die chinesischen Blog-Einträge, die spanischsprachigen Videos. In einem polyglotten Internet gibt es täglich mehr zu lesen und – für uns als Einzelne – täglich weniger zu verstehen. Wir haben große Fortschritte dabei gemacht, jedem die Möglichkeit zu geben, sich online zu äußern, seine Worte in die Cloud hinauszuschicken, aber wir haben viel weniger dafür getan sicherzustellen, dass wir auch verstehen, was jeder von uns zu sagen hat.

In einer Welt, in der viele, wenn nicht alle, online schreiben können, benötigen wir mehr denn je Redakteure, Gatekeeper und Filter. Wir experimentieren mit neuen Techniken, um die Cloud zu durchforsten und auszusortieren, was uns interessiert. Wir entwickeln Tools, die uns zeigen, was unsere Freunde interessant finden, und User darüber abstimmen lassen, was auf der Titelseite erscheinen soll. Mit vielen Augen sehen wir einen größeren Ausschnitt der Cloud. Letzten Endes aber ist unser Blickwinkel nicht breiter als der der Menschen, von denen wir uns beim Browsen leiten lassen. Wenn wir uns nur mit Gleichgesinnten umgeben – wozu wir nun einmal neigen – riskieren wir, den beglückenden Fund einer kritischen Empfehlung aus Nepal oder Nigeria zu übersehen.

Die Cloud verleitet uns zu dem Glauben, wir seien globaler, als wir wirklich sind. Wenn wir sie uns als eine von der physischen Realität losgelöste Wolke aus Bits vorstellen, die von überall herkommen können, lässt uns das vergessen, dass sich die Infrastruktur noch nicht in jeden Winkel der Erde erstreckt und arme, unfreie, abgeschnittene Orte ausgrenzt. Es lässt uns vergessen, dass sich unsere Aufmerksamkeit eher Sprachgenossen, Landsleuten, Freunden zuneigt und dass wir bewusst und ständig daran arbeiten müssen, uns von unserer Gruppe loszumachen und einer größeren Welt zuzuwenden.

Kurz vor dem Ersten Weltkrieg prophezeite der Radiopionier Marconi ein Radio, das Krieg unmöglich machen würde, weil wir damit die Stimmen anderer Völker vernehmen könnten und erkennen würden, wie sinnlos es ist, sie anzugreifen und zu töten. Neun Jahrzehnte später prophezeite der Internet-Enthusiast John Perry Barlow eine Welt ohne Grenzen, in der Staaten sinnlos geworden sind und die Menschen sich auf neue egalitäre Weise über das Internet organisieren. Barlows und Marconis Prophezeiungen haben sich zwar nicht erfüllt, aber sie waren beide ausgezeichnete Propheten. Die Aufgabe des Propheten ist nicht zu sagen, was eintreten wird, sondern was eintreten könnte, würde man daran arbeiten.

Die Cloud ist eine Prophezeiung. Sie ist ein schöner Traum von einer Zukunft, in der jeder Winkel der Welt miteinander verbunden sein wird. Sie fordert uns auf, Sprachbarrieren zu überwinden, aus unseren üblichen Bahnen und vertrauten Kreisen auszubrechen und neue, globale, vernetzte Lösungen für neue, globale, vernetzte Probleme zu finden. Wir müssen uns diese Zukunft vorstellen, um sie Wirklichkeit werden zu lassen. Aber wir dürfen dabei nicht vergessen, was Vorstellung und was Wirklichkeit ist. Wir müssen uns ständig neuen Herausforderungen stellen statt uns einfach nur einer nützlichen Illusion hinzugeben.

(Aus dem Englischen von Wilfried Prantner)

1   *Anm. d. Übers.:* Anspielung auf Richard Brautigans Gedicht „All Watched Over by Machines of Loving Grace" aus seinem gleichnamigen Gedichtband von 1967.

Pablo Flores

Education for an Inclusive Cloud

If the cloud was just another technological invention, we would expect it to bring real changes to the world. As is the case with many other tools, it would make life better in some ways only for a group of people—either a bigger or a smaller group—and the rest would just be unaffected by it.

However, the cloud is not a gadget or a popular website. It is a new way of intelligence, built in a collective way that gets some of what we think, how we feel and what we do, providing new tools everyday to share, elaborate together and act upon. Cloud intelligence is about people connected in real life and in cyberspace, who have new chances to work and act together.

For some people, it is just a good way to get some knowledge in their areas of interest, not only by reading books or watching videos, but also by interacting with people around the world who share the same interests and may contribute to their experience. For a smaller group, it may also be a way to follow their vocation and their dreams, in ways that classical instances of interaction would never have allowed.

Not everyone has been invited to join this club yet. In fact, most of the people in this world are excluded from almost every technological advance, including old Graham Bell's telephone. Even when we leave out the poorest areas of the world, Internet access and the knowledge needed to use computing devices are still relatively limited.

What can cloud intelligence do to change this?

Probably the first social movement that demonstrated the possibilities of cloud intelligence was the free software one. This is not the place to describe the history of free software and open source movements, but it is well worth looking at their results. You can find ready-to-use libraries, examples or useful documentation for almost any piece of software you may need to develop, new challenges generate energetic discussions that sometimes become alienating on the web, blogs, forums, collaborative portals, open repositories—they all become part of a cloud that once again has the intelligence to resolve the most complex software needs.

It is somehow natural to find a software developer's movement to be a pioneer in building and using cloud intelligence—they have the knowledge to use all the available tools and to develop those that are needed. But fortunately software and technologies are not the only interests of people who are in the cloud—and you may find different spaces for team working on many of this world's social worries, such as ecology, peace culture and education, as well as many others.

A special focus has to be given to education—one of the social concerns that may gain the attention of more people around the world. Inclusive education is much needed to allow more people to get into the cloud. Using computers and Internet to help educate our children gives them the opportunity to use this unlimited tool for their lives and gives them the opportunity to join the club. It will not happen automatically, just because of the presence of the technology. Teachers have to guide their education, and the cloud is an excellent support for them. The participation of other social organizations is also recommended.

Giving teachers tools to teach, children tools to learn, and the community tools to lend support are some of the best investments we can make to create a more inclusive, useful and intelligent cloud.

Pablo Flores

Tools zum Lernen

Wäre die Cloud nur eine weitere technologische Erfindung, würden wir Veränderungen für die Welt erwarten. Wie bei vielen anderen Tools würden diese das Leben nur für eine – größere oder kleinere – Gruppe in erleichtern und die Übrigen hätten nichts davon.

Doch die Wolke ist weder ein Gerät noch eine beliebte Website, sondern eine neue Form von Intelligenz; im Kollektiv entstanden, lebt sie von dem, was wir denken, fühlen und tun und stellt täglich neue Werkzeuge zum Austausch, zur gemeinsamen Weiterentwicklung und Nutzung zur Verfügung. *Cloud Intelligence* dreht sich um Menschen, die im realen Leben und im Cyberspace in Kontakt stehen und neue Möglichkeiten der Zusammenarbeit haben. Für einige stellt es eine Gelegenheit dar, sich Wissen im jeweiligen Fachgebiet anzueignen, indem sie nicht nur Bücher lesen oder Videos ansehen, sondern mit Menschen rund um den Globus interagieren, die das gleiche Interesse teilen und ihren Horizont erweitern wollen. Für eine kleinere Gruppe mag es sogar eine Chance sein, ihre Berufung und ihren Traum auf eine Weise zu verwirklichen, wie es mit herkömmlichen Kommunikationsformen niemals möglich gewesen wäre.

Noch hat nicht jeder eine Einladung in diesen Club erhalten. Tatsächlich ist die Mehrheit der Menschen von fast allen technischen Errungenschaften – wie auch dem guten, alten Telefon von Graham Bell – ausgeschlossen. Selbst wenn wir die ärmsten Regionen der Welt nicht berücksichtigen, sind der Zugang zum Internet und das Wissen im Umgang mit Rechnern noch immer ziemlich eingeschränkt. Wie kann *Cloud Intelligence* das ändern?

Die Freie-Software-Bewegung war wohl die erste soziale Bewegung dieser Art, die die Möglichkeiten der *Cloud Intelligence* aufzeigte. Die Geschichte der Freien-Software- und Open-Source-Bewegungen sollen hier nicht erörtert werden, aber deren Ergebnisse allemal. So finden sich gebrauchsfertige Bibliotheken, Beispiele oder nützliche Dokumentationen für fast jede Art von zu entwickelnder Software. Neue Herausforderungen führen zu angeregten Diskussionen – die im Web gelegentlich befremdlich wirken – in den Blogs, Foren, Kollaborationsportalen, offenen Repositorien – sie alle werden Bestandteil einer Wolke, die die Intelligenz besitzt, selbst die komplexesten Programmierbedürfnisse zu befriedigen.

Es mutet fast schon natürlich an, dass eine Bewegung von Softwareentwicklern zu Pionieren bei der Gestaltung und Nutzung von *Cloud Intelligence* wird – sie verfügen über die Kenntnisse, all die verfügbaren Tools einzusetzen und die noch benötigten zu entwickeln. Zum Glück sind Software und Technik nicht die einzigen Interessen der Menschen in der Wolke: Der Ausbildung ist besondere Beachtung beizumessen, ist sie doch eines der sozialen Anliegen, dem immer mehr Menschen auf der Welt Beachtung schenken. Eine umfassende Ausbildung ist notwendig, damit möglichst viele Zugang zur Cloud erlangen. Computer und das Internet sind Hilfsmittel bei der Ausbildung unserer Kinder, die ihnen die Möglichkeit bieten, diese Tools unbegrenzt zu nutzen und dem Club beizutreten. Dazu braucht es aber Lehrer, die deren Ausbildung gestalten und die von der Cloud dabei unterstützt werden. Auch die Teilnahme anderer sozialer Organisationen wird befürwortet. Eine der besten Investitionen zur Entwicklung einer umfassenden, nützlichen und intelligenten Cloud wäre es, den Lehrern Werkzeuge zum Unterrichten zu geben, den Kindern Tools zum Lernen und der Gemeinschaft Tools zur gegenseitigen Unterstützung zu geben.

(Aus dem Englischen von Michael Kaufmann)

Juliana Rotich

African Environmentalism Online

I would like to briefly discuss environmentalism online, particularly in Africa. I look at it in the context of online expression and organization.

African culture has always been about respect for the earth, for people and for the animals. There is an ancient Adinkra symbol of providence and divinity of mother earth, *Asase Ye Duru* which represents the importance of the earth in sustaining life.

The key to having more environmental activism online is for Africans to rediscover that living a lifestyle that embodies the age-old values of respecting the earth is something to embrace. For instance, recycling is not a white Anglo Saxon value; it's as African as "fufu" (a common staple food in western Africa, made out of maize flour). Re-using materials is a part of life in many parts of Africa. Many examples of this can be found on the popular group blog *Afrigadget*. What examples exist that exhibit environmentalism in the cloud? How might that level of environmentalism change in the next couple of years—if at all?

The Cloud as is understood in the context of this conference, is a metaphor for the Internet. It helps to look at the origin of the words *Cloud Computing*. Ramnath K. Chellapa is said to have originally defined cloud computing as a computing paradigm where the boundaries of computing will be determined by economic rationale rather than technical units. Companies make the decision to use the Amazon EC2 Service instead of running server farms. It still comes down to the economics of connectivity, and the cost of services—who can afford it, and who cannot. The boundaries of participation would still be cost. Even though there are platforms that can aggregate information received via SMS (*Ushahidi*) and relay it to the cloud (in the form of a mashup), there is still a cost component to getting on the cloud. Internet connectivity in Africa has largely been a case of not enough bandwidth, and too high a connection price. This is about to change, with several undersea cables being planned that will connect West, Southern and East Africa in a way that has not been possible over the last 10 years.

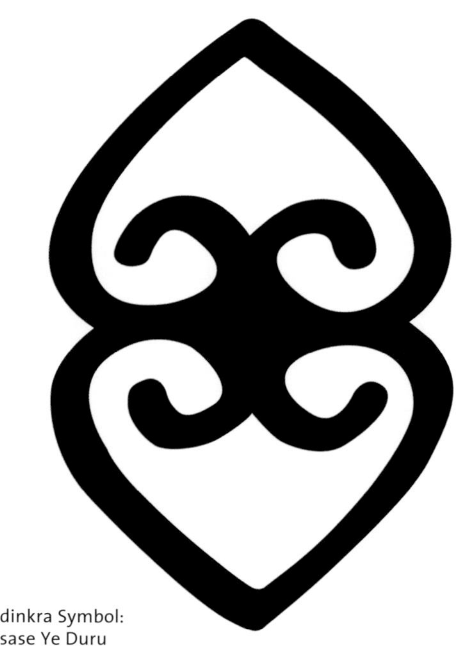

Adinkra Symbol:
Asase Ye Duru

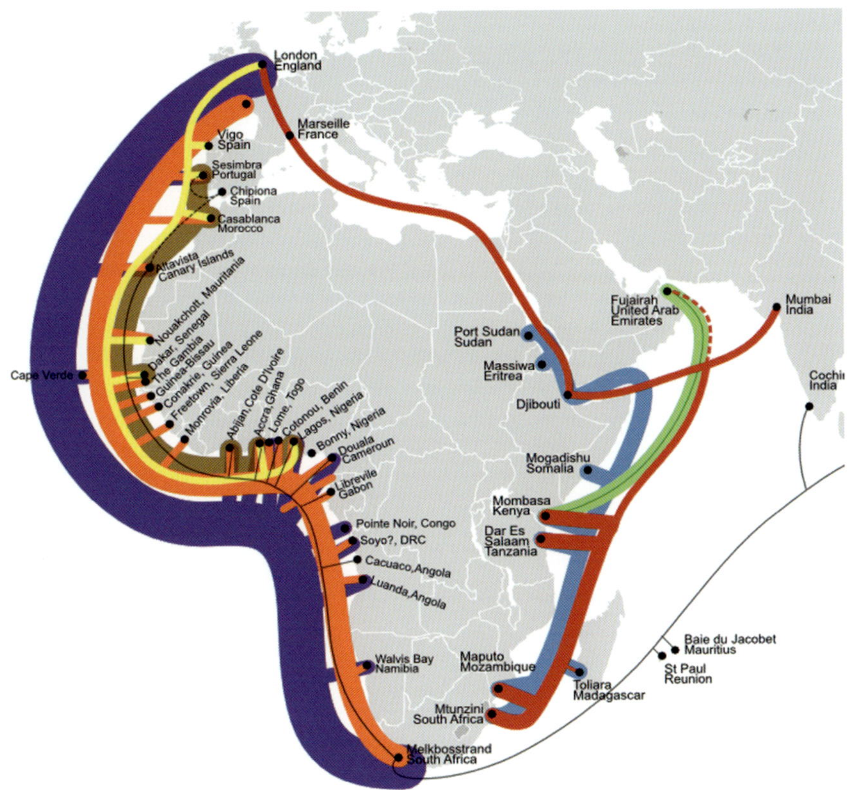

SSA Undersea Cables by Steve Song, *http://manypossibilities.net/african-undersea-cables/*

In 2009 alone, it is expected that the fibre optic cable line reaching Kenya could reduce the cost of Internet connectivity by more than 50%. Of course that will only happen if ISP pass along the savings reaped from having access to bigger and cheaper pipes onto the consumers. When this happens, the once excluded populace will find it within reach to be connected to the cloud, to participate in it and express themselves online. Will this expression include environmental activism?

The shift of information from offline media like newspapers, even water cooler conversations, to blogs, Twitter, Facebook walls, fan pages and countless other web applications, have brought to light what matters to many people. Our collective anxiety as it were, our fears, and our exasperations. People are live streaming with pictures, video, and 140 character messages. Some brave activists are using web 2.0 technologies to document environmental degradation and, in some cases, pollution. In Egypt, Trust Chemical Company sued Tamer Mabrouk, author of the blog *El Hakika* for slander. This was because he took pictures that showed how the company was polluting the Manzalla River. Sadly, we found out through *Global Voices Online* in early 2009 that there are laws in Egypt that resulted in Tamer having to pay the chemical company a fine. As more people get online in different countries, legal questions such as those highlighted by the Tamer case also crop up. How can people use the cloud for activism without having negative on-the-ground consequences? This case in Egypt shows that laws differ greatly from country to country and this might cause problems for activists who express themselves online.

When it comes to environmental matters, we see bloggers in South Africa expressing their misgivings about nuclear energy, genetically modified foods (GMO) and the destruction of trees to make way for World Cup 2010 related construction. As part of *Global Voices Online* we see bloggers who care about pesticides in food and the source of what they eat. Candice, an avowed locavore in Cape Town South Africa, inspires others through her blog *The Aspirant Locavore* that includes a directory for others to find green businesses—from local organic food shops and restaurants to accommodation. Dax Villanueva of the blog *Relax with Dax* often reviews organic restaurants. Africa is expressing its green choices online. Obviously South Africa is better connected and many more people have Internet access than in Kenya, but it is still interesting to see how many bloggers in Cape Town consistently write about the green lifestyle and environment. If connectivity in East Africa increases will we see more bloggers writing about the environment? If we take the case of Kenya, where the blogosphere is rather extensive, the answer to these questions will become apparent in the coming years as connectivity is expected to vastly improve with the advent of the undersea fibre optic cable. In the past year more Kenyan voices with environmental themes have emerged, but that increase does not rival the enviro-blogosphere of Cape Town.

What can be done to encourage online citizens to participate in environmental activism through whatever platforms they use? The noted futurist Kevin Kelley writes about the rules of the new economy, succinctly stating: "If it is not connected, connect it". In the case of Kenyan bloggers who write about the environment, they are lone voices out in the blogosphere. There is a need to aggregate, curate and highlight their voices, ideas and actions. To train the next generation of web users who will be coming online how to use all the tools at their disposal to express themselves and join the global conversation. This is something that Global Voices Online does very well.

The next step after self-expression is connecting with others who share similar viewpoints, acting as an individual who is part of a smart group. Some nascent ideas of self-organization can be found on Facebook, initiatives that go beyond what Evgeny Morozov, a blogger for Foreign Policy calls "Slacktivism". Was a tree planted because you joined the group? This slacktivism is saying something about our behaviour on the cloud. We just expect activism to be as easy as signing up with the click of a mouse and expecting someone else to make the changes we seek. Clearly that is not going to help us deal with any of the tough global problems we face. Interestingly, the corollary to this slacktivism can be found in Facebook. There are two examples that stand out from Sub Saharan Africa. One is the group Just Add Heart in Cape Town. The group of aforementioned bloggers decided to organize themselves online for offline impact. They pick a cause, be it visiting an orphanage, with one of them calling ahead to find out what they need, bringing the donations to their meet up and proceeding to the orphanage to spend part of their day there. On World Oceans day they self-organized a trip to the Save Our Seas Shark Centre and found out just why the shark species have declined greatly. Dax wrote:

> I think that what many people don't understand is that every animal is part of an ecosystem and if you take away that animal, things get out of balance and the whole ecosystem disintegrates. While some people might like the idea of a sea with no sharks in it, they won't like the idea of a sea with no life in it whatsoever. That is what the end result would be if there were no sharks. The Save Our Seas Shark Centre's (SOSSC) mission is to encourage awareness, protection, conservation and the sustainable use of sharks worldwide through research, education and awareness. The SOSSC is a "Rethink the Shark" experience that inspires a shift from the inherent negative perceptions of sharks to one of awe and wonder.

The second group in Facebook that has taken environmental activism to heart is the Friends of Lembus Forest in Nairobi called The Rhino Charge. They ended up planting 100 trees in a section of a forest that was heavily deforested and which is part of the complex Mau forest system. There are many other people who read about the deforestation going on in Kenya, the drying up of water catchment areas, yet this group of less than 100 people decided to act. They used the cloud to self-organize and deliver on environmental action. Can these two examples be replicated in the world? Granted others have other types of environmental problems, but can the same self-organizing idea be used? Absolutely. The cloud makes it easier for you to wake up, tell others about your cause, and actually lead like-minded thinkers who agree with your cause to act. It makes it easier for people to collaborate on whatever level they would like, be it local, regional or even international.

In the guiding text of the *Cloud Intelligence* conference, Isaac Mao and David Sasaki asked whether it is possible to craft a new connected consciousness to tackle global problems collectively and equitably. I say yes, absolutely, and because our environmental degradation is one of the foremost challenges we face in this century, we must. What is needed to start crafting this global environmental movement?

First, we have to start at home. We have to start with our own lifestyles; we have to act in one way or the other to do something, one thing for the environment. Then use the cloud to organize and inspire others to join in. We need to remember that if we invite others to join, we have to be willing to share. Joi Ito of Creative Commons observed recently, that we are failing to share if we do not reduce the legal cost of getting approval to remix or build upon others' work. The future has a copyright framework, and that framework is Creative Commons. Any sort of global consciousness for environmental change will need to use the Creative Commons for it to thrive. If we get mired in copyright issues, how are we to inspire others if we hug our data—in the case of scientists—or our images—in the case of artists?

Here is one idea I would like to leave you with, for the one thing you chose to do for the environment, take a picture or document it in any way you would like, tag it with "greensouls" or tweet with the tag "greensouls" on whichever online platforms you use. I truly believe that we can utilize the cloud to curate global action on the environment and create a global movement for environmental change.

Juliana Rotich

Online-Umweltschutz

Adinkra Symbol:
Asase Ye Duru

Ich möchte in diesem Beitrag auf den Online-Umweltschutz, wie er sich vor allem in Afrika äußert und organisiert, eingehen.

In der afrikanischen Kultur ging es schon immer um Respekt vor der Erde, den Menschen und den Tieren. Das Adinkra-Symbol *Asase Ye Duru* steht seit alters her für die weise Fürsorge und Heiligkeit von Mutter Erde und weist auf ihre lebenserhaltende Bedeutung hin.

Um den Online-Umweltaktivismus zu fördern, müssen die Afrikaner wieder erkennen, dass sie ihren alten Lebensstil, der die Erde respektiert, aufgreifen sollten. So ist z. B. das Recycling kein Wert in der weißen, angelsächsischen Welt – es ist so afrikanisch wie *fufu*, ein in Westafrika gängiges Nationalgericht aus Maismehl. In vielen Teilen Afrikas ist Wiederverwertung ein Teil des Lebens, wofür man im Gruppenblog *Afrigadget* viele Beispiele findet. Welche Beispiele zeugen von Umweltschutz in der *Cloud*? Wie könnte sich das Bewusstsein für Umweltschutz in den nächsten Jahren ändern – falls überhaupt?

Die Cloud bzw. Wolke ist im Kontext dieser Konferenz eine Metapher für das Internet. Es ist in diesem Zusammenhang hilfreich, sich den Ursprung des Begriffs Cloud Computing anzusehen. Ramnath K. Chellapa soll diesen ursprünglich als Rechenparadigma eingeführt haben, das die Rechnergrenzen eher durch wirtschaftliche Überlegungen als durch technische Einheiten definiert. Firmen entscheiden sich für die Nutzung des EC2-Diensts von Amazon statt Serverfarmen zu betreiben. Dennoch lässt sich alles auf die Wirtschaftlichkeit der Netzanbindung und die Dienstkosten reduzieren – wer es sich leisten kann und wer nicht. Immer noch stellen die Kosten eine Hürde für eine Teilnahme dar. Und obwohl es Plattformen gibt, die per SMS empfangene Informationen aggregieren (*Ushahidi*) und diese (als Mashup) an die Wolke weiterleiten, spielen die Kosten bei der Anbindung an die Wolke noch immer eine Rolle. In Afrika war die Internetdurchdringung meist eine Frage zu geringer Bandbreite und zu hoher Anbindungskosten. Das ändert sich durch die in Planung befindlichen Unterseekabel, die – wie es in den letzten zehn Jahren unmöglich war – West-, Süd- und Ostafrika vernetzen werden.

Allein 2009, wenn die Glasfaserverbindung Kenia erreicht, rechnet man mit einer Halbierung der Verbindungskosten zum Internet. Natürlich nur, wenn die Internetdienstanbieter die durch den Zugang zu stärkeren und billigeren Leitungen erzielten Einsparungen an die Konsumenten weitergeben. Dann allerdings ist die Verbindung zur Cloud für die Bevölkerung in Reichweite, dann kann sie daran teilnehmen und sich online Ausdruck verschaffen. Werden sie sich für Umweltaktivismus stark machen?

Die Verschiebung des Informationsgewinns weg von Offline-Medien wie Zeitungen oder den Gesprächen am Wasserspender hin zu Blogs, Twitter, Facebook, Fan-Websites und zahllosen weiteren Webapplikationen brachte ans Licht, was für die meisten Menschen zählt – ihre kollektiven Sorgen, Ängste und ihren Ärger. Bilder, Videos und Nachrichten mit 140 Zeichen werden zu

Live-Streams über sie. Einige mutige Aktivisten setzen auf Web-2.0-Technologien, um die ökologische Krise oder auch die Verschmutzung der Umwelt zu dokumentieren. Die ägyptische Firma Trust Chemical Industries verklagte Tamer Mabrook, den Autor des Blogs *El Hakika*, wegen Rufschädigung, weil er deren umweltverschmutzenden Praktiken am Manzala-See fotografierte. Anfang 2009 mussten wir über *Global Voices Online* traurig zur Kenntnis nehmen, dass Tamer aufgrund der Gesetzeslage in Ägypten zur Zahlung einer Entschädigung an das Chemiewerk verurteilt wurde. Rechtliche Fragen, wie jene zu Tamers Fall, nehmen mit der zunehmenden Zahl von Internetusern in aller Herren Länder ebenfalls zu. Wie lässt sich die Wolke für Aktivisten ohne konkrete negative Konsequenzen nutzen? Dieser Fall in Ägypten hat gezeigt, dass sich die Gesetze von Land zu Land oft signifikant unterscheiden, was wiederum den Aktivisten Probleme bereiten kann, die online ihre Stimme erheben.

Im Zusammenhang mit Umweltthemen äußern südafrikanische Blogger ihr Unbehagen über Atomenergie, genetisch modifizierte Lebensmittel und die Abholzung im Rahmen der Bauarbeiten für die Weltmeisterschaft 2010. Auf *Global Voices Online* erfahren wir von Bloggern, die sich Gedanken zu Pestiziden in der Nahrung und zur Herkunft ihrer Lebensmittel machen. Candice,

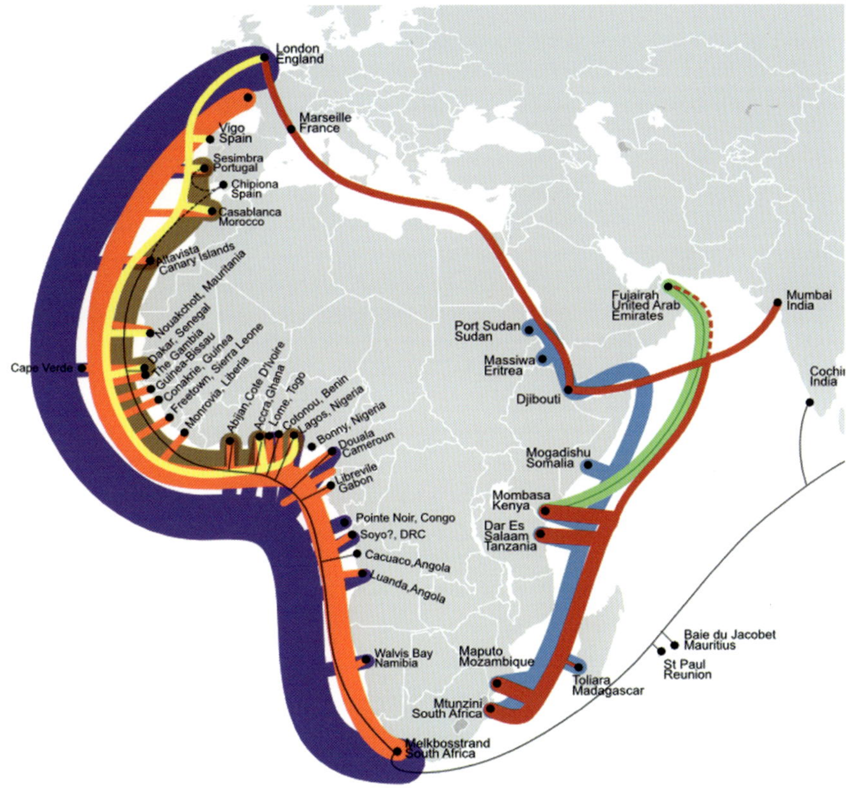

Abbildung 1: Unterseekabel von Steve Song (http://manypossibilities.net/african-undersea-cables/)

Juliana Rotich

eine bekennende Anhängerin der Locavore-Bewegung[1] aus Kapstadt, Südafrika, inspiriert mit ihrem Blog *The Aspirant Locavore* andere User und bietet ein Verzeichnis Biobetrieben – von regionalen Läden mit Bioprodukten über Restaurants bis hin zu Beherbergungsbetrieben. Dax Villanueva bespricht in seinem Blog *Relax with Dax* oft Biorestaurants. Afrika schreibt also online über seine Entscheidung für grüne Lösungen. Südafrika hat offensichtlich eine bessere Connectivity, hier haben mehr Menschen einen Internetzugang als in Kenia, dennoch ist es interessant nachzuvollziehen, wie viele Blogger in Kapstadt ständig über grünen Lebensstil und über die Umwelt schreiben. Werden noch mehr Blogger über die Umwelt schreiben, wenn die Internetanschlüsse in Ostafrika zunehmen? Im Fall von Kenia, wo die Blogosphäre ziemlich ausgeprägt ist, werden wir die Antworten in den nächsten Jahren erfahren, wenn die Zugangsmöglichkeiten zum Internet durch die geplanten Untersee-Glasfaserkabel deutlich verbessert werden. Im letzten Jahr haben sich zwar immer mehr kenianische Stimmen zu Umweltthemen geäußert, doch kann sich dieser Zuwachs nicht mit der Umwelt-Blogosphäre von Kapstadt messen.

Wie kann man die Online-Gemeinde ermutigen, sich – welche Plattform auch immer sie nutzt – für den Umweltaktivismus einzusetzen? Der bekannte Futurist Kevin Kelley bringt die Gesetze der New Economy auf den Punkt: „Wenn es nicht angeschlossen ist, schließ es an." Die kenianischen Umweltblogger sind einsame Rufer in der Blogosphäre. Ihre Stimmen, Ideen und Handlungen müssen gebündelt, geordnet und mit Nachdruck präsentiert werden. Die nächste Generation, die online geht, braucht Unterweisung im Einsatz aller zur Verfügung stehenden Tools, um sich ausdrücken und in die globale Konversation einsteigen zu können. Darin ist *Global Voices Online* sehr gut.

Hat man sich Ausdruck verschafft, sollte man sich als nächsten Schritt mit Gleichgesinnten zusammentun, um als Individuum innerhalb einer gut organisierten Gruppe zu handeln. Auf Facebook keimen schon Ideen zur Selbstorganisation auf, Initiativen, die über den von Ewgenij Morozow, einem Blogger mit Fokus Außenpolitik, geprägten „Slacktivism" hinausgehen. Wurde ein Baum gepflanzt, weil du dich einer Gruppe angeschlossen hast? Dieser Slacktivism sagt etwas über unser Verhalten in der Wolke aus. Wir erwarten, dass Aktivismus so einfach wie ein Mausklick ist, und gehen davon aus, dass jemand anderer die von uns erhofften Änderungen herbeiführt. Das ist mit Sicherheit keine Hilfe angesichts der knallharten globalen Probleme. Interessanterweise findet sich die logische Fortsetzung des Slacktivism auch auf Facebook. Zwei Beispiele aus Subsahara-Afrika stechen hervor. Eines ist die Gruppe *Just Add Heart* in Kapstadt: Die Blogger beschlossen, sich online zu organisieren, um offline etwas zu bewirken. Sie planen ein Vorhaben, z. B. den Besuch eines Waisenhauses; rufen vorher an, um herauszufinden, was gebraucht wird; legen ihre Spenden für das Benötigte zusammen, gehen damit zum Waisenhaus und verbringen einen Teil ihres Tags dort. Am Weltmeerestag organisierten sie eine Fahrt zum Save Our Seas Shark Centre (SOSSC) und lernten, warum die Spezies Hai so stark dezimiert wurde. Dax schrieb:

> Ich glaube, die meisten Menschen verstehen nicht, dass jedes Tier Teil eines Ökosystems ist. Eliminiert man dieses Tier, gerät alles aus dem Gleichgewicht, und das Ökosystem zerfällt. Auch wenn einigen vielleicht die Vorstellung eines Meers ohne Haie gefällt, können sie einem völlig leblosen Meer sicher nichts abgewinnen. Das wäre aber das Endergebnis, wenn es keine Haie mehr gibt. Die Aufgabe des SOSSC ist

es, durch Erforschung und Bildung das Bewusstsein, den Schutz, die Bewahrung und den nachhaltigen Umgang mit Haien weltweit zu fördern. Das SOSSC möchte zum Überdenken der Erfahrung Hai anregen und die inhärent negativen Assoziationen mit Haien in Bewunderung und Begeisterung verwandeln.

Die zweite Gruppe auf Facebook, die sich im Umweltaktivismus engagiert, sind die *Friends of Lembus Forest* in Nairobi, die sich *The Rhino Charge* nennen. Sie pflanzten schließlich hundert Bäume in einem stark gerodeten Gebiet des komplexen Mau-Waldgebiets. Es gibt viele andere, die über die Rodungen und das Austrocknen von Wassereinzugsgebieten in Kenia lesen, aber nur diese Gruppe von nicht einmal hundert Mitgliedern hat sich entschieden zu handeln. Sie nützten die Wolke, um sich zu organisieren und eine Aktion für die Umwelt zu starten. Können diese beiden Beispiele wiederholt werden? Kann dieser Gedanke der Selbstorganisierung auch für andere Umweltprobleme anderswo umgesetzt werden? Mit Sicherheit. Die Wolke fördert Bewusstseinsprozesse, erleichtert es, andere von der eigenen Sache zu überzeugen und Gleichgesinnte zum Handeln zu bewegen. Die Zusammenarbeit auf lokaler, regionaler oder sogar internationaler Ebene wird um vieles einfacher.
Im Einleitungstext zur fragen Isaac Mao und David Sasaki (siehe S. 20), ob ein vernetztes Bewusstsein zum gemeinsamen und fairen Herangehen an die globalen Probleme geschaffen werden kann. Ich bejahe das auf jeden Fall, es ist sogar unerlässlich, da die Umweltzerstörung eine unserer größten Herausforderungen in diesem Jahrhundert darstellt. Was braucht es zur Schaffung dieser weltweiten Umweltbewegung?
Wir müssen zu Hause anfangen, bei unserer eigenen Lebensweise – und zumindest eine Tat für die Umwelt setzen. Und dann die Wolke dazu nutzen, um andere zum Mitmachen zu motivieren. Allerdings dürfen wir dabei nicht auf den Austausch vergessen, wenn wir andere einladen mitzumachen. Joichi Ito von Creative Commons bemerkte kürzlich, dass ein Austausch nicht möglich ist, wenn wir die rechtlichen Kosten nicht senken, um eine Erlaubnis zum Remix oder zur Weiterentwicklung der Arbeit eines anderen zu erlangen. Die Zukunft hat einen Urheberrechtsrahmen – und der stammt von Creative Commons. Jede Form globalen Bewusstseins für Umweltänderung braucht Creative Commons, um zu florieren. Wenn wir uns in Urheberrechtsthemen verzetteln, wie sollen wir für andere motivierend sein, wenn wir unsere Daten – im Fall von Wissenschaftlern – oder Bilder – im Fall von Künstlern – nicht aus der Hand geben?
Eine Anregung möchte ich noch weitergeben: Fotografieren oder dokumentieren Sie auf beliebige Weise etwas, das Sie für die Umwelt tun und verschlagworten Sie es mit *greensouls* auf welcher Plattform auch immer. Ich bin überzeugt, dass die Wolke zum Ordnen der weltweiten Handlungen für die Umwelt herangezogen und eine globale Bewegung zur Änderung des Umweltbewusstseins geschaffen werden kann.

(Aus dem Englischen von Michael Kaufmann)

---

1   Anm. d. Übers.: Mit *Locavore* bezeichnen sich Menschen, die bewusster und kritischer mit ihren Lebensmitteln umgehen und sich nur noch von lokal (in einem Umkreis von rund 100 Meilen) angebauten, kultivierten oder hergestellten Produkten ernähren.

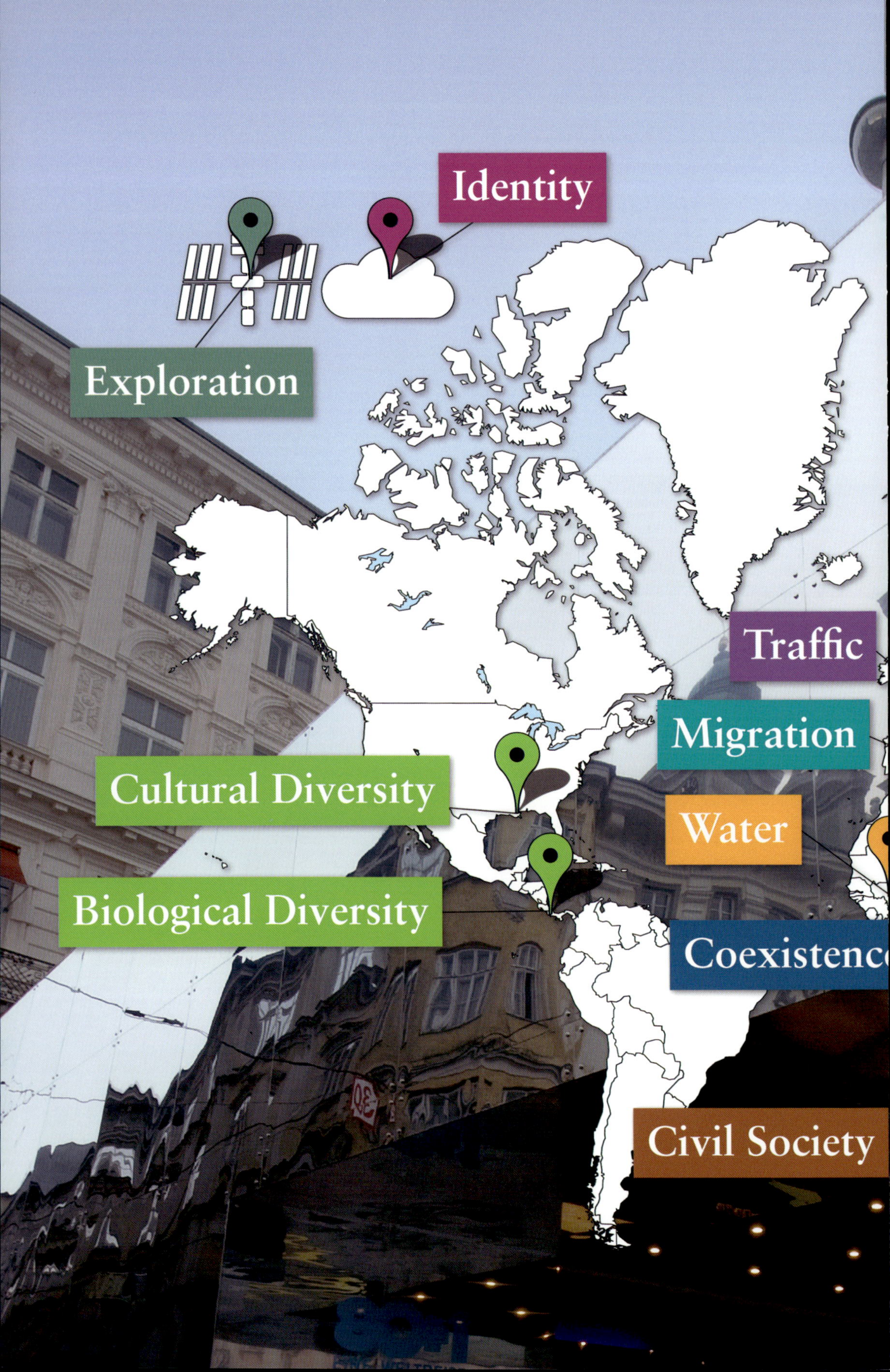
Identity
Exploration
Traffic
Migration
Cultural Diversity
Water
Biological Diversity
Coexistence
Civil Society

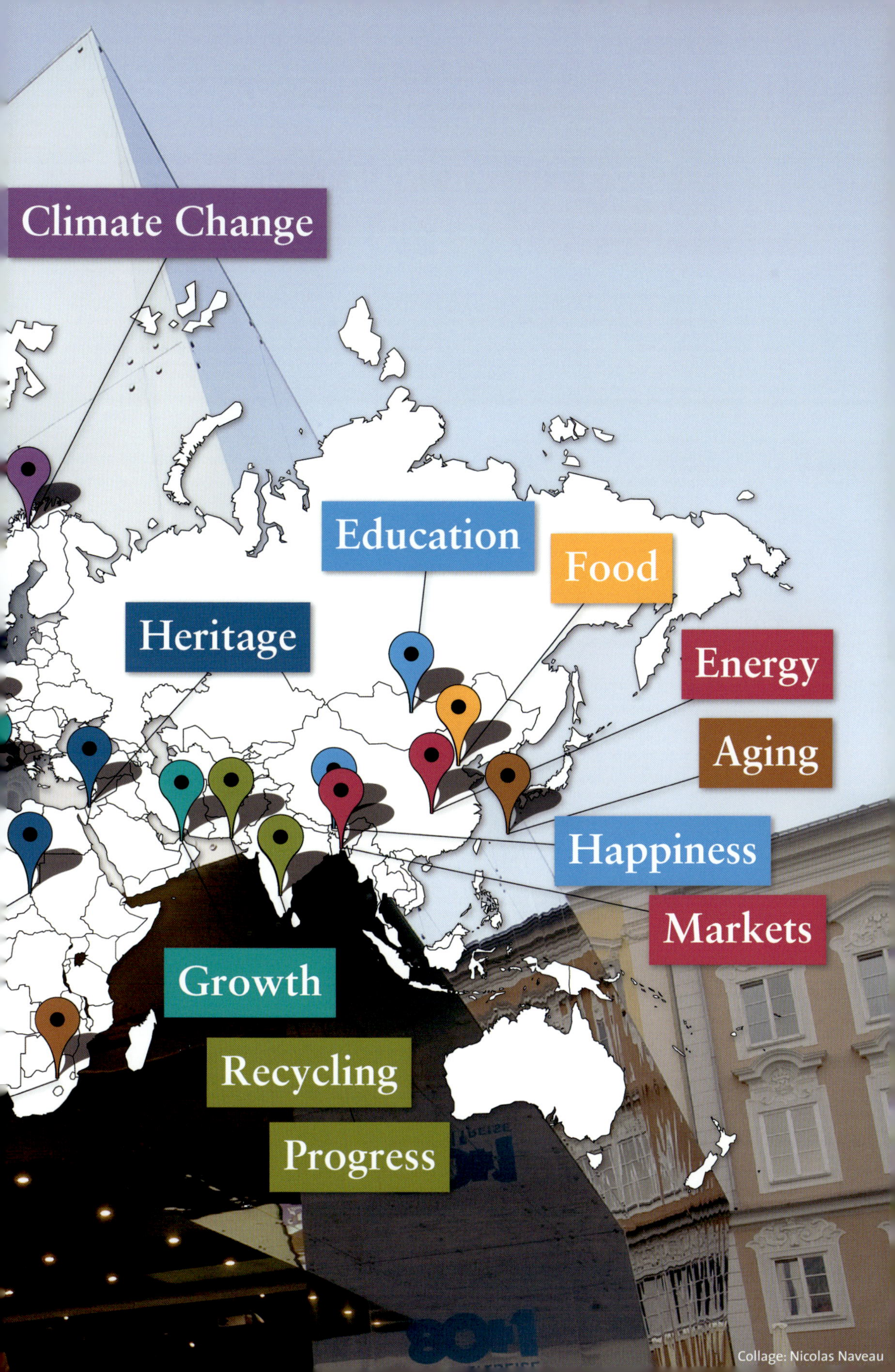

Climate Change
Education
Food
Heritage
Energy
Aging
Happiness
Markets
Growth
Recycling
Progress
Collage: Nicolas Naveau

80+1—A Journey around the World

http://www.80plus1.org/

Inspired by Jules Verne's famed novel "Around the World in 80 Days," Ars Electronica, voest-alpine and Linz09 set off on June 17, 2009 on a global expedition. *80+1 — A Journey around the World* will be on the go until September 5, 2009. But it won't entail any physical travel—this is a virtual expedition via satellite linkup and fiber optic cable. The itinerary takes us to 20 locations that represent issues of essential importance to our future.

80+1—The Base Camp

The hub of this project's data flows is the 200-m² Base Camp on Hauptplatz. Literally mirroring its surroundings, the Base Camp's architecture is meant as a metaphor of a way of seeing the world, the results of which always ultimately depend on ones own point of view. "'Movement' and 'communication' are the essential terms of our concept," is how Michael Grugl of any:time Architects explained the Base Camp's design. "The floor and roof surfaces of a cuboid structure are turned towards one another. All exterior walls are steel-clad, and thus covered in the material that absolutely bespeaks the City of Linz. Their reflective surfaces produce surprising optical effects. Depending on how light hits them and the observer's own perspective, 'the world' is continually reflected anew."

80+1—Participation

We've come up with wide array of activities designed to effectively mediate installation visitors' and traveling companions' encounters with 80+1's 20 topics. Active participation—whether directly on Linz's Hauptplatz or online at *www.8oplus1.org*—is absolutely vital to this project. After all, how else are we to make an impact on the future?

80+1—Traveling Companions and Project Partners

In spite of it being summer recess, we've succeeded in recruiting enthusiastic students from about 20 local schools to participate in 80+1. We've also lined up about as many partner schools worldwide. After all, when it comes to the future, young people above all deserve to be heard and to have input into decisions that will affect them. Plus, international experts and highly motivated local interest groups are helping us to make complex background information about the various themes more easily understandable. They're also providing key data and hosting activities.

80+1—Live Bits

In 2008, we issued a call for the submission of ideas for artistic tele-presence projects. What has emerged from this are 15 ways of getting Linz linked up with the respective destinations on our global itinerary.

80+1—Pin Hole—Live out of the Box

An empty transport box is being sent on a journey. But this isn't just a common, everyday flight case; rather, it's a sort of mobile object for interventions in the public sphere. When you open it up, mount it on the tripod that comes along for the ride, and set up a PC including internet connection and webcam inside it, what you have is a light- and weather-controlled video chat situation. Three of these PIN HOLEs have been produced, and two of them dispatched on 'round-the-world trips. The PIN HOLE that remains in Linz is hooked up just about every day to one of the other two located somewhere on the face of this planet.

80+1—Hopes & Fears

Hopes and Fears is a project developed especially for the Global Window. In cooperation with Dolores Labs, a Web 2.0 marketing firm, Mechanical Turk and other social network websites are being used to line up volunteers to knock on our Global Window and spend some time with us in video chats elaborating on their hopes and fears about our future. Any and all forms of live interaction (singing, dancing, a speech, poetry,…) are welcome. Contributors will be compensated for taking part.

80+1—Rope in Space

Rope in Space turns a length of cable into a connector between two human beings far removed from each other. This time, the sister city is Vienna, and the Architecture Center in the Austrian capital's Museumsquartier is the partner venue. This project, developed by the Ars Electronica Futurelab in cooperation with voestalpine's apprenticeship workshop, the University of Linz's Department of System Software and the Festo Company, invites installation visitors to engage in a tug-of-war via video linkup. Is this matter of pulling together to achieve an objective or a test of strength between two cities?

80+1—Collage Table (Office of Tomorrow)

The desk of the future is a lot more than a flat surface on which to set up office equipment. The desk itself becomes a computer and a graphics display. This tabletop developed at the Hagenberg Campus of the Upper Austria University of Applied Sciences is a high-resolution projection surface that's connected to an interactive presentation screen. The entire desktop can be used as a digital graphics tablet. On it, ideas and concepts can be sketched with a wireless stylus—and even combined with pre-existing children's drawings about our future and inserted into a collage. The drawings can be uploaded to the project website via an infrared interface.

(Text: Gerfried Stocker, Manuela Pfaffenberger, translated from German by Mel Greenwald)

80+1—A Journey around the World

is a project that spans the globe. Many men and women have worked on it.
Co-organizers: Ars Electronica Linz, voestalpine AG, Linz 2009 European Capital of Culture
Steering Group: Martin Heller (Linz09), Hannes Leopoldseder (AEC), Michael Sterrer-Ebenführer (voestalpine) und Gerfried Stocker (AEC)
Project directors: Michael Naimark, Steve Clark, Manuela Pfaffenberger
Architects: Michael Grugl / any : time architects
Project managers: Richard Baldinger, Yu-Han Chen, Cyrus Farivar, Ingrid Fischer-Schreiber, Dominique Hölzl, Sigrid Hofmeister-Watanabe, Carmen Lauss, Angelika Rainer, Maria Seidl, Susi Windischbauer
Technical production: Alexander Böhmler, Tim Grabham, Michael Probst, John Reason, Chris Reason, Chris Sheehan
An updated list of everyone involved is online at *http://www.80plus1.org/de/about/credits*.
Among the many works that have inspired and served as models for this project, we'd like to single out two for special mention: *Hole in Space*, 1977, by Sherry Rabinowitz and Kit Galloway
The World in 24 Hours, 1982, initiated by Robert Adrian X

80+1 – Eine Weltreise

http://www.80plus1.org/

Inspiriert von Jules Vernes weltberühmtem Klassiker, sind Ars Electronica, voestalpine und Linz09 am 17. Juni 2009 zur großen Reise aufgebrochen. *80+1 – Eine Weltreise* ist eine bis 5. September 2009 anberaumte Expedition – keine physische, sondern eine virtuelle Reise via Satellitenverbindung und Glasfaserkabel, die an 20 Orte führt, die für zentrale Fragen der Zukunft stehen.

80+1 – Das Basislager

Auf ca. 200 Quadratmeter präsentiert sich das Basislager von 80+1 mitten am Linzer Hauptplatz, in dem alle Daten zusammenfließen. Rundum verspiegelt, versteht sich dessen Architektur als Metapher einer Weltbetrachtung, deren Ergebnis letzten Endes immer vom eigenen Standpunkt abhängt. „Bewegung und Kommunikation sind die Schlüsselbegriffe unserer Konzeption", erläutert Michael Grugl von any:time Architekten die Formgebung des Basislagers: „Boden- und Dachfläche eines rechtwinkeligen Quaders werden gegeneinander gedreht, alle Außenwände mit Stahl und damit einem für Linz prägenden Material verkleidet. Dessen reflektierende Oberfläche erzeugt überraschende optische Effekte – je nach Einfallswinkel des Lichts und der eigenen Perspektive spiegelt sich ‚die Welt' hier immer wieder anders."

80+1 – Partizipation

Um die 20 Themen den interessierten BesucherInnen und Mitreisenden näherzubringen, haben wir uns unterschiedliche Aktivitäten einfallen lassen. Aktive Teilnahme – ob direkt am Hauptplatz in Linz oder über die Web-Plattform *www.80plus1.org* – ist für dieses Projekt von extremer Wichtigkeit, denn wie kann sonst Zukunft gestaltet werden?

80+1 – Reise- und ProjektpartnerInnen

Fast 20 Schulen aus Linz und Umgebung konnten trotz Ferienzeit für die Teilnahme bei 80+1 begeistert werden. Und fast ebenso viele Partnerschulen wurden in der Welt gefunden. Denn wer, wenn nicht unsere Jugend, hat so viel Gehör und Mitbestimmung zu unserer Zukunft verdient? Internationale ExpertInnen sowie ambitionierte lokale Interessengruppen helfen uns des Weiteren, die Hintergründe zu den Themen verständlicher werden zu lassen, und liefern wichtige Informationen und Aktivitäten.

80+1 – Live Bits

Eine internationale Ausschreibung für künstlerische Telepräsenzprojekte fand 2008 statt, und daraus sind 15 Projekte hervorgegangen, die Linz mit den virtuellen Zielen unserer Weltreise verbinden werden.

80+1 – Pin Hole – Live out of the Box

Eine leere Transportbox wird auf die Reise geschickt. Doch es handelt sich dabei nicht nur um ein herkömmliches Flightcase, sondern um eine Art mobiles Interventionsobjekt für den öffentlichen Raum. Öffnet man das Objekt, montiert man es auf dem mitgelieferten Stativ und platziert man einen PC inkl. Internet-Verbindung und Webcam darin, hat man eine licht- und wetterkontrollierte Videochat-Situation. Drei dieser Pin Holes wurden produziert und zwei davon auf die Reise um die Welt geschickt. Die Pin Hole in Linz ist fast täglich mit einer anderen Pin Hole in der Welt in Verbindung.

80+1 – Hoffnungen und Ängste

Hoffnungen und Ängste ist ein Projekt, das speziell für das Global Window entwickelt wurde. Gemeinsam mit dem Web2.0-Marketing-Unternehmen Dolores Labs werden über Mechanical Turk und andere Social-Network-Plattformen Personen akquiriert, die sich freiwillig zur Verfügung stellen, um via Videochat am globalen Fenster anzuklopfen und über ihre Hoffnungen und Ängste bezüglich unserer Zukunft zu sprechen. Jede Form der Live-Interaktion (Singen, Tanzen, Vorträge, Gedichte, ...) ist willkommen, und die beteiligten Personen werden für ihre Mitarbeit bezahlt.

80+1 – Rope in Space

Bei „Rope in Space" wird ein Seil zu einem weltweiten Verbindungskabel zwischen zwei Menschen an unterschiedlichen Orten. In diesem Fall ist Wien Partnerstadt – mit dem Architekturzentrum im Wiener Museumsquartier als Partnerort von Linz. Das Projekt, das vom Ars Electronica Futurelab gemeinsam mit der Lehrwerkstätte der voestalpine, dem Institut für Systemsoftware der Johannes-Kepler-Universität und der Firma Festo erarbeitet wurde, lädt ein zum Tauziehen via Videoverbindung – ein gemeinsames Ziehen am Seil oder Kräftemessen zwischen zwei Städten?

80+1 – Collage Table (Office of Tomorrow)

Der Schreibtisch der Zukunft ist viel mehr als eine Abstellfläche für Geräte: Er wird selbst zum Computer und zur Grafikoberfläche. Diese von der FH Hagenberg entwickelte Tischplatte ist eine hochauflösende Projektionsfläche, die mit einer interaktiven Präsentationswand verbunden ist. Die gesamte Tischfläche kann als digitales Grafiktablett benutzt werden. Ideen und Konzepte sowie bereits bestehende Kinderzeichnungen zu unserer Zukunft werden mit drahtlosen Stiften skizziert und collagiert. Über eine Infrarot-Schnittstelle werden die Zeichnungen zur Website gesendet.

(Text: Gerfried Stocker, Manuela Pfaffenberger)

80+1 – Eine Weltreise

ist ein weltumspannendes Projekt, an dem zahlreiche Personen mitwirken.
Organisatoren: Ars Electronica Linz, voestalpine AG, Linz 2009 European Capital of Culture
Steuerungsgruppe: Martin Heller (Linz09), Hannes Leopoldseder (AEC), Michael Sterrer-Ebenführer (voestalpine)
und Gerfried Stocker (AEC)
Projektleitung: Michael Naimark, Steve Clark, Manuela Pfaffenberger
Architekten: Michael Grugl / any : time architects
ProjektmanagerInnen: Richard Baldinger, Yu-Han Chen, Cyrus Farivar, Ingrid Fischer-Schreiber,
Dominique Hölzl, Sigrid Hofmeister-Watanabe, Carmen Lauss, Angelika Rainer, Maria Seidl, Susi Windischbauer
Technik: Alexander Böhmler, Tim Grabham, Michael Probst, John Reason, Chris Reason, Chris Sheehan
Eine aktuelle Liste aller Beteiligten ist zu finden unter *http://www.80plus1.org/de/about/credits*.
Unter den vielen Inspirationen und Vorbildern für dieses Projekt möchten wir zwei ganz besonders
hervorheben: *Hole in Space*, 1977, by Sherry Rabinowitz und Kit Galloway
Die Welt in 24 Stunden, 1982, initiiert von Robert Adrian X

AGING / OKINAWA (JAPAN)

The average worldwide human life expectancy has nearly doubled in the last few decades to about 66 years. As this number continues to rise, how do our societies cope with a population that can live longer and may have more sustained medical needs?

BIOLOGICAL DIVERSITY / LA GAMBA (COSTA RICA)

In many ways, it's the extreme complexity of life on Earth that makes the entire ecosystem so stable and beautiful. However, biological diversity is threatened by the human need to eat and expend energy. We'll take a look at the challenges to other animal species created by the presence of modern humans.

CIVIL SOCIETY / JOHANNESBURG (SOUTH AFRICA)

Civil Society represents the non-governmental elements of a given society. Often it represents the non-business and non-public elements in a particular regional or national area.

CLIMATE CHANGE / KILPISJÄRVI (FINLAND)

After an exhaustive international study we as a species can now definitively say that human-induced climate change is real. We will particularly focus on how new technologies, particularly technologies of simulation and visualization, can help us with this new and profound understanding.

COEXISTENCE / BREIDJING CAMP (TCHAD)

Coexistence is particularly difficult when there is strained history to overcome. How can peoples that have fought each other overcome their differences?

CULTURAL DIVERSITY / NEW ORLEANS (USA)

Cultural Diversity is one of our topics very simply because most cultures on a worldwide scale are under threat from a handful of dominant cultures. What does it take, for example, to convince children to be as proud and interested in the music and food of their grandparents as they are of what they see on television?

EDUCATION / MONGOLIA

We have included education as a topic largely to explore learning in the context of new technologies, and we are particularly interested in "constructionism," which means, more or less, learning by doing. We will look at both education in schools and education in the DIY (do it yourself) context.

ENERGY / THREE GORGES (CHINA)

Human energy use, perhaps more than any of our other topics, is undergoing a change fast enough that we see it within our lifetimes. Traditional energy sources are being rapidly depleted as new energy sources are being developed, and at the same time, many individuals are beginning to question how they use energy in their everyday lives.

EXPLORATION / INTERNATIONAL SPACE STATION

Exploration has been a natural desire among nearly every animal species, especially humans. In the last half century, humans have overcome terrestrial boundaries and have begun to probe space itself. What is the relationship between self-exploration and the exploration of outer worlds?

FOOD / BEIJING (CHINA)

As much as many of us would like to seize the topic of food to discuss organic products, buying local, and eating fresh, such topics hardly address how to feed the almost seven billion people presently living on our planet. We will use the topic of food to ask the difficult question of how to feed the world in an environmentally friendly way.

80+1
A JOURNEY AROUND THE WORLD

GROWTH / DUBAI (UNITED ARAB EMIRATES)
Growth encompasses both fixed resources, such as urban growth, and unlimited resources, such as intellectual or spiritual growth. Often, the line between the two is blurred.

HAPPINESS / BHUTAN
Given the state of the world today, it's tempting to keep our journey focused on the enormous problems and challenges that confront us. But we equally believed that it's important to balance the serious with things on the lighter side. Additionally, today happiness is considered a science, with a great deal of research toward understanding deeper issues. Our exploration of Happiness will take us both places.

HERITAGE / JERUSALEM (ISRAEL)
Though heritage may be about the past, it's all too often the source of friction between cultures. How can different heritages be mutually appreciated?

IDENTITY / INTERNET
The Internet has totally transformed the definition of identity. What does it mean to have an identity when one's language, culture and media are communicated on a vast, dynamic, global network?

MARKETS / DHAKA (BANGLADESH)
During the planning stages for 80+1, we envisioned the topic of markets to span, compare, and contrast the micro-credit stories emerging from less industrialized nations with novel methods of understanding world economy. We still plan to, but much has changed in the past year, and our exploration of markets will confront the difficult and volatile issues of the global economic crisis.

MIGRATION / LAMPEDUSA (ITALY)
Most humans, throughout most of human history, died close to where they were born. Exceptions, on a mass scale, are always noteworthy—people migrate for reasons of famine, war, religious persecution, and climate change. Though modern transportation may have made migration easier, the reasons remain noteworthy, and we have chosen migration as a topic to explore these deeper underlying forces.

PROGRESS / BANGALORE (INDIA)
Progress is an ideal not shared by all people and all cultures. How can we come up with a definition that fits our own society? What can we learn by comparing these definitions?

RECYCLING / GADANI (PAKISTAN)
Recycling is a process by which we as a human society can better take into account what it is that we consume and what we leave behind as waste. By recycling our waste, we can affect save money, reduce our energy use, and preserve our environment.

TRAFFIC / ST. GOTTHARD (SWITZERLAND)
Traffic sounds like such a mundane problem, so everyday and so close to home—it's often easy to overlook. This is precisely why we selected it as one of our topics. We'll examine several scientific and industrial studies that offer unusual, even drastic solutions to traffic problems.

WATER / MALI
Water is something you either take for granted or you don't, depending on where you live. It's also, like air, an important indicator of planetary wellness. We will explore daily lifestyles different from our own to open up a global discussion on water usage.

ALTERN / OKINAWA (JAPAN)
Die durchschnittliche menschliche Lebenserwartung hat sich in den letzten paar Jahrzehnten auf etwa 66 Jahre verdoppelt und ist nach wie vor im Steigen begriffen. Wie gehen verschiedene Gesellschaften damit um, dass die Bevölkerung länger lebt und mehr medizinische Versorgung benötigt?

BIODIVERSITÄT / LA GAMBA (COSTA RICA)
In vielerlei Hinsicht ist es gerade die extreme Komplexität des Lebens auf Erden, die die Ausgewogenheit und Schönheit des Ökosystems ausmacht. Die biologische Vielfalt ist allerdings durch die Übernutzung der Ressourcen bedroht. Wir beschäftigen uns in diesem Kontext mit Tierarten, die durch die moderne Lebensweise bedroht werden.

KLIMAWANDEL / BREIDJING CAMP (TSCHAD)
Einer groß angelegten internationalen Studie zufolge steht nunmehr fest, dass der Klimawandel eine vom Menschen verursachte Realität ist. Wir beschäftigen uns in diesem Kontext hauptsächlich damit, wie wir mit dieser Erkenntnis umgehen und welchen Beitrag neue Technologien, insbesondere jene der Simulation und der Visualisierung, leisten können.

KOEXISTENZ / KILPISJÄRVI (FINNLAND)
Koexistenz ist insbesondere dann schwierig, wenn eine konfliktträchtige Geschichte überwunden werden muss. Wie können Völker, die einander bekämpft haben, ihre Differenzen überwinden?

KULTURELLE VIELFALT / NEW ORLEANS (USA)
Kulturelle Vielfalt haben wir aus dem einfachen Grund als Thema gewählt, weil die meisten Kulturen weltweit von einigen wenigen dominiert und dadurch gefährdet werden. Wie kann man beispielsweise Kinder davon überzeugen, dass die Musik und die kulinarischen Traditionen ihrer Großeltern ebenso interessant sind, wie das, was im Fernsehen geboten wird, und dass sie darauf stolz sein können?

BILDUNG / MONGOLEI
Wir haben das Thema Bildung aufgenommen, um Lernen im Kontext neuer Technologien zu thematisieren, wobei unser Interesse insbesondere der „konstruktivistischen Lerntheorie", also dem *learning by doing*, gilt. Wir werden uns sowohl mit dem Schulunterricht als auch mit der Do-it-Yourself-Methode auseinandersetzen.

ENERGIE / DREI SCHLUCHTEN (CHINA)
Der Energieverbrauch unterliegt, mehr als alle anderen Probleme, die wir hier aufgreifen, einem Wandel, der sich so rasch vollzieht, dass wir mit den Konsequenzen noch zu Lebzeiten konfrontiert werden. Die traditionellen Energiequellen werden in absehbarer Zeit erschöpft sein, neue Energiequellen werden entwickelt und viele Konsumenten hinterfragen bereits ihren alltäglichen Energieverbrauch.

EXPLORATION / INTERNATIONAL SPACE STATION
Fast alle Tierarten und natürlich auch der Mensch haben einen natürlichen Forschungsdrang. In den letzten fünfzig Jahren haben die Menschen terrestrische Grenzen überwunden und begonnen, den Weltraum zu erforschen. Welche Beziehung besteht zwischen Selbsterforschung und der Erforschung äußerer Welten?

NAHRUNGSMITTEL / BEIJING (CHINA)
Auch wenn viele beim Thema Ernährung gerne über Bio-Lebensmittel, Einkauf in der Region und frische Produkte diskutieren würden – diese Diskussionen blenden das Problem aus, wie die fast sieben Milliarden Menschen ernährt werden können. Wir werden uns dem Thema daher über die schwierige Frage nähern, wie die Ernährung der gesamten Menschheit in umweltverträglicher Weise gewährleistet werden könnte.

WACHSTUM / DUBAI (VEREINIGTE ARABISCHE EMIRATE)
Wachstum bot sich als Thema an, weil es sowohl ein begrenztes Wachstum wie etwa das einer Stadt als auch unbegrenzte Ressourcen wie etwa spirituelles Wachstum und geistige Entwicklung umfasst. Die Grenzen sind hier häufig fließend.

GLÜCK / BHUTAN
In Anbetracht des Zustands der Welt ist man versucht, insbesondere die enormen Probleme und Herausforderungen, vor denen wir stehen, zu thematisieren. Wir halten es aber für wichtig, dabei eine gewisse Balance zwischen Ernsthaftigkeit und Leichtigkeit zu halten. Glücksforschung ist heute auch eine wissenschaftliche Disziplin, die sich intensiv mit den Voraussetzungen des Glücklichseins auseinandersetzt.

80+1
EINE WELTREISE

KULTURERBE / JERUSALEM (ISRAEL)
Obwohl man Kulturerbe mit Vergangenheit assoziiert, ist es nur allzu oft ein Konfliktpotential zwischen unterschiedlichen Kulturen. Wie können sich verschiedene Traditionen wechselseitig anerkennen?

IDENTITÄT / INTERNET
Das Internet hat den Identitätsbegriff grundlegend neu definiert. Was heißt es, eine Identität zu haben, wenn Sprache, Kultur und Medien in einem gigantischen, weltumspannenden Netzwerk kommuniziert werden?

MÄRKTE / DHAKA (BANGLADESCH)
In der Planungsphase für 80+1 hatten wir vor, in Zusammenhang mit dem Topos Märkte Kleinkreditprogramme in Entwicklungsländern neuen Theorien zum Verständnis der Weltwirtschaft gegenüberzustellen. Das Thema interessiert uns nach wie vor, doch hat sich im vergangenen Jahr vieles grundlegend geändert, sodass wir uns in diesem Kontext auch mit den schwierigen und komplexen Fragen auseinandersetzen werden, die die globale Wirtschaftskrise aufwirft.

MIGRATION / LAMPEDUSA (ITALIEN)
Wie die Geschichte zeigt, starben die Menschen meist in der Nähe ihres Geburtsortes. Signifikante Ausnahmen von dieser Regel sind als Warnsignale zu verstehen – Menschen verlassen ihre Heimat aufgrund existenzieller Bedrohung: wegen Hungersnöten, Krieg, religiöser Verfolgung oder Klimawandel. Obwohl moderne Transportmittel die Migration erleichtert haben mögen, sind die Ursachen nach wie vor klärungsbedürftig, weshalb wir Migration als Topos gewählt haben.

FORTSCHRITT / BANGALORE (INDIEN)
Fortschritt ist nicht für alle Menschen und Kulturen ein Ideal. Wie finden wir eine Definition, die unserer eigenen Gesellschaft entspricht? Was lässt sich durch den Vergleich unterschiedlicher Definitionen lernen?

RECYCLING / GADANI (PAKISTAN)
Recycling ist ein Prozess, durch den einer Gesellschaft bewusst werden kann, was sie konsumiert und welchen Abfall sie zurücklässt. Durch das Recycling unserer Abfälle können wir Geld sparen, unseren Energieverbrauch reduzieren und unsere Umwelt erhalten.

VERKEHR / ST. GOTTHARD (SCHWEIZ)
Das Verkehrsproblem ist so selbstverständlich, alltäglich und allgegenwärtig, dass es leicht zu übersehen ist. Gerade deshalb haben wir uns des Themas angenommen. Wir werden in diesem Kontext mehrere wissenschaftliche und industriellen Studien prüfen, die ganz und gar nicht alltägliche, ja drastische Lösungen des Verkehrsproblems vorschlagen.

WASSER / MALI
Wasser ist entweder etwas Selbstverständliches oder etwas Kostbares – je nachdem, wo man lebt. Die Qualität des Wassers ist wie jene der Luft ein wichtiger Indikator für den Zustand unseres Planeten. Wir entschieden uns für das Thema Wasser, um uns mit Formen des Alltags auseinanderzusetzen, die sich stark von unserer Lebensweise unterscheiden, und um eine globale Diskussion über die Wasserverwendung auszulösen.

ZIVILGESELLSCHAFT / JOHANNESBURG (SÜDAFRIKA)
Der Begriff Zivilgesellschaft hat in der heutigen wissenschaftlichen und öffentlichen Diskussion im Wesentlichen zwei Bedeutungen: Zum einen bezeichnet er einen Bereich innerhalb einer Gesellschaft, der zwischen staatlicher, wirtschaftlicher und privater Sphäre entstanden ist – oder auch: zwischen Staat, Markt und Familie. Der Bereich wird als öffentlicher Raum gesehen, den heute eine Vielzahl vom Staat mehr oder weniger unabhängiger Vereinigungen mit unterschiedlichem Organisationsgrad und -form bilden – etwa Initiativen, Vereine, Verbände. Der Begriff soziale Bewegung bezeichnet Teile solcher Organisationen.

Pierre Proske

Grand Mutual Smiles

In a response to accusations in 1987 by a journalist from UK's Financial Times that the pace of development in Bhutan was slow, the then King of Bhutan is quoted to have replied, "Gross National Happiness is more important than Gross National Product." This statement signalled his commitment to building an economy based on Buddhist spiritual values that was appropriate to Bhutan's culture and has since served as a unifying vision for the country's developmental strategies. In a survey in 2005, 45 percent of Bhutanese reported being very happy, 52 percent reported being happy and only three percent reported not being happy.
(Source: http://en.wikipedia.org/wiki/Bhutan)

While the Gross National Happiness of Bhutan has been criticised for being naïve and an attempt to deflect attention from the material poverty of its people, there is no doubt that its citizens have benefited from the emphasis on well-being and the environment their king has instituted. The advent of television and the Internet has nevertheless raised questions of the fragility of this so-called "Last Shangri-La". Part of the success of the King's GNH is based on the preservation of traditional customs and culture, which the spectre of materialism inherent in both online and broadcast media threatens to unravel.

Grand Mutual Smiles is a two-way interactive installation that communicates between two parties through the transmission of images of smiling faces. Progressively captured pictures of smiling people are displayed on screens at each installation site. The motivation is to encourage users to communicate across the Internet in a non-verbal and humoristic way, by smiling. The project presents a real-time updating set of people's faces ("smile-board") at each of the locations—Linz in Austria and Thimphu, the capital of Bhutan. There are two "smile-boards" at each location, one representing the remote location and one representing the local location. Each smile-board is realised in practice by either a screen or a video projector.

At each installation site, a camera is connected to a computer running custom smile detection software. The software continually captures the faces of people interacting with the installation. If the software detects what it considers to be a smile, it saves the image to the respective smile-board. As a local smile-board acquires new images, it sends those new images across the Internet to the corresponding board in the remote location. The software also keeps track of smile statistics, indicating how many smiles are tracked per country, per hour and per day.

Grand Mutual Smiles therefore creates a simple but effective Internet powered real-time index of happiness at the specific sites in both Austria and Bhutan.

Pierre Proske—*Concept, Aesthetics, Programming. http://www.digitalstar.net*
Damian Stewart—*Computer Vision Programming*
Arturo Castro—*Software Architecture and Network Programming*
Thanks / Supporters
A warm thank you to the following people who were vital to the realisation of this project: Michael Rutland OBE, chairman of the British Bhutanese Society, Dr Claus Walter and Franz Leuthner from the Austrian Bhutanese Society, Dorji Wangchuck and Dr. Michael Schneeberger. Voluntary Artists Studio Thimphu (VAST) (Bhutan)
Austrian Bhutanese Society (Austrian/Bhutan)

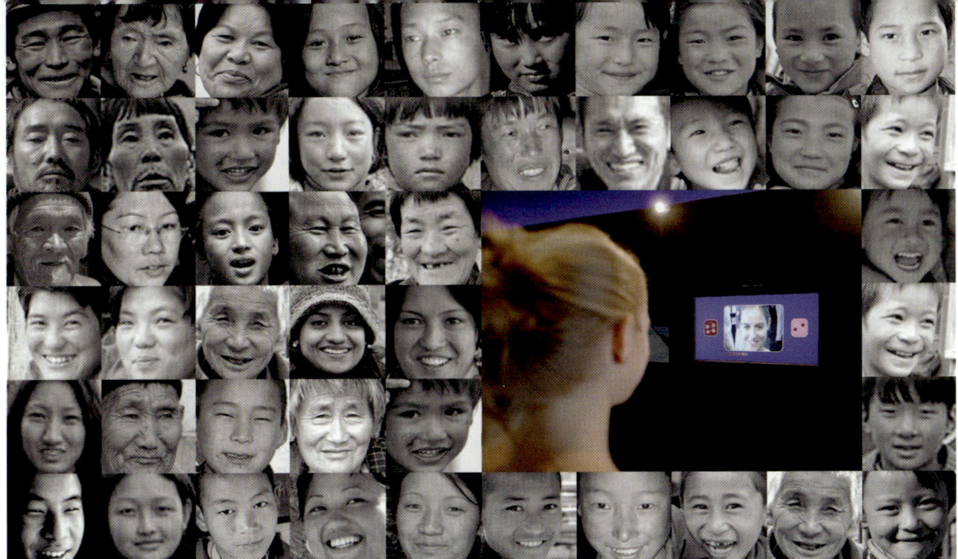

Pierre Proske

Grand Mutual Smiles

Das Bruttosozialglück in Bhutan wurde als naiv kritisiert, als ein Versuch, die Aufmerksamkeit von der Armut der Bevölkerung abzulenken, doch besteht kein Zweifel, dass die Bürger durch die vom König gesetzten Prioritäten – Wohlbefinden und Umweltschutz – profitiert haben. Die Einführung von Fernsehen und Internet zeigte jedoch, auf welch fragilem Fundament das „letzte Shangri-La" begründet ist. Der Erfolg des Bruttosozialglücks basiert teilweise auf der Bewahrung traditionellen Brauchtums und kultureller Werte, die durch das Schreckgespenst des Materialismus, der sowohl Online- als auch anderen Massenmedien zu eigen ist, ausgehöhlt zu werden drohen.

Grand Mutual Smiles ist eine interaktive Installation, bei der zwei Parteien mittels der Übertragung von Bildern lächelnder Gesichter kommunizieren. An den beiden Standorten der Installation werden Bildserien lächelnder Menschen auf Bildschirmen gezeigt. Ziel ist es, die User zu ermutigen, über das Internet in nonverbaler und humorvoller Weise – eben durch ein Lächeln – zu kommunizieren. Im Rahmen des Projekts werden an beiden Standorten – Linz, Österreich, und Thimphu, Bhutan – zwei in Echtzeit aktualisierte Porträtserien präsentiert. An jedem Ort gibt es zwei „Smile-Boards", wobei eines die fremde Stadt und das andere die eigene repräsentiert. Bei den „Smile-Boards" handelt es sich entweder um Monitore oder Videoprojektionen.

An jedem der beiden Orte ist eine Kamera mit einem Computer verbunden, auf dem eine Smile-Detection-Software – eine Software, die ein Lächeln erkennt – installiert ist. Sie nimmt die Gesichter der Teilnehmer auf, speichert das Bild auf dem jeweiligen Smile-Board, sobald sie ein Lächeln entdeckt, und übermittelt es via Internet zum entsprechenden Board in der Partnerstadt. Die Software legt auch Smile-Statistiken an, die dokumentieren, wie viele User in einem Land pro Stunde und pro Tag gelächelt haben.

Grand Mutual Smiles ist ein einfacher, aussagekräftiger Glücksindikator, der mithilfe des Internets in Echtzeit die Zufriedenheit an bestimmten Orten in Österreich und Bhutan ermittelt.

(Aus dem Englischen von Martina Bauer)

Eugene Ahn, Hye Ki Min

LinkCube

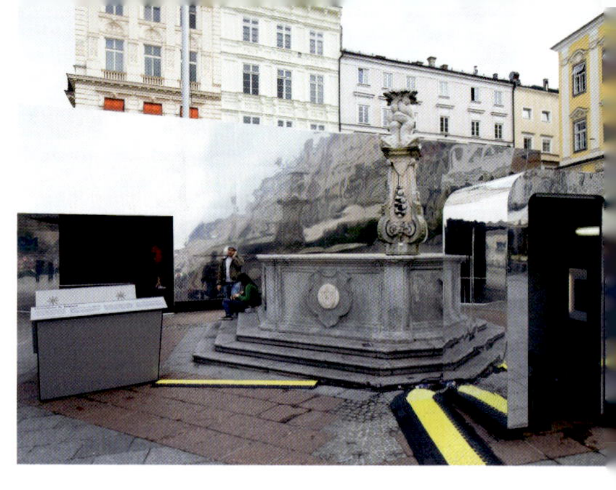

LinkCube is a network of units stationed in public spaces between New York and Linz, Austria. The project allows people in remote locations to take pictures together at the same time. *LinkCube* allows users to develop a personal connection with anonymous people from around the world. The resulting picture serves as a memento of the shared experience.

The user draws a curtain to enter the booth and closes it for privacy. The interior is a well-lit white environment. The user can immediately see himself/herself on the screen. The participants from the other unit appear on the screen soon after. The users from both locations move around in their respective booths, experimenting with movement and location in order to establish the perfect pose. Either user can then press a button to initiate the camera shot. The process begins when the user on the other side of the unit hits the button as a sign of agreement. When each button from the two stations is pressed, the camera shoots 4 photos, approximately 2 seconds apart. Pictures are displayed on screen after they are taken, so poses can be adjusted and smiles perfected. Seconds later, the pictures are printed with different backgrounds.

Our aim is to create an immersive experience—one of being together with people who happen to be in affiliated photo booths, elsewhere in the world. In this space, the users, who are geographically distant, are presented on screen as if they were right next to each other. This closeness lets users get momentarily acquainted with human beings to whom they would not otherwise be exposed. *LinkCube* fosters a sense of global connectedness as users in disparate locations collide in one photograph.

LinkCube allows the user to take a photo with people who are not physically present, but visible via a screen located in the booth. As the two parties appear in the same picture plane on screen, they position themselves appropriately, posing together in an effort to take a successful photograph. What results is a set of playful interactions. The ultimate photographs serve as a tangible record of this memorable virtual experience.

Technical Description

Each station has an IP camera grabbing image of the users in front of the screen. The video image of the users captured by the cameras at each station is transferred to a web server in real-time. The video data are then edited automatically via a video-editing algorithm. An algorithm separates the person or the group of people in front of the camera from the background and creates an image statistic from the silhouette. The scales of people derived from the image statistic values are compared in order to establish perspective. The manipulated images are then juxtaposed together in one picture plane in the video. This final video from the web server continuously streams to each station through QuickTime broadcaster. As live streaming videos are being played, the user chooses the moment to take a picture together by pressing a button on a simple, user-friendly control panel. The generated still image of the users is printed out from a built-in printer for photograph output.

Sponsored by the Embassy of the United States of America

Eugene Ahn, Hye Ki Min

LinkCube

LincCube basiert auf vernetzten Fotokabinen, die in New York und Linz im öffentlichen Raum aufgestellt sind. Das Projekt ermöglicht Menschen, die geografisch getrennt sind, eine persönliche Beziehung zueinander zu entwickeln und ein gemeinsames Foto aufzunehmen. Das dabei entstehende Bild ist eine bleibende Erinnerung an eine gemeinsame Erfahrung.

Der Teilnehmer öffnet einen Vorhang, betritt die Kabine – einen gut beleuchteten weißen Raum – und schließt den Vorhang wieder hinter sich, um sich von der Außenwelt abzuschirmen. Er sieht sich sofort auf dem Monitor. Kurz danach erscheinen auch die Mitspieler aus der anderen Kabine auf dem Monitor. Beide Parteien bewegen sich in ihren Kabinen, experimentieren mit Bewegungen und Posen, um sich perfekt in Szene zu setzen. Jeder der Teilnehmer kann nun per Tastendruck die Kamera auslösen. Der fotografische Prozess beginnt, sobald der zweite Teilnehmer ebenfalls die Taste betätigt, um sein Einverständnis zu signalisieren. Die Kamera nimmt nun im Abstand von etwa zwei Sekunden vier Fotos auf. Die Bilder erscheinen unmittelbar nach der Aufnahme auf dem Monitor, sodass die Posen noch aufeinander abgestimmt werden können und das schönste Lächeln aufgesetzt werden kann. Ein paar Sekunden später werden die Bilder mit unterschiedlichem Hintergrund ausgedruckt.

Das Projekt will mittels vernetzter Fotokabinen eine eindringliche Erfahrung von Nähe ermöglichen. Die örtlich getrennten Teilnehmer erscheinen auf dem Bildschirm, als ob sie nebeneinander stünden. Diese virtuelle Nähe macht Menschen miteinander bekannt, die sich sonst nie getroffen hätten. *LinkCube* fördert ein Gefühl globaler Verbundenheit, indem Teilnehmer aus verschiedenen Kulturkreisen in einer Fotografie zusammenfinden.

LinkCube ermöglicht dem Teilnehmer, ein Foto mit Menschen aufzunehmen, die zwar nicht anwesend, aber auf dem Bildschirm in der Kabine zu sehen sind. Wenn die beiden Mitspieler auf derselben Bildebene erscheinen, nehmen sie entsprechende Posen ein, damit das Foto auch gelingt. Das Ergebnis sind spielerische Interaktionen. Die daraus resultierenden Fotos sind konkrete Aufzeichnungen einer einprägsamen virtuellen Erfahrung.

Technische Beschreibung

In jeder Station ist ein mit einer Web-Kamera aufgenommenes Bild der jeweiligen Teilnehmer auf dem Bildschirm zu sehen. Diese Videobilder werden in Echtzeit an einen Internet-Server übertragen. Die Videodaten werden dann mithilfe eines Algorithmus automatisch bearbeitet, der die vor der Kamera posierende Person oder Gruppe vom Hintergrund freistellt und eine Bildstatistik der Silhouette erstellt. Um ein perspektivisch korrektes Bild zu erstellen, werden die aus den Kennwerten der Bildstatistik abgeleiteten Maße der Personen miteinander verglichen. Die manipulierten Bilder werden dann auf einer Bildebene im Video wiedergegeben. Das daraus resultierende Video wird vom Web-Server kontinuierlich mittels QuickTime Broadcaster an die einzelnen Stationen übermittelt. Während das Video als Livestream zu sehen ist, wählt der Teilnehmer den optimalen Augenblick für das gemeinsame Foto, indem er auf einer einfachen, benutzerfreundlichen Bedienkonsole auf eine Taste drückt. Das so erzeugte Bild wird von einem integrierten Fotodrucker ausgedruckt.

(Aus dem Englischen von Martina Bauer)

8gg interactive

Blowing—Blow The Air From Beijing To Linz

This is a single-way interactive device realized by the Internet; however, it wishes to give people at the two ends of the world a feeling of mutual exchange.

In Beijing, we install a *blowing* sensor and connect it to the computer and get it online. At the main square in Linz we install a huge blowing fan and connect it to the computer with real time Internet. The fan not only creates strong wind, it is also pre-installed with "spicy hot pot" scent.

The ultimate effect is that the participants in Beijing blow strongly into the *blowing* sensor, which will activate the electronic fan in Linz to release the scents with the powerful wind. Viewers in Beijing see that amazingly they can blow away the people in Linz. At the same time people in Linz can see the blower in Beijing on the screen and if they are close enough to the fan they can also smell a particular scent.

The installed scent—the spicy hot pot scent—is collected and obtained in advance in Beijing. We place the *blowing* sensor in a restaurant and invite the diners to take part in the project.

This project enables the viewers to experience a trip of scents on this journey around the world.

We discover that the scents we perceive while traveling are extremely important for our memories of a city. They even call to mind our feelings towards a place that we have visited—and Beijing is a city filled with strong and abundant scents.

With widespread modern technology and transmitting, people are no longer satisfied with just the visual and audio senses, because they can already watch millions of films about a place before actually visiting it. Nevertheless, the smell of a place cannot be experienced without making an actual trip and this is the main purpose of our project. We allow 80+1 participants to gain an almost genuine experience of Beijing.

Concept: 8gg interactive (Fu Yu, Jia Haiqing)
Tech: Shan Yang, Sun Zhongyi
Assistance: Er Mao, Ding Ying
Special thanks to: Gai Yunong, Wang Zhaofang, EON

Blowing – Der Duft der großen weiten Welt

Diese interaktive Installation versucht, Menschen aus unterschiedlichen Kulturkreisen die Möglichkeit eines kommunikativen Austauschs zu ermöglichen.

Wir installieren in Peking einen mit einem Sensor ausgestatteten „Blasebalg" und schließen diesen an einen Computer mit Internet-Verbindung an. Auf dem Hauptplatz in Linz wird ein großer Ventilator aufgestellt, der ebenfalls an das Internet angeschlossen ist und die Daten aus Peking in Echtzeit überträgt. Dieser Ventilator erzeugt nicht nur einen starken Windstrom, sondern kann auch den Duft von „Spicy Hot Pot", einem typischen chinesischen Gericht, verbreiten.

Wenn die Teilnehmer in Peking kräftig in das Gerät „blasen", erzeugt der elektronische Ventilator in Linz starken Wind und setzt Duftwolken frei. Die verblüfften Zuseher in Peking haben den Eindruck, dass sie die Macht haben, den Menschen in Linz den Wind ins Gesicht blasen zu können.

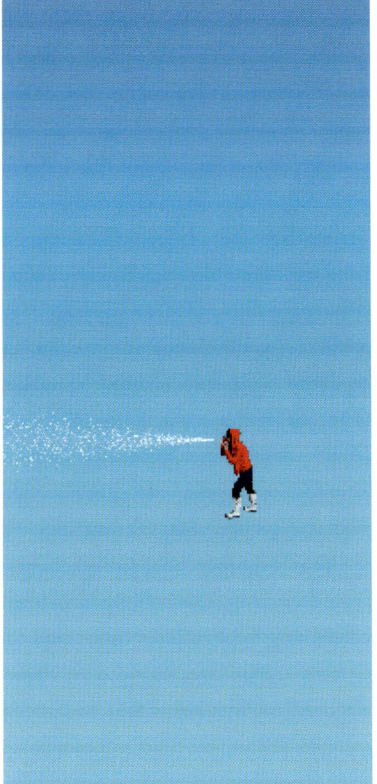

Gleichzeitig sehen die Linzer „den Windmacher" aus Peking auf einem Monitor; stehen sie nahe genug beim Ventilator, können sie auch einen ganz speziellen Duft wahrnehmen.

Der Duft des Spicy Hot Pot wurde vorab in Peking „komponiert". Der „Blasebalg" ist in einem Restaurant aufgestellt, und die Restaurantgäste werden eingeladen, an der Interaktion teilzunehmen.

Dieses Projekt versucht, den Zusehern „den Duft der großen weiten Welt" näherzubringen.

Beim Reisen sind Düfte für die Erinnerungen an eine Stadt von größter Bedeutung. Sie rufen Gefühle wach, die man an einem bestimmten Ort empfand. Peking ist für dieses Projekt besonders gut geeignet, da die Stadt für ihre vielfältigen und intensiven Düfte bekannt ist.

Aufgrund der rasanten Verbreitung moderner Medien und Übertragungstechnologien sind viele Reisende heute nicht mehr mit visuellen und akustischen Eindrücken zufriedenzustellen, weil sie unzählige Filme über einen Ort sehen können, bevor sie ihn besuchen. Wie es an einem Ort riecht, erfährt man aber nur, wenn man tatsächlich dorthin reist, und dies hat uns auch zu diesem Projekt inspiriert. Wir möchten den Besuchern von 80+1 ermöglichen, nahezu authentische Eindrücke von Peking zu gewinnen.

(Aus dem Englischen von Martina Bauer)

Niklas Roy

WIA < > WIA
Water in Africa < > Water in Austria

The "80+1—A Journey around the World" exhibition's project entitled *WIA < > WIA -Water in Africa—Water in Austria*, which was purportedly to have linked up Linz via the internet to an African village's well in order to gather data in real time about African water usage and transmit the data to Linz where it would be used to flush a toilet with the exact same amount of water, was actually completely fabricated. Nor does there exist an artist named Melissa Fatoumata Touré. Both the artist and the entire project are fictions that I invented, and I intentionally did not inform Ars Electronica of this fact. Nevertheless, when doubts began to mount about the reality of this project, it seemed advisable to go public with the truth and state the background facts and circumstances.

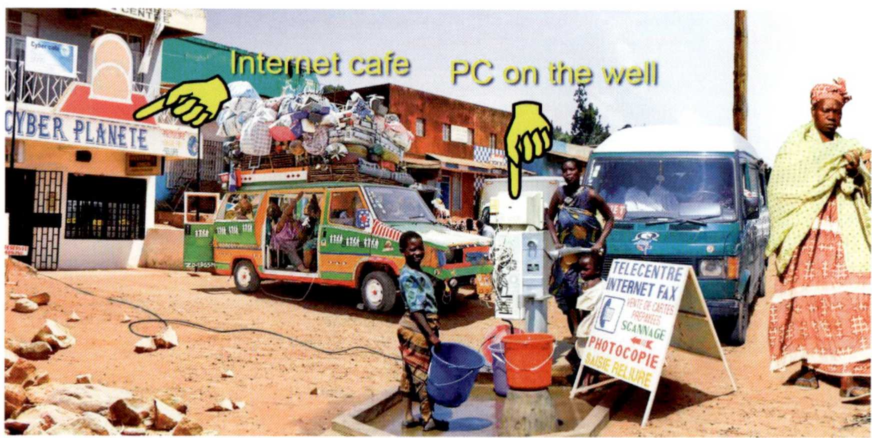

WIA < > WIA: Photo Montage: Niklas Roy

In a public call for the tender of ideas in 2008, Ars Electronica invited artists and scholars to submit proposals for a virtual journey around the world, a medial reinterpretation of the trip protagonist Phileas Fogg took in Jules Verne's novel *Around the World in 80 Days*. The aim is to thereby call attention to important issues that affect the population of the whole world.

I took the journey's belletristic basis (as specified by Ars Electronica itself) as an occasion to consider an installation that would be played out in the realm of fiction just like the novel that gave the whole project its name. The internet as the filter in the communication between Ars Electronica and me played an essential role in this by effectively concealing my true identity for a long time. Inventing and subsequently maintaining a fictional identity by means of digital communication have also simultaneously been the core of my artistic contribution to this exhibition.

The *WIA < > WIA* installation I proposed via a fictitious person named Melissa Fatoumata Touré unfortunately deals with a very serious issue: the fact that not all people in this world have enough clean drinking water at their disposal. The installation is set up in such a way that it puts forth a real solution to this very real problem: the operation of the installation will help to raise money that will be used to subsidize the building of wells in Africa. These facts are not changed in the least by the otherwise fictive character of the installation. The data that are being fed to the toilet in Linz don't come from an African well hooked up to the internet but rather from a random number generator. And the panoramic image of the African village square that adorns the walls of the toilet is actually a Photoshop collage assembled using images freely available online.

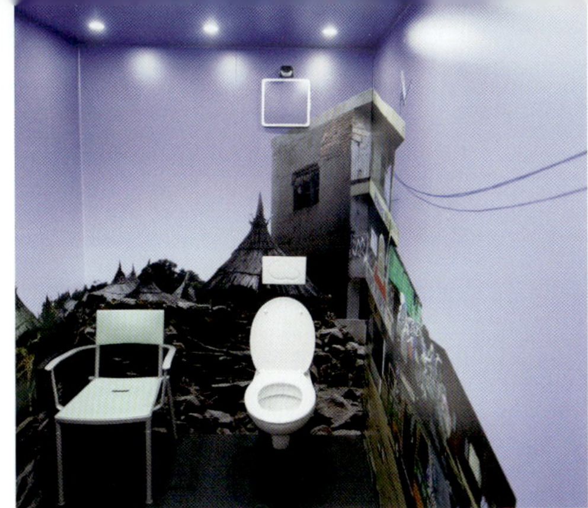
WIA < > WIA: Toilet in Linz

An integral part of a fiction, if it's to be perpetrated in such a way that people will give it credence, is skepticism. What was originally perceived by the project organizer and audiences as a real project by a real person was revealed, at a certain point, to be a deception. From an artistic perspective, I was interested in exploring this borderline. How long does one keep believing in information? At what point does one classify it as false? And how can I, someone who disseminates fictitious information, use my influence to cause it to be believed nevertheless?

This is why the way in which the project is set up calls attention to a problem that, although it has always existed in all media, has been significantly exacerbated by the speed and multi-layered complexity of global digital communications: the increasing importance of being able to autonomously assess the extent to which information is true. Or to put this in different terms: to be cognizant of ones occasional impotence in this regard. After all, one is not always in the enviable situation of being able to correctly classify the quality of a piece of information or its source.

I custom-tailored both the *WIA < > WIA* installation as well as the fictional artist Melissa Fatoumata Touré to the wishes expressed by the project organizers in their published call for submissions. Doing so afforded me the opportunity to very vividly treat the subject of fraudulent identity and falsified information on the basis of a concrete example in an exhibition context since it's my opinion that 80+1—*A Journey around the World*, a project structured precisely in such a way as to take advantage of all modes of electronic data transfer, should also shed light on this dark side of the internet.

I'm pleased that discovery on the part of Ars Electronica has now brought closure to this undertaking. Since sustainably providing all people with clean drinking water is more important than the subject of misinformation in the media—indeed, is truly a matter of life or death—I'm also happy that the installation will remain in operation until the conclusion of 80+1—*A Journey around the World* and will continue to raise donations to finance the construction of actual wells in Africa.

http://www.niklasroy.com/shows/index.htm

Niklas Roy

WIA < > WIA

Water in Africa < > Water in Austria

Das in der Ausstellung *80+1 – Eine Weltreise* präsentierte Projekt *WIA < > WIA -Water in Africa - Water in Austria*, bei dem angeblich ein afrikanischer Dorfbrunnen mit dem Internet verbunden ist und Daten des afrikanischen Wasserverbrauchs in Echtzeit nach Linz übertragen werden, um dort eine Toilettenspülung mit derselben Menge Wasser zu speisen, entspricht nicht der Wahrheit. Genauso wenig existiert eine Künstlerin namens „Melissa Fatoumata Touré". Sowohl bei der Künstlerin als auch bei ihrem Projekt handelt es sich um von mir erdachte Fiktion - wobei Ars Electronica über diese Tatsache von meiner Seite her bewusst nicht informiert wurde. Als sich jedoch die Zweifel an der Realität der Arbeit häuften, schien es daher sinnvoll, mit den wahren Hintergründen des Projektes an die Öffentlichkeit zu treten.

In einem öffentlichen Aufruf hatte sich die Ars Electronica 2008 an Künstler und Wissenschaftler gewandt, um Projektvorschläge für eine virtuelle Weltreise zu erhalten, die laut Ausschreibung die Reise des Helden Phileas Fogg aus Jules Verne's *In achtzig Tagen um die Welt* neu medial interpretieren und hierbei substanzielle Themen aufgreifen, welche die gesamte Weltbevölkerung betreffen.

Die von der Ars Electronica vorgegebene belletristische Grundlage der Weltreise habe ich zum Anlass genommen, über eine Installation nachzudenken, die sich – genau wie die Vorlage – im fiktionalen Raum abspielt. Das Internet als Filter in der Kommunikation zwischen der Ars Electronica und mir hat hierbei eine wesentliche Rolle gespielt, meine wahre Identität über einen längeren Zeitraum effektiv zu verschleiern. Das Erfinden und anschließende Lebendigwerdenlassen einer fiktionalen Identität durch die Mittel der digitalen Kommunikation waren gleichzeitig auch Kern meines künstlerischen Beitrags zur Ausstellung.

Die von mir durch die fiktive Person „Melissa Fatoumata Touré" vorgeschlagene Installation *WIA < > WIA* nimmt sich eines leider sehr ernsten Themas an: dass nicht allen Menschen auf dieser Welt genügend sauberes Trinkwasser zur Verfügung steht. Die Installation ist so aufgebaut, dass sie für dieses reale Problem eine reale Lösung generiert; durch den Betrieb der Installation werden Spenden gesammelt, die wiederum den Brunnenbau in Afrika fördern. An dieser Tatsache ändert auch der ansonsten fiktive Charakter der Installation nichts. Die Daten, die der Toilette in Linz über das Internet zugespielt werden, stammen nicht aus einem an das Internet angeschlossenen Brunnen in

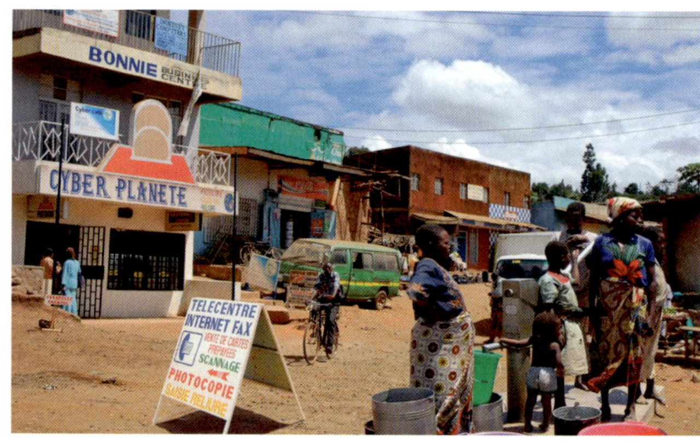

WIA < > WIA: Photo Montage: Niklas Roy

Afrika, sondern von einem Zufallsgenerator. Und das in der Toilette tapezierte Panorama des afrikanischen Dorfplatzes ist in Wahrheit eine Photoshop-Collage, zusammengesetzt aus frei im Internet verfügbaren Afrika-Fotos.

Ein integraler Bestandteil der Fiktion, wenn sie denn als bare Münze verkauft wird, ist die Skepsis. Was anfangs vom Veranstalter und vom Publikum als reales Projekt einer echten

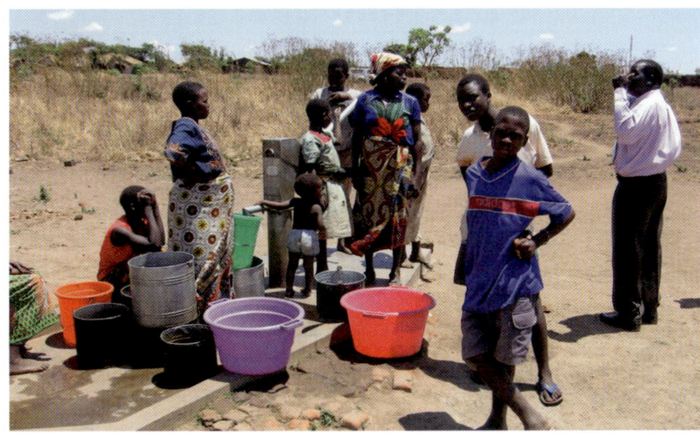

Brunnen in Kawale / Sence (Malawi).
Quelle: flickr, http://www.flickr.com/photos/khym54/287032344/
User: khym54. Published under a Creative Commons Licence

Person wahrgenommen wurde, hat sich ab einem gewissen Punkt als Täuschung entpuppt. Aus künstlerischer Perspektive war ich an der Erforschung dieser Grenzlinie interessiert: Wie lange schenkt man einer Information Glauben? Ab welchem Punkt stuft man sie als falsch ein? Und wie kann ich als jemand, der fiktive Informationen streut, Einfluss darauf nehmen, dass ihnen dennoch geglaubt wird?

Deshalb weist das Projekt in seiner Machart auf ein Problem hin, das medienübergreifend zwar schon immer bestand, durch die Geschwindigkeit und Vielschichtigkeit globaler digitaler Kommunikation jedoch drastisch an Schärfe gewinnt: Es geht um die zunehmende Wichtigkeit, den Wahrheitsgehalt von Informationen autonom einschätzen zu können. Oder andersherum gesagt: Es geht darum, sich der gelegentlichen eigenen Ohnmacht diesbezüglich Gewahr zu werden. Denn nicht immer ist man in der glücklichen Lage die Qualität einer Information bzw. einer Quelle richtig einstufen zu können.

Sowohl die Installation *WIA < > WIA*, als auch die fiktive Künstlerin „Melissa Fatoumata Touré" habe ich direkt auf die in der Ausschreibung geäußerten Wünsche der Organisatoren zugeschnitten. Dadurch hatte ich die Möglichkeit, das Thema der gefälschten Identität und der gefälschten Information im Ausstellungskontext am praktischen Beispiel plastisch zu verhandeln, denn ich bin der Meinung, dass das Projekt *80+1 – Eine Weltreise*, dessen struktureller Aufbau alle Register elektronischer Datenübertragung zieht, auch diese Schattenseite beleuchten sollte.

Ich freue mich, dass dieses Projekt durch die Aufdeckung seitens der Ars Electronica nun einen runden Abschluss gefunden hat. Da die nachhaltige Versorgung aller Menschen mit sauberem Trinkwasser allerdings noch wichtiger als das Thema medialer Fehlinformationen ist, ja, im wahrsten Sinne des Wortes *lebenswichtig* ist, freue ich mich darüber hinaus, dass die Installation bis zum Ende von *80+1 – Eine Weltreise* weiter betrieben wird und weiterhin Spenden für einen tatsächlichen Brunnenbau in Afrika sammelt.

http://www.niklasroy.com/shows/index.htm)

Shahjahan Siraj

80+1 days around Dhaka
Live Bits from Dhakai Markets

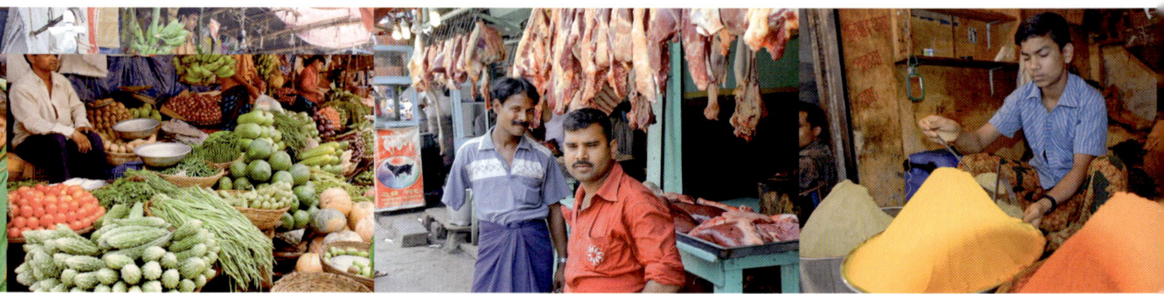

About Dhaka

Dhaka, the capital city of Bangladesh, is a city of rickshaws and mosques. This metropolis is one of the most densely populated cities of the world, with a population of over 12 million. Although it is a megacity, Dhaka itself is like a market. From bazaars to parks, slums to five star localities—there is a touch of production and marketing about everything. With the fast growing market economy, the bazaars, shops and consumerism are rapidly changing—largely due to the influence of global media and culture. The modern fast food, coffee shops, multistoried shopping malls and entertainment-based consumerism are hitting small business and forcing change. Although old Dhaka still has historical traditions in commerce, food and culture, it is now losing its community spirit. Life in new Dhaka has been updated and influenced by global culture, which reveals the spirit of individualism. Above all Dhaka is inheriting the love, life and the cultural lineage of modern Bangla society, which leads to the spread of updated life information and consumerism around the country.

Motivation

In the spirit of Jules Verne, the virtual journey "80+1 days around Dhaka" can be undertaken. One by one the major market spots are visited and the audience is guided through this virtual tour. The live video from the spot is a web cast via wireless Internet connectivity. A favorable mode is created to unite the audience with the people, culture and lifestyle of Dhaka—something that has never been done before. On the 1st day the journey starts from New Market and it will end at ULAB (University of Liberal Arts) at the 80+1 days' victorious closing ceremony.

The market spots along the journey are selected according to the goods and popularity, with special consideration for the diversity of Dhakai life styles. Along with formal markets, entertainment spots, performance and contemporary art and culture, events and practices will also be web cast. We will also do live bits from Dhaka's famous restaurants to stream Dhaka's food market, culture and hospitality.

Artist: Shahjahan Siraj; *Assistance:* Jahangir Alam, Raihath Sohel, Farhad Hossain, Kamrul Hasan, Junaed Shihriar, Matsuzaki Misuzu

Shahjahan Siraj

80+1 Tage in Dhaka
Live Bits von den Märkten in Dhaka

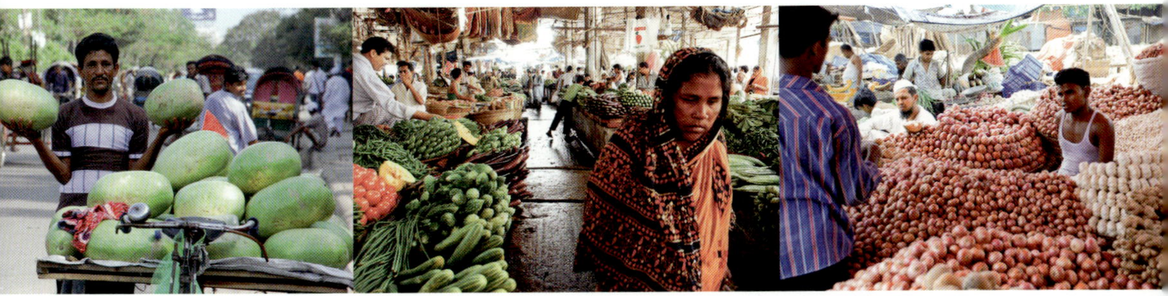

Über Dhaka

Dhaka, die Hauptstadt Bangladeschs, wird als Stadt der Rikschas und Moscheen bezeichnet. Die Metropole zählt mit mehr als zwölf Millionen Einwohnern zu den bevölkerungsreichsten Städten der Welt. Ganz Dhaka ist ein Markt. Vom Basar bis zu den Parkanlagen, von den Slums bis zu den Fünf-Sterne-Hotels – überall werden Produkte feilgeboten. Manche der von Läden und Kaufhäusern gesäumten Straßen und Gassen sind für ganz bestimmte Produkte und Händler bekannt. Mit der rasanten Entwicklung der Marktwirtschaft und unter dem Einfluss der globalen Medienkultur haben sich Basare, Läden und Konsumverhalten schlagartig verändert. Fast Food, Coffee Shops, mehrgeschossige Einkaufszentren und eine auf Unterhaltung basierende Konsumkultur verdrängen die Kleinunternehmen und sind Motoren der Veränderung. Das Leben in New Dhaka ist beeinflusst von der globalen Kultur, in der vor allem Individualismus zählt. Auf dem New Market sind internationale Luxusprodukte erhältlich. Dhaka steht nach wie vor für die traditionelle Lebensweise und das kulturelle Erbe Bangladeschs, treibt aber gleichzeitig Erneuerung, Medienkultur und Konsum im ganzen Land voran.

Motivation

Die virtuelle Reise „in 80+1 Tagen um Dhaka" ist eine Hommage an Jules Verne. Wir besuchen die wichtigsten Märkte der Stadt, wobei die virtuelle Rundfahrt das Publikum durch digitale Momentaufnahmen in Echtzeit führt. Die Videos werden live vom jeweiligen Ort über eine drahtlose Internetverbindung übertragen. Die Fahrt beginnt am ersten Tag am New Market und endet bei der ULAB (University of Liberal Arts) bei der feierlichen Schlussveranstaltung am 81. Tag. Kriterien für die Auswahl der Märkte waren die dort angebotenen Produkte sowie ihre Popularität, wobei besonderes Augenmerk auf die Diversität des Lebensstils in Dhaka gelegt wurde. Neben Märkten, Vergnügungsvierteln, Performances und zeitgenössischer Kunst und Kultur zeigen die Webcasts auch landestypische Besonderheiten. Live-Streams aus berühmten Restaurants vermitteln einen Eindruck vom kulinarischen Angebot, der Kultur und Gastfreundschaft der Stadt.

(Aus dem Englischen von Martina Bauer)

Zhu Handong

The Three Gorges of the Future

The Three Gorges of the Future is an integrated art project that builds up the connection between a virtual platform of Second Life and the real space. The project is composed with the documentary *New Three Gorges*, a virtual island in Second Life, and the on-site installation in Linz. The backgrounds of the documentary and the creation of Second Life are human and historical landscapes, the natural ecological environment and relocated villages and towns in the Three Gorges reservoir area. They aim to present the history and current situations of the Three Gorges, which also explore the contradictory relationship between the development of new energies and the preservation of cultural heritage. The viewers can experience the virtual world of the project while realizing interactions via real time images from Linz and from the Three Gorges area.

Documentary

It keeps records of the influences and changes upon upstream cities and cultural sceneries caused by the rise of water level in the Three Gorges reservoir area. It also reflects the status quo of ordinary people's lives along the shore.

Virtual Island

The main elements of the island are current situations as well as historical architectures in the Three Gorges reservoir area. It is divided into three regions: *Underwater:* The submerged cultural heritage along the water route and the ruins of relocated cities and towns. *Surface:* An artistic representation of the existing architectures and artificial sceneries in the Three Gorges reservoir area. *Air:* The creation of an imaginary future of the Three Gorges area.

Daily Live Connection

During the presentation of the project, local residents from six locations in the Three Gorges reservoir area are invited to realize online interactions with people in Linz. Visitors in Linz can travel through Second Life and communicate online with local Chinese residents who are floating on the water surface. At the same time there are live broadcasts of the documentary along with real-time images sent from the Yangtze River presented in the Base Camp on the main square of Linz. The visitors at two ends of the planet can experience the virtual and the real world of Three Gorges through Second Life, the documentary and the real-time images.

Concept: Zhu Handong. *Photographer:* Liao Hongbo. *Second Life Technician:* Zhao Ken. *Project Assistant:* Zhang Han

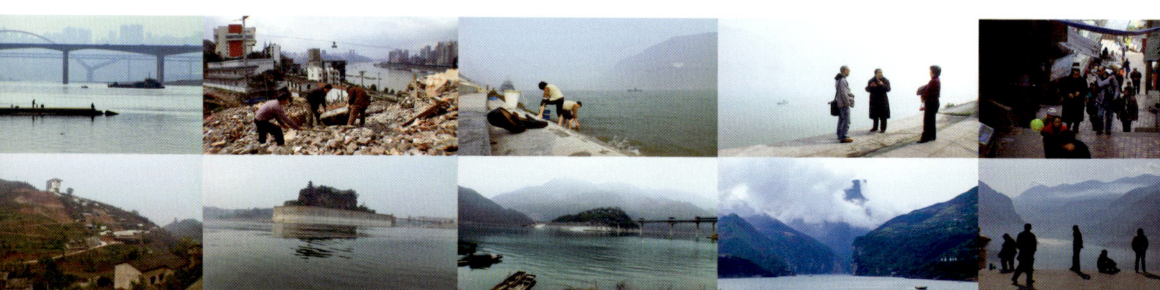

Zhu Handong

Die Drei Schluchten in der Zukunft

The Three Gorges of the Future ist ein mehrteiliges Kunstprojekt, das eine virtuelle Second-Life-Plattform und die reale Welt miteinander in Verbindung setzt. Das Projekt besteht aus dem Dokumentarfilm „New Three Gorges", einer virtuellen Insel in Second Life sowie einer standortspezifischen Installation in Linz. Den Hintergrund des Dokumentarfilms und der Second-Life-Simulation bilden künstlich geschaffene und historische Landschaften, die ökologische Umwelt sowie die umgesiedelten Dörfer und Städte im Gebiet des Drei-Schluchten-Staudamms. Sie zeigen die Geschichte und aktuelle Entwicklung der Region und thematisieren den Konflikt zwischen der Entwicklung neuer Energiequellen und der Bewahrung des kulturellen Erbes. Die Zuseher tauchen in die virtuelle Welt des Projekts ein, während sie gleichzeitig über Echtzeitbilder aus Linz und der Drei-Schluchten-Region interaktiv miteinander kommunizieren können.

Dokumentarfilm

Der Film zeigt Einflüsse und Veränderungen in den Städten und Kulturlandschaften, die auf den Anstieg des Wasserspiegels im Gebiet des Drei-Schluchten-Staudamms zurückzuführen sind, sowie den Alltag der Menschen, die hier leben.

Virtuelle Insel

Die wesentlichen Gestaltungselemente der Insel sind aktuelle Szenarien sowie historische Bauwerke in der Drei-Schluchten-Region. Die Insel ist in drei Bereiche unterteilt:
Unter-Wasser-Bereich: das überflutete Kulturerbe entlang des Wasserwegs und die Ruinen von Städten und Dörfern, deren Bewohner umgesiedelt wurden;
Land: eine künstlerische Darstellung der bestehenden Bauwerke und künstlichen Landschaften in der Drei-Schluchten-Region;
Luft: eine Zukunftsvision für die Drei-Schluchten-Region.

Tägliche Live-Verbindung

Während der Präsentation des Projekts werden Bewohner aus sechs Orten der Drei-Schluchten-Region eingeladen, interaktiv mit den Besuchern der Stadt Linz zu kommunizieren. Die Linzer können durch die virtuellen Landschaften in Second Life reisen und online mit den Bewohnern des Gebiets kommunizieren. Gleichzeitig werden der Dokumentarfilm sowie Echtzeit-Bilder vom Jangtse im Basislager auf dem Linzer Hauptplatz gezeigt. Die Mitwirkenden in China und Österreich können die virtuelle und reale Welt der Drei-Schluchten-Region über Second Life, den Dokumentarfilm und Echtzeit-Bilder erleben.

(Aus dem Englischen von Martina Bauer)

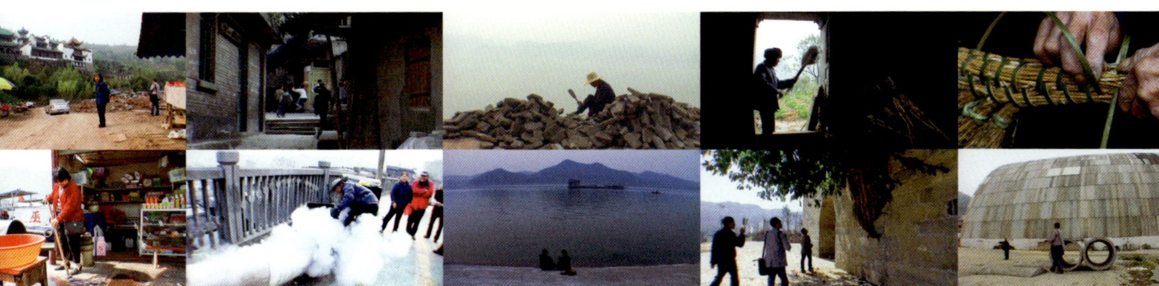

Noah Shibley, Hyunjoo Oh

Net Topology

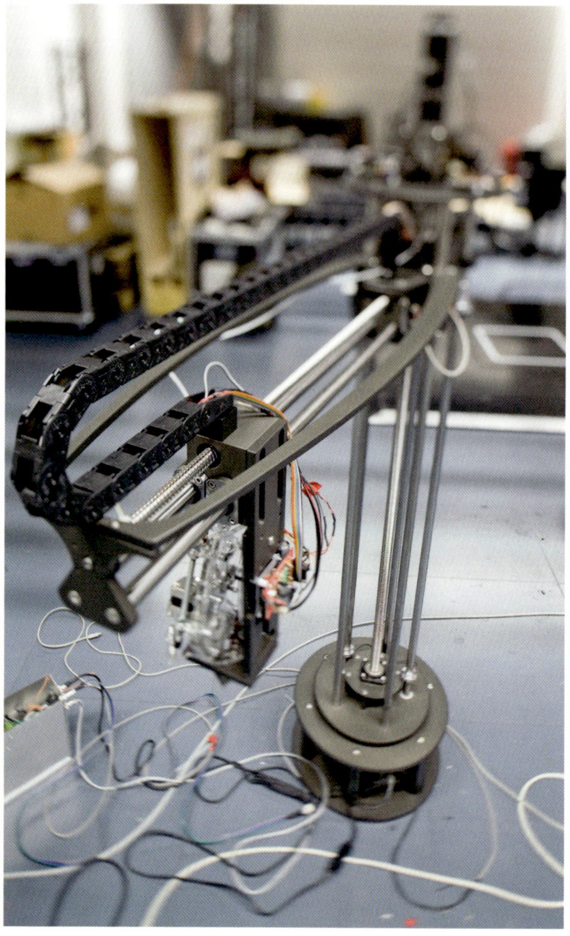

Because of organisational reasons related to the actual financial crisis, the project *Topology of Dubai* couldn't take place. In the meantime the artists developed already a new concept which we are publishing here instead.

Net Topology focuses on the topic of growth and in particular on the growth of the internet. Nothing says growth like the internet, and sometime in 2010 the number of computers that can be uniquely addressed will reach its limit. With only one year to go, this is the perfect time to think about this problem and, in so doing, think about our future. *Net Topology* uses HDPE plastic to graph out the continued growth of the internet in each of the world's five internet regions. This data is used by a 3D printer created by the artist to construct unique sculptural record of the internet's growth.

Concept: Noah Shibley, Hyunjoo Oh
Mechatronic Engineering: Michael Grant
Database and embedded programming: Andrea Bianchi
Printing algorithm design assistance: Will Craig,
Facilities and Digital Resources: Sogang Unviersity Art & Tech Department
Software for getting the IPV4: Takashi Muzohata
http://socialhardware.net

Noah Shibley, Hyunjoo Oh

Net Topology

Die Arbeit *Topology of Dubai* konnte aufgrund organisatorischer Hindernisse in Dubai, die auf die Finanzkrise zurückzuführen waren, nicht stattfinden. Die Künstler haben mittlerweile ein neues Konzept erarbeitet, das hier stellvertretend, beschrieben wird:

Net Topology thematisiert das Thema Wachstum und im besonderen das Wachstum des Internet. Man sagt, dass nichts so sehr wächst wie das Internet. Irgendwann in 2010 wird die Zahl der Computer, denen eine eindeutige Adresse zugeteilt werden kann, an ihre Grenze stoßen. Da es bis dahin nur noch ein Jahr ist, ist dies der perfekte Zeitpunkt, über dieses Problem und damit auch über unsere Zukunft nachzudenken. *Net Topology* verwendet HDPE-Plastik, um das fortgesetzte Anwachsen des Internet in jeder der fünf Internet-Regionen grafisch darzustellen. Die Daten werden von einem eigens kreierten 3D-Drucker verarbeitet, der ein plastisches Modell des Internetwachstums erstellt.

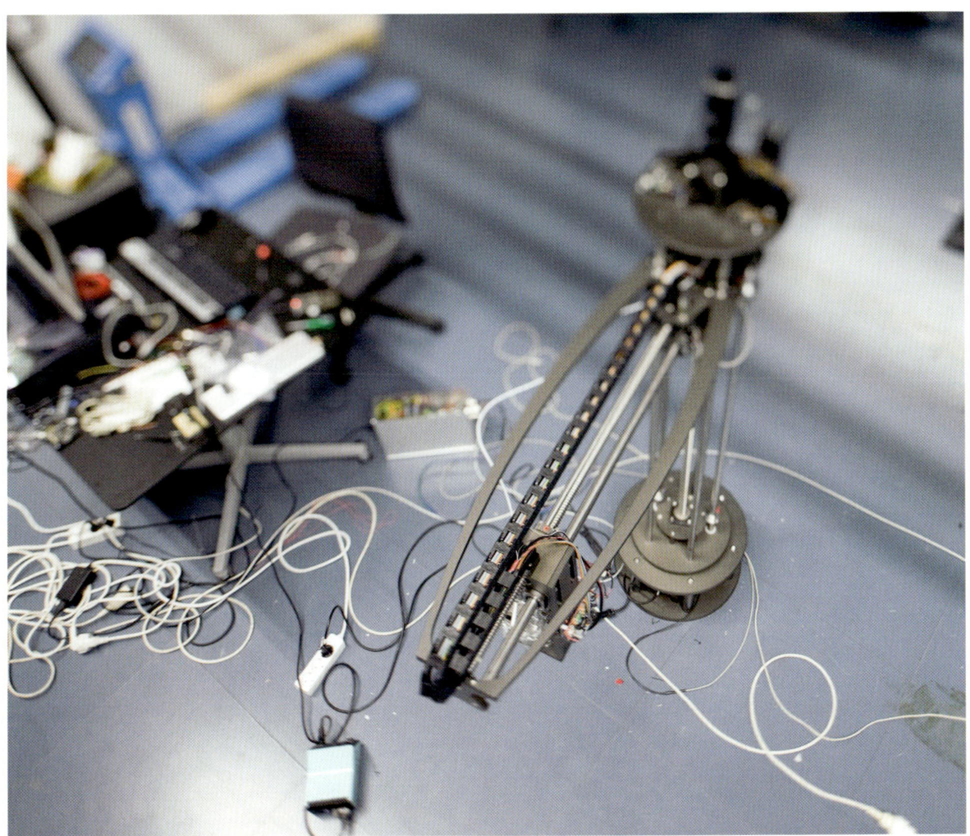

Team 4040

White Shadow

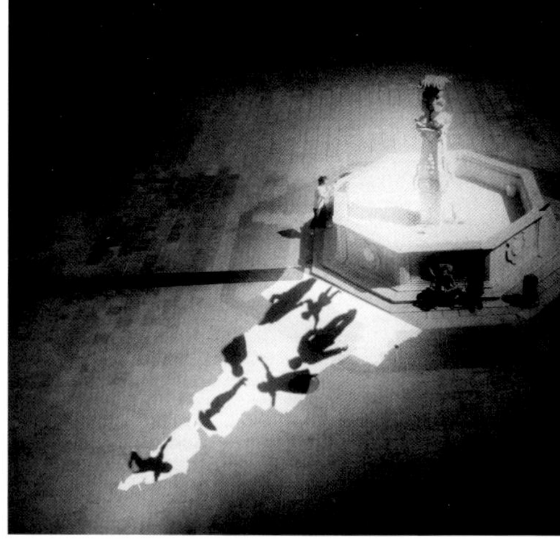

White Shadow is an interactive art installation composing a telematic sundial that connects people on two remote locations via a monument's shadow. A white shadow of the Monument to Cuauhtémoc in Mexico City is remotely cast at the Hauptplatz in Linz, matching the original shadow's shape. This white shadow is then populated in real-time by the shadows of Mexico City inhabitants.

The tradition of constructing sundials goes far back to the obelisks built in 3500 BC and has played an important role in the developments in various fields of science, which led to our current state of knowledge regarding science and technology. Today's technology is able to bring us closer to things situated on the other side of the world almost in real-time. Distance and time are interpreted as things that we can skip with the help of modern communication networks. What we acknowledge as "reality" has changed and extended far beyond what exists in our field of vision. Today, distance is not only the space between us and objects, but also a modifier of how we can relate to these objects and a conditioner of the dynamic experience generated. We can reduce the time needed to access far away locations, but we are also altering our perception of that place.

White Shadow embodies a play between the changing of our perception of time and distance and issues related to human migration. The Monument to Cuauhtémoc, the last Aztec ruler, proudly casts its shadow during daytime in Mexico City, the shape and orientation of its shadow changing with (and marking) the passing hours. At the same time, night has fallen in Linz and the main square is illuminated by the white shadow of Cuauhtémoc's Statue, bounding the distance in time and space between the two locations.

Furthermore, the white shadow becomes a channel which allows the inhabitants of Mexico City to also bound this time-space gap via their shadows, enabling them in a way to be remotely present in Linz but also anonymizing each individual and limiting his/her presence in both time and space.

To achieve this, a camera is placed in Mexico City to capture images of people passing by during daytime. A computer then extracts the silhouettes of people from the background. These silhouettes are then streamed over to Linz, where it is nighttime (geographically 8 hours difference from Mexico City). This allows for projecting images in the open space of the Hauptplatz. The streamed silhouettes of Mexico inhabitants are received by a computer in Linz and composited in black against a white shadow of the Cuauhtémoc Monument, rendered so as to match the shadow being cast at the same time by the monument in its original location. The resulting image is then projected on the ground of the Hauptplatz, in a way that the white shadow seems to be cast by another structure of different shape—namely the fountain in the south part of the square.

Concept and Production: Jesus Cabrera Hernandez (ES), Jona Hoier (AT), Ulrike Gollner (AT), Ebru Kurbak (TR), Sho Kuwabara (JP), Tiago Martins (PT), Michael Probst (AT), Jeldrik Schmuch (AT), Onur Sönmez (TR)
Supported by Frima Green Lemon—*http://www.green-lemon.com/*
Supported by Festival de México en el Centro Histórico, Museo de Antropologias

White Shadow

White Shadow ist eine interaktive Kunstinstallation, die auf einer telematischen Sonnenuhr basiert und Menschen an zwei verschiedenen Orten durch den Schattens eines Denkmals miteinander verbindet. Der weiße Schatten des Denkmals für Cuauhtémoc in Mexico City wird auf den nächtlichen Linzer Hauptplatz projiziert. Durch diesen weißen Schatten wandern in Echtzeit die Schatten der Einwohner von Mexico City.

Die Geschichte der Sonnenuhren geht auf die 3500 v.Chr. errichteten Obelisken zurück und spielte eine bedeutende Rolle bei der Entwicklung verschiedener wissenschaftlicher Disziplinen, die unseren heutigen wissenschaftlichen und technischen Wissenstand maßgeblich beeinflussten. Die Technik kann uns heute nahezu in Echtzeit Dinge näherbringen, die sich auf der anderen Seite der Welt befinden. Distanz und Zeit werden als Kategorien interpretiert, die mithilfe moderner Kommunikationsnetzwerke aufgehoben werden können. Was wir als „Realität" betrachten, hat sich verändert und weit über unsere Wahrnehmungsgrenzen hinaus erweitert. Distanz ist heute nicht nur der Raum, der uns von Objekten trennt, sondern definiert auch unsere Beziehung zu diesen Objekten neu und bedingt die dabei entstehende dynamische Erfahrung. Wir können die für die Erreichung bestimmter Ziele erforderliche Zeit reduzieren, aber auch unsere Wahrnehmung dieser Orte verändern.

White Shadow ist ein Spiel zwischen der Veränderung unserer Zeit- und Raumwahrnehmung und dem Thema Migration im weitesten Sinn. Das Denkmal für Cuauhtémoc, den letzten Herrscher der Azteken, wirft tagsüber stolz seinen Schatten auf Mexico City, wobei sich Form und Ausrichtung mit dem Sonnenstand verändern und dadurch die Tageszeit anzeigen. In Linz bricht zeitgleich die Nacht herein – der weiße Schatten des Cuauhtémoc-Denkmals erhellt den Hauptplatz und überbrückt die zeitliche und räumliche Distanz zwischen den beiden Städten.

Dieser weiße Schatten wird zu einem Kommunikationskanal, der es den Einwohnern von Mexico City ermöglicht, durch ihre Schatten die weite Spanne von Raum und Zeit zu überbrücken und im fernen Linz präsent zu sein, wobei der einzelne Passant anonymisiert und seine Präsenz zeitlich und räumlich begrenzt wird.

Zur Realisierung des Projekts wurde in Mexico City eine Kamera installiert, die Bilder der tagsüber dort flanierenden Menschen aufnimmt. Mithilfe einer speziellen Software werden die Silhouetten vom Hintergrund gelöst, freigestellt und nach Linz übertragen. Der Zeitunterschied beträgt acht Stunden, in Linz wird es also gerade Nacht, wodurch es möglich ist, Bilder auf die Freifläche des Hauptplatzes zu projizieren. Die Silhouetten werden auf einem Computer in Linz bearbeitet und in Schwarz auf den weißen Schatten des Denkmals projiziert, der genau so wiedergeben wird, wie er an seinem ursprünglichen Ort fällt. Das daraus resultierende Bild wird dann so auf den Hauptplatz projiziert, dass es den Anschein erweckt, der weiße Schatten stamme von einem anderen Bauwerk – nämlich dem Brunnen im südlichen Bereich des Platzes.

(Aus dem Englischen von Martina Bauer)

Sabine Haerri, Yvonne Weber
In Collaboration with the Ars Electronica Futurelab

Movement & Impact

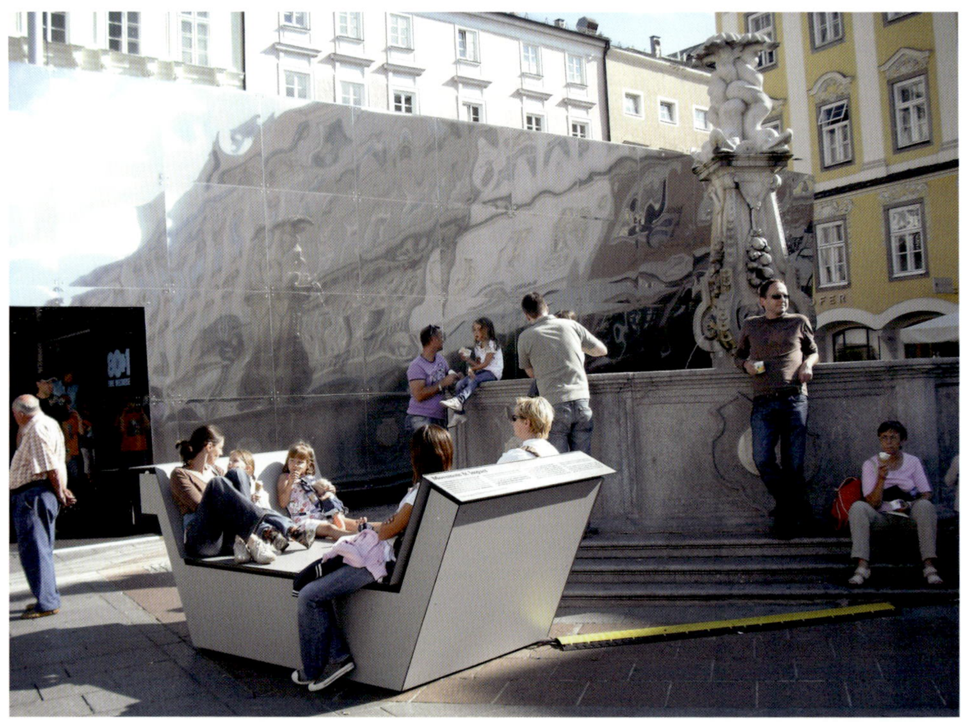

The Gotthard Tunnel is a major traffic bottleneck. The *Movement and Impact* installation lets visitors to *80+1* in Linz experience this massive confluence of vehicles with their own bodies. The Gotthard Road Tunnel is Switzerland's most important north-south transalpine traffic artery. It connects Northern and Southern Europe as well as northern Switzerland with the southern flair of the Tessin region. The Gotthard is the link between north and south, cold and warm, work and vacation, business suit and bathing suit. An average of six million cars and trucks pass through the tunnel each year—at peak times causing traffic jams extending for miles.

Switzerland's Federal Bureau of Statistics has set up traffic monitoring devices to count every passing vehicle and register its speed and make. This information corresponding to the events transpiring in the Gotthard Tunnel is communicated to the installation visitors reclining on the platform in Linz via simultaneous vibrations.

This installation is designed to increase awareness of the impact of this "avalanche of steel" on the alpine region, and to make people cognizant of the consequences of a globally network-linked world and increasing mobility.

Sabine Haerri, Yvonne Weber
In Zusammenarbeit mit Ars Electronica Futurelab

Movement & Impact

Die Installation *Movement and Impact* lässt BesucherInnen von *80+1* in Linz ein Gefühl für die Masse an Fahrzeugen am Nadelöhr des Gotthard-Straßentunnels unmittelbar am eigenen Körper erleben. Der Gotthard-Straßentunnel ist die wichtigste Nord-Süd-Alpentransversale der Schweiz, verbindet Nord- und Südeuropa ebenso wie den Norden der Schweiz mit dem südländischen Flair des Tessins. Der Gotthard steht als Bindeglied zwischen Nord/Süd, kalt/warm, Arbeit/Urlaub und Business-/Badeanzug. Jährlich rollt eine Blechlawine von durchschnittlich sechs Millionen Fahrzeugen durch den Tunnel und verursacht zu Spitzenzeiten kilometerlange Staus durch die Landschaften.

Das schweizerische Bundesamt für Statistik erfasst mit Verkehrszählern jedes vorbeifahrende Fahrzeug, dessen Geschwindigkeit und Typ. Diese Informationen werden den in Linz auf der Plattform liegenden BesucherInnen zeitgleich zu den Ereignissen am Gotthard mittels entsprechenden Vibrationen vermittelt.

Die Installation möchte die BenutzerInnen auf die Auswirkungen der Blechlawine in der Alpenregion aufmerksam machen, ein Bewusstsein schaffen für die Auswirkungen einer Global vernetzen Welt und immer größer werdenden Mobilität.

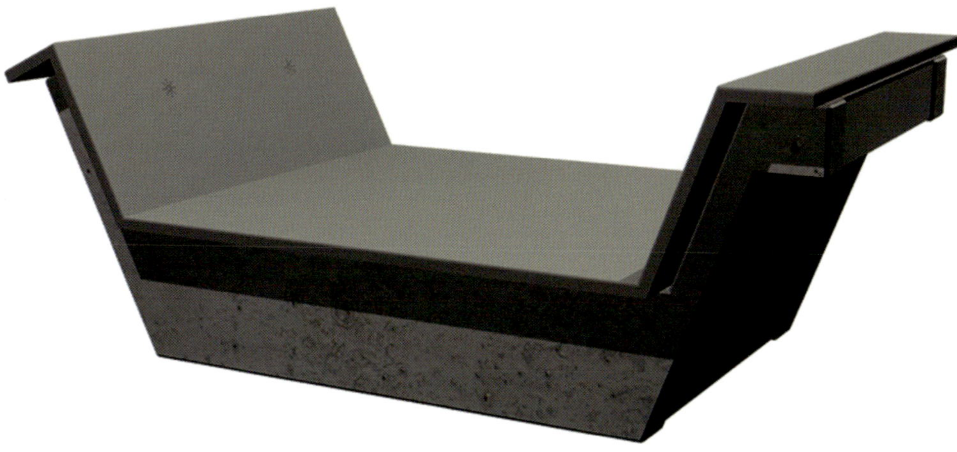

Extra Europa Schweiz – Kooperation von Linz 2009 und der Schweizer Kulturstiftung Pro Helvetia

Bundesamt für Straßen ASTRA

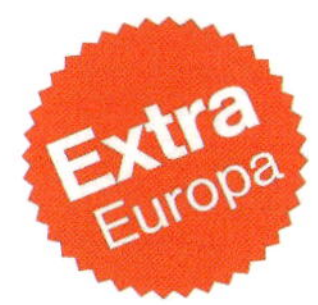

Gabriela Golder

Arrorró

Buenos Aires—Linz / Linz—Buenos Aires

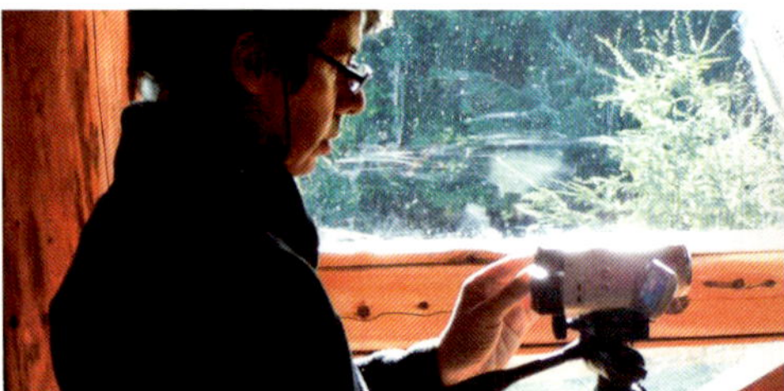 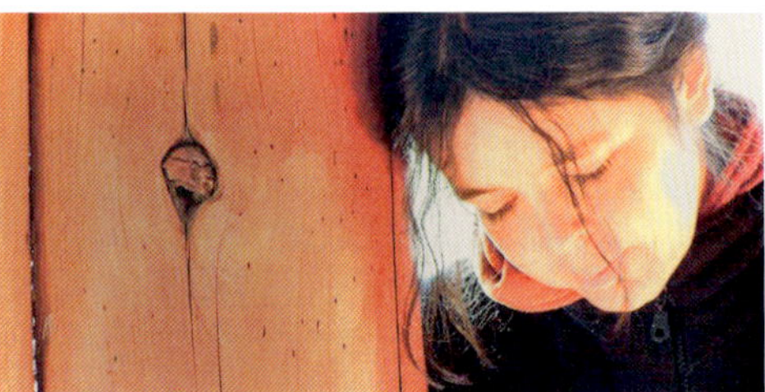

Arrorró is a project about cultural diversity that proposes the creation of a technological bridge that builds a bond between different realities. Two cities are connected in real time, hundreds of people will share dreams, traditions and languages through lullabies. These songs talk about our identity that is diverse, plural. In each country the language of the lullabies is the most diverse, as it corresponds to established traditions, to the history or to knowledge passed on from generation to generation.

The Project. Dynamics

Over a period of approximately three months, testimonies of people singing lullabies were gathered from all over our country. We have created a website where these audiovisual recordings are kept: *http://www.arrorrolullabies.com.ar.* Users are able to contribute to this site. Therefore there are recordings that we have recorded and other recordings that have been contributed by other users. There is an urban video installation, a screen with hundreds of lullabies interrupting the landscape.

Live

For a whole hour the people of Buenos Aires broadcast live and share lullabies across thousands of miles with the people of Linz. In return, the people of Linz are invited to sing lullabies back to the people of Argentina.

Artist: Gabriela Golder
Realization: Gabriela Golder,
and Escuela de Comunicación Multimedial de la Universidad Maimónides [Argentina]
Production: Abel Cassanelli
Design, website and connectivity: Violeta Gau / José Allona
Editing: Santiago Pedroncini
Team: María Fernanda Amenta, Facundo Colantonio, Guido Gardini, Violeta Cassanelli, Tiago Espírito Santo, Valeria Evdemón, Pablo Martín Fernández, Guido Ceratto, Ars Electronica [Austria]
Sponsored by: Universidad Maimónides.
http://www.arrorrolullabies.com.ar/

[1] *Arrorró* is the most well known lullaby in Spanish speaking countries.

Arrorró
Buenos Aires – Linz / Linz–Buenos Aires

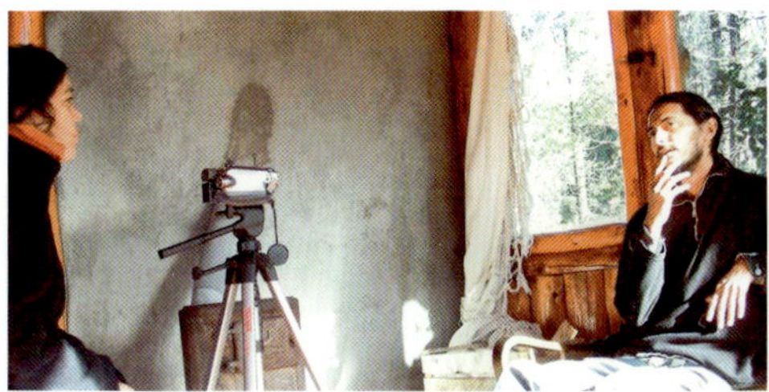 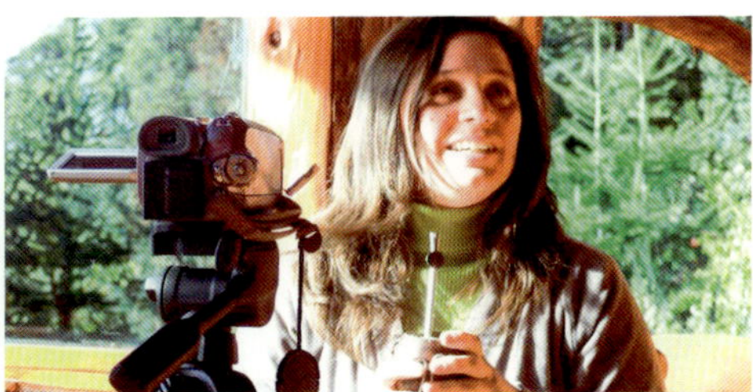

Das Projekt *Arrorró* thematisiert kulturelle Vielfalt und versucht, mittels Technologie eine Brücke zwischen verschiedenen Wirklichkeiten zu schlagen. Wiegen- und Schlaflieder haben Rhythmen und Klänge, die über sprachliche und andere Barrieren hinweg verstanden werden. Zwei Städte werden in Echtzeit miteinander verbunden und geben so ihren Bewohnern die Möglichkeit, Träume, Traditionen und Sprachen über den Austausch von Wiegenliedern miteinander zu teilen. Wiegenlieder erzählen von unserer vielfältigen, pluralen Identität. Die Sprache von Wiegenliedern ist in jedem Land völlig anders, sie entspricht alten Traditionen, einer Geschichte oder einem Wissen, das von Generation zu Generation weitergegeben wird.

Das Projekt. Dynamiken

Drei Monate lang haben wir im ganzen Land Material für das Projekt gesammelt, indem wir Menschen filmten, die Wiegenlieder sangen. Wir haben eine Website eingerichtet, auf der diese Videos veröffentlicht werden: *http://www. arrorrolullabies.com.ar*. Die User können auswählen, welchen Song aus welchem Land, in welcher Sprache etc. sie hören möchten, und auch einen eigenen Beitrag auf der Website präsentieren. Eine Videoinstallation im Stadtraum, eine Projektionswand, auf der Hunderte Interpreten von Wiegenliedern zu sehen sind, durchbricht den städtischen Alltag.

Live

In einer einstündigen Live-Übertragung haben die Bewohner des fernen Buenos Aires den Linzern während des Projektes *80+1 – Eine Weltreise* Wiegenlieder vorgesungen. Die Linzer waren eingeladen, den Argentiniern ebenfalls ein Wiegenlied vorzusingen.

Realisation: Gabriela Golder
Escuela de Comunicación Multimedial de la Universidad Maimónides (AR).
Produktion: Abel Cassanelli; Design, Website und Vernetzungstechnologie: Violeta Gau /José Allona; Schnitt: Santiago Pedroncini; Team: María Fernanda Amenta, Facundo Colantonio, Guido Gardini, Violeta Cassanelli, Tiago Espírito Santo, Valeria Evdemón, Pablo Martín Fernández, Guido Ceratto, Alexis Wurstein, Ars Electronica
Gesponsert von: Universidad Maimónides
http://www.arrorrolullabies.com.ar/

[1] *Arrorró* ist der Titel des bekanntesten Wiegenlieds in spanisch sprechenden Ländern.

(Aus dem Englischen von Martina Bauer)

Alon Chitayat, Lila Chitayat

TaxiLink

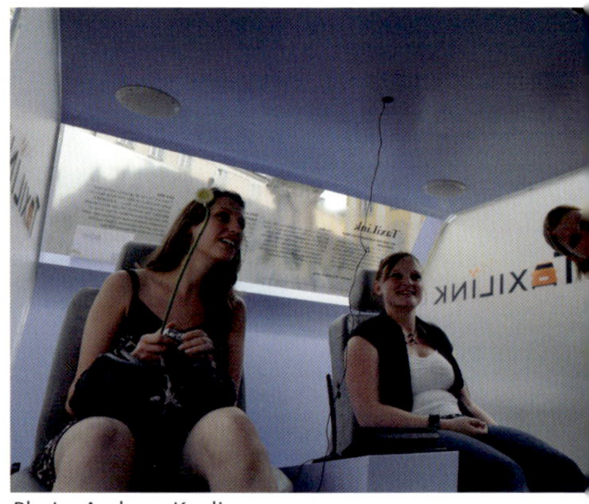

Photo: Andreas Keplinger

The *TaxiLink Project* is an interactive installation that enables users to experience an authentic distant taxi ride. Sitting in the static *TaxiLink* booth, the passengers join a live ride in and around the old city of Jerusalem, experiencing personal interaction with a real-life taxi driver screened through a rear view mirror.

Jerusalem reflects endless polar diversities composed of the three major monotheistic faiths that coexist in this extraordinary metropolis. The city imbeds extreme cultural ethno zones clustered in a very small place, echoing through national and political conflicts. Over 3000 years old, the holy city manages to encapsulate essences of religions, cultures and histories, woven together in the most delicate way. Thus, the traces of time, layered in every street, house and cobblestone, reveal themselves as visual, cultural, or historic emotional tides.

TaxiLink was developed as a multi-layered experience of an urban virtual tour, offering a brief yet meaningful experience of Jerusalem. The intensity of this encounter is two-fold, since the passengers see the city once through their own eyes and again, as seen through the eyes of an authentic local driver. By recording a personal journey, absorbing, gazing, collecting glimpses along the way, one will end up with an unexpected virtual experience. The users choose their destination, starting the trip at the point where the previous one ended. It is the road that we focus on rather than a given destination. The urban icons become meaningless and the place is exposed to chance and singularity. We decided to work with a taxi after being amazed by the global similarities of the taxi driver's characteristics. They are all urban reflectors that are constantly exposed to unlinked bits of information and amazing stories. As a passenger, you enter a private moving space, usually into a "tornado storm" of political discussions, to a personal family conversation on the phone or to an unexpected music repertoire. You can then choose to join, ignore or convert the conversation for the limited time of a short ride.

On the other side of the globe we build a physical static booth. It is designed to incorporate two riders. Inside the booth a screen projects the live ride from Jerusalem as seen from the front view window. A rear-view mirror is also installed that shows via video the reflection of the eyes of the driver in Jerusalem, and a surround system allows conversations with the driver while listening to the local radio station that is playing in the background.

A small monitor is installed beside the seats and transfers the live ride via GPS. All routes are recorded and the passengers can see where the real taxi is located and choose a nearby destination for the ride.

On the exterior facade of the booth another screen shows a superimposed video of the interiors, connecting the real driver with one or two "static" riders at different locations.

Lila Chitayat: *Architectural and Space Design*. Alon Chitayat: *Visual and Experience Design*. Tal Chalosin: *Technical Director*. Michael Shynar: *Software*
Sponsors: G.M.B.S. (General Management and Business Strategy). Garage Geeks (*http://www.garagegeeks.org/*) Hewlett-Packard. Pelephone. Jerusalem City Hall

TaxiLink

Das Projekt *TaxiLink* basiert auf einer interaktiven Installation, die den Mitwirkenden ermöglicht, eine Taxifahrt in einer fernen Stadt in Echtzeit mitzuerleben. Die Teilnehmer sitzen in einer stationären *TaxiLink*-Kabine und nehmen als virtuelle Fahrgäste an einer realen Rundfahrt durch die Altstadt von Jerusalem teil. Über ein aus der Fahrerkabine übertragenes Live-Video erleben sie die Fahrt gleichsam aus nächster Nähe mit, obwohl sie Tausende Kilometer entfernt sind.

Das Besondere an Jerusalem ist die Vielfalt der Stadt, die von den drei großen monotheistischen Glaubensrichtungen geprägt ist, welche in dieser ungewöhnlichen Metropole nebeneinander existieren. Die Stadt ist auf relativ kleiner Fläche in extreme ethnokulturelle Zonen unterteilt, deren Differenzen sich in nationalen und politischen Konflikten manifestieren. Der 3.000 Jahre alten heiligen Stadt gelingt es dennoch, die Quintessenz unterschiedlicher religiöser, kultureller und historischer Entwicklungen, die auf hochkomplexe Weise miteinander verwoben sind, in sich zu vereinen.

TaxiLink wurde als mehrdimensionale Erfahrung einer virtuellen Stadtführung entwickelt, die einen kurzen, aber aussagekräftigen Eindruck Jerusalems bietet. Die Intensität dieser Erfahrung beruht auf einer Verdoppelung der Wahrnehmung, da die Fahrgäste die Stadt zuerst aus eigener Sicht und dann noch einmal durch die Augen des lokalen Fahrers sehen. Durch die Aufzeichnung einer persönlichen Rundfahrt, die Aufnahme von flüchtigen, intensiven Eindrücken entlang der Route, wird dem Fahrgast eine unerwartete virtuelle Erfahrung geboten.

Die Mitwirkenden wählen ihr Ziel und starten die Fahrt an der Stelle, an der die vorherige Fahrt endete. Im Blickpunkt steht eher die Straße als ein bestimmtes Ziel. Urbane Ikonen werden bedeutungslos, Zufälle und nebensächliche Dinge stehen im Vordergrund.

Die Idee, ein Projekt mit einem Taxi zu machen, entstand aus der Erkenntnis, dass Taxifahrer auf der ganzen Welt gewisse Ähnlichkeiten aufweisen. Sie sind Spiegel des Urbanen, die ständig mit vordergründig zusammenhanglosen Informationseinheiten und erstaunlichen Geschichten konfrontiert werden. Als Fahrgast betritt man einen Privatraum auf Rädern, gerät in hitzige politische Diskussionen, bekommt Privatgespräche am Handy oder unerwartete Musik zu hören. Man kann sich entscheiden mitzumachen, sich zu distanzieren oder das Gespräch auf eine kurze Fahrt beschränken. Auf der anderen Seite der Erdkugel richten wir eine stationäre Kabine ein, in der zwei Fahrgäste Platz finden. Im Inneren der Kabine wird auf einem Monitor die Fahrt aus Jerusalem, durch die Frontscheibe gefilmt, live übertragen. Auch ein Rückspiegel ist installiert, der die Augen des Taxifahrers zeigt, während ein Surround-System es ermöglicht, mit ihm zu plaudern und dem lokalen Radiosender zuzuhören, dessen Programm im Hintergrund zu hören ist. Neben den Sitzen ist ein kleiner Monitor angebracht, der die Fahrt per GPS überträgt. Alle Fahrten werden aufgezeichnet, die Fahrgäste können sehen, wo das Taxi sich gerade befindet, und eine nahe gelegene Destination für ihre Fahrt aussuchen. Auf der Außenwand der Zelle zeigt ein weiterer Bildschirm Videoeinblendungen des Innenraums, die den Fahrer mit einem oder zwei „stationären" Fahrgästen an unterschiedlichen Orten zeigen.

(Aus dem Englischen von Martina Bauer)

Samir Ayyad

Soundshelters

Soundshelters is an interactive multi-channel sound space, which connects people more then 1000 miles away from each other. The multi-channel sound connection exists between Linz and Gaza.

This 'live-bits' sound-connection is established in two locations that are very similar regarding the audio-spatial setup properties, for instance in 2 churches. The "real" sound of the one space is overlaid by the sound traveling from some thousands of kilometers away. This then creates a place of literally mutual understanding, a place of compassion and maybe love...

Within this environment we will also have readings, maybe prayers or just the sounds of shattered glass, crying gunshots or birds and singing...

There are five mobile phones in each location. Each mobile phone speaker is connected to a loudspeaker to create almost the exact spatial sound of the other location.

There is no other image, there is only the sound and maybe the poetic words of the friendly place that is so far away. *Soundshelters* is only a silent listener, a help for families in places like ours, which are often surrounded by stupid violence. It's like surveillance or real-life sound tap-wiring, but offers more privacy and is not as expensive! As a multi-channel installation *Soundshelters* is also very emotional and it provides moral support, because it makes you feel good when you know that friends far away can simultaneously feel in their heart and know what is going on in the other place.

Apart from being beautiful, multi-channel sound space may also offer very effective security for people that live in places like Gaza.

Sponsored by many, many good spirits

IMAGE A.

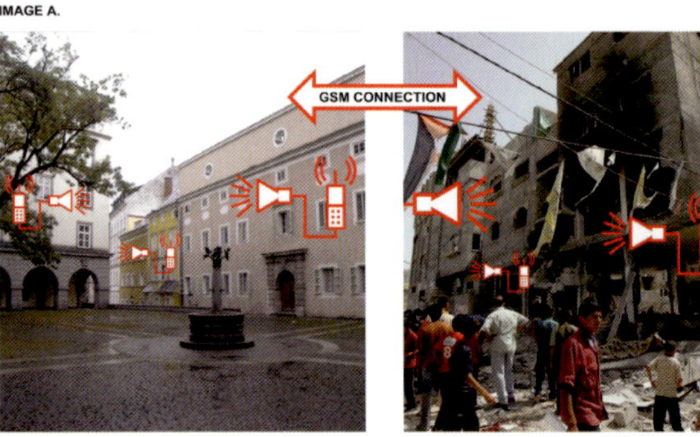

PUBLIC SQUARE IN CITY OF LINZ   PUBLIC SQUARE IN CITY OF GAZA

Soundshelters

Soundshelters ist ein interaktiver Mehrkanal-Klangraum, der Menschen miteinander in Verbindung setzt, die Tausende Kilometer voneinander entfernt leben. Die Mehrkanal-Klangbrücke verbindet die Städte Linz und Gaza.

Zwischen Orten mit ähnlichen akustischen Eigenschaften, wie z. B. Kirchen oder Plätzen, wird eine akustische Echtzeitverbindung eingerichtet. Der aktuelle Sound des jeweiligen Orts wird von Klängen überlagert, die von weither kommen. Ziel des Projekts ist es, einen Raum zu schaffen, in dem Verständnis, Empathie, ja vielleicht sogar Liebe möglich sind ...

In diesem Ambiente finden Lesungen statt, werden vielleicht Gebete gesprochen oder das Klirren von berstendem Glas, das Knallen von Schüssen, Vogelgezwitscher, Gesänge etc. zu hören sein.

An beiden Orte stehen je fünf Mobiltelefone zur Verfügung. Jeder, der eines dieser Mobiltelefone benutzt, bekommt über einen angeschlossenen Lautsprecher die Klanglandschaft des anderen Orts vermittelt. Bilder sind keine zu sehen, der Zuhörer ist auf akustische Eindrücke, vielleicht auch poetische Impressionen des verbündeten Orts in weiter Ferne angewiesen. *Soundshelters* setzt auf stilles Zuhören, das für Familien in Städten wie Gaza, die oft nur von roher Gewalt umgeben sind, sehr hilfreich sein kann. Es erinnert an Überwachung oder das Anzapfen eines realen Klangbilds, hat aber den Vorteil, dass es die Privatsphäre nicht verletzt und darüber hinaus kostengünstig ist. Als Mehrkanal-Installation hat *Soundshelters* nicht zuletzt eine starke emotionale Wirkung. Sobald die Klangbrücke installiert ist, verschafft sie den Menschen moralischen Schutz, weil sie die Sicherheit haben, dass Freunde in der Ferne mitfühlen und wissen, was geschieht.

Abgesehen von ihrer ästhetischen Dimension kann diese Klanglandschaft Menschen, die an Orten wie Gaza leben, eventuell sogar Schutz bieten.

(Aus dem Englischen von Martina Bauer)

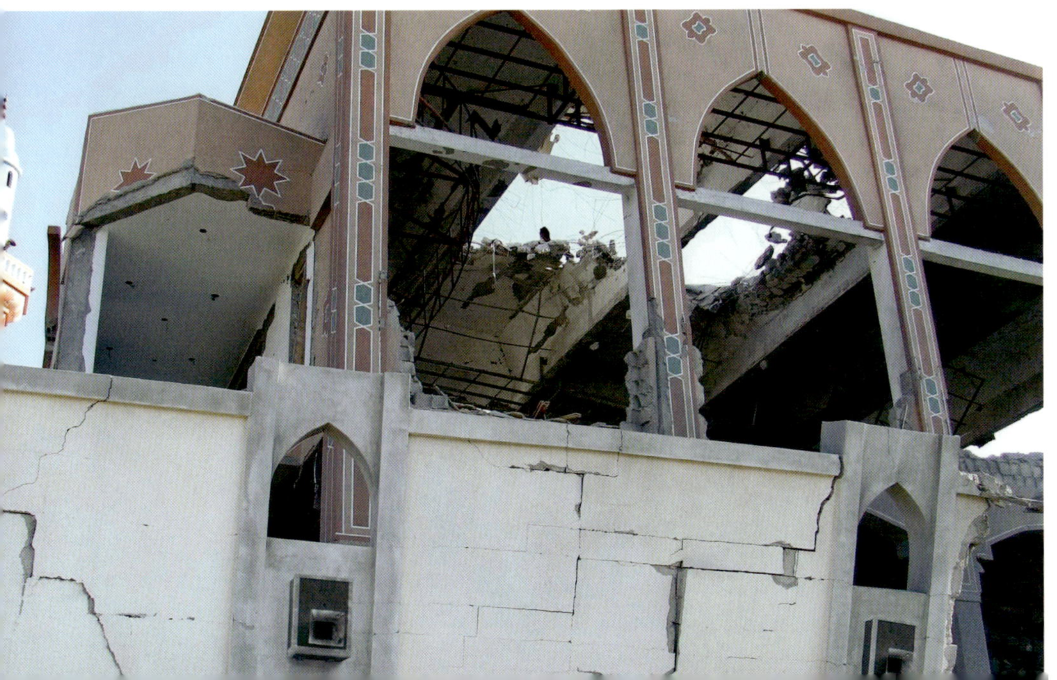

Stephen Hobbs, Marcus Neustetter

Urbanet: Johannesburg—Linz

Responding to the theme of Civil Society during the Johannesburg period of the *80+1* project, Hobbs/Neustetter aim to alert the European audience "looking" at Johannesburg, to the harsh, unusual and often abrasive social and economic conditions that produce a contradictory experience of the city and its varying suburban realities.

As a backdrop to their presentation, the polarities of apartheid and democratic change in South Africa vie for recognition. In other words many conditions within the city today either perpetuate the previous order of the apartheid city or challenge to transform it in a new and confrontational way. This condition is presented by the artists generally as "other" to that of the experience of a European audience. Hence the notion of standing in a European town like Linz and exchanging information with a very different city like Johannesburg is in and of itself extreme and contradictory. And it is in this light that the artists aim to convey a message of stark urban contrasts, ironies and juxtapositions to an audience in Linz, whose frames of reference may or may not exist for a reading of such an urban context as Johannesburg, South Africa.

With the aim of accentuating the psychological and physical difference and distance between Linz and Johannesburg: Hobbs/Neustetter's intervention for the *80+1* programme in Linz, will take the form of an interactive camera and video screen, concealed within the Hauptplatz. Visitors to *80+1* are encouraged to seek out the "surveillance" installation in order to have a one-on-one interaction with a strategic display of visual concepts. This mediation of place through technology and distance or separation is intended to motivate the viewer to make connections or question difference. In the spirit of the contradictions inherent in this project, the architecture of the Hauptplatz in Linz serves as a somewhat ironic window onto Johannesburg.

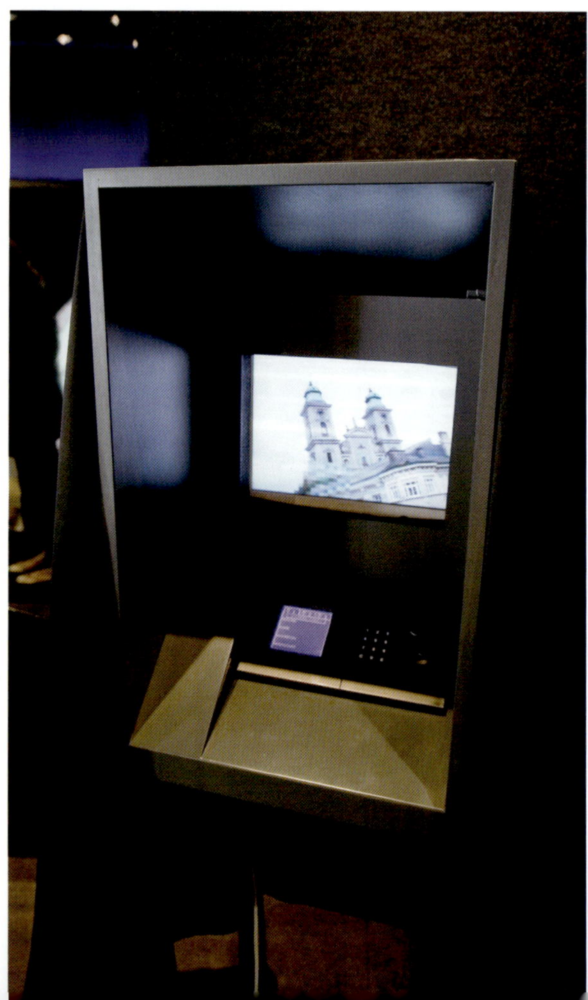

Thanks to
Österreichische Provinz der Jesuiten,
Ignatiuskirche / Alter Dom;
Kunstuniversität Linz;
Uniconsult, Dr. Manfred Lehner;
MitarbeiterInnen der Stadt Linz im Alten
Rathaus

Urbanet: Johannesburg – Linz

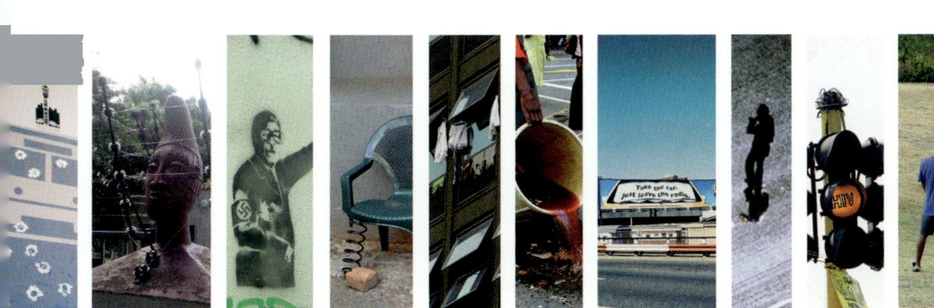

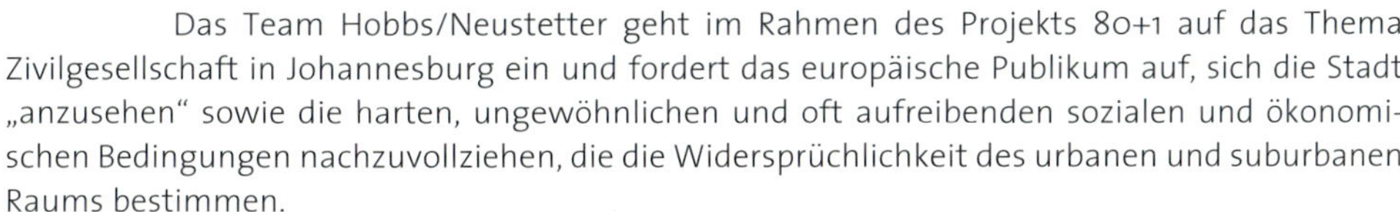

Das Team Hobbs/Neustetter geht im Rahmen des Projekts 80+1 auf das Thema Zivilgesellschaft in Johannesburg ein und fordert das europäische Publikum auf, sich die Stadt „anzusehen" sowie die harten, ungewöhnlichen und oft aufreibenden sozialen und ökonomischen Bedingungen nachzuvollziehen, die die Widersprüchlichkeit des urbanen und suburbanen Raums bestimmen.

Die polaren Gegensätze Apartheid und demokratischer Wandel, die den südafrikanischen Alltag prägen, bilden den Kern der Präsentation. Mit anderen Worten, die gesellschaftlichen Verhältnisse stehen teilweise auch heute noch für die alte Ordnung der Apartheid und zementieren diese, andererseits hingegen für die mitunter kontroversielle Entwicklung einer neuen Gesellschaft. Die Künstler betonen, dass das europäische Publikum solche Zustände nicht kennt. Dass man in Linz auf dem Hauptplatz steht und mit Johannesburg in Verbindung tritt, einer Stadt, die sich von europäischen Städten fundamental unterscheidet, ist an sich schon eine außergewöhnliche und widersprüchliche Erfahrung. Die Künstler vermitteln dem Linzer Publikum krasse urbane Kontraste, ironische Einblicke und Gegenüberstellungen, ungeachtet dessen ob ein Referenzrahmen für die Interpretation des urbanen Kontexts von Johannesburg gegeben ist oder nicht.

Um die psychologische und faktische Differenz und Distanz zwischen Linz und Johannesburg zu akzentuieren, montierten Hobbs/Neustetter eine interaktive Kamera und einen Bildschirm auf dem Linzer Hauptplatz. Die Besucher sind aufgefordert, das „Überwachungssystem" aufzuspüren, um in direkte Interaktion mit strategisch konzipierten visuellen Szenarien zu treten. Diese technische Vermittlung von Ortseindrücken und die Auseinandersetzung mit Distanz und Trennendem soll den Betrachter anregen, Verbindungen herzustellen und Differenzen zu hinterfragen. Die diesem Projekt inhärenten Widersprüche spiegelnd, fungiert die Architektur des Linzer Hauptplatzes als Fenster, das einen ironischen Blick auf Johannesburg freigibt.

(Aus dem Englischen von Martina Bauer)

Flaviu Moldovan

Microblogging Suit for an Industrial Worker

Microblogging Suit for an Industrial Worker provides industrial workers with a way and a voice to verbalize and communicate what their work environment is like. It is also a critical comment on information overflow and an artistic reflection about the big hype of web 2.0 and social networks.

There's just a limited bandwidth of human perception and we should use that wisely! The concept of Twitter and other so-called microblogging services is questionable. Isn't most of the information transmitted via these services beyond meaninglessness? Considering the amount of bulk information that comes upon and is spread by an average western metropolitan office worker, it is questionable whether this communication is not counter-productive and a first sign of decadency and degradation. Romania is not a decadent place! In fact it is the sweatshop of Europe! The vast majority of the population works in either agriculture or in labor intensive industry. Because labor in Romania is even cheaper than the investment in industrial robots, most of the Dacia, Romania's No.1 export, is welded by hand.

For that same reason the textile industry too is a Romanian stronghold. From H&M to D&G; Romania is the most prominent manufacturer of clothes in Europe. None of these workers enjoy the financial luxury and decadence of being able to send around information that nobody needs; primarily because they do not have the money for the devices, but also because they simply do not have a free hand.

Microblogging Suit for an Industrial Worker provides typical manual laborers with custom-built hands-free communication devices to connect them to the mobile Internet. The repetitive work of a car producer, a textile sewer or a checkout person in supermarkets is verbalized as a Twitter tweets. So *Microblogging Suit for an Industrial Worker* aims to give them a voice and attempts to show what his or her work environment is like.

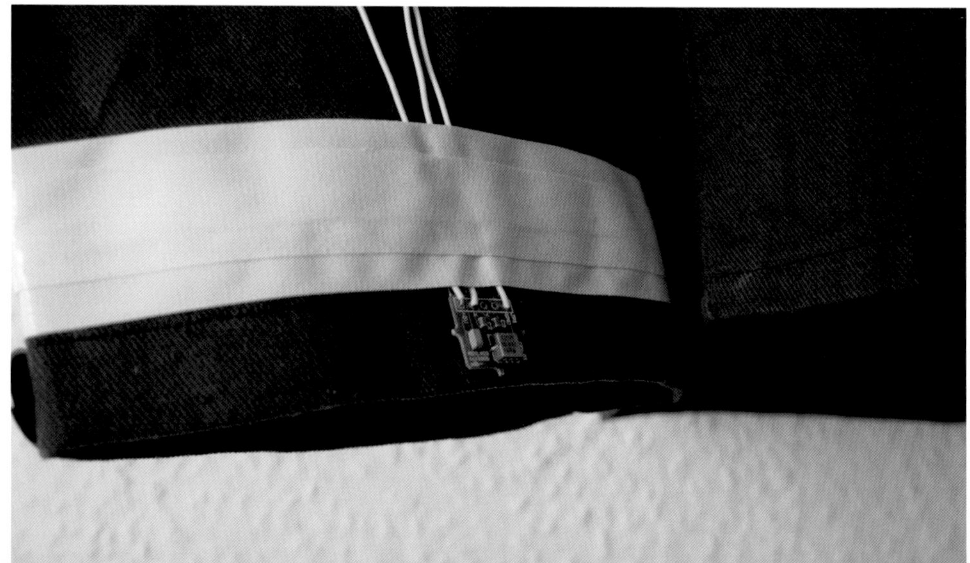

Photo: Flaviu Moldovan

Microblogging Suit for an Industrial Worker

Microblogging Suit for an Industrial Worker verleiht Industriearbeitern eine Stimme, die Möglichkeit sich mitzuteilen und ihr Arbeitsumfeld zu beschreiben. Das Projekt ist darüber hinaus ein kritischer Kommentar zum Informations-Overkill und eine künstlerische Reflexion über den Hype des Web 2.0 und sozialer Netzwerke.

Das menschliche Auffassungsvermögen ist begrenzt, weshalb wir weise damit umgehen sollten! Das Konzept von Twitter und anderer sogenannter Microblogging-Dienste ist daher fragwürdig. Ist nicht der Großteil der Informationen, die über diese Dienste übertragen werden, an Belanglosigkeit kaum zu übertreffen? In Anbetracht der Unmengen an Information, die von einem Büroangestellten in einer westlichen Stadt durchschnittlich verbreitet werden, stellt sich die Frage, ob diese Kommunikation nicht kontraproduktiv und ein erstes Zeichen von Dekadenz und kulturellem Niedergang ist. Rumänien ist so gesehen nicht dekadent! Das Land ist vielmehr der Sweat-Shop Europas! Die Mehrheit der Bevölkerung arbeitet entweder in der Landwirtschaft oder der beschäftigungsintensiven Industrie. Da Arbeitskräfte in Rumänien sogar billiger sind als Investitionen in Industrieroboter, werden die meisten Dacias, Rumäniens Exportartikel Nummer eins, manuell gefertigt.

Aus demselben Grund ist Rumänien auch eine Hochburg der Textilindustrie. Ob für H&M oder D&G, Rumänien ist der wichtigste Standort der Bekleidungsindustrie in Europa! Keiner der dort Beschäftigten kann sich jedoch den dekadenten finanziellen Luxus leisten, Informationen herumzuschicken, die keiner benötigt; in erster Linie, weil das Geld für die Geräte fehlt, aber auch, weil er einfach keine Hand frei hat.

Mithilfe des *Microblogging Suit* werden Industriearbeiter mit speziell angefertigten Freihand-Kommunikationsgeräten ausgerüstet, über die sie Zugang zum Internet haben. Die monotone Tätigkeit von Arbeitern in der Auto- oder Textilindustrie oder der Kassiererin eines Supermarkts wird dann als Twitter-Nachricht in Worte gefasst. Das Projekt verfolgt das Ziel, anonymen Arbeitern eine Stimme zu verleihen und die Verhältnisse an ihrem jeweiligen Arbeitsplatz zu zeigen.

(Aus dem Englischen von Martina Bauer)

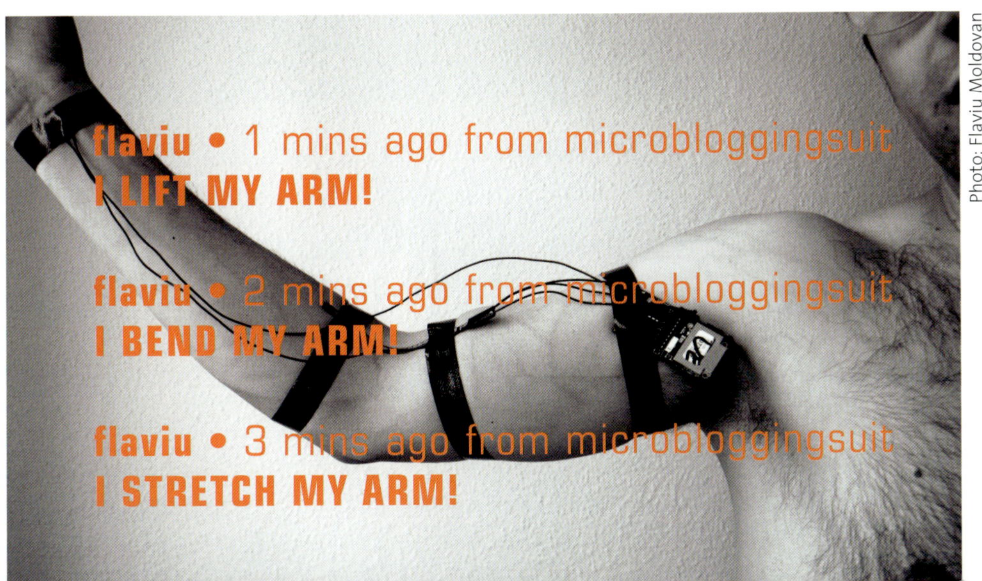

Photo: Flaviu Moldovan

Marianne Schmidt

Digitie

Digitie is a real-time communication channel between Linz and Istanbul. The cities are linked by each one apparat, which enables communication by gesture.

To use them, participants have to put one of their hands into the device. The hands of the users are displayed together in a united image on a screen. Strange people of different languages, ages and cultures and far distant living places, are able to get in touch with each other in this manner.

Both sides can wave, shake hands, try to do hands-wrestling or communicate by spontanious signals. There are no limits for the possibilities of gesticulation and interaction, except those of one's own imagination and expression.

Playful and experimental participants act according to their own form of body language. This becomes a process with it's own internal dynamics, which explores the proceedings of coding and encoding expression styles. An important aspect is to scrutinize our sense of apparent contradictions, such as closeness and distance, familiarity and strange, or the self and oneness. Using the simple example of hands gesticulation, the workings of non-verbal communication are explored, particularly under the influence of digital media technologies.

What are the expresion and interpretion potentialities with digital media?

The project calls into question the significance and possibilities of analog, but technical forms of communication.

And what are the implications of the digital revolution on our human interaction, from the individual up on a global level?

Concept: Marianne Schmidt
Software Engineer: André Bernhardt
Hosted by santralistanbul

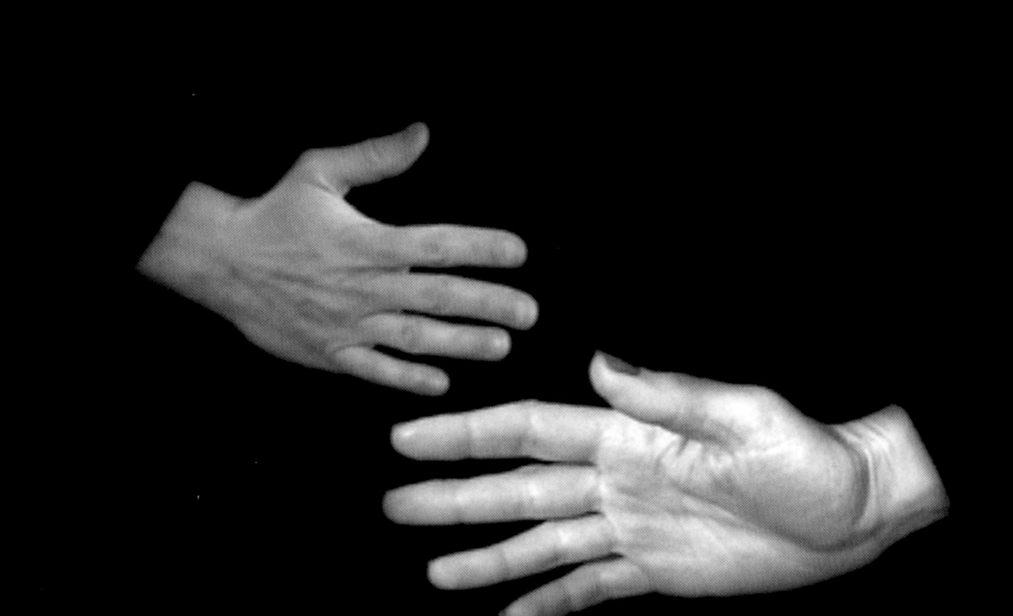

Digitie

Digitie ist ein Kommunikationskanal in Echtzeit zwischen Linz und Istanbul. Beide Städte sind durch jeweils einen Apparat, welcher Verständigung durch Gestik ermöglicht, miteinander verbunden.

Um von diesem Gebrauch zu nehmen, legen Teilnehmer ihre Hand in das Gerät. Die Hände der beiden Benutzer werden auf einem Monitor live miteinander in einem Bild vereint. Fremde Menschen unterschiedlicher Sprachen und Kulturen, deren Lebensräume weit voneinander entfernt liegen, können miteinander auf diese Weise in Kontakt treten.

Beide Seiten können einander zuwinken, die Hände schütteln, sich mit Zeichengesten austauschen oder im Armdrücken versuchen. Der Gestikulation und Interaktion sind keinerlei Grenzen, außer die der eigenen Vorstellungskraft und Ausdrucksweise, gesetzt.

Spielerisch und experimentell handeln die Teilnehmer gemäß ihrer eigene Form der Körpersprache. Es entsteht eine Eigendynamik, welche performativ und selbstreflexiv das Generieren und Rezipieren von Sprachcodes untersucht. Ein wesentlicher Aspekt ist das Verständnis scheinbarer Gegensätze von Nähe und Ferne, Vertrautheit und Fremde oder dem Ich und dem Einssein.

Am Beispiel der Hand werden Funktionsweisen nonverbaler Kommunikation erforscht, insbesondere unter der Wirkung digitaler Medientechnologien. Das Projekt fragt nach der Bedeutung und den Möglichkeiten analoger, dabei aber technischer Kommunikationsformen. Wie werden Informationen durch nonverbale Verständigung, insbesondere mit digitalen Medien, vermittelt und interpretiert?

Und was sind die Auswirkungen der digitalen Revolution auf unser menschliches Miteinander, von der individuellen bis hin zur globalen Ebene?

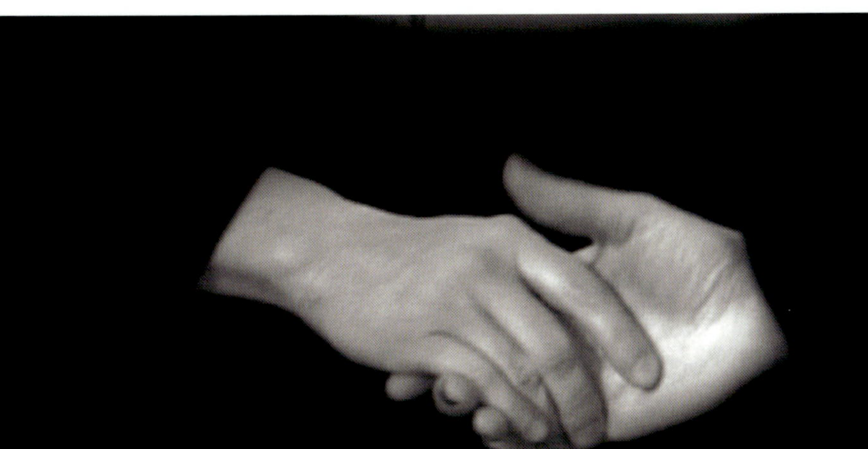

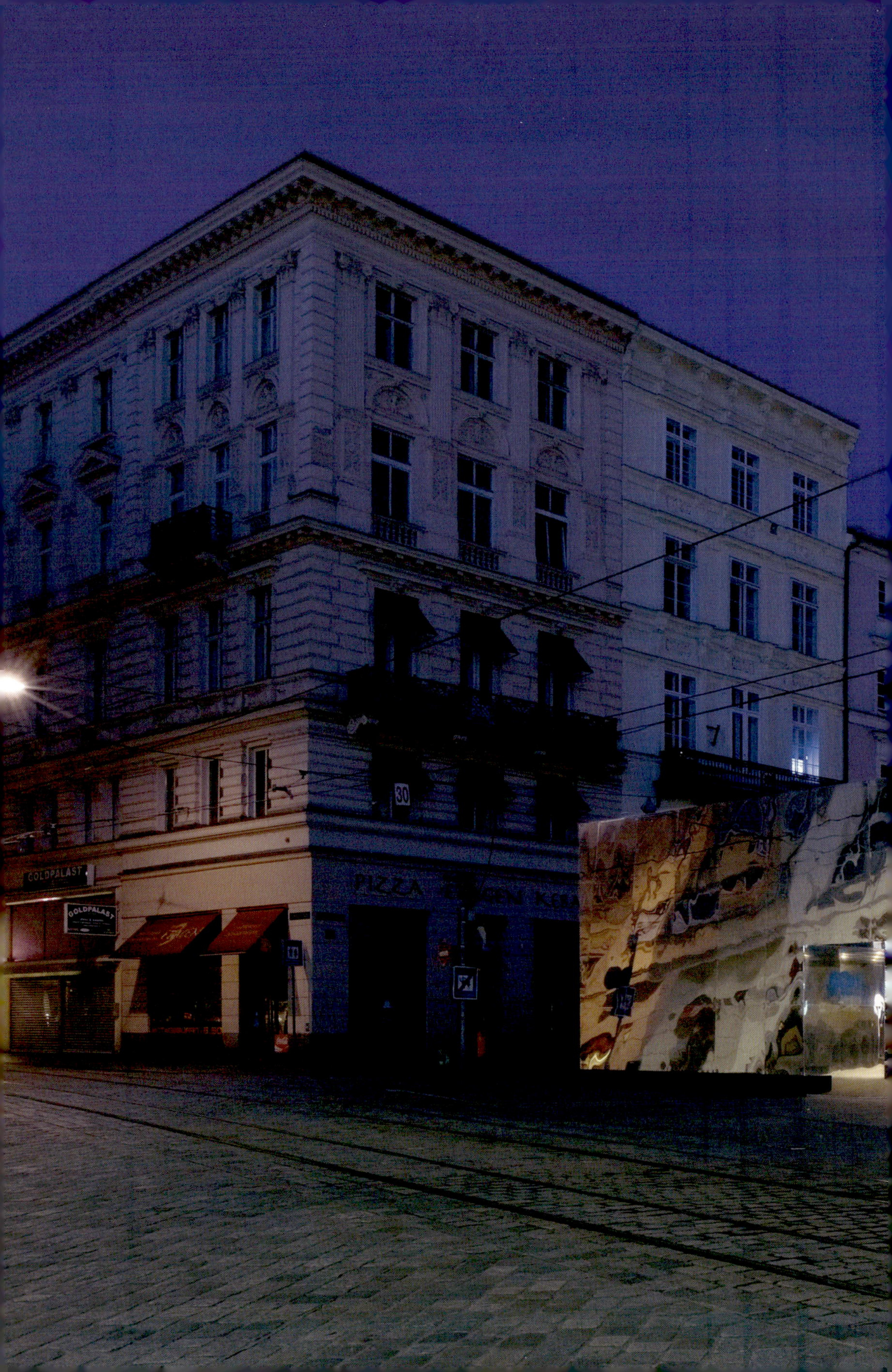
GOLDPALAST
GOLDPALAST
PIZZA
30
7

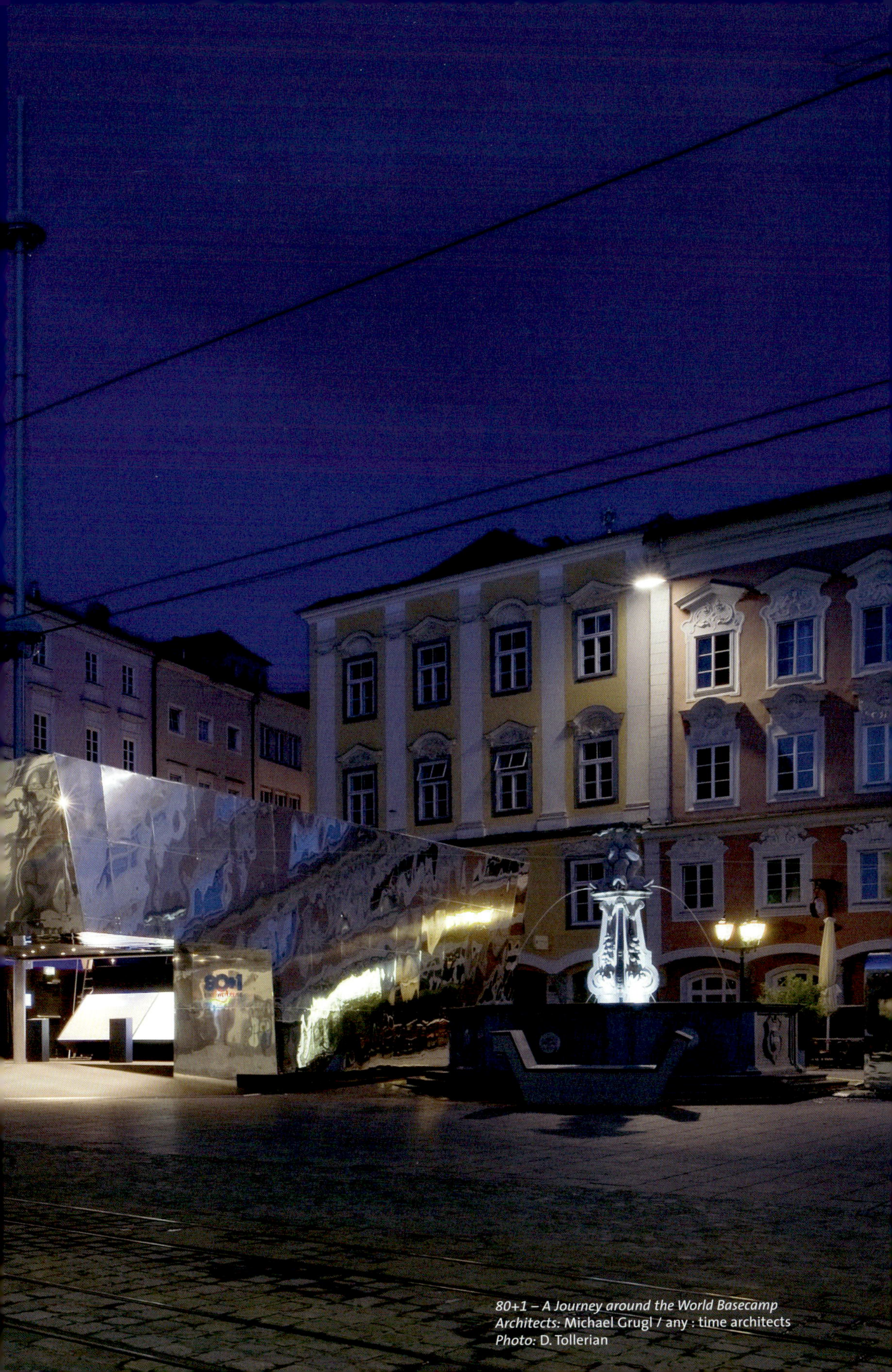

80+1 – A Journey around the World Basecamp
Architects: Michael Grugl / any : time architects
Photo: D. Tollerian

Sternennacht

Ars Electronica Festival Opening

The 2009 Festival's opening is being staged in conjunction with *80+1*, Ars Electronica's contribution to Linz's year as European Capital of Culture and a project that can be seen as having already launched the festival proceedings at mid-year. This virtual journey around the world in *80+1* days departed on June 17th. The extra day—the one that will make it a bit longer than its literary predecessor—will be the day on which the festival kicks off. This 81st day featuring the *Cloud Intelligence Symposium* and *Starry, Starry Night* will wind this trip up on a high note.

80+1 commenced with a look at happiness, scrutinizing joy and satisfaction as key forces driving humankind. It concludes with a consideration of the subject of exploration, focusing on curiosity and the urge to investigate and discover. Amidst the International Year of Astronomy honoring the first use of the telescope for astronomical observations by Galileo Galilei and Johannes Kepler's first geometric description of the solar system in his "Astronomia nova" 400 years ago, and in the year that marks the 40th anniversary of the first lunar landing, the subject of exploration is naturally connected with aspects of these momentous occasions as well.

Starry, Starry Night is the 2009 Ars Electronica Festival's opening event. In addition to the area in and around the Ars Electronica Center, which will primarily be a setting for musical acts, Linz's Main Square (Hauptplatz) is the main venue.

There is probably no more powerful image symbolizing the indivisibility of every person's responsibility for all life on planet Earth than the canopy of stars in the night sky and the view of our own planet from outer space. This thought presumably also played a part in the decision to add another location to the list of 878 UNESCO World Heritage honorees: the starry night sky, or rather Tekapo, the New Zealand village from which it can be seen most clearly due to the least light pollution there. About a fifth of the world's population is no longer able to see the Milky Way from where they live. In light of the cultural-historical consequences attributable to the observation and interpretation of the heavens, the replacement of a view of the stars at night by the mere reflection of that which lies below them—city lights and others emissions of civilization—is indeed a loss of worldview-proportions. (The higher the degree of light pollution, the more encouragement is given to conflating astronomy with astrology.)

Thus, a core concept of *Starry, Starry Night* is to make the night sky visible again. Much of the city's illumination infrastructure will be turned off, and lots of telescopes will be set up on Hauptplatz, where experts and amateur astronomers will aid visitors in exploring the heavens until midnight.

An essential aspect of this event is to get as many people as possible involved—not only by participating as stargazers but also as part of a communal expression of the will of the residents of Linz to make this event possible—that is to say, private households pitching in too by turning off their lights to enable the stargazers to enjoy a view of the heavens from Hauptplatz.

(Text: Heimo Ranzenbacher)

Sternennacht
Ars Electronica Festival Opening

Die Eröffnung des Ars Electronica Festivals 2009 steht im Zusammenhang mit dem Projekt *80+1*, jenem Beitrag der Ars Electronica zum Programm der Europäischen Kulturhauptstadt Linz, durch den das Festival heuer gleichsam schon zur Jahresmitte begonnen hat. Am 17. Juni erfolgte der Aufbruch zur virtuellen Reise um die Welt in *80 + 1* Tagen, wobei an dem Tag, um den diese Reise länger als ihr Vorbild dauert, der tatsächliche Festival-Auftakt erfolgt. Am 81. Tag sind das *Cloud Intelligence Symposium* und die *Sternennacht* Ziel und Höhepunkt der Reise. *80+1* hat mit dem Thema Happyness begonnen, mit Fragen in Sachen Glück und Zufriedenheit als eine der zentralen menschlichen Tiebkräfte. Es endet mit einer Veranstaltung zum Thema Exploration, bei dem die Neugierde, der Forscher- und Entdeckerdrang im Mittelpunkt stehen. Im Internationalen Jahr der Astronomie, das den erstmaligen Gebrauch eines Teleskops für astronomische Beobachtungen durch Galileo Galilei und Johannes Keplers erste geometrische Beschreibung des Sonnensystems in seiner „Astronomia nova" vor 400 Jahren referenziert, und in dem Jahr, da sich das Ereignis der ersten Mondlandung zum 40 Mal jährt, ist das Thema Exploration natürlich auch mit Aspekten dieser Jubiläen verknüpft.

Die *Sternennacht* der Ars Electronica ist das Eröffnungsevent des Festivals 2009. Neben dem unmittelbaren Umfeld des Ars Electronica Center, wo primär musikalische Acts angesiedelt sind, ist der Linzer Hauptplatz der eigentliche Schauplatz des Geschehens.

Es gibt wohl kaum ein zweites so starkes Symbol und Bild für die Unteilbarkeit der Verantwortung aller für alles Leben auf dem Planeten Erde als der umgebende Sternenhimmel und den Blick von außen auf den Planeten. Dieser Gedanke spielt vermutlich auch in die Überlegungen hinein, neben den bisher 878 als UNESCO-Welterbe gekennzeichneten Stätten auch dem Sternenhimmel – bzw. dem neuseeländischen Dorf Tekapo durch dessen bestmögliche Vermeidung der Lichtverschmutzung – dieses Prädikat zu verleihen. Etwa ein Fünftel der Weltbevölkerung kann von ihren Wohnorten aus die Milchstraße nicht mehr erkennen. Angesichts der kulturgeschichtlichen Folgen, die der Betrachtung und Interpretation des Himmels geschuldet sind, ist der Ersatz des Anblicks des Sternenhimmels durch die bloße Spiegelung dessen, was unter ihm liegt, das Licht und die Emissionen der Städte, in der Tat ein Verlust in der Dimension eines Weltbildes. (Je höher der Grad an Lichtverschmutzung, desto mehr Vorschub erhält die Verwechslung von Astronomie mit Astrologie.)

Kernidee der *Sternennacht* ist es daher, den Nachthimmel wieder sichtbar zu machen: Es werden die Beleuchtungsanlagen großflächig ausgeschaltet, und es wird ein Wald von Teleskopen auf dem Hauptplatz installiert, wo Experten und Amateur-Astronomen den Besuchern helfen, bis Mitternacht den Sternenhimmel zu explorieren.

Auch bei diesem „Event" ist die Einbindung einer möglichst großen Zahl an Menschen ein wichtiger Aspekt – nicht nur im Hinblick auf die Teilnahme als „Sternengucker", sondern auch dahingehend, dass es einer gemeinsamen Willensbekundung der Bewohner von Linz bedarf, um das Event zu ermöglichen: Denn die Sichtbarkeit der Sterne hängt nicht zuletzt auch vom Abschalten privater Lichtquellen ab.

Dietmar Hager

Starry, Starry Night on Hauptplatz

UNESCO, in response to an initiative by the IAU—International Astronomical Union, has declared 2009 the International Year of Astronomy (IYA2009). The occasion is provided by the 400th anniversary of telescope astronomy initiated by Galileo Galilei, as well as the publication of Kepler's first two laws. One of the IYA2009's Cornerstone issues is the night sky, which will occupy the focal point of UNESCO's global projects.

Humankind's origins are in outer space. All of the elements that make up the human body were formed billions of years ago, much of it in long-since-extinguished stars. We are the children of these stars. We are cosmic dust.

In conjunction with IYA2009, the Ars Electronica Center hosted an exhibition in July and August that offered visitors a colorful, wide-ranging look at astronomy and space travel (the 40th anniversary of the first manned lunar landing was in July) and also featured works of art related to this theme.

The annual Ars Electronica Festival got underway on September 3. "Starry, Starry Night" was one of the highlights on the first evening's lineup of events.

There were astronomers and scientists present from all over the world to report on their work—some attending in person, others taking part via video conferencing. Astronauts and space photographers gave accounts of their exciting activities. We visited professional photographers' observatories that are remote-controlled via the Internet, and witnessed live remote hookups to the European Southern Observatory and the International Space Station. We also got to experience the launch of a high-altitude balloon.

The highlight was "Starry, Starry Night." After sundown, a large group of amateur astronomers set up dozens of telescopes for public stargazing on Linz's Main Square. At 10 pm, Mayor Dobusch gave the order to shut off all non-essential public lighting in the City of Linz until midnight as a way to bring the darkness back to the cityscape. The soundtrack to this "star-studded party" was provided by Nordwest Music Studio.

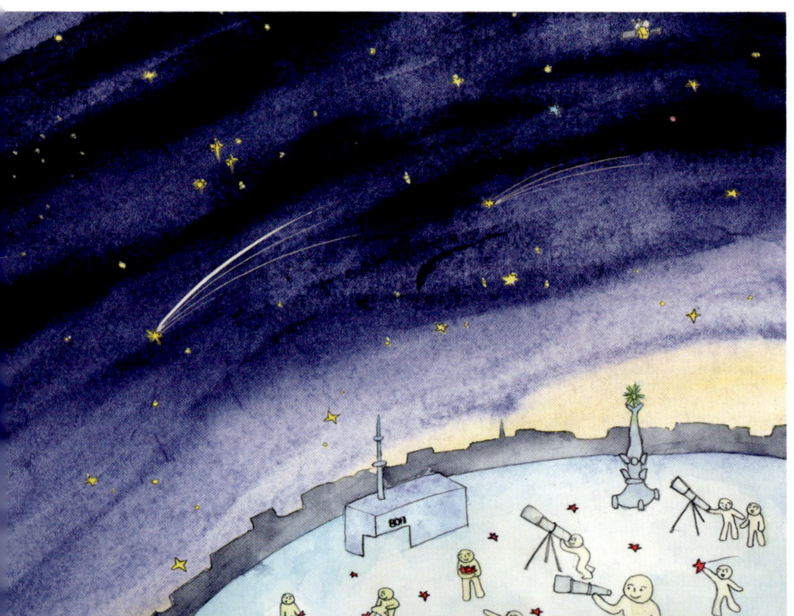

The background of this idea

One of the achievements of human enterprise is nighttime illumination. We need light at night since our culture develops nonstop; it bustles with activity faster and faster, 'round-the-clock. This is reflected by an exponential increase in public lighting of businesses and dwellings. Many cities on this planet are so massively bathed in light at night that their inhabitants can hardly make out anything in the night sky. This is referred to as light pollution. But more and more light-polluting sources of illumination are now found in rural areas too.

Starlight travels up to many billions of light years through space before entering Earth's brightly illuminated atmosphere where, in the final few hundred meters of its journey, it is so completely outshone by man-made light sources that it becomes virtually invisible.

The upshot of this is that the generation growing up today is in danger of being the first to have never even seen the starry night sky with the naked eye. Whereby it is interesting to note that UNESCO's La Palma Declaration states that every Earth-dweller has the right to starlight.

Light pollution is a matter of concern to all of us. And it has wide-ranging implications.

Using modern light sources in streetlights that focus light downwards where it's needed helps cut energy use by 40% and saves money too. Plus, alternative means of illumination do not give off ultraviolet (UV) light that is harmful to the environment. The victims affected most intensely by this are nocturnal animals like insects, bats and migratory birds. UV light itself also damages architectural structures. In addition to the problem of disposing of obsolete existing light sources, all of this gives rise to enormous additional costs that have to be born by the general public. UV light sources are hazardous waste.

In addition to the economy and the environment, human health is also directly affected—for instance, by excessive illumination in people's sleeping quarters.

Research on the human health consequences of nighttime lighting has been going on worldwide for about 18 years.

Located in the human eye right next to the sensors responsible for vision are those that permanently measure the brightness of the immediate surroundings. It is not until these sensors report to the brain that it's dark that this part of the brain triggers the synthesis of melatonin, a hormone of critical importance to human beings. This substance produced in the pituitary gland has a very positive effect on our immune system, is conducive to restful, refreshing sleep, and makes a major contribution to a balanced hormone level. If a person is subjected to too much light at night over an extended period, the production of this hormone drops to an insignificant amount and melatonin cannot produce its positive effects.

It would be very simple to say that people should just pull down the shades that keep out streetlight illumination to make the bedroom totally dark. But isn't eliminating the cause of this problem for the benefit of all preferable to just treating the symptom? After all, it makes more sense to simultaneously save energy, spare the environment and protect people's health by appropriately adjusting sources of illumination.

Light pollution is a matter of concern to all of us.

Additional information on this subject is available online at
http://www.stargazer-observatory.com/print/LV.pdf

(Translated from German by Mel Greenwald)

Dietmar Hager

Die Sternennacht am Hauptplatz

Die UNESCO hat auf Anregung der IAU, der Internationalen Vereinigung der Astronomen, 2009 zum internationalen Jahr der Astronomie – kurz IYA 09 – ausgerufen. 400 Jahre Fernrohrastronomie, eingeleitet durch Galileo Galilei, sowie die Veröffentlichung der ersten beiden Keplergesetze geben Anlass dazu. Eines der „Cornerstone"-Projekte des IYA 09 ist der Sternenhimmel, der in globalen UNESCO-Projekten stark thematisiert wird.

Wir Menschen nehmen Ursprung im Weltall, denn alle Elemente, die unseren menschlichen Körper formen, wurden vor Jahrmilliarden u. a. in Sternen gebildet, welche längst vergangen sind. Wir sind Kinder dieser Sterne, wir sind Sternenstaub.

Das Ars Electronica Center trägt dieser Tatsache Rechnung und bot seinen Besuchern in den Monaten Juli und August eine Ausstellung an, welche einen bunten Querschnitt durch Astronomie und Raumfahrt (im Juli jährte sich die erste erfolgreiche bemannte Mondladung zum 40. Mal), aber auch zum Thema assoziierte Kunst zeigt.

Am 3. September wurde das alljährliche Festival Ars Electronica eröffnet. Und als eines der Highlights wurde an diesem Eröffnungsabend die „Sternennacht" gefeiert.

Astronomen und Wissenschafter aus aller Welt kamen, um über ihre Arbeit zu berichten. Teils als reell anwesende Referenten, teils als Live-Video-Konferenzen. Raumfahrer und Astrofotografen erzählten von ihrer spannenden Betätigung. Wir waren in via Internet ferngesteuerten Sternwarten von Profifotografen zu Gast und haben uns live zur ESO geschaltet, der Europäischen Südsternwarte, sowie zur ISS, der Internationalen Raumstation. Der Start eines Hochatmosphärenballons stellte nur einige der Aktivitäten dar.

Das ganz besondere Ereignis war aber die Sternennacht: Am Abend wurde ein großer Teleskopwald von Amateurastronomen am Hauptplatz eingerichtet; dutzende Fernrohre standen den Besuchern zur Verfügung, als schließlich Herr Bürgermeister Dobusch um 22.00 Uhr alles entbehrliche öffentliche Licht in der Stadt Linz bis 24.00 Uhr abgeschaltet hat, um den Linzern den Sternenhimmel wiederzugeben. Diese „Starparty" wurde musikalisch untermalt vom Nordwest-Musikstudio.

Der Hintergrund

Eine der Errungenschaften menschlichen Strebens ist die nächtliche Beleuchtung. Wir benötigen Licht bei Nacht, da sich unsere Kultur nonstop rund um die Uhr immer schneller entwickelt und emsig beschäftigt ist. Dies bildet sich aber in einer exponentiellen Zunahme der öffentlichen, der Geschäfts- und privaten Beleuchtung ab. Viele Städte auf Erden sind des Nachts so massiv in Licht getaucht, dass die darin wohnenden Menschen vom Nachthimmel kaum mehr etwas sehen können. Man nennt dies „Lichtverschmutzung". Aber auch im ländlichen Bereich finden sich mehr und mehr lichtverschmutzende Beleuchtungsquellen.

Das Sternenlicht ist bis zu viele Milliarden Lichtjahre im Weltraum unterwegs, um auf den letzten paar hundert Metern in unserer hell erleuchteten Atmosphäre derart überstrahlt zu werden, dass es praktisch unsichtbar wird.

Als Konsequenz dessen wächst in unserer Zeit nun die erste Generation an Menschen heran, die Gefahr läuft, den Sternenhimmel überhaupt nicht mehr zur Ansicht zu bekommen. Dabei ist es interessant zu wissen, dass für jeden Erdenbürger sogar das Recht auf Sternenlicht in der La-Palma-Deklaration der UNESCO festgehalten ist.

Lichtverschmutzung geht uns alle an. Und sie zieht weite Kreise: Moderne Lichtquellen in Laternen, welche das Licht streng nur nach unten abstrahlen, helfen zum einen, über 40 Prozent Energie und damit Geld zu sparen. Zum anderen strahlen alternative Beleuchtungsmittel kein UV-Licht ab, welches die Umwelt schädigt: Nachtaktive Tiere wie Insekten, Fledermäuse, Zugvögel und dergleichen sind massiv davon betroffen. UV-Licht selbst schädigt Gebäudestrukturen. All dies verursacht neben der problematischen Entsorgung vorhandener und veralteter Lichtquellen enorme zusätzliche Kosten, welche die Allgemeinheit zu tragen hat.

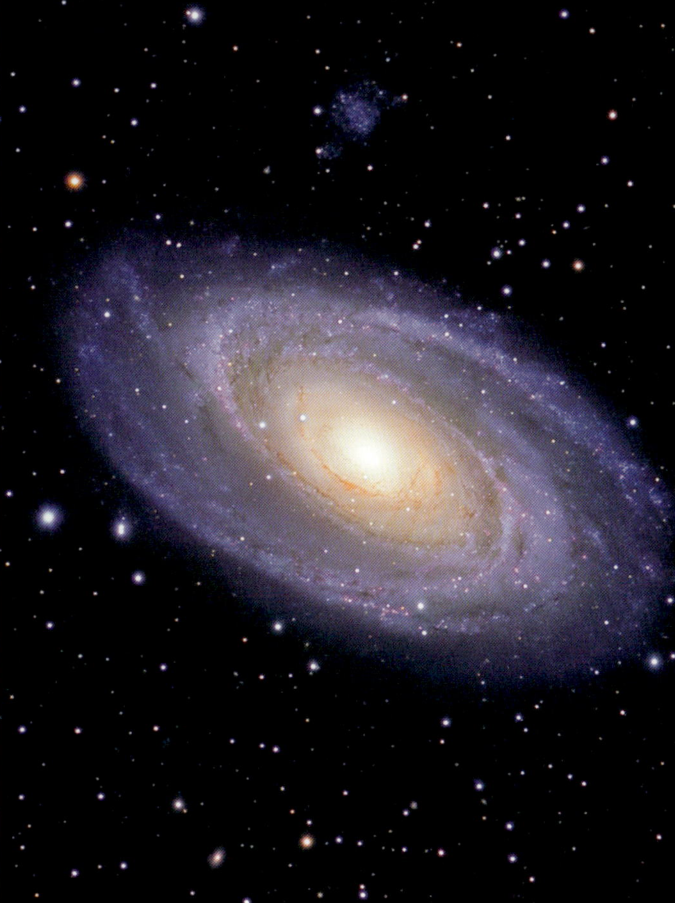
Bode-Galaxie

UV-hältige Leuchtmittel sind Sondermüll.

Neben der Wirtschaft und der Umwelt ist aber auch die menschliche Gesundheit direkt betroffen, etwa von zu heller Beleuchtung am Schlafplatz.

Seit etwa 18 Jahren wird international an den Auswirkungen von Licht bei Nacht auf die menschliche Gesundheit geforscht.

Im menschlichen Auge sitzen neben den Sensoren, die für das Sehen zuständig sind, auch solche, die permanent die Umgebungshelligkeit messen. Erst wenn diese an einen Gehirnabschnitt melden, dass es dunkel ist, beginnt die für uns Menschen so wichtige Synthese von Melatonin, einem Hormon, welches in der Hirnanhangsdrüse gebildet wird, sehr positiv auf unser Immunsystem sowie auf die Entfaltung eines erholsamen Schlafes wirkt und wesentlich zu einem ausgewogenen Hormonspiegel beiträgt. Ist der Mensch langfristig zu viel Licht bei Nacht ausgesetzt, reduziert sich die Produktion dieses Hormons auf irrelevante Mengen, und Melatonin kann seine positiven Effekte nicht entfalten.

Es wäre sehr einfach zu sagen, man möge einfach Jalousien runterlassen, welche das Licht von den Straßenlaternen wegblenden, um es im Schlafzimmer finster zu haben. Dieser Symptombehandlung ist zweifelsfrei eine Ursachenbekämpfung zum Wohle aller vorzuziehen. Denn es ist sinnvoller, gleichzeitig Energie zu sparen, die Umwelt zu schonen und die Gesundheit zu schützen, indem man die Beleuchtungsquellen entsprechend anpasst.

Lichtverschmutzung geht uns alle an.

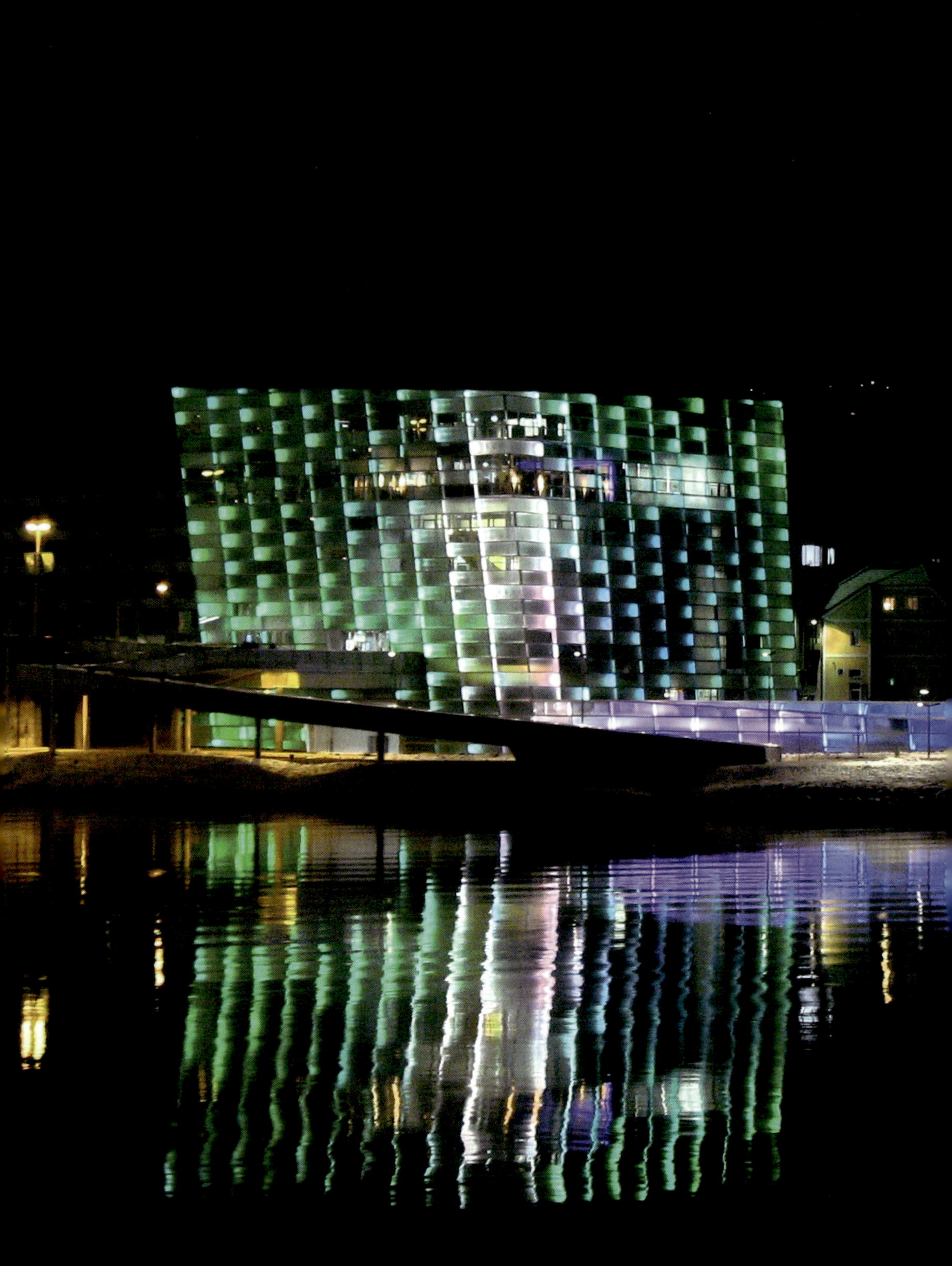

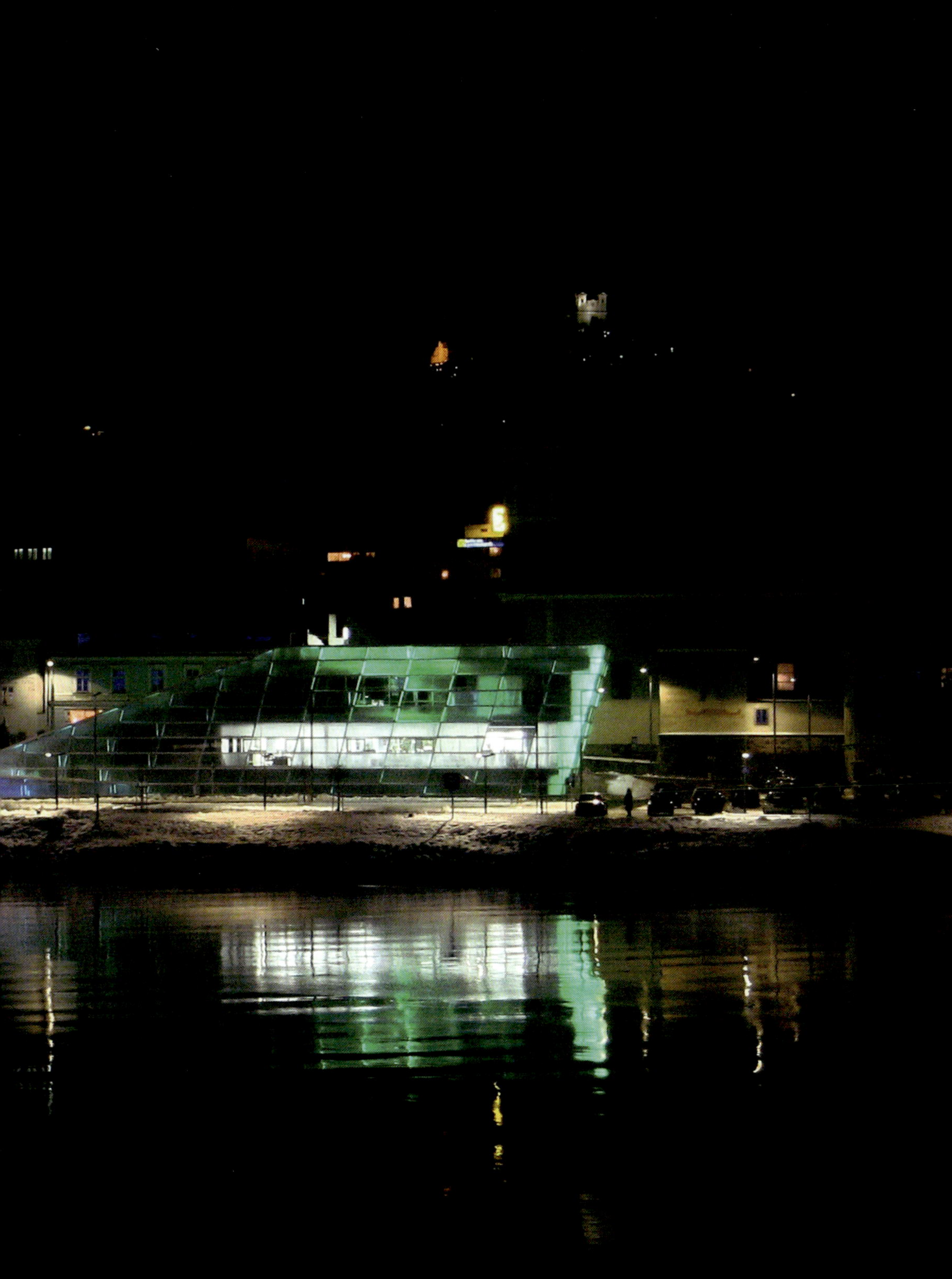

The New Ars Electronica Center

The new and expanded Ars Electronica Center debuted on January 2, 2009, right at the outset of Linz's stint as European Capital of Culture. Following two years of construction, a 6,500-m² facility for exhibitions, educational activities and R&D officially opened its doors. In addition to spacious new halls for exhibits, the new premises house the Ars Electronica Futurelab's ateliers and workshops. The event spaces and food & beverage service area were also substantially enlarged.

The Linz City Council resolution to this effect was passed in 2005; an EU-wide architectural competition in 2006 was won by a Vienna-based firm, Treusch Architecture. The groundbreaking ceremony was held in March 2007. On December 15, 2008, we got the go-ahead to move in and get set up.

The building that Treusch Architecture has created is an attractive and highly functional facility that can host several exhibitions simultaneously.

Along with the new center, there are new fields of thematic focus: the life sciences, genetic engineering, biotechnology and the neurosciences. None of the exhibits from the old AEC are still on display. Center stage is occupied by "New Views of Humankind on exhibit," in approximately 1,000 m² in the Main Gallery. A 450-m² exhibition space adjacent to it is occupied by "GeoCity." It examines the increasing urbanization of our world, highlighting the juxtaposition and interplay of the local and the global.

Additional exhibitions include "Poetry of Motion" and "Artist, Creators, Engineers." Temporary exhibits scheduled for 2009 are "20 Years of Art+Com," "Ars Intrinsica," "Stardust" and "Device Art."

One of the new Ars Electronica Center's top attractions is Deep Space, a spacious projection area for ultra-high-definition worlds of imagery. It features 8 stereo HD projectors that each produce diamond-sharp pictures on a 16x9-meter wall and floor surface. The formats that this infrastructure can accommodate include interactive VR, gigapixel photos and HD videos. The current lineup features 20 productions.

Photo: Michael Frühmann

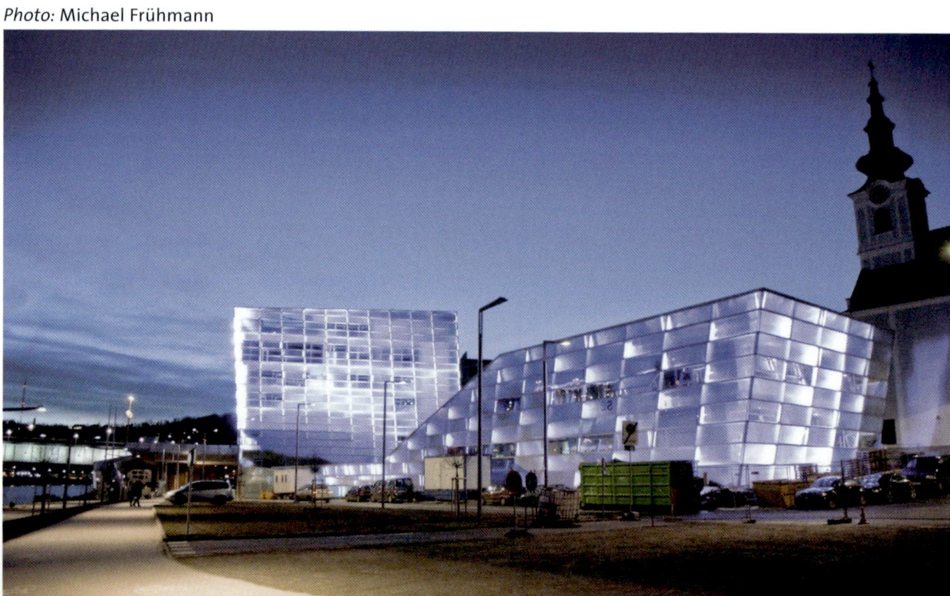

Das neue Ars Electronica Center

Am 2. Jänner 2009, zu Beginn der Europäischen Kulturhauptstadt Linz 2009, wurde das neue, erweiterte Ars Electronica Center eröffnet. Nach zweijähriger Bauzeit stehen nun 6.500 Quadratmeter für Ausstellung, Vermittlung, Forschung und Entwicklung bereit. Neben den großen neuen Ausstellungsflächen findet auch das Ars Electronica Futurelab mit seinen Studios, Werkstätten und Labors im neuen Haus seinen Platz. Aber auch die Veranstaltungs- und

Gastronomieräume wurden großzügig erweitert.

Der Beschluss des Gemeinderats erfolgte 2005, 2006 gab es einen europaweiten offenen Architekturwettbewerb, den Treusch Architecture aus Wien gewann. Im März 2007 fand der Spatenstich statt. Am 15. Dezember 2008 wurde das Gebäude an uns übergeben,

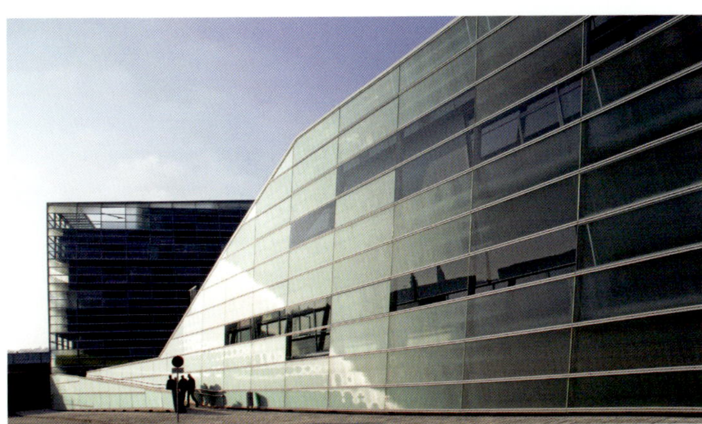

Photo: Martin Mittermayr

um die Ausstellungen einzurichten.

Mit dem neuen Gebäude von Treusch Architecture steht ein attraktives und hochfunktionelles Gebäude zur Verfügung, das die gleichzeitige Präsentation von mehreren Ausstellung ermöglicht.

Für die neuen Ausstellungen wurden auch thematische Bereiche erschlossen, die bislang nicht vertreten waren: Life Sciences, Gen-, Bio- und Neuro-Sciences. Aus den alten Ausstellungen wurde keines der Exponate übernommen. Im Zentrum steht die neue Ausstellung „Neue Bilder vom Menschen", die in der ca. 1.000 Quadratmeter großen Main Gallery untergebracht ist.

Daneben gibt es mit der ca. 450 Quadratmeter großen „GeoCity" einen Ausstellungsbereich, der die zunehmende Urbanisierung unserer Welt thematisiert und die Besucher mit dem Gegen- und Zusammenspiel von lokal und global beschäftigt.

Als weitere Ausstellungen werden „Poesie der Bewegung" und „Artist, Creators, Engineers" gezeigt. Temporäre Ausstellung im Jahr 2009 sind „20 Jahre Art+Com", „Ars Intrinsica", „Sternenstaub"und „Device Art".

Eine Besonderheit des neuen Ars Electronica Center ist der „Deep Space", ein großräumiger Projektionsraum für ultrahochauflösende Bildwelten. Mit acht Stereo-HD-Projektoren wird auf eine jeweils 16 x 9 Meter große Wand- und Bodenfläche projiziert. Von interaktiven VR-Welten über Gigapixelfotos bis zu HD-Videos reichen die Formate, die in diesem Raum optimal präsentiert werden können. Über zwanzig verschiedene Inhalte werden aktuell gezeigt.

New Views of Humankind

This age we live in is one dominated more than ever by science and technology. The new imaging methods used in the neurosciences observe our brain as it thinks. They show us how perception, emotions and intelligence function, and attempt to explain how our consciousness originates. Molecular biologists and genetic engineers are decoding the elementary building blocks of life. They're manipulating life, and creating artificial life forms, many of which also deliver grounds for anxiety.

New cultural techniques are emerging in the ever more tightly-knit global networks of digital technologies. Engineers are constructing machines that imitate human capabilities. And with space-based telescopes, we're peering far beyond our own solar system into the depths of space and time. The findings and insights coming to light thereby are beginning to permanently change our picture of the world and of the people who inhabit it.

"New Views of Humankind" deals with these changes. It shows where these images come from, how they materialize, and how we interpret them. In going about this, art and science are deployed in tandem as two methods that often seem dissimilar to us but are related in many ways. After all, the aim of both has always been to understand and explain the world.

Four labs constitute the exhibition's core: BrainLab, BioLab, RoboLab and FabLab. Via interaction and hands-on experience, visitors get an introduction to the mental and visual worlds of the modern Life Sciences.

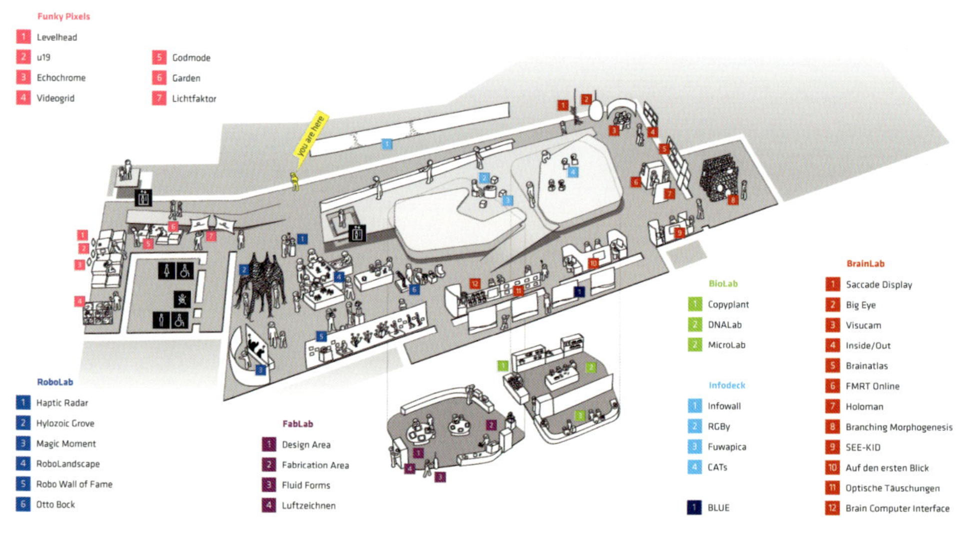

Neue Bilder vom Menschen

Wie nie zuvor leben wir in einer von Wissenschaft und Technologie dominierten Zeit. Die neuen bildgebenden Methoden der Neurowissenschaft beobachten unser Gehirn beim Denken und erweitern damit unsere natürlichen Wahrnehmungsprozesse. Sie zeigen uns, wie Wahrnehmung, Emotionen und Intelligenz funktionieren, und versuchen zu erklären, wie unser Bewusstsein entsteht.

Molekularbiologie und Gentechnik entschlüsseln die elementaren Bausteine des Lebens, können diese manipulieren und eröffnen Möglichkeiten zur Entwicklung neuer, künstlicher Lebensformen, die vielfach auch Grund zur Angst geben.

Neue Kulturtechniken und Produktionsstätten entstehen in den immer dichter werdenden globalen Netzen digitaler Technologien und rücken den Menschen als individuellen Gestalter in den Vordergrund. Maschinen werden konstruiert, die menschliche Fähigkeiten nachahmen, und mit Weltraumteleskopen können wir unseren Blick weit über unser Sonnensystem hinaus in die Tiefen von Zeit und Raum richten. Die Erkenntnisse, die dabei zutage treten, setzen dazu an, unser Welt- und Menschenbild nachhaltig zu verändern.

Der neue Ausstellungsbereich beschäftigt sich mit diesen Veränderungen, zeigt, wo die Bilder herkommen, wie sie entstehen und wie wir sie interpretieren. Dazu werden Kunst und Wissenschaft gemeinsam zum Einsatz gebracht als zwei Methoden, die uns oft unterschiedlich erscheinen, aber in vielfacher Weise miteinander verwandt sind, geht es doch beiden immer wieder darum, die Welt zu verstehen und zu erklären.

Den Kern dieser Ausstellung bilden vier Labs: BrainLab und BioLab führen in die Denk- und Bildwelten der modernen Life Sciences, der Wissenschaften vom Leben. Im RoboLab und FabLab geht es um Körper und Maschine und darum, aus eigenen Ideen reale Objekte zu machen. „Funky Pixels" stellt die kreative Gestaltung der digitalen Medien, Interaktion und spielerisches Erleben in den Mittelpunkt.

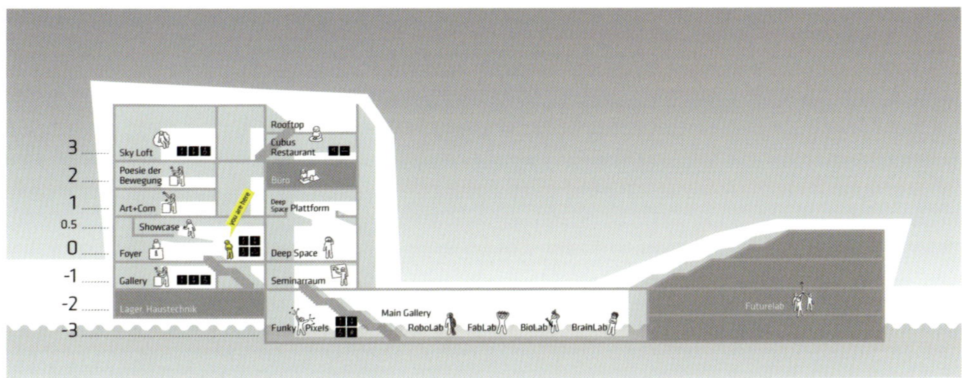

BrainLab

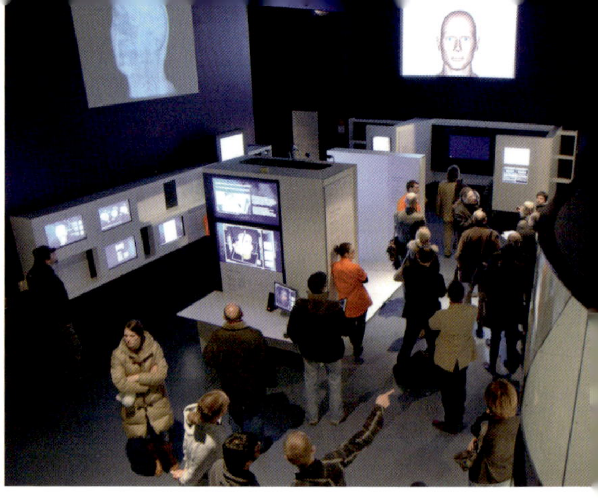

Research on the human brain—the striving to understand how it works when it's healthy and when it malfunctions—is one of the supreme challenges facing science and medicine. This is the human body's most complex organ. And perhaps the most complex structure of all. What can be said with certainty is that it's our most important organ—after all, it not only controls all of our bodily functions (many of them involuntary and subconscious); it's also the site of our ego, our conscious mind. This is where our picture of the world materializes, where what our sensory organs perceive turns into experience and insight, into recollection and memory, into personality and character.

How much of what our brain can do is genetically predetermined? How much is shaped and acquired by means of external influences, via experience and learning? To what extent can we influence this ourselves? How can we diagnose and heal illnesses? Can we deliberately enhance the brain's efficiency and capabilities? These are the questions facing brain research, the field of neuroscience.

Totally new methods are making it possible to investigate all aspects of the nervous system: its structure, development and functions. Imaging procedures like functional magnetic resonance imaging (fMRI) enable researchers to observe a living brain while it's functioning. We can literally watch ourselves think. The countless billions of electrical signals that the brain continuously produces are registered by high-tech devices applied to the scalp. Very powerful computer programs can filter significant patterns out of this deluge of signals and then identify and categorize them. Thus, it's already possible to control a computer, a prosthesis or any household appliance with the power of thought alone.

In addition to insights into imaging techniques and experiments that make use of them, the exhibition's installations deal with the processes of perception that take place in the human brain and methods that enable scientists to observe and understand the brain's activities and cognitive processes (i.e. functional magnetic resonance imaging, electroencephalography, eye tracking).

Considering the fact that many of these possibilities have emerged only in the last few years (now that computer chips and software have made sufficient processing power available), it doesn't take much of an imagination to realize what breakthroughs lay ahead in the coming decades. Findings by no means limited to the physiological nature of the brain; they'll be blazing trails deep into the human being's conception of self. These insights have to do with our worldview and our view of humankind.

The BrainLab in the new Ars Electronica Center gives visitors the opportunity to go along on a journey into the fascinating world of the human brain. From the very moment that a visual stimulus makes contact with our retina, to the complexities of controlling our eye muscles and the subtle processes of perception that take place while we view an image. And even the chance to get hands-on experience controlling a robot by means of a so-called brain-computer interface.

Concept: Gerfried Stocker, Christopher Lindinger, Katharina Maria Hengel *Coordination*: Katharina Maria Hengel *Exhibition Design*: Scott Ritter, Jakob Illera

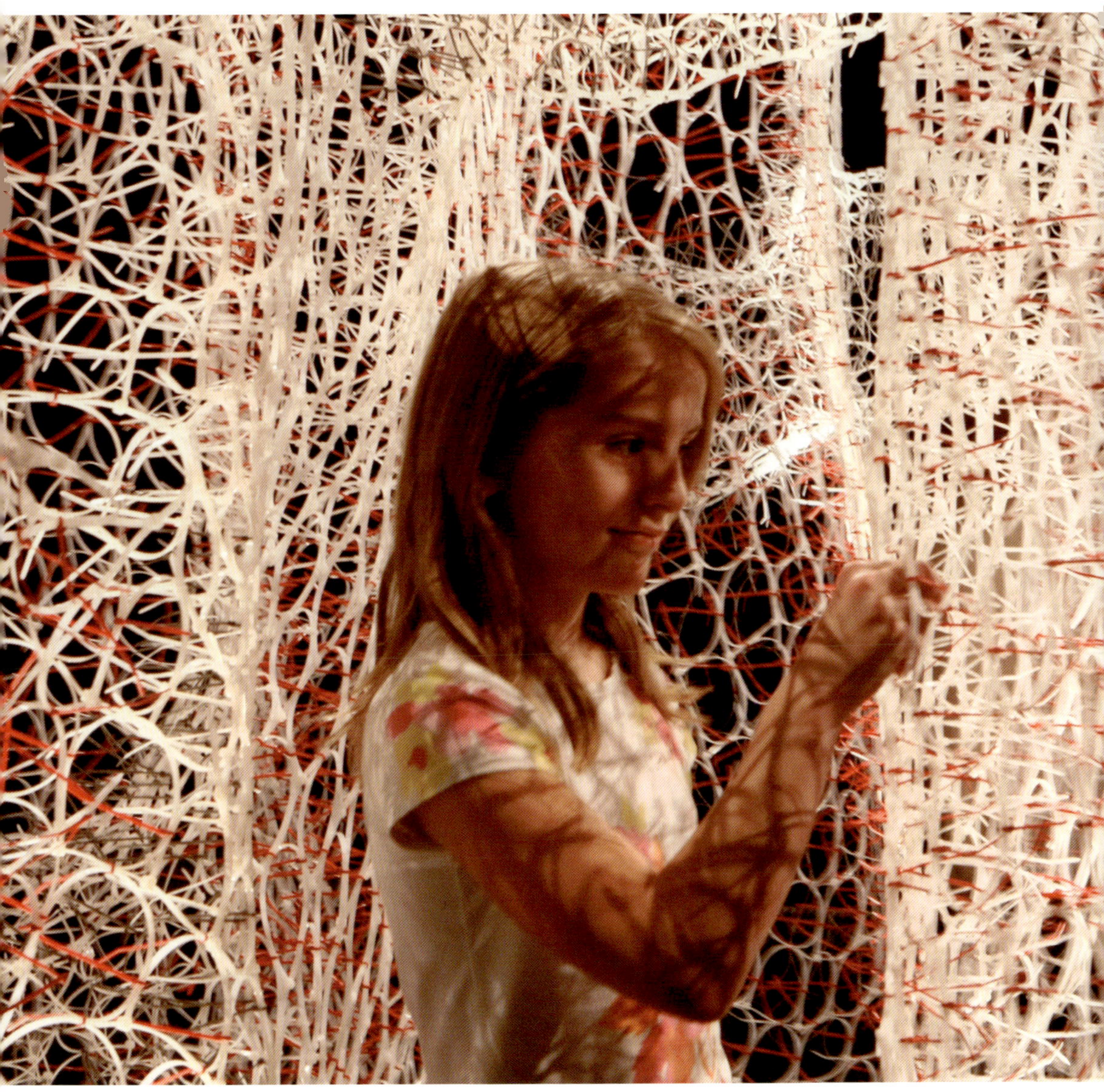

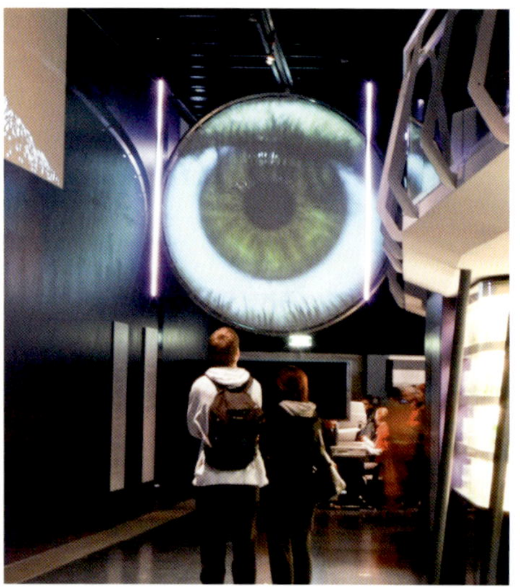

Big Eye / Saccade-based Display

A combination of back-projection and saccade bars serve as the portal to the exhibition.

Running in the background is an imagery sequence that begins with the human eye, proceeds on through it into the brain, then continues with footage of stars and planets in outer space and finally returns to Earth and the human beings who inhabit it.

In front of the installation are two saccade bars on which the image of two eyes can be seen when ones glance quickly sweeps past them. But as soon as the installation visitor focuses on the pictorial impressions, they disappear.

Big Eye: Ars Electronica Futurelab (AT)
Saccade-based Display: Junji Watanabe, Tetsutoshi Tabata, Hideyuki Ando (JP)

Visucam: The Universe on the Retina

Visitors to this installation can produce a picture of their own retina, the part of the eye through which the external world enters the body's internal realm of images and thoughts. In the retina, optical impressions are already pre-processed into initial images that are then forwarded to the brain. Every person's retina looks slightly different; you can e-mail a picture of yours right from the installation to yourself or your friends.

Visucam: Ars Electronica Futurelab (AT); supported by Carl Zeiss GmbH

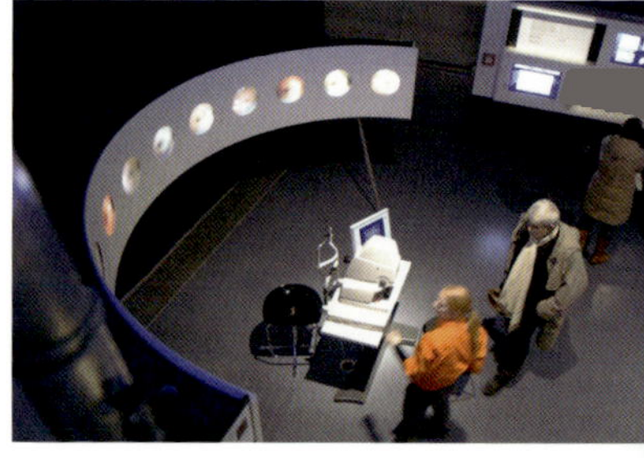

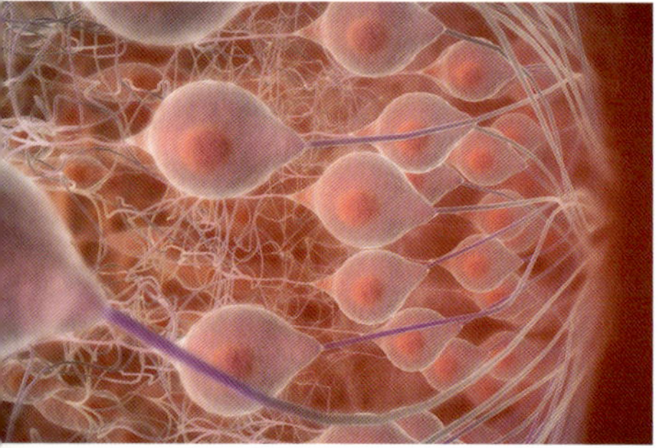

Inside / Out

Several interconnected monitors display animated films, diagrams and information about the neuro-physiological structure of the retina. To get more detailed information, all you have to do is click on one of the touchscreens—you can learn how the eye functions, find out about the most common eye diseases, or even watch an eye surgeon performing an operation at Linz General Hospital.

Inside / Out: Ars Electronica Futurelab (AT); scientific advisor: Prim. Priv.Doz. Dr. Siegfried Priglinger, Linz General Hospital (AT); supported by HP Hewlett Packard

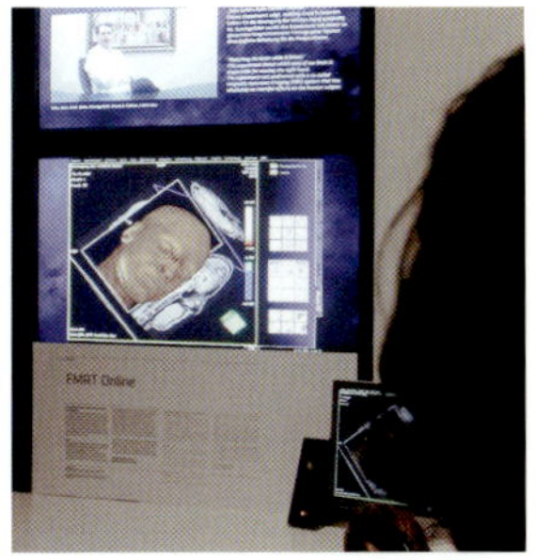

fMRI Online

A direct hookup connects this installation to Linz General Hospital's Radiology Department, which makes it possible to send data from fMRI (functional magnetic resonance imaging) examinations directly to the AEC's workstation, where they're evaluated and used to produce impressive visual representations.

fMRI Online: Ars Electronica Futurelab (AT); supported by SIEMENS Österreich, *scientific advice:* AKH Linz, Prim. Univ.-Prof. (University of Erlangen) Dr. Franz A. Fellner, Linz General Hospital (AT). This cooperative arrangement is also the basis of a new research project at the nexus of art and science that will enable artists to work with fMRI.

Brainatlas

The brain is our most complicated and most important organ. It consists, on average, of about 100 billion neurons, each of which is connected to approximately 10,000 synapses.

Interlinked touchscreens provide an overview of the brain's anatomical structure and its component regions in which the most important sensory impressions are processed.

Brainatlas: Ars Electronica Futurelab (AT), scientific advisor: Prim. Univ.-Prof. (University of Erlangen) Dr. Franz A. Fellner, Linz General Hospital (AT)

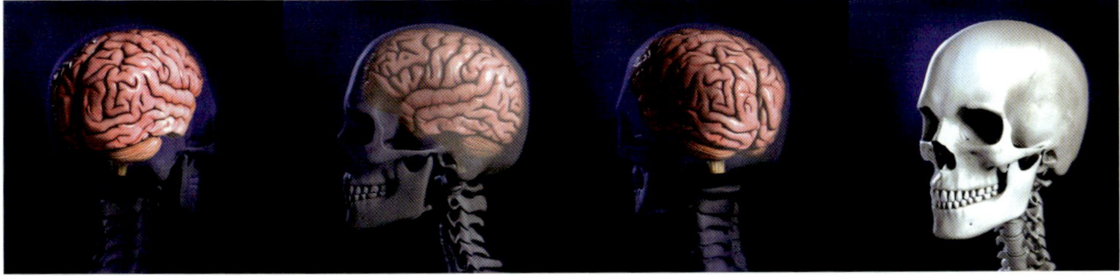

Holoman

On one side, you can see a piece of medical equipment (MRI). Here, you can playfully, interactively explore the body. Step in front of the mirror and discover the fascinating world of human anatomy!

Via IR cameras, the computer registers the installation visitor's outline and scales a highly detailed computer-graphic anatomical model, which it then projects onto a disc that installation visitors can use to apparently scan their own body. Rotating the disc makes it possible to view the respective levels of the anatomical model.

Holoman: Ars Electronica Futurelab (AT)

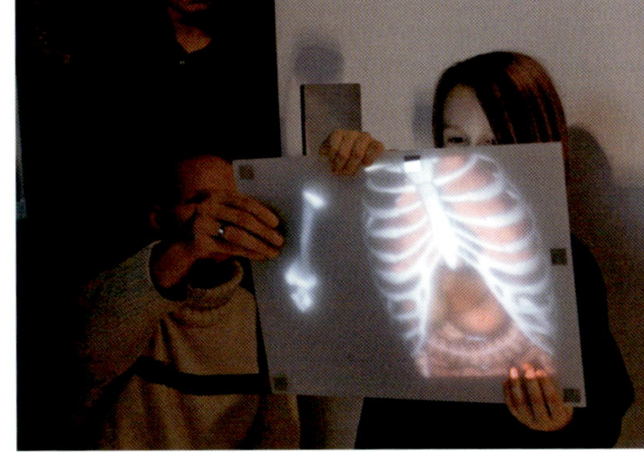

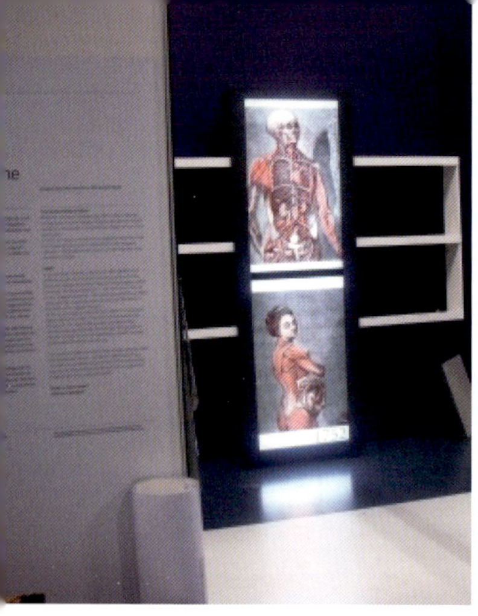

Anatomical Time-Travel

Two large-format monitors display anatomical drawings created over the centuries. These representations let us see how knowledge of the body and its representation with artistic techniques have changed over time.

Anatomical Time-Travel: Ars Electronica Futurelab (AT), *historical images:* U.S. National Library of Medicine, Wikimedia, W.K. Kelloggs Health Sciences Library, Dalhousie University, Halifax.

Branching Morphogenesis

Jenny Sabin observes the structures of cells, their fibrous interconnective tissue and the forces at work among them. These observations inspired her large-scale, walk-through sculpture consisting of 75,000 cable ties. She created it in collaboration with cell biologist Dr. Peter Lloyd Jones. Sabin is both an artist and a researcher. She combines the fascination of science with the beauty of an object, and works on potential architectural applications of biological processes.

Branching Morphogenesis: Jenny E. Sabin, Andrew Lucia, CabinStudio+ (US)

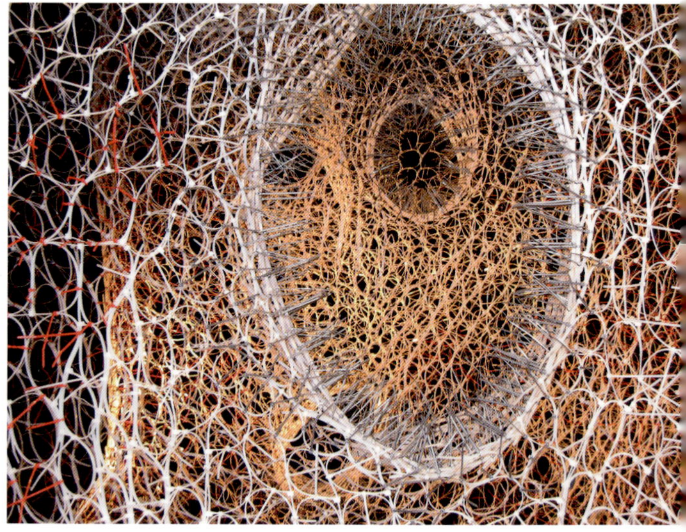

See-Kid

SEE++ is a high-performance computer program that makes it possible to simulate our eyes' complex sequences of movements. With it, operations on the eye muscles can be planned. SEE++ is also used for educational and training purposes.

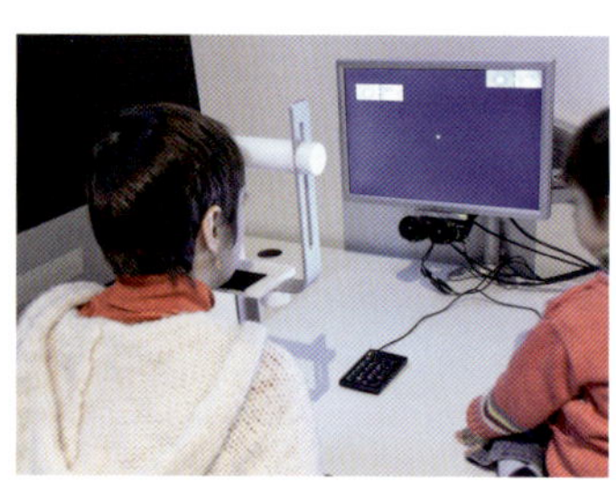

This software is utilized here together with an eyetracker to show visitors how the brain controls the eyes—from intentional observational movements all the way to involuntary, unconscious viewing sequences e.g. when a person sees a face for the first time.

SEE-KID: RISC Software GmbH, Hagenberg (AT), Prim. Prof. Dr. Siegfried Priglinger, DI Dr. Michael Buchberger, DI Thomas Kaltofen (AT)

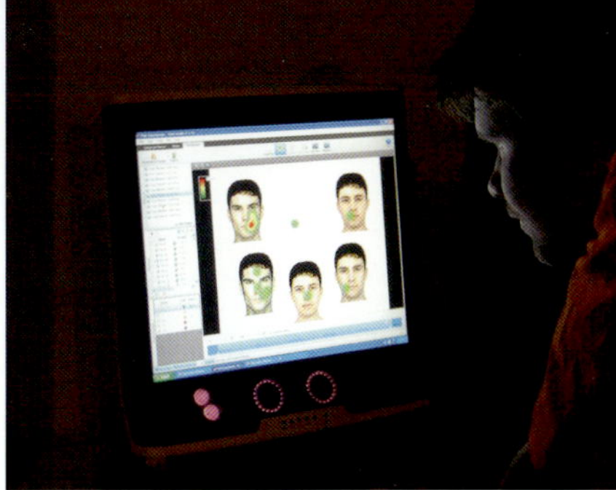

At First Sight

Decision-making processes in the brain are lightning-fast and often proceed unconsciously. Explaining how this works is the aim of several different research fields—from the neurosciences to artificial intelligence all the way to psychology. The human brain has developed over millions of years; numerous instincts and patterns of behavior that have been useful for human beings over the course of our evolution are still present. The activity of the eyes provides an excellent picture of how our brain reacts to its surroundings. The eyetracker recognizes which points our eyes concentrate on (fixation) and how long we look at individual points (duration). This makes it possible to investigate, for example, how we perceive billboards, commercials and websites, which content elements we pay attention to and which we overlook.

Dr. Bernhard Fink, behavioral biologist at the University of Göttingen, has developed pioneering experiments that reveal our preferences for faces, forms and colors. His research work is an effort to understand human behavior from the perspective of evolution. This installation provides a rundown on several of his experiments that deal with the question of what or whom we find attractive, and investigates how human beings select a mate.

At First Sight: Dr. Bernhard Fink, University of Göttingen (DE)

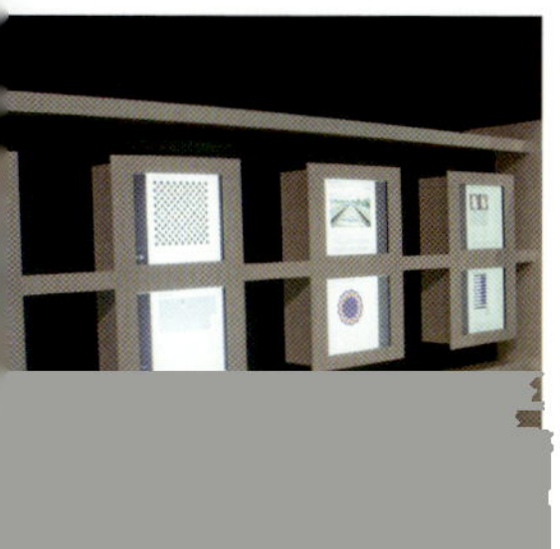

Optical Illusions

These are situations in which you can't even trust your own eyes! Several monitors display optical illusions (some of them interactively). This is designed to be a simple, fun way to bring out that we have to employ our faculties of reflection even when examining scientific images. Just because an image depicts something in logically consistent fashion doesn't necessarily mean that an interpretation derived from it is likewise correct.

Optical Illusions: Prof. Dr. Michael Bach, Prof. Daniel Mojon (DE), Prim. Priv. Doz. Dr. Siegfried Priglinger (Linz General Hospital, AT)

Brain-Computer Interface

The brain-computer interface utilizes an EEG cap to transfer signals from the brain to the computer. Visitors who take the time (about 30 minutes at this installation) can find out for themselves what it's like to control a computer directly with their own brain. Several experiments are possible here—installation visitors can try out control via p300 potential, the SSVEP (steady-state visually evoked potential) procedure, and motor-induced control.

By presenting exhibits and projects like these, the AEC is entering largely unexplored territory in an effort to integrate extremely complex and time-consuming experiments into the Museum of the Future's everyday offerings, and to provide visitors with an up-close-and-personal experience that is as intense as possible.

Brain-Computer Interface: g tech medical engineering GmbH (AT), Ars Electronica Futurelab (AT)

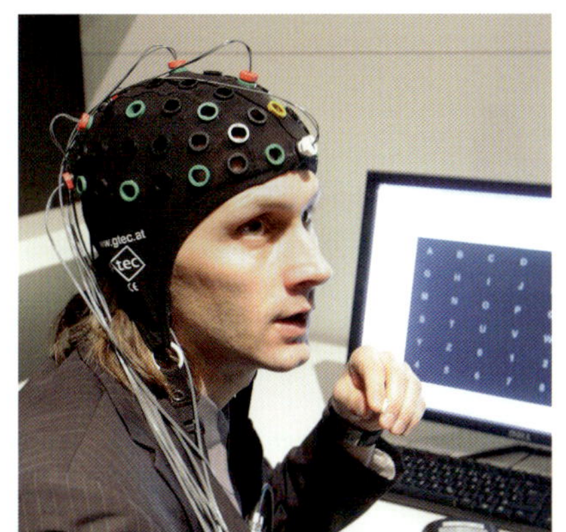

Hardly any area of research has launched as many debates as genetic engineering and microbiology have. The very fact that it has become technically feasible to modify a person's basic genetic makeup and even to clone someone calls into question our worldview and our moral and ethical preconceptions.

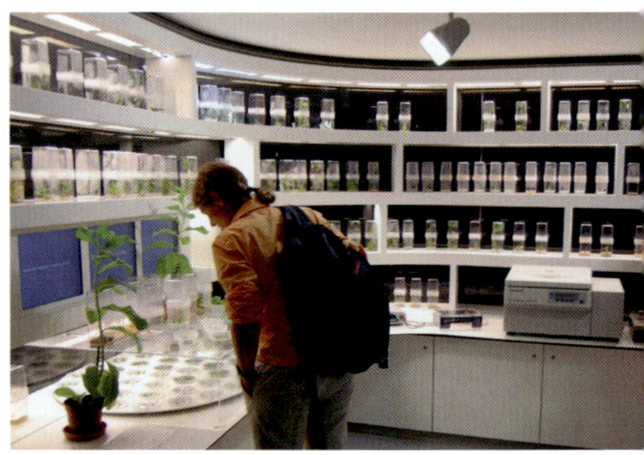

The BioLab delivers insights into the inner structures of life, into the make-up of cells and DNA. Its approach to imparting knowledge and skills is oriented on actual practice in this field, and enables visitors to get into a wide range of related issues. The objective is an intensive encounter—not at a distance, but rather up-close-and-personal perspectives and experiences.

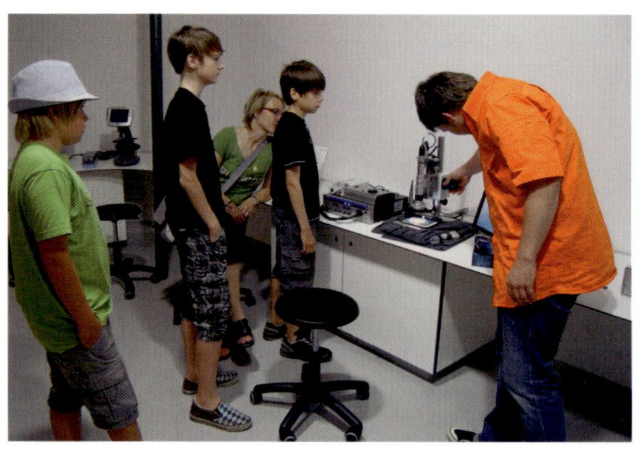

The lab's equipment and setup are professional grade and S1 certified. In addition to opportunities to try out and work with devices, investigational methods and experiments from a scientific research context, visitors also have a chance to deal with legal and ethical questions and the potential risks and rewards of current research.

The lab has two areas: DNA & Cells and MicroWorlds. It's open to all visitors to the AEC, but can also provide a closed setting for workshops. The BioLab's attractions include fun microscope journeys for youngsters age 6–10, brief hands-on experiments, and complex DNA workshops for upper school classes and adults. Content and methods are custom-tailored to the needs of the respective target groups. All attractions have been developed in cooperation with educators and scientists.

The BioLab's technical equipment makes it possible for forensic DNA and SNP analyses to be performed by and on our visitors (with gel electrophoresis as well as PCR and sequencer). There's also an xCELLigence System for cell analysis, and a series of special microscopes such as a digital video microscope, a fluorescence microscope and a raster electron microscope capable of 20,000x enlargement and that is so simple to use that visitors can try it out for themselves. Featured exhibits include anatomical specimens, a wide array of histological and cytological samples, as well as prototypes of a retina implant and a lab-on-a-chip that in only a few years will make it possible to perform fast, easy and cheap DNA analyses.

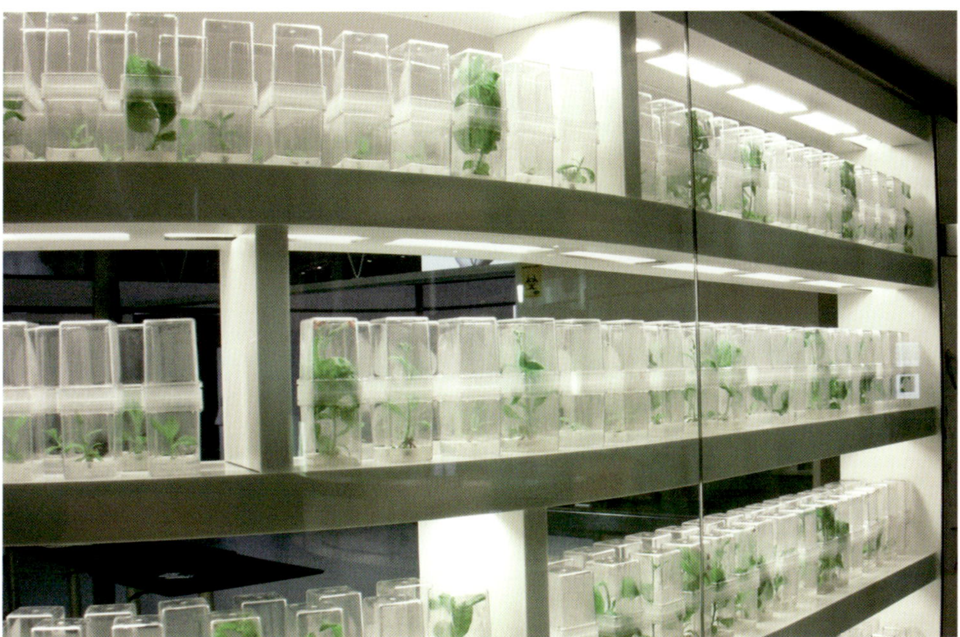

CopyPlant

CopyPlant is an impressive installation consisting of more than 400 genetically identical tobacco plants on plant shelves that are integrated into the wall of the BioLab; visible from both front and rear, it forms a visual and thematic membrane between the lab and the exhibition area. Hooked up to *CopyPlant* is equipment that enables visitors to clone a plant themselves and to thereby continually renew the lab's living wall.

Concept: Gerfried Stocker, Christopher Lindinger, Irene Posch
Scientific advice: Dr. Manuel Selg, Mag. Reinhard Nestelbacher
Coordination: Irene Posch
Exhibition Design: Scott Ritter, Jakob Illera

DNA & Cells: Ars Electronica Futurelab, *supported by:* Eppendorf, Applied Biosystems, Roche Applied Science, Greiner Bio-One GmbH, University of Salzburg Department of Molecular Biology, Upper Austria University of Applied Science, Wels Campus' Bio- and Environmental Technology program

Microworlds: Ars Electronica Futurelab, *supported by:* Hirox, FEI Company, Schäfer Technologie, University of Salzburg Department of Molecular Biology, Nanoident Technologie, Retina Implant AG, Prof. Dr.med. Christian Albrecht May – Medical Faculty Technische Universität Dresden.

CopyPlant – Gerfried Stocker, Reinhard Nestelbacher, University of Salzburg Department of Molecular Biology

What drives us to build robots? The striving for efficiency or the longing to craft machines in our own image? Or even the urge to reproduce nature and improve on it?
The RoboLab has been designed as an open lab situation conducive to a direct, interactive encounter with the installations and exhibits on display.
Here, the lab truly lives up to its name as a site for experimentation and a proving ground for educational settings and presentation possibilities in a museum context. This is a hands-on experimental array; the set-up seeks to show how current issues can be addressed and challenges met in an interactive, visitor-oriented way. In this spirit, the AEC with its special orientation and its unique strategic approach to conveying content constitutes a prototype in its own right.

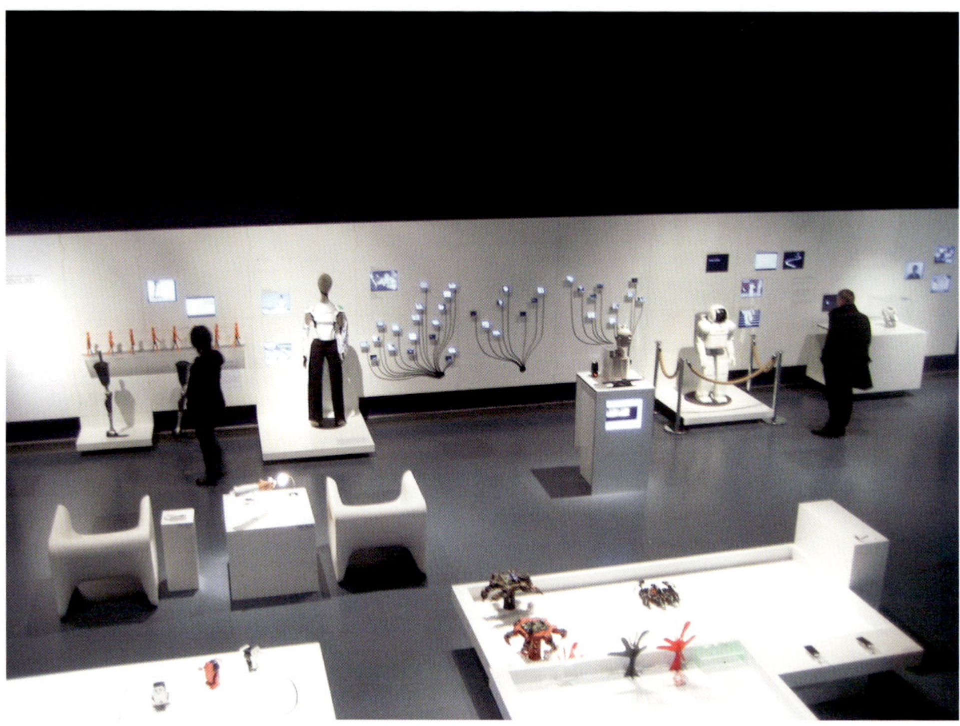

Humanoid Robotics

On the way to developing humanoid—that is, man-like—robots, we learn a lot about ourselves:
What exactly are motion, intelligence, and perception? In doing so, we come to recognize what a
great job nature did constructing human beings. But we also recognize our limitations, technical
limits but also limitations in our understanding of how nature really works.
Juxtaposing a human being to a humanoid robot raises the question: What makes a human
being human? What could make a robot appear to be human? Walking upright on two legs?
Gripping devices that function as well as our hands? Gestures and facial expressions? Even if
there still are no robots that truly come across as human, it's still fascinating to see how easy it
is to bring emotions into play. The suggestion of a face, the hint of a smile, the physical stature
of a child are all it takes for us to stop regarding the robot as a threat and to see it as a friend.

Bionic Prosthetics

The projects shown in this area are a key link at the nexus of neuroscience and robotics thus they
are placed as a transition zone between the BrainLab and the RoboLab. The human body's modes
of functioning are extended into the prosthesis itself.
The next step is the direct linkup of the prosthesis to the body's network of nerves, whereby even
implanting electrodes directly into the human brain is already a reality.

Design and Entertainment, Art and Research

A great deal of the attention that's been paid to humanoid robotics in Japan of late has been
focused on the emotional impact of these robotic machines on human beings. This has motivated designers to get more actively involved not only in creating the robots' look but also in
fine-tuning how they move. Many of these designs feature unmistakable allusions to Japanese
pop culture.

Concept: Gerfried Stocker, Christopher Lindinger, Hide Ogawa, Emiko Ogawa, Katharina Maria Hengel
Coordination: Hide Ogawa, Emiko Ogawa, Katharina Maria Hengel
Exhibition Design: Scott Ritter, Jakob Illera, Katharina Maria Hengel

C-Leg

The C-Leg® developed by Otto Bock is the world's first leg prosthesis with its own completely microprocessor-controlled knee joint. Via constant measurement of the joint momentum, joint angle and joint angle speed, the prosthesis reacts instantaneously to changes in terrain, motion and walking speed, and makes possible a stable bearing as well as a natural gait. Additional security and comfort is provided by the wearer-activated Standing Mode. It stabilizes the C-Leg® without the wearer having to exert muscle power. A special Second Mode has also been developed for varied activities like cycling and cross-country skiing.

C-Leg: Otto Bock Healthcare Products GmbH (DE/AT)

Myoelectrical Arm Prosthesis

An arm prosthesis controlled by the electrical signals of your muscles. Tensing a muscle produces a tiny electrical charge (in the microvolt range). This electricity is conducted via electrodes to the myoelectrical prosthesis where servo motors convert it into the intended movement. With two mobile electrodes, the visitors can control the prosthesis with the play of their muscles.

Myoelectrical Arm Prosthesis: Otto Bock Healthcare Products GmbH (DE/AT)

Photo: Lammerhuber/Ferrando

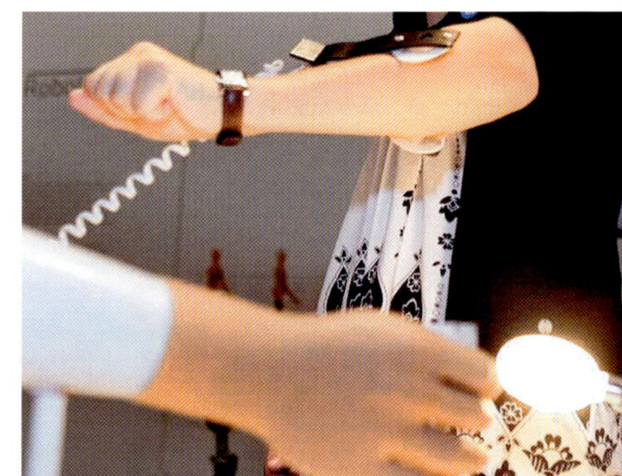

ActiGait

If the control of the musculature by the brain has been impaired, the nervous system can be activated by means of electrical impulses. The stimulation is applied by electrodes either through the skin or, via implantable devices, directly to a nerve.

Stroke patients often suffer weak foot dorsiflexion because the central nervous system is no longer able to activate the peronaeus nerve. The ActiGait® foot lifter stimulator implant assumes the task of initiating the lifting action of the foot when walking. Thanks to restoration of muscle flexion, the patient's ability to walk improves significantly: his/her foot no longer drags when striding.

ActiGait: Otto Bock Healthcare Products GmbH (DE/AT)

Photo: rubra

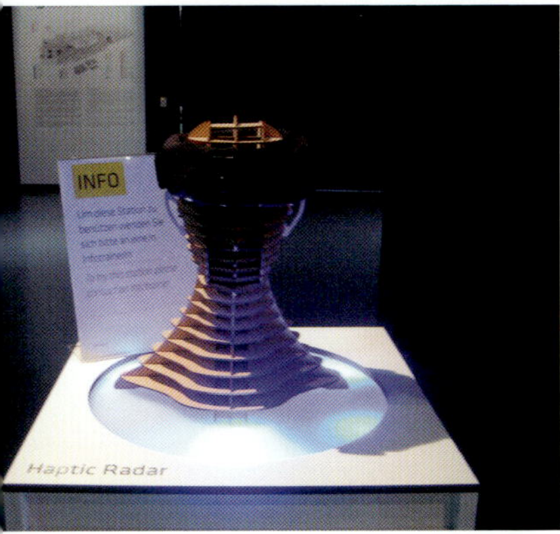

Haptic Radar

Haptic Radar

The *Haptic Radar* expands our senses and enables a totally new experience of space. The headband is composed of an array of optical sensors, which constantly measure the distance to surrounding objects. An analogy in the animal world to this artificial sensory system would be insect antennae or specialized sensory hairs such as cat whiskers. The respective measured distances are converted into vibrations of different intensities. In this way, the user get a tactile "image" of the surrounding space.

Haptic Radar: Alvaro Cassinelli, Alexis Zerroug, MetaPerception Group, Ishikawa-Komuro Laboratory, The University of Tokyo

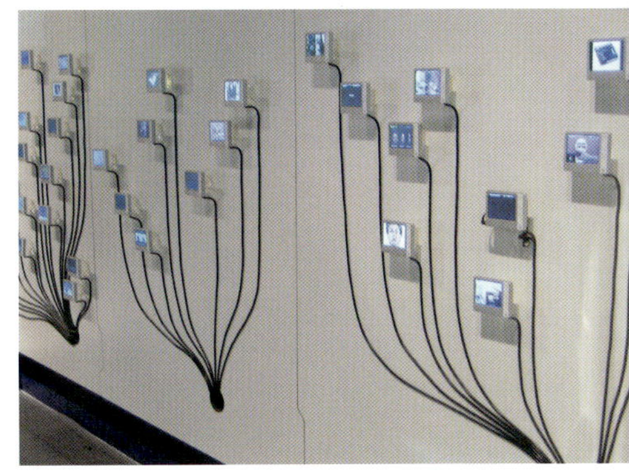

Robowall

An overview of R&D being done all over the world in the field of humanoid robotics is presented on 50 screens. This material brings out the various approaches and the three main challenges—walking upright, hands, and facial features. It also goes into artistic projects in which robots are utilized—for example, as part of a stage set or as cast members.

Robowall: Ars Electronica Futurelab (AT)

Photo: Richie Pettauer

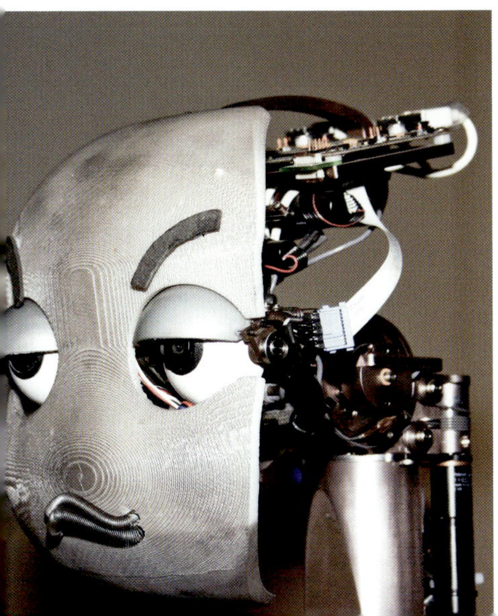

Mertz

A child's voice, big eyes and bushy eyebrows—MERTZ is a "face robot" that evokes empathy. As soon as it notices a human being in its surroundings, it makes contact with him/her. Thanks to its camera sensors and special software, MERTZ can recognize faces. It attempts to interact with as many people as possible, and, in doing so, gathers data about their facial expressions.

Developed by Lijin Aryananda in conjunction with work on her doctorate at the MIT Computer Science and Artificial Intelligence Laboratory; Ph.D. *advisor:* Prof. Rodney Brooks. *Technical design* by Jeff Weber.

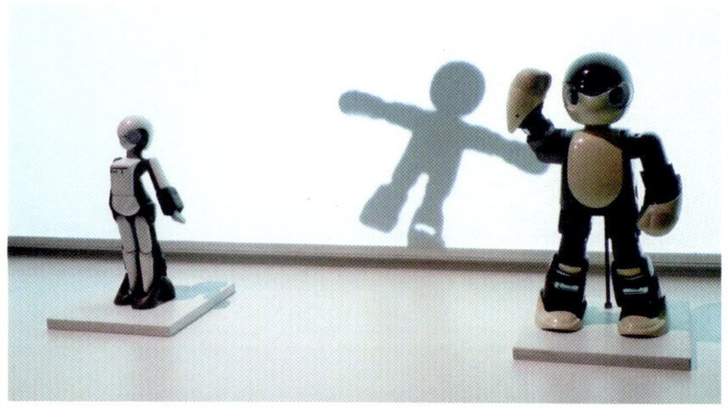

FT and Manoi

Two robots created and developed by Japanese designer and engineer Tomotaka Takahashi combine design artistry with leading-edge technology. Big eyes and a broad forehead convey openness; the expansive chest radiates self-assurance. Whereas FT comes across as very feminine and elegant, Manoi PF01 gives the impression of strength and friendliness. FT is one of the world's first female bipedal robots. Its slim feminine body was a real engineering challenge since there were so many parts that had to fit inside. Plus, a slim build makes it harder to maintain balance. FT's parts were designed especially to evoke a lean, feminine physique. FT is equipped with 23 motors and two gyroscope sensors yet it is still a prototype while Manoi PF01 is already sold as commercial product and equipped with 17 motors and 2 gyroscope sensors.

FT and Manoi: Tomotaka Takahashi
Special thanks to Kyosho Coroporation

Magic Moment

In this interactive installation, conceived by the artists collective h.o, humans and robots can share one special moment. *Shadow* builds a bridge between the real shadows of the installation visitors and the virtual ones of the robots. In the interplay of these shadows, both worlds come together. You're invited to join in on this interplay! Step behind the screen and become part of the shadow world of FT and Manoi PF01.

Magic Moment: Tomotaka Takahashi, h.o (Yuichi Tamagawa), Ars Electronica Futurelab (Emiko Ogawa, Hide Ogawa). *Special thanks:* Kyosho Corporation

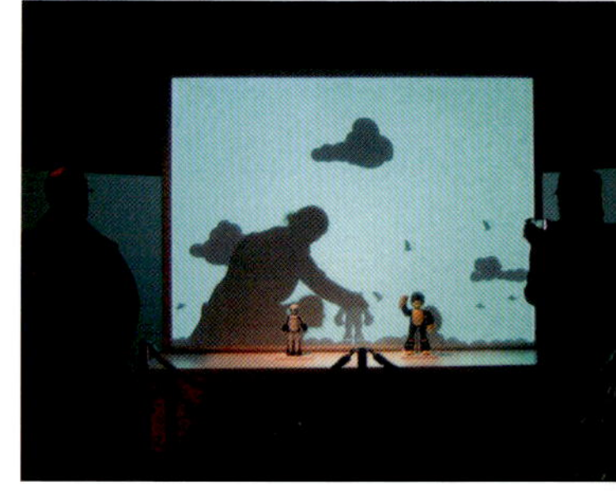

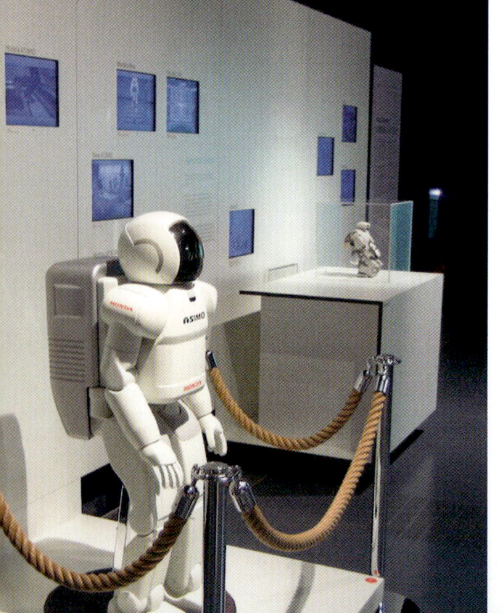

Asimo – Advanced Step in Innovative Mobility

Design study and original mock up of Honda's Asimo robot. Asimo is considered to be the most advanced humanoid robot of our time. It is 1,2 m tall and weighs 54 kilograms. The internal battery pack gives Asimo 40 min of operating time. In its actual version it has 34 degrees of freedom and as one of its sepical features it can run on two feet at speeds up to 6 kmh.

Asimo: Honda Motor Europe Ltd

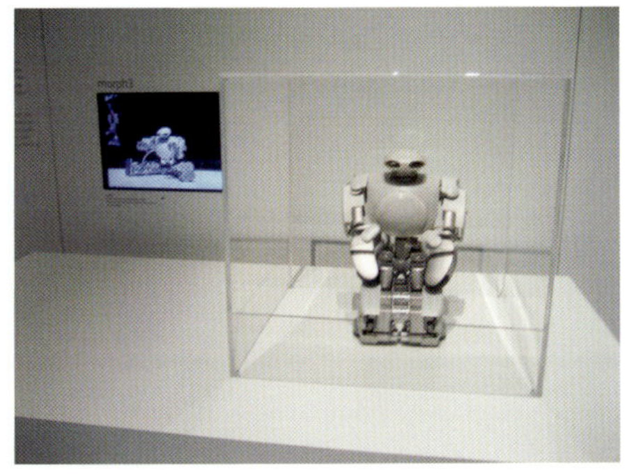

Morph3

Morph3 is a classic among small humanoid robots and superb example of a enormous agility. *Morph3* was developed by Kitano Symbiotic Systems and Leading Edge Design. Not only can morph3 jump; it's also capable of a midair backwards flip! The first public demonstration of its incredible agility was in competition in the first league of humanoid robots at RoboCup 2002.
Morph3 is 38 cm tall, weighs 2.4 kg and communicates via Bluetooth. Its movements are controlled by 138 pressure sensors, 30 motors and 14 processors. On display is one of the first development prototypes of *Morph3*.

Morph3: Future Robotics Technology Center (Chiba Institute of Technology), Shunji Yamanaka (Leading Edge Design), Japan Science and Technology Agency

Robo Playground

A playground for and with robots. Here visitors can play around with many types of robots. Starting with toy-robots from Elekit and the Topobo system from MIT Medialab up to elaborate Designrobots like Plen and Manoi.

Robo Playground: Ars Electronica Futurelab, Elekit, Topobo – MIT Medialab, PicoCricket, RobotEducation Kit Festo

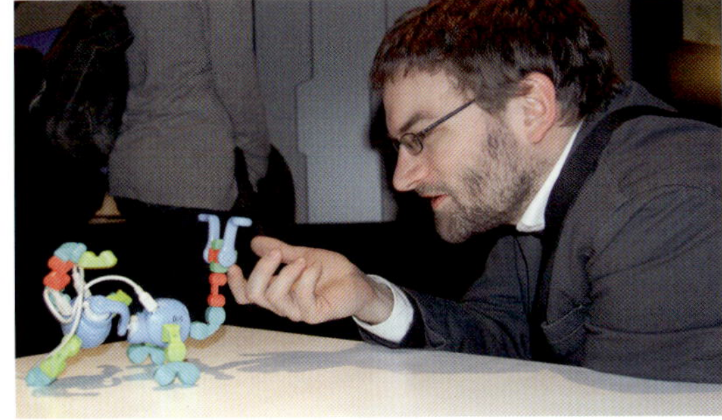

Photo: dleithinger
Photo: rubra

Plen Park

Skating, dancing, playing football—Plen robots are dynamic little dudes capable of some truly amazing feats! The Plens can be controlled by the visitors via PC or cellphone with Bluetooth. Even skating poses absolutely no problem. The heart of a Plen is its 32-bit ARM processor with a clock rate of 33 Mhz. With custom made software visitors can program their own motion patterns and choreographies thus experiencing the complexity of planning and optimising the motion of a machine.

Plen Park: Systec Akazawa

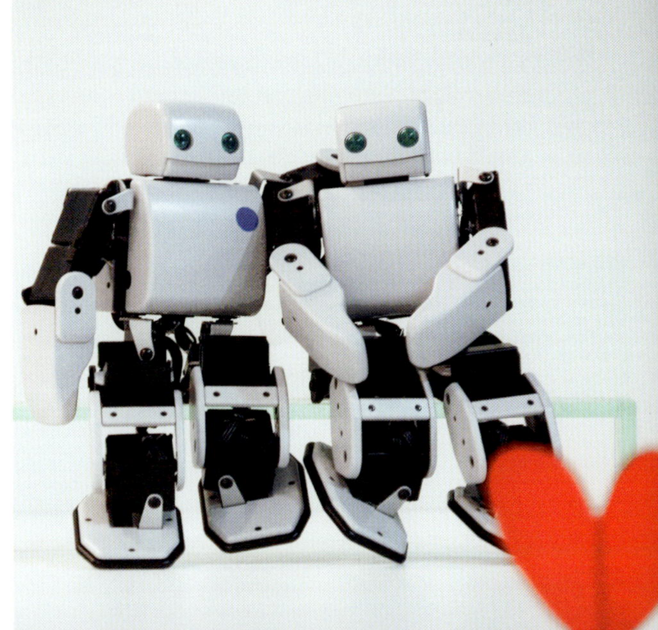

Hexapods

In contrast to the two legged Plens the Hexapods show that 6 legs are much better for robots. It makes them more stable and faster and allows for a much better payload-to-weight ratio. Since visitors can control the hexapods on their own they can experience the challenges of machine based robotic motion. Two different types of Hexapods are on display.

Hexapods: Matt Denton, mircomagic systems ltd. (UK), FH Hagenberg (AT)

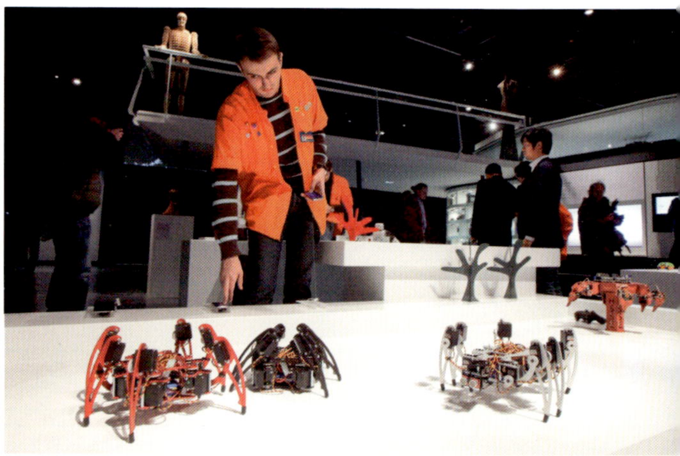

Photo: rubra

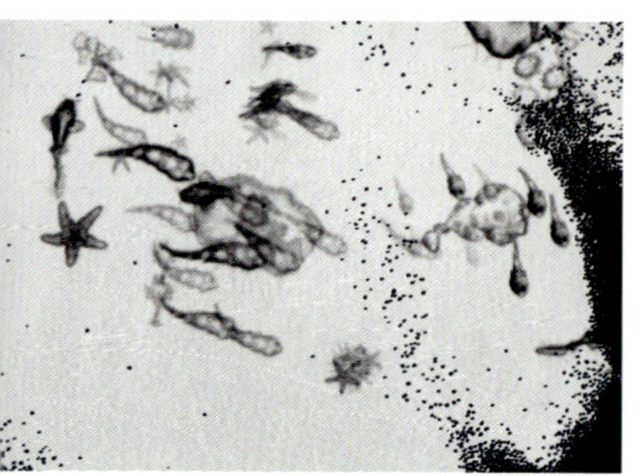

Photo: herr_s

Oasis II

As soon as some of the sand is removed from the surface of a high-resolution monitor, what's brought to light is a virtual pool populated by digital creatures. A computer program controls the behavior of the pool's virtual inhabitants in real time and simulates their swarming behavior. In the exhibition, the artificial creatures of Oasis II are the link between the machines of RoboLab and the BioLab's cloned plants and genetically engineered zebra fish.

Oasis II: Yunsil Heo, Hyunwoo Bang (KR)

Realive

A a robotic suit that supports stroke patients in the rehabilitation of their upper extremities. It consists of sensors and rubber muscles controlled by compressed air. When patients move their unaffected arm, sensors detect the movement and send signals to the rubber muscles that are wrapped around the impaired arm mirroring the movement of the unaffected arm. Through regular, automated training of the impaired extremity, the ability to carry out particular sequences of motions is re-installed in the brain—that is to say, it's actually relearned. This training device goes into commercial distribution in 2009. It will initially be sold to hospitals and rehab centers. The long-term objective is to develop an affordable version for private users.

Realive: Activelink Co., Ltd., Panasonic's in-house R&D division

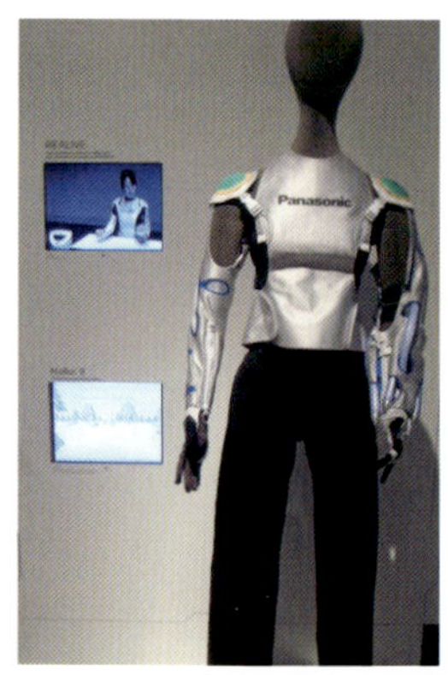

Guest Robots

Many robots are prototypes that their respective R&D labs can make available only for a few days or weeks. Thus, occasionally over the course of the year, the Ars Electronica Center is also able to showcase one-of-a-kind robots in the new exhibition.

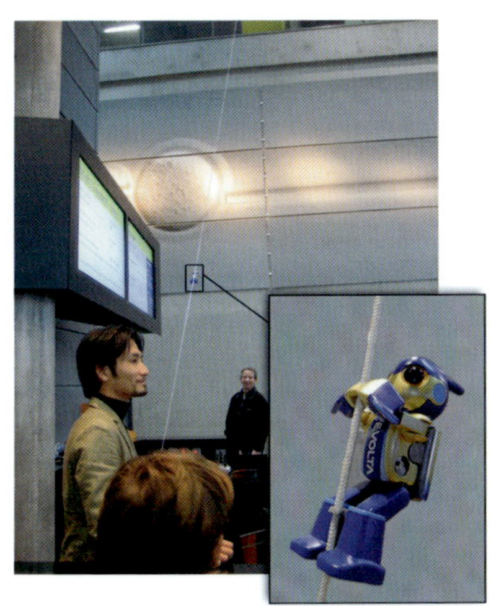

Evolta

In what was perhaps the most impressive publicity stunt of 2008, a 17-centimeter tall, 130-gram Panasonic Evolta robot hoisted itself up a 530-meter length of rope suspended next to a sheer rock wall at the Grand Canyon. The feat took a grueling 6 hours and 45 minutes.

(Guest in the Ars Electronica Center in January 2009)
Evolta: Tomotaka Takahashi

Chroino and FT

Chroino and FT (for female type) are the first two design robots coming out of Tomotaka Takahashi's Robo-Garage. Not only the visual design but even more the pre-programmed motion patterns give the robots their unique and distinctive character.

(Guest in the Ars Electronica Center in January 2009)
Chroino und FT: Tomotaka Takahashi

Photo: rubra

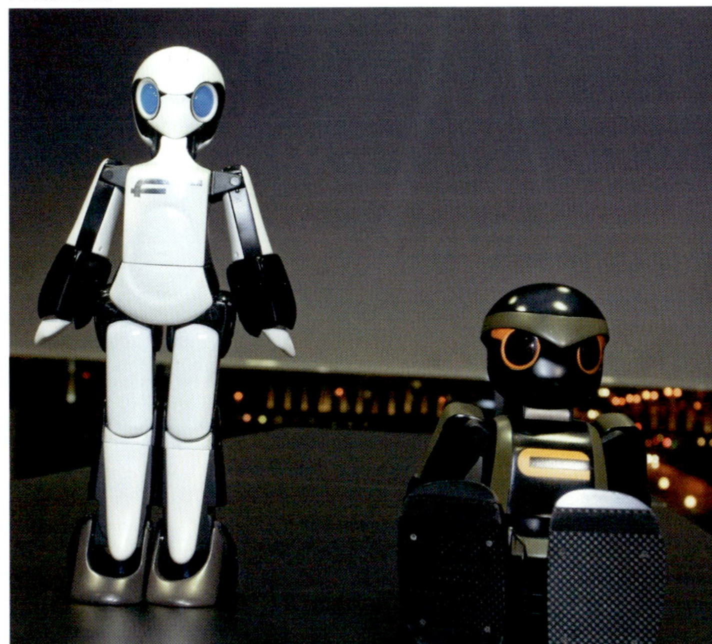

Halluc II

Halluc II is a high-tech prototype of a new generation of robots. A designer was brought on board the development team especially for this project. *Halluc II* amazing legs enable it to move in a variety of ways including rolling, crawling and walking. Each leg is powered by seven motors. The legs are also interconnected. Plus, they can feel their surroundings: 13 sensors measure distances; a pair of lasers detect obstacles.

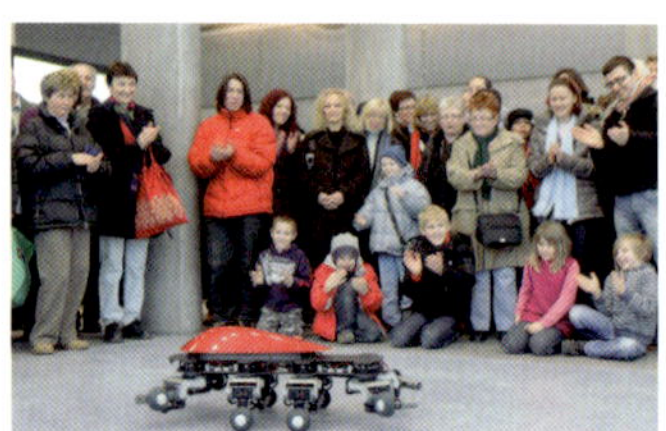
Photo: rubra

(Guest in the Ars Electronica Center in January 2009)
Halluc II: Shunji Yamanaka (Leading Edge Design), Future Robotics Technology Center (Chiba Institute of Technology)

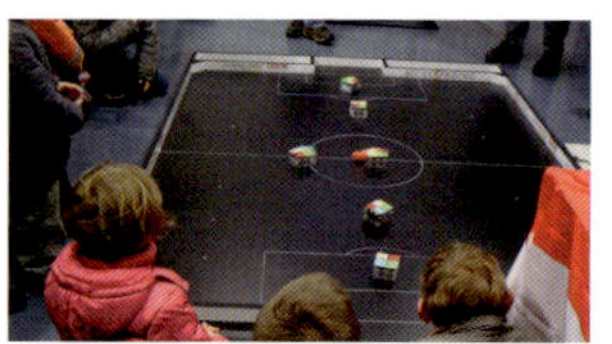

Leonding Micros

The Robo-Soccer-Team of HTL Leonding was demonstrating their skills during the opening days of the new Ars Electronica Center.

(Guest in the Ars Electronica Center in January 2009)
Leonding Micros: HTL Leonding

Murata Boy, Murata Girl

Murata Boy is a bicycle-riding robot. He's capable of riding his bike along a 2-cm-wide balance beam and can even nimbly negotiate tight S-curves. Murata Girl is a unicycle specialist who's equally adept riding forward and in reverse. Both utilize use a gyroscope to maintain their balance and ultrasound sensors to keep their distance from moving objects. A built-in camera is available for orientation purposes, and came in handy during the little daytrips the robots took during their stay at the AEC.

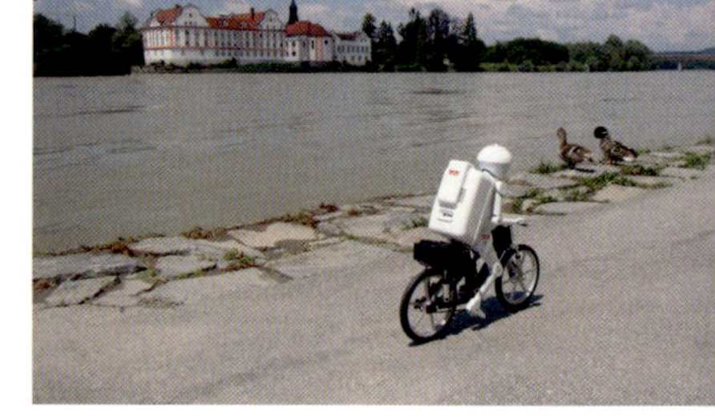

(Guest in the Ars Electronica Center in June 2009)
Murata Boy, Murata Girl: Murata Manufacturing Co., Ltd, Japan

Mars-Rover "Dignity"

Visitors to the "Stardust" exhibition can put a model of the Austrian Space Forum's Mars rover Dignity through its paces and assess its performance.

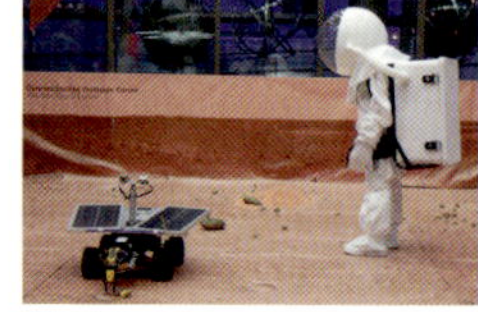

(Guest in the Ars Electronica Center in July and August 2009)
Mars-Rover "Dignity": Österreichisches Weltraum Forum

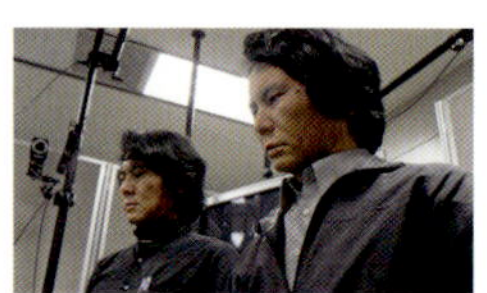

Geminoid

(Guest in the Ars Electronica Center in July and August 2009)
See pp 218–225 in this catalog

Hylozoic Grove

Canadian architect and artist Philip Beesley calls his sculpture "geotextile mesh," that combines nature and technology within an electrokinetic intelligent machine. The installation contains a dense net of proximity sensors, microcontrollers and actuators. When visitors come close, *Hylozoic Grove* responds with waves of motion stirring the air and spreading over the whole structure.

What makes the encounter with *Hylozoic Grove* so striking is the symbiosis of organic forms of behavior with technological materials as well as the dialog that arises between the installation and the visitors—do you watch or are you being watched?

Hylozoic Grove: Rob Gorbet (Engineering Director), Hayley Isaacs, Christian Joakim, Jonah Humphrey, Kirsten Robinson, Jon Cummings (Core Team), with Yoshikatsu Wachi, Manuel Kretzer, William Elsworthy, Eric Bury, David Blackmore, Lawrence Chan

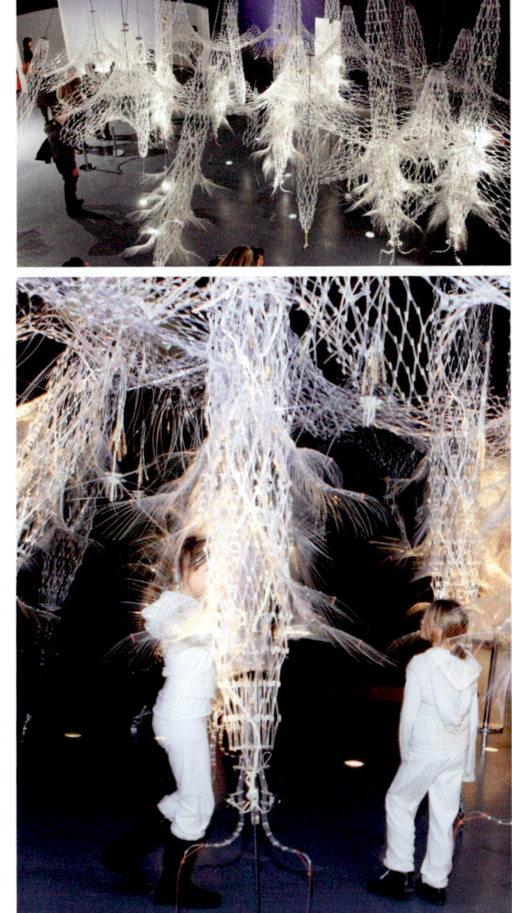

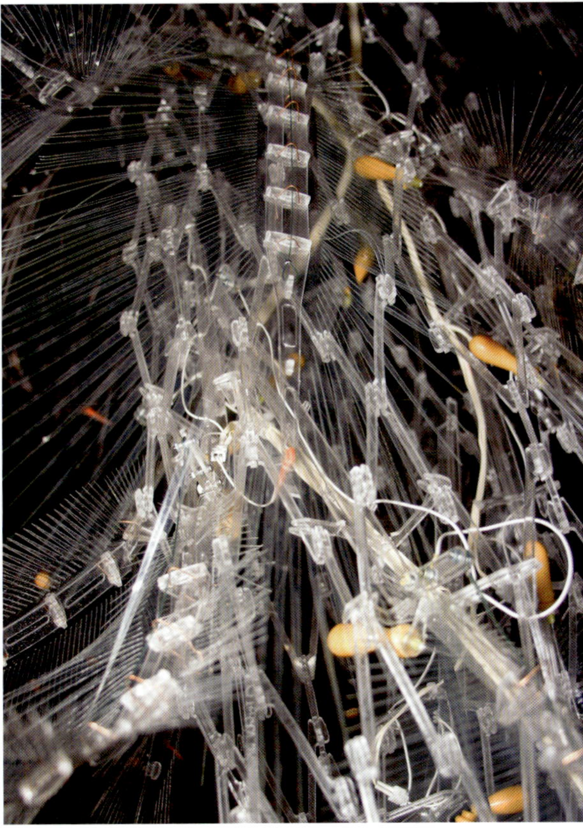

Photos: rubra

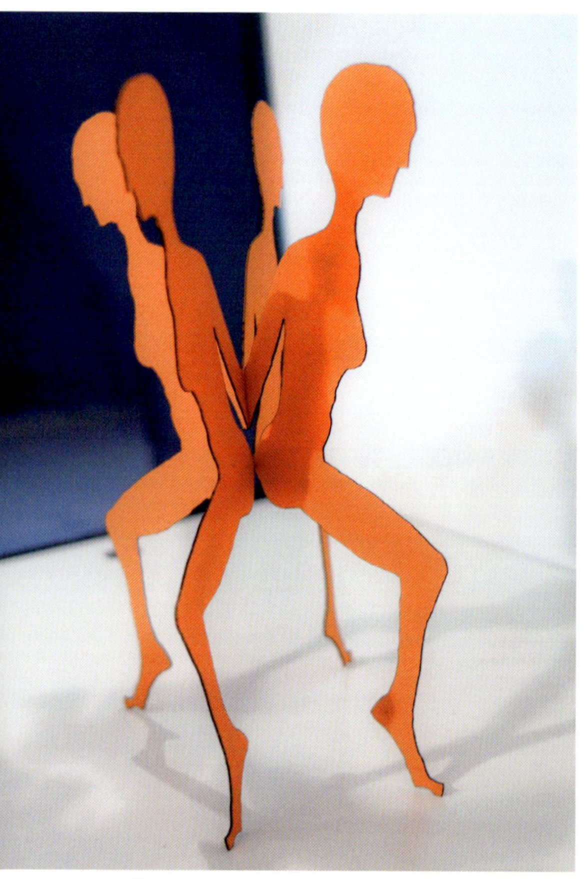

Photo: herr_S

This Lab provides access to new methods already in use in design and production. Rapid prototyping with 3D-printer and laser cutter. The aim is to discuss the visions and the possible impact that comes along with this technology.

Imagine a future in which you no longer buy gym shoes in a store; instead, you print them out at home, use them, and then toss them into the recycling bin when you're done. Downloading objects from the internet and printing them out at home. And not just on paper; as real stuff!

Visualizing individual design concepts on a PC and then transforming them into real-world creations in a home mini-factory—in the future, anyone will be able to be their own designer and mechanical engineer. And maybe even produce their own replacement body parts!

Using the internet makes it possible to disseminate designs for articles of clothing or pieces of furniture just as easily as sharing music and pictures today. What is indeed unimaginable is this technology's impact on established economies, but maybe it is also a step towards democratisation.

The lab's architectural layout dovetails with its educational strategy: it functions as both an open and a closed facility. Its freely accessible, open character invites visitors to engage in hands-on encounters that are supported by Infotrainers. The concepts and skills acquired thereby then develop into real-material prototypes and objects in the context of in-depth workshops.

Special Lab Days, Interactive-Creative Days for kids and young people, design workshops with artists, and workshops and presentations for school classes—the FabLab hosts a highly diversified educational program that facilitates a wide variety of approaches to many different subjects. Bringing out lateral linkages to other labs (e.g. BioLab, RoboLab) and illustrating interdisciplinary modes of work are additional areas emphasized by the AEC's mode of mediating visitors' encounters with content.

Concept: Gerfried Stocker, Christopher Lindinger, Irene Posch, *Coordination:* Irene Posch
Exhibition Design: Ars Electronica Futurelab, Jakob Illera, Scott Ritter
Development: Ars Electronica Futurelab
Special Thanks to: Wacom (*http://www.wacom.eu*), Trotec (*http://www.trotec.net*), fab@home Project (*http://www.fabathome.org*), gach edv agentur (*http://www.gach.biz*)

The FabLab's Input and Output Stations

At eight workstations equipped with Wacom tablets and a selection of rendering & construction programs, visitors can create their own objects. In addition to standard software, specially developed programs and two 3D scanners complement the infrastructure.

Placed at visitors' disposal are a Dimension 3D printer based on ABS plastic and a Trotec laser cutter. A DIY-Fab@Home can be used for experimentation purposes.

System Design and Integration: Ars Electronica Futurelab, elPhantasmo
Fibermesh Modeller based on: FiberMesh System by Takeo Igarashi, Andrew Nealen, Olga Sorking, and Marc Alexa
Rotation Designer: Ars Electronica Futurelab
Plushie System by Takeo Igarashi and Yuki Igarashi
Picture Scanner: Ars Electronica Futurelab
Grafictablets: Wacom Cintiq
3D Laser Scanner: Next Engine
3D Printer: Stratasys Dimension Elite
Laser Cutter: Trotec Rayjet
Fab@Home

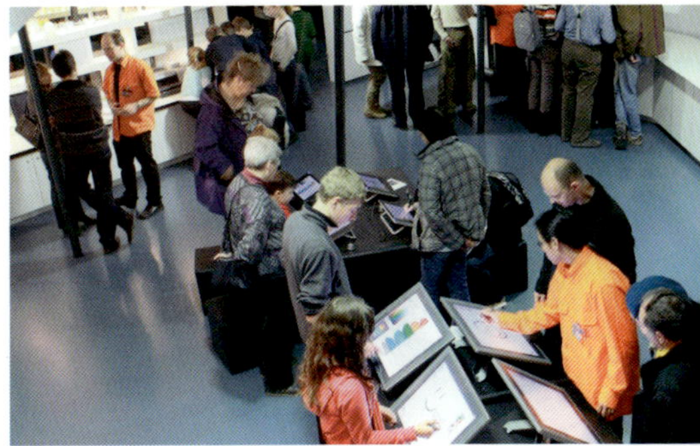

Photo: rubra

Air Drawing

A tracking system (Motion Capturing) registers your gestures and, via special software, transforms them into a three-dimensional object. This model can be edited on a PC and printed out with a 3D printer.

Air Drawing: Ars Electronica Futurelab

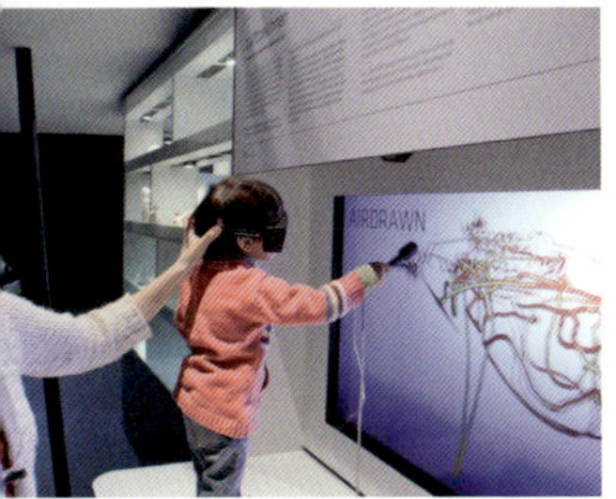

Photo: a_baranoff

Cassius

Fluid Forms takes an original approach to implementing the concept of user-generated designs. To accomplish this, a user-friendly tool has been developed that enables anyone to create an individualized lamp or jewelry: a punching bag.

This device is peppered with sensors. Force and position of each blow and hugs as well are transmitted to the computer model of the punching bag. The software then generates the production data for the production of a real lamp based on the shape you just created. Send this data to Fluid Form and they will produce your individual lamp with a 3D-printer.

Cassius: Stephen Williams, Hannes Walter
http://fluid-forms.com/projects/cassius

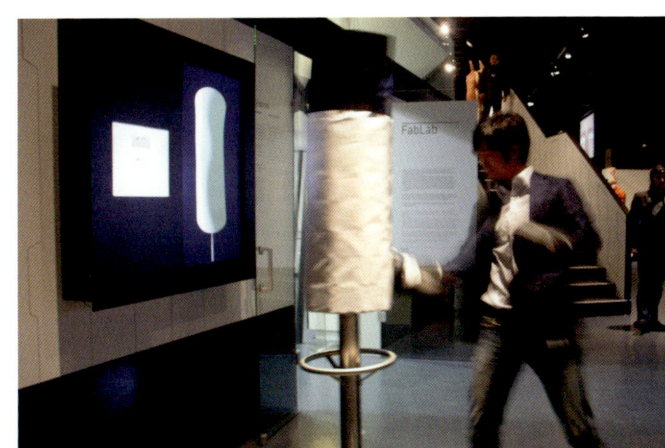

Photo: fluid forms
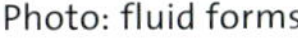

FabLab

FabGallery

The objects on display in this exhibition come from artists, design studios and engineering offices; they're meant to illustrate the various technical methods being used in the field of digital fabrication, current areas of application as well as visions for the future.

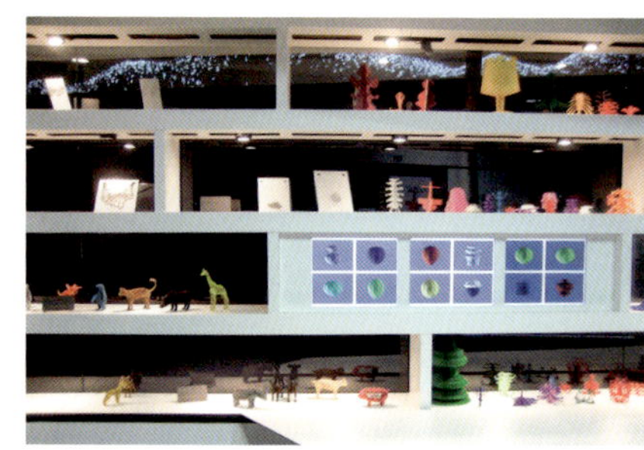

Photo: fluid forms

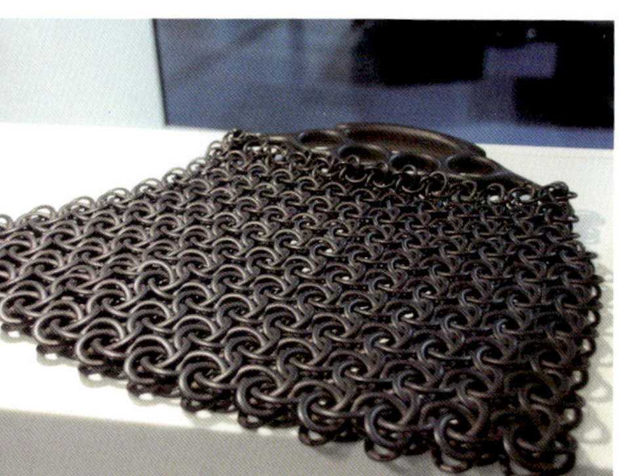

Photo: a_baranoff

FOC – freedom of creation (NL)

FOC is a pioneering design and research company, specialized in designing for rapid manufacturing. The outcome of their work is either part of the FOC collection or commercialized by other design labels.

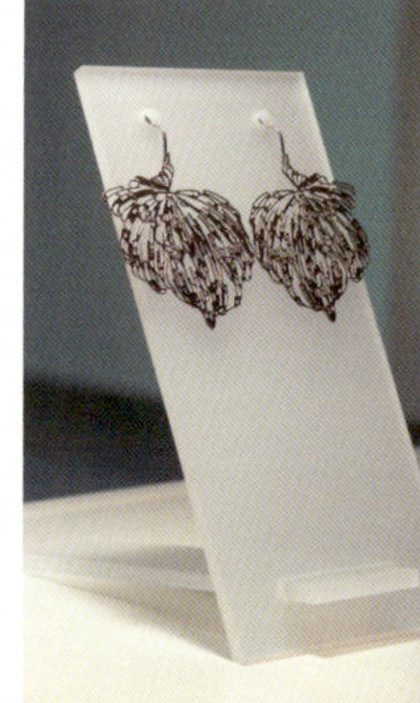

Nervous System (US)

Nervous System creates experimental jewelry, combining nontraditional materials like silicone rubber and stainless steel with rapid prototyping methods.

Photo: fluid forms

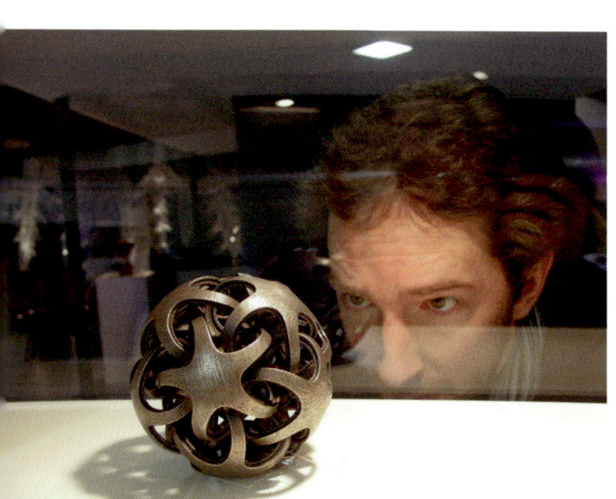

Batshebha Grossmann (US)

As an artist exploring the region between art and mathematics her work is about beauty in geometry and symmetry and balance. On display are some of her objects made with a new direct-metal printing technique, which produces a composite steel-bronze metal with a rich texture.

Photo: fluid forms

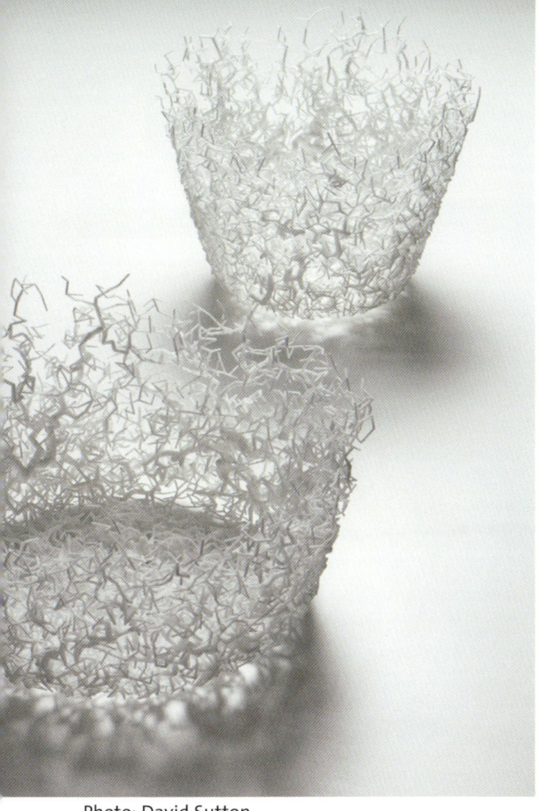

Photo: David Sutton

David Sutton (UK)

His *Diffusion Vessels* are formed through a process called Diffusion Limited Aggregation (DLA) which has been modelled and constrained within a virtual environment and made into real objects with a 3D printer. DLA is usually studied as an example of fractal growth processes such as branching, lightning, snowflakes, mineral deposits and coral.

D-Torso, aki co. ltd. (JP)

D-Torso System is a 3D figurative system developed by Aki Co. ,Ltd. The method is to divide the 3D objects into sliced data which can be cut out of paper or wood with a laser cutter and then reconstructed as solid objects.

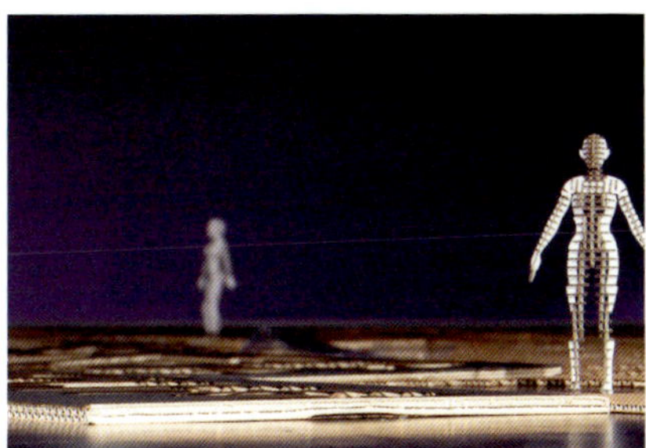
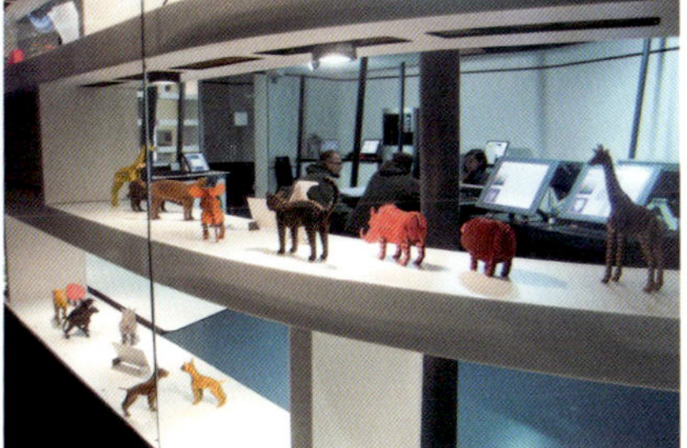

Photo: inflex

Also on display are the *Stranger* wooden robots by Mario Wingert (DE), results of the R&D work being done by Ralf Huttary and Michael Verius at the University Clinic in Innsbruck, two additional works by Fluid Forms (AT), printouts of objects from the "Escher for Real" series by Gershon Elber (IL), mathematical geometrical models by George Hart (US), design studies by zCorp (US) and lots of models created together with our visitors since the opening.

Photo: rubra

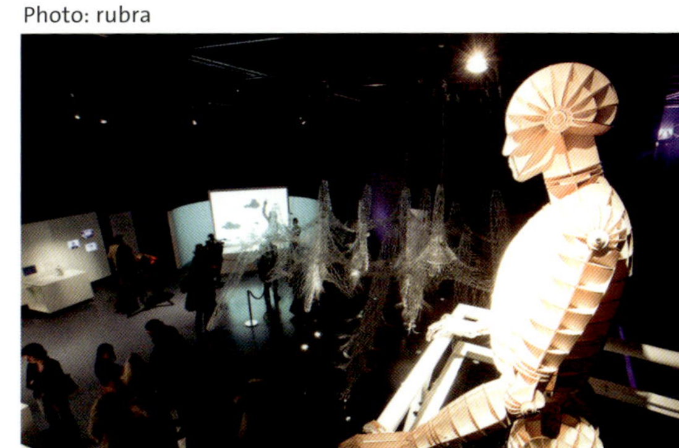

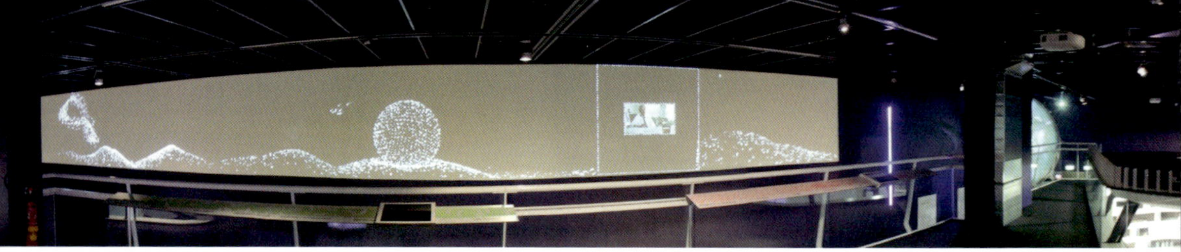

Infodeck

Located directly above the Labs' is a platform that visitors can use as a retreat providing a respite from the hustle & bustle of the Main Gallery's exhibition and interaction areas. The Infodeck is a setting for peace and quiet, but it's also a knowledge portal offering those who seek it out the opportunity to undertake a more profound encounter with a wide array of themes via interactive media stations, mobile devices like e-books, and conventional printed matter too. The Infodeck also serves as an observation platform from which you can see what's transpiring in the Labs and be inspired by what you see.

Concept: Gerfried Stocker, Christopher Lindinger *Coordination:* Irene Posch, Katharina Maria Hengel *Exhibition Design:* Scott Ritter, Jakob Illera

Infowall

The *Infowall*, the exhibition's knowledge databank, consists of two levels. It's visible from the lower Action Level (exhibition spaces, Labs) as well as from the Infodeck. Cameras mounted on the ceiling register visitors' movements and use this material to animate the graphics on the *Infowall*, which consists of 12 projectors. From the Infodeck, users can access a wide array of information via four slide terminals, each assigned to one of the exhibition areas.

The slide terminals are transparent touchscreens that are integrated into the Infodeck's railing. Selecting from a list of keywords enables users to bring up on screen more detailed context menus that provide access to texts, images and videos.

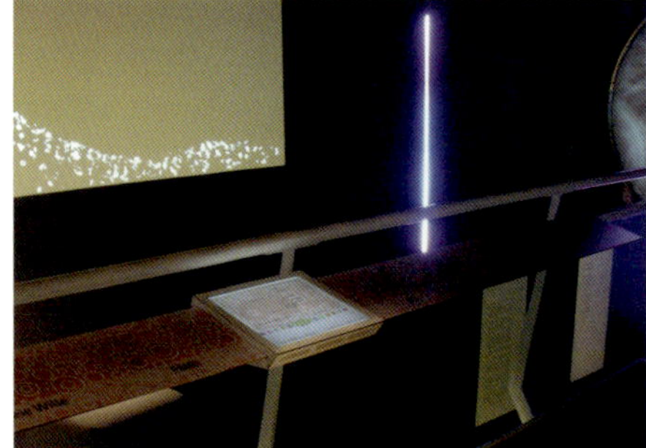

Infowall: Ars Electronica Futurelab, Sebastian Neitsch (DE)

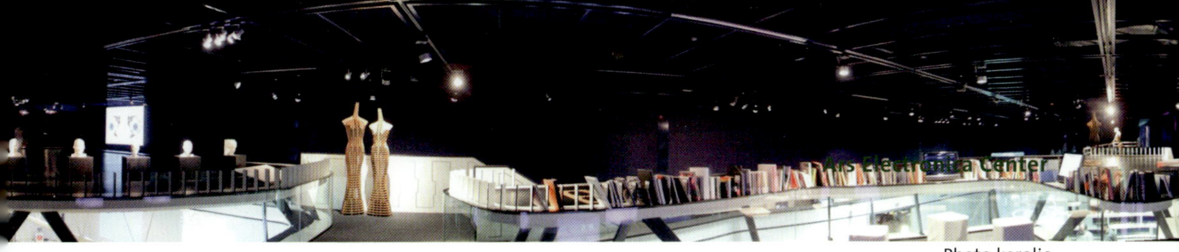

Photo kerolic

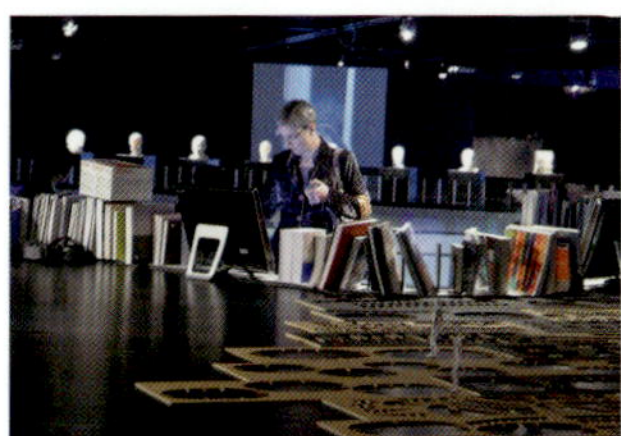

Photo: Andreas Hirsch

Library

In the library visitors can consult a nice selection of science and art books that are directly related to the theme exhibits in the Labs and other objects on display. If experiences on the exhibition level have piqued your curiosity, you can delve a bit deeper into the subject matter—of course, via surf terminals and mobile devices like e-books too.

Library: System Integration: Ars Electronica Futurelab (AT)

Fuwapica & RGBy

Interactive stools designed by Japan's Mongoose Studio invite you to linger a while. They change their color and make sounds when you sit on them.

RGBy are small decorative light sources that can register and reproduce colors from any other surface. Three LEDs (red, green and blue) shine onto the selected surface. A color sensor registers how strongly the individual colors are reflected and, from the interrelationship of the data, calculates the color of the background.

Fuwapica & RGBy: Mongoose Studio, Tokyo (JP)
http://mongoose.proto-type.jp/products/rgby/

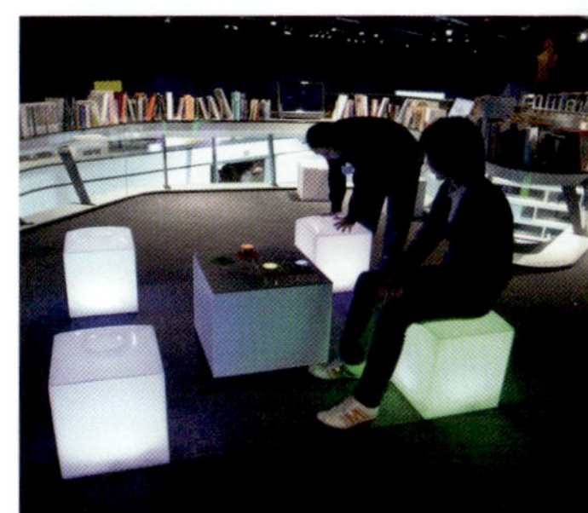

Photo: Andreas Hirsch

CATS

Bilbao combines art and standard medical and industrial engineering tools. Computed Axial Tomography (CAT) data is used here for artistic purposes. The goal is to experiment with the unexplored creative potential of medical hardware and software when applied in combination with 3D modelling software and rapid-prototyping machines. Some of the tasks are entrusted to machines which leave their print on the final work with pixels, scan lines, laser cutting and interferences that resemble the grain of a photograph. Íñigo Bilbao depicts both the changing and perishable outer appearance of the model and the more solid and lasting internal structure of its bone structure.

This work not only constitutes a superb blend of art and science; it also forms an artistic bridge connecting three exhibition areas: Biolab, Brainlab and Fablab.

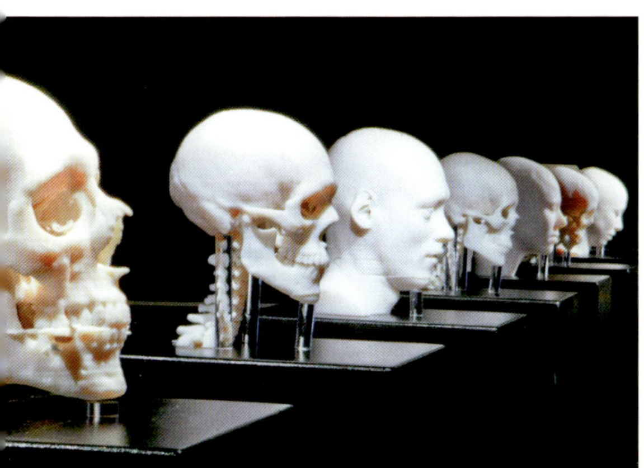

CATS: Íñigo Bilbao; Felix Luque (Sound Design)
The work was produced and first presented within the Projects Office program of LABoral Centro de Arte y Creación Industrial Gijon/Spain.
http://www.ibl3d.com; http://www.othersounds.net

161

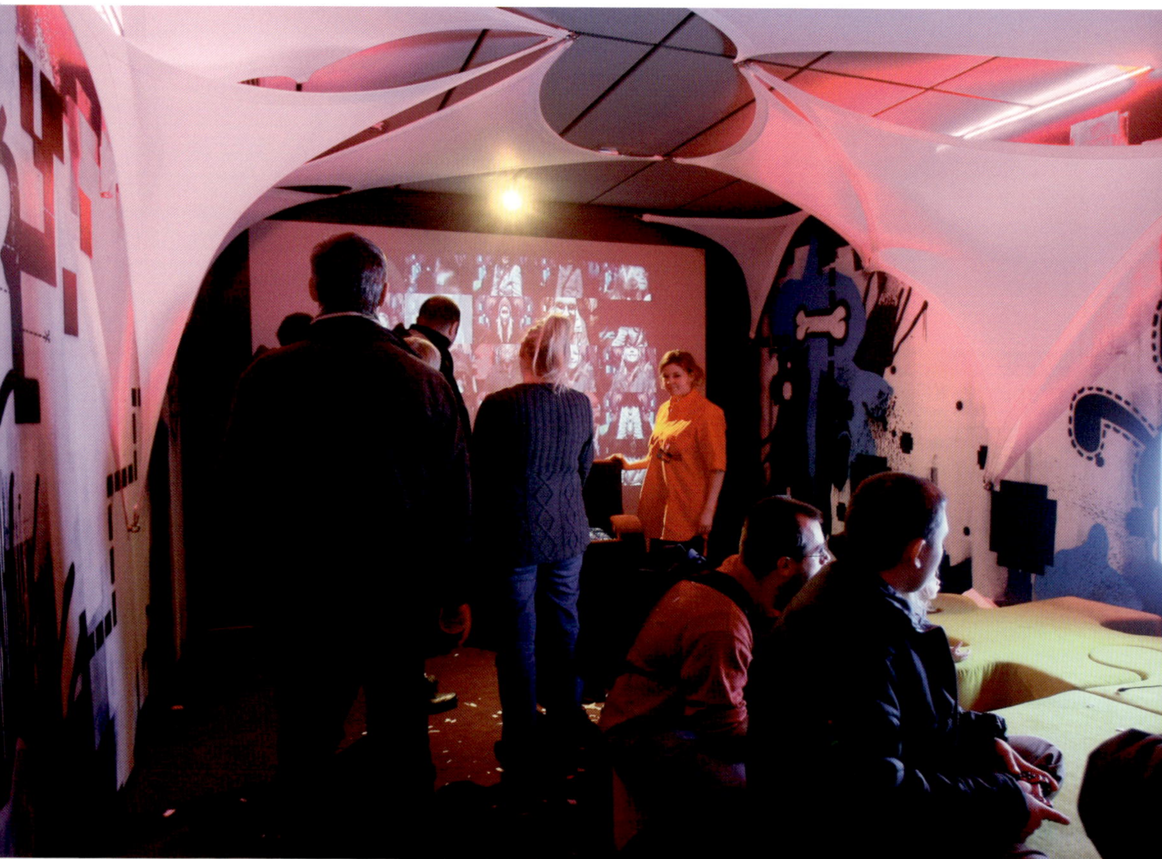

Photo: rubra

The *Funky Pixels* area of the exhibition shifts the focus onto some of Ars Electronica's familiar core themes: creativity and having fun dealing with digital media. It features haptic, tactile interfaces that interconnect the virtual sphere with our real, physical realm of experience. Designed as a shoes-off zone, this area is a favorite of our younger guests.

Concept: Gerfried Stocker, Martin Honzik, Susi Windischbauer
Coordination: Martin Honzik. Susi Windischbauer, Jochen Zeirzer
Exhibition design: Roland Ploner

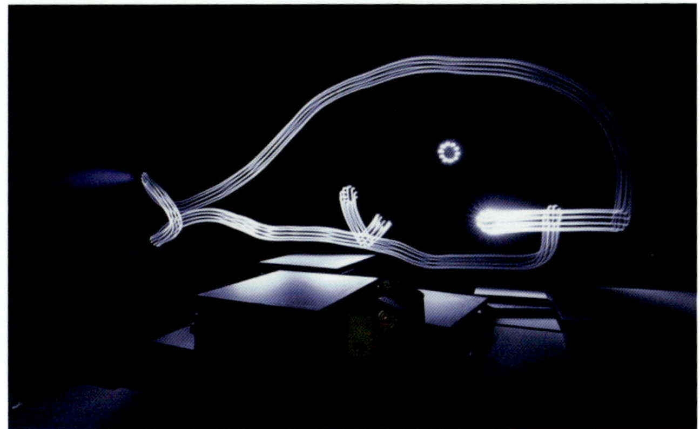

Lichtmaler

Painting with moving light. Visitors can use a palette of lamps to paint on a canvas. Serving as inspiration are impressive examples of such light graffiti created by the Lichtfaktor Crew.

Lichtmaler: lichtfaktor crew (DE)
www.lichtfaktor.eu

Garden

This work of Japanese Artist Kohei Asano needs very active amblers: by throwing scraps of paper into the air, flowers are projected on the floor. The number of flowers become even more, the more scraps of papers are raining down on the vitual flowerbed.

Garden: Kohei Asano, Kosuke Matsuura
http://www.asanokohei.com

Photos: rubra

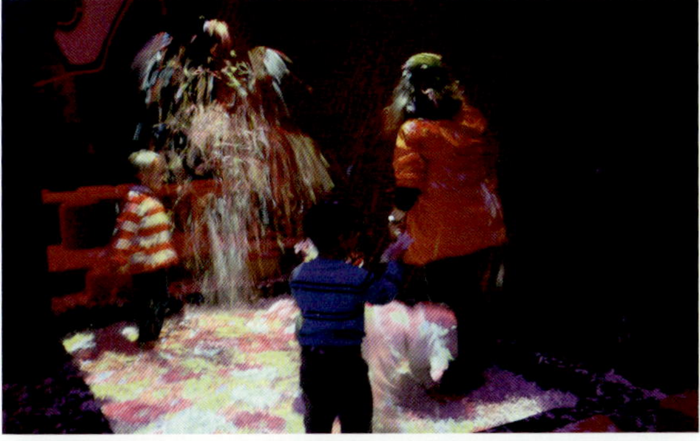

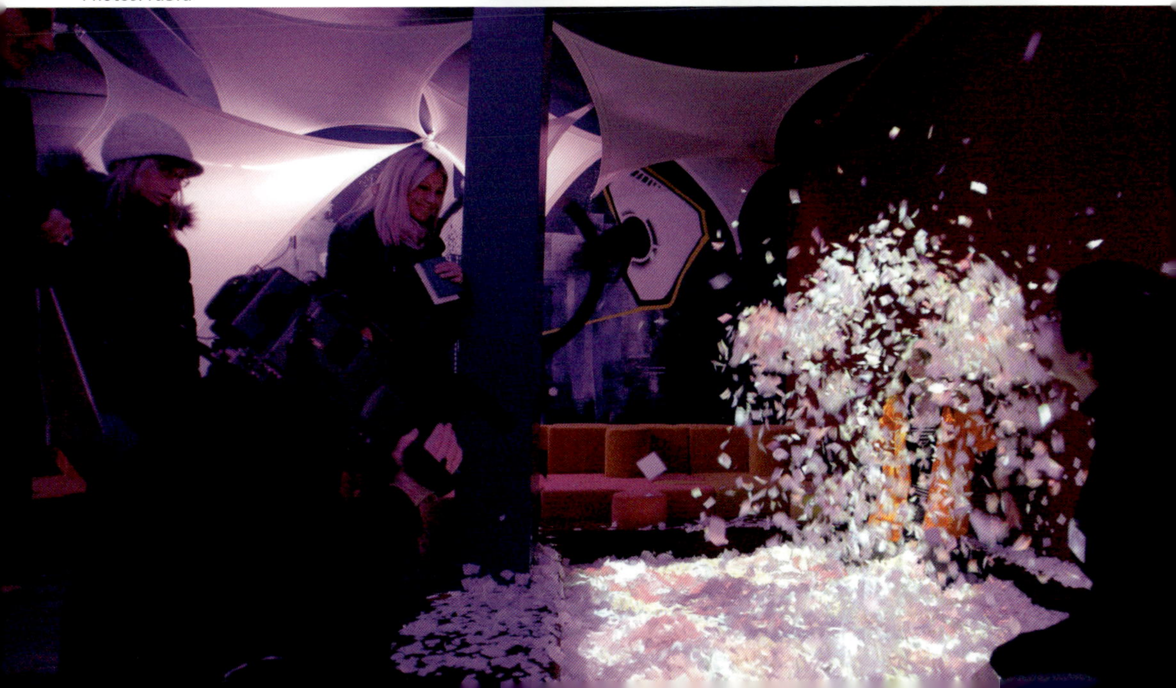

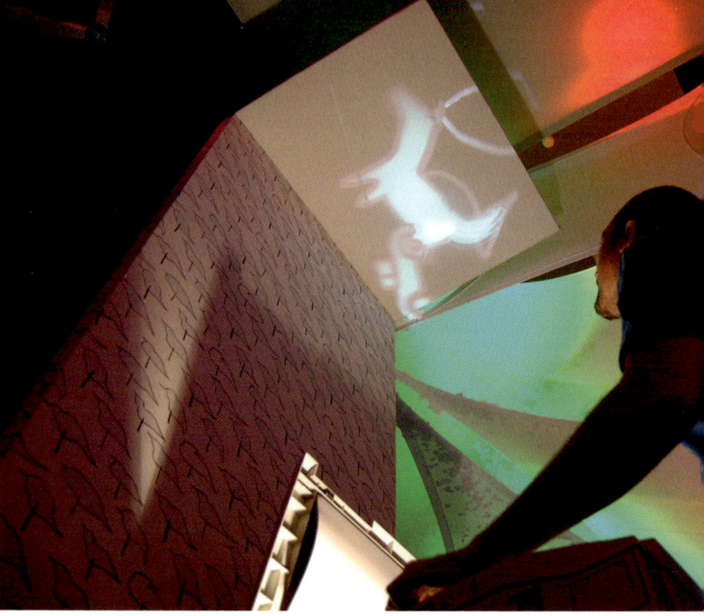

Godmode

Godmode is a customized copier. When you put your own drawing inside, software developed by Tim Knappen animates it and projects it onto the ceiling together with drawings done by other visitors.

Godmode: INDIANEN (Tim Knapen)
http://www.pacesetter2000.be

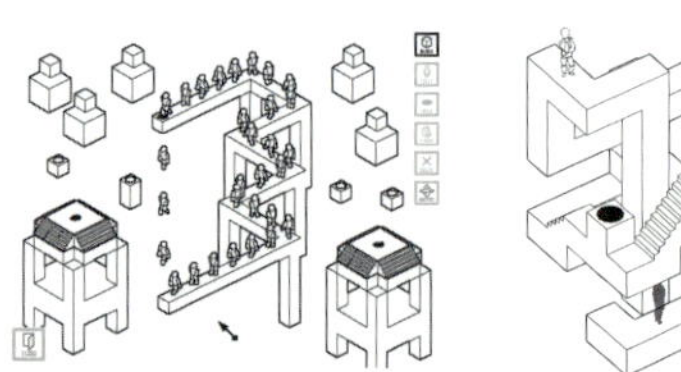

Photo: rubra

levelHead

levelHead is a spatial memory game that's played with plastic cubes you hold in your hand. When you move the cubes in front of a small camera, a screen displays spaces and rooms that seem to be located inside the cubes. The cubes—and thus the spaces—are interconnected; tilting and rotating the cubes lets you manipulate a small human figure as if through a labyrinth. But some of the doors lead nowhere, while others lead back to the room the figure was in at the start.

levelHead: Julian Oliver, developed with support from Medialab Prado.
http://www.julianoliver.com

Echochrome / *Extended Cognitive Tools*

Echochrome is a set of expressive software applications that play with the expansion of human perception. The set consists of three modules. Part 1, Incompatible BLOCK, is a building block-based 3D modeling program that enables users to reposition blocks via dragging and to thus create optically distorted constructions. Part 2, OLE Coordinate System, offers interactive illusions that enable the on-screen figures to perform impossible movements on the blocks and stairways of the virtual 3D world. Part 3, Constellation, is a point-based animation application that creates characters out of dots. The characters then undergo "cognitive morphing."

Echochrome: Jun Fujiki, Taketoshi
Ushiama, Kiyoshi Tomimatsu,
Kyushu University (JP),
http://imposs.ible.jp/fujiki/
applications_e.html
Thanks to Sony's JAPAN Studio

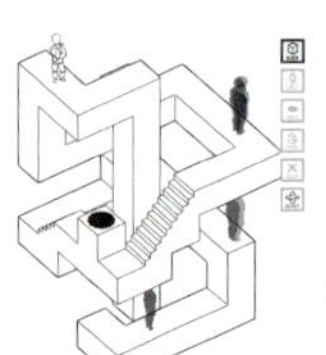

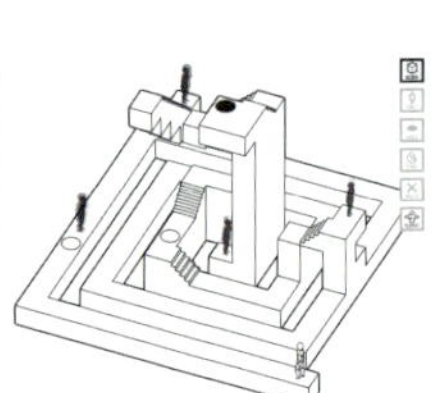

u19 – freestyle computing

u19's inherently broad spectrum and the multifaceted entries submitted to it perennially make it the Prix Ars Electronica's most highly diversified category. *Funky Pixels* presents outstanding examples of animated filmmaking as well as "Dual Mouse" from Christoph Wiesner, one of the most popular games ever submitted for prize consideration to u19.

Prix Ars Electronica u19, Christoph Wiesner

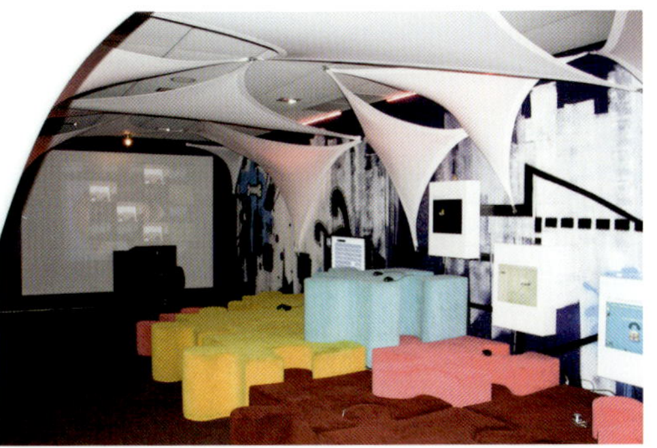

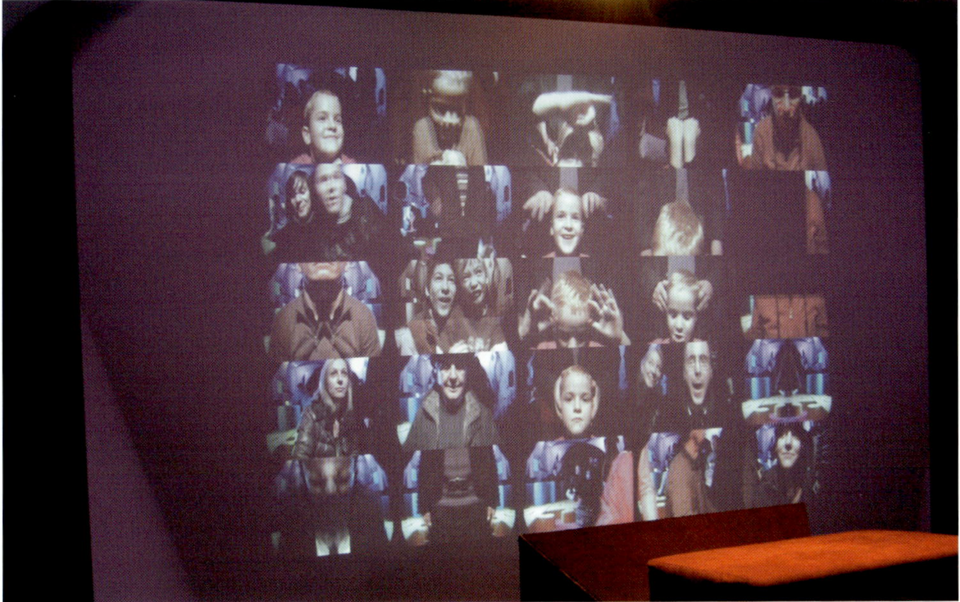

Photo: inflex

Videogrid

An interactive video installation, *Videogrid* consists of a grid of squares (5 x 5) which can each record a one second loop of film. Participants are free to create giant composite moving portraits, simple narratives, group artworks or simply a collage of moving snapshots . The grid starts empty at the beginning of the installation and becomes a constantly changing collaborative artwork that showcases the creativity of visitors through the space.

Videogrid: Ross Phillips, *http://www.rossphillips.me*

Poetry of Movement

In a world whose inhabitants have armed themselves to the teeth with computers, cellphones, GPS receivers and other digital devices, artists have gotten into the swing of things and designed machines that, rather than serving automation and efficiency maximization, showcase mechanical motion as a purely aesthetic experience. They have animated these mechanisms with the breath of life; they give narrative accounts with them, these artfully construed apparatuses that open up realms in which elements of fantasy and imagination can come out and play.

Concept: Gerfried Stocker, Christopher Lindinger, *Coordination:* Jochen Zeirzer, Sofya Yuditskaya
Exhibition Design: Scott Ritter, Jakob Illera

Quartet
Jeff Lieberman, Dan Paluska

Become part of a musical quartet, by entering a short melodic theme, which is then performed as a unique three-minute piece of music by the three robotic members of the *Quartet*: The first is a ballistic marimba, which launches rubber balls 2m in the air, precisely aimed at marimba keys. 35 tuned wineglasses are played by robotic fingers, and an ethnic percussion ensemble round out the quartet. Your performance is broadcast live and

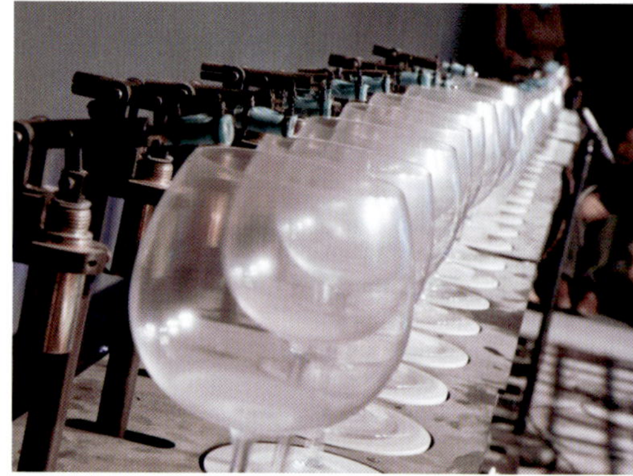

Photo: rubra

archived on the homepage *http://quartet.cc* to share your creation with others. The pieces produced are "open source", and anyone is free to use them.

According to Lieberman and Paluska, the most important quality of interactive art is its capacity to interconnect an incredibly diverse array of people and to foster collaboration.

Quartet: Jeff Lieberman, Dan Paluska (US), V&S Vin & Sprit AB

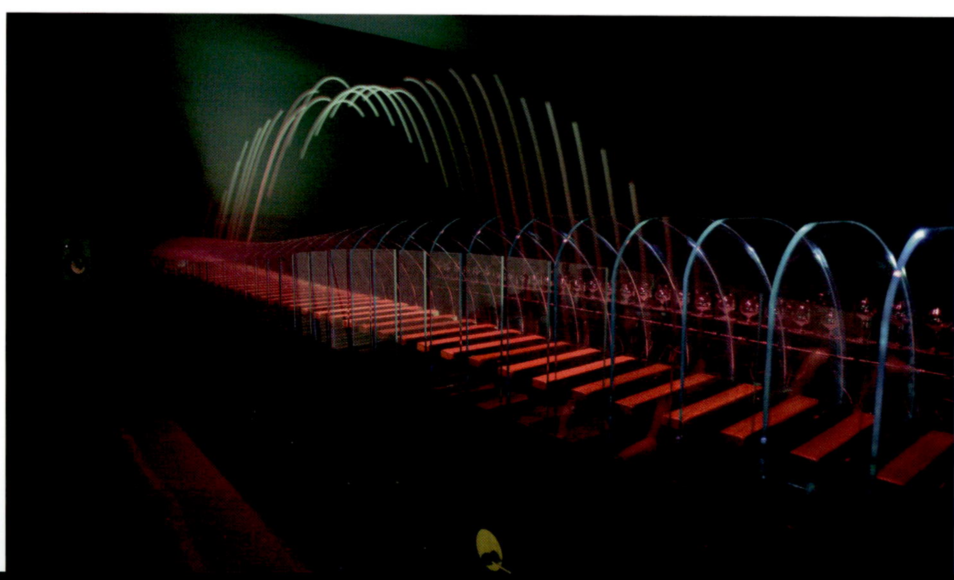

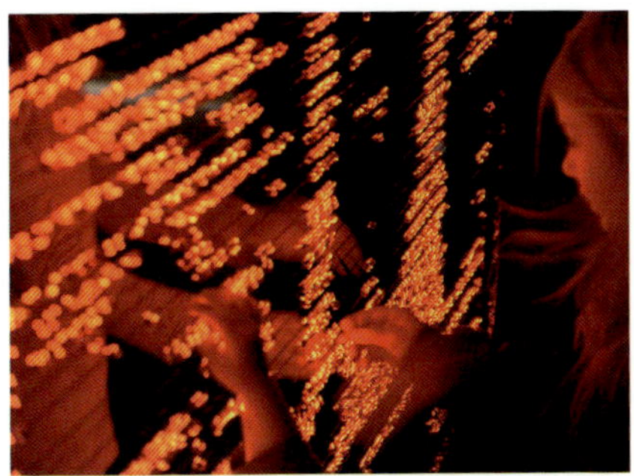

Photo: Andreas Hirsch

L-E-D-LED-L-ED
dilight inc.

Hundreds of tiny bead-shaped light-emitting diodes let you design your own little works of art. Each LED draws its energy from the magnetic field of the wire its strung on. The beads can be moved back and forth along an array of parallel wires, so you can arrange them into any glowing pattern you want.

L-E-D-LED-L-ED: dilight inc. (JP)

Structured Creature
Yosuke Ushigome

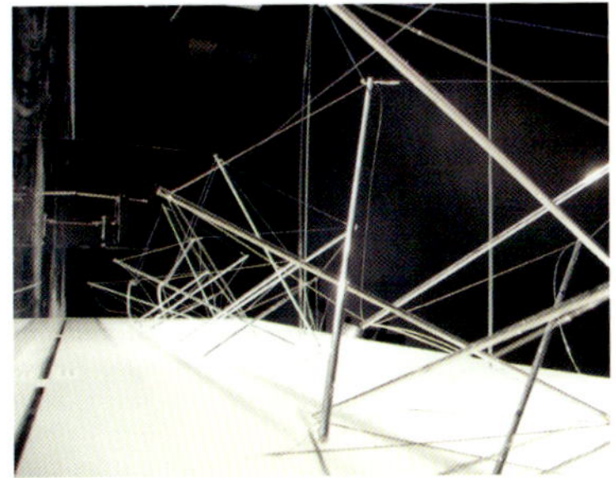

Photo: kerolic

Structured Creature (2008) is a prototype for architectural elements of the future which interact with their surroundings and inhabitants. The organic movement is generated by a "tensegrity" structure, in which fixed elements and ties form equilibrium between tension and compression. It is driven by artificial muscles built from "shape memory" alloy which "remembers" its shape and, after being deformed, can be returned to that shape when heat is applied to the alloy.

Structured Creature (2008): Yosuke Ushigome, Kunihiro Nishimura, Yasuhiro Suzuki and Michitaka Hirose. This artwork is partly supported by JST CREST "Technology to Create Digital Public Art" project.

Bellows
Eric Dyer

Bellows translates the principle of the zoetrope into the 21st century. 200 years ago, viewers peered through slits cut into the walls of a rotating cylinder at a sequence of static images on its interior wall; the cylinder's rotation seemed to animate the images. Now, Dyer has replaced the images with hand-painted 3D computer prints, and the human eye with a camera. Here, though, the speed at which the objects fly by exceeds the eye's ability to see. It is not until the camera images are transferred onto a screen that it becomes possible to register them.

Bellows (2008): Eric Dyer

Photo: rubra

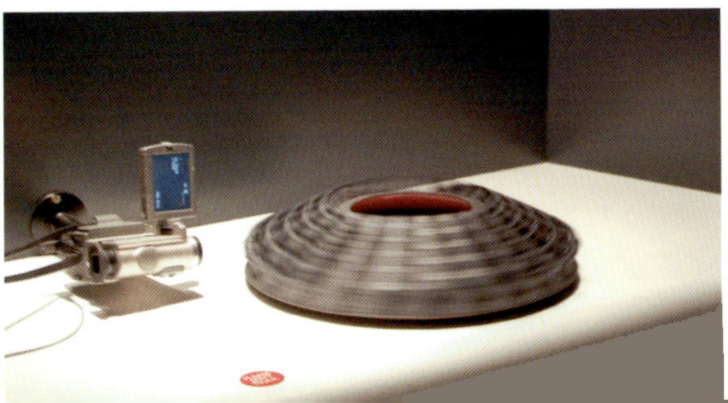

Arthur Ganson

Arthur Ganson has been developing kinetic sculptures for more than 25 years. Fascinated by manual work as well as by computer programming, he has developed works since his college days that combine both interests: accurate manual working and the examination of logical flows of energy within a closed system.

He is particularly fascinated by the question of how motion functions. For Ganson, his sculptures constitute a language all their own. They are not solely mechanical devices; rather, each relates its own story. Characteristic of his way of working is the combination of artificial and natural elements. Thus, in addition to wires and cogwheels, he also uses eggshells, feathers and chicken bones.

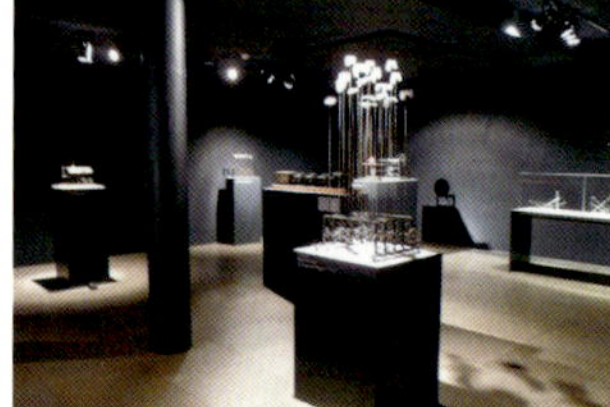

Photo: rubra

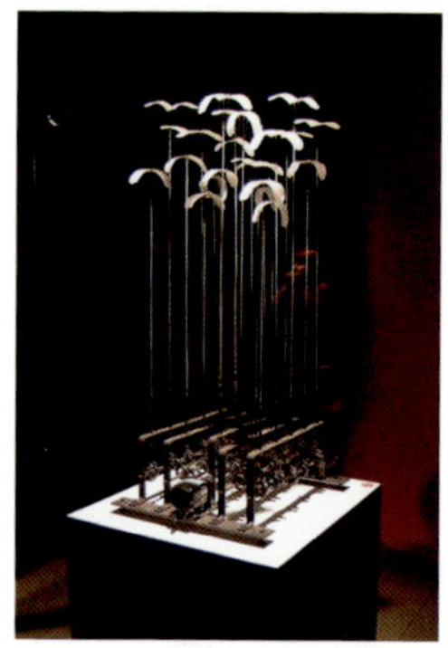

Photo: dleithinger

Machine with 22 Scraps of Paper (# 1 of 5), 2007

A flock of birds, butterflies, or leaves fluttering in the breeze—nature engenders an atmosphere of harmony in utterly simple fashion. This was the source of Arthur Ganson's inspiration. Scraps of paper driven by a finely tuned mechanism are set into gentle motion. In every one of his machines, Arthur Ganson sees in some way a self-portrait. For this piece, the artist has been lead by meditations on the nature of his being. "I am animal and thus am subject to the laws of physics and chemistry. I am spirit and thus am not bound by any physical law. Everything is revealed by the nature of my physicality. Nothing is revealed by the nature of my physicality."

Credits: Arthur Ganson

Machine with Concrete, 1992

The human being is the only creature on Earth capable of building machines that can outlive their creator. The speed at which the cogwheels in *Machine with Concrete* turn is slowed down by 12 pairs of reductors. The last cogwheel needs more than two trillion years to complete one rotation. Whereas the everyday life of modern men and women increasingly seems to be accelerating, changes in the universe take place in time dimensions of billions of years.

Credits: Arthur Ganson

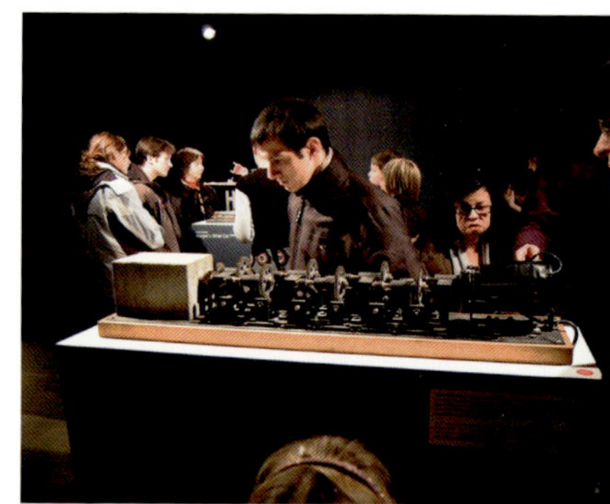

Photo: dleithinger

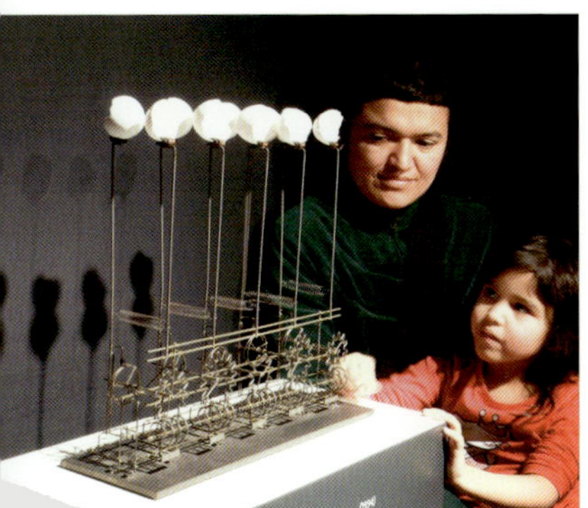

Photo: rubra

Machine with Eggshells, 1994

It is possible to make a toy out of anything. This machine was born out of the impulse to play and the accidental discovery of the sonic potential of the eggshell. It is both a farcical meditation on the complexity of complex gear ratios and a machine for sending a strange and unique 'Morse code' message to the far reaches of the universe. The rhythm of clicks is based on the ratios of the numbers of teeth on the five main gears multiplied together. (The number of revolutions each gear must make before the pattern begins to repeat is stamped below each gear.)

Credits: Arthur Ganson; Courtesy Private Collection

Margot's Other Cat, 1999

The idea that led to *Margot's Other Cat* came to Ganson while he was dealing with a computer program that simulates movements of an object on the Moon. He got the urge to develop a mechanical sculpture that displays motion with the very same elegance. In *Margot's Other Cat*, Ganson seemingly deactivates the laws of nature—here, the gravitational field. While the cat moves uniformly from left to right, the chair completes bizarre movements above it.

Credits: Arthur Ganson

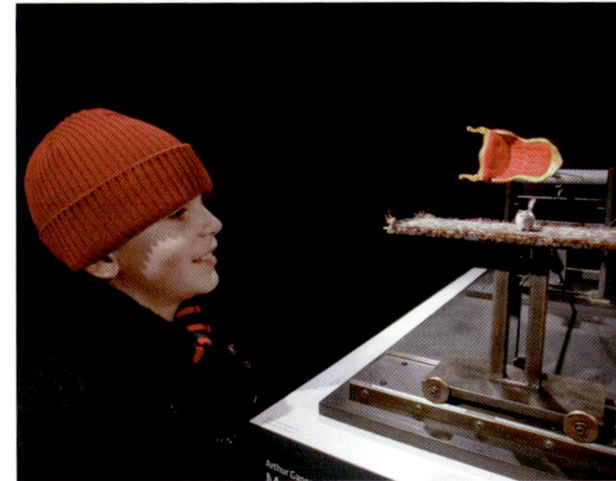

Photo: rubra

Thinking Chair, 2007

Where does inanimate material end and where does life begin? Arthur Ganson lets his *Thinking Chair* straddle the boundary between those two states. Through its movements—which resemble the gait of a human being walking on two legs—the chair exhibits animate traits. Arthur Ganson had the idea that led to this work while taking a walk. Near his studio, there is a small rock outcropping on a trail, which he likes to walk around in slow circles, deep in thought. During this walking meditation, each cycle finds him back in the same physical place but in a slightly different emotional place.

Credits: Arthur Ganson

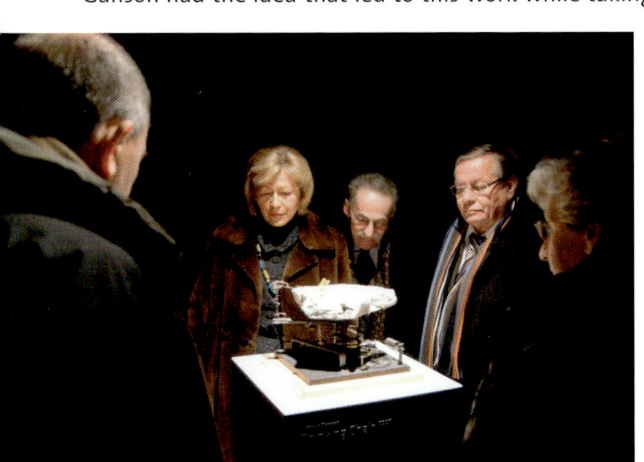

Photo: Andreas Hirsch

Artists Creators Engineers

Three terms that describe an image of the artist, an image that is closely connected to the history of media art and that has occupied the focal point of Ars Electronica's activities for 30 years. Artists, Creators, Engineers: creative artists at the interface of technology and society, who combine an artistic vision with a high level of technical know-how, and provide a key impetus to shaping our modern media-based society.
In this segment of its exhibitions, the new AEC presents people and projects which are best described by their high degree of artistic as well as technical innovation.

Concept: Gerfried Stocker, Christopher Lindinger
Coordination: Jochen Zeirzer, Sofya Yuditskaya

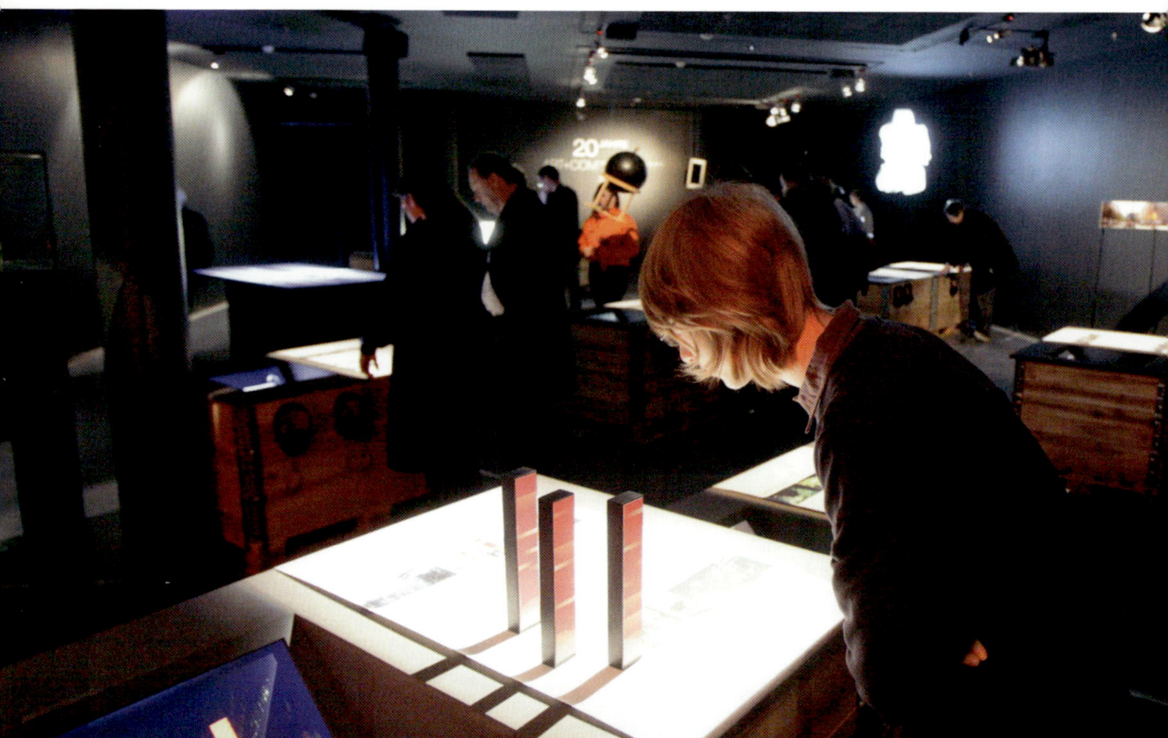

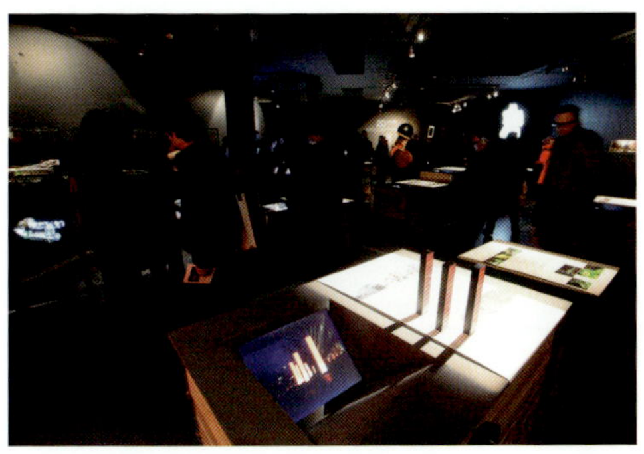

ART+COM – 20 Years of Media Art and Media Design

The personal computer started to become really widespread in the mid-1980s. Back then, it was used almost exclusively as a tool for processing texts and spreadsheets, working with graphics, and doing modeling and animation.

An interdisciplinary group of designers and artists associated with the UdK–Berlin University of the Arts and hackers from the ChaosComputerClub were aware even then of the computer's potential as a mass medium. After some fledgling joint projects, the Berlin group formally established ART+COM in 1988. The aim was to carry out practical R&D on the medium's applicability in the fields of design, art, science and technology.

Over the past 20 years, ART+COM has been at work on the leading edge of this medium's development, conceiving and bringing to fruition forms of communication, design principles and technologies that we now take completely for granted. As far as content is concerned, the spectrum ranges from works of art and design projects all the way to technological developments and inventions. With respect to form, the emphasis has been on four formats: screen-based applications, interactive objects & installations, medial spaces, and medial architecture.

ART+COM is closely associated with the 30-year history of Ars Electronica—including numerous prizes and awards from the Prix Ars Electronica as well as collaboration on the conception of the first Ars Electronica Center. This documentary exhibition running from January 2 to August 23 also provides insights into the further development of the creative deployment media technologies. The following projects are documented by Art+Com:

Zerseher (1992/2008), Terravision (1996/2008), The Invisible Shapes of Things Past (1995–2007/2008), Sensitive Floors (1999–heute), Virtuelles Fahrzeug (1997/2008), timescope (2005/2008), Gardens (2004/2008), Duality (2007/2008), Kinetische Skulptur (2008), Composing the Lines (2002/2008), Mediales Bühnenbild (2002/2008), Sensitive Skins (2004/2008), Das neue Österreich (2005/2008), Reactive Sparks (2008), Sphären (2008).

Concept and Realisation: Art+Com, *Exhibition Design:* Art+Com

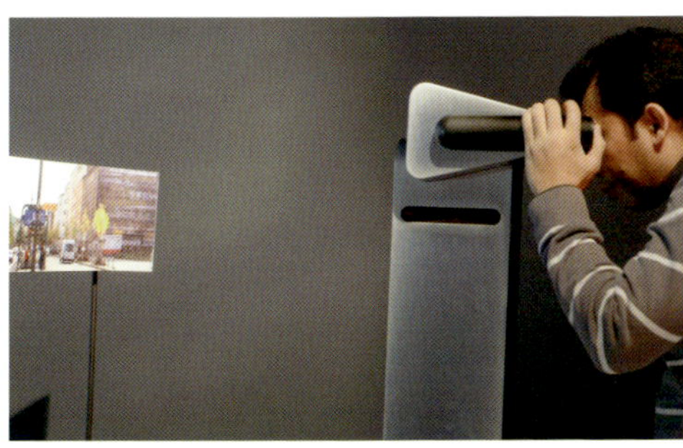

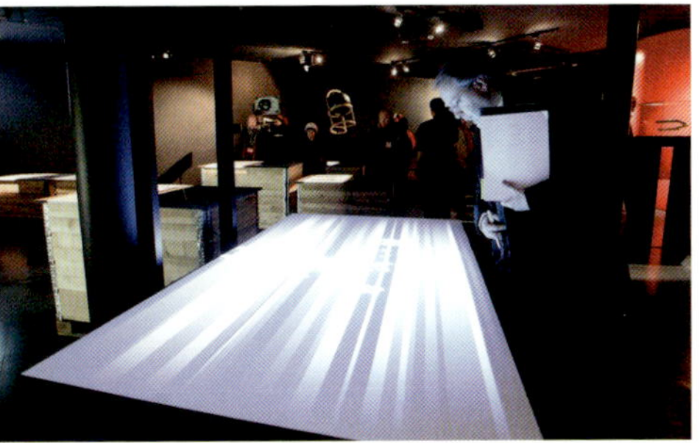

bit.flow
Julius Popp

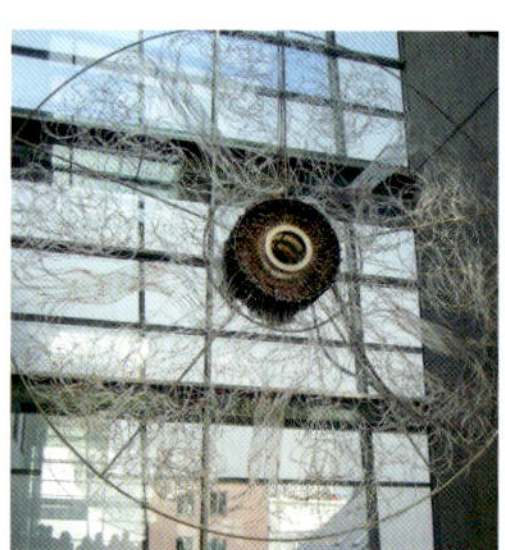

bit.flow deals with the ancient myth of Ariadne's thread: after achieving victory over the Minotaur in the impenetrable labyrinth, Theseus finds his way back out of the maze with the help of Ariadne's thread. *bit.flow* reflects Michel Foucault's interpretation of this myth: What if the famed and rather fragile filament had torn? In *bit.flow* dozens of tiny pieces of the "red thread" coalesce to form a chaotic swarm of particles or bits of information; if you take a closer look, they unexpectedly arrange themselves at a particular point to reestablish the order like Ariadne's thread. Only there do they open up the path to perceptibility.

bit.flow Julius Popp

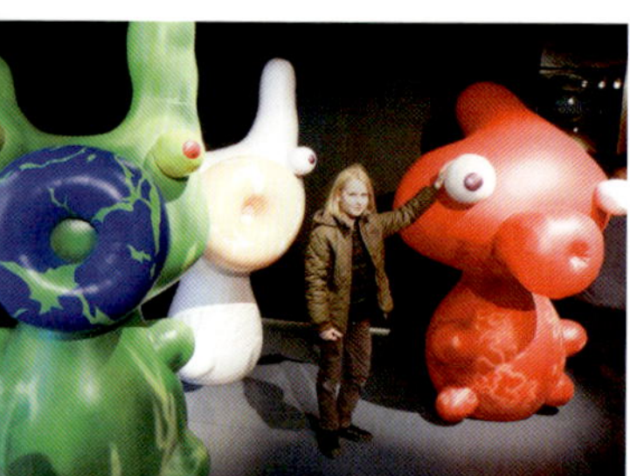

Gemotion Display, Infinite 4D-Fish
Yoichiro Kawaguchi

Yoichiro Kawaguchi is working with the reciprocal interaction of art and science. What he finds particularly interesting is establishing connections between computer graphics and forms that develop in nature, the way shapes, colours and surfaces freely unfold and independently evolve. Already in the 1980s he got a lot of attention for his work at Ars Electronica. A new outcome of these encounters is the *Gemotion Display* that, like an organic being, adapts its form and texture to its respective surroundings. Hundreds of pneumatic actuators deform the projection surface, corresponding to the images being shown. The result is a representation of the world that accommodates our natural perceptive faculties, which take into account factors like perspective, shadowing and surface texture. Conceivable applications are diverse indeed—from cinema to architecture.

Gemotion Display: Yoichiro Kawaguchi, Supported by Kawaguchi Lab. The University of Tokyo

Eggy Boy
Yoichiro Kawaguchi

In Yoichiro Kawaguchi's opinion, conventional robots exhibit two major shortcomings: design artistry and an emotional level in the human-robot interaction. In developing his robots, Kawaguchi combines findings and insights from psychology and neuroscience with technology and art. This approach also manifests itself in his robot designs: cartoon-like shapes, short arms and legs, big eyes and a soft outer surface make a robot come across as harmless and vulnerable. This child-friendly, "emotional" "Eggy robot" is meant to someday be able to socialize with his surroundings and to begin to tremble as soon as someone approaches.

Eggy Boy: Yoichiro Kawaguchi, Supported by Kawaguchi Lab. The University of Tokyo

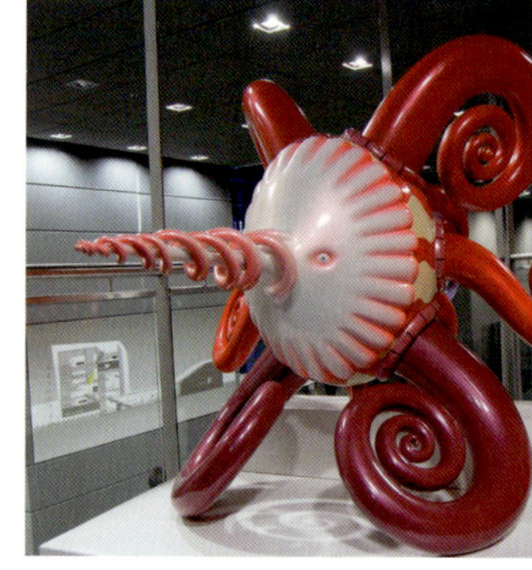

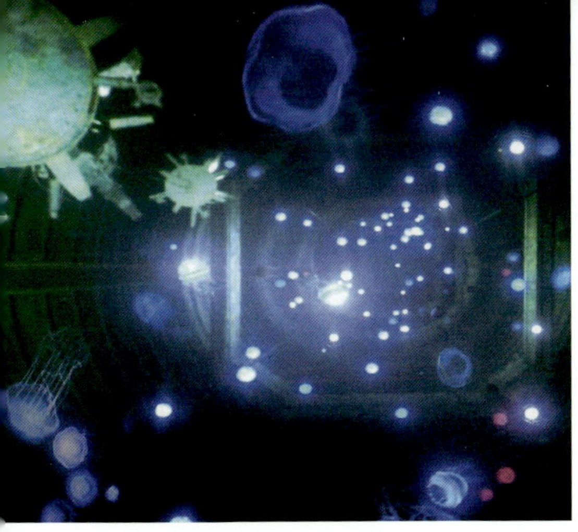

Calamaris – Elevator Installation
Markus Huber

The floor of the visitors' elevator is also a projection screen that displays animated sequences synchronized to the elevator car's movements. Conceived by Roy Ascott for the premiere of the first AEC, this elevator installation has featured new content every year since. In *Calamaris*, a sci-fi short by Markus Huber, the elevator passes through a biotech breeding tank in which fighting jellyfish are being raised.

Calamaris: Markus Huber, FH-Salzburg

Blue
h.o

Blue delivers real-time visualizations of the Danube's flow speed, wave formation and water level. All sorts of bubbles flow in the virtual Danube, and they're constantly combing the internet for info about the river and its environs. When visitors make contact with them, they transfer what they know. *Blue* isn't just a newsroom; it's also a clock that reflects the daily passage of time and the course of the seasons in that the installation changes in accordance with the time of day and the current weather. It reacts to day and night, to rain and snow. *Blue* is set up on the new Main Gallery's exterior wall facing the Danube, and opens up a virtual window on the world in the underground exhibition space.

Blue: h.o (Hide Ogawa, Emiko Ogawa, Satoshi Onodera, Taizo Zushi), Ars Electronica Futurelab (Woeishi Lean, Sebastian Neitsch), Amt der OÖ Landesregierung Hydrographischer Dienst

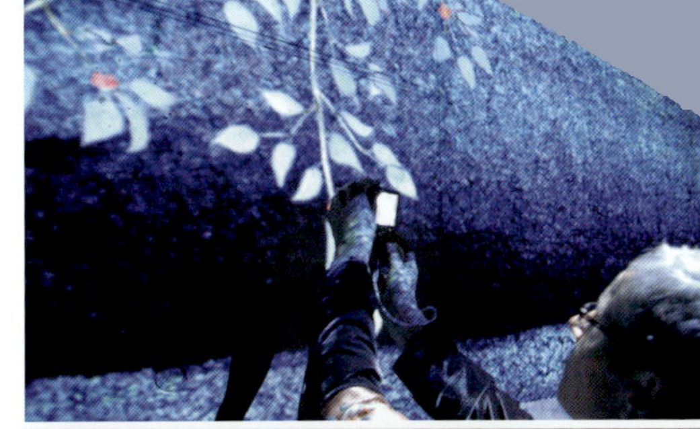

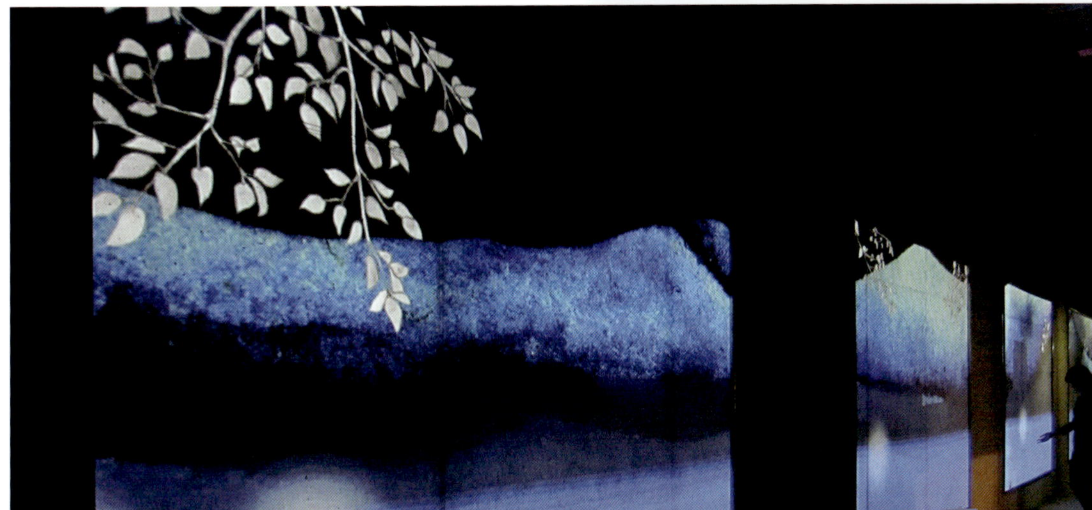

Noriyuki Tanaka

100 Erikas

An Interview with Noriyuki Tanaka

What's the idea behind *100 Erikas*?

How do people form a conscious awareness of other people? What prompts them to decide whether they like or dislike a person? This work takes as its motif what is perhaps the most important determinant of these perceptions, feelings and emotions: the face (or portrait). At the same time the work addresses themes such as the connection between personality and appearance, the problem of memory and identity arising from self-transformation and the desire for bodily manipulation, the collective psychology that leads to the creation of celebrity, the self and the other—or the differentiation and assimilation of history and culture, the issue of ethnicity and community, perceptions of humans resulting from religion or views encompassing their relationships with nature, the relationship between the mythical (as in fantasy stories) and the real, the tension between the recognition of manners and social systems and the expression of the individual, the categories of age and gender and the imagination and so on... Keeping these concerns in mind, I established and gave expression to 100 different characterizations of Erika, as though filling in each of the grid squares in a multi-dimensional matrix.

For example, we have reached a point where a person is able to have two separate identities—one in the real world and the other in virtual space. Maybe by changing your external façade, your way of speaking and gestures, your brain and mind might just adjust to those things, leading to the "overwriting" of your very identity. In *100 Erikas* I have created 100 such potential identities.

How did the work develop?

This work was first exhibited at *Space for Your Future: Recombining the DNA of Art and Design*[1] at the Museum of Contemporary Art, Tokyo. In order to give proper expression to the exhibition

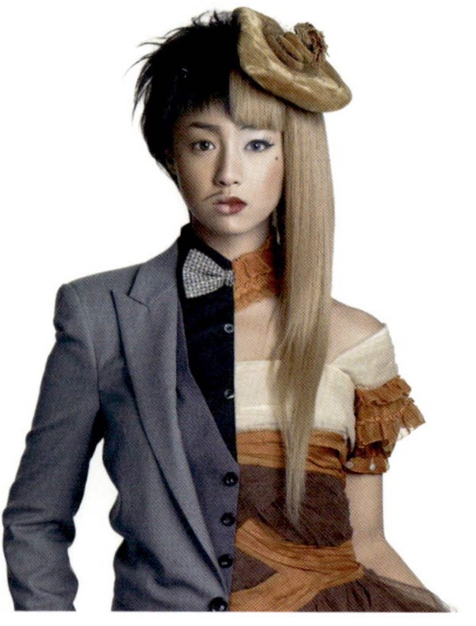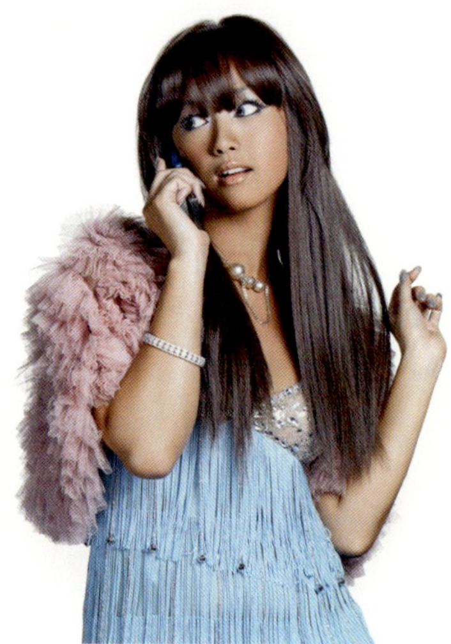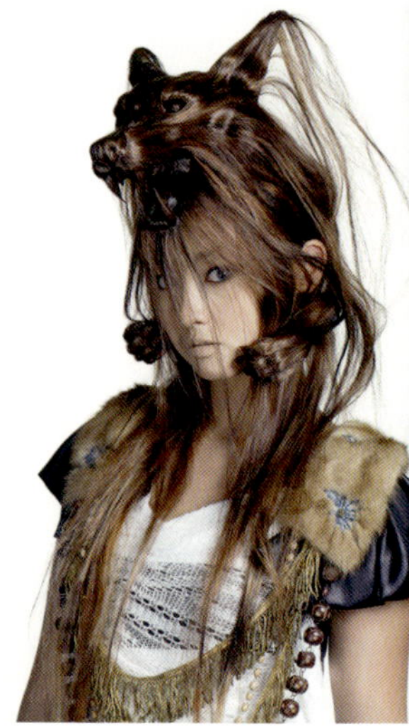

theme, which was the recombination of fine (pure) art and design (applied art) at the "genetic level," I decided a work that genuinely crossed the territories of art and design was necessary. Because it was based on an advertisement for Sony Ericsson mobile phones, *100 Erikas* had a strong commitment, through various media, to society at large and it was also a work that was developing in real time. The model used was Erika Sawajiri, who at the time was an eponymous presence in Japanese media and had a very well recognized identity.[2] I thought that by placing this kind of work into the context of an art exhibition I could visually present the idea of recombining the DNA of art and design. With its links to media and its dynamism, the work would exist beyond the confines of the art museum. And at the same time it would be based around the same question that is at the center of all my creative endeavors: What does it mean to be human? The work represents a wonderful integration of time, space and timeliness. The only thing I miscalculated was quite how difficult it would be to realize the job—the actual labor and the negotiations. (Laughs) You know, every single one of those 100 portraits is a real photograph—made with the model and makeup artists and all. They're not just manipulations on a computer screen.

Nevertheless, by being exhibited in the Ars Electronica Center, the work is removed entirely from the context and circumstances of Tokyo in 2007. I am very interested to see how it will be interpreted there.

Notes

1   *Space for Your Future: Recombining the DNA of Art and Design*: October 27, 2007 till January 29, 2008 / Museum of Contemporary Art, Tokyo / an exhibition of works by artists whose activities span multiple disciplines. By focusing on works made at (or without regard to) the borders between genres, the exhibition sought to propose a new type of creative activity. Participants included Ernesto Neto, Olafur Eliason, Carsten Nicolai and SANAA.

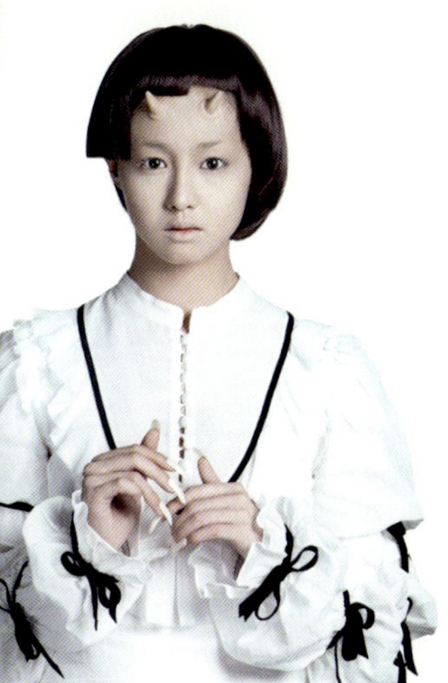

2   Erika Sawajiri: actress. Recipient of many awards, including the Newcomer of the Year Award at the 29th Japanese Academy Awards for her performance in Kazuyuki Izutsu's *Pacchigi!* (2005). Since then her acting ability and media presence have made her a well-established star. In 2007, when *100 Erikas* was made, every aspect of the 20-year-old's life was closely followed by the Japanese mass media. Known simply as Erika-sama (a style of address usually reserved for members of the royal family), Sawajiri was truly an icon of the time. It is easy to imagine that many people who wouldn't normally visit a museum were attracted to *Space for Your Future* just to see the 100 portraits of Erika Sawajiri.

Constructer Photo Collaborator: Erika Sawajiri
Production support: TAKAKI_KUMADA, Indigolight, Tetsuro Nagase, Yasuhiro Watanabe, Shinichi Miter, Toshio Takeda, ShinYa, ABE, Shinji Konishi, COCO, MICHIRU, ASAKO, Yuichi Matsui, Jin Ebashi, Satoshi Wada, Shu Nagasawa, Oichan, MONDO, Rachel D'Amour, ENVY, Sony Ericsson Mobile Communications Japan, Inc., Aoi Advertising Promotion Inc.

Noriyuki Tanaka

100 Erikas

Ein Interview mit Noriyuki Tanaka

Welche Motivation steckt hinter *100 Erikas*?

Wie nimmt man andere Menschen bewusst wahr? Weshalb mag man den einen und den anderen nicht? Ich habe die wohl wichtigste Determinante all dieser Wahrnehmungen, Gefühle und Emotionen als Motiv für dieses Werk gewählt: das Gesicht (bzw. Porträt). Die Arbeit befasst sich aber ebenso mit Themen wie der Verbindung zwischen Persönlichkeit und Erscheinung; dem Problem von Erinnerung und Identität, das durch Selbsttransformation und den Wunsch nach körperlicher Manipulation entsteht; der kollektiven Psychologie, die zur Entstehung von Stars führt; dem Selbst und dem Anderen – oder der Differenzierung und Assimilation von Geschichte und Kultur; der Auseinandersetzung mit Ethnizität und Gemeinschaft; der Wahrnehmung von Menschen aufgrund ihrer Religion oder ihrem Verhältnis zur Natur; der Beziehung zwischen dem Mythischen (wie in fantastischen Geschichten) und dem Realen; der Spannung zwischen dem Anerkennen von Verhaltensregeln und sozialen Systemen und der eigenen Individualität; den Kategorien von Alter und Geschlecht, von Vorstellungskraft und so weiter... Unter Berücksichtigung all dieser Dinge fertigte ich 100 verschiedene Charakterstudien von Erika an, so als ob ich den Raster einer multidimensionalen Matrix ausfüllen wollte.

Heute kann z. B. jemand zwei voneinander unabhängige Identitäten haben – eine im realen Leben und eine andere im virtuellen Raum. Vielleicht lassen sich ja durch das Ändern der äußeren Fassade – wie man spricht und sich gibt – Hirn und Verstand daran anpassen und so die eigenen Identität „überschreiben". Mit *100 Erikas* schuf ich 100 potentielle Identitäten.

Welche Entwicklungsschritte machte das Werk durch?

Die Arbeit wurde erstmals im Rahmen der Ausstellung *Space for Your Future: Recombining the DNA of Art and Design*[1] im Museum für Zeitgenössische Kunst in Tokyo (MOT) gezeigt. Um das Ausstellungsthema – die Rekombination von schöner (reiner) Kunst und Design (angewandter Kunst) auf „genetischer Ebene" – entsprechend umzusetzen, entschied ich mich für eine Arbeit, die die Grenzen zwischen Kunst und Design unbedingt überschreiten musste. Da *100 Erikas* ein Werbesujet für Mobiltelefone der Firma Sony Ericsson aufgreift, war die Arbeitmedial stark im Bewusstsein der Gesellschaft verankert und entwickelte sich somit in Echtzeit. Als Modell wurde die namensähnliche Erika Sawajiri eingesetzt, die damals eine starke Präsenz in den japanischen Medien und deshalb einen hohen Wiedererkennungswert hatte[2]. Wenn ich diese Art von Arbeit, so dachte ich, im Kontext einer Kunstausstellung positioniere, könnte ich das Konzept der Rekombination der DNA von Kunst und Design visuell darstellen. Dank der Verbindungen zu den Medien und deren Dynamik, wäre das Werk auch außerhalb der Museumsmauern sichtbar. Gleichzeitig kreiste es um dieselbe Frage, die das Zentrum all meiner kreativen Bemühungen ausmacht: Was heißt es, Mensch zu sein? Die Arbeit integriert auf wunderbare Weise Zeit, Raum und Rechtzeitigkeit. Ziemlich verschätzt hatte ich mich nur beim Aufwand für die Umsetzung – wie viel Arbeit und Verhandlungen dafür nötig waren. (Lacht) Sie müssen wissen, jedes einzelne dieser 100 Porträts ist eine echte Fotografie – mit Model, Visagisten und allem, was dazu gehört. Nicht bloß Computermanipulationen.

Für die Ausstellung im Ars Electronica Center gelten der Kontext und die Umstände von 2007 in Tokyo nicht mehr. Ich bin gespannt, wie die Arbeit hier gesehen und interpretiert wird.

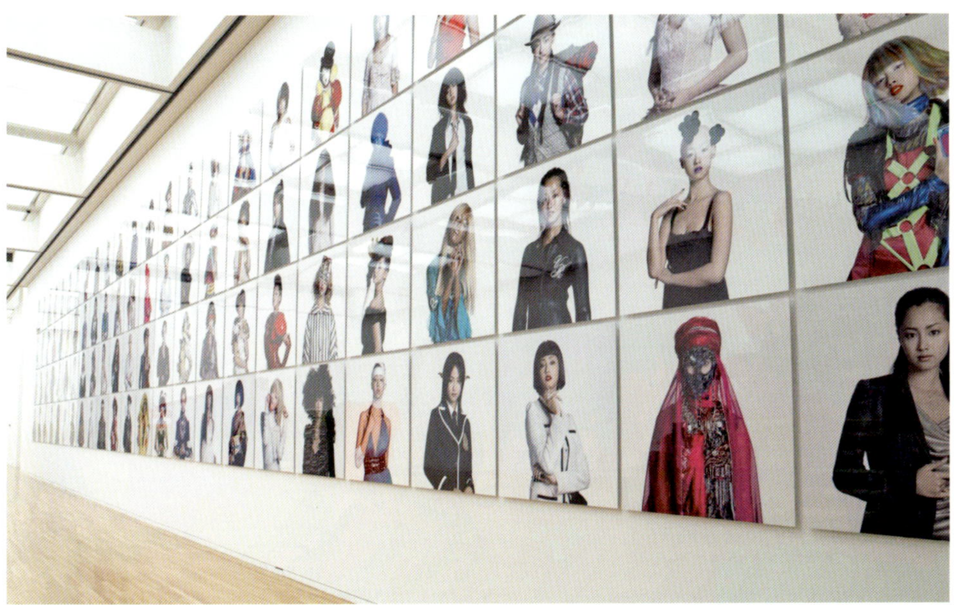

Anmerkungen

1   *Space for Your Future: Recombining the DNA of Art and Design*: 27. Oktober 2007 bis 29 Jänner 2008, Muse
    um für Zeitgenössische Kunst in Tokyo – eine Ausstellung von Werken, deren jeweilige Künstler in mehreren
    Disziplinen tätig sind. Die Ausstellung wollte einen neuen Typ kreativen Schaffens vorstellen, indem sie sich
    auf Werke an den (bzw. unter Nichtbeachtung der) Grenzen zwischen den Genres konzentrierte. Zu den Teil
    nehmern zählten Ernesto Neto, Olafur Eliason, Carsten Nicolai und Sanaa.
2   Erika Sawajiri: Schauspielerin. Vielfach ausgezeichnet, u. a. mit dem *Newcomer of the Year Award* bei den 29.
    Japanese Academy Awards für ihre Leistung in *Pacchigi!* (2005) von Kazuyuki Izutsu. Ihre Schauspielkunst
    und Medienpräsenz haben sie zu einem etablierten Star gemacht. 2007, dem Entstehungsjahr von *100Erikas*,
    wurde jeder Schritt der 20-Jährigen von den japanischen Massenmedien verfolgt. Bekannt als Erika-sama
    (eine der königlichen Familie vorbehaltene Anredeform), war Sawajiri in der Tat eine Ikone dieser Zeit. Daher
    zog es sicherlich viele, die sonst nie ein Museum besuchen, zu *Space for Your Future*, nur um sich die 100
    Porträts von Erika Sawajiri anzusehen.

(Aus dem Englischen von Michael Kaufmann)

The Device Art Project

What is Device Art?
Hiroo Iwata

Device Art is a new form of art that displays the essence of technology through the use of new materials and mechatronic devices. This concept challenges the traditional paradigm of art by its convergence of technology, art and design.
Device Art has three main characteristics:

1. The Device itself is content. The mechanism represents the theme of the piece. Content and tool are no longer separable.

2. Artworks are often playful and can sometimes be commercialized into devices or gadgets for use in everyday life.

3. Refined design and playful features can be traced back to the Japanese tradition of appreciating tools and materials. Traditional Japanese culture, such as the tea ceremony or flower arrangement, uses sophisticated devices. These devices are the roots of device art.

These characteristics are not familiar in Western artwork. For this reason, its novelty draws worldwide attention to Device Art. Significant advances have been observed in the interactive art of Japan over the last few decades. These advances include innovative interface devices used by Device Artists. The concept of Device Art arose when the latest technologies were fused with the traditional Japanese value of art as an inextricable part of life. We hope Device Art provides a model for understanding what it means to live in a world full of new technology.

The *Device Art Project* is funded by Core Research for Evolutional Science and Technology (CREST) of the Japan Science and Technology Agency. Hiroo Iwata is conducting the project, which has the formal title, *Expressive Science and Technology for Device Art*. The name and concept of Device Art came about during the process of its creation in 2004. The goal of this project was to systematize technologies found in Device Art and to establish reasonable methods of evaluating the works. In order to achieve this goal, a new framework named "Gadgetrium", which is composed of a laboratory, exhibition room, and venture business, was constructed. In 2008, we opened the permanent exhibition space, "Device Art Gallery," in the National Museum of Emerging Science and Innovation (Miraikan) in Tokyo. We believe technology will advance and be refined with help from audience feedback and participation.

Collaborators on this project are: Hideyuki Ando, Masahiko Inami, Hiroo Iwata, Machiko Kusahara, Ryota Kuwakubo, Sachiko Kodama, Novmichi Tosa, Kazuhiko Hachiya, Taro Maeda and Hiroaki Yano.

Why Device Art?
Machiko Kusahara

The borders between art and its related fields are no longer clear-cut. Device Art explores new ways of bridging art, design, technology, science and entertainment. Using both the latest and everyday technologies and material, these media artworks enable users/viewers/interactors to enjoy and understand what media technologies mean to us.
In theorizing the nature of Device Art, elements of Japanese culture such as the importance of "tools", the continuity between art, design and entertainment, and the pervasive influence of popular culture become key issues. These elements have been consciously (re)examined and used in Device Art.
Appreciation of playfulness is deeply embedded in Japanese culture accompanied by *mitate*, the tradition of using metaphors, associations, and double meanings in a playful manner. Viewers are invited to read through a multitude of layers of representation to discover the real themes, while the quality of the top layer remains equally important as a self-contained work. Playfulness also contributes by bringing art outside of museums and galleries, enabling the commercial production and distribution of artwork to reach a wider public.
At the same time, Device Art is part of a worldwide phenomenon. It is a logical extension of art movements such as Dadaism, Surrealism, Bauhaus and Fluxus. In these movements, as well as in Device Art, artists from multiple disciplines responded to new media technologies, exploring them and thus expanding the border of art. Today we live in the age of digital (re)production and communication technologies, in which the traditional norms for making, marketing, and appreciating art are challenged. Not only artists, but also designers and architects are highly aware of this trend and are taking action. Device Art responds to such conditions from both a contemporary and a historical perspective, proposing a new approach to media art, and to art itself.

Media Vehicle
Hiroo Iwata

The *Media Vehicle* is a mode of transportation for moving simultaneously around real and virtual worlds. It is composed of a small white dome, in which the rider sits, mounted on a four-legged robot. Inside the dome, the rider views a dome screen displaying video captured by a wide-angle camera situated outside the dome. The four legs "walk" the dome screen through the real world like a motion platform. The legs are fitted with wheels, similar to a car, and can move by up to six degrees of freedom in any direction, stimulating the vestibular sensation of the rider.
The *Media Vehicle* provides the rider with complex and unique experiences through the combination of visual perception and physicality. One example is "Cross-active System". In "Cross-active System," two participants experience unusual communication by dividing the sensory feedback from the motion input of a participant in the *Media Vehicle* and of a participant outside. The camera is equipped with a position sensor. The outside participant holds the camera, which tracks his/her hand motion by way of the position sensor. The image and motion data are transmitted to the vehicle. A slight motion of the camera results in a large motion of the vehicle. This causes the rider to feel as if his/her eyes are separated from their body and put into the hands of the other person. The rider experiences being moved around like a puppet by someone else, a truly dissociative ride.
Another example of the combination of image and motion can be shown to the rider while traveling on a road or field. In this case, the camera is mounted under the body of the dome. As the *Media Vehicle* moves forward, the image projected on the dome screen resembles what a small animal might see. The rider feels as if his/her eyes are actually nearer to the ground. He/she experiences what it is like to be a small animal.
The *Media Vehicle* is inspired by the Japanese comic "Ghost in the Shell". The vehicle in the

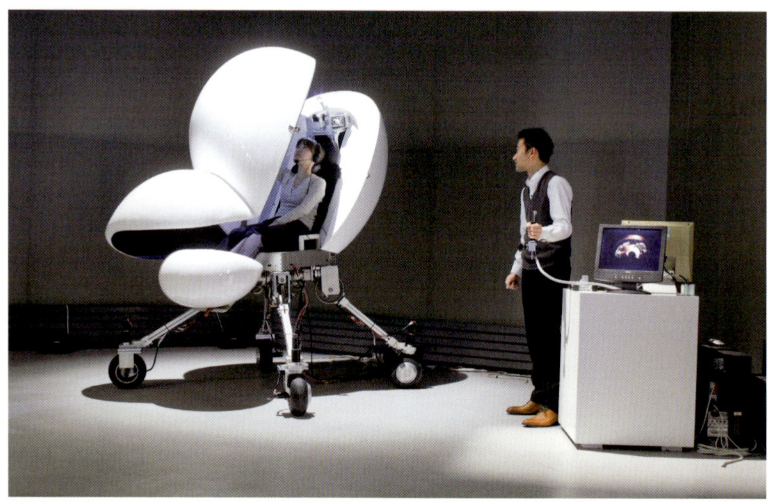

comic named "Fuchikoma" performs both as a terminal for cyber space and as a car for the real world. Imaginary machines that realize virtual experiences have been conceived in virtual worlds, while in the real world the evolution of current cars continues to progress towards realizing "informatic" machines, such as employing cameras and sensors for safe driving in real life. Vehicles in the real world and in the virtual world move further toward coalescence. The *Media Vehicle* symbolizes such a trend.

Knock! Music Program
Novmichi Tosa

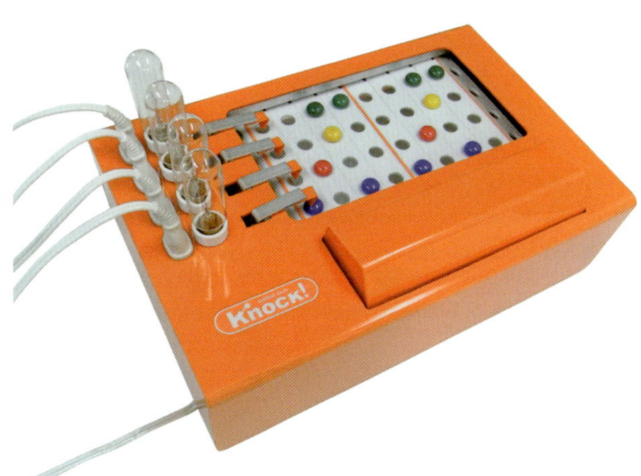

The *Knock! Music Program* offers a new way to play music with unique musical instruments (devices). In steps, the program educates players about technological evolution and digital technology. Each stage of development corresponds to a specific historical advance in technology, so that users naturally retrace technological progress over the course of the program.

Step 1. Knock with Ton Ton Kun!
Attach the "Knocker" to anything that makes an interesting noise. Make a knock with the large "Ton Ton Kun" button.

Step 2. Knock with the "Fun Button"!
Make the button with a simple design. Knock by connecting it to "MIDI-TAP"!

Step 3. Knock with Ele-Beat!
Use the magnetic type sequencer "Ele-Beat," and practice how to type in to *Knock*!

Step 4. Knock with the Computer!
After you experience how to "type in" with the computer, just feel the rhythm of that *Knock* and dance!

Nicodama
Ryota Kuwakuba

Affix the *Nicodama*, and a face appears.

In my early childhood, my mother once decorated the top of my packed lunch so that it resembled a face, but sadly, I was unable to eat it. The face is a shape that people have a special perception of. Even man-made objects can resemble faces. As a natural human response, once something starts to look like a face, one develops inherent feelings towards it. If the objects around us that we don't usually pay much attention to suddenly started to grow faces, what would they try to tell us?

A *Nicodama* is an "eyeball" equipped with an infrared transceiver and magnetic mechanism. When you attach two *Nicodamas* to an object, suddenly you've created a face! Immediately, the eyes communicate and begin blinking together at random intervals. No external conditions influence the behavior of the blinking so that you can see clearly how this singular aspect of a face (eyes) differs according to the object you've put it on.

The project allows us to empathize with mundane objects and to confront our own circumstances in a way that was previously impossible. Ideally, it should be applied within your own world—your neighborhood, your room or your belongings—to ensure a more personal experience. The idea is derived from the traditional Japanese thought that all things have spirit and should thus be respected, regardless of whether they are animate or inanimate. Today, we share a more objective and scientific relationship to objects. While this system is certainly important, our capacity for empathy is equally so. These ideas are not mutually exclusive and can work together in harmony.

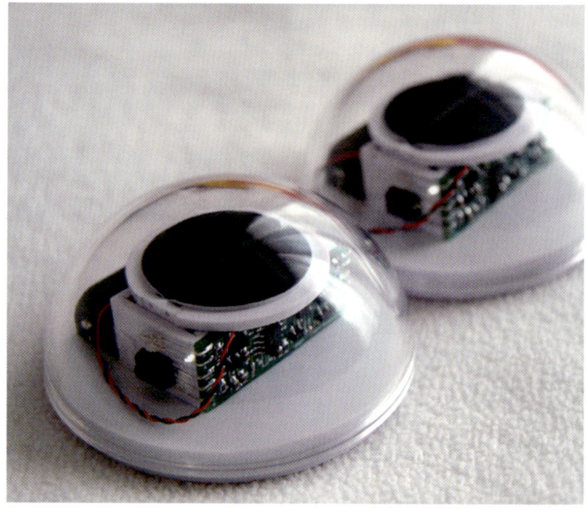

"Morpho Tower" series—toward a responsive and dynamic form of morphing art
Sachiko Kodama

My first project, *Protrude, Flow*, in which ferrofluid was used, was presented in the Ars Electronica Center from 2003 to 2006. The electromagnets used in this work occasionally prevented visitors from viewing the moving liquid.

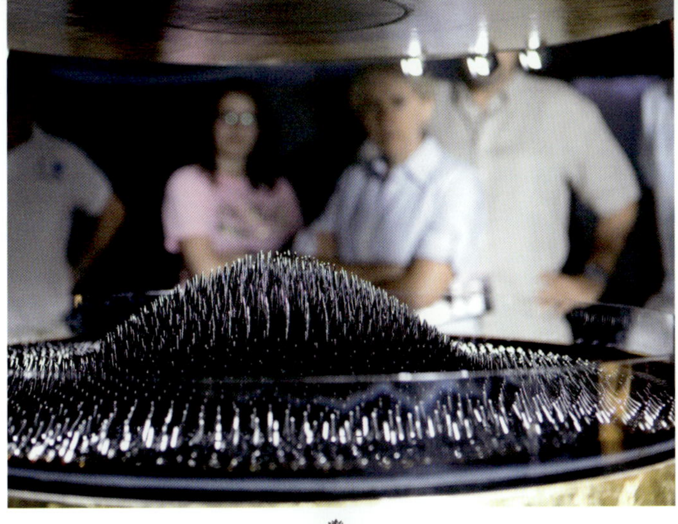

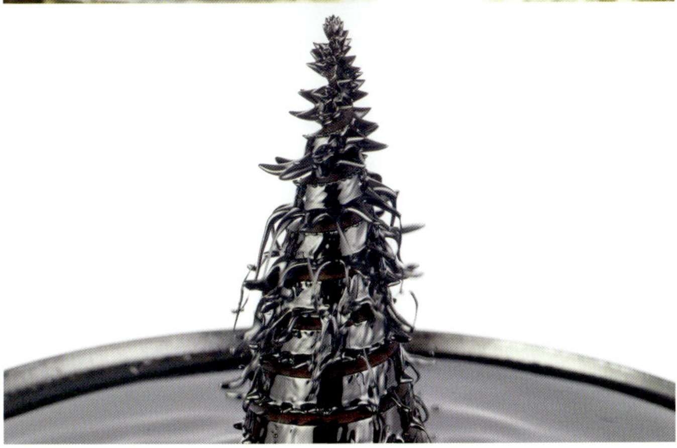

Protrude, Flow 2008, photo: Mario Martin //
Morpho Tower in detail

To solve this problem, I created a larger version of *Protrude, Flow* for the *Museo Nacional Centro de Arte Reina Sofía* in Madrid. While trying to devise a larger and sturdier installation that could be exhibited as public art, I also investigated how to create a smaller morphological art device. Consequently, I discovered a technique called "ferrofluid sculpture." This technique enables artists to create more dynamic sculptures using fluid materials. It involves using an electromagnet with an extended iron core that is sculpted into a particular shape. The ferrofluid covers the sculpted surface of the three-dimensional iron shape. The movement of the spikes in the fluid on the surface is dynamically controlled by adjusting the power of the electromagnet. This can be easily integrated with communication from a computer or inputs from sensors.

In *Morpho Tower/Spiral Swirl*, the helical shape of the iron body located in round-shaped black granite is designed to allow the fluid to move to the top of the helical tower when the magnetic field is sufficiently strong. I find that the spiral is an essential feature in order to cause the liquid to move upward on the sculpture's surface, against the force of gravity. In my opinion, the spiral is an important principle in art. We can observe the rhythm of the spiral in Botticelli's *La Primavera*, Gogh's *Cyprés*, Robert Smithson's land art and Richard Serra's sculpture. All of these works have influenced me as a person. Therefore, I was keenly interested in identifying and incorporating small spirals in my project, and this led to the creation of the new *Morpho Tower* project. The ferrofluid movement in the *Morpho Tower* can be also synchronized with a pleasant natural sound.

In *Morpho Tower/Two Standing Spirals*, an installation I recently completed for the National Science and Technology Museum in Taiwan, one can see two morphing spiral towers standing on a gold plate in a black sea. The motifs for this work are oceans, tornadoes and lightning.

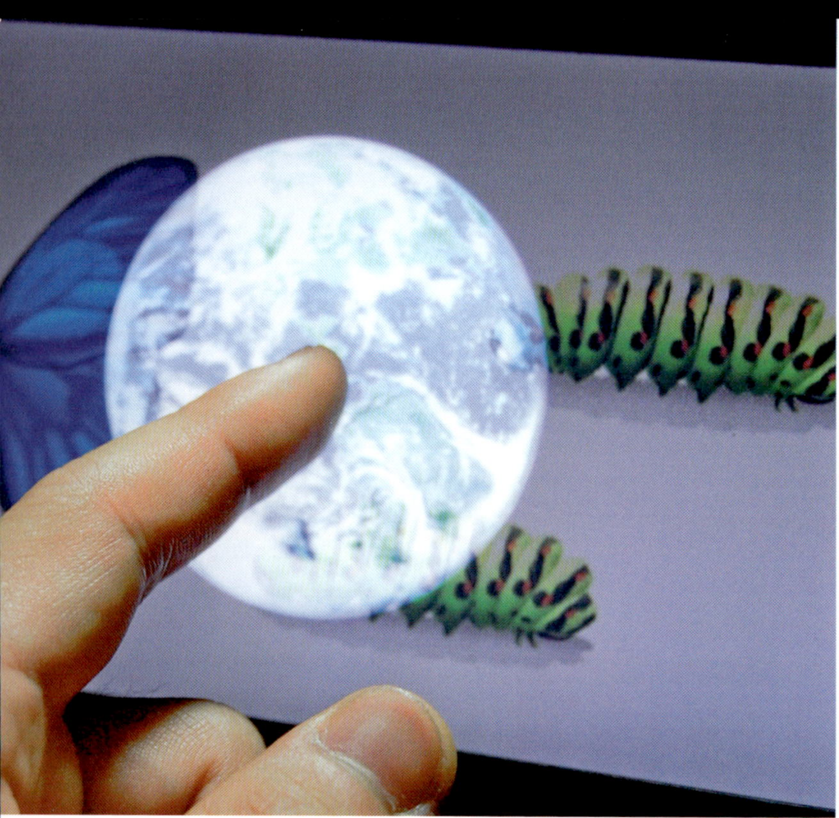

Touch the small world
Hideyuki Ando

Our first access to the world is through touch. We are certain of the existence of objects, i.e. what, when, where, and how they are, by touching them. Touch also establishes communication with things. If we touch something, it reacts to us and we feel its response again through physical contact. Our daily life, as humans, is greatly defined by our sense of touch.
When we trace our finger over a surface, the act unconsciously evokes something representative in our mind. Our internal photo frame fills with the lives of organic / inorganic substances. These visible, invisible, touchable or untouchable creatures co-exist in this small world. All of these assert their existence. And, we feel it...
When tracing the finger pad, the vibration given to the finger is perceived not as vibration but as texture. Based on this perceptual illusion, we have developed a novel interface that can superimpose tactile information onto images displayed on a photo frame. The interface is composed of a vibration panel on the photo frame and sensors to measure the finger position.
The panel is supported by four lever piezo transducers. Different textures are generated by driving these transducers.
The vibration on the panel is controlled in response to the finger motion estimated from the sensors. The vibration can be perceived as the stimulus through the finger pad, not as the stimulus from the panel.

Surrounding of Firefly
Masahiko Inami

Most phenomena in the world have their own frequency. However, we cannot perceive their frequencies because of the limits of our perception. But, if you can choose to see only one specific frequency through a filter, you can perceive new information.
Surrounding of Firefly is an application of Stop Motion Goggle (SMG). SMG functions as the filter to expand visual perception by allowing users to perceive visual information selectively through high-speed liquid crystal shutters.
Early applications of SMG have been used to observe moving objects, which cannot be perceived clearly by the naked eye. Usually, in order to take a clear picture of a moving object, you would adjust an exposure time of your camera to a suitable one. SMG works similarly to this. SMG corrects visual information by adjusting its shutter frequencies and duty cycle.
Not only for moving objects, SMG provides remarkable effects when viewing luminous objects such as projector images, displays, luminaries and so on. Many luminous objects have their own rate of flickering, while SMG also has its own shutter frequencies. If you watch a luminous object through the SMG, you will perceive a blink due to interference between these frequencies.
Surrounding of Firefly is based on this phenomenon. It can alter a night view to appear as if fireflies are blinking. SMG could be useful in sending personal messages, including advertising. For instance, it is easy to send secret messages with SMG by simply providing certain phases of frequency. By providing filters for particular frequencies, personalized messages could be sent secretly.
This demonstration shows that SMG provides a novel visual experience, just as a telescope changes our perception of remote objects.

Stop Motion Goggle

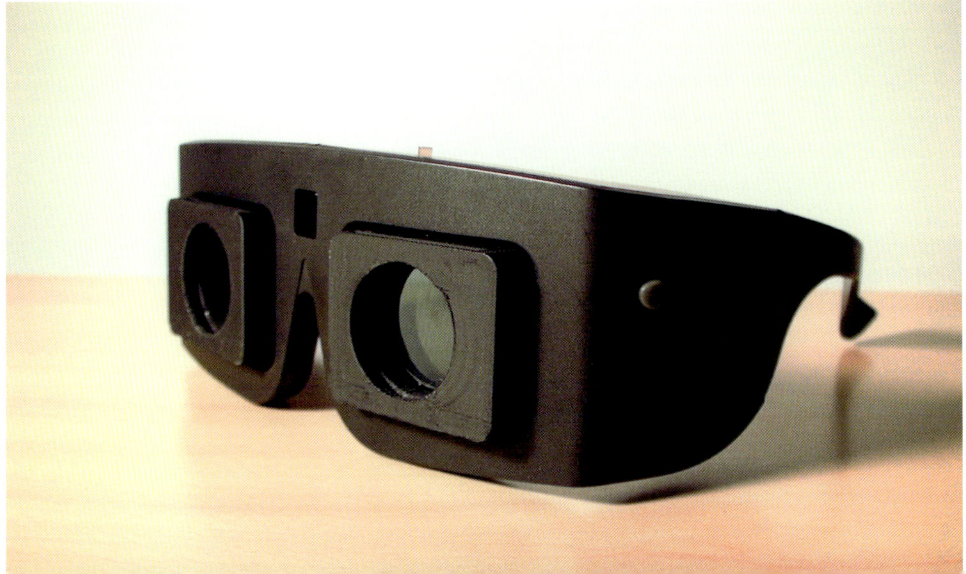

Fairy Finder Series—It Could Be Magic …
Kazuhiko Hachiya

"Any sufficiently advanced technology is indistinguishable from magic,"—so wrote Arthur C. Clarke, the science fiction writer who recently passed away. In other words, genuinely perfected technology is something that ought at first glance to look like magic. If the technology that we currently have at our disposal doesn't yet appear to be magical, that implies that it has yet to reach full maturation. It lacks something—beauty, perhaps, or romance, something that ties people across the world together, or strikes a nerve within them. Here lies the idea of fusing art with science.

Fairy Finder 3
Table of the Colobockle (2006)
This work dates back to three years ago, when I became a father. I felt the urge to make this after noticing how my own child laughed and laughed while playing peek-a-boo, apparently without ever becoming bored.
The work is also influenced by a series of stories written by Satoru Sato. The series depicts Colobockles, clever little creatures who quietly live amongst us. His Colobockle stories are based on legends in the northern part of Japan. While it is fantasy, I can't help but long for it all to be real.

Fairy Finder 4
Mermaid in the Window (2007)
The other day, I took a trip to an island on the ferry. Venturing out onto the deck in the night, and looking at the dark and rain-swept sea that seemed to spread out infinitely, I started to experience a sort of horror. I have a feeling that the nocturnal ocean is the nearest thing to the afterworld. And what is really bizarre is that despite this, it also somehow invokes nostalgia.
Standing in front of a bar table with an antiquated window that looked as though it has been salvaged from a shipwreck, the audience glances over their shoulder, and they find Lorelei, the mythical mermaid, in the mirror behind them. That is the atmosphere you will find in this work.

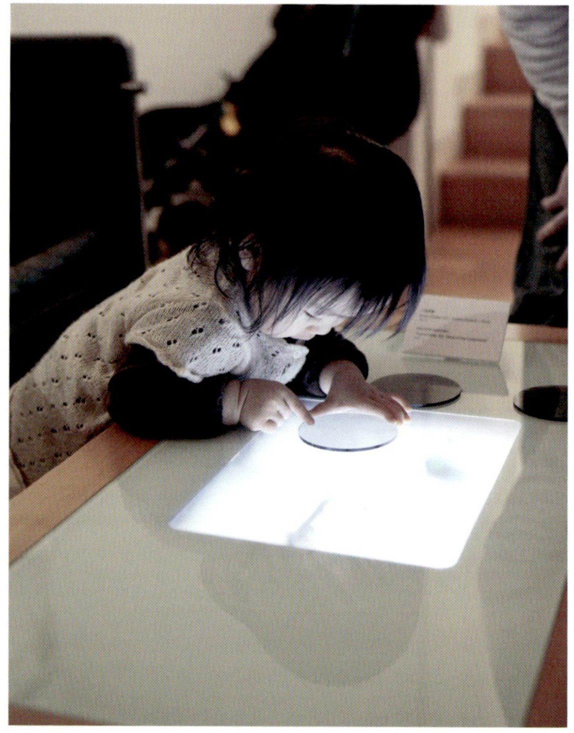

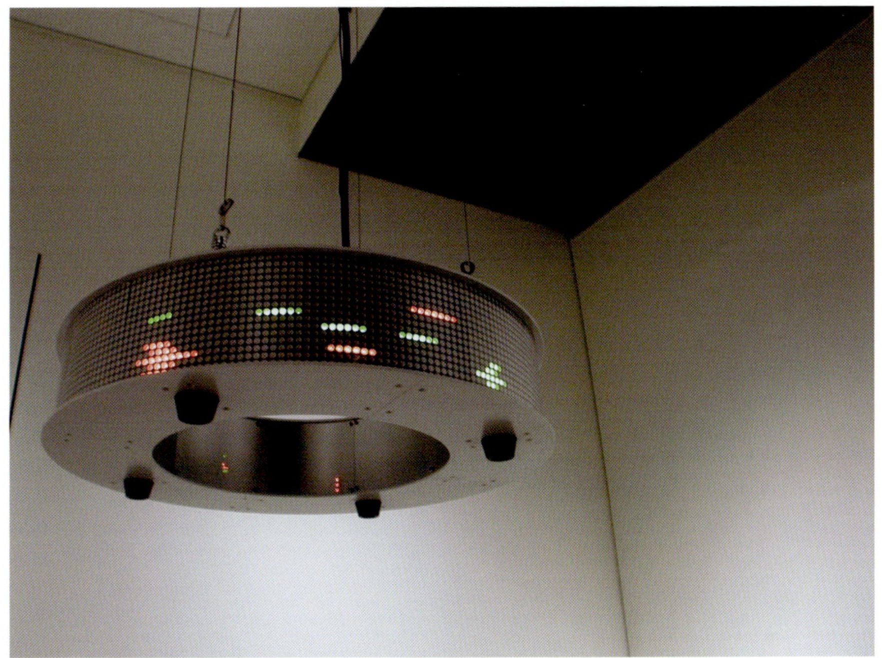

LoopScape
Ryota Kuwakuba

What will happen if the flat display of a video shooting game, which is supposed to have "this side" and "the other side" for the match, is in a cylindrical shape? This artwork appears to be an unusual battle game where two players move around the cylindrical display when they play. With this circular loop display, you must be cautious not to shoot more than necessary, otherwise you will expose yourself to danger. If the bullet you shoot does not hit the opponent, it will go round the circle and attack you from behind. In addition, you must move around the circular display to follow yourself and the opponent while manipulating the controller. The two players can enjoy this game and move their bodies as if they were playing a sport. With a change in thinking that connects "this side" and "the other side," the nature of the battle game is drastically changed from the conventional one.

Deep Space

Deep Space is a large-format projection space for interactive, stereoscopic and high-definition content. The architectural concept and system design of *Deep Space* are meant to go overcome the limitations of previously used VR systems, above all in the context of multi-user interactive storytelling. 16x9-meter wall and floor projections and 4-fold full HD (4K) resolution make *Deep Space* a spacious vehicle in which to travel through space and time. In *Deep Space*, groups of 30-90 persons can experience a broad spectrum of visuals: artistic productions on the basis various different imaging techniques, interactive narratives featuring new approaches to interaction, and art historical, architectural and astronomical visualizations.

Genesis

In its conception and implementation, *Deep Space* has to be seen as the upshot of prior developments at the Ars Electronica Futurelab in the area of projection-based virtual reality infrastructure and human-computer interaction. In this spirit, *Deep Space* serves as both an exhibition space for members of the public touring the Museum of the Future as well as an R&D platform for the Futurelab staff.

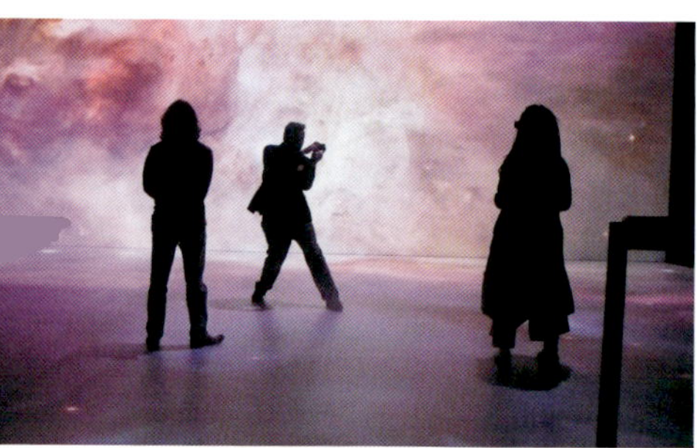

Photo: Régine Debatty

Space

Featuring two 16x9-meter floor and wall projections, *Deep Space* is also suitable for very large groups. It is possible to walk across the floor projection; its size (approximately 145 m²) is intentionally taken advantage of in the screening to foster physical movement. The freedom achieved in this way for individual persons and groups to move about the space has an impact on how the immersion in virtual worlds is experienced, since the virtual elimination of spatial boundaries can also be perceived in a real space thereby.

Five meters above the floor is a wrap-around viewing platform from which observers get a considerably different perspective of the projected content and the audience milling about below. Thus, due to participants' varying positions in space, they can also assume different roles in interactive and collaborative scenarios.

System Design

The technical core of *Deep Space* consists of an ultra-high-definition active stereo-capable projection system and a flexible high-end platform that makes it possible to implement a wide array of applications with minimal effort. In addition to virtual reality and 3D cinema, non-stereoscopic applications that place high demands on the system's computing power can also be utilized.

Projection System

This is a multi-projection system consisting of eight full HD (1080p) and active stereo-capable Barco Galaxy NH12 projectors, each with 12,000 ANSI lumens. Hardware-based edge blending produces two homogeneous picture surfaces with a resolution of 2,160x3,840 pixels (4K) each for the space's wall and floor. A frame rate of 120 Hz for generating stereoscopic images makes possible a flicker-free 3D impression. The projection technology was planned and installed in cooperation with PV Planungs und Veranstaltungstechnik GmbH & Co. KG.

Stereoscopic System

The Ars Electronica Futurelab developed on the basis of a circuit board and high-output infrared emitters a solution to providing active stereo in large-format VR environments like *Deep Space* that is considerably less expensive than systems available on the market and, furthermore, delivers maintenance-free support of several types of glasses while using the same infrastructure.

Computer System

The key determinant that was taken into consideration in designing the computer system was the flexibility to be able to depict different types of content beyond just VR applications. At present, the systems uses 13 Dell Intel Core 2 Quad CPU Q9550 2.83GHz computers distributed among three feeder systems (VR Cluster, Mosaic Cluster, 3D/HD Cineplayer) and several support processors.
In order to have a mobile and multifunctional control unit, an application was developed on the technological basis of the Apple iPod Touch, which supports both application control as well as navigation within the application. The control data generated by the use of the touch-sensitive surface and the acceleration sensor mechanism are transmitted via WLAN to the VR cluster or a central control PC.

Audio System

The 5.1 audio system is complemented in *Deep Space* by HSS (HyperSonic Sound) loudspeakers. The HSS speakers make it possible for music, voices and sounds to be directed with pinpoint accuracy to particular persons or groups within the space.

Software

Deep Space is designed to be open for many different software systems. For VR-applications the preferred system so far is Virtools, for Gigapixel photos and 3D/HD films the Ars Electronica Futurelab developed special software.
DeepImage is an OpenGL based software that allows the user to zoom in and pan to select and enlarge even minute portions of such images. This Gigapixel viewer refreshes portions of the image ad hoc and synchronously across several picture surfaces with a total resolution of 2,160x3,840 pixels.
The 3D/HD Cineplayer allows to play full-HD stereo videos synchronously across several picture surfaces.

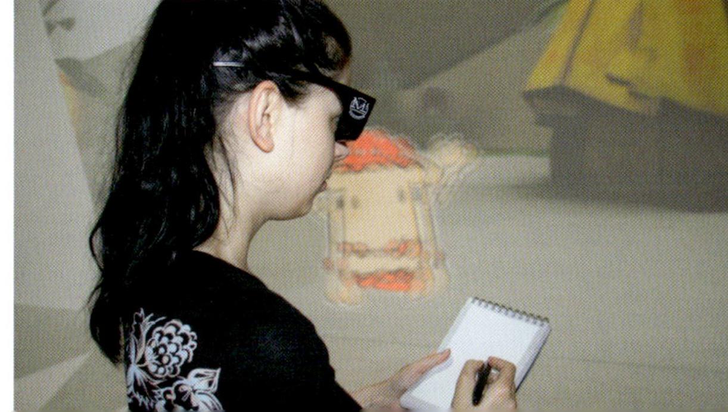

Deep Space

Deep Space ist ein großformatiger Projektionsraum für interaktive, stereoskopische und hochaufgelöste Inhalte. Das architektonische Konzept und das System Design des *Deep Space* sollen den Grenzen bislang verwendeter VR-Systeme vor allem im Kontext von Multi-User Interactive Storytelling begegnen. Wand- und Bodenprojektionen mit einer Größe von je 16 mal 9 Metern und einer Auflösung von jeweils 4-fach FullHD (4K) verwandeln den *Deep Space* in ein geräumiges Vehikel, um durch Raum und Zeit zu reisen. Gruppen von 30 bis 90 Personen können im *Deep Space* eine Bandbreite von Projekten erleben – von künstlerischen Produktionen auf der Basis verschiedener Bildtechniken über interaktive Narrative mit neuen Interaktionsansätzen bis hin zu kunsthistorischen, architektonischen und astronomischen Visualisierungen.

Genesis

In Konzeption und Umsetzung muss *Deep Space* als Konsequenz aus vorausgehenden Entwicklungen des Ars Electronica Futurelab im Bereich projektionsbasierter Virtual-Reality-Infrastrukturen und Human Computer Interaction gesehen werden. So dient *Deep Space* zugleich als öffentliche Ausstellung für geführten Publikumsbetrieb und als Forschungs- und Entwicklungsplattform des Ars Electronica Futurelab.

Space

Mit zwei 16 mal 9 Meter großen Boden- und Wandprojektionen ist *Deep Space* auch für sehr große Gruppen geeignet. Die Bodenprojektion ist begehbar und wird aufgrund ihrer Größe (ca. 145 Quadratmeter) in der Bespielung bewusst zur Förderung physischer Bewegung eingesetzt. Die dadurch erreichte Bewegungsfreiheit von Einzelpersonen und Gruppen wirkt sich auf die erlebte Immersion in virtuelle Welten aus, da die virtuelle Aufhebung räumlicher Grenzen auch im Realraum nachvollzogen werden kann.

In fünf Metern Höhe befindet sich eine umlaufende Aussichts-Plattform, von der aus sich die Perspektive auf die projizierten Inhalte und ein aktives Publikum maßgeblich ändert. So können aufgrund der unterschiedlichen Positionen von Teilnehmern im Raum auch verschiedene Rollen in interaktiven und kollaborativen Szenarien eingenommen werden.

System Design

Den technischen Kern des *Deep Space* bilden das ultrahochauflösende Active-Stereo-fähige Projektionssystem und eine flexible High-End-Plattform, die es erlauben, mit geringem Aufwand verschiedenste Applikationen zu implementieren. Neben Virtual-Reality- und 3D-Cinema kommen auch rechenintensive nicht-stereoskopische Anwendungen zum Einsatz.

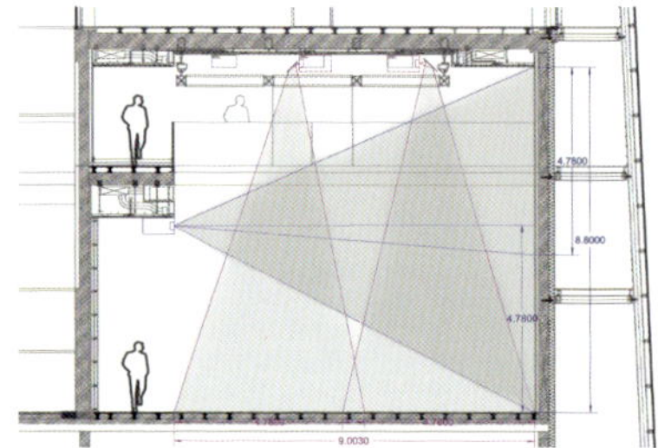

Projektionssystem

Es wird ein Multi-Projektions-System bestehend aus acht FullHD (1080p)- und Active-Stereo-fähigen Barco Galaxy NH12 Projektoren mit je 12.000 ANSI Lumen verwendet. Mittels hardware-basiertem Edge Blending werden für Wand und Boden zwei homogene Bildflächen mit einer Auflösung von je 2160 mal 3840 Pixel (4K) erzeugt. Eine Bildwiederholfrequenz von 120 Hz für stereoskopische Darstellungen erlaubt einen flimmerfreien 3D-Eindruck. Die Projektionstechnik wurde gemeinsam mit der PV Planungs und Veranstaltungstechnik GmbH & Co. KG geplant und realisiert.

Stereoskopisches System

Das Ars Electronica Futurelab entwickelte eine auf einer Steuerplatine und Hochleistungs-Infra-rotstrahlern basierende Lösung für Active Stereo in großformativen VR-Environments wie dem *Deep Space*, die wesentlich preiswerter als am Markt verfügbare Systeme ist und zudem mehrere Brillentypen unter Verwendung derselben Infrastruktur wartungsfrei unterstützt.

Computersystem

Das Computersystem wurde vor allem mit Blick auf die Flexibilität für unterschiedliche darzus-tellende Inhalte, auch über VR-Anwendungen hinaus, gestaltet. Derzeit kommen 13 Computer des Typs Dell Intel Core 2 Quad CPU Q9550 2,83GHz zum Einsatz, die sich auf drei Zuspielsysteme (VR Cluster, Mosaic Cluster, 3D/HD Cineplayer) und mehrere Supportrechner aufteilen.
Für eine mobile und multifunktionale Steuer-Unit wurde eine Applikation auf der technologis-chen Basis des Apple iPod Touch entwickelt, die sowohl die Anwendungssteuerung als auch die Navigation innerhalb von Anwendungen unterstützt. Die Steuerdaten, die unter Nutzung der Touch-sensitiven Oberfläche und der Beschleunigungssensorik erzeugt werden, werden mittels WLAN an den VR-Cluster bzw. einen zentralen Steuer-PC übertragen.

Audiosystem

Ein 5.1-Audiosystem wird im *Deep Space* ergänzt durch HSS (HyperSonic Sound) Lautsprecher. Die HSS-Speaker ermöglichen, Musik, Stimmen und Geräusche nur für bestimmte Personen oder Personengruppen im Raum auftauchen und verschwinden zu lassen.

Software

Deep Space ist offen für verschiedenste Softwaresysteme ausgelegt. Bislang wird für VR-Welten vor allem Virtools verwendet.für Gigapixel Fotos und 3D/HD Filme wurden eigene Softwaresys-teme entwickelt. Als Gigapixel-Viewer wurde die auf OpenGl basierende Software „DeepImage" entwickelt, die es erlaubt, mittels Zoom und Pan selbst winzige Bildausschnitte von Gigapixel Fotos auszusuchen und zu vergrößern. Dabei können Bildbestandteilen ad hoc und synchron über mehrere Bildflächen mit einer Gesamtauflösung von 2160 mal 3840 Pixel aktualisiert werden. Mit dem 3D/HD Cineplayer können Full HD Stereo Videos ebenfalls über mehrere Bild-flächen synchron abgespielt werden.

Papyrate's Island
**Interactive virtual storytelly
by Ars Electronica Futurelab**
Papyrate's Island is an interactive story that is based on the idea of transferring the physical characteristics of paper into the virtual realm. Two-dimensional objects made of paper are depicted in three-dimensional space and brought to life via animation. Situated at the nexus of VR environment and interactive animation film, *Papyrate's Island* takes a bold new approach to interaction dramaturgy. In collaboration with the Media Interaction Lab in Hagenberg,

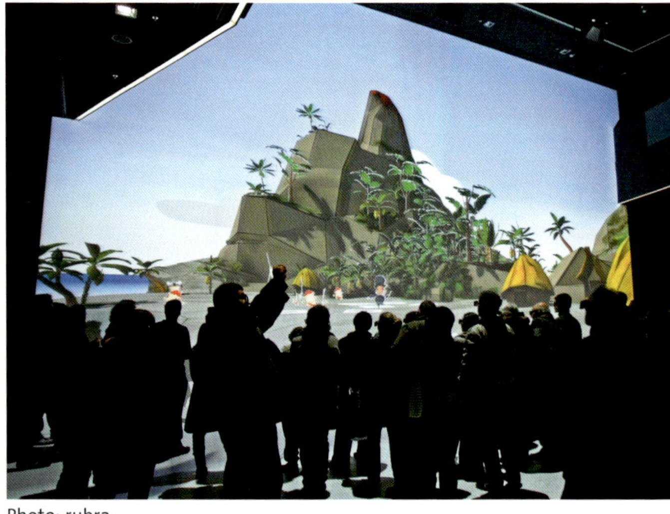
Photo: rubra

Anoto technology was applied for the use of pencil and paper as design tools for interactive virtual storytelling. Thus, multiple users can simultaneously enrich the narrative with additional objects and characters. Real and virtual space are interlinked in a collaboratively produced three-dimensional drawing. The soundtrack was created by Herwig Burghard / Tonburg.

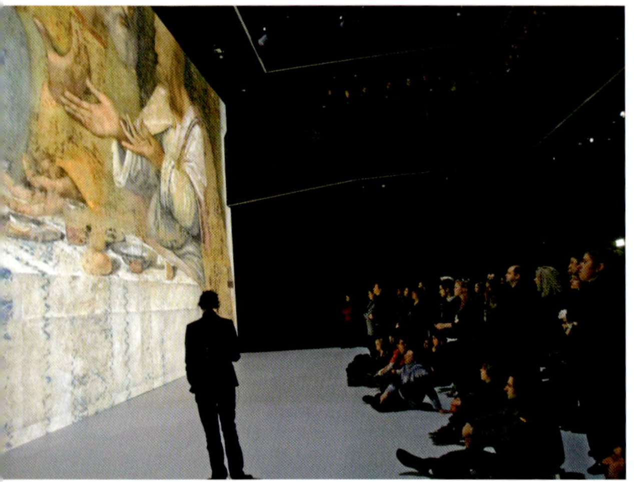
Photo: rubra

The Last Supper
Gigapixel photo by Haltadefinizione
The gigapixel photography of Leonardo da Vinci's *The Last Supper* by the Italian firm Haltadefinizione consists of 172,181 x 93,611 pixels (16 gigapixels) and was produced from 1,677 individual images. Using *DeepImage* the picture was broken down into 18 levels of definition, each with a different number of pixel tiles (the highest definition level consists of 250,182 pixel tiles, each containing 256 x 256 pixels). Then, in *Deep Space* it's possible to focus in on minute details of the original (460 x 880 cm) within a matter of seconds.

Please Stand Back!
by stadtmusik

Please stand back! is a stereographic and interactive version for the "deep space" environment of the short film by stadtmusik with the same name. The work is an exploration of the soundscape of the metro station "Schönhauser Allee" in Berlin.

Contrasting the sounds of human activity from the audio track, the visual layer shows otherworldly, deserted places, where time seems to stand still. Visual elements dissolve and are extracted from the continuum of perception. Given the somnambulistic execution of the pathways of daily routine, most people might be able to relate to this spatial experience.

Attention is constantly refocused, reordering the sensory input. A subway station is a public place with a special space-time structure—a place of waiting, going and coming. Our hearing is different while we are waiting.

Data.Tron [8k enhanced version]
Ryoji Ikeda

This new work of Ryoji Ikeda is an enhanced version of the audiovisual installation *data.tron*, where each single pixel of visual image is strictly calculated by mathematical principle, composed from a combination of pure mathematics and the vast sea of data present in the world. This latest version will flood two giant screens with data, projected on the wall and the ground of Deep Space, thereby heightening and intensifying your perception and total immersion within the work.

Photo: Liz Hingley

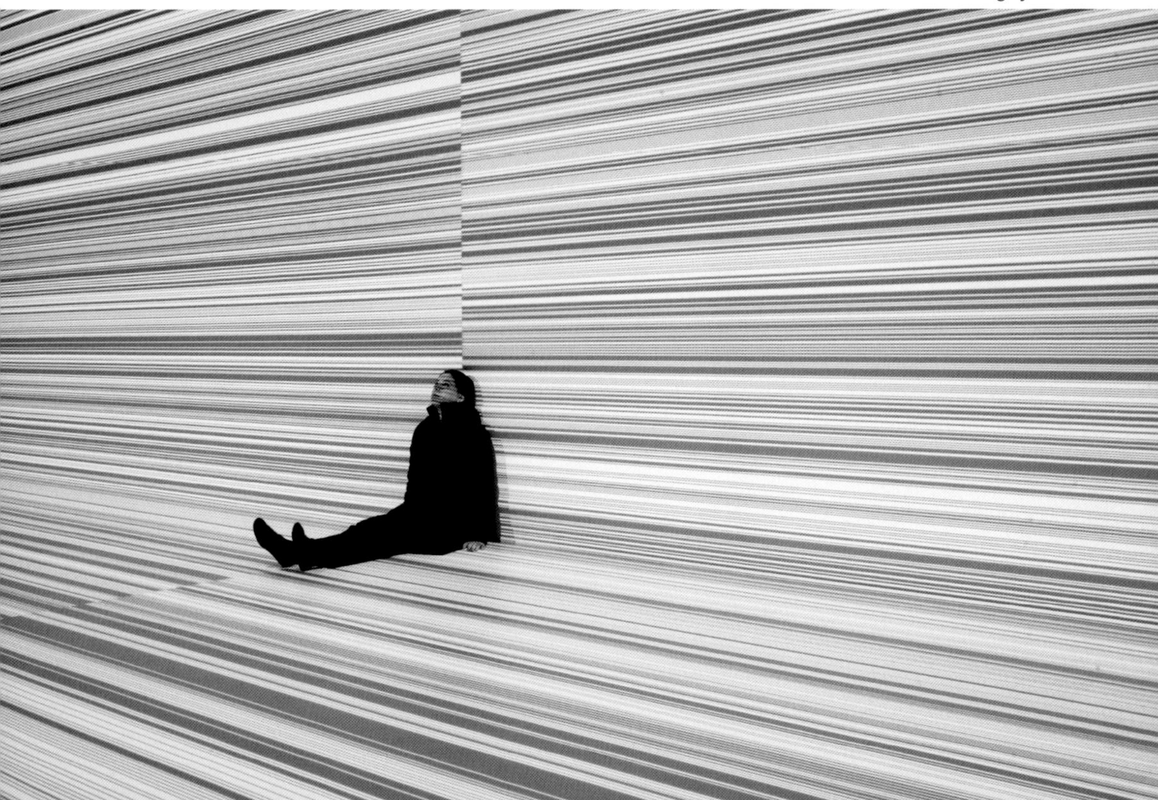

Selections form Ôr'ganic Constructions
Kenneth A. Huff

Inspired by the random, yet structured beauty and minute details of nature (flora, fauna and mineral), his very high resolution images are creating an illusion of reality even while you are gently confronted with the practical knowledge that the objects represented do not exist. At a distance, the familiar, organic forms engage the mind, beginning a journey of examination and interaction. With no reference of scale, you are drawn closer, searching for additional clues which might aid in identification. With each step, the visual structures trigger subliminal reactions based on past experiences. In the end, you are left with indefinable organic connections, suspended in the purposeful ambiguity of the work.

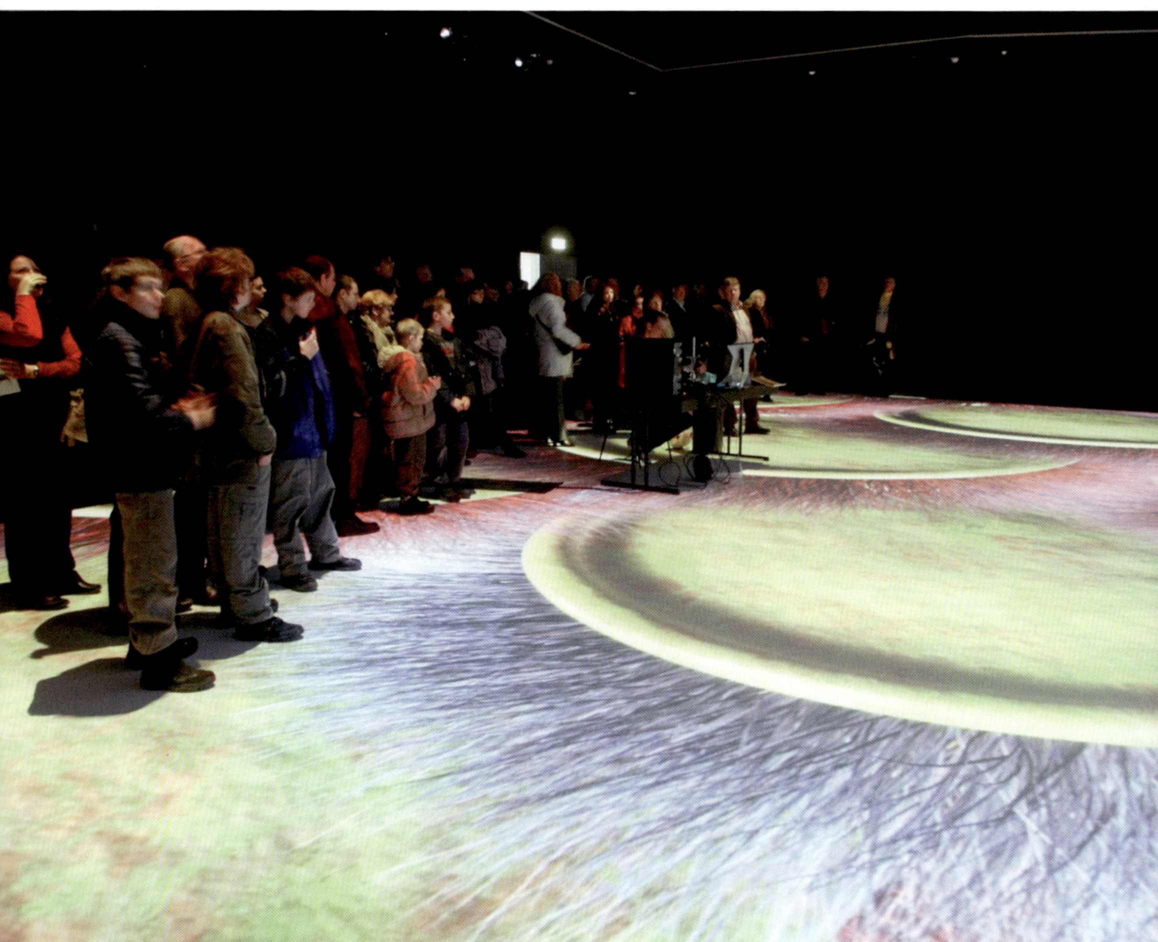

Photo: rubra

Empire of Sleep: The Beach
Alan Price

Empire of Sleep is an exploration of subconscious externalized through narrative and temporal structure of cinema adapted to the medium of real time graphics and user interaction.

Time is emphasized, in which a single moment is in a suspended state, yet you can navigate within the frame on a different scale.

The touch screen installation displays interactive stereoscopic 3D renderings of a surreal landscape haunted by a catastrophic event, sculpting a frozen moment of time in an iterating loop, fading away much like images fracture and lose definition as a dream is forgotten. *The Beach* is the first part of a series.

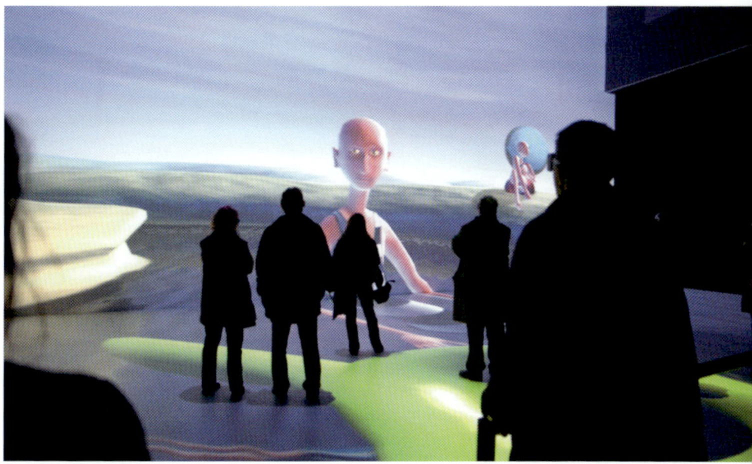

Photo: Andreas Hirsch

Jungle Imperator
The Sancho Plan

Jungle Imperator is an interactive visual and musical experience in which you control a cast of animated musical characters performing as part of an evocative soundtrack that evolves from dark ambience to rich layers of collaborative grooves.

Combining music provided by Vienna-based musicians Tosca (Richard Dorfmeister and Rupert Huber) with rich surrealist imagery inspired by Max Ernst, this uniquely refined installation has been especially crafted to take advantage of the immersive opportunities presented by *Deep Space*. Exploring the theme of collaboration through music (light) versus isolation (dark), the work also exists as a purely enjoyable interactive audiovisual adventure for „musicians" & „non-musicians" alike.

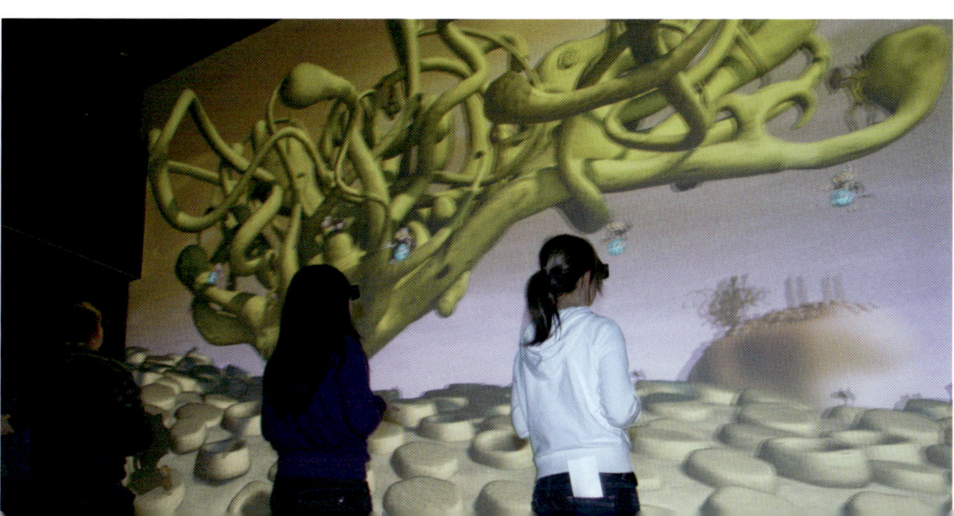

Deep Space

Idea and Concept: Gerfried Stocker, Horst Hörtner, Christopher Lindinger, Daniela Kuka.
Coordination: Daniela Kuka.
Realisation: Ars Electronica Futurelab: Oliver Elias, Ronald Martins, Andreas Pramböck, Otto Naderer, Florian Krebs, Thomas Kollmann, Karl Schmidinger, Michael Badics, Wolfgang Ziegler, Christian Reisenberger, Nicolas Naveau, PV Planungs- und Veranstaltungstechnik GmbH & Co. KG.

Many thanks for the generous support of BARCO, Dessault Systèmes (3DVIA Virtools), GROTHUSEN Audio Video Vertriebs Ges.m.b.H. (Andreas Hammerschmid), PV Planungs- und Veranstaltungstechnik GmbH & Co. KG.

Gigapixel Photography

Alte Meister in neuem Licht – Haltadefinizione (IT)

The Last Supper, Leonardo da Vinci
Santa Maria delle Grazie, Milan
by courtesy of Superintendency Ministero per i Beni e le Attività Culturali, Soprintendenza per i Beni Architettonici e Paesaggistici, Milano & Haltadefinizione
www.haltadefinizione.com
Photography: Mauro Gavinelli, Vincenzo Mirarchi, Agostino Temporelli

Christ's Passion, Gaudenzio Ferrari
Santa Maria delle Grazie, Varallo Sesia (VC)
by courtesy of Comune di Varallo Sesia, Assessorato alla cultura e al turismo & Haltadefinizione;
www.haltadefinizione.com
Photography: Mauro Gavinelli, Vincenzo Mirarchi, Agostino Temporelli

The trompe l'œil ceiling of Sant'Ignazio, Andrea Pozzo
Sant'Ignazio di Loyola, Rome
by courtesy of Haltadefinizione;
www.haltadefinizione.com
The Church is a property of Fondo Edifici di Culto managed by Ministero dell'Interno
Dipartimento per le Libertà civili e l'Immigrazione
Direzione Centrale per l'Amministrazione del Fondo Edifici di Culto
Photography: Mauro Gavinelli, Vincenzo Mirarchi, Agostino Temporelli
Technology Partners: AMD, CLAUSS, De Agostini, I.NET, Moonlab, Nikon, Nital

Landscapes / Cityscapes

xRez in Focus
a selection of images from US Cities / Urban Subjects, Yosemite National Park, Owens Valley, Norway Fjords and Hawaii (Oahu)
xRez Studio, Inc.; Eric Hanson, Greg Downing (US)

Gigapixel Linz
An areal photograph of the whole city with 23,75 gigapixels
Ars Electronica Futurelab, areal photrgraphy FMM,

Marathon Linz
interactive preview of the route of Linz Marathon 2009
Ars Electronica Futurelab, areal photrgraphy FMM, in collaboration with LIVA – Ewald Tröbinger and DORIS.

Scientific Images

Outerspace
HiRes Images from the Hubble Telescope, Nasa, Esa, Dietmar Hager F.R.A.S. (AT)

Nanospheres
HiRes microscopic images, Max-Planck-Institute (DE)

Artistic Images

Ôr'ganik Constructions
Selected images from Kenneth A. Huff (US)

VR Stereo Projects, Interactive Storytelling

Papyrate's Island
Idea & Concept: Daniela Kuka, Pascal Maresch
Concept, Design, 3D-Modeling & Animation:
Andreas Jalsovec, Michael Mayr, Timm Wilks, Leonhard Immervoll
Software Engineering: Ronald Martins, Oliver Elias
Anoto Implementation: Media Interaction Lab FH-Hagenberg (Peter Brandl, Adam Erol Gokcezade)
Music: Herwig Burghard, *Sounddesign: www.tonburg.at*

Empire of Sleep: The Beach
Alan Price (US)

Jungle Imperator
Idea: The Sancho Plan (UK), Daniela Kuka
Director & Audio: Ed Cookson
Lead Environment: Olly Venning
Lead Characters: Gordon Dunn
Background Characters: Edward Dawson-Taylor, Ondrej
Svadlena, Steven Mertens
AV Assistant: Bruno Mathez
System Architecture: Adam Hoyle/ Do Tank Studios
Musical Interfaces: Ian Steele
Music: Tosca (Richard Dorfmeister & Rupert Huber)
Audio Mix: Rupert Huber & Ed Cookson
Narrative Design: Maurice Suckling
*A commission of Ars Electronica, co-production with Ars
Electronica Futurelab:*
Realtime Programming: Michael Heiml (Lead), Oliver
Elias, Ronald Martins, Florian Berger
Realtime 3D: Andreas Jalsovec, Michael Mayr, Wolfgang
Hauer

On-Site by CyArk
An archeological walk-in archive based on 3D laser
sancs made by CyArk (US), showcasing virtual models
of Ancient Thebes, Angkor, Pompeii, Tikal, Cathedral
of Beauvais, Pisa – Piazza del Duomo, Volumnis'
Hypogeum, Mesa Verde, St. Sebald Church.
Sponsored by: Egyptian Antiquities Information Service
(EAIS), INSIGHT, Kacyra Family Foundation (KFF) und
Plowman Craven, National Science Foundation (NSF),
THE SAMUEL H. KRESS FOUNDATION, World Monu-
ments Fund (WMF), CNR-ISTI Visual Computing Lab,
DIAPReM University of Ferrara, Dipartimento di Pro-
gettazione dell'Architettura di Firenze, Leica
Geosystems Italia, Opera della Primaziale Pisana Pisa,
Soprintendenza per i beni architettonici e per il
paesaggio e per il patrimonio storico, artistico e
demoetnoantropologico, Pring Turner Capital Group /
Joe Turner, KCET, PBS, Wired Science and National
Center for Preservation Technology and Training
(NCPTT), Christofori und Partner

Uniview – Scaling the Universe
SCISS AB Norrköping (SE)

Audiovisual Installations

data.tron [8K enhanced version]
Commissioned by Ars Electronica Center for the inaugu-
ration of their Deep Space venue, produced by Forma
Concept, composition: Ryoji Ikeda
Programming: Tomonaga Tokuyama

Please stand back!
a stereographic and interactive short film
Visuals and Music: stadtmusik

HD Films

Linz – A Somewhat Different Perspective
Kamera und Gestaltung – Erich Pröll
Steadicam – Hubert Doppler
Seilbahnkamera – Martin Burger, Christian Dimt
Ergänzende Kamera und Schnitt – Jutta Anna Wirth
Kameraassistenz – Bernhard Gerstmair, Katharina
Glamuzina, Dieter Pröll
Produktion – Pröll Film Production GmbH © 2009
Music: Herwig Burghard, Sounddesign: *www.tonburg.at*

Deep Universe
Dietmar Hager F.R.A.S., Ars Electronica Futurelab,
Musik: Thomas Nordwest

Sternenstaub
Erich Pröll, Dietmar Hager F.R.A.S., Ars Electronica
Futurelab, Musik: Thomas Nordwest

Now that the AEC's exhibition spaces have been considerably enlarged, several exhibits can run simultaneously and it's also possible to feature special added attractions of an artistic as well as a scientific nature.

Ars Intrinsica
13. 5. 2009 – 5. 7. 2009

Ars Intrinsica utilizes state-of-the-art technology to deliver astonishing views of the human body's innermost realms.

Digital x-rays, computer tomography and magnetic resonance imaging are usually deployed to determine the causes of illnesses and to produce detailed, comprehensive diagnoses. But the extraordinary possibilities afforded by these imaging techniques can also be used to create a new artform in which scientific methods are combined with artistic approaches.

The outcome of a collaboration with graphic designer Richard Giesemann is an exhibition of large-format artworks that let viewers peer into the fascinating world deep inside the human body. One of the featured works is an artistically processed magnetic resonance image of the entire body of Linz's own Günter Kohout, a former world champion body builder.

"Put aside preconceptions when viewing the works and encounter them impartially. After all, nothing is more fascinating than life itself." (Dr. Franz A. Fellner, head of the Radiology Department at Linz General Hospital)

Ars Intrinsica is an artistic-scientific project by Dr. Franz A. Fellner, head of the Department of Radiology at Linz General Hospital, in collaboration with graphic designer Richard Giesemann. This project was supported by Siemens Oberösterreich.

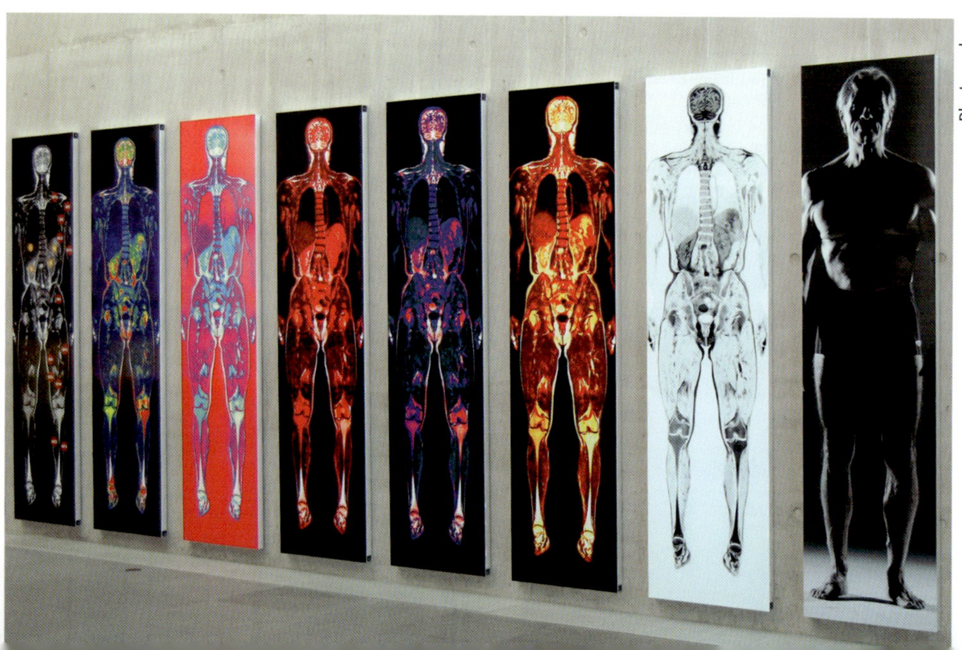

Photo: rubra

Stardust – Astronomy and Outer Space
July 8-August 23, 2009

On the occasion of the International Year of Astronomy and the 40th anniversary of the first Moon landing, exhibits on astronomy and space exploration are being featured on several floors of the new AEC.
This exhibition invites visitors to shift into active discovery mode! Drive a replica of the Mars Rover Dignity in the Lobby and try on prototypes of space suits of the future.
The *Spacelab* is the spot to marvel at a genuine Moon rock and use high-powered microscopes to get a close-up look at it and other long-distance space travelers like meteorite fragments and cosmic dust.

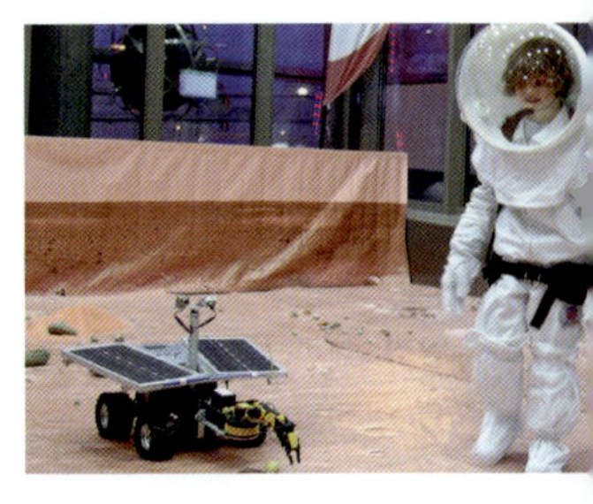

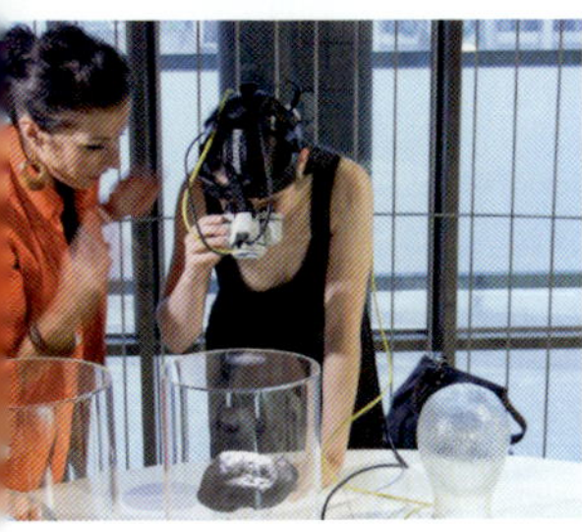

In the *Apollo Lounge*, extensive documentation tells the story of the race to the Moon and the successful mission of Apollo 11. Stop by *Space Cinema* to watch screenings of impressive computer simulations about dark matter and get updated about an important issue: so-called light pollution.

Along the way, you can admire works by 25 Austrian artists that make up *The rolling stars and planets*, an exhibition initiated by Elisabeth Ledersberger-Lehoczky.

Sure to be one of your most unforgettable highlights is *Uniview,* a 3D stereo simulation of the entire known universe. You can experience this incredible VR world produced by the Swedish firm SCISS in *Deep Space*, the new Ars Electronica Center's big interactive projection space.

To get into the mood for this journey across the heavens, you can watch a film that transports you from the microcosm of the human eye to the macrocosm of the universe. Shot by Erich Pröll, famed director of nature films for the *Universum* TV series, and micro-surgeon and astronomical photographer Dietmar Hager, this film shows what goes into the making of these breathtaking images of outer space.

An extensive program consisting of guided tours, workshops, speeches and presentations is accompanying this exhibition. And the focus on astronomy continues even after the exhibition closes: "80+1 – A Trip around the World" running from August 31 to September 4, 2009 deals with the subject of exploration in the form of artistic projects, discussions and workshops.

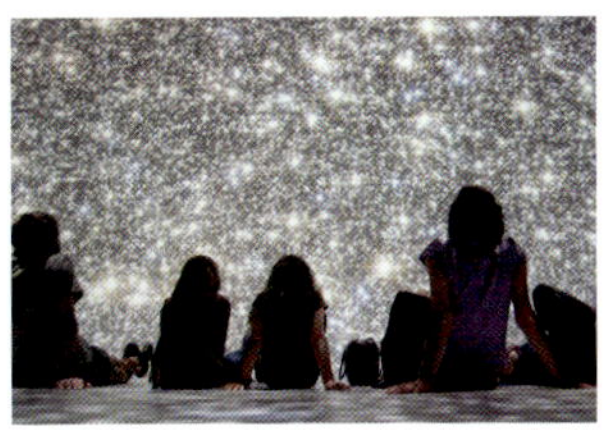

Concept and astronomical advice: Dietmar Hager (F.R.A.S.), Projectmanagement: Irene Posch, Ars Electronica Futurelab
We wish to express our sincere thanks to the following institutions for their cooperation:
Dietmar Hager (Fellow of the Royal Astronomical Society), the Austrian Space Forum, the Department of Astronomy of the University of Vienna, SCISS Uniview, the Professional Association of Austrian Visual Artists and the Linz Astronomers' Society, Teleskop- und Sternwartenzentrum Linz, Abteilung für Unfallchirurgie AKh Linz, Thomas Nordwest, Erich Pröll, Wolfgang Schober, Elisabeth Ledersberger-Lehoczky.

GeoCity

GeoCity went into operation on June 16, 2009. This exhibition/laboratory deals with life in a permanently globally-networked world from the perspective of digital media. The aim is to make people aware of the simultaneity of local and global phenomena, to focus attention on Spaceship Earth, and to offer insights into the dynamic organism of a city—Linz, the one in which we live.

To achieve this, the Ars Electronica Futurelab has conceived and executed various media-technological scenarios for geo- and data-visualization. Geocity has been conceived as a three-year pilot project. Over this time, the technical infrastructure's capacity to get across the meaning of complexly interrelated data sets will be assessed and enhanced. These data sets will be continuously expanded and updated. An additional aim is to assess how well visitors interact with this installation and to derive new application possibilities for the interfaces deployed here on the basis of this experience.

Concept: Gefried Stocker, Horst Hörtner, Michi Badics, Christopher Lindinger, Jonathan Hoyer
Execution: Ars Electronica Futurelab
Exhibition architecture: Scott Ritter, Jakob Illera, Ars Electronica Futurelab

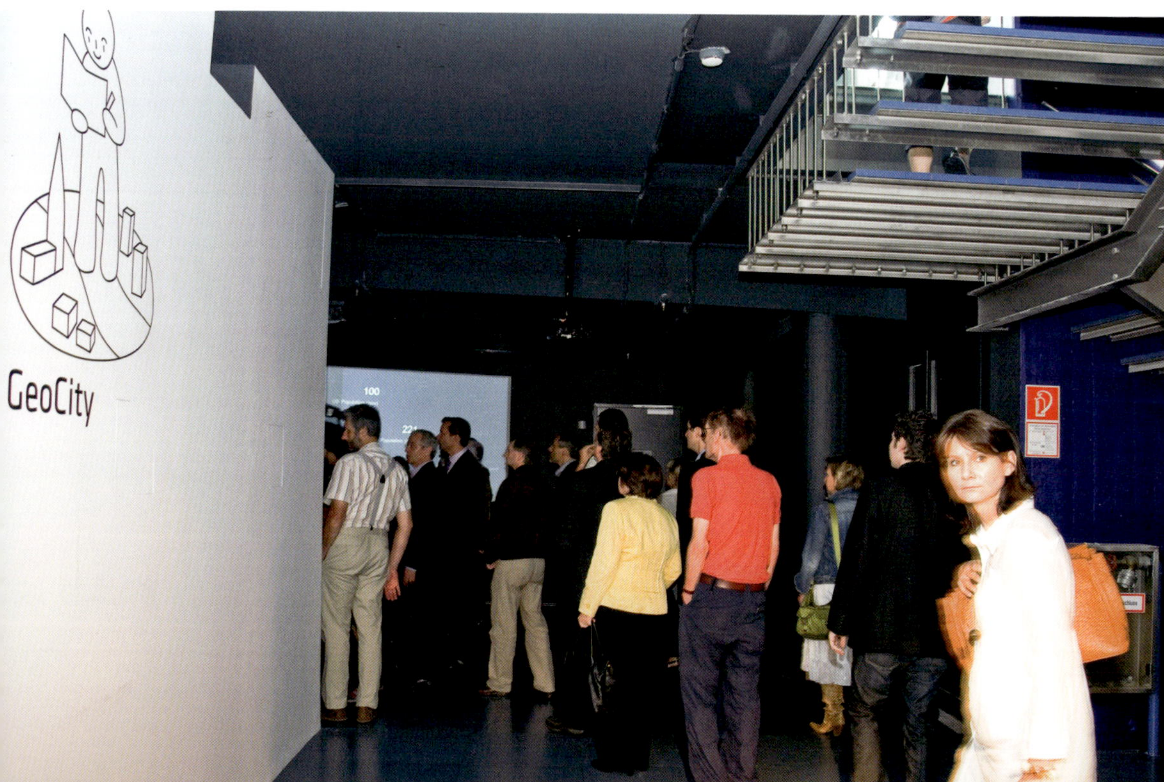

Pixel City

Every city is just as distinctive as each of its inhabitants, whose respective personalities, histories and cultures are unique, integral parts of the urban mosaic

189,355 plastic blocks (one for each inhabitant of the City of Linz) are placed at the disposal of GeoCity visitors to construct their own cityscapes and urban architecture. More than two tons of these Lego-like blocks thus form this exhibition's constantly evolving backdrop.

Pixel City: Ars Electronica Futurelab

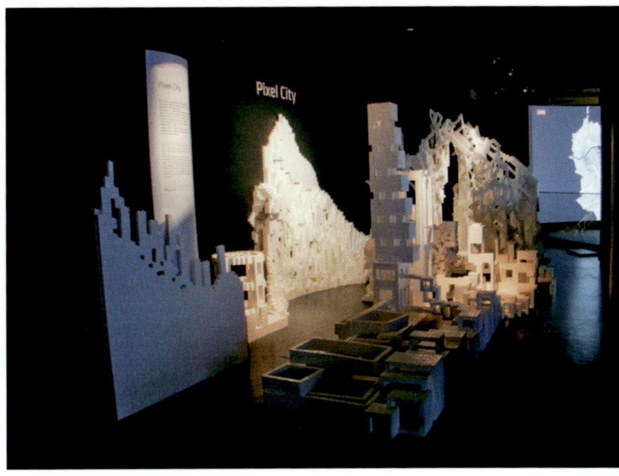

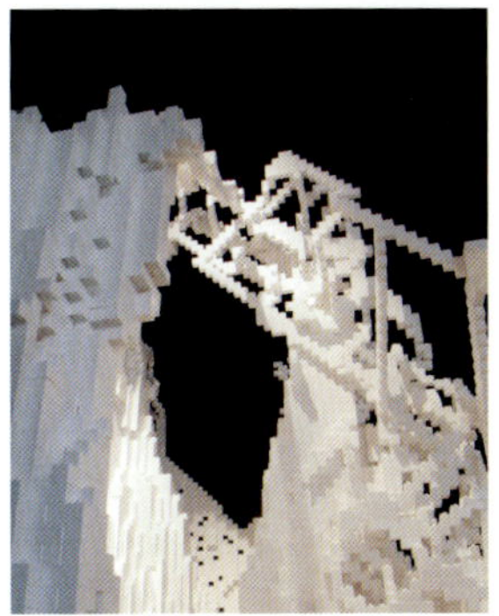

Pixel Windows

Installation visitors can use mobile micro-beamers to project imagery onto a portion of a cityscape constructed of pixel-cubes and thus open up virtual windows and peer behind walls. What this brings into view are stories and pictures—both true-to-life and completely fabricated—of life in the big city.

Pixel Windows: Ars Electronica Futurelab

Procedural City

Every city is just as distinctive as each of its inhabitants. By using a fingerprint scanner one can create an individual "ground plan" of a city. An algorithmic program then uses this as the blueprint for an urban structure comprised of building blocks similar to the plastic cubes used in "Pixel City". You can freely navigate through the city conjured up in this way and e-mail screenshots of what you see during your explorations.

Procedural City: Procedural, Ars Electronica Futurelab

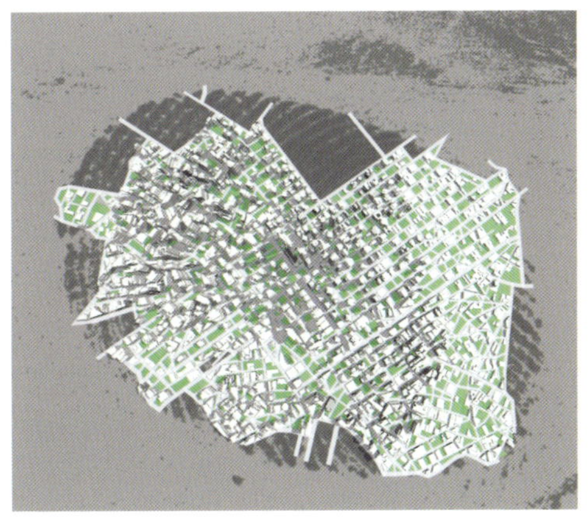

SimLinz

SimLinz is a futuristic prototype of an interactive urban- and geo-information system that—on the basis of Linz—provides interesting and unusual insights into the city and its functions. Exemplary data from the 1950s to the present let users follow Linz's development over time.

The spatial changes that the cityscape has undergone can be observed on the basis of aerial images and city maps dating back to 1824. *SimLinz* also uses current and historical photos as well as statistical extrapolations and real-time data fed from various sources directly into the exhibition.

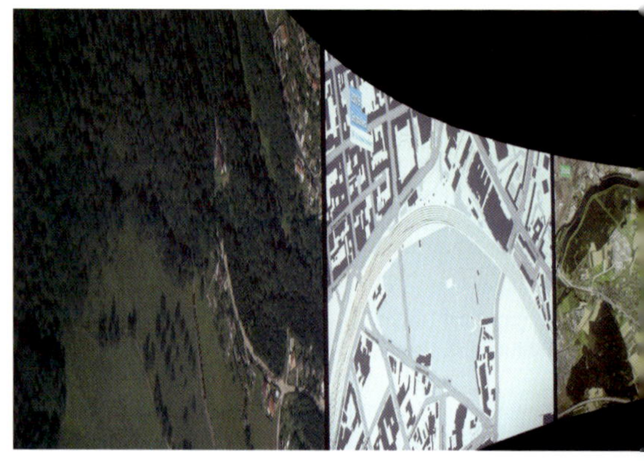

SimLinz has been conceived as a walk-through database that utilizes new means of communication to get across complex, interrelated information in an intuitive way. Whether it's a book or a city map—everything morphs into an interactive surface. Analog and digital elements react to each other—pencil and paper unite with computer and projection.

An approximately 6 x 3 meter city map of Linz generated on the basis of Anoto technology (incidentally: the largest one-piece Anoto print ever produced) serves as visitors' primary navigation tool. Providing an overview of the variously combinable data sets are filofax folders containing interactive data sheets. These can be used to select data; the necessary control elements and explanations are also printed on them.

Thus, the same pencil can be used to select information from the folders, to assign it to a particular geographical area, and to navigate on the city map.

Three different data-streams can be depicted simultaneously via an 11-meter-wide panorama projection.

SimLinz: Ars Electronica Futurelab
With the support of: Media Interaction Lab, FH Hagenberg, Michael Haller; numerous government agencies of the City of Linz, IKT-Linz and Linz AG; FMM; the Province of Upper Austria; Via Donau

Populouscape

This virtual, high-definition flight over Earth in which cities are depicted as columns (higher or lower, depending on their population) is an aesthetically impressive way to show the human species' presence on our planet.

Populouscape: Hiroshi Ota, Kaori Ito, Tomohiko Okabe, Ksuke Fukushima, Kohske Kawase, Kazuma Yamao (JP)

City Prints

High-resolution aerial photos generated by the surveillance flyover of Linz staged in conjunction with Ars Electronica 2007 are exhibited together with text visualizations on the subject of the city.

City Prints: Photo editor: Dietmar Tollerian (AT), Text visualizations: MF Redman (DE)

Global Pulse

Here's something that's sure to make an impression on you! Seeing the speed at which the Earth's population is growing: 2.6 human beings per second! And when you're also able to see how much faster the population of India is growing in comparison to China, Europe and the USA, how many cars, bicycles, PCs etc. are being produced at the moment, the number of new cases of HIV infection, how much oil we're using and how much CO2 we emit etc. etc., then a few glances are all it takes to get a powerful impression of the global dimension of our life. Dynamically visualized by Zach Lieberman, these statistical rhythms of the world constitute the thematic and spatial portal to GeoCity.

Global Pulse: Zachary Lieberman, Ars Electronica Futurelab

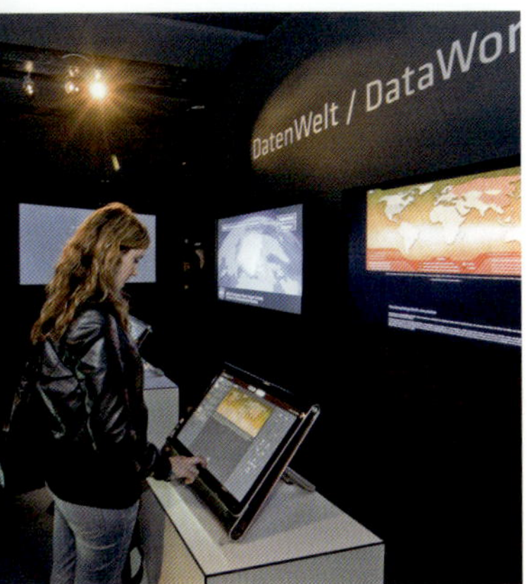

Data World and Data Floor

Two touchscreen terminals full of information about our planet—impressive images and animated films made by NASA, wonderful historical cityscape views and maps, evocative geo-imaging and very telling data visualizations. These highly diversified information offerings and data sets—all gleaned from the internet—once again attest to this fantastic collective storehouse of knowledge that constitutes a new way to access the world.

Images from this world of data are projected onto the floor as animated sequences and thereby impart to the exhibition space an additional touch of the atmosphere of a global observatory.

All those people who are sharing their knowledge on the Internet

Exhibits also include: global air traffic, visualised by the swiss Air Traffic Team; animated infographics of the human rights declaration created by Seth Brau; Google Earth Specials, *www.worldmapper.org*; historical maps from the university of Texas; Space Debris, ESA, *Antarctic Plumbing:* Lake Englehardt's Subglacial Hydraulic System, NASA; Total Solar Eclipse, NASA; A Short Tour of the Cryosphere, NASA; www.urban-age.net; CIA Factbook; Breathing Earth; Global HealthMap; *www.tenbyten.org*; *www.192021.org*; Antipodes Map

80+1 Travellog

80+1 is a virtual 'round-the-world journey being staged by Ars Electronica and voestalpine for Linz 2009 European Capital of Culture. State-of-the-art telecommunications technology set up on Hauptplatz is the mode of travel and the link connecting Linz to the whole wide world. The geographic/thematic destinations that make up this trip's itinerary can be accessed via this interactive globe.

This installation also features data depictions—for example, all air traffic at the world's 20 busiest airports and details of current seismic and volcanic activity.

80+1 Travellog: Ars Electronica Futurelab, 80+1 Team
Supported by: voestalpine, Linz09 and many other partners

Emiko Ogawa, Hideaki Ogawa

Hand Drawing for the New Ars Electronica Center

In my drawings, there's always a drawing of a "human".
The human isn't just decoration for me; rather, it's the important factor to show both the concept and the interaction with artwork in a non-verbal way. When people see the picture, they will immediately understand how they can interact. This human drawing has a cute personality to create an atmosphere beyond the normal explanation of an artwork.

This drawing methodology has been developed through the activities of "h.o", a media art group I belong to. At the beginning of the activity, when we had a presentation, we would just write the descriptions directly with the work and environments. Through successive presentations, we found a more natural way to use these human drawings and let people more clearly visualize our plan.

This signage project in the new Ars Electronica Center was an experimental and exciting collaboration using these hand drawings. This approach makes sense only in the Ars Electronica Center, where visitors feel and experience things through interactive experiences. Through this project, we encountered a new dimension in which this method is used in the communication for both hosts and visitors.

The process of this methodology starts by personally experiencing the scenarios of each project. We imagine the guided tours, where visitors can enjoy the environment. What is the form of the work? How do visitors interact with each work? Is it altogether fun, philosophical and amazing? How is the relation to the next work after this one? Based on these observations, the design of the human icon changes in the distance from the work, in the facial expressions and the interaction with the work. This process sometimes influences the layout of the exhibition.

If a regular museum used this hand drawing style for signage, it wouldn't make sense, because visitors would find a boring floor map with quadrilateral paintings. There the drawings would contain less information than the text.

In our project, we also made some small indication signs such as "Don't Touch" and "No Entry!" The "Out of Order", for example, was designed not only for the meaning as "Sorry" for visitors, but also the message that it's currently undergoing repairs for you. The drawings allow people to feel positive, even when the situation is negative.

When you walk around the Ars Electronica Center, you will definitely meet the small humans somewhere. We would be happy if they bring you more fruitful experiences in the museum of the future.

Special thanks to Nicolas Naveau, Stefan Eibelwimmer, Christian Korherr & Sini Zein

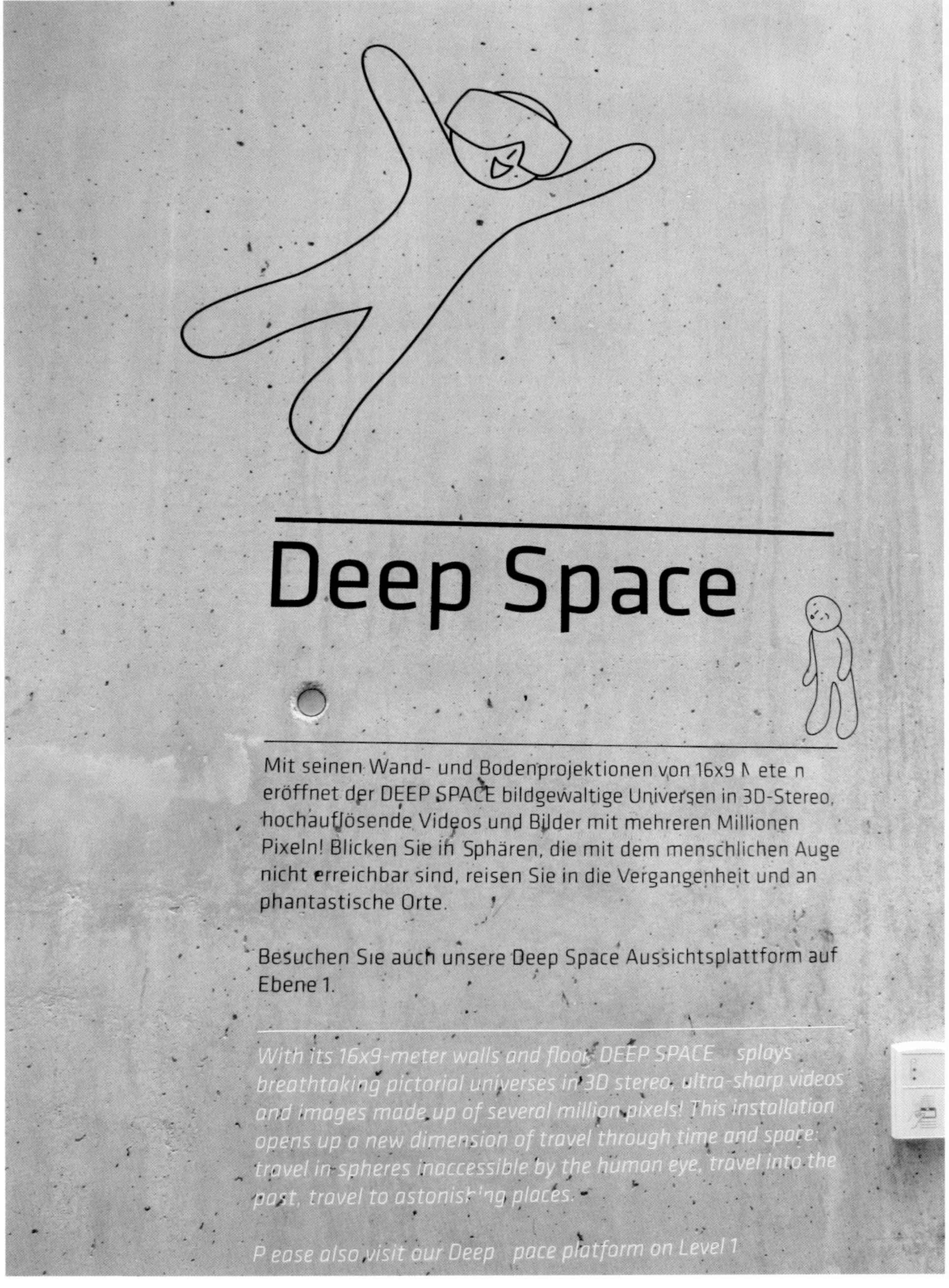

Mit seinen Wand- und Bodenprojektionen von 16x9 Meten
eröffnet der DEEP SPACE bildgewaltige Universen in 3D-Stereo,
hochauflösende Videos und Bilder mit mehreren Millionen
Pixeln! Blicken Sie in Sphären, die mit dem menschlichen Auge
nicht erreichbar sind, reisen Sie in die Vergangenheit und an
phantastische Orte.

Besuchen Sie auch unsere Deep Space Aussichtsplattform auf
Ebene 1.

With its 16x9-meter walls and floor, DEEP SPACE splays
breathtaking pictorial universes in 3D stereo, ultra-sharp videos
and images made up of several million pixels! This installation
opens up a new dimension of travel through time and space:
travel in spheres inaccessible by the human eye, travel into the
past, travel to astonishing places.

Please also visit our Deep Space platform on Level 1.

Emiko Ogawa, Hideaki Ogawa

Zeichnungen als Leitsystem für das neue Ars Electronica Center

In meinen Zeichnungen stelle ich stets auch „Menschen" dar.

Der Mensch, dargestellt als kleines piktogrammartiges Wesen, dient nicht nur Illustrationszwecken, sondern soll den Besuchern das hinter einem Kunstwerk stehende Gesamtkonzept auf einen Blick veranschaulichen und auf nonverbale Weise verdeutlichen, wie man als Besucher mit einer Installation in Interaktion treten kann. Wer das Bild betrachtet, versteht sofort, was von ihm erwartet wird. Die Männchen in den Zeichnungen sind als freundliche Wesen dargestellt; sie schaffen so eine spezielle Atmosphäre und ein besonderes Verständnis der ausgestellten Werke, die über herkömmliche textbasierte Formen der Werkbeschreibung hinausgehen. Dieser Ansatz einer auf Zeichnungen basierenden Form der Beschilderung wurde von *h.o.* entwickelt, einem Kollektiv von Medienkünstlern, dem ich angehöre. Anfangs beschrieben wir Projekte, die wir in Ausstellungen präsentierten, auf traditionelle Weise. Im Lauf der Zeit erkannten wir aber, dass Besucher das hinter den präsentierten Arbeiten stehende Konzept mittels symbolhafter Zeichnungen weitaus besser erfassen können.

Die Gestaltung des Beschilderungsleitsystems im neuen Ars Electronica Center war ein experimentelles, spannendes Projekt, für das wir solche Zeichnungen entwarfen. Ein derartiger Zugang macht nur in einem Ausstellungsambiente wie dem Ars Electronica Center Sinn, wo Besucher verschiedene Phänomene interaktiv erfahren und erleben. Durch dieses Projekt eröffnete sich uns eine neue Dimension, in der unsere Zeichnungen zur Kommunikation sowohl mit den Ausstellungsträgern als auch den Besuchern genutzt werden.

Bei der Erarbeitung derartiger symbolhafter Zeichnungen beginnen wir damit, dass wir mit den verschiedenen Szenarios Erfahrungen sammeln. Wir stellen uns Führungen durch die Ausstellung vor, bei denen Besucher die Installationen und das Ambiente auf sich wirken lassen. Wie sieht das Werk aus? Wie interagieren Besucher mit den verschiedenen Installationen? Sind die präsentierten Projekte unterhaltsam, werfen sie philosophische Fragen auf oder bieten sie einfach eine verblüffende neue Perspektive? In welchem Zusammenhang stehen sie zu anderen in ihrer unmittelbaren Umgebung präsentierten Installationen? Auf der Basis dieser Überlegungen werden die dargestellten Männchen bildnerisch erarbeitet; so ändern sich vielleicht die

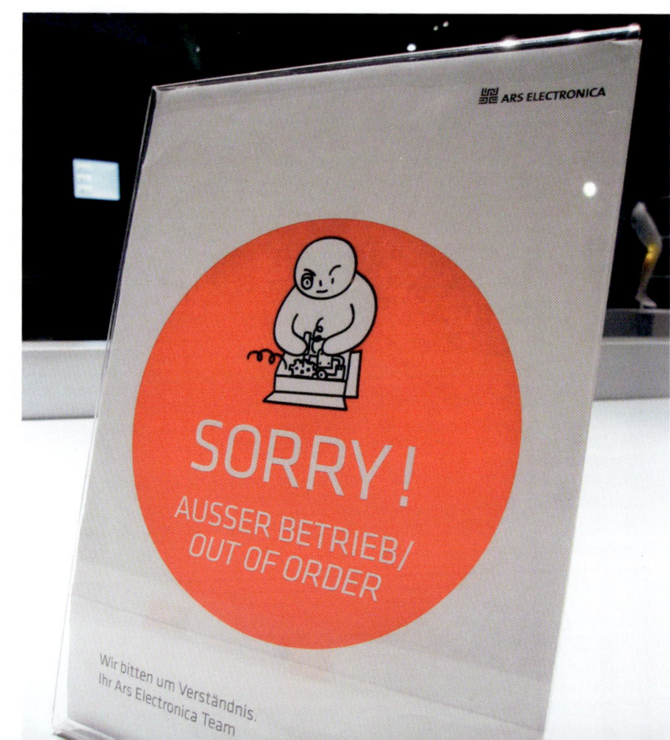

Abstände, der Gesichtsausdruck oder der Bezug zum Werk. Dieser Prozess beeinflusste teilweise auch die Gestaltung der Ausstellung.

Es wäre wenig sinnvoll, derartige Zeichnungen zur Beschilderung in einem traditionellen Museum zu verwenden, da die Besucher sich mit einem langweiligen Etagenplan mit viereckigen Bildern zufriedengeben müssten. Die Zeichnungen würden weniger Information liefern als die Begleittexte.

Bei unserem Projekt fertigten wir auch einige Hinweisschilder an, wie etwa „Bitte nicht berühren" und „Eintritt verboten!". Das „Außer Betrieb"-Schild wurde beispielsweise so konzipiert, dass Besucher das Schild nicht nur im Sinne von „Es tut uns leid!" interpretieren, sondern dass darüber hinaus vermittelt wird: „Dieses Werk wird gerade für Sie restauriert!" Durch solche Zeichnungen entsteht bei den Besuchern ein positiver Eindruck, auch wenn der Anlass für die Anbringung des Schilds vielleicht auf wenig Gegenliebe stößt.

Wenn Sie das Ars Electronica Center durchstreifen, werden Sie sicher irgendwo auf unsere kleinen Symbole stoßen. Wir würden uns freuen, wenn die Ausstellung für Sie durch unsere Zeichnungen zu einem Museumserlebnis der besonderen Art wird.

Unser besonderer Dank gilt Nicolas Naveau, Stefan Eibelwimmer, Christian Korherr und Sini Zein.

(Aus dem Englischen von Sonja Pöllabauer)

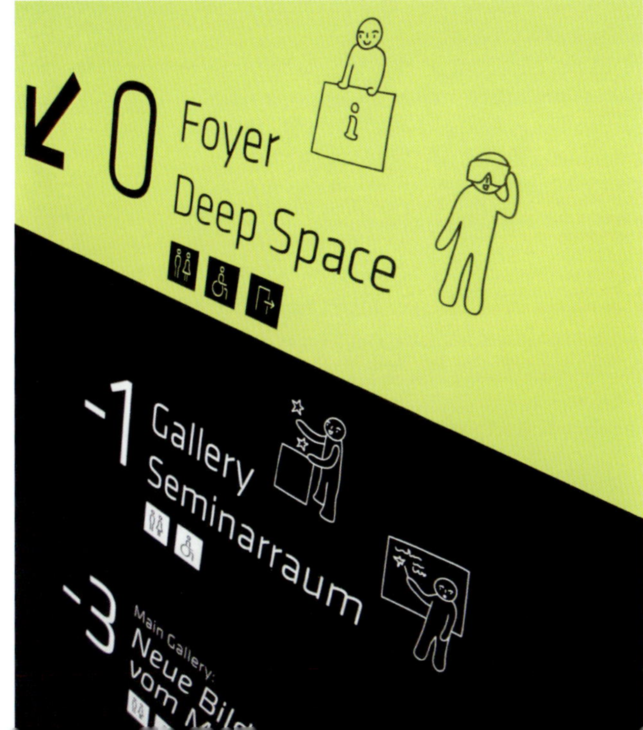

Architectures of the New Ars Electronica Center

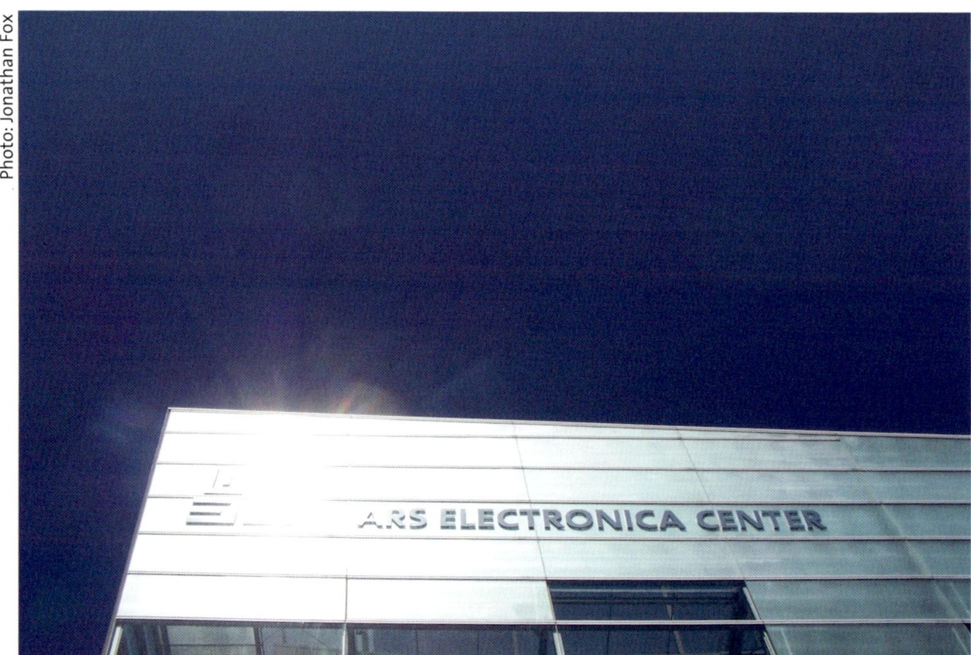

The new building's design by Viennese architect Andreas Treusch was the winner of an EU-wide architectural competition. His bureau, Treusch Architectures, was also responsible for the general planning of the construction project.

It was completed promptly under the supervision of Harald Jakober and Herbert Poscher of ILG (Immobilien Linz GmbH) as project organizer. Thanks to highly motivated and thoroughly professional cooperation on the part of all government agencies and private firms involved, this extremely complex project was completed on time and without incident.

Many of the items on the client's wish list of functional features as well as certain design preconditions were already very clearly set forth in the call for entries to the architectural competition. First of all, the preexisting structure was to be preserved for the most part, but the add-on was to be planned in such a way that it would give the impression of a holistic unit. Furthermore, the view to the historical architectural ensemble and the church had to be unimpaired.

Treusch's design complies with these preconditions and implements the client's wishes in an outstanding way; above all, it was the superb exterior effect of the glass & light façade that won over the jury.

Fortunately, during the timeframe when this project was being planned, the cost of LED lighting fell dramatically. This meant that, instead of the fluorescent tube illumination that was originally planned, it would be feasible to install a futuristic, energy-efficient LED façade that can be directly controlled by computer and is thus an attractive design medium to boot. In this connection: a tip of the hat to the Multivision Company and Mr. Scherenhuber for their committed efforts.

An important design element of the new Ars Electronica Center complex is its spacious plaza, the *Maindeck* with its inviting steps/grandstand. This is an urban setting for alfresco socializing and just hanging out, as well as a dramatic venue for a wide variety of events and activities.

The eastern end of the Ars Electronica Center where the building emerges above ground houses the labs, studios and workshops of the Ars Electronica Futurelab. In the spirit of all that Ars Electronica has come to represent in its 30-year history, this facility accommodates exhibitions, events and R&D.

The architecture and design of the new exhibitions are almost entirely the work of two Viennese practitioners, Scott Ritter und Jakob Illera. The Funky Pixels area was designed by Herbert Ploner. The Ars Electronica Futurelab was intensively involved in the design process right from the outset in order to insure optimal integration of the technical infrastructure into the architectural design.

One particular challenge was the orchestration of the large new exhibition hall, the *Main Gallery*. The aim was to juxtapose the exhibit area and the lab operations without strictly segregating them from one another. The integration of two lab pavilions that display a high degree of transparency but can nevertheless provide a modicum of privacy for intensive workshops and courses, as well as the positioning of the Infodeck on the labs' ceilings so to speak, structure the *Main Gallery* in an ideal way and permit a highly diversified dramaturgy of the visitors' encounters with content on their way through the new AEC.

The themes of the exhibition—digital fabrication, for instance—and its laboratory character that is at the core of the message it's attempting to get across are ingeniously reflected by the formal vocabulary of the exhibition architecture.

One particularly illustrative example of this is the design of the entry control stations conceived and developed by Jakob Illera. Instead of conventional turnstiles, the new Ars Electronica Center uses three pneumatically operated elements that roll in as soon as a visitor holds his/her admission ticket up to the reader.

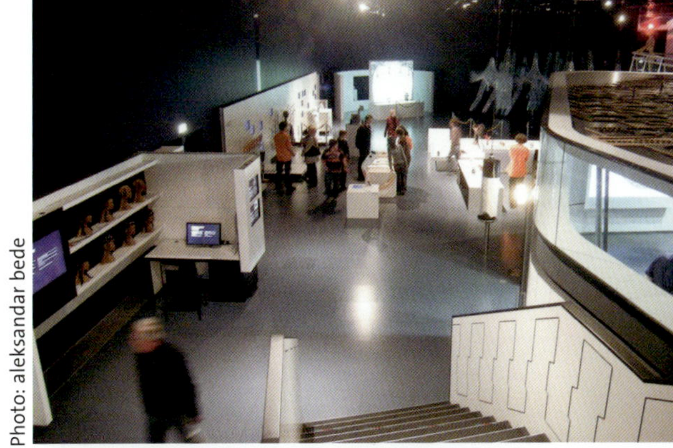

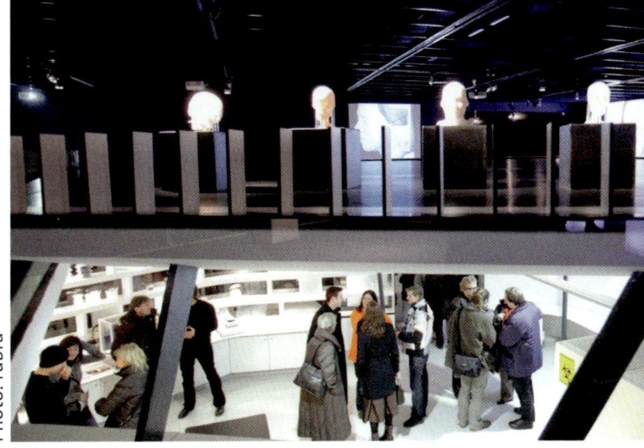

Architekturen des neuen Ars Electronica Center

Das neue Gebäude wurde als Siegerprojekt eines offenen europaweit ausgeschriebenen Wettbewerbs vom Wiener Architekten Andreas Treusch, der mit seinem Büro Treusch Architectures auch die Generalplanung überhatte, entworfen. Es wurde in äußerst kurzer Zeit unter der Bauleitung von Harald Jakober und Herbert Poscher von der ILG (Immobilien Linz GmbH) als Bauträger errichtet. Der hoch motivierten und professionellen Zusammenarbeit aller zuständigen Stellen und Firmen ist es zu verdanken, dass dieses baulich komplexe Projekt zeitgerecht und ohne Zwischenfälle fertig gestellt wurde.

In der Wettbewerbsausschreibung waren viele der funktionalen Nutzerwünsche bereits sehr klar vorgegeben, ebenso wie bestimmte gestalterische Rahmenbedingungen. So galt es, das alte Gebäude im wesentlich gleich zu belassen, den Zubau aber so zu planen, dass dennoch der Eindruck eines zusammenhängenden Gebäudes entstehen sollte. Ebenso musste z. B. die Sicht auf das Altstadtensemble und die Kirche freigehalten werden. Der Entwurf von Treusch setzt diese Vorgaben und Nutzerwünsche in ausgezeichneter Weise um und überzeugte die Jury vor allem auch durch die großartige Außenwirkung der Glas und Lichtfassade.

Zum Glück fielen im Zeitraum der Projektplanung die Kosten für LED-Beleuchtungen maßgeblich, so dass nicht die ursprünglich geplante Beleuchtung mit Leuchtstoffröhren, sondern eine zukunftsweisende und energiesparende LED-Fassade realisiert werden konnte, die durch direkte Computersteuerung auch ein gestalterisch attraktives Medium ist. Dafür ist auch dem engagierten Einsatz der Firma Multivision von Herrn Scherenhuber zu danken.

Ein wichtiges gestalterisches Moment des neuen AEC ist der neu entstandene große Vorplatz, das „Maindeck" mit der einladenden Freitreppe – ein urbaner Platz, der sich für entspanntes Verweilen genauso eignet wie für ein breites Spektrum von Events und Aktivitäten.

Im östlichen Teil, wo das Gebäude wieder aus dem Boden heraustritt, befinden sich nun die Labors, Studios und Werkstätten des Ars Electronica Futurelab. Das Gebäude bietet so ganz im Sinne der 30-jährigen Arbeit von Ars Electronica Raum für Ausstellungen, für Events und Veranstaltungen ebenso wie für Forschung, Entwicklung.

Photo: Pertlwieser / Stadt Linz

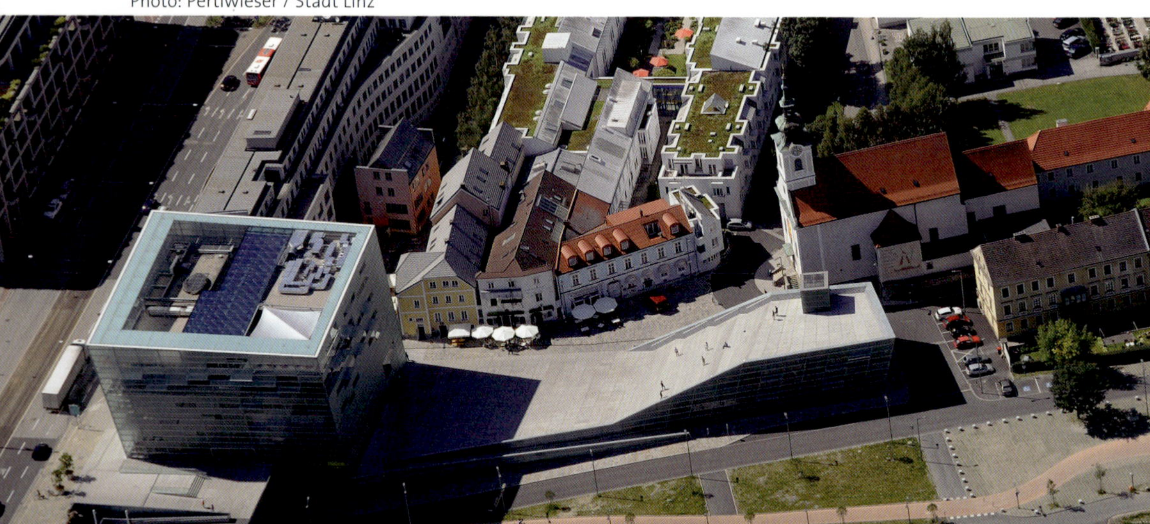

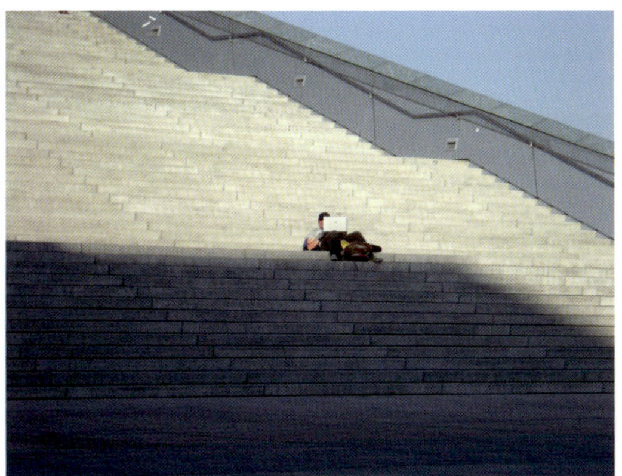

Photo: Aleksander Bede

Ausstellungsarchitektur und -design der neuen Ausstellungen kommen fast zur Gänze von Scott Ritter und Jakob Illera aus Wien. Der Bereich *Funky Pixels* wurde von Herbert Ploner gestaltet. Das Ars Electronica Futurelab hat an den Entwürfen von Anfang an intensiv mitgearbeitet, um so eine optimale Integration der technischer Infrastruktur in die Designs zu ermöglich.

Besonders in der neuen großen Ausstellungshalle, der *Main Gallery*, stand man vor der großen Herausforderung, Ausstellungs- und Laborbetrieb miteinander zu ermöglichen, ohne die Labs vom Ausstellungsbereich abzutrennen. Die Integration von zwei Labor-Pavillons, die eine hohe Transparenz aufweisen und dennoch als Rückzugsort für intensive Workshops und Kurse taugen, und das gewissermaßen auf den Labordächern angesiedelte Infodeck strukturieren die große Halle in optimaler Form und erlauben eine abwechslungsreiche Dramaturgie der Besucherwege.

Themen der Ausstellung wie z. B. Digital Fabrication oder auch der Laborcharakter der neuen Ausstellung finden sich in der Formensprache der Ausstellungsarchitektur kongenial wieder.

Ein besonderes Beispiel dafür sind die von Jakob Illera erdachten und entwickelten Zutrittskontrollen. Statt standardmäßiger Drehkreuze finden sich nun drei pneumatisch betriebene Elemente die sich einrollen, sobald der Besucher seine Eintrittskarte in den Kartenleser steckt.

Photo: rubra

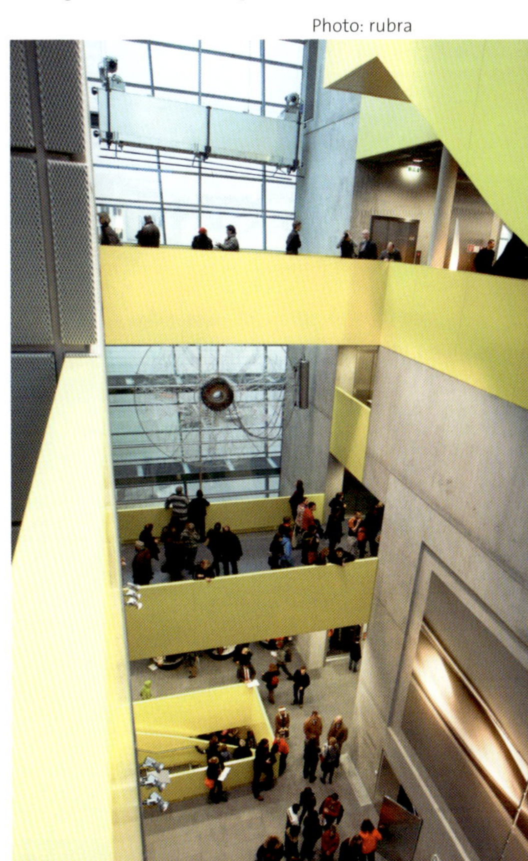

Ars Electronica Center
Bauträger: ILG (Immobilien Linz GmbH)
Geschäftsführer: Christian Strasser, Werner Penn
Projektleitung: Harald Jakober (ILG)
Örtliche Bauaufsicht: Herbert Poscher (Landauer-TB GmbH)
Architektur und Generalplanung:
TREUSCH architecture ZT GmbH

Die Kosten der Errichtung wurden von Stadt Linz (21 Mio Euro), und Land Oberösterreich (9 Mio Euro) getragen.

The Façade of the New Ars Electronica Center

38,500 LEDs are built into the Ars Electronica Center's 5,100-m2 glass shell. Every one of the façade's 1,100 glass panels thus becomes what amounts to a pixel that can be individually controlled. Each of the LED beams used here includes red, green, blue and white LEDs, which makes available a very wide color spectrum.

In order to minimize technical access impediments, the Ars Electronica Futurelab created a special development environment with which façade projects can be realized in a simple way with widely available tools (e.g. Max/MSP, Processing, VVVV) that lots of users are familiar with. An application made available free of charge thus enables artists and developers to work out their ideas offline at their own workstations and to simulate the visual results before they're displayed live on the façade.

In die 5.100 Quadratmeter große gläserne Hülle des neuen Ars Electronica Center sind 38.500 LEDs eingebaut. Jede der 1.100 Fensterflächen wird so zu einem Pixel und kann direkt angesteuert werden. Die zum Einsatz kommenden LED-Balken sind jeweils mit roten, grünen, blauen und zusätzlich weißen LEDs bestückt, damit steht ein äußerst breites Farbspektrum zur Verfügung.

Um die Gestaltung der Lichtfassade möglichst vielen Künstlerinnen zugänglich zu machen, wurde eine spezielle Entwicklungsumgebung geschaffen, mit der auf einfache Art und Weise – mit weit verbreiteten Tools (Max/MSP, Processing, VVVV ...) - Projekte auf der Fassade realisiert werden können. Dieser Fassadensimulator wird frei zur Verfügung gestellt und erlaubt es, Ideen und Projekte offline zu entwickeln und das visuelle Ergebnis zu simulieren, bevor es live auf der Fassade gezeigt wird.

Photo: rubra

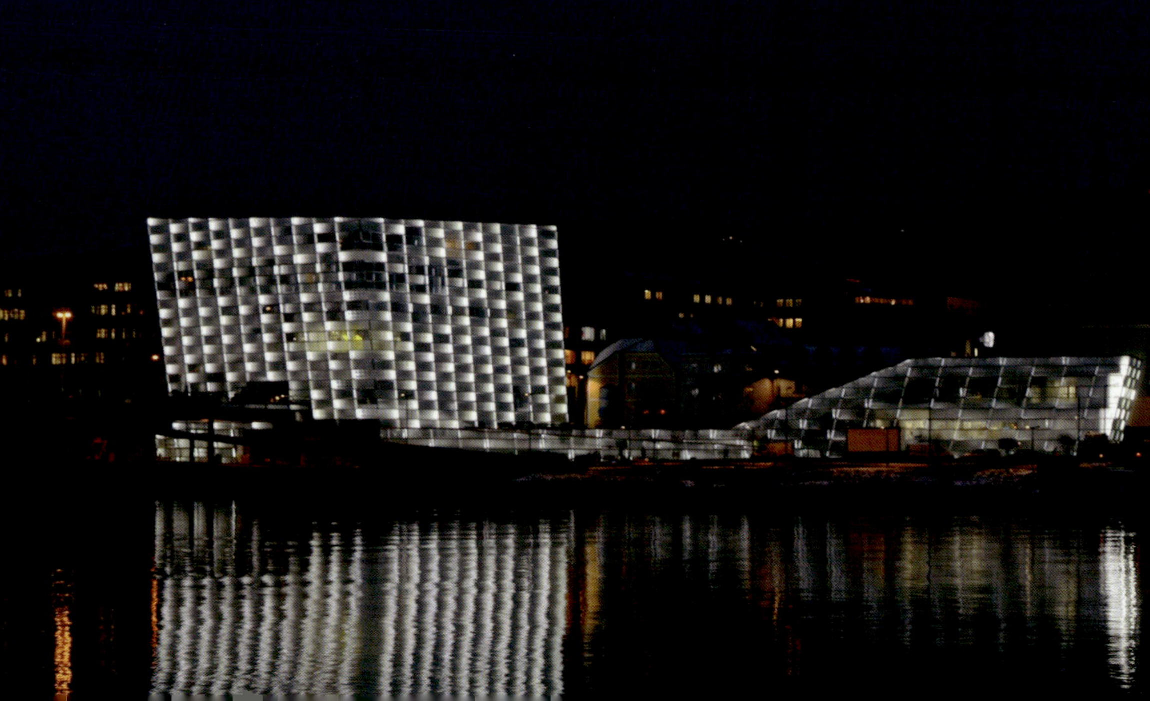

Lights On

For the opening of the new AEC, Zachary Lieberman and Daito Manabe were invited to be the first to put the façade through its artistic paces before an audience. What came out of this was a 10-minute visualization accompanied by a soundtrack that cuts in at particular moments, as well as a work based on the concept of a planetary clock that can be presented on an ongoing basis. The orbits of the planets control the movements of the colors on the façade while image of the surface of the sun produced by research satellites contribute dynamic lighting effects.

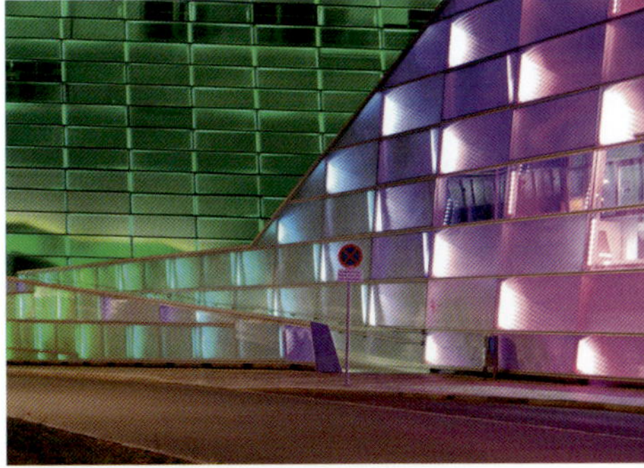
Photo: Severin Mayr

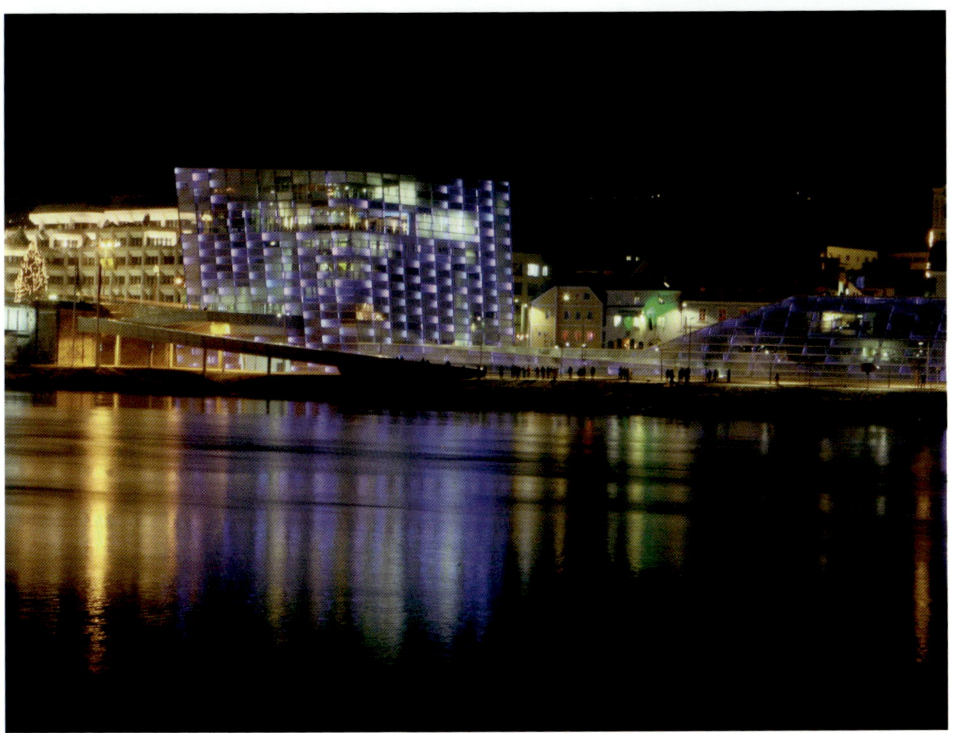

SMS Façade

Another prime option for putting the façade into action is direct interaction. Ars Electronica Futurelab staffers developed an SMS interface that can be used to control the façade's colors and patterns of movement. Of course, users can also send text messages to the façade.

Playing the Façade

Loudspeakers have also been integrated into the façade, which provides a simple way to stage a brief, daily façade event (comparable to an old-fashioned glockenspiel on the Main Square of some European cities). Specially commissioned musical artworks can be used; it's also possible to hook up an MP3 player to the façade and let prerecorded commercial music control the play of the colors. At these events, the SMS control feature will be turned on and the façade turned over to the audience.

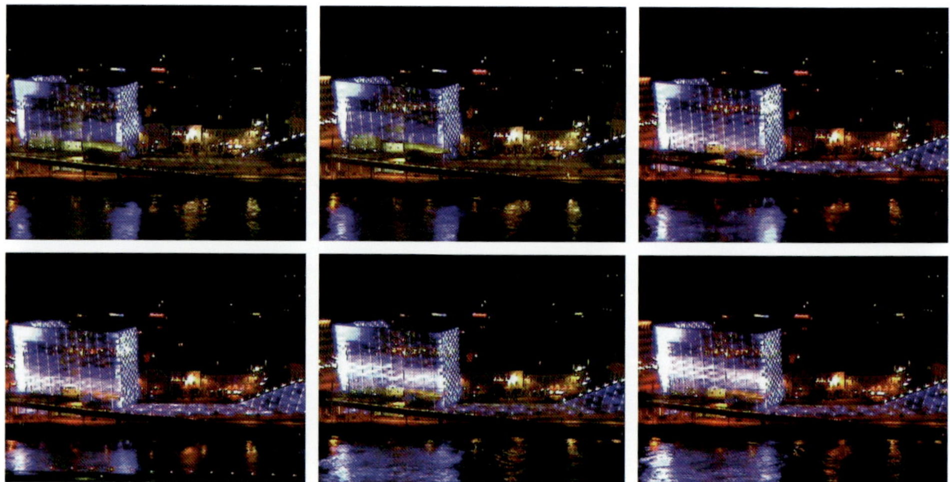

Pictures from the webcam constantly focused on the façade

Midnight Sun / Kilpiscope

In conjunction with *80+1 – A Journey around the World*, AEC has had the opportunity to work together with Laura Beloff, Erich Berger and other artists in Finland who spent some time at a research station in Kilpisjarvi, Lapland. There, they installed a webcam that's transmitting images of the midnight sun direct to the AEC façade in Linz. Although the façade's doesn't have high enough resolution to display images, it can give an impression of the shift of colors and the moods that creates.

Images from the webcam constantly aimed at the façade

Kilpisjärvi project development team: Beloff Laura, media artist, researcher; Berger Erich, media artist, curator; Järvinen Antero, professor at Helsinki University, director of the Kilpisjärvi Biological Station; Osva Anu, artist with science background

Partners: The Finnish Bio Art Society and the Kilpisjärvi Biological Station, Helsinki University

Façade Festival at Ars Electronica 2009

In conjunction with the 2009 Festival, the façade will become a large-scale public proving ground for interesting artistic approaches to the AEC's interactive media façade.

Five institutions of higher education (Linz Art University, Upper Austria University of Applied Sciences – Hagenberg Campus, Vienna University of Technology, University of Applied Arts Vienna and the St. Pölten University of Applied Sciences) as well as several individual artists have accepted our invitation and developed projects that will be presented on the façade of the Ars Electronica Center on the evenings of the Ars Electronica Festival. Every evening of the Façade Festival, we'll showcase different projects that illustrate the very broad spectrum of approaches to this creative challenge. They're subsumed under three main programmatic headings: Facade Music, Interact! and Visual Experiments.

Project supervision: Ars Electronica Futurelab, Christopher Lindinger, Maria Eschlböck; *project technical director:* Andreas Pramböck; *software development:* Andreas Pramböck, Roland Haring, Robert Hnatyk, Lukas Hostynski, joreg; *technical infrastructure:* Markus Schernhuber / Multivision; *individual artists:* Zachery Lieberman, Daito Manabe, Roland Haring, Andreas Gruber, Erich Berger

Vienna University of Technology, Department of Art & Design, University of Applied Arts Vienna, Department of Digital Art, *program directors:* Thomas Lorenz, Nicolaj Kirisits, Klaus Filip.
Projects by: Tim Blechmann, Juan C. Carvajal and Martin Grödl, Peter Linhart, Florian Gruber, Clemens Hausch and Peter Moosgard, Ulrich Kühn and Robert Zimmermann, Simon Repp, Achim Stromberger, Corinne Studer, Kathi Stumreich, Conny Zenk

University of Art and Industrial Design Linz, Interface Cultures, *program directors:* Dietmar Offenhuber, Mahir Mustafa Yavuz.
Projects by: Jayme Cochrane, Javier Lloret, Tim Devine, Sabina Dallu, Stefan Bandalac, Ulrike Gollner, Michael Probst, Basia Jol, Mar Canet-Sol

St. Pölten University of Applied Sciences, Department of Media Technology, *program directors:* Markus Seidl, Klaus Temper
Projects by: Kerstin Blumenstein, Thomas Eitler, Martin Grubinger, Roman Kuba, Maurice Wohlkönig

Upper Austria University of Applied Sciences - Hagenberg Campus, Digital Media masters program, *program directors:* Eno Henze, joreg
Projects by: Andreas Opferkuch, Anna Gruber, Bernadette Fellner, Christiane Eckl, Christoph Einfalt, Claudia Leeb, Claus Helfenschneider, Dominik Gottherr, Ingrid Stürmer, Johannes Eichberger, Karl Bergthaler, Kathrin Eder, Maria Hauer, Martin Lenzelbauer, Martin Pernsteiner, Nicole Pilkenroth, Philipp Horwath, Remo Rauscher, Stephan Müller, Veronika Pauser, David Steiner, Michael Markschläger, Ralph Windischhofer, Skoczylas Sven, Wolfgang Schroeck

The New Ars Electronica Center

Artistic Director
Gerfried Stocker

General Project Manager
Christopher Lindinger

Project and Production Managers:
Michael Badics, Florian Bauböck, Maria Eschelböck, Stefan Fuchs, Katharina, Maria Hengel, Gerold Hofstadler, Martin Honzik, Horst Hörtner, Thomas Kollmann, Wolfgang König, Daniela Kuka, Emiko Ogawa, Hideaki Ogawa,Irene Posch, Florian Wanninger, Sofya Yuditskaya, Sini Zein, Jochen Zeirzer.

Exhibition Design
Scott Ritter, Jakob Illera, Roland Ploner, Art+Com, Ars Electronica Futurelab

Architecture of the new building
TREUSCH architecture ZT GmbH

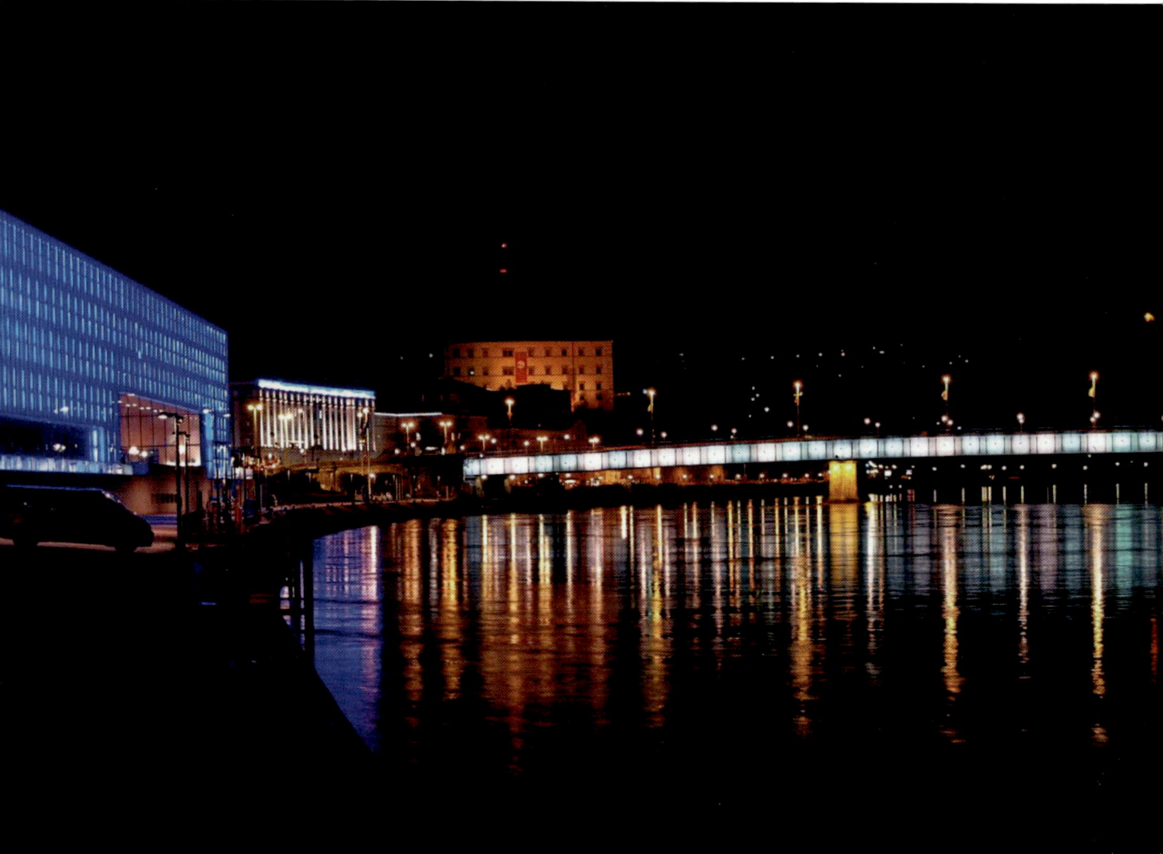

Photo: Andreas Keplinger

Construction Management of the new Building
Immobilien Linz GmbH, Landauer-TB GmbH

The Ars Electronica Center is a facility of the City of Linz and is supported by the Province of Upper Austria and sponsors from the private sector:

Many thanks to:
3DVIA Virtools, Activelink Co., Ltd., Amt der OÖ-Landesreg.Hydrographischer Dienst, Applied Biosystems, Art+Com, BARCO, Bene, BFI, CyArk, D-Torso, Elekit, Eppendorf, fab@home project, FEI Company, Festo GmbH, FH Oberösterreich Campus Wels – Bio- und Umwelttechnik, Future Robotics Technology Center, g tech medical engineering GmbH, gach edv agentur, Greiner Bio-One GmbH, Haltadefinizione.com, Hirox, Honda Europe, HP Hewlett-Packard GmbH, HTL Leonding, JST CREST, LIWEST, Mongoose Studio, Otto Bock Healthcare Products GmbH, PV Planungs- und Veranstaltungstechnik GmbH & Co. KG, RISC Software GmbH Hagenberg, Roche Applied Science, Schäfer Technologie, SIEMENS Österreich, Systec Akazawa, The University of Tokyo , Kawaguchi Lab, Ishikawa Lab, Trotec GmbH, Univ. Salzburg – Fachbereich Molekulare Biologie, voestalpine, Wacom, xRez Studio, Inc.

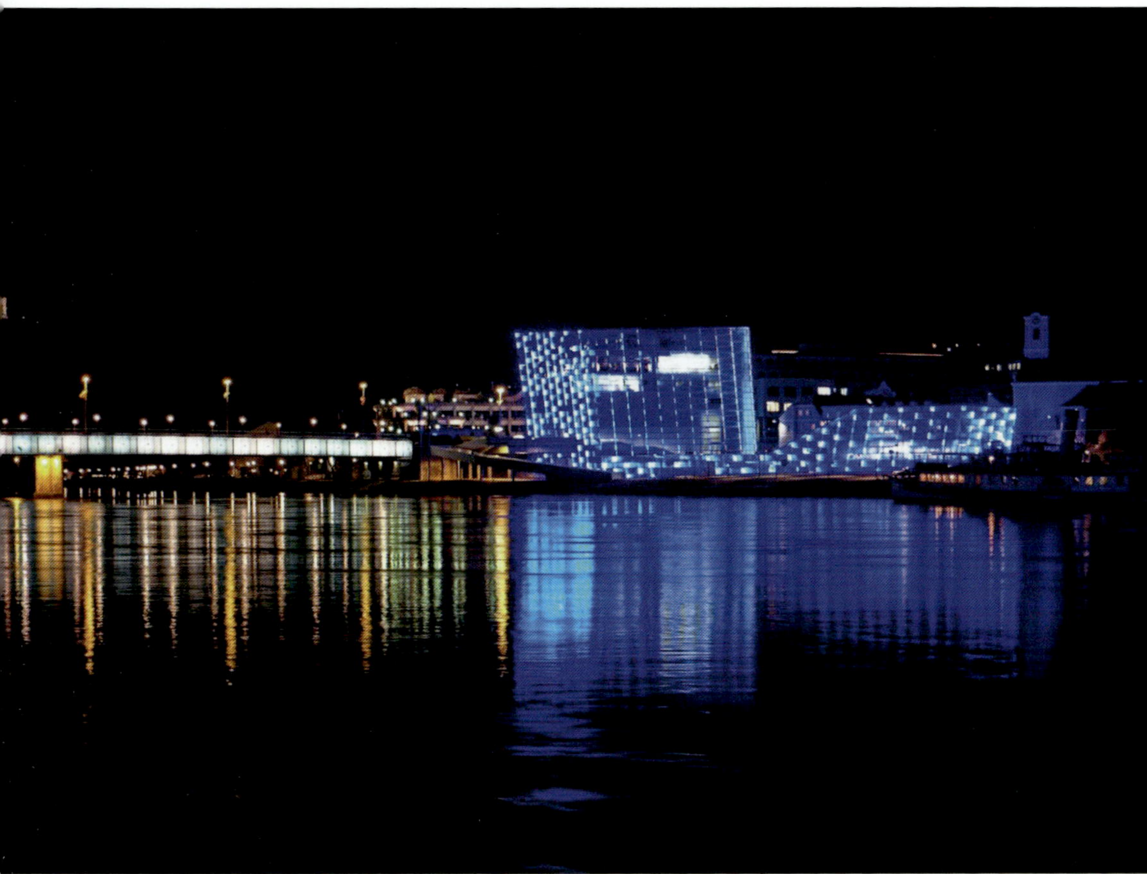

Geminoid HI-1

Why do we feel another person's presence? How can this presence be captured, revived, and transmitted? To tackle these mysteries, we have developed a new artificial being, *geminoid*. The word "geminoid" comes from the Latin *geminus*, meaning "twin" or "double," and a postfix *oides* which means "similarity". As the name suggests, a geminoid is a robot that will work as a duplicate of an existing person. Because they are closely connected by network and sensor technology, a geminoid not only appears but also behaves just like its source person.

Geminoid belongs to a new category of robots, which were originally planned to be test-beds for studying the individual nature of human beings. Whilst humanoid robots are good for studying the effectiveness of having a human-like body, and androids are used for seeking the general nature of humans, studies using geminoids focus on investigating the nature of individuality. Geminoids allow us to examine personal aspects, such as presence or personality traits, tracing their origins and implementing them into robots. Differences among people enable us to distinguish individuals and they emerge from complex combinations of various elements, such as appearance, facial expression, or ways of speaking. We intuitively know this from our daily experience, but until now scientific ways to examine this complex interplay have been rather limited. By using geminoids, we can systematically investigate the essentials of what makes a person an individual.

The first Geminoid prototype HI-1, created in 2006, was modeled on Dr. Hiroshi Ishiguro, Professor of Osaka University and visiting group leader of ATR Intelligent Robotics and Communication Laboratories. Since then numerous studies have been performed. Research with Geminoid takes two approaches: The first one follows the engineering approach that focuses on aspects such as the development of an effective teleoperation interface and the generation of natural human-like motion. The second follows the cognitive modeling approach to study aspects of human nature, such as "human presence". These two approaches in combination will eventually lead to both advanced robots that closely resemble humans and new insights on human nature.

Appearance of Geminoid

The appearance of a geminoid is based on an existing person and does not depend on the imagination of designers. Currently, two factors are considered: how a geminoid looks and how a geminoid moves. Similarity to the original person can be measured by comparing these two factors with those of the original. Also the existence of a real person analogous to the robot enables us to easily perform comparison studies. As HI-1 presented here is modeled after a researcher, we even have access to the source person's most personal subjective impressions. These insights are especially important at the very first stage of a new field of study.

In creating the first geminoid prototype HI-1, efforts were concentrated on making a robot that appears not just to resemble a living person, but also to be a copy of the original person. Silicone skin was molded using a cast taken from the original person; shape adjustments and skin textures were painted manually based on magnetic resonance imaging scans and photographs. Fifty pneumatic, i.e. air-pressure driven, actuators let the robot generate smooth and quiet

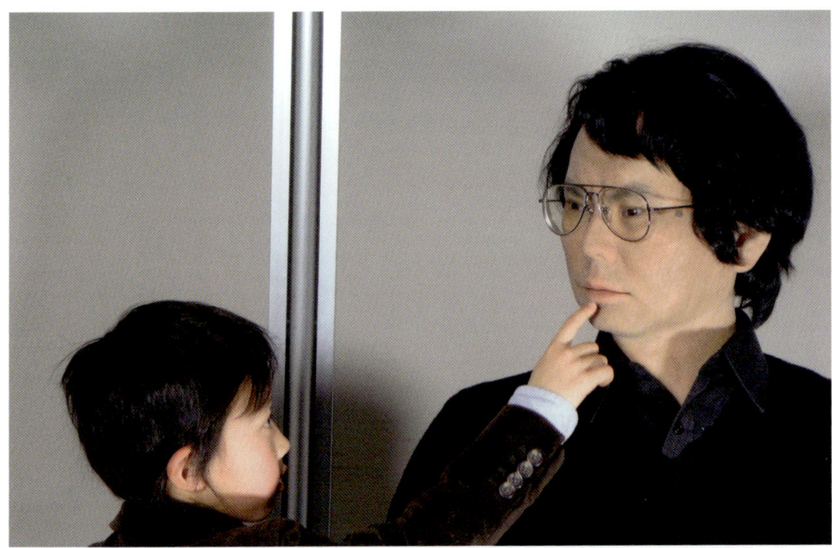

movements, which are important attributes when interacting with humans. The allocation of actuators was used so that the resulting robot can effectively show the necessary movements for human interaction and also allow for the recreation of the original person's personality traits. Of the 50 actuators, 13 are embedded in the face, 15 in the torso, and the remaining 22 move the arms and legs. The softness of the silicone skin and the compliant nature of the pneumatic actuators also provide safety while interacting with humans.

Teleoperation

So far several androids have been developed. Although these androids enabled us to conduct a variety of cognitive experiments, their functionality was still quite limited. The bottleneck in interaction with humans is an android's inability to perform long-term conversations. Robots equipped with artificial intelligence cannot yet perform at a level comparable to that of adult humans and still respond in a simple manner. This heavily constrains research on human-robot interaction. Thus, our solution to this problem lies in combining androids with teleoperation technology. Using teleoperation, we can immediately start researching and implementing high-level human interaction, shedding light on mysteries such as human presence.

The teleoperation system with which every geminoid is equipped also allows us to tackle a more philosophical question: whether a human's "mind" is separable from his or her "body". In geminoids, the operator (mind) can easily be exchanged, while the robot (body) remains the same. In addition, the strength of connection—that is how much information of which kind is exchanged between a geminoid's body and an operator's mind—can easily be reconfigured. This is especially important when taking a top-down approach that adds or deletes elements from a person to discover the "critical" elements that constitute a human's character. Before the era of geminoids, this research methodology was impossible.

Some operator movements are captured, converted and transmitted to drive geminoids. These include, for example, lip motions while speaking and head movements while looking around. The operator can also explicitly send commands for controlling android behavior using a simple graphical user interface. Several selected movements, such as nodding, opposing, or staring in a certain direction, can be triggered with a single mouse click. This relatively simple interface was

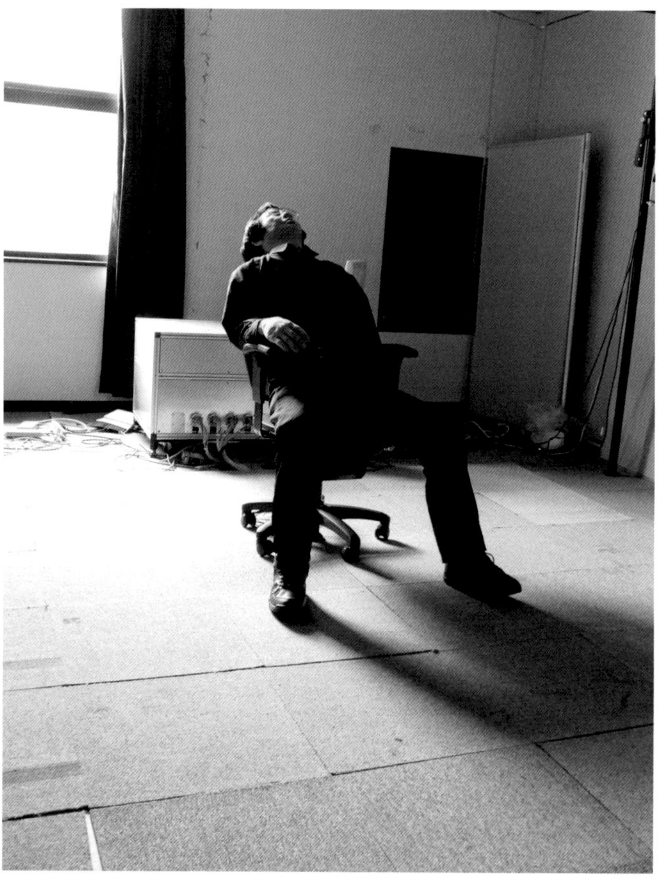

used because the robot has 50 degrees of freedom, which make it one of the world's most complex robots. This huge amount of actuators cannot be manipulated manually in real time. Thus, a simple, intuitive interface was conceived so that the operator can concentrate on the interaction itself and does not have to think much about how to drive the androids' behavior. Despite its simplicity this interface enables the operator to generate natural humanlike motions for the robot, with the help of the geminoid management system.

The teleoperation system also maintains the state of interaction and generates autonomous movements for the robot, which are driven unconsciously in humans. With a robot's appearance nearly matching that of a human, its behavior should also become suitably sophisticated to retain a "natural" look. A human never stops breathing or eye blinking, because these easily observable kinds of behavior are driven unconsciously by the autonomic nervous system. Most robots, however, lack these movements. Thus, to increase a geminoid's naturalness, the geminoid management system emulates a human's autonomic nervous system by automatically generating these micro-movements, depending on the state of interaction. When the android is "speaking," its micro-movements are different from those triggered when it is "listening" to others. These automatic robot motions, generated without an operator's explicit orders, are merged with explicit operation commands from the teleoperation interface.

Android Science

If we could build an android that is very similar to a human, how can we distinguish a real human from an android? The answer is not trivial. While interacting with androids, we cannot see their internal mechanisms and thus we may simply believe that they are human.

We propose to use androids that behave similarly to humans for studying what it essentially means to "be human", i.e. the mystery of human nature. Androids and geminoids are artificial humans that allow us to investigate human nature by means of psychological and cognitive tests, which we conduct during interaction with people. This new approach for understanding humans is called *Android Science*.

Current robotics research builds upon findings from the field of cognitive science, especially in the area of human-robot interaction. Robotics researchers try to adopt mechanisms underlying successful human-human interaction to create robots that people can easily communicate with. At the same time, cognitive scientists have begun to utilize robots. As the scientific understanding of complex, higher-level human functions steadily increases, expectations will rise for robots to function as easily controlled machines with communicative ability. However, the contribution from robotics to cognitive science has not been adequate because the appearance and behavior of current robots cannot be separately handled. Since traditional robots look quite mechanical and very different from human beings, their appearance strongly influences a human's expectations. As a result, researchers cannot clarify whether a specific finding reflects the robot's appearance, its movement, or a combination of both.

We expect to solve this problem using androids, which closely resemble humans in their appearance and behavior. To achieve this goal, an objective, quantitative means to measure the effect of appearance is required, which forms part of our research endeavor.

In summary, our motivation is twofold: On the one hand, a major robotics issue in the construction of androids is the development of humanlike appearance, movements, and perception functions. On the other hand, cognitive scientists are aiming to gain insights into the processes leading to "conscious and unconscious recognition." The goal of android science is to realize a humanlike robot and to find the essential factors for representing human likeness. How can we define human likeness? Further, how do we perceive human likeness? It is commonly assumed that humans have conscious and unconscious recognition. When we observe others, various brain areas are activated. Each of them matches sensory input with human models, thereby modulating our response behaviors. These unconscious processes let us, for example, treat an android as if it were a human partner in conversation, although we consciously recognize it as what it is: a robotic system with very humanlike appearance. This is a fundamental issue for both engineering and scientific approaches. It will be an evaluation criterion in android development and helpful for understanding the mechanisms of human brains that make us social and emotional creatures.

Geminoid HI-1

Warum spüren wir die Präsenz anderer Menschen? Wie können Präsenz und Wesenszüge eines Menschen erfasst, simuliert und auf Roboter übertragen werden? Zur Lösung dieses Rätsels haben wir ein komplexes künstliches Wesen geschaffen, den Geminoiden. Das Wort „Geminoid" setzt sich aus dem Lateinischen *geminus* (Zwilling, Pärchen) und dem Suffix *-oides* zusammen. Wie schon der Name erahnen lässt, ist ein Geminoid ein Roboter, der als Klon eines real existierenden Menschen geschaffen wurde. Weil Roboter und Mensch dabei durch eine innovative Netzwerk- und Sensorentechnologie eng miteinander vernetzt sind, sieht ein Geminoid nicht nur wie sein Vorbild aus Fleisch und Blut aus, sondern verhält sich auch so.

Geminoide sind eine neue Klasse von Robotern, die ursprünglich als Objekte zur Erforschung der menschlichen Individualität eingesetzt werden sollten. Während humanoide Roboter zur Untersuchung eines möglichst effizienten Einsatzes derartiger menschenähnlicher Maschinen eingesetzt werden, werden Androide allgemein zur Erforschung der menschlichen Natur genutzt. Studien auf der Basis von Geminoiden untersuchen hingegen das Wesen der menschlichen Individualität. Mit Geminoiden können typisch menschliche Eigenschaften, etwa Präsenz oder Persönlichkeitsmerkmale, untersucht werden; es wird versucht, den Ursprung individueller menschlicher Wesenszüge ausfindig zu machen und auf Roboter zu übertragen. Unterschiede zwischen den Menschen erlauben uns, zwischen Individuen zu unterscheiden; diese Unterschiede entstehen aus dem komplexen Zusammenspiel verschiedener Faktoren, etwa Aussehen, Gesichtsausdruck und Sprechweise. Aus Erfahrung wissen wir intuitiv, dass es derartige Unterschiede gibt. Bis jetzt gab es jedoch wenig Möglichkeiten, dieses komplexe Zusammenspiel verschiedener Eigenschaften wissenschaftlich zu erfassen. Mithilfe von Geminoiden können wir systematisch untersuchen, was einen Menschen zu einem Individuum werden lässt.

Für den ersten Prototyp eines Geminoiden, HI-1, stand 2006 Hiroshi Ishiguro Modell, Professor an der Universität Osake und Gastgruppenleiter der *ATR Intelligent Robotics and Communication Laboratories*. Seit 2006 werden Geminoide für verschiedene Forschungszwecke genutzt. Bei der Geminoid-Forschung können zwei Ansätze unterschieden werden: Der eine ist techniklastig und konzentriert sich auf die Entwicklung eines funktionellen Fernsteuerungsmechanismus und die Programmierung möglichst natürlicher menschenähnlicher Bewegungen. Der andere konzentriert sich auf kognitive Modellierung zur Untersuchung typischer Eigenschaften der menschlichen Natur, etwa der „menschlichen Präsenz". Die Kombination dieser beiden Ansätze führt schließlich zur Entwicklung ausgereifter Roboter, die dem Menschen stark ähneln und neue Einblicke in die menschliche Natur gewähren.

Aussehen eines Geminoiden

Das Aussehen eines Geminoiden ist einem lebenden Menschen nachempfunden und bleibt nicht der Fantasie der Designer überlassen. Zwei Faktoren sind maßgebend: wie der Geminoid aussieht und wie er sich bewegt. Der Grad der Ähnlichkeit mit dem Original kann durch einen Vergleich dieser beiden Aspekte (Aussehen und Bewegung) mit dem Original ermittelt werden. Durch eine Gegenüberstellung mit gleichzeitig anwesenden „echten" Menschen können auf einfache Weise Vergleichsstudien durchgeführt werden. Da HI-1 in seiner aktuellen Ausgestaltung einem Forscher nachempfunden wurde, haben wir sogar Zugang zu persönlichen, subjektiven Eindrücken des Originals aus Fleisch und Blut. Für ein neues Forschungsfeld wie die Geminoid-Forschung sind derart subjektive Einblicke überaus wichtig.

Bei der Entwicklung des ersten Geminoid-Prototypen HI-1 wurde versucht, einen Roboter zu schaffen, der einer lebenden Person nicht nur ähnelt, sondern als Kopie des Originals durchgehen könnte. Das Skelett wurde mit einer Silikonhaut überzogen, die von einem Abdruck des menschlichen Vorbilds angefertigt wurde; Form und Textur der Haut wurden auf der Grundlage von MR-Bildern und Fotografien manuell nachbearbeitet. Fünfzig pneumatische Aktuatoren lassen die Bewegungen des Roboters geschmeidig und ruhig aussehen, was für eine Interaktion mit dem Menschen ein entscheidender Aspekt ist. Die Aktuatoren wurden so verteilt, dass der Roboter alle für eine Interaktion mit dem Menschen nötigen Bewegungsabläufe beherrscht; darüber hinaus wurden auch die typischen Persönlichkeitsmerkmale des Vorbilds repliziert. Von den 50 Aktuatoren sind 13 im Gesicht angebracht, 15 am Rumpf, und die restlichen 22 dienen der Steuerung von Armen und Beinen. Die Weichheit der Silikonhaut und die Nachgiebigkeit der Pneumo-Aktuatoren machen eine Interaktion mit dem Menschen gefahrlos.

Teleoperation

Es wurden bereits mehrere Androide entwickelt. Obwohl mit diesen verschiedene kognitive Experimente durchgeführt werden konnten, war ihre Funktionalität noch relativ beschränkt. Das größte Hindernis bei der Interaktion mit dem Menschen ist die Unfähigkeit von Androiden, ein Gespräch über einen längeren Zeitraum aufrechtzuerhalten. Mit künstlicher Intelligenz ausgestattete Roboter interagieren noch nicht auf einem Niveau, das demjenigen erwachsener Menschen entspricht, ihre Antworten sind relativ einfach. Diese Tatsache schränkt die Forschung zur Mensch-Roboter-Interaktion stark ein. Die Lösung sind mit einem Teleoperationsmechanismus ausgestattete Androiden. Durch Teleoperation können wir komplexe menschliche Interaktion erforschen und nachahmen und so Licht in lange gehütete Geheimnisse der Menschheit bringen, etwa die menschliche Präsenz.

Das Teleoperationssystem, mit dem alle Geminoiden ausgestattet sind, führt uns auch zu einer ungleich philosophischeren Frage: Kann der menschliche „Geist" von seinem „Körper" losgelöst werden? Bei Geminoiden kann der Operator (Geist) einfach ausgetauscht werden, während stets derselbe Roboter (Körper) zum Einsatz kommt. Die übertragene Datenmenge, d.h. wie viele und welche Informationen zwischen dem Körper des Geminoiden und dem Geist des Operators ausgetauscht werden, kann einfach neu konfiguriert werden. Das ist besonders bei einem Top-down-Zugang wichtig, wenn bestimmte menschliche Eigenschaften neu hinzugefügt oder gelöscht werden, um die entscheidenden Attribute herauszufiltern, die den menschlichen Charakter ausmachen. Vor der Entwicklung der ersten Geminoiden war dieser methodische Zugang nicht denkbar.

Manche Körperfunktionen des Operators werden zur Steuerung des Geminoiden aufgezeichnet, adaptiert und an den Roboter übertragen, etwa Lippenbewegungen beim Sprechen oder Kopfbewegungen beim Umsehen. Über ein einfaches grafisches User-Interface kann der Operator auch direkt Befehle zur Steuerung des Verhaltens des Androiden geben. Bestimmte Bewegungen wie etwa Nicken, Verneinen oder Starren in eine Richtung können mit einem einzigen Mausklick aktiviert werden. Dieses relativ einfache Interface wurde erarbeitet, weil der Roboter über 50 verschiedene Freiheitsgrade verfügt, was ihn zu einem der komplexesten Roboter weltweit macht. Es wäre nicht möglich, diese große Zahl von Aktuatoren manuell zu steuern. Daher wurde ein einfaches, intuitiv bedienbares Interface entwickelt, damit der Operator sich auf die Interaktion selbst konzentrieren kann und nicht übermäßig mit der Steuerung des Verhaltens des Androiden befasst ist. Trotz der einfachen Struktur des Interface kann der Operator mithilfe des Steuersystems möglichst natürliche menschenähnliche Bewegungsabläufe generieren. Das Teleoperationssystem hält die Interaktion aufrecht und generiert auch autonome Bewegungen und Funktionen, die beim Menschen willkürlich erfolgen. Der Roboter ähnelt im Aussehen dem Menschen sehr stark, weshalb auch sein Verhalten entsprechend komplex und „natürlich" wirken sollte. Beim Menschen werden bestimmte unwillkürliche Körperfunktionen wie die Atmung oder Lidbewegungen über das vegetative Nervensystem gesteuert und können nicht direkt beeinflusst werden. Den meisten Robotern fehlen diese Funktionen. Zur Maximierung der Natürlichkeit der Bewegungen von Robotern kopiert das Steuersystem des Geminoiden das menschliche vegetative Nervensystem und generiert, je nach Art der Interaktion, automatisch derartige Mikrobewegungen. Wenn der Roboter „spricht", unterscheiden sich diese Mikrobewegungen von jenen, die ausgelöst werden, wenn der Roboter anderen „zuhört". Diese Roboterbewegungen erfolgen automatisiert und können nicht vom Operator generiert werden; sie werden in der Interaktion durch direkte Befehle, die der Operator über das Teleoperationsinterface gibt, ergänzt.

Android Science

Wenn wir einen Androiden schaffen könnten, der dem Menschen stark ähnelt, wie können wir dann einen echten Menschen von einem Androiden unterscheiden? Die Antwort auf diese Frage ist nicht einfach. Bei der Interaktion mit Androiden können wir die internen Mechanismen, die den Roboter steuern, nicht sehen und glauben daher vielleicht, dass es sich um einen Menschen handelt. Wir propagieren zur Untersuchung typisch „menschlicher" Eigenschaften die Nutzung von Androiden, die ein menschenähnliches Verhalten aufweisen, um so dem Geheimnis der menschlichen Natur auf den Grund zu gehen. Androide und Geminoide sind künstliche Wesen, die mithilfe psychologischer und kognitiver Tests, die während der Interaktion mit dem Menschen durchgeführt werden, die Erforschung der menschlichen Natur ermöglichen. Dieser neue Ansatz zur Erforschung der Natur des Menschen kann als *Android Science* bezeichnet werden.
Die moderne Roboterforschung baut auf Erkenntnissen aus dem Bereich der Kognitionswissenschaften auf, besonders auf der Forschung zur Mensch-Roboter-Interaktion. Forscher versuchen, jene Mechanismen, die einer erfolgreichen Mensch-Mensch-Interaktion zugrunde liegen, auf Roboter zu übertragen, um so Roboter zu schaffen, mit denen der Mensch einfach kommunizieren kann. Zeitgleich haben nun auch Kognitionswissenschaftler begonnen, sich für Roboter zu interessieren. Die Wissenschaft gewinnt stets neue Einblicke in komplexe, vielschichtige menschliche Funktionen; damit steigen auch die Erwartungen an Roboter: Diese sollen möglichst einfach zu bedienen sein, aber dennoch über die Fähigkeit zur Kommunikation verfügen. Weder die Roboterwissenschaft noch die Kognitionswissenschaft können allein zufriedenstellende Ergebnisse liefern, da Aussehen und Verhalten von Robotern nicht voneinander losgelöst betrachtet werden können. Da traditionelle Roboter nach wie vor ein sehr mechanisches Aussehen haben und sich stark vom Menschen unterscheiden, beeinflusst ihr Erscheinungsbild stark die menschlichen Erwartungen. Forscher können daher nicht sicher feststellen, ob ein spezifisches Ergebnis auf das Aussehen eines Roboters, seine Bewegungen oder eine Kombination dieser

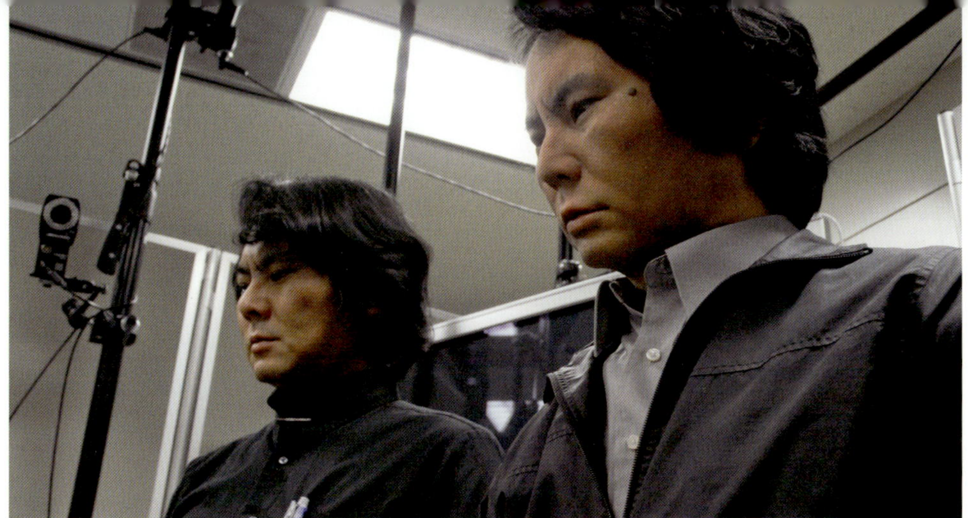

beiden Aspekte zurückzuführen ist. Wir hoffen, dass wir dieses Problem durch die Nutzung von Androiden lösen können, die dem Menschen sowohl im Aussehen als auch im Verhalten stark ähneln. Zur Umsetzung dieses Ziels benötigen wir auch objektive, quantitative Möglichkeiten zur Messung des Einflusses, den das Aussehen von Robotern auf das menschliche Verhalten ihnen gegenüber hat – dies ist Teil unserer Forschung.

Wir verfolgen dabei zwei Ziele: Zum einen ist die Entwicklung eines möglichst menschenähnlichen Aussehens, menschlicher Bewegungen und Wahrnehmungsfunktionen ein zentraler Aspekt bei der Entwicklung von Androiden. Zum anderen versuchen Kognitionswissenschaftler neue Einblicke in jene Prozesse zu gewinnen, die „bewusstes und unbewusstes Erkennen" steuern. Das Ziel der Android-Forschung ist die Schaffung eines möglichst menschenähnlichen Roboters und die Erforschung der für eine möglichst große Menschenähnlichkeit zentralen Faktoren. Wie kann man Menschenähnlichkeit definieren? Wie nehmen wir Menschenähnlichkeit wahr? Es wird allgemein angenommen, dass Menschen Reize sowohl auf einer bewussten als auch einer unbewussten Ebene wahrnehmen. Wenn wir andere beobachten, sind verschiedene Gehirnareale aktiv. Sensorischer Input wird dabei automatisch mit bereits bekannten menschlichen Vorbildern verglichen; dadurch werden unsere Reaktionen gesteuert. Diese unbewussten Prozesse führen dazu, dass wir beispielsweise einen Androiden behandeln, als wäre er ein menschlicher Gesprächspartner, obwohl wir auf einer bewussten Ebene erkennen, was unser Gegenüber ist: ein Robotersystem mit einem stark menschenähnlichen Aussehen. Dies ist eine zentrale Frage, sowohl für die Robotertechnik als auch für verschiedene andere wissenschaftliche Disziplinen. Die Antworten darauf können als Kriterien für die Entwicklung von Androiden dienen und Aufschluss über jene Prozesse des menschlichen Gehirns geben, die uns zu sozialen und emotional gesteuerten Wesen machen.

(Aus dem Englischen von Sonja Pöllabauer)

Shen Shaomin
Bones of Contention

Shen Shaomin's skeletons of imaginary creatures send one's thoughts back to the debates generated by Charles Darwin's "dangerous idea", and forward to the Faustian ambitions of contemporary science. The bones of humans and animals we dig from the earth are the most basic and poignant proofs of existence. They testify to the act of being, and—in the hands of forensic scientists—provide clues as to the physical appearance and properties of the living creature. They do not, however, tell us anything about the mind or the personality that was once contained by that carriage of bones. Science deals in facts and leaves art to provide the imaginative and sentimental elements. It is one of the abiding conceits of Shen's work that the artist mimics the role of the natural scientists. He presents us with a museum of relics that seem, at first glance, to have been excavated by archaeologists. We look upon a skeletal menagerie that has never truly existed, although the bones and bone meal he uses have been drawn from real animals. This gives his creations an uncanny verisimilitude—they are eerily reminiscent of Dr. Frankenstein's experiments in stitching together a new life from remnants of the dead.

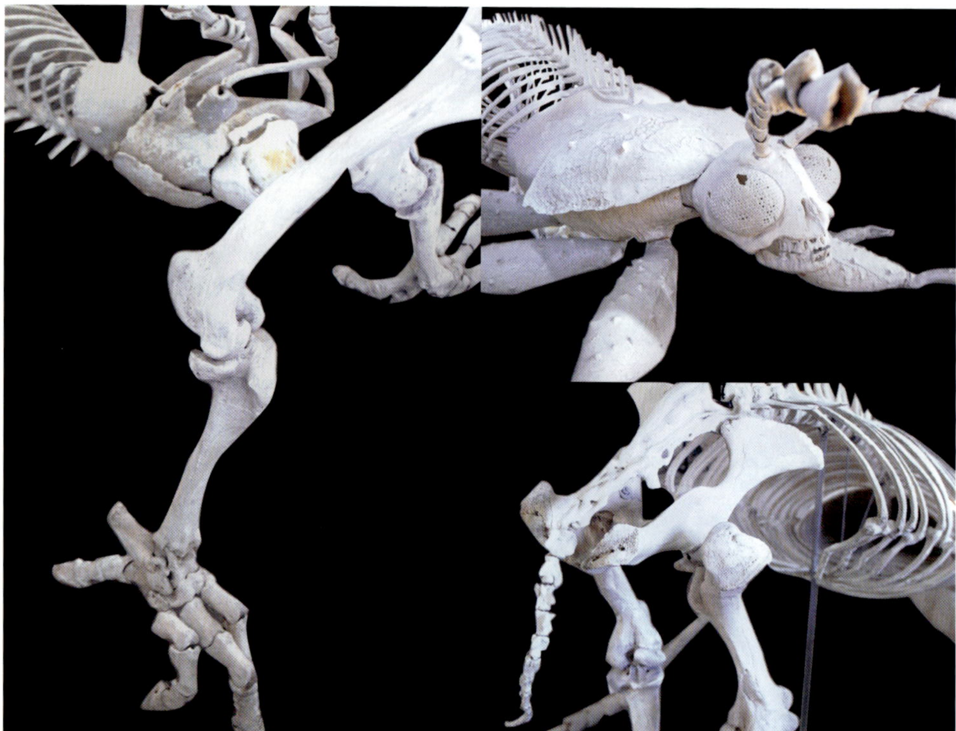

Unknown Creatures No. 2

Part of the impact of Shen's work comes from his willingness to create strange hybrids between species and to upset conventional expectations about scale. Some of his creatures resemble gigantic insects, in the manner of the bug-eyed monsters of the B-movies, yet they may have elements suggestive of fish or animal forms. The many small pieces in installations such as Experimental Field No.2, are combinations of animal and vegetable, as though small, sharp-clawed creatures were growing from between the leaves of a Chinese cabbage. In another work, the skeletal infants have been nurtured inside cocoons that look like huge pea pods. These clustered sculptures are even more disturbing than the large individual pieces, insofar as they portray a deliberate breeding program, with some anonymous intelligence at work behind the scenes.

There is a warning here about science running out of control, but also a delight in theatrical detail—in the sense that each piece acts as a prop in some unknown narrative. Shen never aims to capture a completely lifelike illusion, in the manner of a sculptor such as Ron Mueck, he shows us only the relics of life. His creatures are not only dead, they have been frozen stiff by some sudden disaster, as bodies were embalmed by volcanic ash during the destruction of Pompeii. He apparently suggests that there are deathly consequences when scientists go wading boldly into the gene pool.

There is a double irony in these works being made by a Chinese artist, because China, of all nations, has had one of the most ruthless attitudes towards the exploitation of the natural world. Mao's Promethean vision saw Nature as an unruly resource that had to be subdued at all costs, and parts of the country will long suffer the effects of pollution. With the introduction of a market economy, and China's rapid ascension to the point where it is now the world's largest industrial consumer of raw materials, there may be much worse to come. It is, perhaps, a further irony that Shaomin makes these works in an old factory in a northern industrial city, playing foreman to a team of assistants.

As China's industrial and trading might continues to grow, it also continues to send exhibitions of archaeological finds to international museums. Even during the worst days of the Cultural Revolution, Chinese authorities were always ready to conjure up a show of recently-discovered relics, to suggest an ongoing concern with national heritage. In more open and friendly times, these shows have flourished. Many who viewed Shen's sculptures when shown at Gallery 4a in Sydney, in June 2004, may have seen an exhibition of Chinese dinosaur bones last year at the Australian Museum. It is difficult to know whether one should emphasise the differences between the two shows or the similarities. In one sweeping gesture, Shaomin satirises the overwhelming hubris of science, and the timeless appeal of the touring dinosaur show. He points out where science and popular culture intersect—in our fascination with the skeletons of vanished behemoths and those small but sinister genetic experiments waiting to be born.

(Text: John McDonald)

Shen Shaomin
Bones of Contention

Shen Shaomins Skelettskulpturen imaginärer Wesen erinnern an die von Darwins „gefährlicher Idee" ausgelösten Debatten und gemahnen an die Faust'schen Umtriebe der modernen Wissenschaft. Die bei Ausgrabungen gefundenen Knochenreste von Menschen und Tieren sind zentrale und nachhaltige Beweise für deren Existenz. Sie dienen als Beleg für menschliches und tierisches Leben und in den Händen der Forensiker liefern sie Aufschluss über Aussehen und Körpereigenschaften jener Wesen, deren Körper sie einst stützten. Sie liefern jedoch keine Informationen über die Wesenszüge oder die Persönlichkeit, die diese Knochen einst umhüllten. Wissenschaft basiert auf Fakten; sie überlässt es der Kunst, sich mit Gedankenkonstrukten und Gefühlen auseinanderzusetzen. Shaomins Arbeiten sind insofern vermessen, als der Künstler die Rolle des Naturwissenschaftlers übernimmt. Er führt uns in ein Museum der Relikte, die, so scheint es auf den ersten Blick, aus archäologischen Funden stammen. Wir sehen eine Menagerie von Skeletten vor uns, die in dieser Form nie existierten, auch wenn Knochen und Tiermehl der Skulpturen von echten Tieren stammen. Dies verleiht den von ihm geschaffenen Geschöpfen eine verblüffende Echtheit. Sie erinnern auf unheimliche Weise an Frankensteins Experimente, der aus den Überresten von Toten neues Leben schaffen wollte.

[...]

Shens Werke sind beeindruckend, weil er seltsam anmutende Hybride aus verschiedenen Arten kreiert und mit den gängigen Erwartungen an die Größe dieser Wesen bricht. Manche seiner Skulpturen ähneln – wie die glupschäugigen Monster aus B-Movies – riesigen Insekten; und erinnern gleichzeitig oft an Fische oder andere Tiere. Die vielen kleinen Komponenten von Installationen wie *Experimental Field No. 2* sind Hybride aus Tieren und Gemüsesorten, etwa als ob den Blättern eines Chinakohlkopfs kleine Wesen mit scharfen Klauen entspringen würden. In einem anderen Werk zeigt Shen Säuglingsskelette in Kokons, die wie riesige Erbsen anmuten. Diese Cluster-Skulpturen sind ungleich verstörender als die großen Einzelwerke, da sie ein von anonymen Kräften im Hintergrund gelenktes Zuchtprogramm andeuten.

Diese Werke dienen als Warnung vor einer außer Kontrolle geratenden Wissenschaft. Ihre Gestaltung zeigt aber ebenso eine unglaubliche Liebe zum Detail, wie bei einem Theaterstück: Jedes Exponat fungiert als Requisite in einer uns unbekannten Erzählung. Shen möchte nie eine völlig lebensechte Kopie schaffen, wie

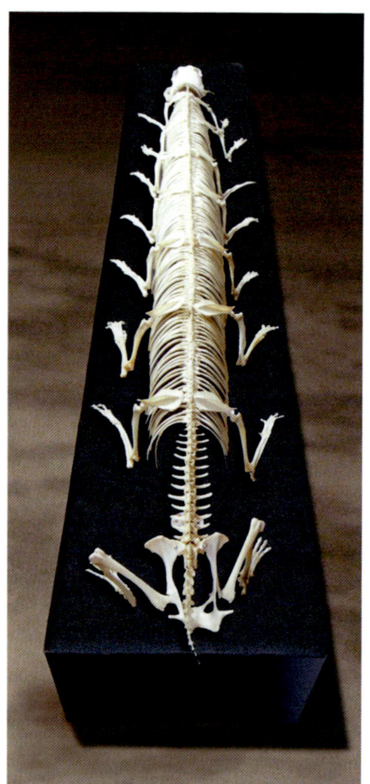

Unknown Creature No. 18. Multiped 18

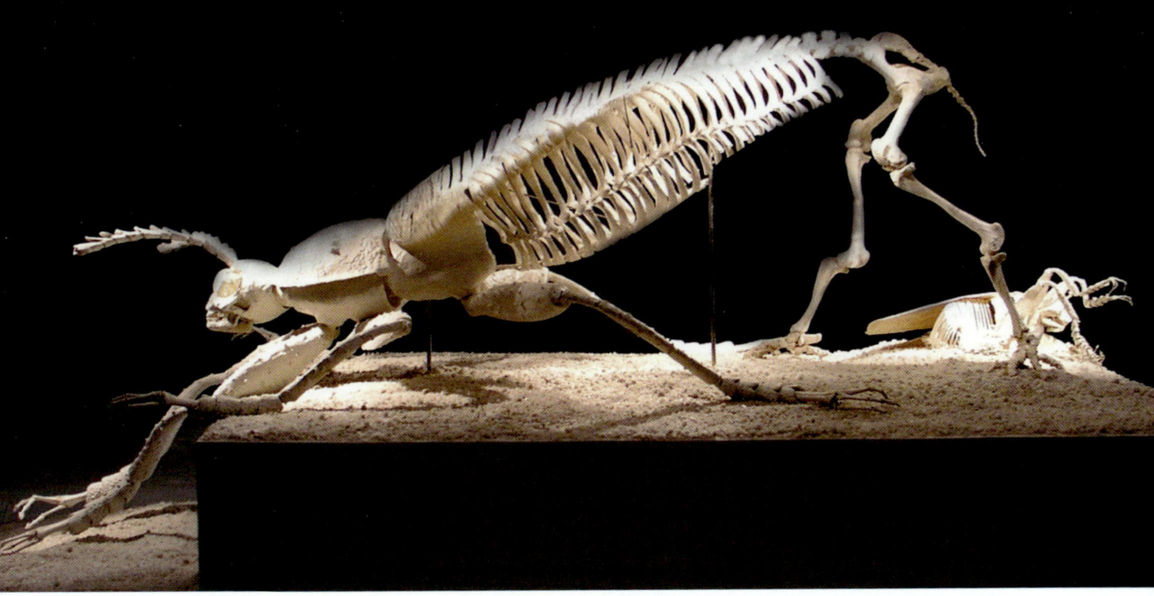

Unknown Creatures No. 2

dies manche Bildhauer, etwa Ron Mueck, versuchen – er zeigt lediglich die sterblichen Überreste des Lebens. Die von ihm geschaffenen Wesen sind nicht nur tot, sondern wurden wie bei einer plötzlichen eintretenden Katastrophe petrifiziert, wie beim Ausbruch des Vesuvs in Pompeji die Menschen in der Vulkanasche konserviert wurden. Er will damit vor den potentiell tödlichen Folgen warnen, die eintreten könnten, wenn Wissenschaftler leichtsinnig mit dem globalen Genpool experimentieren.

In den Werken dieses chinesischen Künstlers zeigt sich eine doppelte Ironie, da ausgerechnet China zu jenen Ländern zählt, in denen die Naturressourcen der Erde rücksichtslos ausgebeutet werden. Maos prometheusartige Vision sah die Natur als widerspenstige, unbändige Ressource, die sich der Mensch mit allen Mitteln untertan machen muss. Große Teile Chinas werden noch lange an den Folgen der Umweltverschmutzung leiden. Mit der Einführung der Marktwirtschaft und dem raschen Aufstieg Chinas zu einem der größten industriellen Rohstoffkonsumenten könnte sich die Situation noch wesentlich verschlimmern. Eine weitere Ironie dieser Werke ist vielleicht, dass Shen als Vorarbeiter eines Teams von Helfern seine Skulpturen in einer alten Fabrik in einer Industriestadt im Norden Chinas herstellt.

Handel und Industrie könnten in China weiter zulegen. China vermittelt internationalen Museen auch weiterhin Sammlungen archäologischer Funde. Sogar während der schlimmsten Phasen der Kulturrevolution waren die chinesischen Behörden stets bereit neu entdeckte Funde in Ausstellungen zu präsentieren, um ihrem Interesse am chinesischen Nationalerbe Ausdruck zu verleihen. In offeneren und freundlicheren Zeiten florieren derartige Veranstaltungen. Viele Besucher, die im Juni 2004 Shens Skulpturen in der Gallery 4a in Sydney sahen, besuchten vielleicht letztes Jahr auch eine Ausstellung chinesischer Dinosaurierknochen im Australian Museum. Es ist schwierig zu entscheiden, ob man die Unterschiede oder die Ähnlichkeiten zwischen diesen beiden Ausstellungen unterstreichen soll. Shaomin parodiert auf beeindruckende Weise die anmaßende Überheblichkeit der Wissenschaft und den zeitlosen Reiz der Dinosaurierausstellung. Er zeigt anschaulich die Schnittflächen zwischen Wissenschaft und Volkskultur auf – unsere Faszination für die Skelette bereits ausgestorbener Ungeheuer und jene kleinen, unheimlichen Genexperimente, die noch ihrer Umsetzung harren.

(Text: John McDonald, aus dem Englischen von Sonja Pöllabauer)

Chance = Change
On the Work of Lawrence Malstaf

The first time I was confronted with the work of Lawrence Malstaf was at a theatre performance. *Sauna in exile* was a project he had done with Mette Edvardsen, Heine Avdal and Liv Hanne Haugen. It had a lasting impression on me. As is the case with all work from Lawrence Malstaf, the starting point is very clear and simple. In the middle of the room there was a sauna that was surrounded with all kinds of chill out zones where you could listen to music, see video performances or just have a drink. But the real heart of the performance is the sauna itself—the genuine article because the visitors have to get into his or her bathrobes to enter the installation. Once naked you surrender yourself to the hot air—and before you know it an equally naked actor introduces you to the use of vihta, tree branches that stimulate your blood flow. A few people even evaporate on the scene and minutes later you witness the start of a choreography.

That choreography also evaporates into the heat and sweat. And right here is the essence of the work: evaporation. Being naked and in bathrobes all difference between "visitor" and "actor" disappears. I am in the sauna, naked and I am on the scene, evaporating. Maybe I even look like an actor if seen from the bar on a higher floor? But is this even important? Isn't this work just all about your own experience? Nothing in this theatre needs to be told, shown or imagined. It is about different things. The observation of the body by the body and by the people surrounding you. It is the intensity of the senses. How heat and cold change your body and your reactions. This is experience theatre in which you as audience create your own theatre space, in which you are free to do as you please. Theatre on your naked skin.

Central to this experience is the visitor surrendering to the successive heat and cold waves, just like in any real sauna. But this is a sauna squared, a sauna in the fictional theatre space. It is in fact just a representation of a sauna, but this is precisely the deciding factor that provides the extra experience. Being exposed (in different ways) creates different side effects. The visitor enters a liminal zone of seeing and being seen that influences perception and action. It has a delicate and widespread effect on your body that is felt in your smallest veins. It is corporeal because of its sensory perception, but it also influences your self-image and projection. It is a kind of melting consciousness of the self within the context of an interactive installation in which everybody is equal.

This hyper-activation of all your receptors touches the heart of the alchemy of the theatrical representation. The experience is as real and as false as any other theatre night, but it is more violent because of the melting processes that occur and the evaporation of the difference between observation and participation. The fear of being exposed, the consciousness of observing, but especially the observation of the body lead to more inner reflection. It is a kind of corporeal seeing in which every stimulation is experienced by the theatrical display you are a part of. It can be compared to meditating in the rush hour. Trying to reach your inner self in the middle of chaos. It is not just the sauna that is in exile—it is also the visitor that is in and out of his or her body at the same time.

Malstaf did not only design the sauna but also some of the surrounding installations. *Shaft* is one of them: a plastic tube that works like a vacuum cleaner and sucks up different objects.

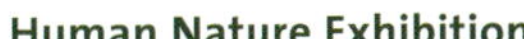

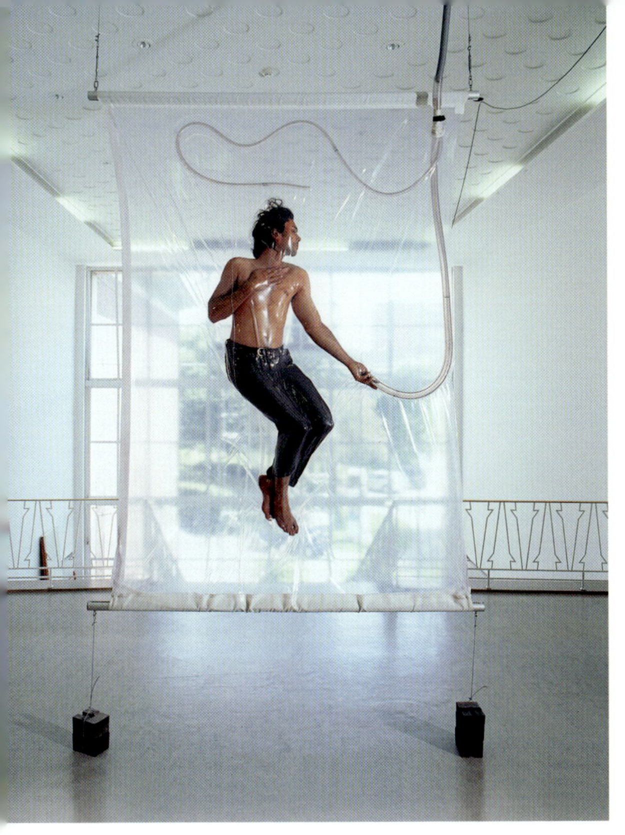

The visitor lies on the sofa underneath the tube and watches as plates float on air until they hit each other and break into pieces. The tension in this installation is created by the contrast between your relaxed body and the floating and breaking plates above your head. Calm and danger delicately balanced. One can see the installation as a metaphor for a comparable situation during a psychiatric session, but the raw effect on the body seems more important here. Relaxation and stress combined. What happens in your perception? Which muscles are tense and which ones are not? How do you channel your fear? These changes in perception are always at the heart of the works of Lawrence Malstaf. He smoothly attacks your skin, ears, balance and vision. He makes you lose your balance and control and gets you breathing differently. In the very moment that your heart skips a beat, Malstaf strikes.

Shaft is exemplary for most of the works of Lawrence Malstaf. They are all aimed at sensory deception. Not like Escher with his visual rebus work, but by immersing and exposing the visitor to contrasting impulses. Malstaf invites you to his twilight zone where your pre-programmed perception is challenged. In anthropology this is known as limen (Victor Turner): a transitional stage with its very own rules in which new situations are prepared and tested. These moments are stuck between reality and fiction and are used by Turner to describe the particularity of rituals. Richard Schechner applies liminality to the theatre in which transitional stages are used to see how we can look at man and world. Malstaf approaches liminality in the same way as these great thinkers, he also saves a stage that is different but not detached from reality. He erects glass walls through which you can still vaguely see that reality. In this free stage he invites you to be vulnerable. His installations require submission and sensitivity. Leave your clothes in the dressing room and enter into a world of possibilities.

Dramaturgy of the machine

Malstaf's interactive installations have their own dramaturgy. They look friendly and comfortable. They look inviting and contemporary. Neatly designed, light and transparent. And then suddenly something inside starts to growl and the friendly installation becomes a mean machine and starts to hiss, suck and turn. The air pressure changes. Invisible valves and pumps start to work. The calm that was is sucked into a turbine, reduced to atoms and spat out. And then suddenly the machine becomes silent yet again, too silent. And you are back in the calm and comfortable surroundings you were in before. Was that just the wind? Or was it someone else who caused my inner storm?

Malstaf's installations are notably theatrical. Just like Greek drama. Life becomes a mess in just a few minutes. All it takes is a little passion and the whole thing starts to shake. It becomes uncontrollable and everything falls apart. One minute it is caressing you and the next it wants to destroy you. A gentle breeze turns into a hurricane. What looked like a mirror now explodes like a tsunami. The momentum is of the essence, the exact point in time when everything changes. Malstaf stages time like a rotation mechanism. Something starts to shake and sets a whirlpool in motion. It comes to life and starts breathing. The rest is all tragedy.

Malstaf installations deceive the eye. The visitor is always part of the picture. The machine requires a direction of view. In front, underneath or right in the middle. Very rarely above. Malstaf turns the visitor into the object, the submissive part. The machine forces you to take position and then undermines your contemplation. Your mirror image is shattered into a thousand pieces, like in *Mirror* (2002). A renaissance portrait of a woman is sucked away by a vacuum pump, turning the mouth into an outlet pipe of a bath (*Whirlpool*, 1999). Everything around you starts to twirl as if you are in the eye of the storm (*Nemo Observatorium*, 2000). Walls start to move and the room becomes a labyrinth (*Nevel*, 2003). All these tragic machines have their moment of rage, a kind of blindness that reflects the flaws in your own view. This is how they invite you to look inside. But once the rage is over they become vulnerable, drained, and powerless. And then you sit down with some form of shame, in front, inside or underneath. Waiting for that moment when everything changes again.

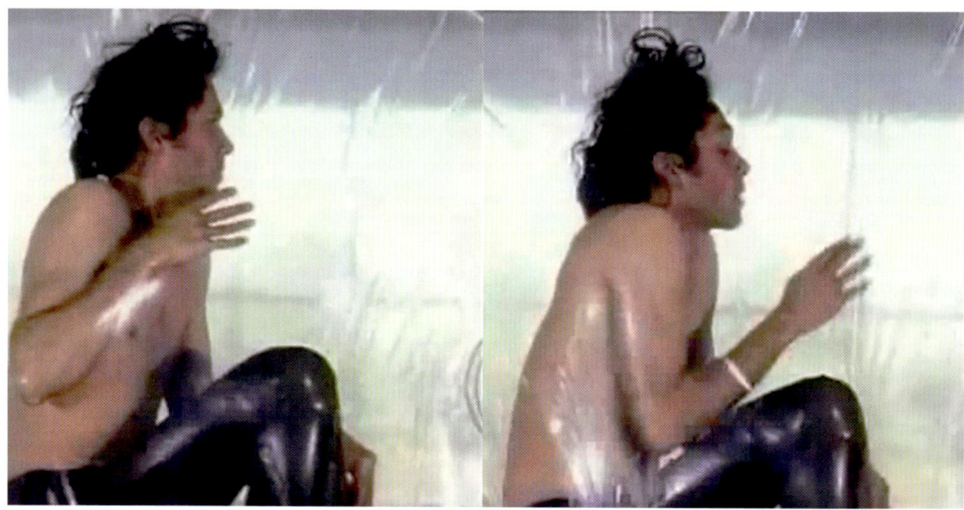

The Bible and the motor

Sandbible is the work that strikes me the most in the Malstaf exposition "Freestate". It is an older work from 1999 that is not an interactive installation. Underneath a sheet of glass you see an open book with a rectangle cut out. In that rectangle there is some sand. Suddenly the machine starts and the sand starts to tremble, forming new figures over and over again. And then the machine stops and the sand finds its peace once again. This clash between that most holy of books and the machine that puts everything in motion is fascinating. The motor strikes at the heart of the Bible. The grains of sand follow their own path in the Bible, forming strange signs, hieroglyphics waiting for the creative reader. The work has several layers in several ways. Some will really feel the hole in the Bible; others will cherish the unlimited amount of signs in the sand.

This work defines Malstaf's artistic creed because it displays the new technological condition: the motor controls the Bible. The core of Malstaf is the technology he uses. The image is changed by any number of technological applications; it is alienated from its static expression and constantly searches transformation. There is constant experimentation with new technology to show its effect on perception. From that angle the use of all these machines is much more than a gimmick. A work like *Sandbible* hints at a change of paradigm: the laws of physics substitute the law of God. But Malstaf's metaphysics are exciting and interesting because they are ruled by coincidence. The plates in *Shaft* follow their own path, the grains of sand in *Sandbible* write their own signs. And thus Malstaf's artistic practice is closely related to the research of physicist Ilya Prygogine and his famous formula: chance = change.

(Text: Luk Van den Dries)

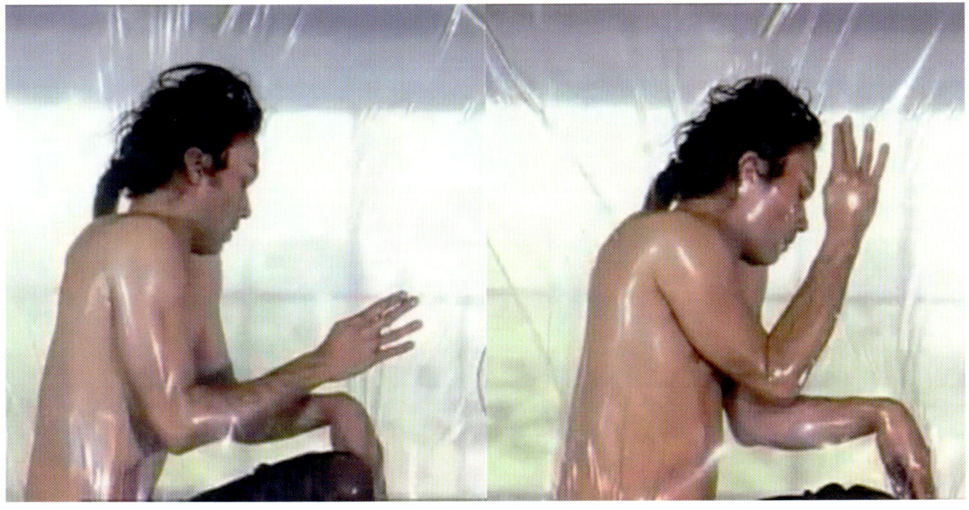

Mit dem Werk von Lawrence Malstaf wurde ich erstmals bei einer Theater-Performance konfrontiert. *Sauna in exile* war ein Projekt, das er mit Mette Edvardsen, Heine Avdal und Liv Hanne Haugen realisiert hatte. Es hinterließ einen bleibenden Eindruck.

Wie in allen seinen Arbeiten geht Lawrence Malstaf von einem sehr klaren und einfachen Konzept aus. In der Mitte eines Raumes befindet sich eine Sauna, die von allen möglichen Entspannungsbereichen umgeben ist, wo man Musik hören, Videos ansehen oder einfach nur einen Drink nehmen kann. Im Zentrum der Performance steht aber die Sauna selbst, eine richtige Sauna, die Besucher müssen sich entkleiden und dürfen die Installation nur im Bademantel betreten. Nackt gibt man sich der Hitze hin – und bevor man weiß, wie einem geschieht, führt einen ein ebenfalls nackter Schauspieler in den Umgang mit Birkenzweigenbüscheln (*vihta*) ein, die die Blutzirkulation anregen. Einige Besucher scheinen sich in der Hitze gleichsam aufzulösen – dann beginnt die Choreografie.

Auch die Choreografie scheint sich in Hitze und Dunst aufzulösen. Und dies ist auch das zentrale Thema der Arbeit: Verdunstung, Evaporation. Nackt oder im Bademantel verschwindet jede Differenz zwischen „Besuchern" und „Performern". Ich bin in der Sauna, nackt, und ich bin auf der Bühne im Begriff mich aufzulösen. Vielleicht wirke ich aus der etwas höher gelegenen Bar betrachtet auch wie ein Schauspieler? Aber spielt dies überhaupt eine Rolle? Geht es in dieser Arbeit nicht einfach nur um die eigene Erfahrung? In diesem Theater muss nichts gesagt, gezeigt oder imaginiert werden. Es geht um andere Dinge. Die Beobachtung des Körpers durch den Körper und die Menschen um mich herum. Es geht um die Intensität der Sinnesempfindungen. Wie Hitze und Kälte den Körper und die eigenen Reaktionen verändern. Erfahrungstheater, bei dem sich das Publikum den eigenen Theaterraum schafft, in dem man tun kann, was man will. Ein Theaterstück über die nackte Haut.

Eine zentrale Rolle bei dieser Erfahrung spielt der Besucher, der sich wie in einer echten Sauna den Hitze- und Kältewellen hingibt. Aber wir haben es hier mit einer potenzierten Sauna zu tun, einer Sauna in einem fiktiven Theaterraum. Eigentlich handelt es sich nur um die Repräsentation einer Sauna, gerade dadurch aber entsteht die besondere Erfahrung. Exponiert zu sein (in mehrerer Hinsicht), zeitigt Nebeneffekte. Der Besucher bewegt sich in einem Grenzbereich zwischen Sehen und Gesehen-Werden, der Wahrnehmung und Handlungen beeinflusst und eine subtile, weitverzweigte, bis in die feinsten Verästelungen zu spürende Wirkung auf den Körper ausübt. Aufgrund der Sinneswahrnehmungen ist dieser Zustand in erster Linie ein körperlicher, er beeinflusst aber auch das Selbstbild und das Projektionsverhalten. Das Selbstbewusstsein zerfließt im Kontext einer interaktiven Installation, in der alle gleich sind.

Die Hyperaktivierung aller Rezeptoren rührt direkt an die Alchemie der Theatervorstellung. Die Erfahrung ist so real und künstlich wie jeder andere Theaterabend, aber intensiver – aufgrund der Erfahrung des Zerfließens und der Auflösung der Differenz zwischen Beobachtung und Partizipation. Die Angst, sich zu exponieren, das Bewusstsein, beobachtet zu werden, insbesondere aber die Beobachtung des Körpers führen zu einer gesteigerten Innenschau. Es ist eine Art körperlichen Sehens, bei dem jede Stimulierung im Rampenlicht der Bühne intensiviert erfahren wird. Es lässt sich mit einer Meditation in der Rush Hour vergleichen. Mit dem Versuch, mitten im Chaos Zugang zum inneren Selbst zu finden. Nicht nur die Sauna ist im Exil – auch der Besucher, der sich gleichzeitig inner- und außerhalb seines Körpers zu befinden meint.

Malstaf entwarf nicht nur die Sauna, sondern auch einige der um sie herum aufgebauten Installationen, etwa *Shaft*: ein transparentes Kunststoffrohr, das wie ein Staubsauger funktioniert und diverse Objekte aufsaugt. Der Besucher liegt auf einem Sofa unterhalb des Rohrs und beobachtet Platten, die durch die Luft schweben, bis sie kollidieren und in Stücke zerbrechen. Die Spannung dieser Installation entsteht durch den Kontrast zwischen dem entspannten Körper und den unmittelbar über dem Kopf schwebenden und berstenden Platten. Ruhe und Gefahr in subtiler Balance. Man kann die Installation als Metapher für die Couch in der Psychotherapie betrachten, wobei die Wirkung auf den Körper hier im Vordergrund steht. Entspannung kombiniert mit Stress. Wie verändert sich die Wahrnehmung? Welche Muskeln sind angespannt und welche nicht? Wie geht man mit der Angst um? Solche Wahrnehmungsveränderungen stehen immer im Zentrum von Lawrence Malstafs Arbeiten. Geschickt attackiert er Haut und Ohren, Gleichgewichts- und Sehsinn. Er lässt einen die Balance und die Kontrolle verlieren und anders atmen. Genau dann, wenn der Herzschlag aus dem Takt gerät, schlägt Malstaf zu.

Shaft ist beispielhaft für die meisten Arbeiten des Künstlers. Sie zielen alle auf die Täuschung der Sinne ab. Nicht durch Bildrätsel wie Escher, sondern durch gegensätzliche Impulse, denen der Besucher ausgesetzt ist. Malstaf führt einen in eine Grauzone, in der die gewohnte Wahrnehmung herausgefordert wird. In der Anthropologie ist dieses Phänomen als *limen* (lat.: Schwelle; Victor Turner) bekannt: ein Übergangsstadium mit eigenen Regeln, in dem neue Situationen vorbereitet und erprobt werden. Es sind Momente, die zwischen Realität und Fiktion schweben, und mit denen Turner die Besonderheit von Ritualen beschreibt. Richard Schechner überträgt die Liminalität auf das Theater, wo Übergangszonen eingesetzt werden, um das Menschen- und Weltbild zu hinterfragen. Malstaf begreift Liminalität ähnlich wie diese Denker, auch er interessiert sich für diese Zone, die sich von der Realität unterscheidet, aber nicht von ihr losgelöst ist. Er errichtet Glaswände, durch die die Realität nach wie vor verschwommen zu sehen ist. In dieser Zone der Freiheit lädt er einen ein, Verletzbarkeit zuzulassen. Seine Installationen erfordern Unterwerfung und Sensitivität. Lassen Sie Ihre Kleider in der Umkleidekabine, und betreten Sie eine Welt voller Möglichkeiten.

Dramaturgie der Maschine

Malstafs interaktive Installationen haben ihre eigene Dramaturgie. Sie wirken freundlich und angenehm, einladend und zeitgemäß. Sind elegant designt, hell und transparent. Doch plötzlich beginnt etwas im Inneren zu fauchen, und die freundliche Installation wird zu einer tückischen Maschine, die sich zischend und saugend zu verwandeln beginnt. Der Luftdruck verändert sich. Unsichtbare Walzen und Pumpen beginnen zu arbeiten. Die Stille, die eben noch herrschte, wird in eine Turbine gesogen, atomisiert und wieder ausgeworfen. Dann setzt die Maschine plötzlich aus, es wird still, zu still. Und man befindet sich wieder in dem ruhigen und angenehmen Ambiente wie zuvor, als wäre nichts geschehen. War das nur der Wind? Wer hat diesen inneren Sturm ausgelöst?

Malstafs Installationen sind auffällig dramatisch. Sie erinnern an das griechische Drama. Das Leben wird innerhalb weniger Minuten zum Chaos. Ein Funke Leidenschaft – und schon gerät alles aus den Fugen, wird unkontrollierbar und zerfällt. Gerade noch umschmeichelt, läuft man schon Gefahr, vernichtet zu werden. Eine sanfte Brise wird zu einem Hurrikan. Was wie ein Spiegel aussieht, explodiert mit der Gewalt eines Tsunami. Das Momentum ist das Wesentliche, der exakte Zeitpunkt, an dem die Dinge sich verändern. Malstaf inszeniert Zeit wie einen Rotationsmechanismus. Etwas beginnt zu beben und löst einen Tumult aus. Es erwacht zum Leben und beginnt zu atmen. Der Rest ist Tragödie.

Malstafs Installationen täuschen das Auge. Der Besucher ist immer Teil des Bildes. Die Maschine gibt die Blickrichtung vor. Vorne, unten oder in der Mitte. Selten oben. Malstaf verwandelt den Besucher in ein Objekt, weist ihm den untergeordneten Part zu. Die Maschine zwingt einen, Stellung zu beziehen und unterminiert dann, was man sich zurechtgelegt hat. Das eigene Spiegelbild zersplittert in tausend Stücke wie in *Mirror* (2002). Ein Renaissanceporträt einer Frau wird von einer Vakuumpumpe aufgesaugt, wodurch der Mund wie ein Abfluss erscheint (*Whirlpool*, 1999). Ringsum beginnt alles zu wirbeln, als befände man sich im Auge eines Orkans (*Nemo Observatorium*, 2000). Wände setzen sich in Bewegung, und der Raum wird zu einem Labyrinth (*Nevel*, 2003). Alle diese tragischen Maschinen haben einen Moment des Aufruhrs, eine Art Blindheit, die die blinden Flecken der eigenen Wahrnehmung widerspiegelt. Dadurch laden sie einen zur Innenschau ein. Sobald der Aufruhr vorüber ist, werden sie verletzlich, erschöpft, machtlos. Dann setzt man sich irgendwie beschämt vor sie hin, oder in sie hinein oder darunter. In Erwartung des Augenblicks, der wieder alles verändert.

Die Bibel und der Motor

Sandbible ist für mich die faszinierendste Arbeit von Malstafs Ausstellung „Freestate". Es ist eine ältere Arbeit aus dem Jahr 1999, die nicht interaktiv ist. Unter einer Glasplatte sieht man ein offenes Buch mit einem ausgeschnittenen Viereck. In diesem Viereck befindet sich Sand. Plötzlich setzt sich die Maschine, in Gang und der Sand beginnt zitternd Figuren zu bilden. Dann stoppt die Maschine und der Sand kommt wieder zur Ruhe. Der Gegensatz zwischen dem heiligsten aller Bücher und der Maschine, die alles in Bewegung versetzt, ist faszinierend. Der Motor greift das Innerste der Bibel an. Die Sandkörner bahnen sich ihren eigenen Weg durch die Bibel, bilden seltsame Zeichen, Hieroglyphen, die auf einen kreativen Leser warten. Das Werk ist in mehrfacher Hinsicht vielschichtig. Manche werden vor allem auf das Loch in der Bibel fixiert sein, andere werden die vielen in Sand geschriebenen Zeichen bewundern.

Dieses Werk umreißt Malstafs künstlerisches Credo, weil es unsere neue technologische Befindlichkeit aufzeigt: Der Motor kontrolliert die Bibel. Das Wesentliche an Malstafs Kunst ist die Technologie, die er verwendet. Das Bild wird durch eine Reihe technischer Verfahren verändert; es entfernt sich von seinem statischen Ausdruck und verlangt permanent Transformation. Ständig wird mit neuer Technologie experimentiert, um deren Wirkung auf die Wahrnehmung aufzuzeigen. So gesehen ist die Verwendung dieser Maschinen mehr als eine Spielerei. Eine Arbeit wie *Sandbible* zeigt einen Paradigmenwechsel an: Die Gesetze der Physik ersetzen das Gesetz Gottes. Malstafs Metaphysik ist insbesondere deshalb spannend und interessant, weil sie vom Zufall gesteuert wird. Die Platten in *Shaft* gehen ihren eigenen Weg, die Sandkörner in *Sandbible* schreiben ihre eigenen Zeichen. Malstafs künstlerische Praxis ist demnach mit den Forschungen des Physikers Ilya Prigogine und seiner berühmten Formel verwandt: *chance = change*.

(Text: Luk Van den Dries, aus dem Englischen von Martina Bauer)

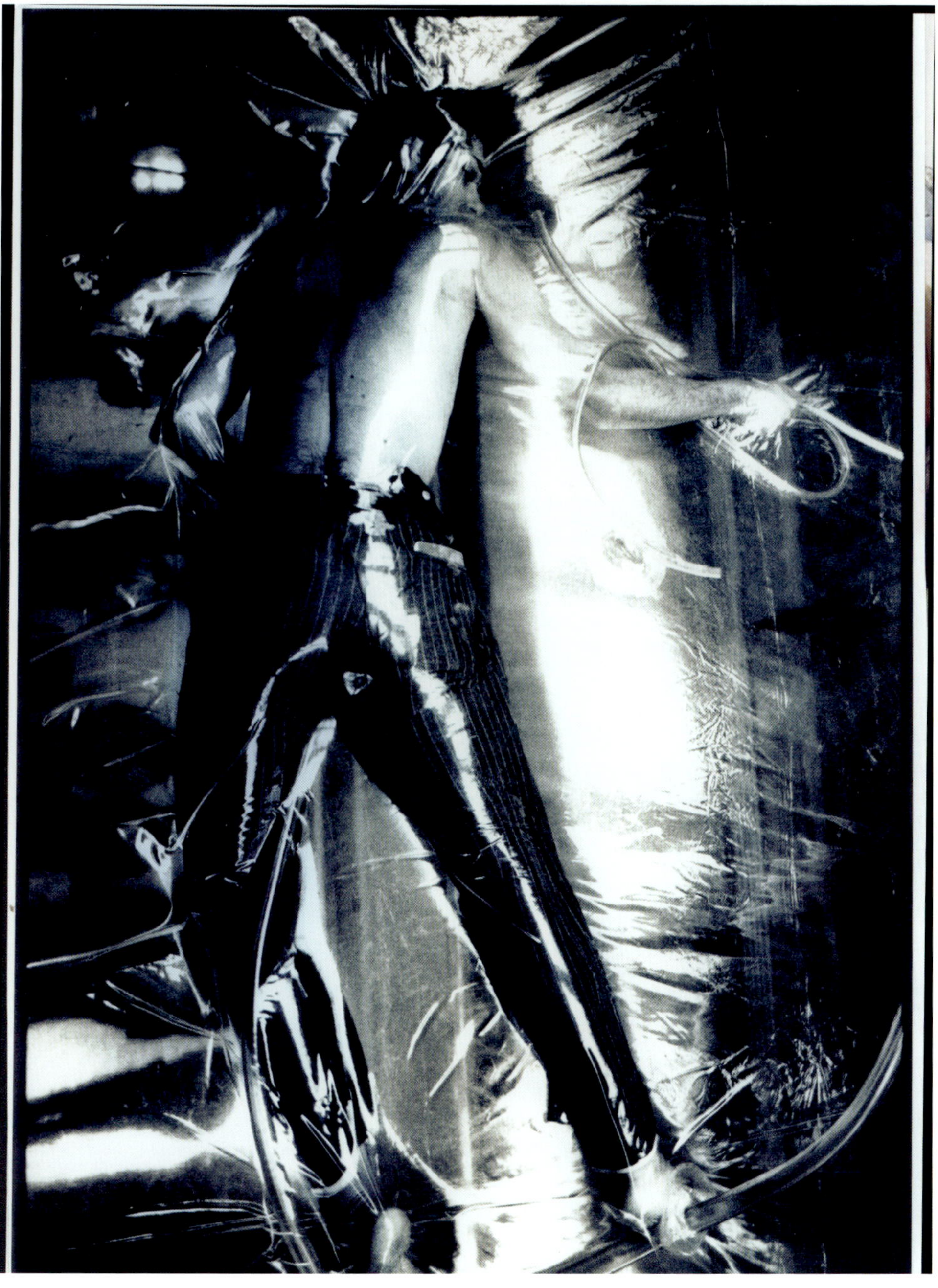

etoy. CORPORATION

MISSION ETERNITY—a digital death ritual for the information age

All cultures need to dispose of the dead and share the loss of friends and family connected with the challenge of remembering and forgetting. *MISSION ETERNITY* (*M*∞) trespasses the norms of a civilization obsessed with data storage and transportation of cargo. Existing architecture and rituals are inadequate when facing death today.

Independent of religious beliefs and scientific speculations, etoy explores life after death. The operation is based on facts: all we know for sure is that we leave behind mortal remains and a massive body of electrical information. The art group exploits computer technology and global transportation networks to process, distribute and revive human remains.

The key to this long-term project is TIME. etoy decided to invest 32 years into *M*∞: after the Internet hype of the 90s it is time to radically slow down and to investigate the sustainable impact of digital media in full depth. etoy.AGENTS carefully approach the memory issue from an emotional, a technical and an artistic perspective. Once again they face organizational, ethical, legal, spiritual, economical and aesthetical challenges. At the heart of *M*∞ stands the creation and long-term conservation of ARCANUM CAPSULES. They are hosted in the shared memory of thousands of networked computers and mobile devices of *M*∞ ANGELS, people who contribute a part of their digital storage capacity[1] to the mission. The *M*∞ ANGEL APPLICATION stores and publishes capsule content forever.

The ARCANUM CAPSULE is a digital portrait of a *M*∞ PILOT—a data swarm that travels space and time forever. It contains digital fragments of a person's life: ASCII text, statistics, voice samples, electrocardiograms, photos and other records from government and family archives or online sources. The launch of an ARCANUM CAPSULE requires the active presence of a living PILOT and involves interaction with trained etoy.AGENTS. An ARCANUM CAPSULE is defined by a unique 16 digit alphanumerical ID (e.g. F718 34AA 6A9A 6586) assigned to each PILOT. This system is used to identify, search and evoke the dead and their info sphere. The available IDs provide a stable base for the first (short-term[2]) phase of the mission: potentially 18.447 quadrillion ARCANUM CAPSULE IDs can be assigned to active users (expressed in the short scale numerical system). In other words, etoy.AGENTS could encapsulate 7 billion individuals per second for more than 83 years.

The ritual of the encapsulation process culminates in the file upload. At the *M*∞ GATE (*http://www.missioneternity.org/gate*), PILOTS hand over their data and the control over them to eternity. The GATE scrambles the file names and then distributes and publishes the data online through the ANGEL APPLICATION (free software). From this point forward, the data cannot be changed or revoked. The act of uploading is end and beginning. Every file that is injected into *M*∞ receives a new (scrambled) file name consisting of a 32 digit alphanumeric hash plus the individual CAPSULE ID of the PILOT. For example:

54ef830fda55ead3303082c0e0525e77054eoc7e-E20C1977B82F6C26.jpg

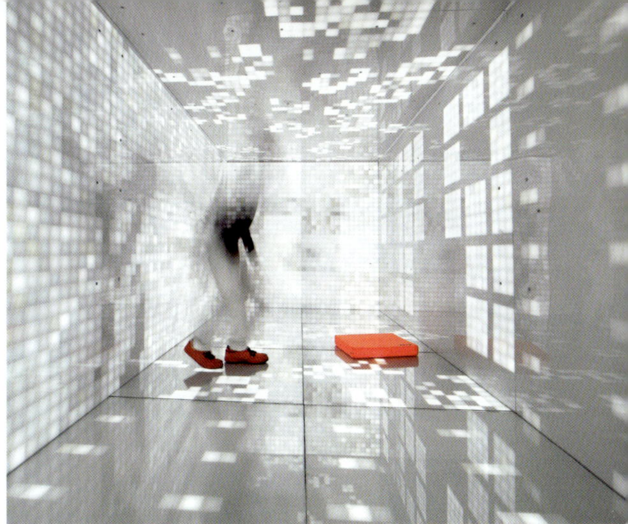

SCRAMBLING destroys the deceptive intelligibility of file names and thus unmasks the illusion of order in computer networks and guarantees the sanctity of each file: the risk of overwriting files is minimized because the total amount of file names that can be generated with this method exceeds earthly measures. $M\infty$ recognizes that search will henceforth be the task of machines. The search for a specific PILOT'S digital remains comes down to a search for their CAPSULE ID (e.g. the entry into a search engine such as Google). ARCANUM CAPSULES are globally distributed and publicly accessible. PILOTS cross the ultimate boundary to investigate afterlife, the most virtual of all worlds.

After uploading the digital heritage, the integration of the mortal remains (the hardware) of a PILOT complements the death ritual.

The TERMINUS, a cube-shaped plug, molds the ashes of a PILOT with cement. During a ceremony the TERMINUS is installed in the SARCOPHAGUS: a 20 foot cargo container outfitted with 17,000 LEDs that displays ARCANUM CAPSULE content of up to 1000 human beings who passed away. The interactive and networked sculpture links the community of the living and the dead. It serves as a BRIDGE that connects human memory and electric impulses with mortal remains and functions as a mobile, final resting place. Hence, it re-unites biomass with digitised data.

At the moment etoy works with two TEST PILOTS. Sepp Keiser, a pioneer of microfilm technology born in 1924, collaborates with etoy since 2005 to design an encapsulation process leading to his own ARCANUM CAPSULE. Further, on May 26, 2007, etoy transferred the mortal remains of Timothy Leary into the multiuser SARCOPHAGUS. A key figure of the information society, Leary experimented with the expansion of the human mind with the drug LSD and interpreted his own death as a last trip in his book *'Design for Dying'*[3]. $M\infty$ is open to selected PILOTS, pioneers of the information age. In addition to that, etoy.AGENTS encapsulate STOWAWAYS during workshops around the world. The wider public can access $M\infty$ content, use the open sources of $M\infty$ and create their own ARCANUM CAPSULE and death rituals.

http://www.missioneternity.org; http://www.etoy.com

1   Lev Manovich. *Art After Compression*. Lecture at ZHdK (Zurich University of the Arts), Zurich, 2005.
2   "For $M\infty$ the definition of short-term" covers the first 32 years. This is the period in which etoy.CORPORATION has to establish and evaluate the technical and cultural fundament for eternal coexistence of the living and the dead. etoy initiates a number of rituals that facilitate sharing and storing personal digital files for the long term. In the year 2037 (beginning of the mid-term time count) the average age of the currently active etoy. AGENTS will be around 60 years.
3   Timothy Leary with R.U. Sirius. *Design for Dying*. San Francisco: HarperEdge, 1997

In cooperation with Swiss Arts Council Pro Helvetia,
Linz 2009 European Capital of Culture – Extra Europa Schweiz.

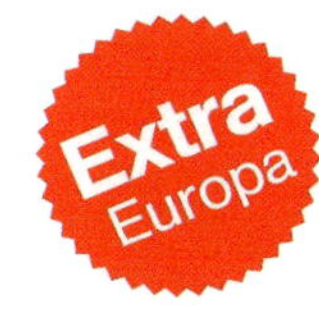

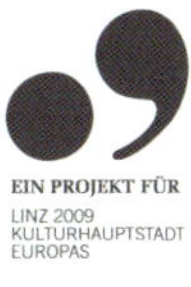

etoy. CORPORATION

MISSION ETERNITY – Ein digitales Totenritual für das Informationszeitalter

Menschen in allen Kulturen müssen leblose Körper entsorgen, die Trauer um ihre Verstorbenen teilen und gleichzeitig die Herausforderung von Vergessen und Erinnern meistern. *MISSION ETERNITY* (M∞) überschreitet die Normen einer von Datenspeicherung und Güterverkehr besessenen Zivilisation: Bestehende Architektur und Rituale sind inadäquat, wenn es darum geht, das Totenreich, die virtuellste aller Welten, zu erschließen.

Unabhängig von religiösen Vorstellungen und wissenschaftlichen Spekulationen erforscht etoy das Leben nach dem Tod. Die Operation basiert auf Fakten: Alles, was wir mit Sicherheit wissen, ist, dass Menschen sterbliche Hüllen und elektrische Infosphären hinterlassen. Die Kunstgruppe nutzt Computertechnologie und das globale Transportnetzwerk, um menschliche Überreste zu prozessieren, zu verteilen und ihnen zu ewigem Leben zu verhelfen.

Zeit ist der Schlüssel zu diesem langfristigen Projekt. etoy investiert 32 Jahre in M∞: Nach dem Internet-Hype der 90er Jahre ist es an der Zeit, die nachhaltige Wirkung der digitalen Medien auszuloten. etoy.AGENTS untersuchen das Memory-Problem aus der emotionalen, technischen und künstlerischen Perspektive und werden wieder mit organisatorischen, ethischen, rechtlichen, spirituellen, wirtschaftlichen und ästhetischen Herausforderungen konfrontiert. Im Zentrum von M∞ steht die Erschaffung und langfristige Erhaltung von ARCANUM CAPSULES. Sie werden abgelegt auf hunderten von vernetzten Rechnern und Mobiltelefonen von M∞ ANGELS - User, die bereit sind, einen Teil ihrer reichlich vorhandenen Speicherkapazität[1] zur Verfügung zu stellen. Die M∞ ANGEL APPLICATION (Freie Software) versucht, die Daten von speziellen PILOTS für immer zu speichern und öffentlich abrufbar zu machen.

Eine ARCANUM CAPSULE ist ein digitales Porträt eines M∞ Piloten – ein Datenschwarm, der für immer durch Raum und Zeit reist. Sie enthält digitale Fragmente eines Lebens: ASCII-Text, Statistiken, Stimmproben, Elektrokardiogramme, Fotos und andere Aufzeichnungen aus Regierungsdatenbanken, Familienarchiven und Online-Quellen. Die Initiierung einer ARCANUM CAPSULE erfordert die aktive Präsenz des lebenden Piloten und entsteht in Zusammenarbeit mit etoy.AGENTS. Jedem Piloten (und damit seiner Datenkapsel) wird eine 16-stellige alphanumerische Kennnummer (z.B. F71834AA6A9A6586) zugeordnet. Dieses System dient später zur eindeutigen Identifikation, Suche und Evokation der Toten und ihrer Infosphäre und bildet eine stabile Basis für die Erreichung der kurzfristigen[2] Ziele der Mission: 18.447 Quadrillionen IDs können generiert werden. Das heißt, etoy kann über 83 Jahre hinweg sieben Milliarden ARCANUM CAPSULES pro Sekunde aktivieren.

Das Ritual der Verkapselung eines Menschen kulminiert im Hochladen der persönlichen Files. Am M∞ Gate (*http://www.missioneternity.org/gate*) übergibt der PILOT seine Daten und die Kontrolle darüber der Ewigkeit. Vom GATE werden die Informationen zerhackt und an die weltweit verteilten M∞ ANGEL APPLICATIONS übermittelt. Die Daten können fortan nicht mehr zurückgerufen oder verändert werden: Der Akt des Hochladens ist Ende und Anfang. Jedes Dokument, das so ins System injiziert wird, erhält eine neue Bezeichnung, die sich aus einem 32-stelligen alphanumerischen Hashwert und der individuellen Kennnummer der Kapsel zusammensetzt. Beispiel:

54ef830fda55ead3303082c0e0525e77054e0c7e-E20C1977B82F6C26.jpg

Das Scrambling zerstört die vermeintliche Interpretierbarkeit der ursprünglichen File-Namen, entlarvt damit die Illusion von Ordnung in Computernetzwerken und garantiert die Unantastbarkeit jedes Files: Die Gefahr des Überschreibens ist minimal, weil die Gesamtzahl der möglichen Dateinamen mit dieser Methode alle irdischen Maße übersteigt. M∞ anerkennt, dass das Finden von Information fortan die Aufgabe von Suchmaschinen ist. Das Aufspüren digitaler Überreste von PILOTS beschränkt sich auf die Suche nach den Kennnummern ihrer ARCANUM CAPSULES (die Eingabe einer ID, z.B. in Google, führt direkt zum Erbe).

Nach dem Hochladen der digitalen Hinterlassenschaft vervollständigt der Einbezug der sterblichen Überreste der PILOTS das Totenritual.

Der Terminus, ein kubusförmiger Stecker – gegossen aus Beton und menschlicher Asche –, wird in einer Zeremonie im SARCOPHAGUS installiert: Ein 20–Fuß-Frachtcontainer, ausgerüstet mit 17.000 Leuchtdioden, zeigt die Daten der verstorbenen PILOTS und bietet Platz für rund 1.000 Pilots. Die vernetzte und interaktive Skulptur ist nur eine mögliche BRIDGE, die Erinnerungen (elektrische Impulse gespeichert in Gehirnen, auf Datenträgern und in Netzwerken) mit den sterblichen Überresten der Piloten verbindet. Die virtuellen und die physischen Spuren bilden eine fragile Verbindung und definieren einen Raum für die Begegnung der Lebenden und der Toten. Der SARCOPHAGUS reist als Teil des weltweiten Containerverkehrs durch den geografischen Raum wie die ARCANUM CAPSULES als Datenpakete durch das Internet.

Bisher arbeitet etoy mit zwei TEST-PILOTS: Sepp Keiser aus Zug wurde 1924 geboren und gilt als Pionier der Mikrofilmtechnologie. Seit 2005 werden mit ihm künstlerische Verfahren zur Erfassung seiner ARCANUM CAPSULE erprobt. Und am 26. Mai 2007 wurde ein Teil der sterblichen Überreste von Timothy Leary in den Multi-User-Sarkophag überführt. Leary, eine Schlüsselfigur der Informationsgesellschaft, experimentierte mit der Erweiterung des menschlichen Bewusstseins unter Nutzung von LSD und interpretierte seinen eigenen Tod als letzte aufregende Reise im Buch „Design for Dying" [3]. Eine derart umfassende Porträtierung erwägt etoy gegenwärtig nur für ausgewählte Pioniere der Informationsgesellschaft. In Workshops schickt etoy aber auch zahlreiche STOWAWAYS (blinde Passagiere) auf die ewige Reise. Außerdem hat jedes Individuum die Möglichkeit, auf die offenen Quellen von M∞ zurückzugreifen und seine eigene ARCANUM CAPSULE und Totenrituale zu realisieren.

http://www.missioneternity.org
http://www.etoy.com

1   Lev Manovich. Art After Compression. Lecture at ZHdK (Zurich University of the Arts), Zurich, 2005.
2   Kurzfristig definiert sich für M∞ als die ersten 32 Jahre. In dieser Zeit muss etoy.CORPORATION die technische und kulturelle Basis der Koexistenz der Lebenden und der Toten evaluieren und etablieren. Dazu gehört auch die Lancierung verschiedener Rituale, welche das Teilen und langfristige Erhalten persönlicher Dokumente vereinfachen. Im Jahr 2037 (Beginn mittelfristiger Zielrechnung) wird das Durchschnittsalter der heute aktiven etoy.AGENTS bei etwas mehr als 60 Jahren liegen.
3   Timothy Leary with R.U. Sirius. *Design for Dying*. San Francisco: HarperEdge, 1997

In Kooperation mit Schweizer Kulturstiftung Pro Helvetia, Linz 2009 Kulturhauptstadt Europas – Extra Europa Schweiz.

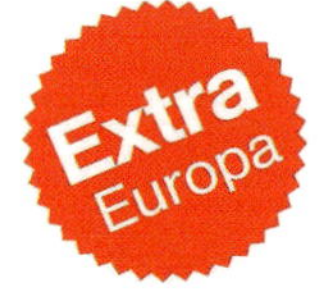

Adam Brandejs

Genpets Series 01

http://www.genpets.com

In 1985, the US Patents and Trademarks Office (PTO) affirmed the legal precedent, ruling that genetically engineered plants, seeds and plant tissue could all be patented. Today, agricultural crops are being modified and organisms with built-in obsolescence are being sold as commodities. Life itself is quickly becoming a processed commodity in the privatization of nature. Biological engineering by large companies, outside of nature, has become a terrifying reality for my generation to contend with.

Today, we are well within the process of desensitizing an upcoming generation towards accepting bioengineering as "natural". I see this generation slowly and systematically being desensitized towards owning and manipulating life through toys that mimic living creatures but carry no weight of responsibility with them. Individually these objects are harmless, however when analyzing the trends in consumption on a larger scale, we can see that with every new toy the envelope is pushed a little further. Bioengineered pets would not have been acceptable yesterday, but they could be today. Boundaries have been eroded.

My belief is that this is leading us even further down the path of objectifying living matter and *Genpets* is my interpretation of how such a relationship would take form as we continue to artificially separate ourselves from nature and treat it more as a 'product'.

Any new technology can bring with it both positive and negative ramifications. Thus it is important that we be critical of both sides and ask questions every step of the way. I see how we treat the life already surrounding us, which we have no moral claim over, and I fear for any life brought into the world through the act of genetic manipulation—life that would inherently have patented DNA. It would not be far fetched to assume that any such creation would have no rights of its own and be subject to whatever treatment deemed necessary upon it. Whether by testing, or packaging, this life would be a commodity of less value than any we have today. *Genpets* is meant to ask questions about a great deal of issues by providing a tangible example of a possible future.

Thanks to Rob Sherwin: Rob was an immense help throughout this piece and he was my third and fourth hands near the end when I needed it. (Thanks Buddy).
Crystal Pallister: Handled the makeup on *Genpets* that added a true level of realism to the creatures.

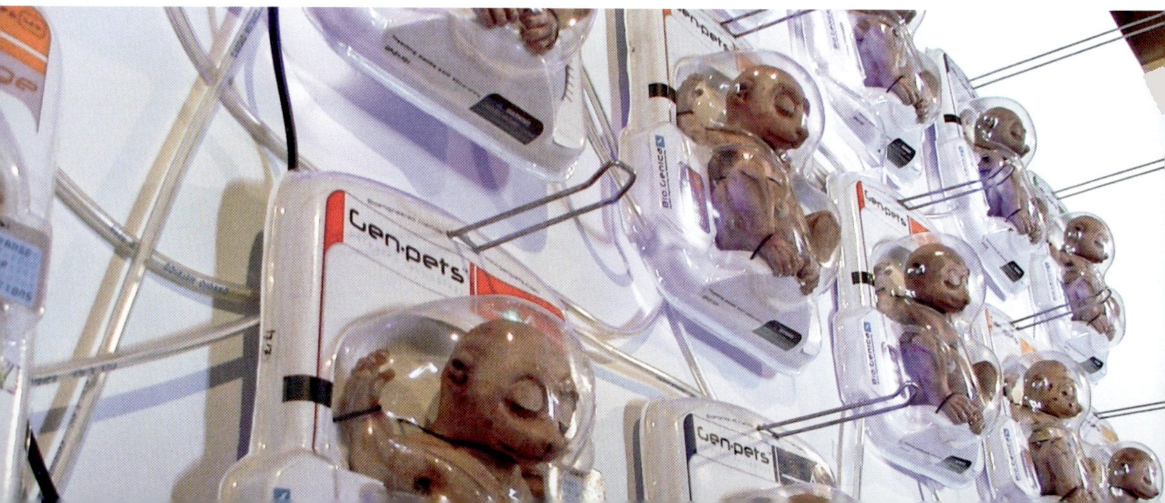

Adam Brandejs

Genpets Series 01

http://www.genpets.com

1985 bestätigte das US-Patentamt (*US Patents and Trademarks Office*, PTO) den vom Obersten Gerichtshof der USA entschiedenen Präzedenzfall und befand, dass genmanipulierte Pflanzen, Samen und pflanzliches Gewebe patentiert werden dürfen. Pflanzen werden immer häufiger gentechnisch verändert, und Organismen mit künstlicher Obsoleszenz werden bereits als Konsumgüter verkauft. Das Leben selbst wird immer mehr zu einer Ware im fortwährenden Kreislauf der Privatisierung der Natur. Meine Generation muss sich heute damit abfinden, dass Konzerne auf Methoden der Biotechnologie setzen und die Natur nicht länger die Oberhand hat.

Die nächste Generation wird zunehmend desensibilisiert und wächst damit auf, dass Genmanipulation und Bioengineering etwas „Natürliches" sind. Sie ist einem langsamen systematischen Prozess der Desensibilisierung ausgesetzt, der so weit geht, dass der Besitz und die Manipulation von Spielzeug, das echten Lebewesen ähnelt, den Besitzern jedoch wenig Verantwortung abverlangt, mit Leben gleichgesetzt wird. Für sich allein sind derartige Produkte harmlos; betrachtet man jedoch die Konsumtrends vor einem größeren Hintergrund, zeigt sich, dass mit jedem neuen Spielzeug der Bogen etwas weiter überspannt wird. Genimanipulierte Haustiere wären gestern unvorstellbar gewesen – heute sind sie denkbar. Die bislang geltenden Grenzen erodieren immer stärker.

Ich bin der Ansicht, dass diese Entwicklung uns immer weiter in Richtung einer Vergegenständlichung von Lebewesen bringt; mit *Genpets* versuche ich darzustellen, wie derartige Beziehungen gestaltet sein könnten, wenn wir uns immer weiter von der Natur entfernen und jene immer stärker als rein künstliches „Produkt" betrachten.

Jede neue Technologie hat positive und negative Folgen. Es ist daher wichtig, dass wir beide Seiten kritisch beleuchten und uns den Fragen stellen, die mit jedem neuen Entwicklungsschritt auftauchen. Ich beobachte mit Sorge, wie wir mit dem Leben um uns, auf das wir keinerlei rechtmäßigen Anspruch haben, umgehen, und jenen Lebewesen, die mittels Genmanipulation geschaffen werden – Leben, das patentierte DNA in sich tragen würde. Die Annahme, dass solcherart gezeugten Lebewesen keinerlei Rechte zugestanden und sie jeder denkbaren, für nötig befundenen Behandlung unterworfen würden, scheint nicht länger utopisch.

Dieses Leben, ob es nun in Versuchsreihen getestet oder für den Verkauf verpackt wird, wäre eine Ware, die viel weniger wert ist als andere Produkte unserer heutigen Welt. *Genpets* soll Fragen zu zentralen Themen aufwerfen, indem auf anschauliche Weise dargelegt wird, wie das Leben in Zukunft aussehen könnte.

Dank an Rob Sherwin: Rob war mir stets eine sehr große Hilfe; er war meine dritte und vierte Hand, als ich sie gegen Ende des Projekts dringend benötigte. (Vielen Dank dafür, Kumpel.)
Crystal Pallister: Zeichnet für das Make-up der *Genpets* verantwortlich, durch sie sahen diese erst lebensecht aus.

(Aus dem Englischen von Sonja Pöllabauer)

Adam Brandejs

Animatronic Flesh Shoe
Moving, twitching, pulsating

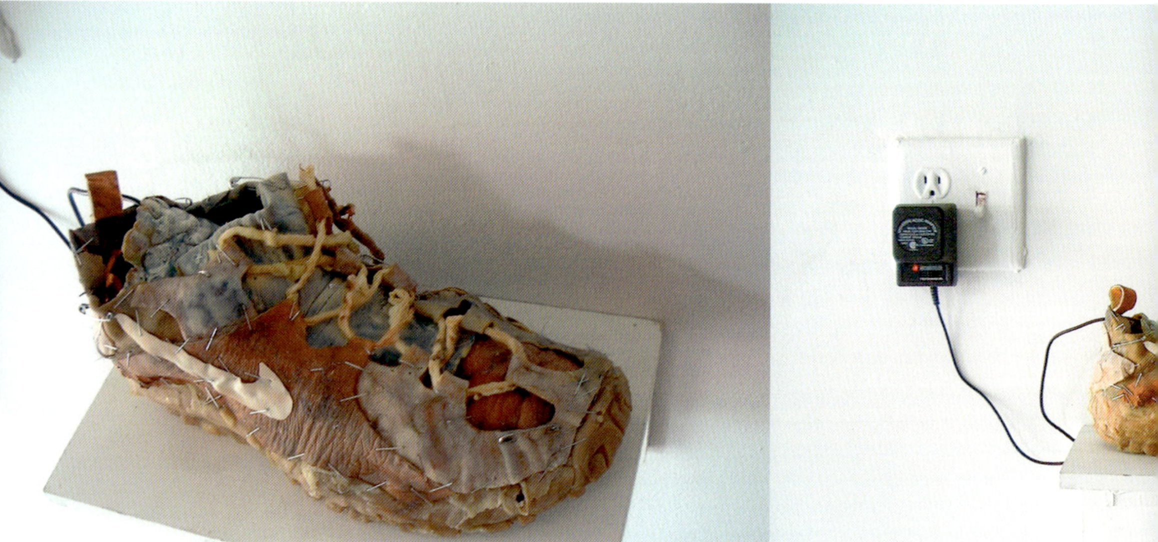

In our modern world of fast and easy consumption we rarely pay any thought to where products actually come from and how they were produced. Many times we assume mass produced items were simply built by a series of machines. Unfortunately the reality is that we usually exploit other humans to produce goods as cheaply as possible. We place our well being over that of others, and usually for trivial objects.

As this piece deals with issues of sweatshop labor and content ownership, each piece of skin is different in color, size, and texture and the Nike Logo is done in white and placed prominently overtop.

This moving and twitching shoe is stitched together with multiple pieces of latex rubber, cast out of molds made from my own skin. The shoe's toe and heel raise and lower as it occasionally vibrates/pulsates, and twitches on the floor as if it were still alive.

While the flesh is disturbing the reality behind the issue is far more disturbing. We live in a culture that is disconnected from what it is doing to itself and others and we choose to ignore rather than deal with the reality we have created for ourselves.

Adam Brandejs

Animatronic Flesh Shoe

Ein Schuh, der sich bewegt, zuckt, pulsiert

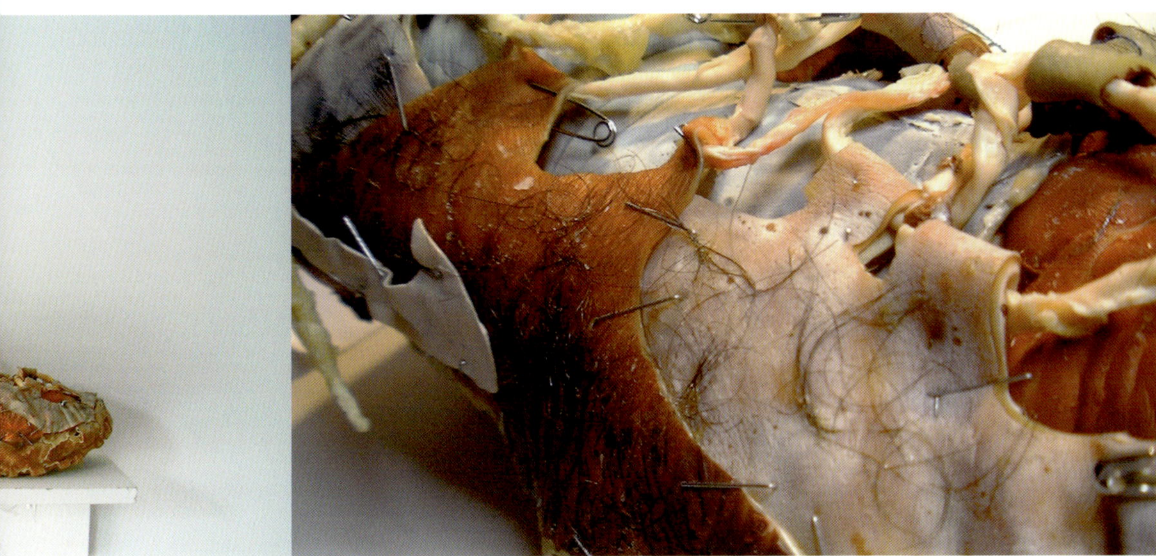

In unserer schnellen und einfachen Konsumwelt fragen wir selten nach dem Herkunftsort und den Produktionsbedingungen von Gütern. Sehr oft nehmen wir stillschweigend an, dass Massenprodukte maschinell hergestellt werden. Dies ist allerdings ein Trugschluss, denn sehr oft wird die Arbeitskraft von Menschen ausgebeutet, damit Waren so billig wie möglich produziert werden können. Wir stellen das eigene Wohlbefinden über das der anderen – für oft vollkommen triviale Produkte.

Dieses Projekt setzt sich mit der Ausbeutung von Arbeitskraft und Fragen von Besitz auseinander: Der sich bewegende, zuckende Schuh wurde aus verschiedenen Latexteilen zusammengestückelt, die nach Abdrücken meiner Haut gegossen wurden. Jedes Hautstückchen hat eine andere Farbe, Größe und Textur; das Nike-Logo ist weiß und an gut sichtbarer Stelle am Schuh platziert.

Spitze und Ferse des Schuhs heben und senken sich, während der Schuh gelegentlich leicht pulsiert und auf dem Boden hin- und herzuckt, als lebte er.

Die Hautfetzen wirken verstörend, doch die Realität hinter dem Projekt ist ungleich verstörender. Wir leben in einer Welt der Ignoranz, in der wir keinen Gedanken darauf verschwenden, was wir ihr oder anderen antun – lieber ignorieren wir diese Realität, als dass wir uns ihr stellen.

(Aus dem Englischen von Sonja Pöllabauer)

Britta Riley, Rebecca Bray

Drink.Pee.Drink.Pee.Drink.Pee

The project *Drink.Pee.Drink.Pee.Drink.Pee* reconsiders urine as a rich source of nutrients instead of a waste product. The Urine Fertilizer Lab transforms your urine into fertilizer for your houseplants, removing elements that are toxic to the waterways where your urine ends up. Participants pee in a jar, learn about urine and its role in the water cycle, perform a multi-stage reaction, and walk away with a dry fertilizer derived from their own bodies.

The project was born of the question: how might we thoughtfully and actively participate in our ecosystems and better manage the impact of human presence on the planet?

Human urine traverses ecosystems. When we flush our pee down the toilet, its powerfully concentrated nutrients pollute aquatic ecosystems. Because urine is not fully treated by current sewage treatment plants, excess nitrogen and phosphorus in human urine cause suffocating algae overgrowth in waterways. Our medications can cause sterility or mutation in other life forms. Traces of human medicines remain in the bodies of water from which we all eventually drink.

However, this liquid by-product of our daily lives need not be a pollutant. Urine can be a rich food source if it gets into the RIGHT part of the right ecosystem.

The way we deal with our urine across the globe exemplifies unnatural management. The latest innovations in environmentally responsible sewage treatment attempt to recycle nutrients back to fertilizer. However, like most attempts to mass-manage the ecosystem, the sheer size of the project creates its own problems. Mass solutions involve long-distance pathways, huge volumes of man-made material infrastructure, and vast amounts of energy.

Potentially what lies ahead is a softening and dispersal, a naturalization of agency in which we evolve away from centralized mass-management of ecosystems. Instead of sending our pee through miles of new pipes and then buying fertilized food grown from pee-derived fertilizer, we might recycle our urine for our own houseplants, shrinking the sprawl of the nutrient exchange to a size appropriate for our own sphere of responsibility. The *Drink.Pee.Drink.Pee. Drink.Pee* project asks participants to look at their own urine as something beyond waste, and instead as a potentially rich nutrient that can be thoughtfully managed in their own ecosystems.

Perhaps we can evolve from passive supporters of centralized mass-management into a network of sentient ecosystems. If put into the hands of the masses, future innovations in technologies such as nanotechnology, biochemistry and sensing might allow us all to better convert materials within our immediate surroundings, rather than simply consuming and then disposing of them. We can be more active humans at the center of our own microenvironments, enthusiastically brokering ever-new opportunities for exchanges of hyper-local organic materials and intelligently managing our own role in continuous natural cycles.

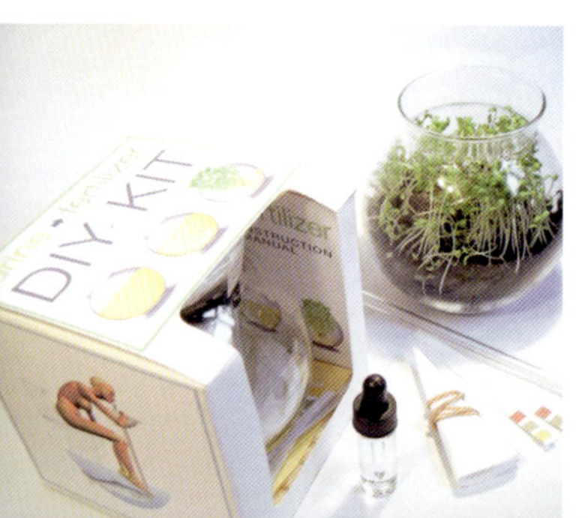

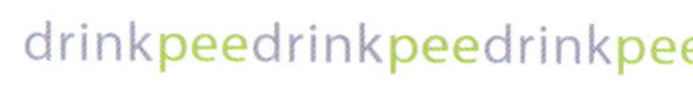

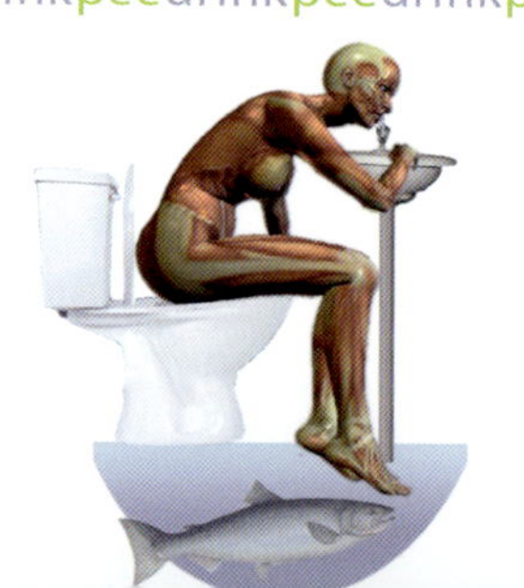

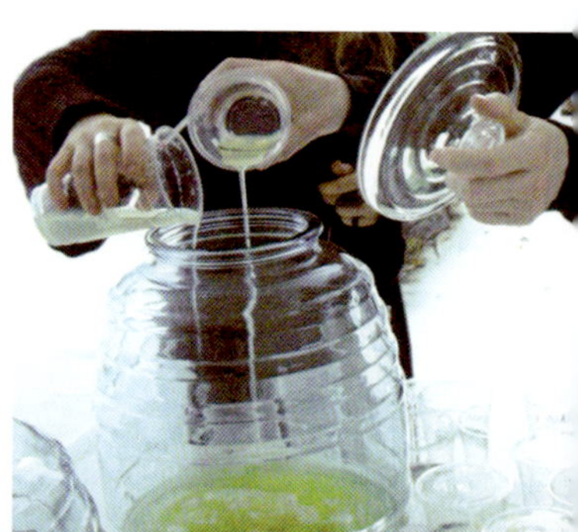

Britta Riley, Rebecca Bray

Drink.Pee.Drink.Pee.Drink.Pee

Das Projekt *Drink.Pee.Drink.Pee.Drink.Pee* betrachtet Urin nicht als Abfallprodukt, sondern als reichhaltige Nährstoffquelle. Das *Urine Fertilizer Lab* verwandelt ihn in Dünger für Zimmerpflanzen und entfernt dabei jene Stoffe, die sich schädlich auf die Gewässer auswirken, in denen der Urin normalerweise landet. Man pinkelt in einen Behälter, erfährt etwas über die Rolle von Urin im Wasserkreislauf, wartet eine Reihe chemischer Reaktionen ab, und erhält am Ende einen aus dem eigenen Körper gewonnenen Trockendünger.

Das Projekt entwickelte sich aus der Frage nach einem rücksichtsvollen, aktiven Umgang mit unserem Ökosystem, der die Auswirkungen unserer Präsenz auf den Planeten mildert.

Menschlicher Urin wirkt ökosystemübergreifend. Wenn wir ihn die Toilette hinunterspülen, gelangen seine hochkonzentrierten Nährstoffe in den Wasserkreislauf. Da Urin in heutigen Kläranlagen nicht restlos abgebaut wird, kommt es durch überschüssigen Stickstoff und Phosphor zu unmäßigem, alles erstickendem Algenwuchs. Medikamentenrückstände können zur Sterilisierung oder Mutation anderer Lebensformen führen. Spuren davon bleiben auch in den Wasserreservoiren zurück, aus denen wir letztlich wieder trinken.

Allerdings muss dieses flüssige Nebenprodukt unseres täglichen Lebens nicht zwangsläufig umweltschädlich sein. Urin kann auch eine reiche Nährstoffquelle darstellen, wenn es in den richtigen Teil des richtigen Ökosystems gelangt.

Unser globaler Umgang mit Urin ist ein Beispiel für nicht naturgemäßes Wirtschaften. Die neuesten Formen umweltfreundlicher Abwasseraufbereitung versuchen, die Nährstoffe zu Dünger zu recyceln. Doch wie die meisten Versuche, das Ökosystem im großen Maßstab zu managen, bringt das seine eigenen Probleme mit sich. Großlösungen sind mit langen Wegen, riesigen Volumina an materieller Infrastruktur und gewaltigem Energieverbrauch verbunden.

Vor uns liegt eine potentielle Aufweichung und Aufteilung – eine Naturalisierung – der Handlungsmacht, die uns von einer zentralisierten Großbewirtschaftung von Ökosystemen wegführt. Statt den Urin kilometerweit durch neue Rohrsysteme zu schicken, aufzubereiten und damit gedüngte Lebensmittel zu kaufen, könnten wir ihn gleich für unsere eigenen Zimmer- und Gartenpflanzen recyceln und damit den Nährstoffaustausch auf einen Bereich einschränken, der unserem Verantwortungsbereich entspricht. Mit dem Projekt *drink.pee.drink.pee.drink.pee* fordern wir dazu auf, Urin nicht nur als Abfallprodukt, sondern als potentiell reichhaltigen Nährstoff zu sehen, der im eigenen Ökosystem verwaltet werden kann.

Vielleicht können wir uns von passiven Förderern zentralisierter Großbewirtschaftung zu einem Netzwerk intelligenter Ökosysteme entwickeln. Wenn wir künftige Innovationen in Bereichen wie Nanotechnologie, Biochemie und Sensorik in die Hände der Allgemeinheit legen, schaffen wir vielleicht bessere Möglichkeiten, Materialen in unserer unmittelbaren Umgebung selbst umzuwandeln, statt sie einfach zu konsumieren und wegzuwerfen. Wir können aktive Gestalter im Zentrum der eigenen Mikroumgebung werden, die begeistert immer neue Austauschmöglichkeiten von hyperlokalen organischen Materialien finden und intelligent mit ihrer Rolle in natürlichen Kreisläufen umgehen.

(Aus dem Englischen von Wilfried Prantner)

Bibi Nelson, Matt Johnson, Isabel Lizardi, Becky Pilditch

Bare—Skin Safe Conductive Ink

Bare—Skin Safe Conductive Ink is the result of a graduate project at the Royal College of Art, created by Bibi Nelson, Matt Johnson, Isabel Lizardi and Becky Pilditch. This project began as an experimental investigation of parasitic technology, and developed into an exploration of the possibilities for bridging the gap between electronics and the body. *Bare* is an innovative and unique material that allows users to interface with electronic devices directly through gesture, movement and touch. The final formula was developed through a design-led material exploration. A thorough study of the history of body art and ornamentation led to the creation of an ink that humanizes wearable technologies and provides a sensuous method of applying electronics to the body through customized circuitry.

In its current form, *Bare* can be applied with a brush, stamp, or spray, and has been used to send information between people, people and computers, and to power small devices such as LEDs. The ink is currently best suited to low power, information-lean applications such as switching and simple data transfer. However, other potential application areas include dance, music, computer interfaces, communication and medical devices. The ink has the potential to sensually replace and augment existing technologies where wires are cumbersome or undesirable.

Temporary, non-toxic and water-soluble, this material is composed of non-metallic conductive particles suspended in food and cosmetic additives. This combination is the result of extensive research into a wide array of inert and non-toxic ingredients allowing for the safe application directly on the skin. The development process behind *Bare* generated over 120 different material samples before reaching the final formula. Connections between the ink and electronic devices are made through small electrodes placed directly on the skin that can transmit data either wirelessly or via cables.

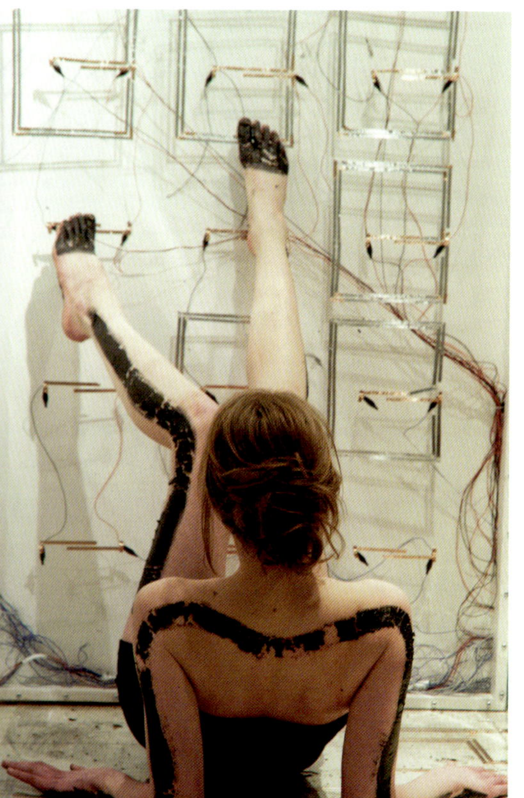

Bare has been used to either power small devices directly, such as LEDs or to interface with the computer. The most poignant interface demonstration allows a dancer to use the surface of their skin as a musical instrument, simultaneously choreographing dance and composing music. In this performance, *Bare* is used as a conductive medium, bridging between electrodes placed on surfaces around a space (typically walls and floor). As different parts of the dancer's body touch between these contacts, musical notes and patterns are created. The dynamic properties of the material allow for a wide variety of musical expression through manipulation of tone and rhythm. The result of this direct interaction between movement and sound is a unique and compelling performance.

Bibi Nelson, Matt Johnson, Isabel Lizardi, Becky Pilditch

Bare – Skin Safe Conductive Ink

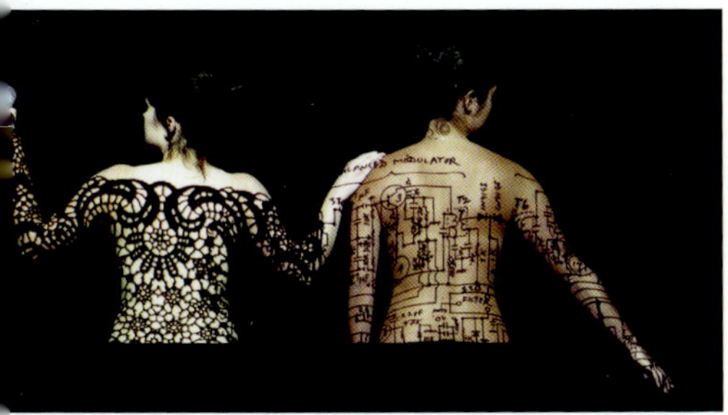

Bare–Skin Safe Conductive Ink ist das Resultat eines Diplomprojekts von Bibi Nelson, Matt Johnson, Isabel Lizardi und Becky Pilditch am Royal College of Art. Es begann als experimentelle Untersuchung parasitischer Technologien und entwickelte sich zu einer Suche nach Möglichkeiten, die Kluft zwischen Elektronik und Körper zu überwinden. *Bare* ist ein innovatives, einzigartiges Material, mit dessen Hilfe sich elektronische Geräte direkt durch Gesten, Bewegungen und Berührungen ansprechen lassen. Die endgültige Formel wurde in einem designgesteuerten Materialentwicklungsprozess gefunden. Ein gründliches Studium der Geschichte der Körperkunst und des Körperschmucks bereitete den Weg zur Entwicklung einer Tinte, die der Wearable-Technologie einen menschlichen Aspekt verleiht und es ermöglicht, Elektronik auf sinnliche Weise über maßgeschneiderte Schaltkreise mit dem Körper zu verbinden.

In seiner gegenwärtigen Form kann *Bare* mittels Pinsel, Stempel oder Sprühdose aufgetragen werden. Es wurde bereits zum Versenden von Informationen zwischen Personen bzw. Personen und Computern sowie zum Betreiben kleiner Geräte wie LEDs verwendet. Die Tinte ist derzeit am besten für informationsarme Kleinststromanwendungen wie Schaltvorgänge und einfache Datenübertragung geeignet. Mögliche Anwendungsbereiche sind u. a. Tanz, Musik, Computerinterfaces, Kommunikation und medizinische Geräte. Die Tinte hat das Potential, existierende Technologien dort zu ersetzen oder zu ergänzen, wo Drähte hinderlich oder unerwünscht sind.

Das temporär einsetzbare, ungiftige, wasserlösliche Material besteht aus in Nahrungsmittel- oder Kosmetikzusatzstoffen schwebenden nichtmetallischen leitfähigen Teilchen. Die Verbindung ist das Ergebnis umfassender Untersuchungen auf dem weiten Feld inerter, nicht-toxischer Trägerstoffe, die sich gefahrlos auf die nackte Haut auftragen lassen. Bis zur endgültigen Formel wurden über 120 verschiedene Materialien erprobt. Die Verbindungen zwischen Tinte und elektronischen Geräten werden mittels kleiner, direkt auf der Haut angebrachter Elektroden hergestellt, die die Daten per Draht oder Funk übertragen.

Bare wurde bisher dazu eingesetzt, entweder kleine Geräte wie LEDs direkt mit Strom zu versorgen oder aber Verbindungen zu Computern herzustellen. Bei der markantesten Interfacedemonstration verwendet ein Tänzer seine Hautoberfläche als Musikinstrument und kann so gleichzeitig choreografieren und komponieren. In dieser Performance wird *Bare* als Leitermedium zu im Raum verteilten (meist an Wand und Boden angebrachten) Elektroden verwendet. Berühren sich verschiedene Körperteile des Tänzers zwischen diesen Kontakten, werden Töne und musikalische Muster generiert. Die dynamischen Eigenschaften des Materials erlauben die Erzeugung einer breiten Palette musikalischer Ausdrucksformen durch die Manipulation von Ton und Rhythmus. Durch diese direkte Interaktion zwischen Bewegung und Sound entsteht eine einmalige, außergewöhnliche Performance.

(Aus dem Englischen von Wilfried Prantner)

Michael Burton

Nanotopia

Nanotopia envisages the promises of nanotechnology in socio-economic extremes. It creates a far future scenario building on the prequel, *Future Farm*. It takes the possibilities of manipulating matter on a nano-scale and questions the utopian vision that is predicted for its application. Experts like Richard Jones, writer of *Soft Machines: nanotechnology and life*, believe the true potential of the technology is when fused with living cells to take on self-replicating properties. Reflecting this research, the imaginary world of *Nanotopia* presents a far future application of the technology once released into the everyday world, but raises the question, who is this utopia intended for?

Nanotopia predicts an unexpected outcome of the nanotech age with a widening gap between rich and poor. It presents a scenario drawn from the current desperate reality of severely deprived people who reconsider their body as a site of financial income. Whereas today it is possible to legally or illegally profit from the trade of human organs, eggs, sperm and hair, *Nanotopia* predicts a future scenario where people grow and produce new clinical and pharmaceutical products on the body. Here technology enters into the same materiality as our bodies.

In *Nanotopia*, people are presented as farms with growths cultivated, incubated and harvested on the body. These growths predict the practice of synthetically bioengineering viruses and bacteria, which are modified to form useful and desirable products. In this case the Human Papilloma Virus (HPV), commonly known as the wart virus, is engineered to result in a pharmaceutical product. After incubation the growths are harvested for consumption further up the social class hierarchy.

In comparison at the upper extremity of the socio-economic scale, in the rich and elite classes, the impact of the body farms spur new bodily aesthetics towards growth-free bodies and natural protection systems against free viruses in the environment. In pursuit of protection against the abundance of modified HPVs, which are advantageous and prolific under ideal circumstances, the body's natural protection barriers like the eyelashes and nasal hair are enhanced. These enhancements are embraced to become desirable statements of cleanliness, purity and wealth.

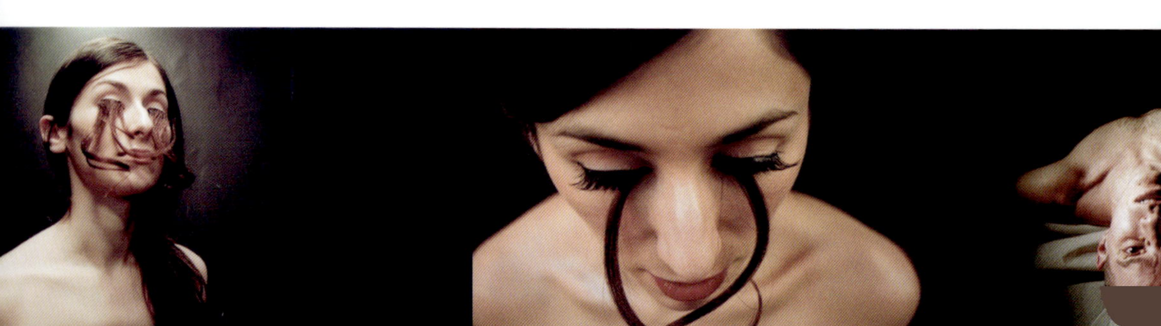

Michael Burton

Nanotopia

Nanotopia befasst sich mit den Verheißungen der Nanotechnologie und ihren Auswirkungen an den Rändern der Gesellschaft. Es entwirft ein fernes Zukunftsszenario, das auf dem Projekt *Future Farm* aufbaut. *Nanotopia* geht von der Möglichkeit aus, Materie im Nanomaßstab zu manipulieren und hinterfragt die utopischen Vorstellungen, die in Hinblick auf die Anwendung dieser Technologie vorherrschen. Experten wie Richard Jones, der Autor von *Soft Machines: Nanotechnology and Life*, glauben, dass das technologische Potenzial erst ausgeschöpft wird, wenn sie mit lebenden Zellen kombiniert wird und selbstreplizierende Eigenschaften entwickelt. Die imaginäre Welt von *Nanotopia* präsentiert eine in ferner Zukunft angesiedelte Einsatzmöglichkeit dieser Technologie, die vielleicht einmal selbstverständlich sein wird, wirft dabei aber auch die kritische Frage auf, für wen diese Utopie eigentlich gedacht ist.

Nanotopia antizipiert eine unerwartete Folgeerscheinung des Nanozeitalters, nämlich dass sich die Kluft zwischen Arm und Reich noch vergrößern wird. Es zeigt ein Szenario, das die ausweglose Situation sozial Benachteiligter unserer Zeit extrapoliert, die gezwungen sind, ihren Körper zu vermarkten. Während es heute bereits möglich ist, legal oder illegal aus dem Handel mit menschlichen Organen, Eizellen, Spermien und Haaren Profit zu schlagen, entwirft *Nanotopia* ein Zukunftsszenario, in dem die Menschen neue Arzneimittel und pharmazeutische Produkte auf ihrem Körper kultivieren und produzieren. Die Technologie wird hier identisch mit der Materialität unseres Körpers.

Nanotopia zeigt Menschen als Farmen, die Gewächse auf ihrem Körper züchten und ernten. Diese Gewächse sind eine Vorwegnahme synthetisch, biotechnisch erzeugter Viren und Bakterien, die in Zukunft zu nützlichen und erwünschten Produkten modifiziert werden. Konkret werden humane Papillomviren (HPV), besser bekannt als Warzenviren, gezüchtet und in ein pharmazeutisches Produkt umgewandelt. Nach der Inkubation werden die Kulturen geerntet, um in höheren sozialen Schichten konsumiert zu werden.

Am oberen Rand der sozioökonomischen Skala, in der Klasse der Reichen und der Eliten, entstehen durch die Körperfarmen neue Ästhetiken, deren Ideal glatte, wachstumsfreie Körper mit natürlichen Schutzsystemen gegen Viren sind. Auf der Suche nach einem wirksamen Schutz vor den modifizierten Papillomviren, die auf den Körperfarmen nützlich und fruchtbar sind, werden natürliche Schutzbarrieren des Körpers wie Wimpern und Nasenhaar verstärkt. Diese „Extensions" werden betont und als erwünschte Symbole von Sauberkeit, Reinheit und Wohlstand kultiviert.

(Aus dem Englischen von Martina Bauer)

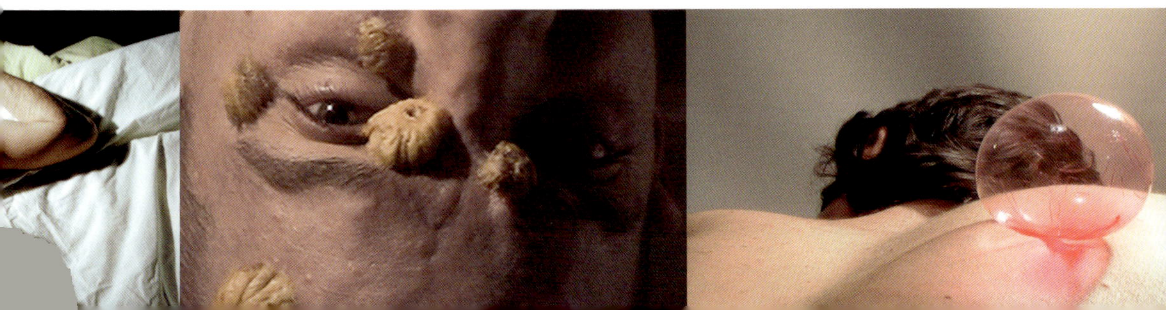

Michael Burton

Future Farm

Future Farm presents the unintentional use of new technologies like bio and nanotech once released from the lab and explores the consequential socio-economical pressures these create. The project investigates how these new technologies give radically new perceptions of ourselves, extending the possibilities of the human body and ultimately having a great impact on our human nature.

Context

Stem Cell research is the current scientific Holy Grail and starting point of the *Future Farm* project. Stem Cells hold the body's genetic blueprints and can be coaxed into replicating, *in vitro*, into most of the body's different cell types. Current research is developing the manipulation of these cells to create muscles, bones, whole organs including hearts and most recently and controversially, even sperm.

Stem Cells are found in regions throughout the human body, but an accessible and readily available site to find adult stem cells is adipose fat tissue. Whereas fat was once seen as an undesirable bodily by-product, it could be a future valuable raw material for the medical industry.

Concept

Future Farm presents the scenario of legalized trade in Stem Cell production. As a precursor to *Nanotopia* (sister project), it predicts an instance where people in need of an economic income use their bodies to produce and sell adipose fat stem cells. *Future Farm* reflects the current body farm practice that thrives due to the success of organ transplant surgery and the subsequent tourist industry grown to transport patients to people willing to sell parts of their body.

For Future Farmers who harvest their adipose tissue sites, they push their bodies for optimum productivity and create the ultimate obesogenic domestic environments. In this context, larger body types and genes favoring greater fat accumulation are more successful and desirable.

As Future Farmers push their body mass index higher, they create more body surface area to host clinical trials and growth sites for nanotechnological products. In the *Future Farm* project these include trials of new, synthetically engineered human papilloma viruses on the back and feet.

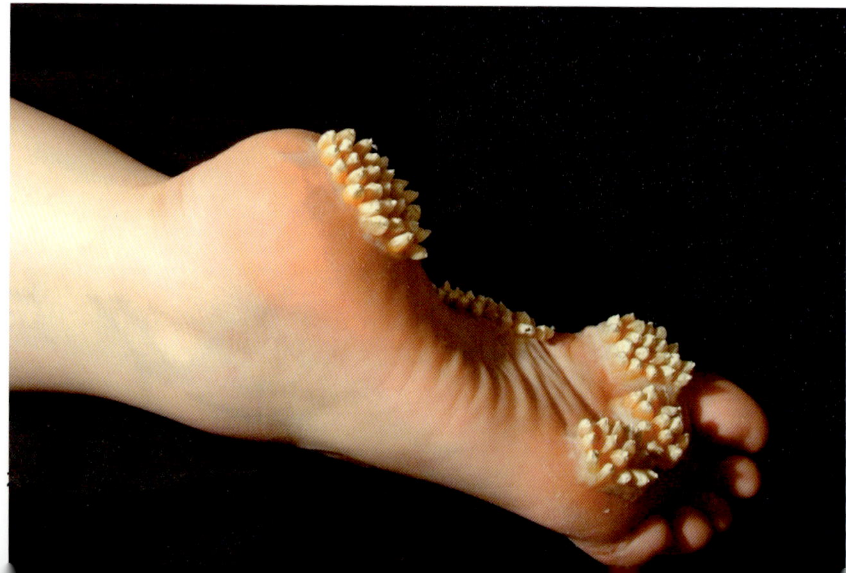

Michael Burton

Future Farm

Future Farm zeigt auf, dass neue Technologien wie die Bio- und die Nanotechnologie unvorhergesehene Anwendungsfelder finden, sobald sie aus dem Labor auf den Markt gelangen, und setzt sich mit den daraus resultierenden sozioökonomischen Spannungen auseinander.
Das Projekt untersucht die radikale Veränderung unseres Selbstbilds, die diese neuen Technologien bewirken, die erweiterten Möglichkeiten des menschlichen Körpers und die tiefgreifenden Auswirkungen auf die menschliche Natur.

Kontext

Ausgangspunkt des Projekts *Future Farm* ist die Stammzellenforschung, die derzeit der Heilige Gral der Wissenschaft ist. Die Stammzellen enthalten den genetischen Bauplan des Körpers und sind in der Lage, sich *in vitro* in die verschiedenen Zelltypen des Körpers auszudifferenzieren. Derzeit arbeitet die Wissenschaft an der Manipulation dieser Zellen, um Muskeln, Knochen, ganze Organe wie etwa das Herz und seit Kurzem sogar Spermien herzustellen, was kontroversielle Diskussionen ausgelöst hat.
Stammzellen finden sich überall im menschlichen Körper, besonders einfach und in großer Menge lassen sich adulte Stammzellen jedoch aus adipösem Gewebe gewinnen. Wurde Fett einst als unerwünschtes Nebenprodukt des Körpers betrachtet, könnte es in Zukunft wertvolles Rohmaterial für die medizinische Industrie sein.

Konzept

Future Farm entwirft das Szenario eines legalen Handels mit Stammzellen. Als Vorläufer des Schwesterprojekts *Nanotopia* antizipiert es die Tendenz, dass Menschen auf der Suche nach einer Einkommensquelle ihren Körper vermarkten und adipöse Stammzellen produzieren und verkaufen. *Future Farm* untersucht aktuelle Praktiken des Organhandels, der aufgrund der Erfolge in der Organtransplantation und der damit verbundenen Tourismusindustrie – Patienten werden zu Menschen gebracht, die bereit sind, Körperteile zu verkaufen – floriert.
Um adipöses Gewebe ernten zu können, sorgen *Future Farmers* für optimale Produktivität ihrer Körper, indem sie bestmögliche Voraussetzungen für die Fettleibigkeit schaffen. In diesem Kontext gelten ein massiver Körperbau und Gene, die Fettdepots begünstigen, als ertragreicher und stellen daher das Ideal dar.
Future Farmers erhöhen ihren Body-Mass-Index, um eine größere Körperoberfläche für klinische Versuche und Anbauflächen für nanotechnische Produkte zu erzielen. Konkret geht es bei *Future Farm* um Versuche zur synthetischen Herstellung von Papillomviren auf dem Rücken und auf den Füßen.

(Aus dem Englischen von Martina Bauer)

The Earth Angel

The Earth Angel is a brand new, innovatively designed adult toy that was designed and developed in Ireland. It is the first ever adult toy to contain "green" technology. Over the last few years there have been attempts made to produce a 100% environmentally friendly sex toy, but so far none have lived up to expectations. "Green" sex toy manufacturers are focusing more on the materials used in their toys than on the operation of the toys. There have been some offerings of solar powered and moon powered toys, but these are not without their disadvantages.

The Earth Angel has all the benefits and none of the disadvantages. Unlike traditional "green" toys it will never require replacement batteries as it houses its own patented power core. Intense vibrations from the word go. A specially adapted key is fitted within the base and is extracted and turned to initiate the power core. A few quick turns … and hey presto!! … you have a fully charged, incredibly intense vibrator. All elements of *The Earth Angel* have been used with the environment in mind—from the internal parts to the outer packaging. We have only produced our vibrator in one colour, white, in keeping with the concept behind the product. *The Earth Angel* is manufactured exclusively for Caden Enterprises to the highest quality control standards and has been given a medical certificate of quality. We have designed our packaging to display *The Earth Angel* to its best advantage.

Clear, clean and 100% recyclable …

When developing *The Earth Angel,* we wanted to produce an environmentally friendly sex toy that appealed to all consumers regardless of gender, age or ethnicity. *THE EARTH ANGEL* has been in its development stage for the past two years and we are excited that our vision has become reality. We will only ever produce environmentally friendly sex toys using our patented technology. Every industry has an obligation to do as much as it can to reduce the effects of climate change, and by developing this new technology we hope that others will follow suit and look for alternative ways to design and manufacture their products.

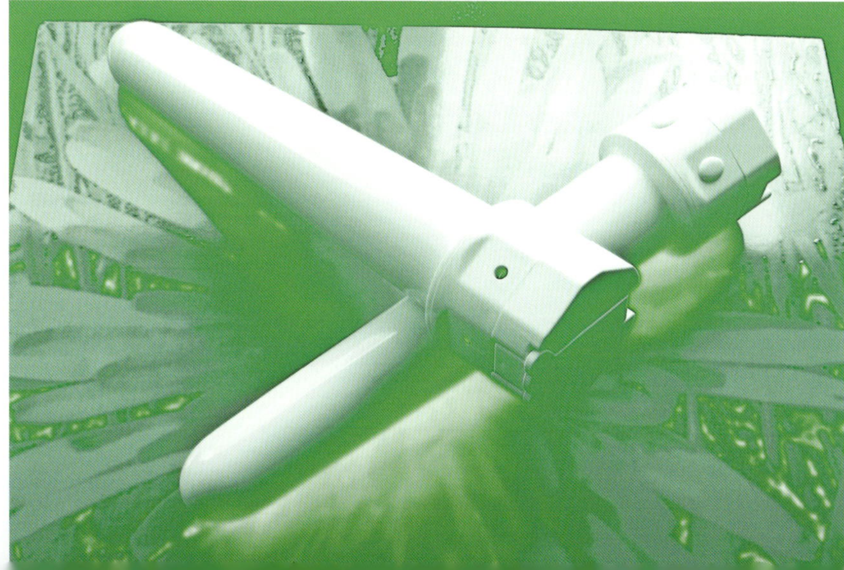

The Earth Angel

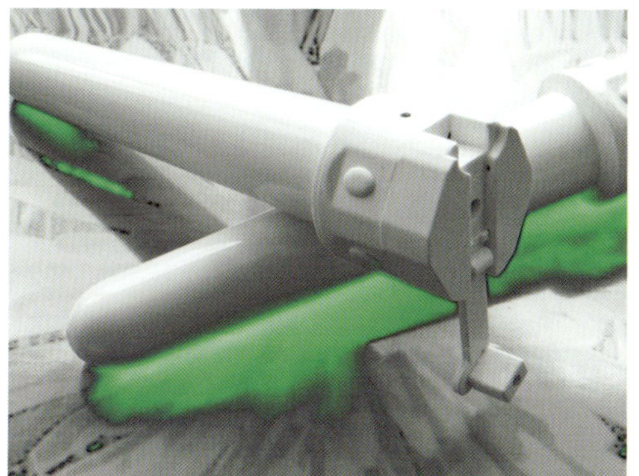

The Earth Angel ist ein brandneues, innovatives Erwachsenenspielzeug, das in Irland entwickelt und hergestellt wird. Das Gerät ist der erste Vibrator, der auf umweltfreundliche Technologie setzt. In den letzten Jahren kamen verschiedene Vibratoren auf den Markt, die als hundertprozentig umweltfreundlich angepriesen wurden. Allerdings konnte keines dieser Produkte diesen Anspruch bislang erfüllen. „Grüne" Hersteller von Sexspielzeug konzentrieren sich meist auf die Unbedenklichkeit der verwendeten Materialien statt auf einen möglichst umweltfreundlichen Betrieb ihrer Produkte. Es gibt zwar einige solar- oder mit Mondlicht betriebene Produkte, die jedoch allesamt gewisse Schwachstellen aufweisen.

The Earth Angel vereint alle Vorteile von umweltfreundlichen Vibratoren und bringt keine Nachteile mit sich. Anders als bei herkömmlichen „grünen" Vibratoren müssen die Batterien nie ausgetauscht werden, da das Gerät über einen patentierten integrierten Akku verfügt, der erregende Momente garantiert. Mit der im Boden eingebauten Kurbel kann der Akku rasch aufgeladen werden. Einige Umdrehungen mit der Kurbel und schon steht Ihnen ein voll aufgeladener Vibrator mit verschiedenen Vibrationsstufen zur Verfügung. Sämtliche Bestandteile des *Earth Angel* – von den Bauteilen bis zur Verpackung – erfüllen strengste Umweltschutzkriterien. Aus Gründen des Umweltschutzes ist der Vibrator nur in einer Farbe (Weiß) verfügbar. Das Gerät wird unter Einhaltung strengster Qualitätskontrollen exklusiv für *Caden Enterprises* produziert; ein Zertifikat attestiert dem Gerät höchste Qualität und medizinische Unbedenklichkeit. Die Verpackung soll die Vorzüge des *Earth Angel* bestmöglich unterstreichen.

The Earth Angel: einfach, sauber und hundertprozentig wiederverwertbar.

Unser Ziel war es, ein umweltfreundliches Sexspielzeug zu entwickeln, das Konsumenten unabhängig von Geschlecht, Alter oder Herkunft anspricht. In den letzten zwei Jahren haben wir beharrlich an der Umsetzung unserer Pläne gearbeitet und freuen uns, dass unsere Vision nun Realität wurde. Wir werden auf der Grundlage unserer patentierten Technologie auch in Zukunft umweltfreundliches Sexspielzeug herstellen. Jede Branche hat die Verpflichtung, so viel wie möglich zur Reduktion der Folgen des Klimawandels beizutragen. Wir hoffen, dass andere unserem Beispiel folgen und umweltfreundliche Alternativen für das Design und die Produktion ihrer Produkte suchen.

(Aus dem Englischen von Sonja Pöllabauer)

Daan van den Berg

Merrick

"From an unknown location, I break into Ikea's computer server. In this nerve centre, the CAD files for every Ikea product are stored and downloaded worldwide. By infecting the CAD files with the 'Elephantiasis virus' I have just designed, I can hack the entire range of products. The virus causes random deformities, like lumps, cracks and humps, which only show up when the customer prints his product at home with his 3D printer."
The *Merrick* originated during a fantasy about the development described above. The *Merrick* is a digital file infected with the human Elephantiasis virus and then converted into a tangible product by using a 3D printer. Every lamp that is printed will therefore be different.
Three-dimensional printing at home might sound like science fiction. But it is far from unthinkable. Consumer 3D printing is still in its infancy, but is expected to touch off a new revolution.

Daan van den Berg

Merrick

„Ich hacke mich von einem unbekannten Ort aus in den Ikea-Server. Hier sind die CAD-Dateien aller Ikea-Produkte gespeichert und von dieser Zentrale werden sie weltweit heruntergeladen. Infiziere ich die CAD-Dateien mit dem von mir soeben entwickelten „Elephantiasisvirus", kann ich die gesamte Produktlinie verändern. Der Virus verursacht nach dem Zufallsprinzip Deformationen wie Klumpen, Risse und Höcker, die sich jedoch nur manifestieren, wenn der Kunde das Produkt zu Hause auf seinem 3D-Drucker ausgibt. *Merrick* entstand im Verlauf von Gedankenspielereien zu oben beschriebener Entwicklung. *Merrick* beschreibt eine Datei, die mit dem menschlichen Elephantiasisvirus infiziert und dann mittels 3D-Drucker in ein greifbares Produkt umgewandelt wird. Jede ausgedruckte Lampe sieht daher anders aus.
Dreidimensionales Drucken zu Hause mag wie Science-Fiction klingen, ist aber durchaus denkbar. 3-D-Druck für den Consumer-Bereich steckt noch in den Kinderschuhen, verspricht aber eine revolutionäre Entwicklung auszulösen.

(Aus dem Englischen von
Michael Kaufmann)

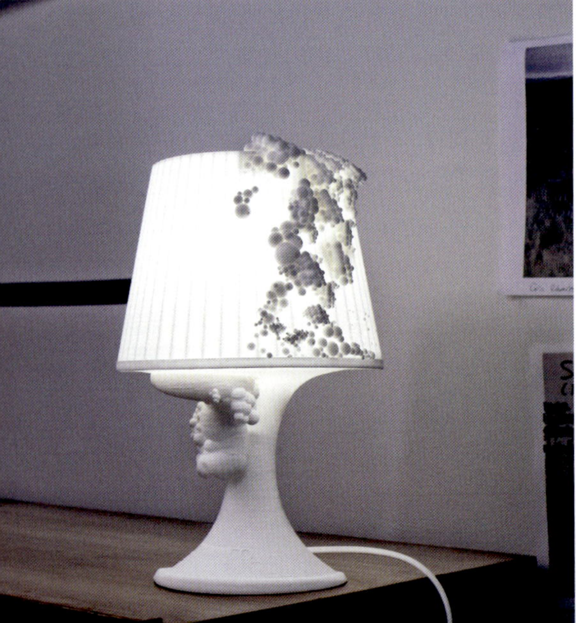

Foto: Maarten Willemstein

Marieke Staps

Soil Clock

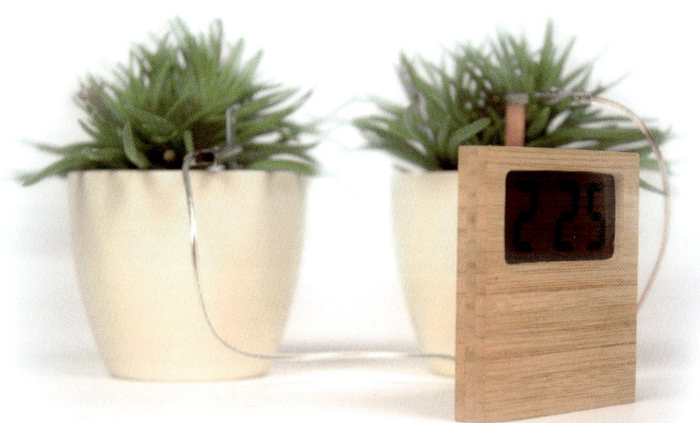

This clock runs on mud and is called an earth battery. An earth battery is a pair of electrodes made of two dissimilar metals, such as zinc and copper, and these metals are buried in the soil. The bacteria in the soil can create webs of electrical wiring that transform the soil into an environmentally friendly source of energy. The copper and zinc transport the energy to the clock. The pair of plants can deliver 1.5 v, and the more cells you have, the more electricity you can create. The soil needs to be moist so that the metal has enough friction. So make sure that you water the plants!
Free and environmentally friendly energy forever and ever.

Marieke Staps

Soil Clock

Diese Uhr läuft mit Erde und wird daher Erdbatterie genannt. Sie besteht aus einem Elektrodenpaar aus zwei verschiedenen Metallen, wie Zink und Kupfer, die in die Erde gesteckt werden. Die Bodenbakterien erzeugen ein Geflecht elektrischer Leiter, die aus dem Boden eine umweltfreundliche Energiequelle machen. Die Energie gelangt über die Kupfer- und Zinkelektroden zur Uhr. Ein solches Pflanzenpaar liefert ca. 1,5 Volt; je mehr Zellen man einsetzt, desto mehr Strom wird generiert. Die Erde muss feucht sein, damit das Metall genügend Reibung hat. Vergessen Sie daher nicht, Ihre Pflanzen zu gießen!
Kostenlose und umweltfreundliche Energie für immer und ewig.

(Aus dem Englischen von Michael Kaufmann)

Werner Jauk + Heimo Ranzenbacher

Moving Mountains

The installation consists of four elements: a triptych made of two monitors flanking a sort of petri dish and a plot of grass. The left monitor displays a private lawn and its (real estate) value. The right monitor shows the search by the system for correspondences to the subjective estimated value of and/or the esteem accorded to this plot of turf by installation visitors on the globe and the area of correspondence.

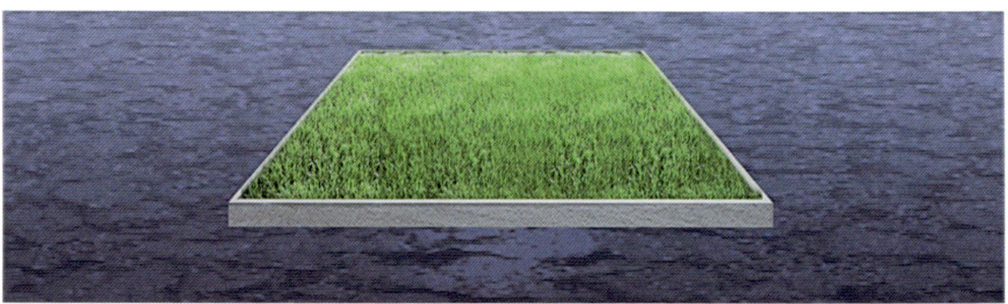

In the central object, a highly reactive fungus culture is stimulated by a fluid, the quality of which approximates the estimated value. Installation visitors make known their value estimations by the length of time they spend on the plot of grass in front of the triptych. The reaction of the fungus culture is not only a consequence of the estimation of value; it is also integrated into the functional context as a psychological (emotional) interface. It counteracts the computer screen aesthetic and has a feedback effect on the evaluation by means of perception.
The expression "to move mountains" is used to indicate the possibility that "something slight" (faith, love, …) can set mighty things in motion. The reference to the emancipation of art from nature is meant to bring this "supernatural" metaphor together with the concept of culture.
Serving as cultural-historical references are the postmodern-pragmatic world of experience of ones own piece of turf and Albrecht Dürer's *The Great Piece of Turf* (especially the way in which this watercolor painting proceeds to extract a portion of nature in order to translate it into an artificial, geometric system of reference). For Postmodernism, culture is the artificial, hedonic process of charging nature with significance; for Modernism, the abstraction of nature is an artificial system of reference. Our basic orientation is that the conversion of nature into meaning-neutral codes constitutes, as emancipation from nature, a precondition for culture, and that the process of charging codes with significance and turning them into systems of meaningful signs can be described as the transpersonal process of the creation of culture. The arbitrariness of the organization of codes and the possibility of charging them with meaning define culture as a dynamic process controlled by (hedonic) valuation.

Software development: Michael Augustyn
Thanks to: Franz Brunner, Department of Geography and Spatial Research of the University of Graz; Walter Buzina, Department of Hygiene, Microbiology and Environmental Medicine / Medical University of Graz; Jauk-Hinz, grelle musik, Department of Musicology of the University of Graz
Subsidized by: Stadt Graz-Kultur + Land Steiermark-Kultur

Werner Jauk + Heimo Ranzenbacher

Berge versetzen

Die Installation besteht aus vier Einheiten – aus einem Triptychon, gestaltet aus zwei Monitoren, die eine Art Petrischale flankieren, und einem Rasengeviert. Der linke Monitor zeigt ein privates Rasenstück und dessen (Immobilien-)Wert. Der rechte Monitor zeigt die Suche des Systems nach Entsprechungen des subjektiven Schätzwertes bzw. der Wertschätzung dieses Rasenstücks durch Betrachter auf dem Globus und das Gebiet der Übereinstimmung.

In dem zentralen Objekt wird eine hochreaktive Pilzkultur durch Flüssigkeit animiert, deren Menge aus der Wertschätzung folgt. Betrachter bekunden ihre Wertschätzung durch die Verweildauer auf dem Rasengeviert vor dem Triptychon. Die Reaktion der Pilzkultur ist nicht nur Folge der Wertschätzung, sondern als psychologisches (emotionales) Interface in den Funktionszusammenhang eingebunden: Sie konterkariert die Bildschirmästhetik und wirkt durch die Wahrnehmung auf die Wertung zurück.

Die Wendung „Berge versetzen" wird im Deutschen gebraucht, um die Möglichkeit zu bezeugen, dass durch „Geringfügiges" (Glaube, Liebe ...) Großes bewegt werden kann. Mit Bezug auf die Emanzipation der Kunst von Natur soll diese Metapher „Übernatürliches" mit der Vorstellung von Kultur zusammenführen.

Als kulturhistorische Referenz dienen die postmodern-pragmatische Erlebniswelt des eigenen Rasenstücks und Albrecht Dürers *Das große Rasenstück* (insbesondere die dem Bild zugrunde liegende Vorgangsweise, aus der Natur ein Stück herauszulösen, um es grafisch in ein künstliches, geometrisches Bezugssystem zu übersetzen). Für die Postmoderne ist Kultur die künstliche, hedonische Aufladung von Natur, für die Moderne die Abstraktion von Natur in ein künstliches Bezugssystem. Wir orientieren uns daran, dass die Konvertierung von Natur in bedeutungsneutrale Codes als Emanzipation von der Natur eine Bedingung von Kultur darstellt, und dass die Bedeutungsaufladung von Codes zu Zeichensystemen als der transpersonale Prozess der Schaffung von Kultur beschrieben werden kann. Die Willkürlichkeit der Organisation von Codes und die Möglichkeit zur Bedeutungsaufladung definieren Kultur als einen dynamischen Prozess – gesteuert durch (hedonische) Wertschätzung.

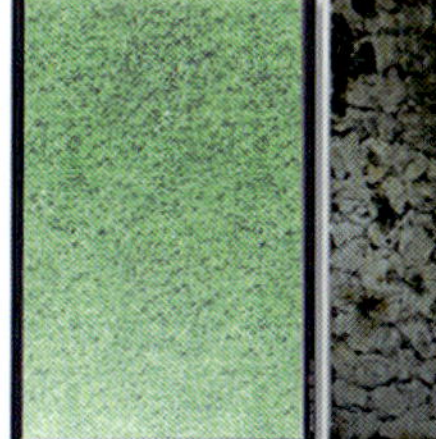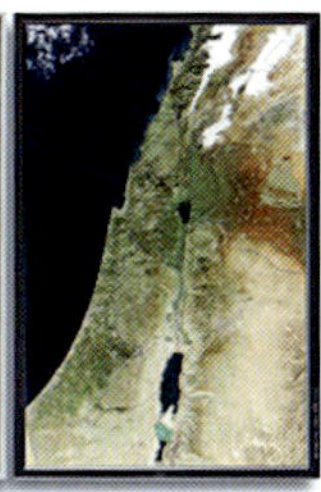

Software-Entwicklung: Michael Augustyn
Dank an: Franz Brunner, Institut für Geographie und Raumforschung / KFUni-Graz; Walter Buzina, Institut für Hygiene, Mikrobiologie und Umweltmedizin / Meduni-Graz; Doris Jauk-Hinz, grelle musik, Institut für Musikwissenschaft, KFUni-Graz.
Gefördert durch: Stadt Graz – Kultur + Land Steiermark – Kultur

History Lounge

The Lobby of the Brucknerhaus is the setting for a retrospective with prospective traits. In the History Lounge here, installations and a series of History Talks will spotlight 30 years of Ars Electronica. But the focus won't be on flashbacks reviewing the chronology of events and the historical development of media art; instead, the accent will be on highly subjective snapshots based on individuals' experiences and insights.

The artistic framework includes four works by the group art+com that was featured in an extensive show at the Ars Electronica Center earlier this year. The current exhibit showcases their efforts singled out for recognition by the Prix Ars Electronica and documents the group's latest project, a kinetic sculpture for the BMW Museum in Munich. Other references to areas of concentration over the course of Ars Electronica's history are *Life Writer* (2006) by Christa Sommerer and Laurent Mignonneau, and network visualizations by Dietmar Offenhuber and Co. Screenings, animated films and video documentations round out the setting in which the History Talks are taking place.

These get-togethers of Ars Electronica protagonists will get into individual points of view, experiences and reminiscences having to do with content and events. For example, guests will be elaborating on their favorite projects and justifying their selections on the basis of material culled from the Festival Archive. Guests are invited to go though the whole catalog of superlatives: their biggest disappointments, most moving experience and most inspiring moment.

The History Lounge is intentionally designed to be a mosaic of highly subjective contributions collectively manifesting what exactly made Ars Electronica what it has become over the past 30 years, and spotlighting the tremendous commitment, energy and inspiration displayed by individuals from the three groups—organizers, artists and audience members—whose perspectives will be represented over the course of the discussions and in the exhibits in the space in which those discussions are being held.

(Text: Heimo Ranzenbacher, translated from German by Mel Greenwald)

History Lounge

Das Foyer des Brucknerhauses ist Schauplatz einer Retrospektive mit prospektiven Zügen: 30 Jahre Ars Electronica werden in der *History Lounge* durch Installationen und in Form von Gesprächsrunden, *History Talks*, und Vorträgen blitzlichtartig beleuchtet. Im Zentrum stehen nicht historische Rückblenden auf die Chronologie der Ereignisse oder die medienkünstlerische Entwicklung, sondern vielmehr subjektive, von individuellen Erfahrungen und Einsichten getragene Schnappschüsse.

Den künstlerischen Rahmen markieren unter anderem vier Arbeiten der Gruppe art+com, die schon im ersten Halbjahr mit einer Werkschau im neuen Ars Electronica Center vertreten war. Dabei handelt es sich um ehemalige preisgekrönte Einreichungen zum Prix Ars Electronica und um die Dokumentation ihres jüngsten Projekts, der *Kinetischen Skulptur* für das BMW-Museum in München. Ebenfalls auf bestimmte Schwerpunkte im Lauf der Geschichte der Ars Electronica verweisen Christa Sommerers und Laurent Mignonneaus Arbeit *Life Writer* aus dem Jahr 2006 und Dietmar Offenhubers Netzwerkvisualisierungen. Screenings, Animationen und Video-Dokumentationen vervollständigen ein Environment, in dem die *History Talks* über die Bühne gehen. Thema der Gespräche sind individuelle Blickpunkte, Erfahrungen und Erinnerungen von Protagonisten und Besuchern der Ars Electronica an Projekte und Geschehnisse. Die Gäste werden beispielsweise nach ihren Lieblingsprojekten gefragt und anhand von Materialien aus dem Archiv des Festivals gebeten, näher auf die Umstände einzugehen, die für diesen Stellenwert im persönlichen Ranking den Ausschlag gaben. Der Fragenkatalog umfasst die Superlative des Gegenteils, die größte Enttäuschung, ebenso wie die bewegendste Erfahrung oder den am meisten inspirierenden Augenblick.

Beabsichtigt ist mit der *History Lounge* der Entwurf eines Mosaiks aus höchst subjektiven Beiträgen, in dem sich manifestiert, was Ars Electronica in den vergangenen 30 Jahren zu dem gemacht hat, was sie heute ist – das große Engagement, die Energie und Inspiration der einzelnen Personen – aus dem Kreis der Veranstalter und der KünstlerInnen ebenso wie aus dem Publikum, jenen drei Gruppen, aus denen sich die Gäste der *History Talks* und die Gestalter der *History Lounge* rekrutieren.

(Text: Heimo Ranzenbacher)

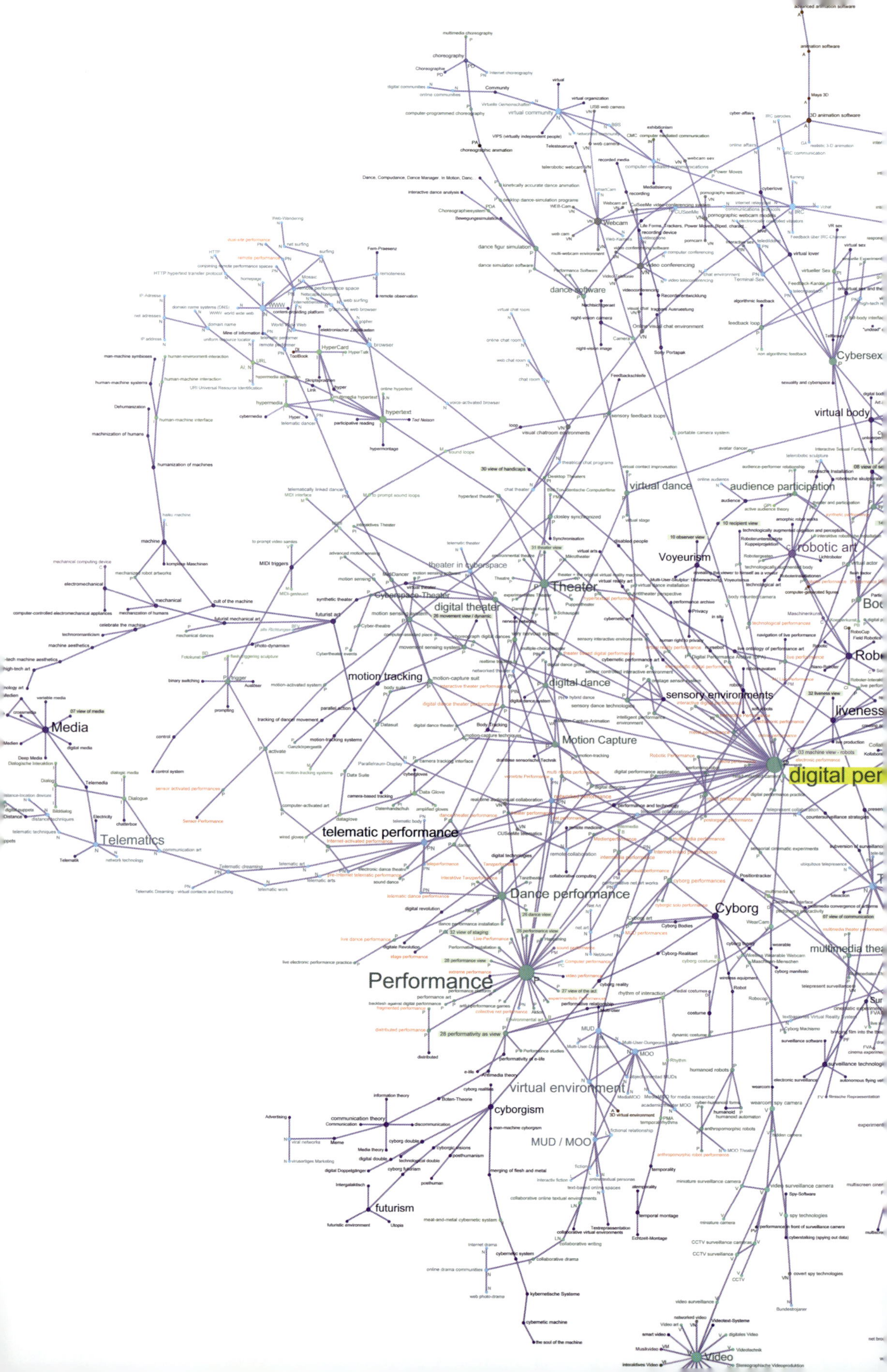

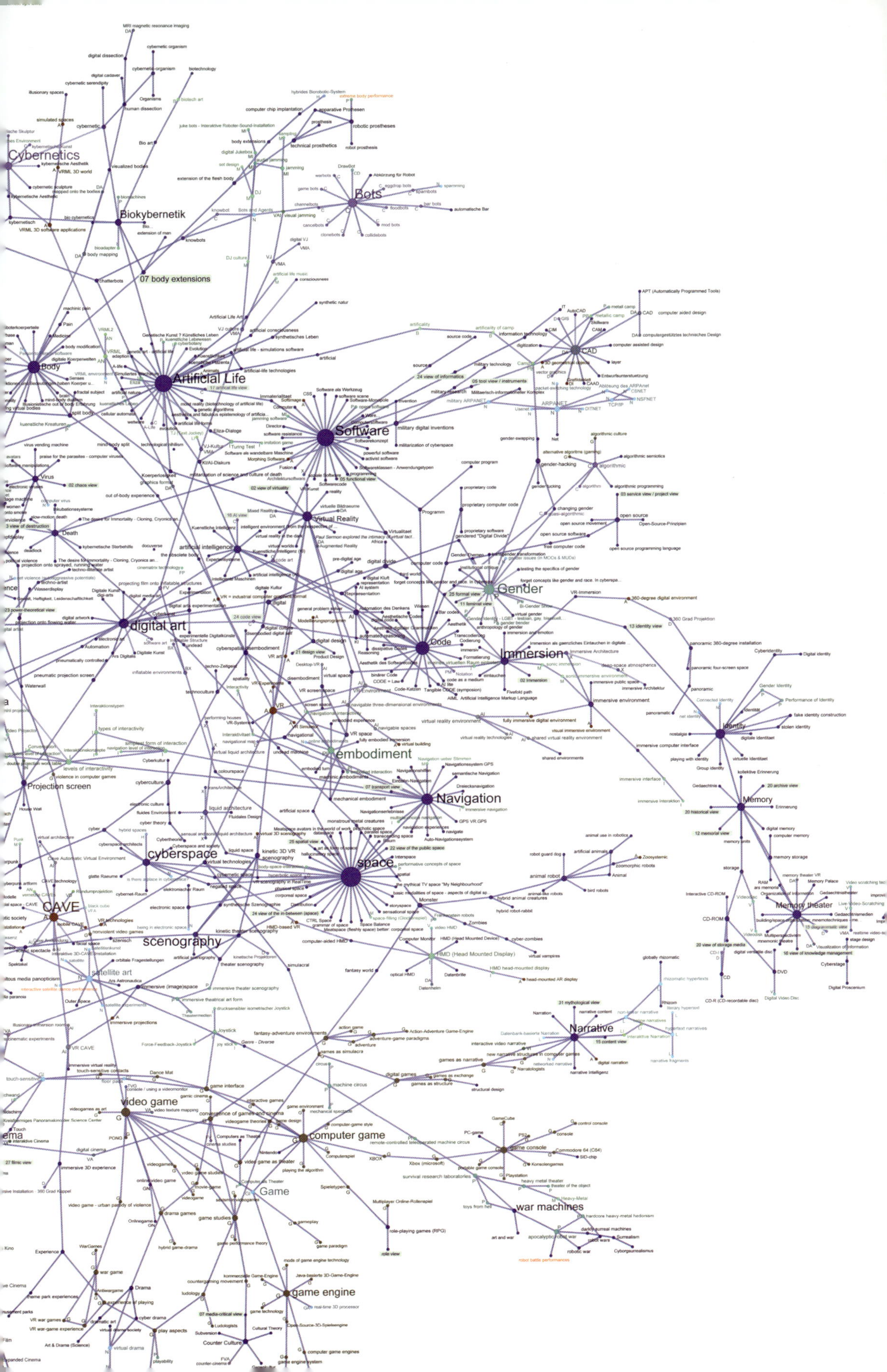

Cybernetics
Biokybernetik
Body
Artificial Life
Bots
Software
CAD
ARPANET
Virus
Death
artificial intelligence
Virtual Reality
Gender
Code
Immersion
Identity
digital art
VR
embodiment
Navigation
Memory
Projection screen
cyberspace
space
CAVE
scenography
Memory theater
satellite art
Narrative
video game
computer game
Game
war machines
game engine
07 body extensions

Mapping the Ars Electronica Archive

Ars Electronica and the Ludwig Boltzmann Institute Media.Art.Research have jointly set up in the AEC's new facility an archive that constitutes one of the world's most comprehensive resources detailing the history of media art. It encompasses recordings and documents from the 30 years of the Ars Electronica Festival, as well as an extensive collection of descriptions and documents relating to works submitted since 1987 to the Prix Ars Electronica. Plus, the holdings include much documentation of Ars Electronica's own in-house productions, exhibitions and other activities. There is also a large collection of institutional material—above all, press kits and the like released by Ars Electronica and the Austrian Broadcasting Company ORF—and documentation of the ensuing coverage by various media outlets.

Transferral of the documents assembled over the years into an archive helped set the stage for the scholarly processing and analysis of these holdings. Moreover, the Ludwig Boltzmann Institute Media.Art.Research has gone about organizing, cataloging and preserving this material, whereby the work has focused on entries to the Prix Ars Electronica competition. All Prix Ars Electronica submissions are collected in a digital archive designed for research purposes. All prizewinning projects are elaborately documented, e.g. additional information concerning their content and technology, including texts and images as well as audiovisual resources, all of it digitized.

The scholarly review and analysis of the Ars Electronica Archive's holdings is one of the most important research projects being conducted by the Ludwig Boltzmann Institute Media.Art.Research. For scholars engaged in visualization, computer science, cultural studies and the arts & humanities, this work is opening up new approaches to and yielding new insights into a field that has been exploring the boundaries of art for the last 30 years and also one that has itself manifested a process of transition that has transcended the art world and made an impact on all facets of life. *(Gabriele Blome)*

In this paper, we will elaborate on three examples of analytic approaches to the holdings of the Ars Electronica Archive and the visualization tools used for this purpose.

Approaches to Quantitative Art History

Despite the fact that it is not feasible to gather detailed information about the motivations, aspirations and agendas of the media artists, designers and computer scientists who have submitted work for prize consideration to the Prix Ars Electronica, published information enables us to analyze several aspects of this.

Registering and processing data about the works submitted each year makes it possible to ascertain how often individuals or groups submitted entries, in which years or over what time spans such entries were submitted, and which categories were considered relevant for the respective works. Entrants active over longer periods of time submit entries to two or three different categories over the years, whereby certain combinations and sequences that correlate to developments in media technology are highly typical. Thus, we observe transitions from computer graphics to works of animation, the transition from interactive art to net art in more than 680 cases, and the transition from the music category to interaction in more than 370 cases.

With respect to the categories in which the submissions were entered, it is possible to formulate certain generalizations about entrants, which could be drawn upon as the basis for an initial structuring process. A survey of the entrants' nationalities and the number of submissions per year from the respective countries permits us to draw conclusions about educational opportunities, subsidy situations, and the Prix's level of "brand recognition" in the respective lands. Following an initial phase of slow familiarization, there has been steady, across-the-board increase in participation. Even the mood prevailing in the wake of the bursting of the so-called Internet Bubble left behind quantitative traces in the Prix submission figures.

Combining prizewinner data with submission data permits us to derive so-called success patterns. Regular submission is a precondition for "visibility" and presence in the Archive, but is by no means a guarantee for recognition.

From approximately 30,000 entrants, we were able to filter out more than 13,000 individuals and groups that appeared promising for further comparison. Diverse data available online made it possible to further narrow down this group to approximately 3,500 persons who have made a name for themselves as media artists in other contexts as well. The names of more than 1,300 persons come up in at least four relevant contexts, and over 550 artists display six mentions or more. This is the company in which we find a significant proportion of those singled out for recognition by the Prix and—hardly surprising—those artists who are accorded significant space in catalogs and reference works.

The inclusion of literature for specialists in this field can also contribute to further refining the process of classification to a particular category. This allows us to reclassify performance artists, and also to come up with a list of more than 170 names for a not yet "prize-worthy" game category. This, in turn, makes it possible to refine the view of interaction and to observe the connection between electronic media arts and performance art.

Thanks to the catalog texts, we are able to reconstruct the educational background of many of the prizewinners. It would be very revealing to be able to conduct research on which institutions in which countries are of significance in media artists' career paths.

This quantitative analysis has just started. The data sets yielded by these initial analyses will aid the detailed media and art historical analyses to follow. In times of online presence, quantitative analyses should not be dismissed as the odd undertakings of dry-as-dust number crunchers; rather, this is a matter of bringing in experts to refine our methods of analysis and visualization.
(Gerhard Dirmoser)

Media Art as Social Process—Network Analysis of the Makeup of the Juries and Their Decisions

The annual jury sessions to determine the prizewinning projects constitute another interesting topic. This raises the question of the extent to which there is a correlation between the substantive development of media art and the social structures of the protagonists involved: the artists and the jurors. The places on the respective juries are filled with new faces each year. And the categories themselves have undergone a constant process of change: old ones are retired or programmatically redefined and new ones introduced. Employing the methods of social network analysis seems to be the obvious solution here. Now, when all the jurors who served throughout the history of this competition are linked to their respective jury sessions, the result is a bi-partite network that can subsequently be investigated.

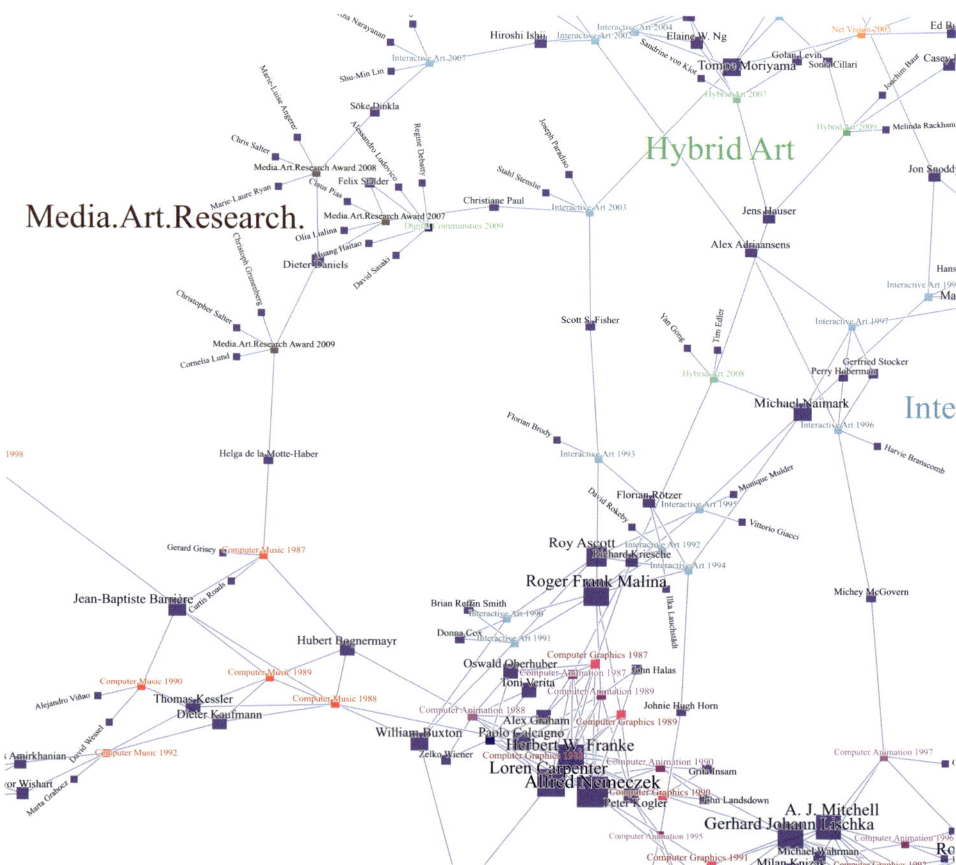

It's interesting to note that this network is a single, contiguous, unitary affair and, for instance, does not break up into various sub-networks corresponding to the Prix categories. This means that there have been no jury sessions (with one single exception[1]) without overlapping personnel with respect to a prior jury and, of considerably greater importance, that various individuals served as jurors in different categories over the years. This is an insight that becomes immediately evident when we examine the network visualization, but would have been much less obvious if the material had been considered on a textual basis only. The network visualization also shows that some categories are clearly delimited from the others and are dominated by key protagonists, whereas others are more strongly interwoven and do not seem to have core personnel. The use of the "centrality mass" concept from network analysis makes it possible to differentiate among various roles of the jurors involved. Some jurors seem to dominate a single category, whereas others appear in several contexts and function as bridges between different categories. The practice of inviting prizewinning artists to serve as jurors the following year additionally brings their contacts and knowledge contexts into play, and contributes to expanding the scope of and adding new facets to the categories.

These interdisciplinary junctions are also present in the counterpart to the jury network: the network of prizewinning artists. Here too, there is a surprisingly high degree of network linkup. This area is dominated by two sub-networks (that are-still?-not interconnected): on the one hand, the "microcosm" of the U19 category for young people and the Next Idea competition, and, on the other hand, the remaining Prix Ars Electronica categories. If one reduces the entire network to individuals with several awards, then the substantive bridges among the categories become clearly evident. The information content of these relations should, of course, not be over-interpreted; nevertheless, the existing networks provide a surprisingly multifaceted and richly detailed picture that persons familiar with the material can appreciate and confirm on the basis of their own experience. *(Dietmar Offenhuber)*

Taxonomies for New Media Art (History): Case Study Interactive Art

Furthermore, the extensive documentary material accompanying the entries to the Prix Ars Electronica allows for a detailed art-historical analysis. Classification systems are subject to criticism, as they neglect the specific characteristics of individual works. However a terminological classification can also lead to a differentiated vocabulary, advancing the description of individual characteristics of single works. Granular categorization enables linguistic accuracy and variety. Furthermore databases allow for the interrelation of different systems of concepts. This facilitates a break with the tradition of linear art(ist) histories and chronological paradigms in favor of parallel interrogations of various commonalities and differences. The term "interactive art", for example, embraces a broad spectrum from net-based literature and media performances to interactive installations. While a generalizing description of these works as interactive art alone is obviously restrictive and reduces the value of the term to a canned genre name, taxonomies help to differentiate but also relate. Differentiated classification systems uncover heterogeneities within one genre, but may also indicate parallels across genres that might otherwise remain unnoticed.

To do justice to the variety of possible approaches to the multidisciplinary field of media art research, we differentiated four perspectives, each containing up to three broader terms for a classification of the works[2]:

Formal perspective

The first broader term "form of artwork" is meant to give a general idea of the physical manifestation of a work, or, as the case may be, its performative or immaterial character. The second broader term "range of artwork" allows us to specify their "spatial" qualities, e.g. if an artwork is stand-alone or networked, to be located in public space or realized on mobile devices. Furthermore the potential "interaction partners" are specified within a third category.

Technological Perspective

Concerning works of new media art, on the one hand, technology can be argued to play a seminal role for the projects. On the other hand, the actually implemented devices and operating systems may be exchangeable. This makes the documentation of the media chosen at the time of production all the more pertinent. In the categories "media" and "processing technology", we encourage the collection of a broad variety of terms that will enable more detailed research into technological questions in the future.

Ludwig Boltzmann Institute Media.Art.Research.

Aesthetic Perspective

Interactive art touches upon a completely new form of aesthetics, as it is based on the active realization of artistic offers by the audience, resulting in an action-based aesthetic experience. We suggest describing whether "the visitor/performer does": observe, explore, activate, control, select, navigate, participate, leave traces, and so on. But there is also another part of the interaction process, originating from the work itself. "The work does": tell or narrate something, document or inform, visualize or sonify; it may be designed to enhance perception or to offer a game, to monitor something or to serve as an instrument, to transform, to collect and store, to process or mediate.

Contextual Perspective

Though we had to acknowledge that taxonomies reach their limits when aiming at a contextualization of works, we decided to include two categories: "catchwords" and "topic". While catchwords are often short-dated buzzwords that may allude to possible functions and application areas, but also to subjective intentions and societal discourses, they turned out to be a perfect way to include intentional, context-based views into a taxonomic approach, exactly because of their fuzzy nature. Though works of media art are often self-referential, they may also reflect on societal, political, economic or environmental processes. Therefore, identifying topics of works is possible and expedient, also because it introduces further points of comparison with non-interactive works.

The taxonomy was integrated into the Prix Ars Electronica online submission tool, so that, since 2008, the submitters themselves have been invited to apply it directly to their works. Furthermore, it was used to retrospectively classify the approximately 300 prizewinning projects from the years 1990–2009. This retrospective classification is visualized and can be interactively explored by means of the Themelandscape (see below). *(Katja Kwastek)*

Visualization Tools

In order to investigate and depict various aspects of the Prix Ars Electronica, several visualization programs were developed for the Ludwig Boltzmann Institute Media.Art.Research:

SemaSpace

SemaSpace is a compact graphics editor and browser for creating and analyzing semantic networks. Its key benefit is that it enables fluid manipulation of large and complex bodies of data. The program has been actively developed since 2004 by Dietmar Offenhuber and Gerhard Dirmoser, and was used to analyze jury networks. Gerhard Dirmoser also used Semaspace to construct and visually design the Ars Electronica Thesaurus comprising 24,000 relations.

Themelandscape

From 1990 to 2009, about 300 works were honored with a prize in the Interactive Art category. Katja Kwastek's art-historical analysis produced a taxonomy of interactive art, which attributed approximately 150 terms (catchwords) to these works, whereby each individual work was described by 20–30 catchwords. The resulting implicit similarities among the works can now be depicted (coded as geometric distances) in a "similarity space."
Through the use of a multidimensional scaling algorithm (MDS), the works are projected onto

a two-dimensional surface according to their relative thematic correspondence. Detailed information about the individual works can be compared on the basis of their forms of visual representation. The terms attributed to each work are depicted metaphorically as flower petals, whereby each catchword corresponds to its own petal shape. The individual forms that result enable the user to easily recognize similarities and differences. *(Evelyn Münster)*

X by Y

The "X by Y" visualization series created by Moritz Stefaner in cooperation with the Ludwig Boltzmann Institute Media.Art.Research constitutes a visual analysis of submissions to the Prix Ars Electronica. The visual representation of the combinations of attributes (such as categories by country or entrants by year) and the respective number of submissions makes it possible not only to survey the history of the Prix, but also to generate hypotheses about the mechanisms at work in this "World of Ars." *(Moritz Stefaner)*

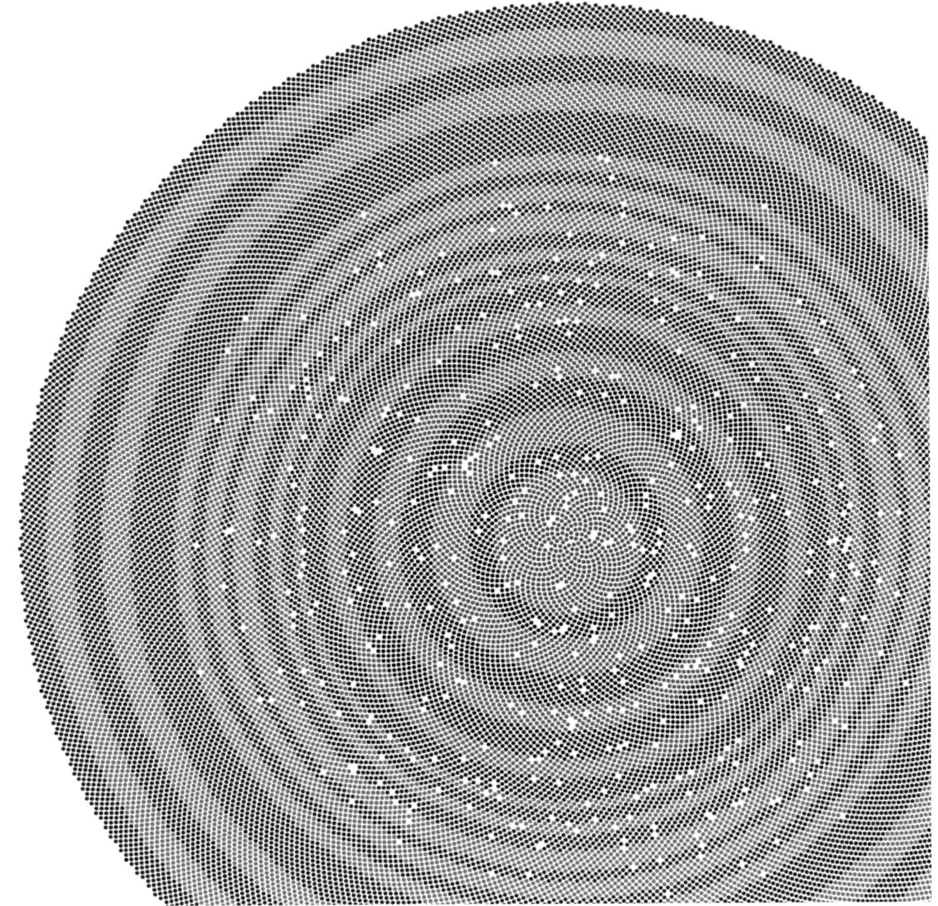

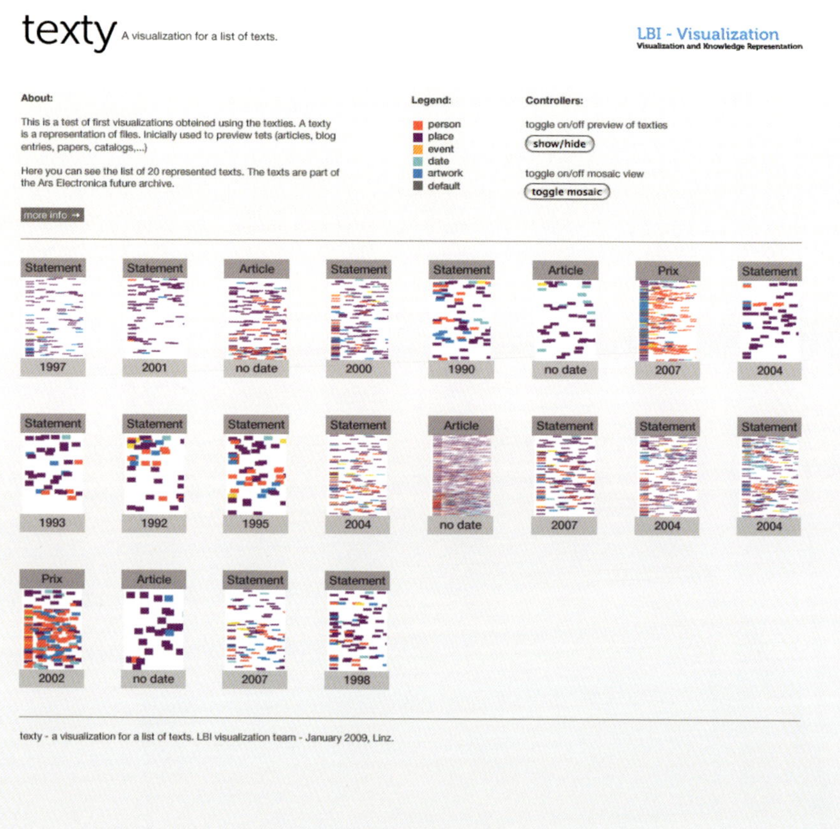
texty
A visualization for a list of texts.
LBI - Visualization
Visualization and Knowledge Representation

About:
This is a test of first visualizations obteined using the texties. A texty is a representation of files. Inicially used to preview tets (articles, blog entries, papers, catalogs,...)

Here you can see the list of 20 represented texts. The texts are part of the Ars Electronica future archive.

more info →

Legend:
person
place
event
date
artwork
default

Controllers:
toggle on/off preview of texties
show/hide

toggle on/off mosaic view
toggle mosaic

Statement
1997
Statement
2001
Article
no date
Statement
2000
Statement
1990
Article
no date
Prix
2007
Statement
2004

Statement
1993
Statement
1992
Statement
1995
Statement
2004
Article
no date
Statement
2007
Statement
2004
Statement
2004

Prix
2002
Article
no date
Statement
2007
Statement
1998

texty - a visualization for a list of texts. LBI visualization team - January 2009, Linz.

AREA: colors of the data

AREA is a visualization tool that allows graphical browsing of data. AREA makes it possible to correlate two different variables for bivariate and univariate analysis. AREA is a non-hierarchical visualization; all the information entities of a representation share a unique visual level with the same visual weight. AREA gives you an image of the whole content of the Prix Ars Electronica submissions database at a single glance. *(Jaume Nualart)*

Tools for Text Analysis

Text.ass is a visual tool for working with annotated text on screen. It is employed for the analysis of the Prix Ars Electronica jury statements. The full text is augmented with a) a network visualization of its main concepts and references and b) thumbnails of its annotation structure. These "texties" can give a super-fast idea about what you will get if you decide to read the text. This can be useful, for example, to get an overview of a large number of search results from a text archive. In order to achieve a meaningful set of annotations, we rely on a workflow combining manual annotation, existing methods for automatic text analysis and keyword extraction as well as our own developments, such as "Proximantics." It is a method for harvesting semantic relationships between annotations based on their spatial proximity as well as their set of co-occurrences. Is it possible to extract semantic meaning from a text's linguistic codes? That's what Proximantics is all about. *(Jaume Nualart)*

1   The Digital Communities Jury, 2008
2   Research project conducted by Katja Kwastek together with Ingrid Spörl, Heike Helfert and Nicole Sudhoff. See also: Katja Kwastek: "Classification vs. Diversification—the value of taxonomies for new media art", in: Peter Gendolla, Jörgen Schaefer (eds.): *Beyond the Screen*, Bielefeld: transcript (forthcoming).

A project of the Ludwig Boltzmann Institute for **Media.Art.Research.**
Data collection and analysis: Gabriele Blome, Gerhard Dirmoser, Katja Kwastek, Theresa Schubert-Minsky, Ingrid Spörl
Databank development: Sandor Herramhof, Günther Kolar
Visualizations: Gerhard Dirmoser, Evelyn Münster, Jaume Nualart, Dietmar Offenhuber, Moritz Stefaner, Mar Canet Sola, *http://vis.mediaartresearch.at*
X by Y: Moritz Stefaner
SemaSpace: Dietmar Offenhuber & Gerhard Dirmoser
Themelandscape: Evelyn Münster, Anika Hirt; content advisor: Katja Kwastek
Area, Proxemantics: Jaume Nualart
Text.ass: Jaume Nualart, Anika Hirt & Dietmar Offenhuber
Ars Thesaurus & Submission Similarity Matrix: Gerhard Dirmoser
Ars Timeline: Mar Canet Sola & Dietmar Offenhuber
Graphic Design: Mahir Javuz, Ule Münster

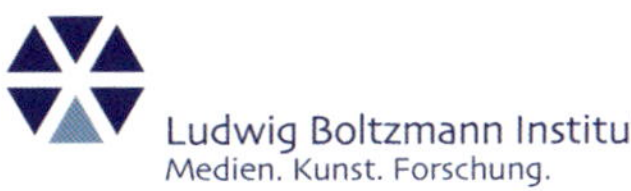

Mapping des Archives der Ars Electronica

In ihrem neuen Haus hat die Ars Electronica in Zusammenarbeit mit dem Ludwig Boltzmann Institut Medien.Kunst.Forschung. ein Archiv eingerichtet, das eine der weltweit umfassendsten Ressourcen zur Geschichte der Medienkunst darstellt. Es umfasst Aufzeichnungen und Dokumente aus 30 Jahren Festival Ars Electronica und enthält eine umfangreiche Sammlung von Beschreibungen und Dokumenten zu Arbeiten, die seit 1987 zum Prix Ars Electronica eingereicht wurden. Darüber hinaus finden sich im Bestand zahlreiche Dokumentationen von eigenen Produktionen, Ausstellungen und anderen Aktivitäten der Ars Electronica. Zusätzlich wurde eine umfangreiche Sammlung an institutionellem Material vor allem zur Öffentlichkeitsarbeit von Ars Electronica und ORF sowie zum Medienecho angelegt.

Mit der Überführung der über die Jahre gesammelten Dokumente in ein Archiv wurde eine wesentliche Grundlage für die wissenschaftliche Bearbeitung des Bestandes geschaffen. Zugleich nahm das Ludwig Boltzmann Institut Medien.Kunst.Forschung. die Erschließung und Erhaltung des Materials in Angriff, wobei der Fokus der Arbeit auf den Einreichungen zum Prix Ars Electronica lag. In einem digitalen Archiv sind für Forschungszwecke alle zum Prix Ars Electronica eingereichten Projekte erfasst. Sämtliche ausgezeichnete Projekte sind darin umfassend dokumentiert, indem zusätzlich inhaltliche bzw. technische Informationen, Text- und Bilddokumente sowie teilweise auch audiovisuelle Ressourcen digital abrufbar sind.

Die wissenschaftliche Aufarbeitung und Analyse des Bestandes des Ars-Electronica-Archivs ist – neben anderen Forschungsprojekten – ein wichtiges Ziel des Ludwig Boltzmann Instituts Medien.Kunst.Forschung. Damit werden – aus der Perspektive der Visualisierung, der Informatik und den Kultur- und Geisteswissenschaften – jeweils neue Zugänge und Erkenntnisse über ein Feld möglich, in dem nicht nur über dreißig Jahre immer wieder die Grenzen der Kunst ausgelotet wurden, sondern in dem sich auch ein Wandlungsprozess manifestiert, der weit über die Künste hinaus alle Bereiche des Lebens verändert hat. *(Gabriele Blome)*

Im Folgenden werden exemplarisch drei analytische Zugänge zum Datenbestand des Ars-Electronica-Archivs sowie die hierfür verwendeten Visualisierungswerkzeuge vorgestellt.

Ansätze eine quantitativen Kunsthistorik

Auch wenn die Motivationen und Ansprüche der beim Prix Ars Electronica einreichenden Medien-KünstlerInnen, -GestalterInnen und -InformatikerInnen im Detail kaum geklärt werden können, lassen sich aus den publizierten Nennungen einige Aspekte im Detail analysieren.

Durch die Erfassung und Zusammenführung aller Einreichjahrgänge lässt sich studieren, wie oft einzelne Personen oder Gruppen eingereicht haben, in welchen Jahren bzw. über welche Zeiträume hinweg Einreichungen erfolgt sind und welche Kategorien für die jeweiligen Werke als relevant erachtet wurden. Über längere Zeiträume aktive EinreicherInnen schaffen über die Jahre Beiträge für zwei bis drei Sparten, wobei im Zusammenhang mit den medientechnischen Entwicklungen bestimmte Kombinationen und Abfolgen sehr typisch sind. So sind Übergänge von der Computergrafik zu Animationsarbeiten beobachtbar, der Übergang von der *Interaktiven*

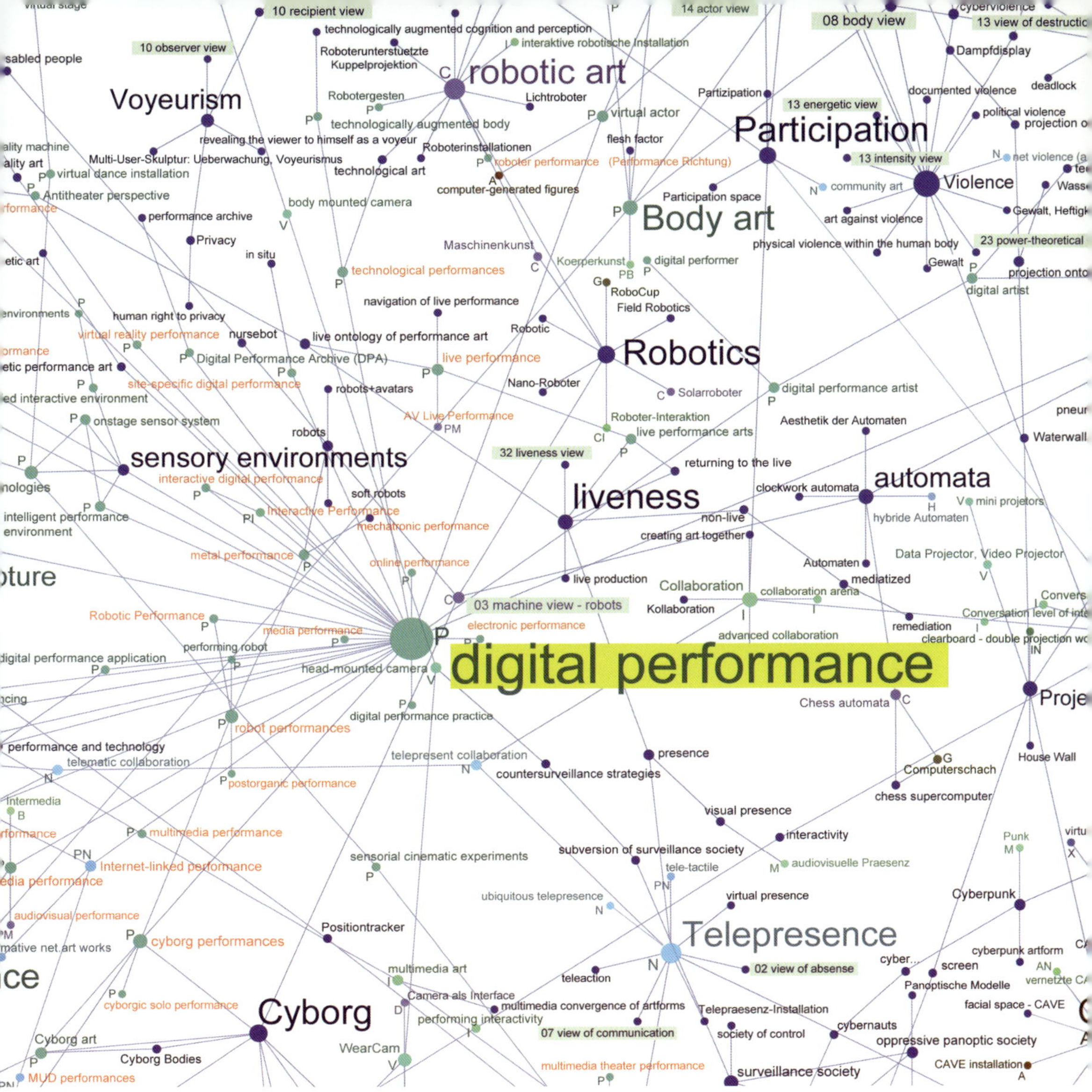

digital performance

Kunst zur *net art* in über 680 Fällen und der Übergang von der Musiksparte in den Bereich der Interaktion in über 370 Fällen zu sehen.

Über die Spartenzuordnungen lassen sich Ähnlichkeitsprofile der einreichenden Personen bilden, die als Grundlage für eine erste Strukturierung herangezogen werden können. Der Blick auf die Ursprungsländer und die Anzahl der Einreichenden je Jahrgang lässt Rückschlüsse auf Ausbildungsmöglichkeiten, Förderungskontexte und den Bekanntheitsgrad des Prix in den jeweiligen Ländern zu. Nach ersten zaghaften Annäherungen sind jeweils gleichmäßige Beteiligungszuwächse zu verzeichnen. Sogar die Stimmungslage im Zusammenhang mit dem Platzen der „Netz-Blase" lässt sich als quantitative Spur bei den Einreichungen nachvollziehen.

Durch die Kombination der Preisträger-Daten mit den Einreichungsdaten lassen sich „Erfolgsmuster" nachzeichnen. Regelmäßiges Einreichen ist Voraussetzung für die „Sichtbarkeit" und Präsenz im Archiv, aber keine Garantie für eine Anerkennung.

Aus den ca. 30.000 Einreichenden lassen sich über 13.000 Personen/Gruppen herausfiltern, die für weitere Vergleiche erfolgversprechend sind. Mithilfe diverser am Internet verfügbarer Datenquellen lassen sich aus dieser Grundgesamtheit ca. 3.500 Personen ermitteln, die auch in anderen Kontexten als Medien-KünstlerInnen wahrgenommen wurden. Über 1.300 Personen sind zumindest in vier relevanten Kontexten nachweisbar, und über 550 KünstlerInnen finden sich jenseits der Schwelle von zumindest sechs Nennungen. In dieser Region findet man auch einen wesentlichen Anteil der beim Prix ausgezeichneten Personen und – kaum überraschend – jene KünstlerInnen, denen in Katalogen und Fachbüchern breiter Raum gegeben wird.

Durch das Einbeziehen von Fachliteratur kann auch die Spartenzuordnung weiter verfeinert werden. So lassen sich Performance-Künstler nachklassifizieren und auch die noch nicht „preiswürdige" Game-Sparte mit über 170 Namen bestücken. Damit lässt sich wiederum die Interaktionssicht verfeinern und der Zusammenhang der elektronischen Medienkünste mit der *performance art* beobachten.

Für die Preisträger ist dank der Katalogtexte in vielen Fällen der Ausbildungszusammenhang rekonstruierbar. Es wäre sehr aufschlussreich, je Länder-Kontext zu recherchieren, welche Institutionen für den Werdegang der MedienkünstlerInnen von Bedeutung waren.

Damit soll zum Ausdruck gebracht werden, dass wir bzgl. der quantitativen Analysen erst ganz am Anfang stehen. Die im Zuge dieser ersten Analysen entstandenen Datenbestände sollten den medien- und kunsthistorischen Detailanalysen als stützendes Material „zur Seite" gestellt werden. Quantitative Analysen sollten in Zeiten der Internet-Präsenz nicht als seltsame Versuche zahlenverliebter Datenknechte abgetan werden, vielmehr gilt es, fachsemantisch versierte Kräfte für die Verfeinerung der Analyse- und Visualisierungsmethoden zu gewinnen.

(Gerhard Dirmoser)

Medienkunst als sozialer Prozess
Netzwerkanalyse der Jurybesetzungen und -entscheidungen

Die jährlichen Jurysitzungen zur Ermittlung der Gewinnerprojekte bilden ein weiteres interessantes Themenfeld. Es stellt sich die Frage, inwieweit die inhaltliche Entwicklung der Medienkunst mit den sozialen Strukturen der involvierten Akteure – KünstlerInnen und JurorInnen – in Zusammenhang stehen.

Die Jurys werden jährlich neu besetzt, aber auch die Kategorien selbst unterliegen zeitlichen Veränderungen: Bestehende Sparten werden abgeschafft, neue eingeführt und andere programmatisch umdefiniert. Der Einsatz von Methoden aus der sozialen Netzwerkanalyse scheint naheliegend. Werden nun, über den gesamten Zeitraum betrachtet, die JurorInnen ihren jeweiligen Jurysitzungen zugeordnet, entsteht ein bi-partites Netzwerk, das im Folgenden näher untersucht wurde.

Bemerkenswert ist, dass dieses Netz aus einem einzigen zusammenhängenden Stück besteht und nicht etwa in unterschiedliche Teilnetze, entsprechend den Prix-Kategorien, zerfällt. Dies bedeutet, dass es (mit einer einzigen Ausnahme[1]) keine Jurysitzung ohne personelle Überschneidungen mit einer vorhergehenden Jury gab und, wesentlich wichtiger, dass verschiedene JurorInnen über die Jahre in mehreren Kategorien vertreten sind. Eine Erkenntnis, die bei der Betrachtung der Netzwerkvisualisierung sofort ins Auge fällt, auf textlicher Basis jedoch sehr viel weniger offensichtlich wäre. In der Netzwerkvisualisierung zeigt sich weiters, dass manche Kategorien klar abgegrenzt hervortreten und von zentralen Akteuren dominiert werden, während andere Kategorien stärker miteinander verwoben sind und kein personelles Zentrum zu besitzen scheinen. Unter Verwendung der Zentralitätsmasse aus der Netzwerkanalyse kann man auch verschiedene Rollen der beteiligten Juroren unterscheiden. Während manche Juroren eine einzelne Kategorie zu dominieren scheinen, tauchen andere Personen in mehreren Kontexten auf und fungieren als Brücken zwischen verschiedenen Kategorien. Die Praxis, ausgezeichnete KünstlerInnen in den folgenden Jahren als Juroren einzuladen, bringt zusätzlich deren Kontakte und Wissenskontexte ins Spiel und trägt zur Ausdifferenzierung der Kategorien bei. Diese interdisziplinären Schnittstellen findet man auch im Gegenstück zum Jurynetzwerk, dem Netzwerk der ausgezeichneten Künstler. Auch hier ergibt sich ein überraschend hoher Vernetzungsgrad. Es dominieren zwei Teilnetze, die – noch? – unverbunden sind: der „Mikrokosmos" der Nachwuchswettbewerbe U19 und Next Idea und die übrigen Kategorien des Prix Ars Electronica. Reduziert man das gesamte Netzwerk auf Personen mit mehreren Auszeichnungen, treten die inhaltlichen Brücken zwischen den Kategorien klar zutage. Der Informationsgehalt dieser Relationen darf natürlich nicht überinterpretiert werden, dennoch liefert das entstehende Netzwerk ein überraschend reichhaltiges und differenziertes Bild, das für mit der Materie vertraute Personen nachvollziehbar ist und in dem eigene Erfahrungen wiedergefunden oder bestätigt werden. *(Dietmar Offenhuber)*

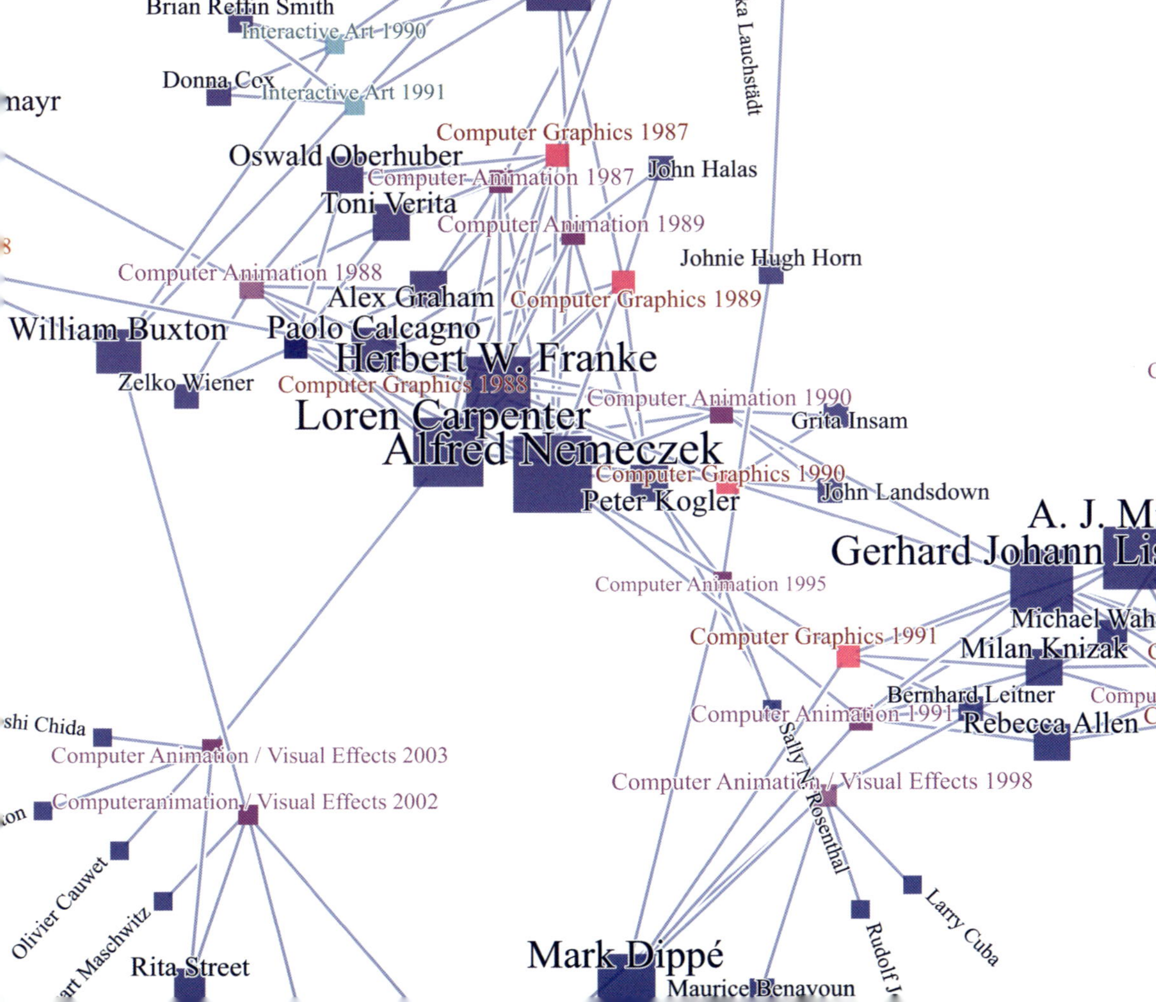

Taxonomien zur Erfassung der Medienkunst(geschichte): Fallstudie interaktive Kunst

Der umfassende Bestand an begleitendem Dokumentationsmaterial zu den zum *Prix Ars Electronica* eingereichten Arbeiten kann als Korpus für eine fundierte kunsthistorische Analyse genutzt werden. Klassifikationssysteme sind stets kritisch zu betrachten, da sie das Besondere einzelner Arbeiten nicht zu erfassen vermögen. Eine terminologische Klassifikation kann allerdings die Ausbildung eines differenzierten Begriffsfeldes zur Folge haben, wodurch bestimmte Eigenschaften einzelner Werke genauer erfasst und beschrieben werden können: Eine granulare Kategorisierung verspricht sprachliche Genauigkeit und Vielfalt. Datenbanken erlauben auch Rückschlüsse auf Verbindungen zwischen verschiedenen Begriffssystemen. Dies führt zu einem Bruch mit der traditionellen, linear ausgerichteten Kunst- bzw. Künstlerhistorik und chronologisch orientierten Paradigmen zugunsten einer parallelen Analyse von Gemeinsamkeiten und Unterschieden. Zur „interaktiven Kunst" zählt z.B. ein breites Spektrum unterschiedlicher Werke, von Literaturarbeiten im Netz über Medien-Performances bis hin zu interaktiven Installationen. Im Gegensatz zu einer generalisierenden Beschreibung dieser Werke als „interaktive Kunst", die zu eng ist und den Begriff auf eine reine Genrebezeichnung reduziert, ermöglichen Taxonomien eine Differenzierung und die Herstellung von Querverbindungen: Differenzierte Klassifikationssysteme decken nicht nur Heterogenitäten innerhalb eines Genres auf, sondern verweisen auch auf Parallelen zwischen verschiedenen Bereichen, die sonst vielleicht übersehen würden.
Um der Vielzahl möglicher Ansätze im multidisziplinären Feld der Medienkunstforschung entgegenzukommen, unterscheiden wir vier verschiedene Forschungsperspektiven, die jeweils bis zu drei verschiedene grobe Kategorien zur Klassifikation der Werke umfassen[2].

Formale Perspektive

Die erste grobe Kategorie, „Form oft artwork", soll die physischen Eigenschaften bzw. den performativen oder immateriellen Charakter eines Werks näher beschreiben. Die zweite Kategorie „Range of artwork", dient der Spezifizierung der „räumlichen" Eigenschaften des Werks, etwa ob ein Kunstwerk für sich allein steht oder in ein Netzwerk eingebunden ist, ob es im öffentlichen Raum präsentiert oder auf mobilen Geräten umgesetzt wurde. In der dritten Kategorie werden mögliche „Interaction partner" genannt.

Technische Perspektive

Es kann argumentiert werden, dass Technik für Werke der Medienkunst eine zentrale Rolle spielt. Andererseits sind die tatsächlich genutzten Geräte und Betriebssysteme oft austauschbar. Dies macht es umso wichtiger, dass genau dokumentiert wird, welche Medien bei der Konzeption und Umsetzung des Werks genutzt wurden. Unter den Kategorien „Media" und „Processing technology" können eine Vielzahl von Schlagworten erfasst werden, die für eine spätere wissenschaftliche Aufarbeitung technischer Aspekte genutzt werden können.

Ästhetische Perspektive

Interaktive Kunst bringt eine völlig neue Form der Ästhetik mit sich: Sie gründet auf der aktiven Umsetzung eines künstlerischen Angebots durch das mitwirkende Publikum und initiiert eine handlungsbasierte ästhetische Erfahrung.

Unter der Kategorie „Type of interaction/the visitor (performer) can" kann daher angegeben werden, in welcher Weise die Besucher aktiv werden (beobachten, erforschen, aktivieren, überwachen, auswählen, navigieren, mitwirken, Spuren hinterlassen etc.). Der Interaktionsprozess umfasst darüber hinaus jedoch eine weitere Dimension, die aus dem Werk selbst entsteht. Die Kategorie „Strategy of interaction/the work (project) does" gibt an, ob das Projekt/Werk eine Geschichte erzählt oder über einen Sachverhalt berichtet, etwas dokumentiert oder informiert, Inhalte visualisiert oder in Klang umsetzt, die Wahrnehmung schärft oder ein Spielerlebnis bietet, etwas überwacht oder als Instrument zur Transformation, Erfassung und Archivierung, Bearbeitung oder Vermittlung dient.

Kontextuelle Perspektive

Auch wenn wir eingestehen müssen, dass Taxonomien für eine Kontextualisierung von Werken nur beschränkt geeignet sind, haben wir uns doch für die Aufnahme der folgenden zwei Kategorien entschieden: „Buzzwords" und „Topic".
Obwohl Schlagwörter oft kurzlebige Modewörter und abgedroschene Phrasen sind, die auf mögliche Funktionen und Anwendungsgebiete bzw. auf subjektive Intentionen und soziale Diskurskonventionen schließen lassen, erweisen sie sich gerade aufgrund ihrer Unschärfe als gute Methode zur Erfassung von intentionalen, kontextbasierten Beschreibungen im Rahmen eines taxonomischen Systems. Zwar sind Medienkunstprojekte nicht selten selbstreferenziell, doch spiegeln sie oft auch gesellschaftliche, politische, wirtschaftliche und Umweltthemen. Es ist daher möglich und sinnvoll, auch das Thema eines Werks zu erfassen, zumal dies auch zusätzliche Vergleichsmöglichkeiten mit nicht interaktiven Werken eröffnet. Unser Klassifikationssystem wurde in das Online-System für die Einreichung von Beiträgen zum Prix Ars Electronica integriert. Die einreichenden Künstler selbst kategorisieren seit 2008 ihre Werke mithilfe des von uns entwickelten Kategoriensystems. Die Taxonomie wurde des Weiteren auch für eine retrospektive Klassifizierung der ca. 300 Siegerprojekte aus den Jahren 1990 bis 2009 verwendet. Die Ergebnisse dieser retrospektiven Klassifikation wurden mithilfe des Visualisierungsprogramms *Theme-landscape* (s. u.) visualisiert und können interaktiv erforscht werden. *(Katja Kwastek)*

Visualisierungswerkzeuge

Um diese unterschiedlichen Aspekte des Prix Ars Electronica zu untersuchen und darzustellen, wurden im LBI für Medien.Kunst.Forschung. verschiedene Visualisierungsprogramme entwickelt:

SemaSpace

SemaSpace ist ein kompakter Graphen-Editor und Browser für die Erstellung und Analyse semantischer Netzwerke. Hauptschwerpunkt ist die flüssige Manipulation sehr großer und komplexer Daten. Das Programm wird seit 2004 von Dietmar Offenhuber und Gerhard Dirmoser aktiv entwickelt und wurde zur Analyse der Jurynetzwerke eingesetzt. Der 24.000 Relationen umfassende Ars-Electronica-Thesaurus von Gerhard Dirmoser wurde ebenfalls mit Semaspace konstruiert und visuell aufbereitet.

Theme-landscape

In der Einreichkategorie der interaktiven Kunst wurden im Zeitraum von 1990 bis 2009 ca. 300 Werke mit einem Preis ausgezeichnet. Im Zuge der kunsthistorischen Aufarbeitung von Katja Kwastek entstand eine Taxonomie der interaktiven Kunst, die diesen Werken ca. 150 Begriffe als Schlagworte zuordnet, wobei jedes Werk durch 20 bis 30 Schlagworte beschrieben wurde. Die sich daraus ergebenden impliziten Ähnlichkeiten der Werke können wir nun – als geometrische Distanzen codiert – in einem „Ähnlichkeitsraum" darstellen.

Mittels eines Multidimensional Scaling Algorithmus (MDS) werden die Werke entsprechend ihrer relativen thematischen Übereinstimmung auf eine zweidimensionale Fläche projiziert. Detailinformationen der einzelnen Werke können anhand ihrer visuellen Darstellungsform verglichen werden. Die zugeordneten Begriffe werden metaphorisch als Blütenblätter für jedes Werk dargestellt, wobei jedem Schlagwort eine eindeutige Blattform entspricht. Die individuellen Formen, die sich daraus ergeben, lassen den Betrachter Unterschiede und Analogien mühelos mit dem Auge erkennen. *(Evelyn Münster)*

X by Y

Die Visualisierungsserie „X by Y" von Moritz Stefaner in Zusammenarbeit mit dem Ludwig Boltzmann Institut für Medien.Kunst.Forschung. stellt eine visuelle Erforschung der Einreichungen zum Prix der Ars Electronica dar. Die visuelle Repräsentation von Attributkombinationen (wie z. B. Kategorien über Länder oder Einreicher über die Jahre) und der jeweiligen Menge der Einreichung erlaubt es nicht nur, die Historie des Preises Revue passieren zu lassen, sondern auch Hypothesen über die Mechanismen der „Welt der Ars" zu generieren. *(Moritz Stefaner)*

AREA: Farben der Daten

AREA ist ein Visualisierungsprogramm für grafisches Durchsuchen von Daten, das die Korrelation zweier verschiedener Variablen für eine bivariate und univariate Analyse erlaubt. Die Visualisierung der Daten ist nicht hierarchisch, alle Informationseinheiten einer Darstellung sind auf der gleichen visuellen Darstellungsebene mit dem gleichen visuellen Gewicht angeordnet. *AREA* bietet einen raschen Überblick über den gesamten Inhalt der Datenbank der Einreichungen zum Prix Ars Electronica. *(Jaume Nualart)*

Programme zur Textanalyse

Text.ass ist ein Visualisierungsprogramm für die Arbeit mit annotierten Texten am Bildschirm und kann zur Analyse der Jury-Entscheidungen über die Vergabe des Prix Ars Electronica eingesetzt werden. Der Volltext wird ergänzt um a) eine Netzwerkdarstellung der Hauptkonzepte und Referenzen und b) Thumbnails der Annotationsstruktur. Diese „Texties" geben sehr rasch Aufschluss über die Inhalte eines Beitrags. Das ist vor allem dann sinnvoll, wenn die Suche im Textarchiv eine große Anzahl von Treffern liefert. Um zu möglichst sinnvollen Annotationen zu gelangen, verwenden wir eine Mischung aus händischer Annotation, bekannten Methoden automatisierter Textanalyse und Schlagwortextraktion sowie eigenen Entwicklungen wie „Prosemantics". Bei Letzterer handelt es sich um eine Methode zur Erfassung semantischer Verbindungen zwischen Annotationen auf der Grundlage ihrer räumlichen Nähe und ihren Konkurrenzen. Kann aus dem Sprachcode eines Textes semantische Bedeutung extrahiert werden? Mit dieser Frage beschäftigt sich „Proximantics". *(Jaume Nualart)*

(Aus dem Englischen von Sonja Pöllabauer)

1   Die *Digital Communities Jury* 2008.
2   Von Katja Kwastek gemeinsam mit Ingrid Spörl, Heike Helfert und Nicole Sudhoff realisiertes Forschungsprojekt. Siehe auch: Kwastek, Katja: „Classification vs. Diversification - the value of taxonomies for new media art",
     in Gendolla, Peter und Schaefer, Jörgen (Hg.): *Beyond the Screen*, transcript, Bielefeld (im Druck).

Ein Projekt des Ludwig Boltzmann Instituts für Medien.Kunst.Forschung.
Datensammlung und Aufarbeitung: Gabriele Blome, Gerhard Dirmoser, Katja Kwastek, Theresa Schubert-Minsky, Ingrid Spörl
Datenbank-Entwicklung: Sandor Herramhof, Günther Kolar
Visualisierungen: Gerhard Dirmoser, Evelyn Münster, Jaume Nualart, Dietmar Offenhuber, Moritz Stefaner, Mar Canet Sola. *http://vis.mediaartresearch.at*
X by Y: Moritz Stefaner
SemaSpace: Dietmar Offenhuber & Gerhard Dirmoser
Themelandscape: Evelyn Münster, Anika Hirt; inhaltliche Betreuung: Katja Kwastek
Area, Proxemantics: Jaume Nualart
Text.ass: Jaume Nualart, Anika Hirt & Dietmar Offenhuber
Ars Thesaurus & Submission Similarity Matrix: Gerhard Dirmoser
Ars Timeline: Mar Canet Sola & Dietmar Offenhuber
Graphic Design: Mahir Javuz, Ule Münster

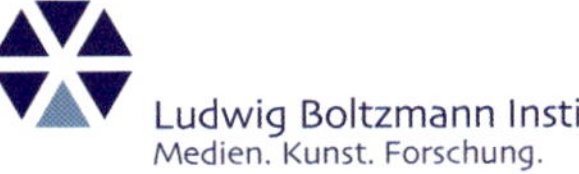

The Ars Electronica Archive
A Work in Progress

Approximately 43,000 entries have been submitted to the Prix Ars Electronica since 1987. There is also a wealth of material documenting the events and protagonists at the Ars Electronica Festival since it debuted in 1979. And thousands of pieces are added annually.

This rapidly growing archive is not only a representative cross-section of the broad field of media & digital art; it is also a historical catalog of the data storage media and formats that in many cases significantly determine the appearance of the works preserved on them. Scholarly articles on computer graphics, computer animation, computer & digital music, interactive art, Web-based- & net-art, software, mixed realities, virtual reality applications, media performance, bio-cybernetic & genetic art, robotics and video art explicitly document the aesthetic strategies used in these fields as well as, implicitly, the technical conditions on which they are based.

However, the Ars Electronica Archive is not only of interest from a scholarly-historical perspective; it also represents an urgent task in view of the brief "half-life" of the data storage media it contains. The video collection includes a multiplicity of formats, the availability of which is progressively diminishing amidst the ongoing proliferation of technological alternatives. The same applies to the programming languages in which art projects are developed, and their various storage media—from diskettes to CDs to websites and their addresses. If material from the early years of the Festival and the Prix Ars Electronica is not transferred to other data storage media in the very near future, then there is a clear and present danger of it being irretrievably lost.

Ars Electronica has vigorously moved forward with the task of securing and digitizing this material and making it available to scholars and interested members of the public. Very high-quality work is being done in cooperation with the Ludwig Boltzmann Institute Media.Art.Research.

The AE Archive: Facts & Figures as of August 2009

Since moving into the new AEC facility, the Archive has had air-conditioned storage rooms available for the first time, and plenty of space for its enormous collection of material documenting 30 years of media art.

258 Meters of Prix Ars Electronica

A major portion of the Archive's holdings consists of 42,889 works submitted for prize consideration since the inception of the Prix Ars Electronica in 1987. The entry forms alone fill 829 files and take up 67 meters of shelf space. The accompanying documentation submitted by entrants with their works has also been preserved on an additional 191 meters of shelf space.

In addition to audio and video tapes as well as digital data storage media in all formats imaginable (and there have been many formats and standards indeed over the years), this collection also includes descriptions, sketches, scores, art catalogs, models and much more.

3,175 Video and Audio Tapes in 20 Different Formats

The Archive's second major category of holdings is documentary material that has been prepared since 1979. In this connection, the role of the ORF-Austrian Broadcasting Company as committed Festival co-organizer is especially important since an extraordinary large amount of material was already documented in the early years.

Still remaining from these early years are 246 1-inch video tapes. The ORF copied these tapes onto MII long ago, and the Ars Electronica Archive staff has completely digitized these MII tapes in recent years.

The works in the audio and video archive are in the following formats: DV CAM, Mini DV, HDV, HD CAM, Digital Betacam, DVC Pro, Betacam SP, Hi8, U-matic, VHS, S-VHS, 1-inch B video tape, MII, DAT, ADAT, MiniDisk, MC, and of course in PAL, NTSC and SECAM

The Archive also contains 1,123 CDs and DVDs, Syquest cartridges, Zip disks, MODs, floppy disks and more than 12,000 photographs, negatives and slides, as well as an extensive collection of printed materials dating back to 1979: Prix & Festival catalogs, special editions, press clippings, press kits, Festival programs, invitations, posters, stickers, postcards, newspaper supplements, flyers etc. (a total of approximately 16,300 archived pieces of documentary material).

The digital archive contains approximately 2,000 hours of video material (as of August 2009; including metadata) requiring a memory capacity of 25 terabytes. 800 tapes have been digitized; an additional 1,000 are to be digitally conserved and archived by the end of 2010.

Thus, the lion's share of the digitization effort will have been completed by December 31, 2010. The next big job, which we intend to tackle in the coming years, is to begin making this material available online.

Ars Electronica Archiv Team: Martina Wagner, Jutta Schmiederer, Heinz Sambs, Elvis Pavic, Jürgen Wiesner. Technical realization: Ars Electronica Futurelab / Michael Badics, Christoph Hofbauer, Fadil Kujundic, Mar Canet-Sola. Special thanks to: Michael Huemer / ORF OÖ, Ludwig Boltzmann Institut Medien.Kunst.Forschung. / Katja Kwastek, Gabriele Blome, Theresa Schubert-Minsky, Ulrike Pimminger, Nina Wenhart. Technical consultance, digitization: Joachim Smetschka

(Text: Gerfried Stocker, translated from German by Mel Greenwald)

Rund 43.000 Arbeiten sind bislang alleine beim Prix Ars Electronica seit 1987 eingereicht wurden, dazu kommen zigtausende Dokumente, die das Geschehen und deren Protagonistinnen bei der Ars Electronica seit der Gründung des Festivals im Jahr 1979 dokumentieren – und jedes Jahr kommen Tausende hinzu.

Dieses gewachsene Archiv bietet nicht nur einen repräsentativen Querschnitt des weiten Feldes der Medien- und digitalen Kunst, sondern auch einen historischen Abriss ihrer Trägermedien und -formate, aus denen die Arbeiten vielfach ihre Erscheinungsform beziehen. Mit Beiträgen zu den Themenbereichen Computergrafik, Computeranimation, Computer- und digitale Musik, interaktive Kunst, Web-basierte und Netz-Kunst, Software, Mixed Realities, Virtual-Reality-Anwendungen, Medien-Performance, Bio Cybernetic & Genetic Art, Robotik und Videokunst werden einerseits explizit ästhetische Strategien und implizit die ihnen zu Grunde liegenden technischen Bedingungen andererseits dokumentiert.

Das Ars Electronica Archiv ist jedoch nicht nur von wissenschaftlich-historischem Interesse, sondern ein dringliches Aufgabengebiet im Hinblick auf die kurze Halbwertszeit der Datenträger. Bereits der Video-Bereich umfasst eine Vielzahl an Formaten, deren Verfügbarkeit im Maß der Proliferation ihrer aktuellen Alternativen zunehmend verschwindet. Gleiches gilt für Programmiersprachen, in denen Kunst-Projekte entwickelt werden, und die diversen Speichermedien, von der Diskette über CD bis hin zu Websites und deren Adressen. Für Material aus den frühen Jahren des Festivals und des Prix Ars Electronica besteht heute die akute Gefahr seines unwiederbringlichen Verlustes, sollte es nicht gelingen, es in nächster Zeit auf andere Speichermedien zu übertragen.

Die von Ars Electronica forcierte Sicherung, digitale Erschließung und Bereitstellung dieses Materials für Forschung und interessierte Öffentlichkeit konnte in Zusammenarbeit mit dem Ludwig Boltzman Institut für Medienkunstforschung auf sehr hohem Niveau vorangetrieben werden.

Einige Zahlen zum AE-Archiv – Stand August 2009

Seit dem Umzug in das neue Gebäude stehen dem Ars Electronica Archiv erstmals eigene klimatisierte Räumlichkeiten zur Verfügung, in denen zigtausende Archivalien aus bereits 30 Jahren Medienkunst Platz finden.

258 Laufmeter Prix Ars Electronica

Einen wesentlichen Teil des Archivs stellen die 42.889 Einreichungen seit Gründung des Prix Ars Electronica im Jahr 1987 dar. Allein die Einreichformulare füllen 829 Ordner und belegen 67 Laufmeter der Regalanlage. Die Unterlagen, die von den Künstlerinnen jeweils mitgeschickt wurden, sind ebenfalls aufbewahrt worden und füllen weitere 191 Laufmeter. Neben Ton- und Videobändern sowie digitalen Datenträgern in allen erdenklichen Formaten – und in all den Jahren gab es enorm viele Formate und Standards – sind es auch Beschreibungen, Skizzen, Partituren, Kunstkataloge, Modelle etc. die hier versammelt sind.

3175 Video- und Audiobänder über 20 verschiedenen Formaten

Der zweite große Bestand des Archivs sind die Dokumentationsmaterialien, die seit 1979 angefertigt wurden. Dabei ist die Rolle des ORF als engagierter Mitveranstalter von besonderer Bedeutung, da dadurch vor allem in den frühen Jahren schon außergewöhnlich viel dokumentiert wurde. Aus diesen frühen Jahren sind noch 246 1-Zoll-Videobändern erhalten. Diese Bänder wurden bereits vor längerer Zeit im ORF auf MII umkopiert, und diese MII-Bänder wurden im letzten Jahr vom Archivteam des Ars Electronica Center vollständig digitalisiert.

Zu den Formaten des Audio- und Videoarchivs zählen: DV CAM, Mini DV, HDV, HD CAM, Digital Betacam, DVC Pro, Betacam SP, Hi8, U-matic, VHS, S-VHS, 1-Zoll- B Videobänder, MII, DAT, ADAT, MiniDisk, MC, natürlich in PAL, NTSC, SECAM. Weiters lagern 1.123 CDs und DVDs, Syquest Cartridges, Zip-Disks, MODs, Floppy Disks und mehr als 12.000 Fotografien, Negative und Diapositive im Archiv, ebenso eine umfangreiche Sammlung an Printmaterialien von 1979 bis 2009: Prixbücher, Festivalkataloge, Sonderausgaben, Pressespiegel, Pressemappen, Festivalprogramme, Einladungen, Plakate, Aufkleber, Postkarten, Zeitungsbeilagen, Flyer etc. Macht insgesamt 16.300 Archivalien an Dokumentationsmaterial.

Das digitale Archiv umfasst mit Stand August 2009 bereits ca. 2.000 Stunden Videomaterial (mit Metadaten erfasst) – mit einem Speichervolumen von 25 Terabyte. Dafür wurden 800 Bänder digitalisiert. Bis Ende 2010 sollen weitere 1.000 Bänder digital gesichert und archiviert werden. Damit sollte bis Ende 2010 der größte Aufwand hinsichtlich Digitalisierung bewältigt werden. Der zweite wichtige Schritt, der uns die nächsten Jahre beschäftigen wird, ist die Absicht, dieses Archiv auch Zug um Zug online zugänglich zu machen.

(Text: Gerfried Stocker)

Ars Electronica Archiv Team: Martina Wagner, Jutta Schmiederer, Heinz Sambs, Elvis Pavic, Jürgen Wiesner. Technische Umsetzung: Ars Electronica Futurelab / Michael Badics, Christoph Hofbauer, Fadil Kujundic, Mar Canet-Sola. *Besonderer Dank an:* Michael Huemer / ORF OÖ, Ludwig Boltzmann Institut Medien.Kunst.Forschung. / Katja Kwastek, Gabriele Blome, Theresa Schubert-Minsky, Ulrike Pimminger, Nina Wenhart. Technische Beratung Digitalisierung: Joachim Smetschka

Gabriele Blome, Ludwig Boltzmann Institute Media.Art.Research.

Gateway to Archives of Media Art (GAMA)
Network-Linked Archives

http://www.gama-gateway.eu/

The World Wide Web seems to be an inexhaustible source of information about media art; nevertheless, online research is time-consuming and often yields unsatisfactory results. Information has to be sought in a diverse array of sources that are heterogeneous with respect to both character and structure, and that must first be checked in order to establish their reliability.

The launch of the *Gateway to Archives of Media Art* in conjunction with this year's Ars Electronica Festival means the creation of a new website *http://www.gama-gateway.eu* that greatly facilitates the process of locating information about works of media art. Henceforth, it will be possible to perform research at a "one-stop shop" providing access to the holdings of eight European archives and collections. The wealth of material available here includes information about early works of Hungarian network art, video art from Slovenia, media art from the Netherlands, France and other European and non-European countries, comprehensive documentation of the Ars Electronica Festival, and experimental films from Sweden.

Of course, this is just the beginning. Once the technical, conceptual, editorial and design work that goes into setting up this portal has been completed, the project will move on to the next phase. It is foreseen that the website will continue to grow and that the portal will successively make it possible to query more and more media art archives and collections. The launch of the GAMA portal is the debut of a model for network-linked access to multiple archives. Implicit in this are ideas, processes and decisions that are briefly described below.

A Portal to Media Art Archives

The *Gateway to Archives of Media Art* is a new portal that provides access from a single website to several different archives and collections—some up to 30 years old—containing works of media art as well as documents about and documentation of media art. This portal thus makes no claim to offering a homogeneous or comprehensive collection. Inherent in this concept is acceptance of the fact that the participating institutions define the term "media art" differently, as well as that the definition of this term has developed and changed over time. The selection of the artistic projects assembled in these archives and collections is the outcome of curatorial work and institutional activities pursued with varying agendas. Some of them utilize systems of reference that go far beyond the visual arts and include musical and cinematic art.

Preserving Heterogeneity

The profile of an individual collection is closely connected with the mission of the respective institution. Thus, the main interest of the participating distributors is to create a showcase to more effectively feature collections assembled for the purpose of distribution and, thereby, to achieve increased public visibility of the artists they represent and those artists' works. In the case of institutional archives such as Ars Electronica, Les Instants Vidéo and C3, on the other hand, the communication of institutional activities also assumes key significance, so that the works have to be assessed within this system of reference. Whereas distributors generally make available databanks that emphasize works and artists, the databanks of institutional archives tend to exhibit a heterogeneous, wide-ranging structure that is an outgrowth of the respective institution's operations. There are also numerous differences in the details of the information provided—for instance, specifications having to do with time, place names, languages and even how persons' names are spelled. Furthermore, the contents of the databanks not only exhibit differing structures; the subjects are also registered and described in varying degrees of depth. Preserving this heterogeneity and still setting up a portal offering a uniform mode of access to and representation of the information contained in the subsidiary archives and collections has been a core element of this website project's task.

User-Oriented

The process of providing enhanced access to media art encompasses the practical level of research possibilities as well as an orientation that accommodates various different types of users. GAMA offers an overview of all information available in the subsidiary archives and collections about a particular work or artist (biographies, descriptions, photographic & video documentation, speeches, and, in the case of distributors, available formats) as well as the possibility of entering a query in one language and obtaining the results of that query in other languages too. Video indexing and image resemblance search capability supplement text-based searching with research possibilities based on visual criteria. For curators and scholars, the portal makes available a multifaceted search interface; users without in-depth knowledge are provided with brief introductions to selected themes and works. For educational purposes at institutions of higher learning, GAMA offers a media wiki that makes it possible to place the collected works and documents into a discursive, user-defined context.

The *Gateway to Archives of Media Art* thus constitutes an essential contribution to improving online access to media art, which is of great importance to the work being done not only by the staff of the Ludwig Boltzmann Institute Media.Art.Research and other research facilities but also at institutions of higher learning and by scholars and creatives active in all fields of culture and the arts.

Ludwig Boltzmann Institut
Medien. Kunst. Forschung.

GAMA links up the collections of the following institutions:
ARGOS centre for art & media, Brussels (BE), Ars Electronica Linz GmbH (AT), C3 Center for Culture & Communication Foundation, Budapest (HU), Heure Exquise! International center for video arts , Mons-en-Baroeul (FR), Les Instants Vidéo Numériques et Poétiques, Marseille (FR), Nederlands Instituut voor Mediakunst Montevideo/Time based Arts, Amsterdam (NL), SCCA-Ljubljana, Center for Contemporary Arts (SI), Filmform Foundation, Stockholm (SE)

Additional Project Partners
Akademia Górniczo-Hutnicza, Cracow (PL), Akademie der Bildenden Künste, Vienna (AT), Atos Origin s.a.e., Madrid (ES), CIANT International Centre for Art and New Technologies, Prague (CZ), Hochschule für Gestaltung und Kunst Zürich (CH), Hochschule für Künste Bremen (DE), Hogeschool voor de Kunsten Utrecht (NL), IN2 Search Interfaces Development Ltd., Bremen (DE), Ludwig Boltzmann Institut Medien.Kunst.Forschung., Linz (AT), Staatliche Hochschule für Gestaltung Karlsruhe (DE), Technologie-Zentrum Informatik (TZI), Universität Bremen (DE), Universitat de Barcelona—Laboratori de Mitjans Interactius, Barcelona (ES), The set-up of the GAMA portal from November 1, 2007 to October 31, 2009 is being co-financed by the European Union's eContentplus program.

Gabriele Blome, Ludwig Boltzmann Institute Media.Art.Research.

Gateway to Archives of Media Art (GAMA)
Vernetzte Archive

http://www.gama-gateway.eu/

Das World Wide Web scheint eine unerschöpfliche Quelle für Informationen zur Medienkunst zu sein, und doch sind Online-Recherchen zeitaufwändig und häufig nicht zufriedenstellend. Informationen müssen aus diversen Quellen zusammengesucht werden, die hinsichtlich ihres Charakters und ihrer Struktur heterogen sind und auf ihre Zuverlässigkeit geprüft werden müssen.

Mit dem Launch des *Gateway to Archives of Media Art* anlässlich des diesjährigen Ars Electronica Festivals gibt es künftig mit *http://www.gama-gateway.eu* eine neue Adresse, die das Auffinden von Informationen zu medienkünstlerischen Arbeiten wesentlich vereinfacht, insofern die Bestände von acht europäischen Archiven und Sammlungen unter einer Adresse recherchierbar werden. Zu finden sind hier beispielsweise Informationen über frühe Werke ungarischer Netzkunst, Videokunst aus Slowenien, Medienkunst aus den Niederlanden, Frankreich und anderen Ländern inner- und außerhalb Europas, Aufzeichnungen des Ars Electronica Festivals sowie Experimentalfilme aus Schweden.

Freilich ist damit nur ein Anfang gemacht. Nachdem die technischen, konzeptionellen, redaktionellen und gestalterischen Aufbauarbeiten des Portals abgeschlossen sind, geht das Projekt in eine neue Phase. Die Plattform soll weiter wachsen und sukzessive mehr Archive und Sammlungen zur Medienkunst über das Portal recherchierbar machen. Mit dem Launch des GAMA-Portals wird erstmals ein Modell für einen vernetzten Zugang zu mehreren Archiven vorgestellt. Es impliziert Ideen, Prozesse und Entscheidungen, die im Folgenden kurz skizziert werden.

Ein Portal zu Archiven der Medienkunst

Der Titel *Gateway to Archives of Media Art* ist Programm, insofern das neue Portal einen gemeinsamen Zugang zu unterschiedlichen Archiven und Sammlungen darstellt, die medienkünstlerische Arbeiten oder Dokumente und Dokumentationen zur Medienkunst teilweise seit 30 Jahren sammeln. Es besteht also nicht der Anspruch, eine homogene oder vollständige Sammlung zu offerieren. Es wird sowohl akzeptiert, dass die beteiligten Institutionen den Begriff „Medienkunst" unterschiedlich verwenden, als auch dass sich die Definition des Begriffs über die Zeit entwickelt und verändert. Die Auswahl der zusammengefassten künstlerischen Projekte ist das Ergebnis kuratorischen Arbeitens und institutioneller Aktivitäten mit sehr unterschiedlichen Intentionen. Sie bewegen sich zum Teil in Referenzsystemen, die weit über die bildende Kunst hinausreichen und in der Musik oder der Filmkunst verortet sind.

Heterogenität bewahren

Das Profil der einzelnen Sammlungen ist eng mit dem jeweiligen institutionellen Auftrag verbunden. So besteht das Hauptinteresse der beteiligten Distributoren darin, die zum Zweck des Vertriebs aufgebaute Sammlung im Verbund besser zu kommunizieren und damit die Sichtbarkeit der Werke bzw. der vertretenen Künstlerinnen und Künstler zu erhöhen. Bei Institutionsarchiv-

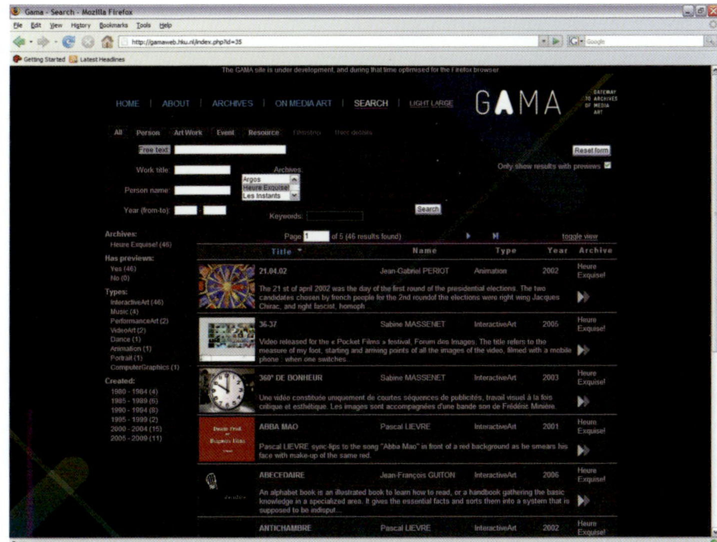

en wie dem der Ars Electronica, von Les Instants Vidéo oder C3 kommt hingegen der Kommunikation institutioneller Aktivitäten ebenfalls eine wesentliche Bedeutung zu, so dass die Werke innerhalb dieses Bezugsystems referenziert werden. Während Distributoren zumeist über Datenbanken verfügen, die Werke und Künstler in den Mittelpunkt stellen, weisen die Datenbanken institutioneller Archive tendenziell eine heterogenere, gewachsene Struktur auf, die sich aus den Notwendigkeiten des jeweiligen institutionellen Betriebs ergibt. Zahleiche Unterschiede bestehen zudem im Detail, wie beispielsweise in der Darstellung von Zeitangaben, bei der Angabe geografischer Namen und Sprachen sowie im Hinblick auf die Schreibweise einzelner Personennamen. Außerdem sind die Inhalte in den Datenbanken nicht nur in unterschiedlichen Strukturen, sondern auch in unterschiedlicher Tiefe erschlossen und beschrieben. Diese Heterogenität zu erhalten und dennoch im Portal einheitliche Zugänge und Darstellungen anzubieten war ein wesentliches Anliegen beim Aufbau der vernetzten Plattform.

Benutzerorientierung

Die Schaffung eines verbesserten Zugangs zur Medienkunst umfasst die praktische Ebene der Recherchemöglichkeiten ebenso wie die Ausrichtung auf unterschiedliche Benutzergruppen. GAMA bietet einen Überblick über die zu einem Werk oder zu einem Künstler/einer Künstlerin im Verbund verfügbaren Informationen (Biografien, Beschreibungen, Bild- und Videodokumentationen, Vorträge, bei Vertrieben auch die verfügbaren Formate) sowie die Möglichkeit, bei Suchanfragen in einer Sprache auch Ergebnisse aus anderen Sprachen zu erhalten. Videoindexierung und Bildähnlichkeitssuche ergänzen die textbasierte Suche um Recherchemöglichkeiten nach visuellen Kriterien. Für KuratorInnen und WissenschaftlerInnen stellt das Portal ein differenziertes Suchinterface bereit, während BenutzerInnen ohne Vorkenntnisse mit kurzen Einführungen an ausgewählte Themen und Werke herangeführt werden. Für die Ausbildung an den Hochschulen offeriert GAMA ein Medienwiki, das es erlaubt, die gesammelten Werke und Dokumente in einen diskursiven, von den BenutzerInnen definierten Zusammenhang zu setzen.

Das *Gateway to Archives of Media Art* stellt also einen wesentlichen Beitrag zur Verbesserung des Zugangs zu Medienkunst im World Wide Web dar, der für Forschung, wie sie am Ludwig Boltzmann Institut Medien.Kunst.Forschung. und anderen Forschungseinrichtungen geleistet wird, gleichermaßen wichtig ist wie für Hochschulen und Kulturschaffende aus allen Bereichen.

Ursula Hentschläger

In memoriam Zelko Wiener. Part II

Zelko Wiener discovered the dynamism of binary media and electronic networks and their possibilities for artistic expression in the early 1980s. He created works for public spaces, was a founding member of the Austrian art & telecommunications group BLIX, and was thus among the first artists to get involved in the area of art and telecommunications. The defining quality of his creative efforts was his development of works in numerous medial formats—art & computer videos, computer animation, computer graphics, digital photography and images, video & computer installations (some real-time) and works in public (telematic) spaces. Over the course of his almost 30-year encounter with new media, he produced an oeuvre that is in equal measure physical and non-material. He thereby numbered among those creatives working in the field of media art, but, at the same time, in the light of his ongoing effort to also juxtapose physically charged positions to the non-binding transience of virtual space, his work is also solidly within classic traditions of the visual arts. In the construction of the strictly binary works he produced since 1986, he experimented with digitally construed bodies in a digital ambience, with real bodies in a construed setting, and construed bodies in seemingly real nature. An intensive confrontation with masculinity runs like a thread through his work, including treatments of a wide variety of themes and in many different formats. In this connection, he was interested in the question of emotional states and processes of change in mediatized societies, in the zone of tension and interplay of proximity and (medial) distance as well as of internal and external (medial) worlds. Zelko Wiener died in 2006 in Vienna.

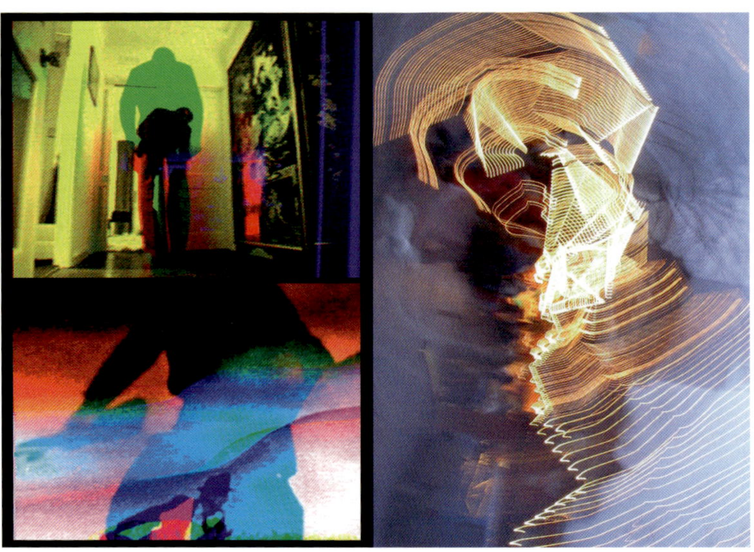

Abb. 1, 2:
„Der verlorene Augenblick. Digitale Photographie Nr. 6 + Nr. 2". Digitale Fotografien 1989

Abb. 3:
„Transmitter 39". Digitale Fotografie 2004

Abb. 1|2 > 1989   Abb. 3 > 2004

On Continuity and Development
Zelko Wiener in conversation with Ursula Hentschläger
(Vienna 1998 | Abridged version 2009)

UH: *You began as a visual artist. What was your approach?*
ZW: The insight that I derived from my studies is: there are no fixed parameters. Neither what constitutes art nor what makes and forms an artist can be definitively specified. This is ultimately a matter of values and decisions that can be reversed in a moment's time. This, of course, fortifies the belief that "ones own" way will eventually turn out to have been the right one. Unfortunately, this attitude tends to lead to a hermetic world view and engenders a similarly deceptive sense of security with respect to ones own creativity that is just like adhering tenaciously to thinking in terms of externally imposed categories. Actually, there's no other choice but to not rely particularly heavily on ones own opinion or on the opinions of others.

UH: *You have dealt especially intensively with art in public spaces. Why?*
ZW: At the time in which public spaces assumed greater significance for me, electronic space simultaneously assumed importance as a public space. (...) Telecommunications itself as well as the founding of the group BLIX had immediate political implications. There were boundaries that could be overcome only under extremely difficult circumstances. Exchange with creative artists from the former Eastern Bloc, for example, or the idea of communicating globally seemed virtually impossible. The works go back to a concept developed by, among others, Canadian and American artists, and were then realized in various contexts—for instance, with BLIX in Vienna as well as with groups from Budapest and East Berlin via telephone lines that were already open at the time. The idea was to transcend borders and get interconnected, to exchange music and images and to communicate.

Abb. 4:
„Lost and Found 1".
Digitale Fotografie
2001

Abb. 5, 6:
„A von 1984".
Kunstvideo 1983
(Stills)

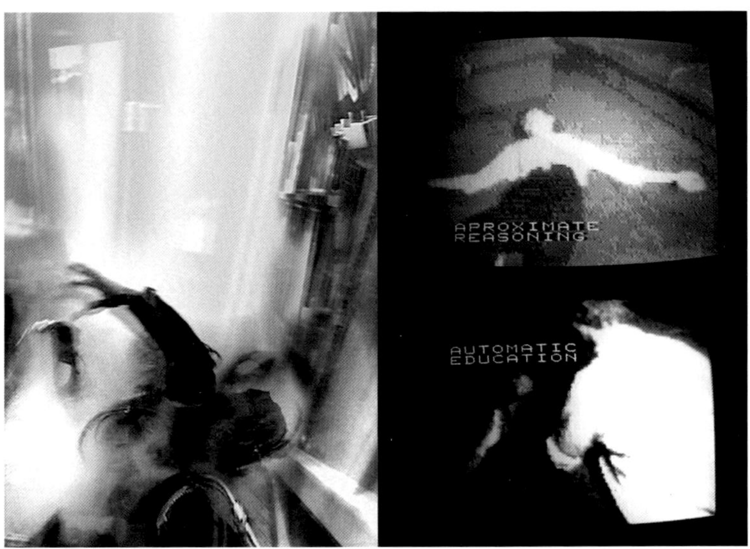

Abb. 4 > 2001   Abb. 5|6 > 1983

In memoriam Zelko Wiener. Part II

UH: What was your first contact with a computer?
ZW: First, there was a so-called slow-scan image-sound converter, a device that could transform video images into sounds and transmit them via telephone lines, and an identical device on the other end received and decoded them. But that wasn't a computer in the current sense of the term. A 1984 work entitled *La Plissure Du Texte* was the first that was truly a case of data communication. The main installation was in Paris, and the project was carried out together with 10 international partner installations. Incidentally, my artist's name also stems from this period. In the network, I was the "Wiener" (the Viennese).

UH: Did you already have your own computer then?
ZW: No. In fact, it was only with great difficulty that we were able to get our hands on a computer for the gallery that served as our headquarters. All the technical equipment we obtained was either via work sharing or solely for the realization of individual projects. I didn't get my first computer until 1985. It was the MUPID. I had gotten started with the development of "Kunst-BTX" and programmed the sites for the Austrian screen text. It was possible to rent it along with the modem that went along with it from the Austrian phone company and hook it up to the telephone line. Both text and image exchange were possible. This was the first computer that was comparable to today's models both with respect to its colors as well as the way it produced images. (…). The digital graphics were closely associated with my new computer, an Amiga 1000. The colors and the graphic capabilities opened up a new field of endeavor. This was truly a matter of the leading edge of visuals. (…). Ultimately, these works launched me in a direction that had been important to me for a long time: an encounter with the question of reality. The approach has to do with self-positioning and the status of the individual within a mediatized society.

UH: You have no inhibitions with respect to messages. What do your latest works say?
ZW: They refer to the anachronism that confronts us wherever we go. We feel or know that things don't fit together, the things that are played out before us or with us. What immediately suggests itself is to define ones own position in terms of rejection, to constantly stress what ought not to be. But in doing so, ones own will, ones personal vision simultaneously slips away. If I have the choice—which I do indeed—then I'd rather be on the side of those who fail than on the side of those who never tried.

Zelko Wiener (1953–2006) started his career with photography and painting. From 1983 to 2006 he developed media art projects in the fields of computer graphics and animations, digital photography, (real-time) installations and art in (telematic) public space. In 1999 he co-founded ZEITGENOSSEN and *www.zeitgenossen.com*. This most recent part of his oeuvre was presented as "In memoriam Zelko Wiener. Part I" at FILE Sao Paulo 2008. *http://www.zelkowiener.net*

Ursula Hentschläger

In memoriam Zelko Wiener. Teil II

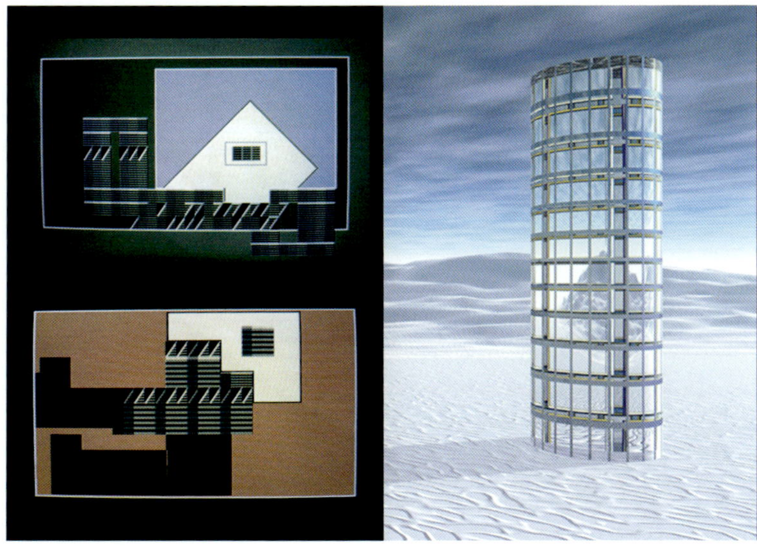

Abb. 7, 8:
„Imaginator". BTX-Computeranimation 1986 (Stills)

Abb. 9:
„RaumSplitter II: Endstation".
Digitales Bild 1997-98 (Ausschnitt)

Abb. 7|8 > 1986

Abb. 9 > 1997|98

Zelko Wiener entdeckte Anfang der 1980er Jahre die Dynamik und künstlerischen Ausdrucksmöglichkeiten binärer Medien und elektronischer Netzwerke. Er agierte im öffentlichen Raum, war Gründungsmitglied der österreichischen Kunst- und Telekommunikationsgruppe BLIX und zählt damit zu den ersten Kunstschaffenden, die sich im Bereich Kunst und Telekommunikation engagierten. Als wesentliche Qualität seines Schaffens gilt der Umstand, dass er in unterschiedlichen medialen Formaten Arbeiten entwickelte. So entstanden Kunst- und Computervideos, Computeranimationen, Computergrafiken, digitale Fotografien und Bilder, Video- und Computerinstallationen (zum Teil in Real-Time) und Arbeiten im öffentlichen (telematischen) Raum. In der beinahe dreißigjährigen Auseinandersetzung mit neuen Medien entstand zudem ein Werk, das gleichermaßen immateriell wie physisch ist. Dabei zählt er mit seinen medialen Arbeiten zu den Medienkunstschaffenden, mit seinem kontinuierlichen Versuch, der Unverbindlichkeit des virtuellen Raumes auch durch physisch aufgeladene Positionen entgegenzutreten, ist er aber ebenso in klassischen Traditionen der bildenden Kunst zu verorten. In der Konstruktion seiner seit 1986 ausschließlich binären Arbeiten experimentierte er mit dem digital konstruierten Körper in digitalem Ambiente, mit realen Körpern in konstruiertem Umfeld oder konstruierten Körpern in scheinbar realer Natur. Thematisch und formatunabhängig zieht sich auch eine intensive Auseinandersetzung mit dem Männerbild durch sein Werk. Damit verknüpft galt sein Interesse der Frage nach emotionalen Befindlichkeiten und Veränderungen in mediatisierten Gesellschaften, dem Spannungsfeld von Nähe und (medialer) Distanz wie auch von Innen- und (medialer) Außenwelt. Zelko Wiener verstarb 2006 in Wien.

Über Kontinuität und Entwicklung.
Zelko Wiener im Gespräch mit Ursula Hentschläger
(Wien 1998 | Kurzfassung 2009)

UH: *Du hast als bildender Künstler begonnen. Welchen Zugang hattest du?*
ZW: Die Einsicht, die ich aus dem Studium gezogen habe, ist: Es gibt keine feststehenden Parameter. Weder was Kunst an sich noch was Künstlerinnen und Künstler ausmacht und formt, ist definitiv festzulegen. Es sind letztlich Wertigkeiten und Entscheidungen, die sich im nächsten Moment umdrehen können. Das bestärkt natürlich den Glauben, der „eigene" Weg werde sich schon als richtig herausstellen. Leider tendiert diese Einstellung zu einem hermetischen Weltbild und schafft eine ähnlich trügerische Sicherheit für das eigene Schaffen wie das Festhalten an dem von außen kommenden Kategoriendenken. Es bleibt eigentlich nichts anderes übrig, als sich weder auf seine eigene Meinung noch auf die Meinung anderer besonders zu verlassen.

UH: *Du hast dich intensiv mit Kunst im öffentlichen Raum beschäftigt. Warum?*
ZW: In dieser Zeit, in der der öffentliche Raum für mich an Bedeutung gewann, wurde gleichzeitig der elektronische Raum als öffentlicher Raum wichtig. (...). Die Telekommunikation selber und auch die Gründung der Gruppe BLIX hatte unmittelbar politische Vorstellungen. Es gab Grenzen, die nur unter extrem schwierigen Umständen zu überwinden waren. Austausch mit Kunstschaffenden aus dem ehemaligen Ostblock zum Beispiel oder die Vorstellung, global zu

Abb. 10:
„VirtWelt: Kraftakt".
Digitales Bild 1998

Abb. 11, 12:
„Passwort
(> Gelb, > Rot)".
Computergrafiken
1987

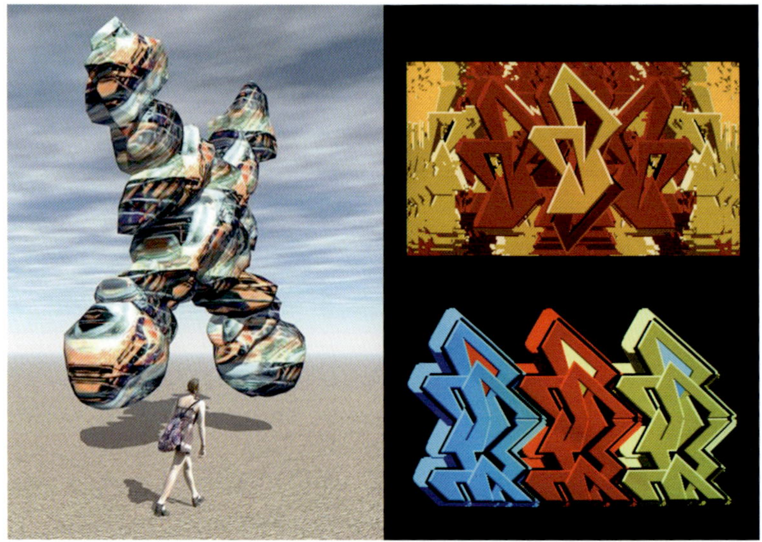

Abb. 10 > 1998   Abb. 11|12 > 1987

kommunizieren, schien beinahe unmöglich. Die Arbeiten gehen auf ein Konzept zurück, das unter anderen die kanadischen und nordamerikanischen Künstler entwickelten und dann in verschiedenen Zusammenhängen, z.B. mit BLIX in Wien, aber auch mit Gruppen aus Budapest und Ostberlin, über Telefonleitungen, die damals schon offen waren, realisierten. Die Idee war, uns über die Grenzen hinweg zu verbinden, Musik bzw. Bilder auszutauschen und zu kommunizieren.

UH: Was war dein erster Kontakt mit einem Computer?
ZW: Am Anfang war ein sogenannter „Slowscan"-Bild-Ton-Wandler; ein Gerät, das Videobilder in Töne übersetzen und über Telefonleitungen verschicken konnte. Am anderen Ende wurden diese von einem gleichen Gerät empfangen und decodiert. Das war allerdings nach dem heutigen Verständnis noch kein Computer. 1984 ging es in „La Plissure Du Texte" erstmals um tatsächliche Datenkommunikation. In Paris war die Hauptstation und gemeinsam mit zehn internationalen Partnerstationen wurde das Projekt durchgeführt. Aus dieser Zeit stammt übrigens mein Künstlername. Ich war der „Wiener" im Netz.

UH: Hattest du zu dieser Zeit bereits einen eigenen Computer?
ZW: Nein, mit großer Mühe konnte überhaupt ein Computer für die Wiener Galerie, von der aus wir agierten, organisiert werden. Alle technischen Geräte wurden entweder als Arbeits-Sharing oder nur für die Realisierung einzelner Projekte angeschafft. Den ersten Computer hatte ich erst 1985. Es war der MUPID. Ich hatte mit der Entwicklung von „Kunst-BTX" begonnen und programmierte die Seiten für den österreichischen Bildschirmtext. Man konnte ihn bei der Post mieten – gemeinsam mit dem dazugehörenden Modem – und an die Telefonleitung stecken. Text- und Bildaustausch war gleichermaßen möglich. Es war der erste Computer, der sich sowohl von seinen Farben als auch von der Darstellungsart mit heutigen Computern vergleichen lässt. (…). Die digitalen Grafiken hingen eng zusammen mit meinem neuen Computer – einem Amiga 1000. Die Farben und Grafikfähigkeiten eröffneten ein neues Arbeitsfeld. Es ging um visuelle Grenzschichten. (…). Letztlich haben mich diese Arbeiten in eine Richtung geführt, die mir schon lange wichtig war: Es geht um Fragen nach Realität. Der Ansatz liegt in der Eigenpositionierung und im Stellenwert des Einzelnen innerhalb einer mediatisierten Gesellschaft.

UH: Du hast keine Hemmung vor Botschaften. Worin liegt die der neuen Arbeiten?
ZW: Im Hinweis auf den Anachronismus, der uns überall begegnet. Wir spüren oder wissen, dass die Dinge nicht zusammenpassen, die sich vor uns und mit uns abspielen. Es liegt nahe, seine eigene Position über die Verneinung zu definieren, das zu betonen, was nicht sein soll. Damit entgleitet aber zugleich das eigene Wollen, die persönliche Vision. Wenn ich die Wahl habe – und die habe ich –, dann bin ich lieber bei denen, die scheitern, als auf der Seite jener, die es nie versucht haben.

Zelko Wiener (1953–2006) begann seine künstlerische Laufbahn mit Fotografie und Malerei. Von 1983 bis 2006 entwickelte er künstleriche Projekte in den Bereichen Computergrafik und -Animation, digitale Fotografie, (Realtime-) Installationen und im (telematischen) öffentlichen Raum. 1999 gründete er gemeinsam mit Ursula Hentschläger die Gruppe ZEITGENOSSEN und *www.zeitgenossen.com*. Das FILE Festival Sao Paulo präsentierte 2008 im Rahmen von „In memoriam Zelko Wiener I" die Arbeiten im „Zeitgenossen"-Kontext. *http://www.zelkowiener.net*

Monika Fleischmann & Wolfgang Strauss

Liquid Views

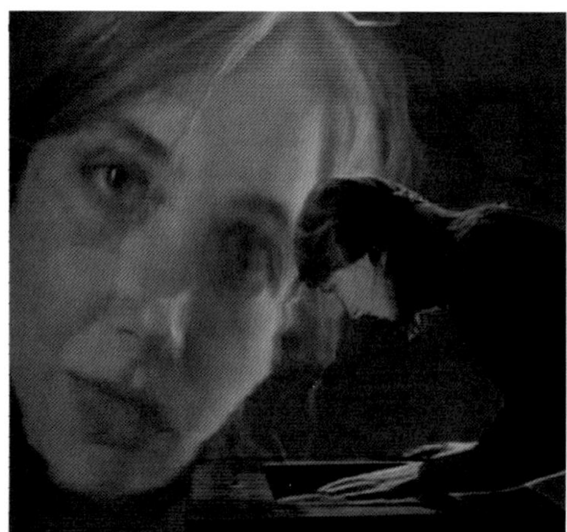 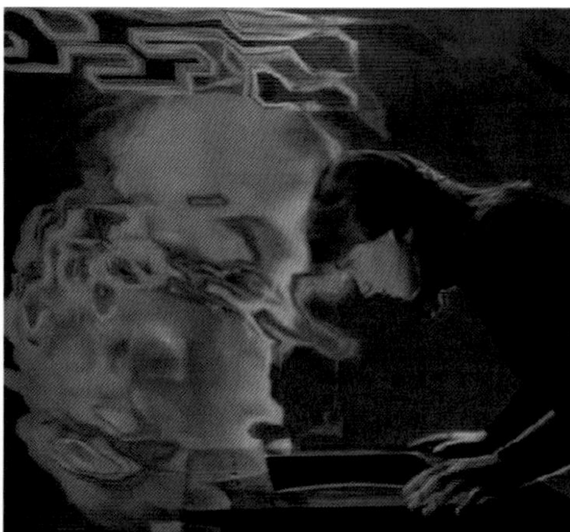

A horizontal screen displays the shimmering surface of a body of water. The sounds made by the water are audible. Coming closer, the observer sees his image reflected in the water. Touching the sensitive screen with ones finger produces waves and causes the image to dissolve. The harder one presses, the more the image disintegrates. When the waves subside, the virtual image appears intact again. Artificial nature is brought to life by artificial intelligence.

At the same time, the surface of the water can be seen to be a large-scale projection. As if through a magnifying glass, the observer sees himself there as an observer of himself. His virtually reflected countenance looks out from there into the space. Thus, the introverted glance beholding ones self seemingly becomes a glance at the Other. At the same time, the intimate act of observation becomes an act of putting an image on public display.

The interactive installation depicts Ovid's parable of Narcissus as an act of reflection of and on oneself, and translates this into a visual and intellectual process of reflection about image and likeness. Digital virtuality and physical presence blend into a mixed reality experience.

Liquid Views summons up the metaphor of water as mirror in which the observer sees himself confronted by himself, and in which the digital universe is reflected. The interface as such is not consciously perceived. The real situation is sensorially interlinked with the virtual one. The real image of the observer in the fictitious image of the water surface accentuates the duality of our observation of the world and of our self as the basis of our construction of reality.

Liquid Views (the 1992–93 version with Christian Bohn) was on exhibit over the course of six years (with three processor replacements) at more than 50 different cultural venues. It brought out the cultural differences among the protagonists. The installation was part of the exhibition staged for the opening of the media museum at the ZKM–Center for Art and Media Karlsruhe in 1997. Since 2008, the reproduced work is being exhibited again.

Monika Fleischmann & Wolfgang Strauss

Liquid Views

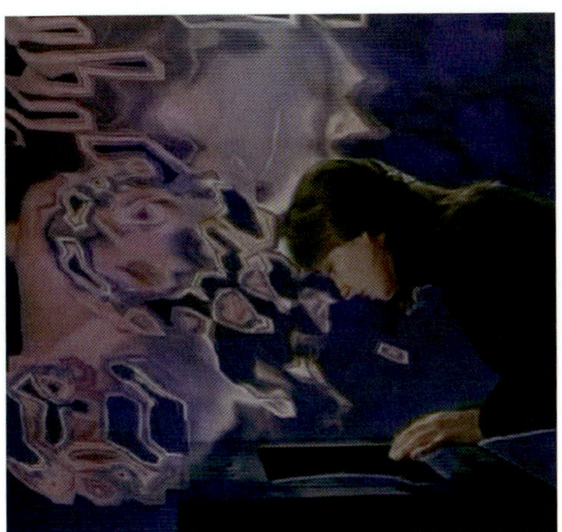

Ein waagerechter Bildschirm zeigt eine schimmernde Wasseroberfläche. Das Geräusch von Wasser ist zu hören. Nähertretend sieht der Betrachter sein Bild im Wasser gespiegelt. Ein Fingertipp auf den sensitiven Bildschirm verursacht Wellen, und das Bild zerfließt. Je stärker die Berührung, umso mehr löst es sich auf. Kommen die Wellen zur Ruhe, erscheint das virtuelle Bild wieder unversehrt. Die künstliche Natur wird durch künstliche Intelligenz belebt. Zeitgleich ist der Wasserspiegel als große Projektion sichtbar. Wie durch ein Vergrößerungsglas sieht sich der Betrachter dort als Beobachter seiner selbst. Sein virtuell gespiegeltes Antlitz blickt von dort aus in den Raum. So wird der introvertierte Blick auf sich selbst scheinbar zu einem Blick auf die anderen. Gleichzeitig wird die intime Betrachtung zu einer öffentlichen Zurschaustellung.

Die interaktive Installation inszeniert die Parabel von Ovids Narziss als einen Akt der Selbst(be)spiegelung und übersetzt sie in eine visuelle und intellektuelle Reflexion über Bild und Abbild. Digitale Virtualität und körperliche Präsenz verschmelzen zu einer Mixed-Reality-Erfahrung.

Liquid Views greift auf die Metapher des Wassers als Spiegel zurück, in dem der Betrachter sich mit sich selbst konfrontiert sieht und in dem sich das digitale Universum reflektiert. Das Interface als solches wird nicht bewusst wahrgenommen. Reale und virtuelle Situation sind sensorisch miteinander gekoppelt. Das reale Bild des Beobachters im fiktiven Bild des Wasserspiegels betont die Dualität von Weltbeobachtung und Selbstbeobachtung als Grundlage der Konstruktion von Wirklichkeit.

Liquid Views war in der Version von 1992–93 (mit Christian Bohn) sechs Jahre und drei Rechnerportierungen lang in mehr als 50 kulturell unterschiedlichen Orten ausgestellt und hat die kulturellen Unterschiede der Akteure zum Sprechen gebracht. Die Installation war 1997 Teil der Eröffnungsausstellung des ZKM | Medienmuseums in Karlsruhe. Seit 2008 wird das reproduzierte Werk wieder ausgestellt.

Laurent Mignonneau and Christa Sommerer

Life Writer

Life Writer is an old-fashioned typewriter that was transformed into a computer interface, where users can interact using the normal functions of the machine. It stands on an old table with a projection from above oriented directly onto the paper. This creates the impression of the paper becoming the computer screen, since the movement of the typewriter's paper tray is seamlessly linked with the movement of the projected image.

When a user writes text on this typewriter, the text transforms into artificial life forms that appear on the paper of the typewriter as if directly emerging from the machine. These spider-like creatures run around frenetically trying to find text to eat. When the user types some more letters, the creatures will quickly snap it up, and once they have eaten enough text, they will reproduce and fill the whole surface of the paper. The user can also kill the creatures by pushing them off the paper or squeezing them back into the machine.

The creatures are programmed with genetic algorithms, so they are semi-autonomous and follow their own internal rules of metabolization and reproduction. The whole process of writing text on *Life Writer* becomes a process of giving life to thoughts and having thoughts themselves evolve, escape and reconfigure.

Life Writer is an extraordinary project, not only in the application of new technologies to sculptural form and in combining old and new technology through a media archaeological interface; it is also an example of an art form in which interactive art begins to evolve towards a "living art" in itself.

The creation and manipulation of fascinating visual images in an interactive environment, where participants also engage in the act of creation, raises fundamental questions about human interaction with increasingly "intelligent" machines and possible levels of human-machine symbiosis.

Acknowledgements
Life Writer is part of the collection of the ITAU Cultural Sao Paulo, Brazil. Originally developed in *2006* for the "All Digital" show at the MOCA Museum of Contemporary Art in Cleveland, curated by Margo Crutchfield.

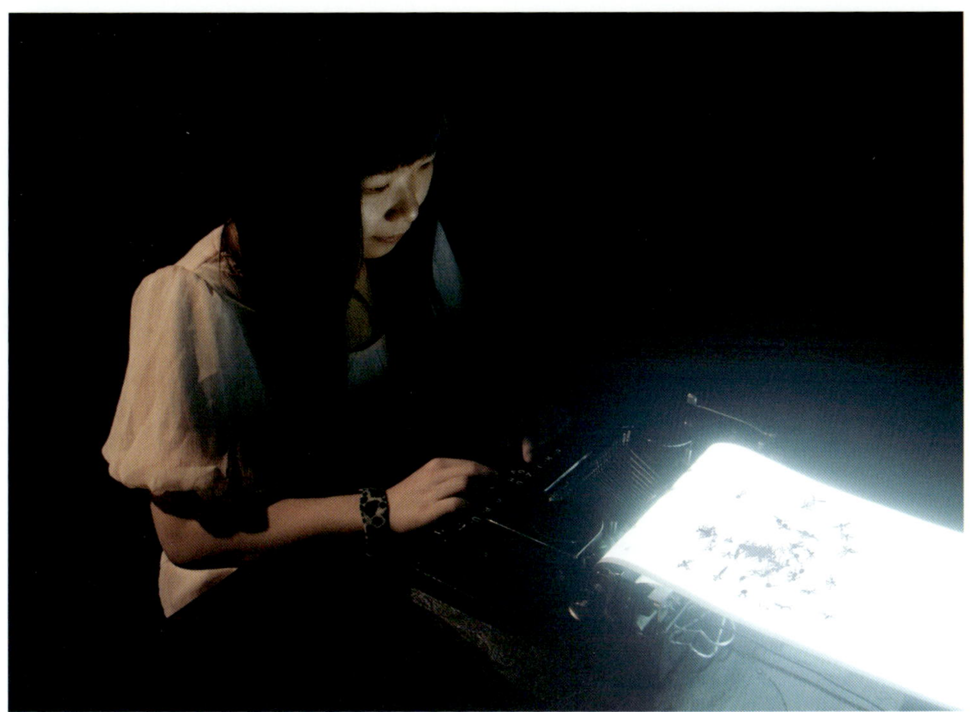

References
C. Sommerer and L. Mignonneau, "Life Spaces II & Life Writer" in *All Digital exhibition catalog*, ed. Margo Crutch-field (Cleveland: MOCA Museum of Contemporary Art, 2006).
C. Sommerer and L. Mignonneau, "Life Writer—Creating life through the act of writing," in *The Gen[H]ome Project* exhibition catalog (Los Angeles: MAK Museum of Contemporary Art, Nov. 2006).
C. Sommerer and L. Mignonneau, "Life Writer," in *Bytes & Bodies—Von Realen Körpern in Digitalen Räumen, Donu-menta* 2006 catalog, ed. Regina Helwig-Schmid (Regensburg: 2006), 39.
C. Sommerer and L. Mignonneau, "Life Writer," in *Feedback: Art Responsive to Instruction, Input, or its Environment*, ed. A.B.D de Corral et al (Gijón, Spain: LABoral Centro de Arte y Creacion Industrial, 2007), 116–119.
C. Sommerer and L. Mignonneau, "Life Writer," in *Genesis—Die Kunst der Schöpfung—The Art of Creation*, ed. F. Eggelhöfer (Berne: Zentrum Paul Klee, 2008), 41–42.
C. Sommerer and L. Mignonneau, "Life Writer," in *YOUniverse Biennial of Contemporary Art of Sevilla (BIACS)*, ed. P. Weibel, W. Rhee and M.A. Brayer (Seville: Fundacion BIACS, 2008), 268–269.
C. Sommerer and L. Mignonneau, "Life Writer," in *Turn and Widen—The 5th Seoul International Media Art Biennale* (Seoul: Seoul Museum of Art, 2008), 140–141.

Laurent Mignonneau and Christa Sommerer

Life Writer

Der *Life Writer* ist eine antik anmutende Schreibmaschine, die zu einem Computer-interface adaptiert wurde: Die Besucher können darauf wie auf einer normalen Schreibmaschine schreiben und treten dabei mit der Installation in Interaktion. Der *Life Writer* steht auf einem alten Tisch; auf das in die Schreibmaschine eingespannte Blatt Papier wird von oben ein Bild projiziert. Die Bewegungen des Papiers und die Projektion sind nahtlos aneinander gekoppelt, wodurch der Eindruck entsteht, dass das Papier zum Computerbildschirm mutiert.

Tippen die Besucher Text auf der Schreibmaschine ein, materialisiert sich dieser in Form von kleinen virtuellen Lebewesen, die plötzlich auf dem Papier herumirren, als ob sie direkt aus der Maschine gekrabbelt wären. Diese spinnenartigen Wesen bewegen sich hektisch über das Papier auf der Suche nach Text, den sie sich einverleiben können. Werden weitere Buchstaben eingetippt, verschlingen die Spinnenkreaturen diese gefräßig. Haben sie sich satt gefressen, pflanzen sie sich fort, und ihre Nachkommen breiten sich allmählich über das gesamte Papier aus. Man kann der Spinneninvasion auch ein Ende setzen, indem man sie vom Papier rutschen lässt oder mit der Walze zurück in die Maschine drängt.

Die kleinen Spinnenwesen werden mittels genetischer Algorithmen programmiert; sie sind halbautonom und folgen ihren eigenen Regeln der Metabolisierung und Fortpflanzung. Durch das Schreiben auf dem *Life Writer* wird Gedanken Leben eingehaucht; diese Gedankengebilde metamorphieren, entschlüpfen ihrer Hülle und materialisieren sich.

Life Writer ist ein außergewöhnliches Projekt, nicht nur, was den Einsatz neuer Technologien für die bildnerische Gestaltung oder die Kombination alter und neuer Technologien mittels eines medienarchäologischen Interface anlangt; *Life Writer* dient gleichzeitig als Beispiel einer Kunst-form, in der interaktive Kunst allmählich zu „lebender Kunst" mutiert.

Die Gestaltung und Verwandlung faszinierender visueller Bilder in einer interaktiven Umge-bung, in der die Besucher selbst am Schöpfungsakt beteiligt sind, werfen einige zentrale Fra-gen auf: Wie interagiert der Mensch mit zunehmend „intelligenten" Maschinen, und welche Möglichkeiten einer Mensch-Maschine-Symbiose tun sich auf?

Danksagungen
Life Writer ist Teil der Kunstsammlung des *ITAÚ Cultural* in São Paulo in Brasilien. Die Installation wurde 2006 ursprünglich für die von Margo Crutchfield kuratierte „All Digital"-Ausstellung am *MOCA Museum of Contemporary Art* in Cleveland entwickelt.

(Aus dem Englischen von Sonja Pöllabauer)

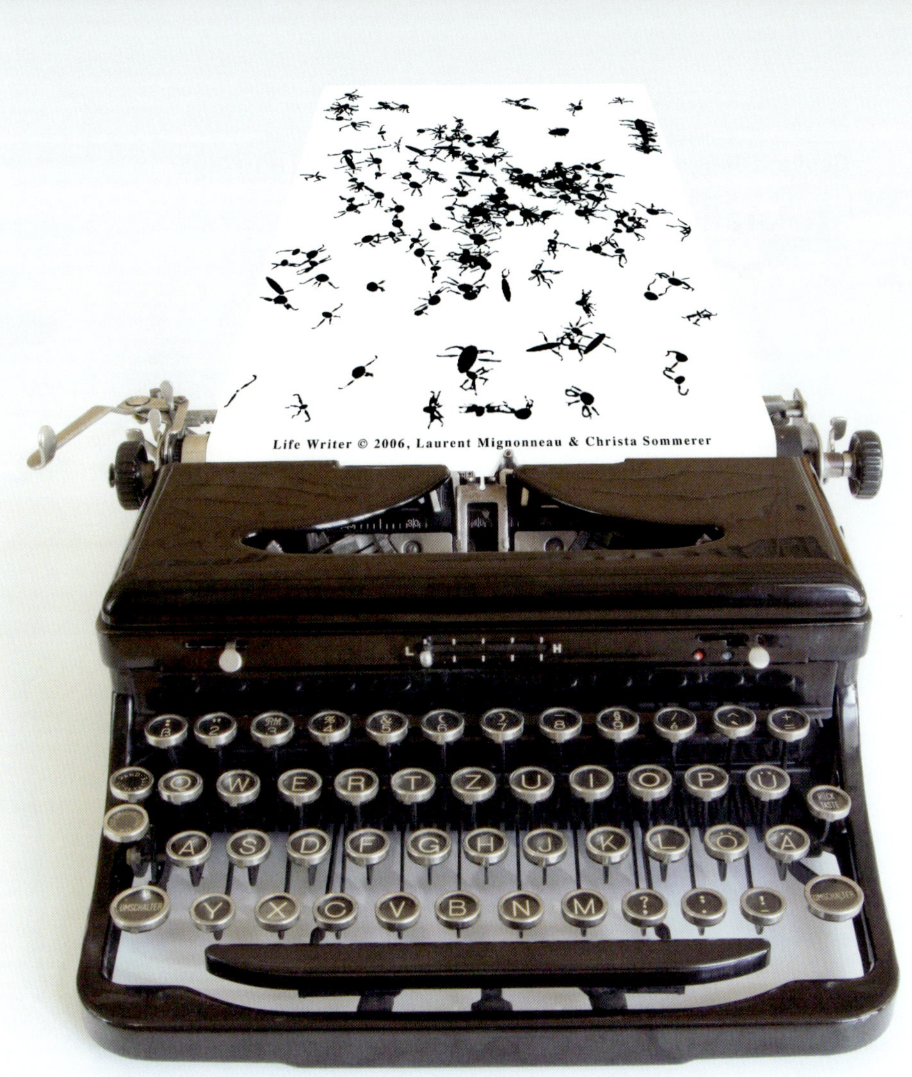

Life Writer © 2006, Laurent Mignonneau & Christa Sommerer

Gebhard Sengmüller, in collaboration with Franz Büchinger

A Parallel Image

In 1880 the French engineer Maurice Leblanc defined for the first time the principle for transmitting images with electricity, which is still valid today.

The basis for this was the idea that an image to be transmitted is broken down into lines; the light impulses are transformed into electrical currents; the sender and receiver of the image must be synchronized; the transmitted electric signals are ultimately transposed into light values on a screen again; and that the picture lines are then recomposed synchronously in time.

The breakdown of images already proposed at that time first became practically possible with the conception of the Nipkow disk by Paul Nipkow in 1883. This was successfully employed for the first time in 1926 by the Scotsman John Logie Baird in an electromechanical television system, the Televisor.

Electronic television, in its form that has remained largely unchanged up to the early 21st century, first presented in 1928 by Philo T. Farnsworth and later commercially standardized by Vladimir Zworykin at RCA, is also based on this principle idea of breaking down images into image lines and the therefore requisite time synchronization between sender and receiver.

This way of chopping up moving images into frames, fields and lines is one of the most universal and powerful continuities in the development of electronic image media. This kind of image transmission can be called serial, because a coaxial cable or radio channel suffices to transmit the image signal from the sender to the receiver.

A Parallel Image starts from the assumption that the development just described never happened.

Would the absence of the idea of breaking down an image into lines have led to the lack of a procedure for live transmission any time soon? Or would the desire of our technological civilization to have an immediate transmission medium have been so great that a completely different, more complicated way would have been accepted?

With this claim I attempt to develop a television format that is useless in its efficiency, but nevertheless technically entirely feasible. My format chooses a parallel transmission of every single pixel, which makes a technically elaborate synchronization in time between sender and receiver superfluous.

To this end, I will design an apparatus that links every pixel on the "camera" side with every pixel on the "monitor" side in the technically simplest way possible. Taking this idea to its logical conclusion, this leads to an absurd system that connects a grid of 2500 photoconductors on the sender side with 2500 small light bulbs on the receiver side, pixel by pixel, using a total of 2500 copper wires.

This results in a relatively gigantic unit consisting of camera, transmission route and monitor, which in its sheer size, complexity and power consumption recalls the mainframes of the early 1940s or old-fashioned electro-mechanical telephone switching centers (telephone exchanges).

Unlike familiar serial image transmission, the technology of *A Parallel Image* is completely transparent even to the lay viewer. An object held in front of the "camera" side of the installation appears as a shadow outline on the "monitor" side. The signal path can be followed simply by

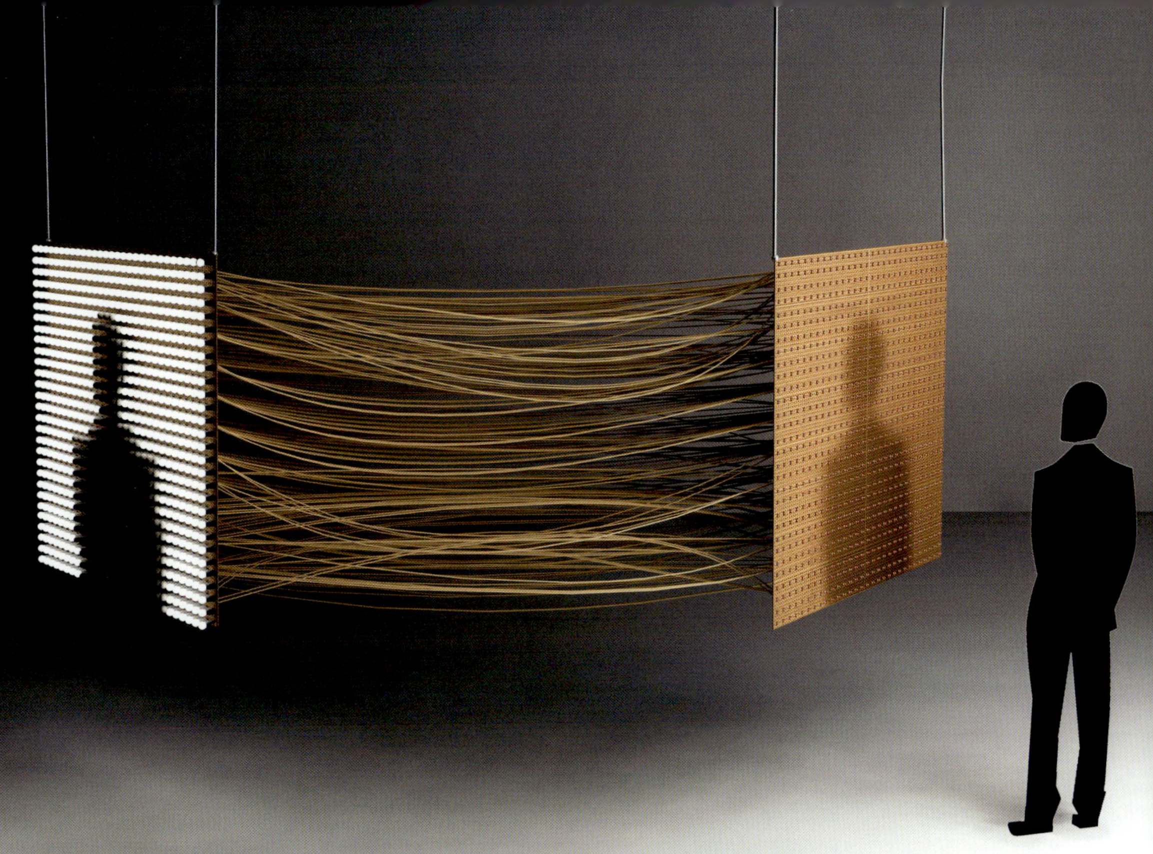

Rendering of the installation (copyright © 2008 by Michael Günther)

tracing the wires from each photoconductor to each light bulb.

The resultant medium has an experiential quality that would be more probably attributed to film. Like film, and contrary to the conventional television system, there is a correspondence here between the real world and the transmission that can be sensually experienced. The television image is imbued with the directness of a film frame without the coding that normally takes place in the transmission of a television signal and does not allow for an easily comprehensible connection between the base image and the recorded signal (e.g. on video tape). In its directness *A Parallel Image* is a radically new live medium that returns the visibility and comprehensibility of the process to electronic image transmission.

Unlike most media systems today, a direct experience is possible with *A Parallel Image*. Visitors can intervene directly in this interactive sculpture: the outlines of their bodies appear without delay on the monitor. It is possible to play with this image by changing the distance to the camera, etc.

Swivelling the photo lens (or projecting a film onto the camera surface) also makes it possible to render bodies and objects in their gradations of brightness and their plasticity. The starkly reduced resolution of this camera obscura leads at the same time to an image that clearly indicates the process it is based on in its quality.

http://www.gebseng.com/08_a_parallel_image/

(Translated from German by Aileen Derieg)

Supported by: *Fels-Multiprint*, Wien

Gebhard Sengmüller, in Zusammenarbeit mit Franz Büchinger

A Parallel Image

Im Jahr 1880 definierte der französische Ingenieur Maurice Leblanc erstmals das bis heutige gültige Prinzip der Übertragung von Bildern durch Elektrizität.

Dem zugrunde lag die Idee, dass ein zu übertragendes Bild in Zeilen zerlegt wird; die Lichtimpulse in elektrische Ströme umgewandelt werden; Bildsender und -empfänger synchronisiert werden müssen; zuletzt die übertragenen elektrischen Signale auf einem Bildschirm wieder in Helligkeitswerte umgesetzt; und die Bildzeilen zeitsynchron wieder zusammengesetzt werden. Praktisch möglich wurde diese bereits damals vorgeschlagene Bildzerlegung erst durch die Konzeption der Nipkow-Scheibe durch Paul Nipkow 1883, die dann erst 1926 von dem Schotten John Logie Baird erstmals erfolgreich in einem elektromechanischen Fernsehsystem, dem Televisor, eingesetzt wurde.

Elektronisches Fernsehen, in seiner bis ins frühe 21. Jahrhundert weitgehend unveränderten Form, die von Philo T. Farnsworth 1928 vorgestellt und später von Vladimir Zworykin bei RCA kommerziell standardisiert wurde, baut ebenfalls auf dieser Grundidee der Zerlegung in Bildzeilen und der dadurch nötigen zeitlichen Synchronisation zwischen Sender und Empfänger auf.

Diese Zerhackung von Bewegtbildern in Frames, Fields und Zeilen ist eine der universellsten und kraftvollsten Kontinuitäten in der Entwicklung elektronischer Bildmedien. Die Art der Bildübertragung kann als seriell bezeichnet werden, weil ein Koaxialkabel bzw. ein Funkkanal genügt, um das Bildsignal vom Sender zum Empfänger zu übertragen.

Detailansicht der Bildschirmseite der Installation: Lochrasterplatte mit Glühbirnen (Ausschnitt, *24* von *2.500* Elementen)

Detailansicht der lackierten Kupferdrähte (*0,4* mm Durchmesser), die bei *A Parallel Image* Sender und Empfänger verbinden (*36* von *2.500* Drähten)

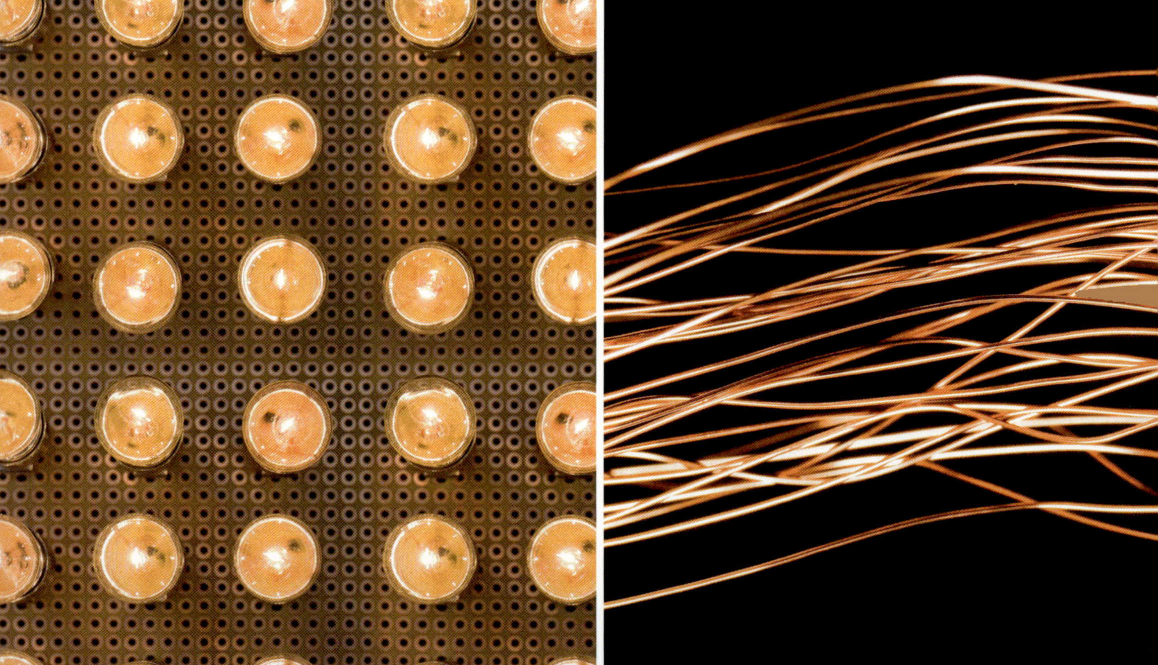

A Parallel Image geht von der Annahme aus, dass die gerade beschriebene Entwicklung nicht stattgefunden hat. Hätte das Ausbleiben der Idee, ein Bild in Zeilen zu zerlegen, dazu geführt, dass sich in absehbarer Zeit kein Verfahren zur Live-Übertragung von bewegten Bildern durchgesetzt hätte? Oder wäre der Wunsch unserer technischen Zivilisation, ein unmittelbares Übertragungsmedium zu besitzen, so groß gewesen, dass auch ein ganz anderer, umständlicherer Weg in Kauf genommen worden wäre?

Ich versuche, mit diesem Anspruch ein zwar in seiner Effizienz unbrauchbares, aber technisch durchaus mögliches Fernsehformat zu entwickeln. Mein Format wählt eine parallele Übertragung jedes einzelnen Bildpunktes, wodurch eine technisch aufwändige zeitliche Synchronisierung zwischen Sender und Empfänger hinfällig wird.

Dazu entwerfe ich eine Vorrichtung, die auf die technisch denkbar einfachste Weise jeden Bildpunkt auf der „Kamera"seite mit jedem Bildpunkt auf der „Bildschirm"seite verbindet. Konsequent zu Ende gedacht führt das zu einem absurden System, das ein Raster von 2.500 Fotowiderständen auf der Senderseite mit 2.500 kleinen Glühbirnen auf der Empfängerseite verbindet, und zwar Bildpunkt für Bildpunkt mit insgesamt 2.500 Kupferdrähten.

Es entsteht so eine einigermaßen riesenhafte Einheit aus Kamera, Übertragungsweg und Bildschirm, die in schierer Größe, Umständlichkeit und Stromverbrauch an Mainframes der frühen 1940er Jahre oder auch an altmodische elektromechanische Telefonvermittlungsstellen (Wählämter) erinnert.

Im Gegensatz zur gewohnten seriellen Bildübertragung ist *A Parallel Image* auch für den laienhaften Betrachter technisch vollkommen transparent. Ein vor die „Kamera"seite der Installation gehaltenes Objekt erscheint als Schattenriss auf der „Bildschirm"seite. Der Signalweg ist durch einfaches Nachverfolgen der Drähte von jedem einzelnen Fotowiderstand zu jeder einzelnen Glühbirne nachvollziehbar.

Das so entstandene Medium hat eine Erfahrungsqualität, die man eher dem Film zuordnen würde. Wie bei diesem, und im Gegensatz zum herkömmlichen Fernsehsystem, ist eine sinnlich erfahrbare Entsprechung zwischen Realwelt und Übertragung vorhanden. Dem Fernsehbild wird die Direktheit des Filmkaders gegeben, ohne die Kodierung, die in der Übertragung eines Fernsehsignals normalerweise stattfindet und keine einfach nachvollziehbare Verbindung zwischen dem zugrunde liegenden Bild und dem aufgezeichneten Signal (z.B. am Videoband) zulässt. *A Parallel Image* ist in seiner Direktheit ein radikales neues Live-Medium, das der elektronischen Bildübertragung die Sichtbarkeit und Verständlichkeit des Prozesses zurückgibt.

Im Unterschied zu den meisten heutigen Mediensystemen ist mit *A Parallel Image* eine direkte Erfahrung möglich. Die Besucher können in diese interaktive Skulptur selbst eingreifen: Ihre Körperumrisse erscheinen ohne Verzögerung auf dem Bildschirm, durch Veränderung des Abstandes zur Kamera etc. kann mit diesem Bild gespielt werden. Durch das Einschwenken der Fotolinse (oder durch die Projektion eines Films auf die Kameraoberfläche) können Körper und Gegenstände auch in ihren Helligkeitsabstufungen und ihrer Plastizität wiedergegeben werden. Die stark reduzierte Auflösung dieser elektronischen Camera Obscura führt dabei zu einem Bild, das in seiner Qualität deutlich auf den zugrunde liegenden Prozess verweist.

http://www.gebseng.com/08_a_parallel_image/

Unterstützt von: *Fels-Multiprint*, Wien

A Parallel Image: Medienkunstpreis des Landes Salzburg 2008, in Kooperation mit
Schmiede Salzburg und Land Salzburg

Pixelspaces 2009: Do it Together!

Pixelspaces 2009 is dedicated to the art of new and not-yet-institutionalized transdisciplinary linkups, and spotlights the innovative new poetic forms of expression engendered by them. The focus here—before the backdrop of converging technologies—is on art and science getting things done together!

The new Ars Electronica Center provides a setting for a new conference format: a nomadic symposium staged along the topography of the facility's exhibits and their component installations. An inspection tour through this exhibition opens up various points of access to the discussion of which forms of reciprocal potential arise when art assumes a leading role within the new convergences involving information and communication technologies, biotechnology and neurotechnology, and other disciplines (such as those emerging in the field of Green technology). And this leads directly to the question of how artistic practices and forms of expression are shifting into this direction.

The casting of this nomadic symposium necessarily brings forth hybrid constellations of presenters and presenter teams. The Ars Electronica Futurelab as well as visiting artists, scientists and media technology experts will be convening in various formats to jointly discuss convergences in the participants' respective fields. The issues that have been raised and put up for discussion are those that can be illustrated by concrete cases of convergence and that, in classical discipline formats, either cannot be adequately answered or do not even come up. The intention is to take an experimental-investigative approach that takes existing facts and circumstances as the point of departure of an effort to derive scenarios with promise for the future.

In addition to innovative solutions for existing tasks, *Pixelspaces* also seeks opportunities to enable the general public to get a comprehensible picture of the process of convergence that is bringing art and science to the very threshold of indistinguishability. *Deep Space*, the new Ars Electronica Center's large-format projection system that's suited to a wide array of forms of depiction and imaging techniques, is quite an up-to-date example. Within the framework of a behind-the-scenes presentation, Deep Space as a physical setting at the interface of publicly accessible lab and exhibition venue will become a stage in its own right. The Ars Electronica Futurelab staffers who developed Deep Space will present this facility's relevant features as illustrated by a broad spectrum of projects from the area of virtual reality and other high-definition, computation-intensive forms of depiction. Artists will also be displaying examples of their work in Deep Space; in this context, Deep Space will morph into a forum for a discussion of new imaging techniques that will seamlessly segue into the exhibition "New Views of Humankind." The convergence of art and science manifests itself here as well on both functional and aesthetic levels.

Experiments performed in cooperation with outside associates in the AEC's four labs—BioLab, FabLab, BrainLab and RoboLab—will illustrate trends and possibilities of shaping nature and human culture via human intervention, whereby each lab will showcase different methods to utilize converging technologies. Hands-on experiences are conducive to micro-discourses that promote wider discussions of related issues—e.g. cloning your favorite plant, creation of everyday objects with a 3D printer, steering a robot with your own brain, and high-tech prostheses.

In *GeoCity*, various high-contrast foils in the form of interactive visualizations and new interface technologies will be applied to Planet Earth and, as a proxy for it, to the City of Linz. What is brought out very clearly by the available data sets and the evaluations of them is the ever-more-urgent challenge to find and implement solutions to global problems such as the energy problem, the water problem, the food problem and the garbage problem. Thus, "do-it-together" reveals itself to be an elementary formula; after all, no single discipline can solve these problems alone. Accordingly, *Pixelspaces* is launching *GeoCity* as a lab for confrontations with the past, present and future of our planet, and as a setting to discuss solution scenarios for existing and looming problems on the basis of a repertoire of converging and Green technologies.

As a natural follow-up to the *Geocity* theme, *Open_Sailing* will present a prototype that is to be regarded as the intermediate result of an ambitious project that Ars Electronica has honored with [the next idea] technology grant. The *Open_Sailing* is building self-organizing pieces of infrastructure that resemble living organisms and are suited for life on the water. In accordance with bionic principles, do-it-yourself technologies are being integrated into an oceanic station that provides its human occupants with all the necessities of life. *Pixelspaces* will showcase *Open_Sailing* as a floating exhibition accompanied by an installation elaborating on some of what's come out of the project experimental approach so far. The prototype's explicit "do-it-together" approach is emblematic of new convergences between disciplines and technologies. *Open_Sailing* not only invites everyone to get involved and pitch in; it's also developing all hardware and software components as open source.

The above-mentioned stations of the nomadic symposium constitute the programmatic core of this year's *Pixelspaces* conference. The agenda also includes various contributions by guest artists and associates who are exhibiting in the Ars Electronica Center. Rounding out the lineup are various evening events such as the Façade Festival that will deliver a behind-the-scenes glimpse at the Ars Electronica Center's massive new individually-programmable LED façade that opens up new prospects for resource-minimizing display technology and the diverse scenarios in which it might be deployed.

In conjunction with this year's *Pixelspaces*, the Ars Electronica Futurelab and Fabrica are jointly offering a series of workshops entitled "Re-imagining the Fashion Retail Store." The background of this initiative is the fact that there's been practically no change in this sub-sector vis-à-vis other shop formats for decades now, which has to be considered in light of the fact that, in the age of eCommerce and multi-functionality-oriented shopping mall concepts, designers and distributors have become all-too-cognizant of the need to rethink not only the cultural rites of "fashion" but also clothing per se and all of its product characteristics—that is, everything from intelligent fabrics to the *mise en scène* of the shopping experience. The workshop's hypothesis is that approaches to this can be sought and found, first and foremost, at the interface of art and converging technologies.

The whole conference and each of the individual contributions to it can be considered an experiment that addresses as well as constitutes new convergences. "Do-it-together" is above all to be seen as a wake-up call for a society that is no longer able to answer its most urgent questions and perform its most pressing tasks within the framework of discrete individual disciplines. In addition to these disciplines, the symposium contributions and exhibition projects are shifting closer together than ever before, a sign that the fields of activity emerging at the nexus of art and science, theory and practice, are blending together into a new functional entity.

(Text: Daniela Kuka, Horst Hörtner)

Pixelspaces 2009: Do it Together!

Pixelspaces 2009 widmet sich der Kunst neuer und noch nicht institutionalisierter Brückenschläge und nimmt die daraus resultierenden neuartigen poetischen Ausdrucksformen in den Blick. Fokussiert wird dabei ein „Do it together" von Kunst und Wissenschaft vor dem Hintergrund von konvergierenden Technologien (Converging Technologies). Das neue Ars Electronica Center bildet dabei die Plattform für ein neues Konferenz-Format: ein nomadisches Symposium, das sich entlang der Topografie der Ausstellung und ihrer Installationen ereignet. Der Streifzug durch die Ausstellung öffnet unterschiedliche Türen in die Diskussion, welche wechselseitigen Potenziale entstehen, wenn die Kunst zu einer Säule innerhalb der neuen Konvergenzen zwischen Informations- und Kommunikationstechnologie, Biotechnologie, Nanotechnologie und Neurotechnologie sowie weiteren Disziplinen etwa im Feld der grünen Technologien wird. Daran knüpft sich auch die Frage, wie sich künstlerische Praktiken und Ausdrucksformen in diese Richtung verändern.

Die Besetzung des nomadischen Symposiums weist dabei zwangsläufig hybride Konstellationen von Präsentatoren und Präsentatorenteams auf. Das Ars Electronica Futurelab sowie externe Künstler, Wissenschaftler und Medientechnologieexperten diskutieren gemeinsam und in unterschiedlichsten Formaten über Konvergenzen in ihren Arbeitsbereichen. Aufgezeigt und zur Diskussion freigegeben werden Fragestellungen, die sich nur anhand konkreter Konvergenzen behandeln lassen und die in klassischen Disziplinformaten entweder gar nicht auftauchen oder nicht zufriedenstellend beantwortet werden können. Der Zugang ist dabei ein experimentell-forschender, der, ausgehend von Bestehendem, Ableitungen für Zukunftsszenarien sucht.

Neben innovativen Lösungen für bestehende Aufgabenfelder sucht *Pixelspaces* auch nach Plattformen, die das sich bis zur Ununterscheidbarkeit ereignende Zusammenrücken von Kunst und Wissenschaft einem breiten Publikum zugänglich machen. *Deep Space*, das großformatige, für verschiedenste Darstellungsarten und Bildtechniken geeignete Projektionssystem im neuen Ars Electronica Center, bildet ein zeitgemäßes Beispiel. Im Rahmen einer Behind-the-Scenes-Präsentation wird *Deep Space* als Plattform an der Schnittstelle von öffentlichem Labor und Ausstellung zu seiner eigenen Bühne. Die Entwickler des *Deep Space* aus dem Ars Electronica Futurelab präsentieren seine plattformrelevanten Eigenschaften anhand unterschiedlicher Projekte aus den Bereichen Virtual Reality und anderen hochauflösenden sowie rechenintensiven Darstellungsformen. Exemplarisch stellen Künstler ihre Arbeiten im *Deep Space* vor. Dabei verwandelt sich *Deep Space* in ein Diskussionsforum über neue Bildtechniken, das sich nahtlos in der Ausstellung „Neue Bilder vom Menschen" fortsetzt. Die Konvergenz von Kunst und Wissenschaft zeigt sich hier nicht nur auf funktionaler, sondern auch auf ästhetischer Ebene.

Im Rahmen von Experimenten in den Laboren BioLab, FabLab, BrainLab und RoboLab werden gemeinsam mit Kooperationspartnern Trends und Möglichkeiten zur Gestaltung der Natur und Kultur des Menschen durch den Menschen aufgegriffen. Jedes Lab stellt dabei unterschiedliche Methoden in der Verwendung konvergierender Technologien vor. Hands-on Experiences bilden exemplarische Mikrodiskurse, die zur Diskussion aufrufen – vom Klonen der Lieblingspflanze über die Kreation von Alltagsgegenständen am 3-D-Drucker, vom Steuern von Robotern mit dem eigenen Gehirn bis zu High-Tech-Prothesen.

In der *Geocity* werden verschiedenste Kontrastfolien in Form von interaktiven Visualisierungen und neuen Interface-Techologien auf den Planeten Erde und, exemplarisch, auf die Stadt Linz angewendet. Was sich anhand der verfügbaren Datensätze und ihren Interpretationen offenbart, ist die immer dringlicher werdende Herausforderung, Lösungen für globale Probleme wie etwa das Energieproblem, das Wasserproblem, das Nahrungsmittelproblem oder das Müllproblem zu finden und zu realisieren. „Do it together" zeichnet sich dabei als elementare Formel ab – es gibt keine Disziplin, die diese Probleme allein lösen kann. So öffnet *Pixelspaces* mit der Geocity ein Labor zur Auseinandersetzung mit der Vergangenheit, Gegenwart und Zukunft unseres Planeten und eine Plattform, um Lösungsszenarien für bestehende und kommende Probleme anhand des Repertoires konvergierender und grüner Technologien zu diskutieren.

Open_Sailing_Crew stellt, im Anschluss an das Thema der Geocity, einen Prototypen vor, der als Zwischenergebnis eines ambitionierten Projekts zu sehen ist: Die Crew des Projekts, das 2009 auch das [the next idea]-Technologiestipendium gewonnen hat, baut sich selbst organisierende, Organismen ähnelnde Infrastrukturen, für ein Leben auf dem Wasser. Bionischen Prinzipien folgend werden Do-it-yourself-Technologien verwoben zu einer Ozeanstation, auf der Menschen unter Verfügbarkeit aller lebensnotwendigen Mittel leben können sollen. Im Rahmen von *Pixelspaces* präsentiert sich *Open_Sailing* als schwimmende Ausstellung mit angegliederten exemplarischen Projektergebnissen. Neben dem experimentellen Ansatz des Projekts steht das explizite „Do it together" prototypisch für neue Konvergenzen zwischen Disziplinen und Technologien: *Open_Sailing* ruft nicht nur jeden zum Mitwirken auf, sondern entwickelt jede Hard- und Softwarekomponente als „Open Source".

Die genannten Stationen des nomadischen Symposiums bilden das Schwerpunktprogramm der diesjährigen *Pixelspaces*-Konferenz. Ihnen angegliedert sind verschiedene Beiträge von externen Künstlern und Kooperationspartnern, die im Ars Electronica Center ausstellen. Verschiedene Abendprogramme wie ein Fassadenfestival, das auch den Blick hinter die LED-Fassade des Ars Electronica Center erlaubt, umrahmen das Programm. Die individuell bespielbare Fassade öffnet dabei auch Perspektiven auf ressourcenschonende Displaytechnologien und die Vielfalt ihrer Einsatzszenarien. Im Rahmen der diesjährigen *Pixelspaces* veranstaltet das *Ars Electronica Futurelab* gemeinsam mit Fabrica, dem Kommunikationsforschungszentrum von Bennetton, ein Symposium und eine Workshopreihe zur Zukunft des Modehandels. Die Initiative beschäftigt sich mit dem Umstand, dass der Einzelhandel im Bekleidungssektor seit Jahrzehnten so gut wie unverändert geblieben ist – dass er keine Digital-, Interaktiv- oder Netzwerktechnologien zur Verbesserung der Kundenbetreuung einsetzt. Die Veranstaltung „The Future of Fashion Retail" geht mit eine Reihe von Rednern der Frage nach, wie der Modesektor auf die Herausforderungen des eCommerce reagieren und sich neue Entwicklungen wie soziales Netzwerken, interaktives Verschlagworten oder persönliche Kommunikationstechnologien zunutze machen kann. Es ist Zeit, nicht nur über die kulturellen Riten der Mode, sondern auch über Bekleidung und ihre Kontextualisierung im Allgemeinen nachzudenken – von intelligenten Textilien bis hin zur Inszenierung des Einkaufserlebnisses. Dabei wird von der Annahme ausgegangen, dass Lösungen vor allem an der Schnittstelle von Kunst und konvergierenden Technologien gesucht werden müssen.

Insgesamt kann die Konferenz ebenso wie jeder einzelne Beitrag als neue Konvergenzen aufgreifendes und auch bildendes Experiment gelesen werden. „Do it together" gilt dabei in besonderer Weise als Aufforderung an eine Gesellschaft, die ihre dringlichsten Frage- und Aufgabenstellungen nicht mehr ihm Rahmen von einzelnen Disziplinen beantworten und lösen kann. Neben den Disziplinen rücken auch die Symposiumsbeiträge und die Ausstellungsprojekte so nah zusammen wie nie zuvor – ein Zeichen dafür, dass in den sich öffnenden Feldern zwischen Kunst und Wissenschaft Theorie und Praxis zu einer neuen funktionalen Einheit verschmelzen.

(Text: Daniela Kuka, Horst Hörtner)

Alois Ferscha

Wearable IT

How Much Technology Can Humankind Bear?

1961: "Beat The Dealer"; mathematician Edward Thorp uses a hidden computer the size of a pack of cigarettes to count cards at casino blackjack tables and thus increase his chances of beating the house in Reno and Las Vegas. 1981: "The World's First Cyborg"; MIT student (and later professor) Steve Mann develops a "rucksack computer" with which he controls cameras that "record his life." In 1994 these become "wearable wireless webcams." 1993: "Private Eye and Twiddler"; MIT student Thad Starner integrates a micro-optical display and a one-hand keyboard operated by a "shoulder bag computer"; he implements a software "remembrance agent" and uses it to defend his doctoral dissertation; in 2002, he presents the system to Linz Art University students. 1996: "Wearables in 2005"; the Defense Advanced Research Projects Agency (DARPA) finances the first scientific conference on wearable computing; the ISWC symposium series is an outgrowth of this. 2001: "Linux Watch"; IBM develops a wristwatch computer that runs on Linux; the first wearable computing manufacturers launch products on the market (Xybernaut, ViA, CDI). 2008: The Zypad "arm computer" integrates a 400 MHz CPU, 3.5" touchscreen, WLAN, BT and GPS. 2009: The University of Linz's Department of Pervasive Computing and the Ars Electronica Center Linz host the 13th International Symposium on Wearable Computing. At this time, 3.2 billion people worldwide are using a wearable computer—their cell-phone—on a daily basis.

Uninspired vision normally leads to uninspired technology! The personal computer, today's "universal machine," and the Internet, today's "uni-versal medium," seem like uninspired building blocks compared to the expectations that have been raised with respect to "intelligent systems" and services custom-tailored to contemporary lifestyles. Could this possibly be a case of the technology coming first and humankind being adapted to its needs?

"Pervasive Computing" takes the human being as the starting point and asks where technology is needed, how much of it is needed, and whether it's even needed at all. Here, work is well underway on the elimination of the "all-purpose computer," whereby the universal machines are increasingly being sent into retirement by task-specific, miniaturized or barely visible (i.e. embedded) computers. "The computer" is not a device; rather, it's the sum of all network-linked items and implements, vehicles, working & living spaces, furniture, and even the very clothes we wear. All of its functions penetrate and pervade the fabric of our lives and thus form a no-longer-visible background intelligence. Minute hidden sensors register what's going on around them; tiny concealed actuators control systems. Information technology "saturates" everything and thereby become "omnipresent." Accordingly, the computer that's closest to us (and that we feel closest to) is a wearable one.

The first epoch of information technological development induced by miniaturization and global networking, "the linkup of all things," has already progressed quite far from a technological point of view. Practically everything can communicate with anything else nowadays, 24/7/365 and uninterrupted, wireless with no line-of-sight required. A global, all-encompassing data network takes care of the long-distance heavy lifting; miniaturized broadcast technology rolls the little waves over the final centimeter of their journey. The question of whether, despite these "possibilities of exchanging data" in a totally network-linked world, things can really be aware of one another—that is, themselves recognize the context of significance of their existence or their interaction with one another and act in accordance with these insights—remains the challenge facing the second epoch (awareness). One of the key challenges of this time will be to come up with technical solutions to facilitate reciprocal "perception" among human beings and things (with computers embedded in them) or things linked up to each other in networks.

Wearable computing is a field of research seeking answers to these questions. What's happening in this field right now will be presented at the 13th International Symposium on Wearable Computing (ISWC '09) set for September 4–7, 2009 in the new Ars Electronica Center in Linz. There will be scientific reporting on impressive technological developments, as well as contributions dealing with such topics as service quality, usability, attention economy and the compatibility of such systems with social norms and values. Not technology but rather solutions and benefits are the central message of ISWC '09.

13th IEEE International Symposium on Wearable Computers
4–7 September 2009, Linz

General Co-Chairs ISWC '09
Alois Ferscha, University of Linz (AT)
Gerfried Stocker, Ars Electronica Center (AT)

Programm Committee Co-Chairs
Kent Lyons, Intel Research, USA
Paul Lukowicz, University of Passau (DE)

Late Breaking Results Co-Chairs
Lucy Dunne, University of Minnesota (US)
Rene Mayrhofer, University of Vienna (AT)
Daniel Roggen, ETH Zurich (CH)

Video Co-Chairs
Antonio Krüger, DFKI Saarbrücken (DE)
Horst Hörtner, Ars Electronica Center (AT)

Design Contest Co-Chairs
Christa Sommerer, University of Art and Design Linz (AT)
Sabine Seymour, Moondial (AT)

Alois Ferscha

Wearable IT

Wie viel Technologie erträgt der Mensch?

1961: „Beat The Dealer": Der Mathematiker Edward Thorp verwendet einen versteckten zigarettenschachtelgroßen Computer, um durch Kartenzählen seine Gewinnchancen beim Black Jack in Casinos in Reno und Las Vegas zu erhöhen. 1981: „The Worlds First Cyborg": Der MIT-Student und spätere Professor Steve Mann entwickelt einen „Rucksackcomputer", mit dem er Kameras steuert, die sein „Leben aufzeichnen". 1994 werden daraus „Wearable Wireless Webcams". 1993: „Private Eye and Twiddler": Der MIT-Student Thad Starner integriert ein mikrooptisches Display und eine Einhandtastatur, betrieben von einem „Schultertaschencomputer", er implementiert einen Software-„Rememberance Agent" und verteidigt damit seine Dissertation (PhD), 2002 präsentiert er das System Linzer Studenten an der JKU. 1996: „Wearables in 2005", DARPA (Defense Advanced Re-search Projects Agency) finanziert die erste wissenschaftliche Konferenz über Waerable Computing, aus der später die Symposiumreihe ISWC wird. 2001: „Linux Watch", IBM entwickelt einen Armbanduhrcomputer, der unter Linux betrieben wird, erste Wearable-Computing-Hersteller treten in den Markt (Xybernaut, ViA, CDI). 2008: Der Zypad „Armcomputer" integriert einen 400 MHz CPU, 3,5" Touch Screen, WLAN, BT und GPS. 2009: Die Universität Linz, Institut für Pervasive Computing und das Ars Electronica Center Linz tragen das 13. Internationale Symposium on Wearable Computing aus. Zu diesem Zeitpunkt nutzen 3,2 Mrd. Menschen täglich tragbare Computer: Mobiltelefone.

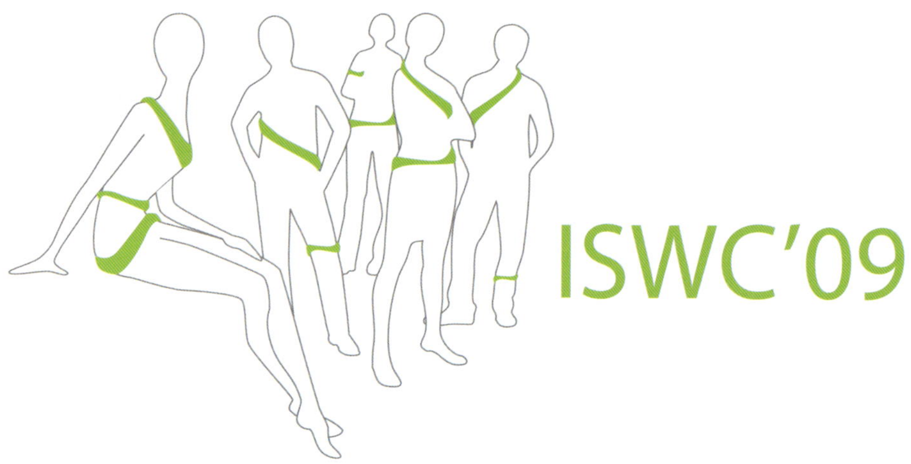

Sujet: Bernadette Emsenhuber

Uninspirierte Vision führt in der Regel zu uninspirierter Technik! Die heutige „Universalmaschine" Personal Computer, das heutige „Universalmedium" Internet erscheinen wie uninspirierte Bausteine, gemessen an der Erwartungshaltung für „intelligente Systeme", und an heutige Lebensstilen angepasste Dienste. Kann es sein, dass hier die Technik zuerst war und dann der Mensch eingepasst wurde?

„Pervasive Computing" beginnt mit dem Menschen und fragt, wo, wie viel und ob er überhaupt Technik braucht. Hier arbeitet man an der Ablöse des „Allzweckcomputers": An die Stelle der Universalmaschinen treten vermehrt aufgabenspezifische, miniaturisierte bzw. kaum sichtbare, d.h. eingebettete Computer. „Der Computer" ist nicht ein Gerät, sondern die Summe aller vernetzten Gebrauchsgegenstände, Fahrzeuge, Arbeits- und Wohnräume, Möbel, ja selbst unserer Kleidung. Alle seine Funktionen dringen in unser „Lebensgewebe" ein und bilden so eine nicht mehr sichtbare Hintergrundintelligenz. Kleinste versteckte Sensoren nehmen ihre Umgebung wahr, kleinste versteckte Aktuatoren steuern Systeme. Die Informationstechnologie „durchdringt" alles und wird dadurch „allgegenwärtig" – der Computer, der uns demnach am nächsten steht, ist der „anzieh- und tragbare Computer" (Wearable Computer).

Die erste Epoche der durch Miniaturisierung und globale Vernetzung induzierten informationstechnologischen Evolution, „die Vernetzung aller Dinge", ist heute aus technologischer Sicht bereits sehr weit fortgeschritten: Nahezu alles kann heute mit allem, jederzeit und ununterbrochen, drahtlos und ohne Sichtverbindung kommunizieren. Ein globales, alles umspannendes Datennetz sichert dabei den Weitverkehrstransport, miniaturisierte Funktechnologie den „letzten Zentimeter". Die Frage, ob die Dinge trotz dieser „Datenaustauschmöglichkeiten" in einer total vernetzten Welt einander auch wirklich gewahr werden können, also den Bedeutungszusammenhang ihres Daseins oder Aufeinandertreffens selbst erkennen und danach handeln können, bleibt die Herausforderung der zweiten Epoche („Awareness"). Diese wird von der Herausforderung technischer Lösungen für eine gegenseitige „Wahrnehmung" zwischen Menschen und Dingen (mit eingebettetem Computer) bzw. von vernetzten Dingen untereinander geprägt sein.

Das Forschungsgebiet des „Wearable Computing" sucht konsequent nach Antworten auf diese Fragen. Die jüngsten Antworten werden im Rahmen des 13. International Symposium on Wearable Computing (ISWC '09) vom 4. bis 7. September 2009 im neuen Ars Electronica Center in Linz gegeben. Die wissenschaftlichen Beiträge zeigen beeindruckende technologische Entwicklungen, gleichzeitig aber auch eindeutig in die Richtung einer Servicequalität, Benutzbarkeit, Aufmerksamkeitsökonomie und Sozialverträglichkeit solcher Systeme. Nicht Technologie, sondern Lösung und Nutzen sind die zentrale Nachricht von ISWC '09.

Christoph Santner, Philippe Souidi

Mission Future @ Ars Electronica
The Initiative to Create Our Tomorrow

"Do or die." The fist-fighter's time-honored watchwords seem to have increasingly become the motto of a creative majority whose members feel they've been ignored, forgotten and betrayed by traditional institutions, enterprises and parties. Something unprecedented is brewing: the creative mass.

Yesterday's class is today's mass. Five years ago, when Richard Florida's bestseller *The Rise of the Creative Class* came out and was immediately hailed as the "breakthrough idea of the year" by *Harvard Business Review*, intense interest was focused on this new work- & lifestyle that might be more appropriately termed a creativity style. Florida described the rapid growth of this class whose way of life was one that, traditionally, only artists and creative scientists had been able to afford. According to his assessment, every third person gainfully employed in the US belonged to this class. Creativity had become the most important factor for success in the economy and the society. Everything—values, business, structures, relations, work, leisure, taste—is changing more rapidly than ever before as a result of this. Uncritical consumers, unassertive burghers and traditional workers are increasingly becoming anachronistic, obsolete models ready to be consigned to the junk heap of history.

On the other hand, the creators and co-creators who playfully engender reality are assuming the mantle of the new role model. More and more, they live according to the watchwords: "The little bit .... that I need [information, music, video, art, design, a firm, and even the useful objects of everyday life], I make myself." New fabricators—that is, personal "nano-factories," are becoming one of the most important tools of the creative mass. Wikipedia, itself an essential tool of this movement, describes it as a "device, designed to make (almost) anything." These three-dimensional "material printers"—also affectionately dubbed fabbers—will soon be as widespread as computer printers once were. Wanna quickly crank out a new handbag or coffee mug based on your own design? No problem!

Today, the majority consisting of technologically-networked creatives that has grown to constitute the creative mass has the power to turn the world as we know it on its head. And that's just what they're doing. It's happening in Iran, where civil disobedience formed overnight via Twitter; the activists include individual "Knights of the Twitter Round Table" like actor Ashton Kutcher, who challenged media giant CNN to a digital duel and emerged victorious in this race to recruit a million "followers." This we-feeling, a new sense of community coupled with technical know-how, is triggering earthquakes in business, politics, culture and the media.

For the first time since the ecology movement, digital culture has brought forth qualitatively new, internet-based political parties—the pirate parties, for instance. The first thoroughly digital generation no longer measures itself according to traditional values, laws and standards; instead, its members define themselves and live according to their own rules. And do so even if they have to upset a few apple carts in the process—for example, the Pirate Bay that first emerged in Sweden. This pro-pirate or anti-copyright movement now has more than 25 million peers who are striking fear into the hearts of music & film industry executives. Despite countless legal proceedings, Pirate Bay continues to grow, to "uphold freedom of speech, freedom of information and the freedom of the internet."

Enterprises that understand this trend and are helping to shape it speak in terms of "our creatives, formerly known as consumers." What's new is that the economy's traditional business models are being turned topsy-turvy. It's not only consumer-generated design becoming everyday reality at leading brands such as Mini, Nokia and Adidas. At sites like Apple's App Store, creatives and programmers can offer their own works, games and software for sale at prices they set themselves. And some are able to make a good living from this, since Apple retains only 30% of the gross revenues. The same holds true for the application programming interfaces on Facebook, Xing & Co, where developers can put their own tools, business software and games online and, thanks to the enormous number people who are members of such social networks, some of these developers have quickly succeeded in launching going concerns.

These new collectives feel committed to the basic principles of open source and sharing. But amidst classic business models as well, mass creativity is making inexorable advances. More and more sectors are following along in the wake of the sharing economy à la Linux, Wikipedia, Flickr and Youtube. Over the last three decades, an essential source of impetus for this development has been Ars Electronica. Swarm intelligence and collective creativity are the driving forces behind projects like Open Moco (mobile communication), Open Design and even Open Cola. Formulas, blueprints and software are being made available to all comers. The production process, formerly the big bottleneck, is no longer the subject of big discussions: either the finished product pops out of the fabricator in accordance with the user's own input or it sails in from China. In the production process, batch size and time hardly play a role any more.

Whether or not you want to refer to this phenomenon as the Participation Age like Sun Microsystems does with respect to Java and lots of other open source solutions, and regardless of whether you call the resulting human clusters communities, networks or tribes, the principle remains the same: We have arrived at a phase of fundamental transformation formerly known as a crisis. In the economy, society and culture, nothing is immune to the effects. The lone wolf has become a discontinued model. What's called for nowadays are rethinking and new forms of collaboration that transcend sector boundaries. And this applies to traditional enterprises too: for instance, Munich Re, a leader in the reinsurance industry, that has taken a position at the forefront of an ambitious consortium named Desertec that's investing the enormous sum of 400 billion euros in solar energy production in North Africa. The Club of Rome was the driving force behind this project's inception. And then there's Mercedes, Smart and energy giant RWE, who are working together with the City of Berlin on a network of E-stations for electric vehicles.

When old authorities cease functioning as well as they once did, more and more people turn to self-organization—thanks to cellphones and affordable netbooks, which have now become very widespread not only among the industrialized nations' (often well educated) welfare recipients, but also to an increasing extent in emerging markets and the so-called developing countries. Whether it's microcredits, self-organized banks, barter exchanges or newly created currency systems like the Chiemgauer in Bavaria, the Crédito in Argentina and the Barter Card in Australia, people are taking matters into their own hands. In line with Hillary Clinton's motto: "Never waste a good crisis!"

MISSION FUTURE—The Initiative to Create Tomorrow was founded three years ago by futurologist Christoph Santner and international trend expert Philippe Souidi. This is the third year that this initiative is working together with Ars Electronica. *http://missionfuture.trendpool.com/*

Christoph Santner, Philippe Souidi

Mission Future @ Ars Electronica
The Initiative to Create Our Tomorrow

„Do – or die": Die alte Boxerregel scheint mehr und mehr zum Motto einer kreativen Mehrheit zu werden, die sich von traditionellen Institutionen, Unternehmen und Parteien nicht mehr gesehen, vergessen und verraten fühlt. Da braut sich etwas noch nie Dagewesenes zusammen – die kreative Masse.

Denn was gestern noch Klasse war, ist heute Masse: Als vor fünf Jahren Richard Floridas Bestseller *The Rise of the Creative Class* erschien und von der *Harvard Business Review* gleich als die „Breakthroug-Idea des Jahres" klassifiziert wurde, rückte dieser neue Lebens- und Arbeits- oder besser Schaffensstil ins Zentrum des Interesses. Florida beschrieb das schnelle Anwachsen dieser Klasse, die ein Leben führt, wie es sich traditionell höchstens Künstler oder kreative Wissenschaftler leisten konnten. Er rechnete jeden dritten US-amerikanischen Erwerbstätigen dieser Klasse zu. Kreativität wurde nun zum wichtigsten Erfolgsfaktor in Wirtschaft und Gesellschaft. Alles – Werte, Wirtschaft, Strukturen, Beziehungen, Arbeit, Freizeit, Geschmack –, alles ändert sich dadurch rapide wie nie zuvor in der Geschichte. Unkritische Konsumenten, unmündige Bürger und traditionelle Arbeiter werden mehr und mehr zum anachronistischen, wegrationalisierten Auslaufmodell.

Dafür entwickeln sich Creators und Co-Creators, die spielerisch Wirklichkeit erschaffen, zum neuen Rollenmodell. Sie leben mehr und mehr nach dem Motto: „Das bisschen, das ich brauche (Information, Musik, Video, Kunst, Design, Firma bis hin zu Gegenständen des Alltags), das mach ich mir selber." Neue Fabricators, also persönliche „Nano-Fabriken", werden zu einem der wichtigsten Werkzeuge der kreativen Masse. Wikipedia, selbst ein zentrales Tool dieser Bewegung, beschreibt sie als „device, designed to make (almost) anything". Diese auch liebevoll „Fabbers" genannten dreidimensionalen „Materie-Drucker" werden bald Alltagsobjekt sein wie einst Computerdrucker. Schnell mal eine neue Handtasche geprintet oder eine Kaffeetasse nach eigenem Entwurf – kein Problem.

Heute hat die zur kreativen Masse angewachsene Mehrheit der technologisch vernetzten Kreativen die Kraft, unsere Welt, wie wir sie kennen, auf den Kopf zu stellen. Und sie tut das auch: Ob sich im Iran per Twitter ziviler Ungehorsam über Nacht formiert, ob einzelne „Ritter der Twitter-Runde" wie der Schauspieler Ashton Kutcher im Alleingang eine Million Followers hinter sich aufbaut gegen den Medien-Giganten CNN, den er zum digitalen Duell herausgefordert hatte: Das neue Community- und Wirgefühl, gepaart mit technischem Know-how, löst in Wirtschaft, Politik, Kultur und Medien wahre Erdbeben aus.

Die digitale Kultur bringt erstmals seit der Ökologiebewegung qualitativ neue, Internet-basierte politische Parteien hervor wie die Piratenparteien. Diese erste rundum digitale Generation misst sich dabei nicht mehr an überkommenen Werten, Gesetzen und Maßstäben, sondern definiert und lebt eigene Regeln. Auch dann, wenn sie einiges auf den Kopf stellt wie etwa die in Schweden gestartete Pro-Piraten- oder Anti-Copyright-Bewegung namens Pirate Bay mit mehr als 25 Millionen Peers, die zum Schrecken der Musik- und Filmindustrie wurde. Trotz zahlloser juristischer Verfahren wächst Pirate Bay weiter, um „Redefreiheit, Informationsfreiheit und die Freiheit des Internets hochzuhalten".

Unternehmen, die diesen Trend verstehen und mitgestalten, sprechen von „our creatives, formerly known as consumers". Neu ist, dass traditionelle Businessmodelle in der Wirtschaft auf den Kopf gestellt werden. Nicht nur Consumer-generiertes Design wird zum Alltag führender Marken wie Mini, Nokia oder Adidas. Auf Plattformen wie auf Apples App Store können Kreative und Programmierer ihre selbst geschriebenen Werke, Spiele und Software zum selbst bestimmten Preis anbieten und fallweise gut davon leben. Denn nur 30 Prozent des Verkaufserlöses bleiben bei Apple. Ähnliches gilt für die Application Programming Interfaces, die offenen Schnittstellen bei Facebook, Xing & Co, wo Entwickler eigene Tools, Business-Software und Spiele online stellen können und bei den riesigen Mitgliederzahlen der sozialen Netzwerke u.U. in kürzester Zeit gut gehende eigene Unternehmen neuen Typs hochziehen.

Diese neuen Kollektive fühlen sich den grundlegenden Prinzipien von Open Source und Sharing verpflichtet. Aber auch in klassische Business-Modelle dringt die Massenkreativität unaufhaltsam vor. Die Sharing Economy à la Linux, Wikipedia, Flickr und Youtube zieht immer mehr Branchen in ihr Fahrwasser. In den letzten Jahrzehnten kamen wesentliche Impulse dafür immer wieder auch aus Linz und der Ars Electronica. Schwarmintelligenz und kollektive Kreativität werden zum Motor von Projekten wie *Open Moco* (Mobile Communication), *Open Design* oder sogar *Open Cola*. Rezepturen, Pläne und Software werden offen zur Verfügung gestellt. Die Produktion, traditionell der Flaschenhals, ist kein Thema mehr. Entweder kommt das fertige Produkt nach eigenen Vorstellungen schlussendlich aus dem Fabricator oder aus China. Stückzahl und Zeit spielen im Produktionsprozess kaum noch eine Rolle.

Ob man dieses Phänomen nun „Participation Age" nennen will wie Sun Microsystems mit Java und viele anderen Open-Source-Lösungen, ob man von den neuen Communities, Netzwerken und Tribes spricht – das Prinzip ist immer das gleiche: Wir sind in einer tief greifenden Transformation, „formerly known as crisis", angelangt. In Wirtschaft, Gesellschaft und Kultur bleibt kein Stein auf dem anderen. Einzelkämpfer werden zu Auslaufmodellen. Neue Kooperationen über Branchengrenzen hinaus und Umdenken sind angesagt. Auch bei traditionellen Unternehmen, wenn sich etwa Munich Re, ein führender Rückversicherer, an die Spitze eines ambitionierten Konsortiums setzt, das sich Desertec auf die Fahnen geschrieben hat, Solarstromerzeugung in Nordafrika, mit einem Investitionsvolumen von 400 Milliarden Euro. Angeregt hat dieses Projekt der Club of Rome. Oder wenn Mercedes, Smart und der Energiegigant RWE gemeinsam mit der Stadt Berlin E-Tankstellen für Elektroautos aufbauen.

Wo alte Autoritäten immer weniger funktionieren, organisieren sich mehr und mehr Menschen selbst – dank Handy und billigem Netbook, die mittlerweile nicht nur bei den (teils gut gebildeten) Sozialhilfeempfängern unserer industrialisierten Länder angekommen sind, sondern mehr und mehr auch auf breiter Basis in den Schwellen- und sogenannten Entwicklungsländern. Ob Mikrokredite, selbst organisierte Banken, Tauschbörsen und neue selbst geschaffene Währungssysteme vom Chiemgauer in Bayern über den Crédito in Argentinien bis zur Barter-Card in Australien: Menschen nehmen ihr Schicksal selbst in die Hand. Frei nach Hillary Clintons Motto: „Never waste a good crisis!"

MISSION FUTURE – The Initiative to Create Tomorrow – wurde vor drei Jahren vom Zukunftsexperten Christoph Santner und vom internationalen Trendexperten Philippe Souidi gegründet. Zum dritten Mal kooperiert diese Initiative in diesem Jahr mit der Ars Electronica. *http://missionfuture.trendpool.com/*

Dieter Daniels, Sandra Naumann
Ludwig Boltzmann Institute Media.Art.Research

See this Sound

Sound-Image Relations in Art and Media

A defining aspect of the world as we experience it nowadays is the omnipresence of audiovisual products and structures in which cultural image and sound production are tightly interwoven (media) technologically, artistically and (marketing) strategically. The *See this Sound* master project is investigating the great current diversity and long history of development of these syntheses and contradictions, this linkup, overlapping and, occasionally, even irreconcilability. The primary objective of the symposium is interdisciplinary exchange among various scholarly fields (including art history, musicology, media & art theory, media archeology and the history of technology) and at the zone of tension and interplay at the nexus of media art and contemporary art. Integrated into the conference agenda will be artistic presentations designed to foster dialog between art and scholarship.

The "See this Sound" Master Project

This is the fifth conference held under the auspices of the Ludwig Boltzmann Institute Media. Art.Research in conjunction with the Ars Electronica Festival. It differs from prior years' efforts in that it is part of the *See this Sound* project being conducted jointly with the Lentos Art Museum Linz and sponsored by Linz 2009 European Capital of Culture. The conference is being accompanied by an extensive exhibition at the Lentos. To elucidate various facets of the project's theme, the Ludwig Boltzmann Institute Media.Art.Research is developing an online archive (*http://www.see-this-sound.at*) containing historical longitudinal sections and systemic cross-sections in the form of approximately 35 lexicon entries that provide an overview of the entire spectrum of audiovisual arts and phenomena. Overarching topics that are being treated at this conference will also be gone into more deeply in detailed and comprehensive essays. Three publications are emerging from this project: an exhibition catalog entitled *See this Sound—Versprechungen von Bild und Ton*, an interdisciplinary lexicon of audiovisual culture entitled *See this Sound—Audiovisualogie 1* and a volume of essays entitled *See this Sound—Audiovisualogie 2: Geschichte und Theorie audiovisueller Medien und Künste*.

Art, Science and Technology

The central significance of the art-science interface for this overall project corresponds to the historical horizon of the thematic field under consideration here. The scientific investigation of and parallel artistic experimentation with acoustic-optical and/or audiovisual relations already commenced in the 18th century, whereby Louis Bertrand Castel's "ocular harpsichord" and the nodal patterns identified by E.F.F. Chladni are two instances of the blurring of the boundary between art and science. A key aspect of this project's multidisciplinary approach is a consideration of the deep-seated changes to auditory and visual culture brought about by technological media over the last 150 years—specifically the telephone, the phonograph and film in the late 19th century and radio, sound film, TV, tape recording and video in the 20th century. The emergence over the last 50 years or so of electronic and digital media has made possible undreamt-of complexity in the blending of sounds and images, a development that has been treated only in cursory fashion by the overviews of this field that have appeared to date.

All these media have reconfigured the Visual and the Acoustic. In the 19th century, they first separated sound and image from one another, only to recombine them in the 20th century. The upshot has been unprecedented diversity of apparative, artificial sound-image relations. Since their appearance, (media) artists have been at work in the interstices between these sound-image techniques, deconstructing their apparent naturalism and recombining their elements in order to thus call into question perception and medium in reciprocal fashion. Digitization ultimately brought about the convergence of all audiovisual media, a fact of fundamental significance both aesthetically and economically. This makes for increasingly fluid borders between art and pop culture, between critical analysis and strategies to achieve domination.

Examples of artistic-scientific-technical work go all the way back to the beginnings of video and computer art in the 1960s, when an international scene of artist-engineers developed audio and video synthesizers as artistic-technical hybrids and promoted these efforts by establishing institutions like Ars Electronica in Linz and the ZKM–Center for Art and Media in Karlsruhe, Germany.[1] Since 1979, Ars Electronica has been closely associated with the *Klangwolke* (Cloud of Sound), an open-air, public musical visualization on a grand scale. Ever since the ZKM was founded in 1989, its Department of Graphic Media and Department of Music and Acoustics have been investigating the range at the interface of these fields. Accordingly, these efforts are an exemplary theme for the programmatic linkup of art, science and technology.

Media Art and Contemporary Art

The situation at present is characterized by the divergence of two fields designated as "media art" and "contemporary art." They have come to differ from one another less with respect to their technical parameters and rather more in terms of cultural context, theoretical discourse and economic value-added as well as the way they come across in the media and their target audiences. The 2001 Ars Electronica, staged under the banner of "Takeover—Who's Doing the Art of Tomorrow," threw down the gauntlet to the art establishment in these terms: "Following the Digital Revolution, there has been a creativity burst (...). The traditional rituals of access to the world of art are irrelevant, and many no longer even bother to seek accreditation from the art establishment."[2] In stark contrast to this position, Stefan Heidenreich announced the end of media art in 2008 in a major German newspaper: "Media art was an episode. Since its institutions don't simply wither away, it lives on as a dinosaur of the '80s and '90s. (...) Artists work with any media they choose, from drawing to the internet. (...) There is enough good art that utilizes media as something taken completely for granted. But there is no media art."[3] This is why the *See this Sound* project is taking an overarching theoretical approach in the conference itself, in the thematic spectrum of the online archive as well as in the selection of works on display at the exhibition in an effort to bring out the common basis of these domains as well as the differences between them. The thematic coupling of graphic arts and science as well as media art and contemporary art corresponds on the institutional level to the collaboration between the Lentos Art Museum Linz and the Ludwig Boltzmann Institute Media.Art.Research, whose staffers have been developing this project jointly from the very outset.

See this Sound—Sound-Image Relations in Art and Media

Music and Visual Art

The history of the relation between music and the visual arts from the 19th to the mid-20th century has already been elaborated on in numerous exhibitions and books.[4]

Crossovers transcending the boundaries separating music from the visual arts by protagonists of classic Modernism (Klee, Mondrian, Richter) was carried on via technical media (Hirschfeld-Mack, Moholy-Nagy, Eggeling, Richter, Ruttmann, Cage) and resulted in the emergence of intermedially functioning artforms. This process of breaking down borders—those separating artistic genres as well as media formats—was elaborately formulated in the 1960s in the practices of "Intermedia," Fluxus and Concept Art.

Video art and sound art, two specialized disciplines that developed along parallel yet separate lines all the way up into the 1980s, have, as an upshot of the intensifying reciprocal interrelationships between audio and video, ultimately become integrated into contemporary art and are no longer subsumed under media art. This might seem to contradict the above-mentioned divergence of media art and contemporary art; nevertheless, only the "classical" media video and audio have gained entrée to the museums' canon and the contemporary art market, and can thus be said to have renounced allegiance to media art and gone over to the established "exhibition media" and "performance media."

On the other hand, the possibilities of arbitrary transformability, manipulability and depictability of digital information have given rise to new forms of production, interaction and interrelation of images and sounds, which have in turn engendered new forms of expression that no longer permit clear attribution to a particular category in the visual arts or music, and can instead only be designated as audiovisual. This development has endowed questions of interdisciplinarity, intermediality and intermodality with new relevance.

Moreover, the democratization of the tools of the trades has even further blurred the dividing lines between consumer and producer, between originality and appropriation, and between "high" and "low", so that aspects of authorship and of the character of the work are once again subjects of debate here.

(Translated from German by Mel Greenwald)

1 Cf. Dunn, David (Ed.): *Die Eigenwelt der Apparate-Welt. Pioneers of Electronic Art* (exhibition catalog), Linz 1992.
2 See *http:www.aec.at/takeover/*
3 Heidenreich, Stefan: Es gibt gar keine Medienkunst!, in *Frankfurter Allgemeine Sonntagszeitung*, January 27, 2008.
4 Three definitive publications have been: Maur, Karin von (Ed.): *Vom Klang der Bilder. Die Musik in der Kunst des 20. Jahrhunderts*, Munich 1985 (exhibition at Staatsgalerie Stuttgart); Centre Pompidou (Ed.): *Sons & Lumières. Une histoire du son dans l'art du XXe siècle*, Paris 2004; Brougher, Kerry / Strick, Jeremy / Wiseman, Ari et al.: *Visual Music. Synaesthesia in Art and Music Since* 1900, New York 2005 (exhibition at the Museum of Contemporary Art, Los Angeles and Hirshhorn Museum and Sculpture Garden)

Ludwig Boltzmann Institut
Medien. Kunst. Forschung.

SEE THIS SOUND
Sound-Image Relations in Art, Media and Perception
Symposium, September 2 - 3, 2009

Organizer: Ludwig Boltzmann Institute Media.Art.Research.
Concept: Dieter Daniels, Sandra Naumann

Opening Performance
Branden W. Joseph in conversation with Tony Conrad followed by a performance by Tony Conrad

Media Art – Visual Art: Divergence or Dialogue?
Christian Höller, author, curator, editor and co-publisher springerin, Vienna:
Deaf Dumb Mute Blind. On artistic ways of dealing with [pop cultural] Image -Sound Relations)

Chris Salter, Assistant Professor of Digital Media Concordia University, Montreal:
Saturation versus Silence: Audio-Visual Perception in the Visual and Media Arts

David Rokeby, Artist, Toronto: *Life in the Feedback Loop*

Art, Science and Technology: Instruments or Artworks?
Birgit Schneider, Dilthey Scholarship of the Fritz Thyssen Foundation, University of Potsdam, Institute of Arts
and Media: *Of hearing eyes and seeing ears. Elements of a history of the media aesthetics of different relations
of sound and image*

Yvonne Spielmann, Chair of New Media, University of the West of Scotland, School of Creative Industries,
Glasgow: *Early Video Tools - Some Reflections on Co-Creativity*

Katja Kwastek, Vice-Director Ludwig Boltzmann Institute Media.Art.Research., Linz, in conversation with
Golan Levin, Artist / Associate Professor of Electronic Art and Director of the STUDIO for Creative Inquiry at
Carnegie Mellon University, Pittsburgh: *On the creation, experience and research of audiovisual interactive art*

Art and Music: Intermediality – Intermodality – Interdisciplinarity?
Branden W. Joseph, Frank Gallipoli Professor of Modern and Contemporary Art, Columbia University, New
York, Department of Art History and Archaeology: *Biomusic and the End of Representation*

Helga de la Motte-Haber, Technical University Berlin, Institute of Language and Communication, Department Musicology: *Augenmusik – Hörbilder. Laudatio für den Preisträger des Media.Art.Research Award
(Eye Music – Audio Images. Laudatio for the prize-winner of the Media.Art.Research Award)*

Winner Media.Art.Research. Award 2009 for "Eye hEar: Music, Art, Film & the Culture of Synesthesia":
Simon Shaw-Miller, Senior Lecturer and Head of School, School of History of Art, Film & Visual Media
Birkbeck College, University of Londons: *Syncretism: Art and Music in the Modern Period*

Closing Performance
Mikomikona (Birgit Schneider & Andreas Eberlein, Berlin): *Fouriertransformation I + II (Fourier Transformation
I + II) Sound-Vision performance with two overhead projectors*

Dieter Daniels, Sandra Naumann
Ludwig Boltzmann Institute Media.Art.Research

See this Sound

Sound-Image Relations in Art and Media

Unsere heutige Erfahrungswelt ist geprägt von einer Allgegenwart audiovisueller Produkte und Strukturen, in denen sich die kulturelle Bild- und Tonproduktion medientechnisch, künstlerisch und marktstrategisch aufs Engste miteinander verschränkt. Die aktuelle Vielfalt und die lange Vorgeschichte dieser Synthesen und Widersprüche, dieser Verkoppelung, Überlagerung und manchmal auch Unversöhnlichkeit untersucht das Gesamtprojekt *See this Sound*. Das Symposium steht im Zeichen des interdisziplinären Austauschs zwischen verschiedenen Wissenschaftsdisziplinen (unter anderem Kunst- und Musikwissenschaften, Medien- und Kunsttheorie, Medienarchäologie und Technikgeschichte) sowie dem Spannungsfeld von Medienkunst und Gegenwartskunst. Eingebunden in den Konferenzverlauf werden auch künstlerische Präsentationen, welche den Dialog zwischen Kunst und Wissenschaft anregen sollen.

Gesamtprojekt „See this Sound"

Die mittlerweile fünfte Konferenz des Ludwig Boltzmann Instituts Medien.Kunst.Forschung. im Rahmen der Ars Electronica unterscheidet sich von den Vorjahren, insofern sie Teil des von Linz 2009 – Kulturhauptstadt Europas geförderten Kooperationsprojekts *See this Sound* mit dem Lentos Kunstmuseum Linz ist. Parallel zur Konferenz findet im Lentos Kunstmuseum Linz eine umfangreiche Ausstellung statt. Zum Themenfeld des Projekts entwickelt das Ludwig Boltzmann Institut Medien.Kunst.Forschung. ein Web-Archiv *(www.see-this-sound.at)*, in dem das gesamte Spektrum der audiovisuellen Künste und Phänomene durch historische Längsschnitte und systematische Querschnitte in zirka 35 Lexikoneinträgen dargestellt wird. Übergreifende Themen, wie sie auf der Konferenz verhandelt werden, sollen außerdem auch in umfangreicheren Essays vertieft werden. Insgesamt erscheinen drei Buchpublikationen zum Projekt (Ausstellungskatalog *See this Sound – Versprechungen von Bild und Ton*, Lexikon *See this Sound – Audiovisualogie 1: Ein interdisziplinäres Lexikon audiovisueller Kultur* und Essayband *See this Sound – Audiovisualogie 2: Geschichte und Theorie audiovisueller Medien und Künste*).

Kunst, Wissenschaft und Technologie

Die zentrale Bedeutung der Schnittstelle von Wissenschaft und Kunst für das Gesamtprojekt entspricht dem historischen Horizont des Themenfelds. Die wissenschaftliche Untersuchung und parallele künstlerische Erprobung von akustisch-optischen bzw. audiovisuellen Relationen beginnt schon im 18. Jahrhundert, wobei seit dem Augenklavier von Louis Bertrand Castel und den Klangfiguren von E.F.F. Chladni immer wieder die Grenzen von Wissenschaft und Kunst verschwimmen. Ein wichtiger Aspekt der multidisziplinären Perspektiven des Projekts sind die tiefgreifenden Veränderungen der auditiven und visuellen Kultur durch die technischen Medien in den letzten 150 Jahren, konkret durch Telefon, Fonograf und Film am Ende des 19. und durch Radio, Tonfilm, Fernsehen, Tonband und Video im 20. Jahrhundert. Seit zirka 50 Jahren ermöglicht die Entwicklung der elektronischen und digitalen Medien eine zuvor ungeahnte Komplexität der Verkoppelung von Bildern und Tönen, die in den bisherigen Überblicksdarstellungen nur am Rande behandelt wird.

All diese Medien haben das Visuelle und Akustische neu konfiguriert. Sie haben Bild und Ton im 19. Jahrhundert zunächst voneinander getrennt, dann im 20. Jahrhundert wieder kombiniert. Damit ist eine neue Vielfalt apparativer, artifizieller Bild-Ton-Relationen entstanden. In den Zwischenräumen dieser Bild-Ton-Techniken arbeiten seitdem (Medien-)Künstler, die ihren scheinbaren Naturalismus dekonstruieren und ihre Elemente neu kombinieren, um so Wahrnehmung und Medium wechselseitig immer wieder infrage zu stellen. Durch die Digitalisierung hat schließlich eine Konvergenz aller audiovisuellen Medien stattgefunden, die ästhetisch wie ökonomisch von fundamentaler Bedeutung ist. Sie verflüssigt zunehmend die Grenzen zwischen Kunst und Populärkultur, zwischen kritischer Analyse und Überwältigungsstrategien.

Die Beispiele einer künstlerisch-wissenschaftlich-technischen Arbeit reichen bis zu den Anfängen der Video- und Computerkunst in den 1960ern zurück, als eine internationale Szene von Künstler-Ingenieuren Audio- und Videosynthesizer als künstlerisch-technische Hybride entwickelte, und forcierte sich in der Gründung von Institutionen wie der Ars Electronica in Linz oder dem ZKM in Karlsruhe.[1] Die Ars Electronica in Linz ist seit 1979 eng mit der *Klangwolke*, einer groß dimensionierten Musikvisualisierung im öffentlichen Raum, verbunden. Seit der Gründung des ZKM in Karlsruhe 1989 sollen ein Institut für Bildmedien und ein Institut für Musik und Akustik die Spannbreite zwischen diesen Feldern untersuchen. Es handelt sich deshalb um ein exemplarisches Thema für die programmatische Verbindung von „Art, Science & Technology".

Medienkunst und Gegenwartskunst

Die heutige Situation ist von einer Divergenz der als „Medienkunst" und „Gegenwartskunst" bezeichneten Felder gekennzeichnet. Sie unterscheiden sich mittlerweile weniger durch ihre technischen Parameter, sondern vor allem durch kulturelle Kontexte, theoretische Diskurse und ökonomische Wertschöpfung sowie durch ihre mediale Vermittlung und ihre Publikumsgruppen. Die Ars Electronica machte 2001 unter dem Motto „Takeover – Wer macht die Kunst von morgen" eine Kampfansage an den Kunstbetrieb: „Der digitalen Revolution folgt ein Creativity Burst (...). Die überkommenen Zugangsrituale zur Kunst sind hinfällig, und viele kommen gar nicht mehr auf die Idee, sich um ihre Beglaubigung durch die Zirkel der Kunst zu bemühen."[2] Demgegenüber verkündet Stefan Heidenreich 2008 in der *Frankfurter Allgemeinen* das Ende der Medienkunst: „Medienkunst war eine Episode. Da ihre Institutionen nicht vergehen, lebt sie als Dinosaurier der 80er und 90er Jahre weiter. (...) Künstler arbeiten mit beliebigen Medien, von der Zeichnung bis zum Internet. (...) Es gibt genug gute Kunst, die ganz selbstverständlich Medien einsetzt. Aber es gibt keine Medienkunst."[3] Deshalb versucht das Projekt *See this Sound* durch einen übergreifenden theoretischen Ansatz sowohl auf der Konferenz wie auch im Themenspektrum des Web-Archivs und in der Werkauswahl der Ausstellung die gemeinsame Basis dieser Bereiche ebenso wie ihre Unterschiede darzustellen. Die thematische Koppelung von bildender Kunst und Wissenschaft sowie von Medienkunst und Gegenwartskunst findet auf der institutionellen Ebene ihre Entsprechung in der Zusammenarbeit von Lentos Kunstmuseum Linz und Ludwig Boltzmann Institut Medien.Kunst.Forschung., die das Projekt von Beginn an gemeinsam entwickelt haben.

Musik und bildende Kunst

Die Vorgeschichte der Relation von Musik und bildender Kunst vom 19. bis zur Mitte des 20. Jahrhunderts wurde bereits mehrfach in Ausstellungen und Buchpublikationen aufgearbeitet.[4] Die Grenzüberschreitungen zwischen Musik und bildender Kunst in der klassischen Moderne (Klee, Mondrian, Richter) wurden mittels technischer Medien fortgeführt (Hirschfeld-Mack, Moholy-Nagy, Eggeling, Richter, Ruttmann, Cage) und hatten die Herausbildung intermedial funktionierender Kunstformen zur Folge. Eine Ausformulierung fand diese Entgrenzung nicht nur der Künste, sondern auch der Medienformate in den 1960er Jahren in den Praktiken „Intermedia", Fluxus und Konzept-Kunst.

Die parallel noch bis in die 1980er als „Videokunst" und „Klangkunst" abgegrenzten Spezialdisziplinen haben sich durch die vermehrten Wechselbeziehungen von Audio und Video schließlich in die Gegenwartskunst integriert und werden nicht mehr der Medienkunst subsumiert. Das könnte scheinbar im Widerspruch zu der oben genannten Divergenz von „Medienkunst" und „Gegenwartskunst" stehen. Doch in den musealen Kanon und aktuellen Kunstmarkt haben nur die „klassischen" Medien Video und Audio Eingang gefunden, sie sind sozusagen von der Medienkunst übergetreten zu den etablierten „Ausstellungsmedien" und „Aufführungsmedien".

Andererseits sind mit der Möglichkeit zur beliebigen Transformierbarkeit, Manipulierbarkeit und Darstellbarkeit von Informationen im Digitalen neue Formen der Produktion, Interaktion und Relation von Bild und Ton entstanden, die Ausdrucksformen hervorgebracht haben, die keine eindeutige Zuordnung zur bildenden Kunst oder Musik mehr erlauben, sondern nur als audiovisuell bezeichnet werden können. In dieser Entwicklung erlangen Fragen der Interdisziplinarität, Intermedialität und Intermodalität neue Aktualität.

Mit der Demokratisierung der Tools haben sich darüber hinaus die Trennlinien zwischen Konsument und Produzent, zwischen Originalität und Appropriation, „high" and „low" weiterhin aufgelöst, so dass hier auch Aspekte der Autorschaft und des Werkcharakters erneut zur Debatte stehen.

1 Vgl. Dunn, David (Hrsg.): *Die Eigenwelt der Apparate-Welt. Pioneers of Electronic Art* (Ausstellungskatalog), Linz 1992.
2 Vgl. *http:www.aec.at/takeover/*
3 Heidenreich, Stefan: Es gibt gar keine Medienkunst!, in: *Frankfurter Allgemeine Sonntagszeitung*; 27.1.08.
4 Drei maßgebliche Ausstellungspublikationen waren: Maur, Karin von (Hrsg.): *Vom Klang der Bilder. Die Musik in der Kunst des 20. Jahrhunderts*, München 1985 (Ausstellung Staatsgalerie Stuttgart). Centre Pompidou (Hrsg.): *Sons & Lumières. Une histoire du son dans l'art du XXe siècle*, Paris 2004. Brougher, Kerry / Strick, Jeremy / Wiseman, Ari u.a.: *Visual Music. Synaesthesia in Art and Music Since* 1900, New York 2005 (Ausstellung The Museum of Contemporary Art, Los Angeles und Hirshhorn Museum and Sculpture Garden).

Ludwig Boltzmann Institut
Medien. Kunst. Forschung.

Sound-Image Relations in Art, Media and Perception
Symposium, September 2 – 3, 2009

Organizer: Ludwig Boltzmann Institute Media.Art.Research.
Concept: Dieter Daniels, Sandra Naumann

Opening Performance
Branden W. Joseph in conversation with Tony Conrad followed by a performance by Tony Conrad

Media Art – Visual Art: Divergence or Dialogue?
Christian Höller, author, curator, editor and co-publisher springerin, Vienna:
Deaf Dumb Mute Blind. On artistic ways of dealing with [pop cultural] Image -Sound Relations)

Chris Salter, Assistant Professor of Digital Media Concordia University, Montreal:
Saturation versus Silence: Audio-Visual Perception in the Visual and Media Arts

David Rokeby, Artist, Toronto: *Life in the Feedback Loop*

Art, Science and Technology: Instruments or Artworks?
Birgit Schneider, Dilthey Scholarship of the Fritz Thyssen Foundation, University of Potsdam, Institute of Arts
and Media: *Of hearing eyes and seeing ears. Elements of a history of the media aesthetics of different relations
of sound and image*

Yvonne Spielmann, Chair of New Media, University of the West of Scotland, School of Creative Industries,
Glasgow: *Early Video Tools - Some Reflections on Co-Creativity*

Katja Kwastek, Vice-Director Ludwig Boltzmann Institute Media.Art.Research., Linz, in conversation with
Golan Levin, Artist / Associate Professor of Electronic Art and Director of the STUDIO for Creative Inquiry at
Carnegie Mellon University, Pittsburgh: *On the creation, experience and research of audiovisual interactive art*

Art and Music: Intermediality – Intermodality – Interdisciplinarity?
Branden W. Joseph, Frank Gallipoli Professor of Modern and Contemporary Art, Columbia University, New
York, Department of Art History and Archaeology: *Biomusic and the End of Representation*

Helga de la Motte-Haber, Technical University Berlin, Institute of Language and Communication, Department Musicology: *Augenmusik – Hörbilder. Laudatio für den Preisträger des Media.Art.Research Award
(Eye Music – Audio Images. Laudatio for the prize-winner of the Media.Art.Research Award)*

Winner Media.Art.Research. Award 2009 for "Eye hEar: Music, Art, Film & the Culture of Synesthesia":
Simon Shaw-Miller, Senior Lecturer and Head of School, School of History of Art, Film & Visual Media
Birkbeck College, University of Londons: *Syncretism: Art and Music in the Modern Period*

Closing Performance
Mikomikona (Birgit Schneider & Andreas Eberlein, Berlin): *Fouriertransformation I + II (Fourier Transformation
I + II) Sound-Vision performance with two overhead projectors*

Amanda Parkes with Hiroshi Ishii

IMPETUS: Works from the MIT Media Lab at the Ars Electronica Festival 2009

Certainly we cannot hope to solve the problems facing us without a greater understanding of the modern world, based on the integration of knowledge. Humanists must be educated with a deep appreciation of modern science. Scientists and engineers must be steeped in humanistic learning. And all learning must be linked with a broad concern for the complex effects of technology on our evolving culture.

Jerome B. Wiesner (Co-founder, MIT Media Laboratory, 1915-1994)

The 2009 Ars Electronica Campus Exhibition features current work of the faculty and students from the MIT Media Lab in Cambridge MA. From its inception almost thirty years ago, the Media Lab has taken an unorthodox research approach to envisioning the impact of emerging technologies on everyday life—technologies that promise to fundamentally transform our most basic notions of human capabilities. The lab attracts designers, computer designers, engineers, artists, and scientists, divergent in background and practice. However, unifying the people of the lab is a particular kind of passion, momentum, drive—the IMPETUS—to create and innovate for change. The depth and breadth of the Media Lab's research areas transcend traditional technology, design or art environments and the lab can be thought of as an ongoing experiment, both physical and intellectual, in facilitating innovation, collaboration and critique. It is an environment where inspiration arises from difference and where the driving force behind creation comes from an inherently transdisciplinary approach.

The MIT Media Lab consists of 30 different research groups including the diverse disciplines of interactivity, robotics, artificial intelligence, education, nanotechnology, music, neuroengineering, material science, visualization, social networking, urban infrastructure, fabrication, and political art all intermingling in joint spaces, courses and projects. Students at the Media Lab generally arrive with a particular area of expertise, but are encouraged to explore new domains to enrich and expand their perspective on their research. In many ways, time spent at the Media Lab becomes an education on the process of innovating in itself. The goal of the lab's work is to develop technologies that empower people of all ages, from all walks of life, in all societies, to design and invent new possibilities for themselves and their communities. Unique to the lab's structure is our pairing with industry sponsors who support the lab's research in a shared intellectual property model and keep the lab connected to the real world issues of the corporate community and society at large.

The idea for the Media Lab came into being in 1980 by Professor Nicholas Negroponte and former MIT President and Science Advisor to President John F. Kennedy, Jerome Wiesner. The Lab grew out of the work of MIT's Architecture Machine Group, and remains within MIT's School of Architecture and Planning. The Media Lab opened the doors to its I. M. Pei-designed Wiesner Building in 1985, and in its first decade was at the vanguard of the technology that enabled the "digital revolution" and enhanced human expression: innovative research ranging from cognition and learning, to electronic music, to holography. In its second decade, the Lab literally took computing out of the box, embedding the bits of the digital realm with the atoms of our physical world. This led to expanded research in wearable computing, wireless "viral" communications, machines with common sense, new forms of artistic expression and innovative approaches to how children learn.

Now, in its third decade, the Media Lab continues to check traditional disciplines at the door. This fall, we will expand into a new building, a Fumihiko Maki-designed atelier style addition to our current space, where we will continue to move forward concept driven research, inventing—and reinventing—how humans experience, and can be aided by, technology.

The Campus exhibition at Ars Electronica features a sampling of current and recent work from the lab—an intersection of cutting edge technology with an appreciation for the power of design and aesthetics to metamorphize an interactive experience, and the desire to position work within a broader social infrastructure to better understand the effects of technology, for better or worse, on the fabric of society. Three subthemes have emerged for this exhibition—community, humanity and materiality—which broadly encompass the conceptual focus of our research and present a cross over between a humanist perspective so central to our approach and the engineering and science for which MIT is so famous.

Community

The development of new media technologies has brought about a revolution in the way we communicate and share knowledge. In recent years the lab has focused on several systems that empower and democratize access to information and reformulate social infrastructure physically and virtually. Some of the systems feature novel methods of mapping information to physicality and temporality while others look at urban transportation and energy processes. Lab researchers have also developed physical and digital platforms that encourage creativity through ease of accessibility to knowledge, transforming educational methods for all ages. Through products and tools that scaffold the process of creation of technologies by amateurs, the lab has helped in fostering the DIY initiative in communities of open source and participatory design. Key to this initiative is the concept of collective intelligence, aggregating knowledge of a diverse community of experts, and allowing for the formation of virtual communities that were never before possible. IMPETUS presents projects that explore how digital technologies have changed our access to and interpretation of information, and in turn empowered the process of learning, making, doing and understanding.

Humanity

Technology has created systems for human augmentation that allow us to expand our physical and sensory capabilities and we have grown accustomed to living in an environment where our digital devices function as an extension of ourselves, both in ability and perception. The design of technological systems with artificial intelligence pushes these boundaries further, where our devices also become a reflection of ourselves—we adapt to technology and in turn create technology that adapts to us. The notion of our relationship with technology is metamorphosizing as the boundary between technology as human augmentation or outside entity shifts, blurring the line between when technological systems become part of us, and where they remain an 'other.' Robotic creations appeal to responses deeply rooted in our human nature, creating a dialogue to persuade, calm, assist or delight, through varying states of anthropomorphized forms and actions, while a vanguard media production questions what it means to be human in the context of an increasingly digital world. Through varying investigative methods, the featured projects seek to challenge and pursue critical inquiry into understanding our own humanity and identity in the context of technology.

Materiality

For all the new dimensions the virtual world has brought us, we still intuitively delight in the physical—the tactile, the graspable, the tangible, the material—allowing us to utilize all of our senses and our inherent bodily knowledge of the world around us. For over a decade, the Media Lab has been at the forefront of understanding and innovating on technology's place within the built environment and the significance of physicality in our experience with digital systems. The idea of *Tangible Bits* was born at the Media Lab, seamlessly coupling the physical and digital world. In many ways, the Media Lab itself embodies the sense of the importance of physicality; it is a culture of learning by doing, a kinesthetic approach by which the physical output of endeavors can embody ideas beyond the imagination. In future visions of interactivity such as programmable matter and radical atoms, material science on the nanoscale begins to merge with concepts of interactivity, envisioning physical materials that are as malleable, programmable, and dynamic as pixels on a screen. Central to the notion of new materiality is also the innovation of fabrication processes that go along with creation, questioning how changing the process of making things also changes the things we make. For the lab's designers, artists and scientists working on novel methods of combining computation and materiality, the challenge becomes how to expand our notion of the possibilities of the material world while creating experiences that remain familiar, comfortable and engaging.

Like everything at the MIT Media Lab, the works presented transcend any one category and show a fusion of the artists' viewpoint, knowledge and personal motivations. Through IMPETUS, we invite you to experience and interpret the diversity and essence of our community.

Amanda Parkes with Hiroshi Ishii

IMPETUS: Arbeiten des MIT Media Lab
Ars Electronica Festival 2009

Die Probleme, vor denen wir stehen, lassen sich mit Sicherheit nicht lösen, wenn wir die moderne Welt, die auf der Integration von Wissen beruht, nicht besser verstehen. Die Ausbildung von Humanisten muss auf einer hohen Wertschätzung der modernen Wissenschaft basieren. Wissenschaftler und Techniker müssen sich ihrerseits an humanistischen Werten orientieren. Und jedes Lernen muss mit einem tiefen Interesse an den komplexen Auswirkungen der Technologie auf die Entwicklung unserer Kultur verknüpft sein.

Jerome B. Wiesner (Mitbegründer des MIT Media Laboratory, 1915-1994)

Die Campus-Ausstellung der Ars Electronica 2009 zeigt aktuelle Arbeiten der Fakultät und der Studenten des *MIT Media Lab* in Cambridge, Massachusetts. Das Media Lab verfolgt seit seiner Gründung vor fast 30 Jahren einen unorthodoxen Forschungsansatz, um die Auswirkungen neuer Technologien auf den Alltag zu antizipieren – Technologien, die eine grundlegende Veränderung der Auffassungen von menschlichen Fähigkeiten versprechen. Das Lab zieht Designer, Softwareentwickler, Techniker, Künstler und Wissenschaftler mit unterschiedlichstem beruflichen Hintergrund an. Um die hier arbeitenden Menschen zu koordinieren, bedarf es einer ganz besonderen Leidenschaft, Schwungkraft, Dynamik – eines kreativen und innovativen *IMPETUS*, um einen Wandel einzuleiten. Die Bandbreite der Forschungsbereiche des Media Lab geht über traditionelle Technologie, Design oder künstlerische Environments hinaus. Man kann das Lab vielmehr als ein permanentes Experimentierfeld verstehen, in dem Innovation, Kooperation und Kritik gefördert werden. Es ist eine Umgebung, in der Inspiration aus Differenz entsteht und der schöpferische Antrieb aus inhärent transdisziplinären Ansatz resultiert.

Das MIT Media Lab besteht aus 30 verschiedenen Forschungsgruppen, die so unterschiedliche Disziplinen wie interaktives Design, Robotik, künstliche Intelligenz, Bildung, Nanotechnologie, Musik, Neurotechnik, Materialkunde, Visualisierung, soziale Netzwerke, urbane Infrastrukturen, Produktion und politische Kunst umfassen, und – unbehindert von Einteilungen in herkömmliche Disziplinen – in gemeinsamen Räumen, Kursen und Projekten zusammenarbeiten. Die Studenten verfügen zwar über spezifische Fachkenntnisse, werden aber ermutigt, neue Bereiche zu erforschen, um ihren Horizont zu erweitern. Während der Ausbildung am Media Lab erfährt man in erster Linie, wie innovative Prozesse ablaufen. Ziel der Arbeit ist es, Technologien zu entwickeln, die Menschen aller Altersstufen, aus allen sozialen Schichten aller Gesellschaften befähigen, selbst neue Möglichkeiten für sich und ihre Gemeinschaften zu entwickeln und zu erfinden. Einzigartig an der Struktur des Lab ist unsere Kooperation mit Sponsoren aus der Industrie, welche die Forschungsarbeit – basierend auf dem Modell gemeinsamer Rechte an geistigem Eigentum – unterstützen und dafür sorgen, dass das Lab den Anschluss an Themen, die sich in der realen Welt im Unternehmensumfeld und der gesamten Gesellschaft stellen, nicht verliert.

Das Media Lab wurde 1980 von Professor Nicholas Negroponte und dem ehemaligen MIT-Präsidenten und wissenschaftlichen Berater von Präsident John F. Kennedy, Jerome Wiesner, konzipiert. Das Lab ging aus der Architecture Machine Group des MIT hervor und gehört nach wie vor zur MIT School of Architecture and Planning. 1985 wurde das Media Lab in dem von

I.M. Pei entworfenen Wiesner Building eröffnet. Im ersten Jahrzehnt übernahm es eine führende Rolle im Bereich der Technologie, die die „digitale Revolution" ermöglichte und die menschlichen Ausdrucksmöglichkeiten förderte: Die innovative Forschung erstreckte sich von den kognitiven Grundlagen des Lernens über elektronische Musik bis hin zur Holografie. Im zweiten Jahrzehnt holte das Lab die Datenverarbeitung aus ihrem Gehäuse und verknüpfte die Bits der digitalen mit den Atomen der realen Welt, was die Forschung in den Bereichen Wearable Computing, drahtlose „virale" Kommunikation, Maschinen mit Bewusstsein, neue Formen künstlerischen Ausdrucks und innovative Lernansätze für Kinder erweiterte.

Auch heute, im dritten Jahrzehnt seines Bestehens, geht das Media Lab nach wie vor über traditionelle Disziplinen hinaus. Im kommenden Herbst werden wir expandieren und unsere Räumlichkeiten um ein neues, von Fumihiko Maki im Stil eines Ateliers entworfenes Gebäude erweitern, in dem wir konzeptgesteuerte Forschung weiterentwickeln und experimentell erproben, wie Menschen Technologie erfahren und nutzen können.

Die Campus-Ausstellung der Ars Electronica zeigt eine Auswahl neuer und aktueller Arbeiten aus dem Lab – einen Querschnitt wegbereitender Technologien, die auf die Kraft von Design und Ästhetik setzen, um interaktive Erfahrungen zu transformieren und zu metamorphisieren. Die Intention dabei ist, die Arbeit in einem breiteren gesellschaftlichen Kontext zu positionieren, um die Auswirkungen der Technik – seien es positive oder negative – auf das soziale Gefüge besser zu verstehen. Für diese Ausstellung boten sich drei Subthemen an – Gemeinschaft, Humanität und Materialität –, die im Großen und Ganzen den konzeptuellen Schwerpunkt unserer Forschung umfassen und einen Brückenschlag zwischen einer humanistischen Perspektive, die zentraler Bestandteil unseres Ansatzes ist, und der Technik und Wissenschaft, die den Ruhm des MIT begründen, ermöglichen.

Gemeinschaft

Die Entwicklung neuer Medientechnologien hat eine Revolution in den Bereichen Kommunikation und Wissensaustausch ausgelöst. In den letzten Jahren arbeitete das Lab an mehreren Systemen, die den Informationszugang fördern und demokratisieren und die soziale Infrastruktur in konkreter und virtueller Hinsicht neu definieren. Einige dieser Systeme setzen auf neuartige Methoden des Information Mapping in Raum und Zeit, während bei anderen urbane Transportsysteme und Energieprozesse im Fokus stehen. Die Forscher des Lab haben auch reale und digitale Plattformen entwickelt, die Kreativität durch erleichterten Zugang zu Wissen fördern, wodurch sich die Ausbildungsmethoden für alle Altersstufen verändern. Das Lab unterstützt die Amateure der DIY-Initiativen der Open-Source Gemeinschaften und im Bereich partizipatorisches Design durch Produkte und Instrumente, die den Entwicklungsprozess von Technologien strukturieren. Charakteristisch für die Initiative ist das Konzept kollektiver Intelligenz, bei dem das Wissen einer heterogenen Expertengemeinschaft gebündelt und auf noch nie da gewesene Weise die Bildung virtueller Gemeinschaften ermöglicht wird. *IMPETUS* präsentiert Projekte, die erforschen, wie digitale Technologien unseren Zugang zu und unsere Interpretation von Information verändern und den Lernprozess, unser Tun und Denken, sowie kognitive Prozesse fördern.

Humanität

Die Technik brachte Systeme zur Erweiterung des Menschen hervor, die es ermöglichen, unsere physischen Fähigkeiten und Sinneswahrnehmungen zu steigern. Wir haben uns daran gewöhnt, in einem Umfeld zu leben, in dem digitale Geräte als Erweiterung von uns selbst, unserer Fähigkeiten und unserer Wahrnehmung dienen. Die Entwicklungen im Bereich der künstlichen Intelligenz verschieben diese Grenzen weiter, sodass unsere Geräte auch zu einer Spiegelung von uns selbst werden – wir passen uns der Technologie an und entwickeln vice versa eine Technologie, die sich uns anpasst. Unsere Beziehung zur Technologie verwandelt sich in dem Maße, in dem sich die Grenze zwischen Technologie als Erweiterung des Menschen oder äußere Entität verschiebt, wodurch die Unterscheidung, wann technische Systeme Teil von uns werden und wann sie als Fremdkörper wahrgenommen werden, aufgehoben wird. Entwicklungen im Bereich Robotik provozieren Reaktionen, die tief in der menschlichen Natur verwurzelt sind; sie initiieren durch anthropomorphisierte Formen und Handlungen einen Dialog des Überzeugens, Beschwichtigens, der Hilfestellung oder des Vergnügens, während eine avantgardistische Medienproduktion hinterfragt, was Menschsein im Kontext einer zunehmend digitalen Welt bedeutet. Durch unterschiedliche Forschungsmethoden versuchen die präsentierten Projekte, kritische Fragen zum Verständnis des Menschseins und unserer Identität im Kontext von Technologie aufzuwerfen.

Materialität

Trotz all der neuen Dimensionen, die uns die virtuelle Welt eröffnete, erfreuen wir uns nach wie vor intuitiv am Physischen – Taktilen, Greifbaren, Berührbaren, am Material –, das uns erlaubt, unsere Sinne und das unserem Körper innewohnende Wissen über die uns umgebende Welt zu nutzen. Seit über einem Jahrzehnt nimmt das Media Lab eine Spitzenstellung ein, was das Verständnis und die Erneuerung der Stellung der Technologie in der gebauten Umwelt sowie die Bedeutung der Physikalität in unserer Erfahrung mit digitalen Systemen anbelangt. Die Idee zu *Tangible Bits*, also Daten zum Anfassen, die die reale und die digitale Welt nahtlos verbinden, entstand am Media Lab. In mancher Hinsicht verkörpert das Media Lab selbst die Bedeutung von Physikalität, es steht für eine Kultur des *learning by doing*, einen kinästhetischen Ansatz, der dadurch gekennzeichnet ist, dass sich als Ergebnis einzelner Bestrebungen Ideen materialisieren, die unsere Vorstellungskraft übersteigen. In Zukunftsvisionen zur Interaktivität, wie programmierbare Materie und radikale Atome, beginnt sich die Materialkunde im Nanobereich mit Konzepten der Interaktivität zu vermischen und Materialien zu antizipieren, die so formbar, programmierbar und dynamisch sind wie Pixel auf dem Bildschirm. Die neue Materialität ist untrennbar mit der Erneuerung von Produktionsprozessen verbunden, wobei sich die Frage stellt, wie die Veränderung des Herstellungsprozesses auch die hergestellten Dinge selbst verändert. Die Designer, Künstler und Wissenschaftler, die am Lab an neuen Methoden zur Kombination von Informationsverarbeitung und Materialität arbeiten, sind herausgefordert, unser Verständnis von den Möglichkeiten der materiellen Welt zu verändern, während sie gleichzeitig Erfahrungen schaffen, die vertraut, angenehm und stimulierend sind.
Wie alle Projekte am MIT Media Lab entziehen sich die präsentierten Arbeiten jeder disziplinären Zuordnung und zeigen eine Verflechtung der Standpunkte, des Wissens und der persönlichen Motivationen der Künstler. Mit der Ausstellung *IMPETUS* sollen die Vielfalt und die wesentlichen Ambitionen der MIT-Gemeinde erfahr- und interpretierbar gemacht werden.

(Aus dem Englischen von Martina Bauer)

Works from the MIT Media Lab

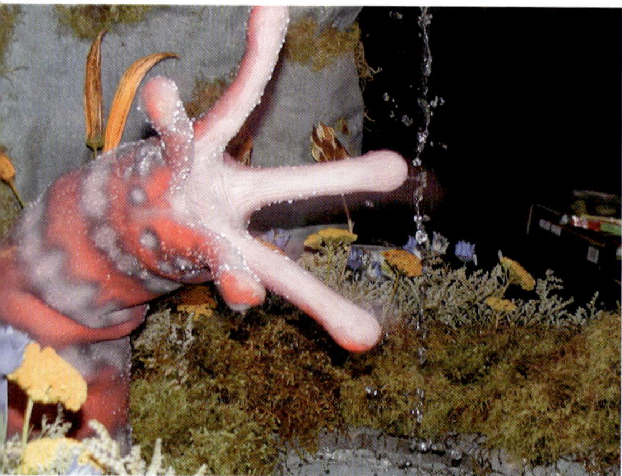

Public Anemone
Personal Robots Group
http://robotic.media.mit.edu/projects/robots/ anemone/overview/overview.html

Inspired by primitive life, *Public Anemone* is a robotic creature with an organic appearance and natural quality of movement. By day, *Public Anemone* is awake and interacts with the waterfall, pond, and other aspects of its surroundings. It interacts with the audience by orienting to their movements using a stereo machine vision system. But if you get too close, it recoils like a rattlesnake.

Cyberflora
Personal Robots Group
http://robotic.media.mit.edu/projects/robots/cyberflora/overview/overview.html

This robotic flower garden is comprised of four species of cyberflora. Each combines animal-like behavior and flower-like characteristics into a robotic instantiation that senses and responds to people in a life-like and distinct manner. Delicate and graceful, *Cyberflora* communicates a future vision of robots that shall intrigue us intellectually and touch us emotionally. The installation explores a style of human-robot interaction that is fluid, dynamic, and harmonious.

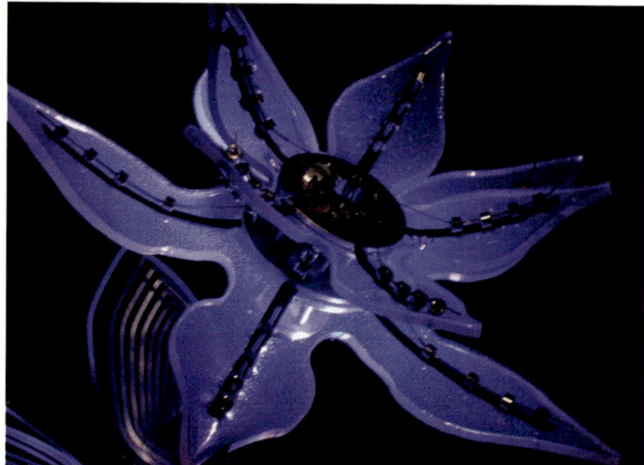

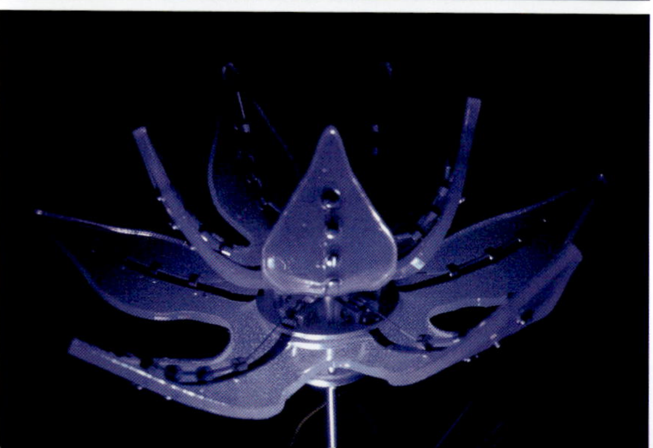

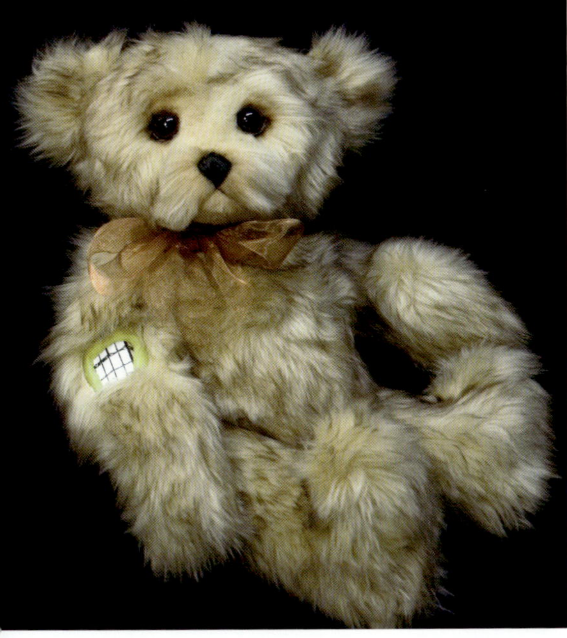

The Huggable
Personal Robots Group
URL: http://robotic.media.mit.edu/projects/robots/huggable/overview/overview.html

The Huggable™ is a new type of robotic companion being developed at the MIT Media Lab for healthcare, education and social communication applications. *The Huggable*™ is designed to be much more than a fun interactive robotic companion. It is designed to function as a team member that is an essential member of a triadic interaction. Therefore, *The Huggable*™ is not designed to replace any particular person in a social network, but rather to enhance that human social network.

Autom
Personal Robots Group
http://robotic.media.mit.edu/projects/robots/autom/overview/overview.html

Autom™ is a robotic weight loss coach designed to help people who are trying to lose or keep off weight. *Autom*™ helps by encouraging you to stick with your diet for long enough to create long-term change and keep extra pounds off. Fifteen robots were used in a controlled clinical trial in the Boston area in the summer and fall of 2007. Results showed that people who worked with *Autom*™ stayed with their diet for twice as long as people using a computer or paper-based diet log.

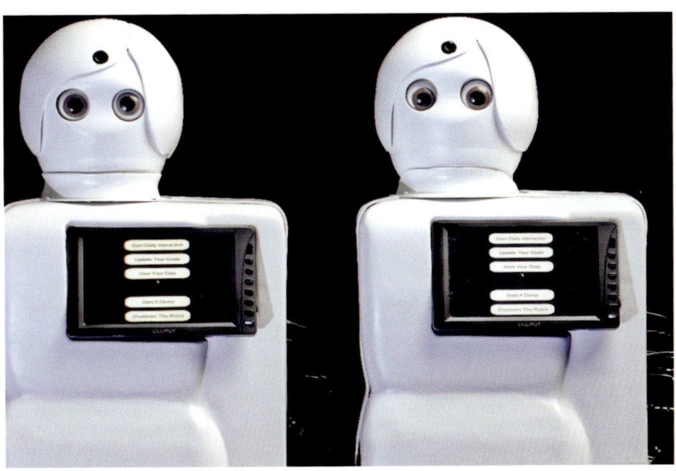

3D Printed Clock
Peter Schmitt &
Robert Swartz

The *3D Printed Clock* is based on the idea of ready assembled 3D printed computational mechanisms and relates to research in the field of rapid prototyping and digital fabrication. The clock was modeled in CAD software after an existing clock, utilizing a weight and a pendulum to keep track of time. The CAD model was created according to the specifications of the 3D printer, assuring suf-

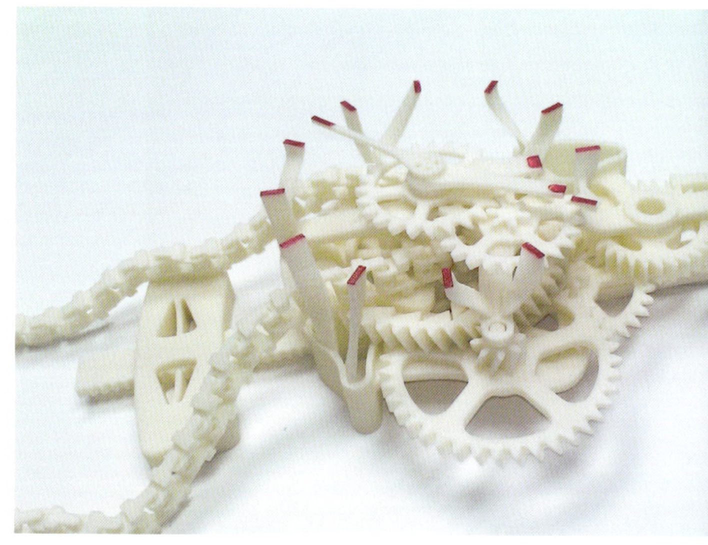

ficient gaps and clearances for the different parts to be separate. In addition support material drainage and perforations were added to allow for the access support material being removed after the print. The *3D Printed Clock* is intended to demonstrate superior capabilities of 3D printing as fabrication process. It should contribute towards a future use of 3D printers to replace injection molding and expensive tooling processes and allow for on demand, customized and "greener" consumer products.

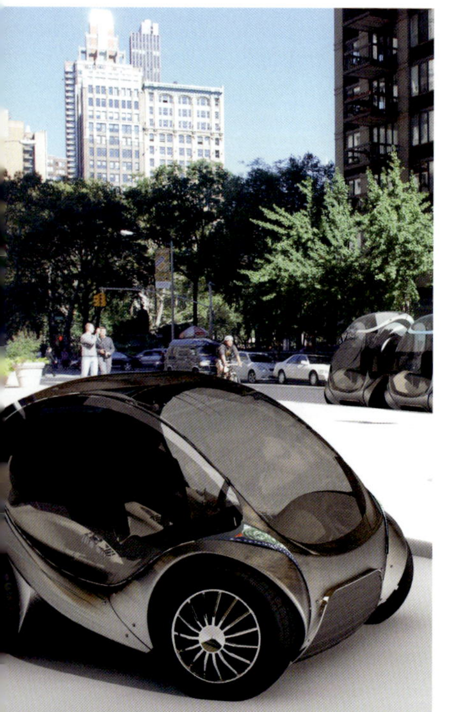

CityCar, RoboScooter, and GreenWheel
Smart Cities Group

The models in this exhibit represent recent work from the Smart Cities group. All were produced by creating 3D digital models and then using deposition printers to generate physical models. Several of the models are of lightweight intelligent electric vehicles—the CityCar developed in collaboration with General Motors, the RoboScooter developed in collaboration with SYM and ITRI, and the GreenWheel electric-assist bicycle. These vehicles are clean, green, and energy-efficient, and they enable new kinds of urban personal mobility systems.

Working models of mechanical devices no longer need to be printed as separate components and then assembled. Using the latest deposition printers, as Peter Schmitt's fully functional printed clock illustrates, they can now be printed in their entirety.

Chameleon Guitar; Physical Heart in a Digital Instrument
Amit Zoran, Marco Coppiardi, Pattie Maes
Credits: Video by Paula Aguilera, Electronics layout design Nan-Wei Gong
http://ambient.media.mit.edu/projects.php?action=details&id=58

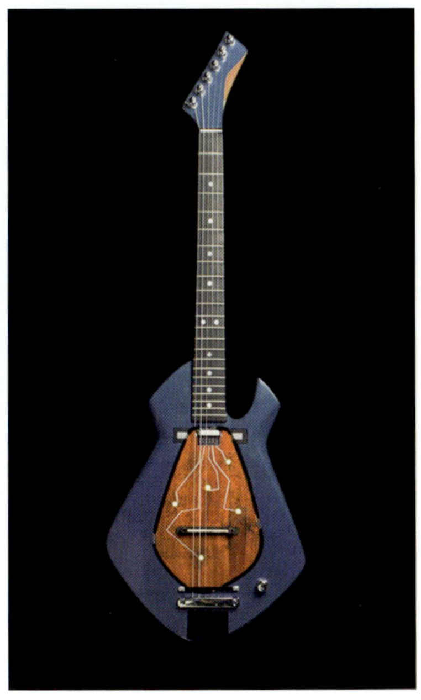

Natural wood, with its unique grain patterns, is what gives traditional acoustic instruments warm and distinctive sounds, while the power of modern electronic processing provides an unlimited degree of control to manipulate the characteristics of an instrument's sound. Now a guitar built by a student at MIT's Media Lab promises to provide the best of both worlds.

The *Chameleon Guitar*—so named for its ability to mimic different instruments—is an electric guitar whose body has a separate central section that is removable. This inserted section, the soundboard, can be switched with one made of a different kind of wood, or with a different structural support system, or with one made of a different material altogether. Then, the sound generated by the electronic pickups on that board can be manipulated by a computer to produce the effect of a different size or shape of the resonating chamber. Several resonators were made, using techniques similar to the guitar body, to demonstrate the acoustic possibilities—from wooden acoustic resonators to experimental ones.

Shutters
Marcelo Coelho
http://ambient.media.mit.edu/projects.php?action=details&id=43

Shutters is a soft kinetic membrane for environmental control and communication. It is composed of actuated louvers (or shutters) that can be individually addressed for precise control of ventilation, daylight incidence and information display. By combining smart materials, textiles and computation, *Shutters* builds upon other façade systems to create living environments and work spaces that are more energy efficient, while being aesthetically pleasing and considerate of its inhabitants' activities.

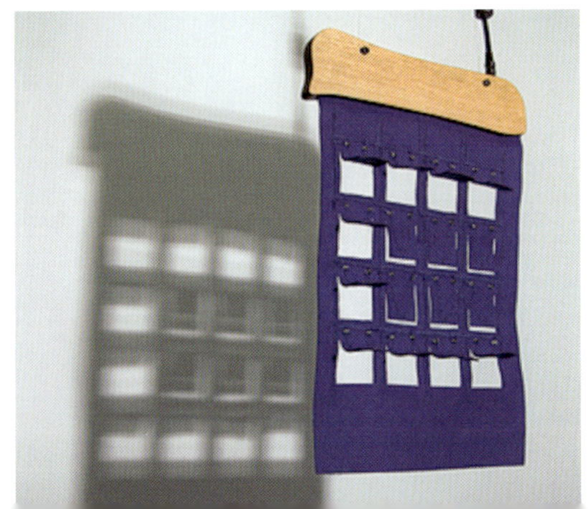

Moving Portrait
Orit Zuckerman & Sajid Sadi
http://ambient.media.mit.edu/projects.php?action=details&id=21

The *Moving Portrait* is based on a set of black and white portraits, comprising a rich library of photographic sequences. The portrait resides in a picture frame and interacts with its viewers using a variety of sensing techniques (vision, ultrasonic, RFID etc.). The sensing architecture enables the portrait to be aware of viewers' presence, identity, distance, speed, and body movements. The cognitive architecture controls the portrait's reaction, taking into account the viewer's behavior, the portrait's mood, as well as memory of previous interactions. All of which contributes to a complex, believable behavior. By adding interaction, dynamics and memory to a familiar portrait, we create a different and more engaging relationship between the viewer and the portrait. The viewer gets to know more about the subject and, in addition, the portrait's responses are adapted to the viewer's behavior and

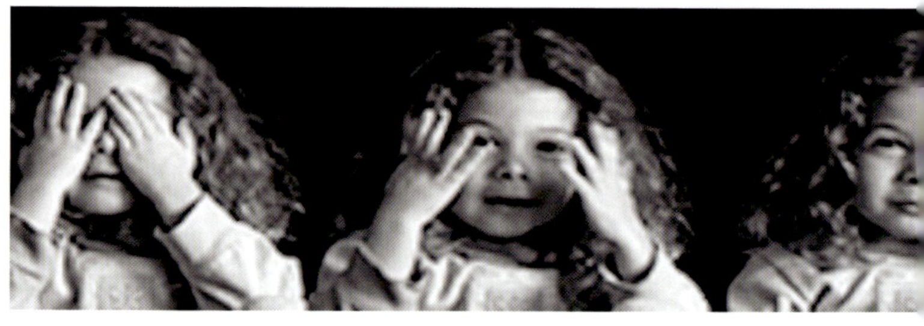

to prior interactions with current and former viewers. Just like in real life, where every person reveals a different side of his/her personality to different people and situations, the evocative portrait reveals different sides of its own personality.

Siftables
David Merrill and Jeevan Kalanithi
http://ambient.media.mit.edu/projects.php?action=details&id=35

Siftables aims to enable people to interact with information and media in a physical, natural manner that approaches interactions with physical objects in our everyday lives. As an interaction platform, *Siftables* applies technology and methodology from wireless sensor networks to tangible user interfaces. *Siftables* are independent, compact devices with sensing, graphical display, and wireless communication capabilities. They can be physically manipulated as a group to interact with digital information and media. *Siftables* can be used to implement any number of gestural interaction languages and HCI applications.

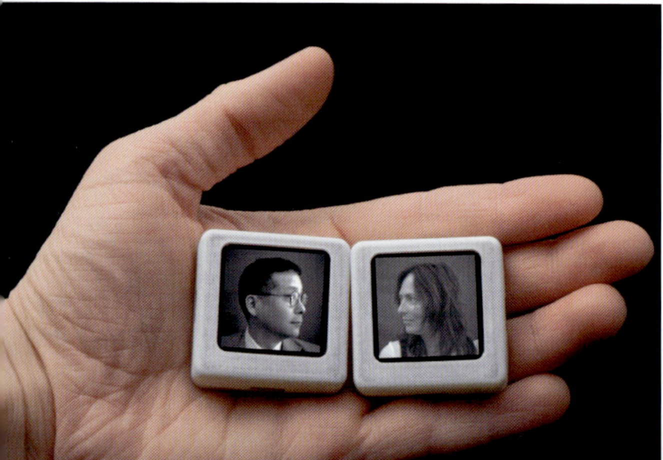

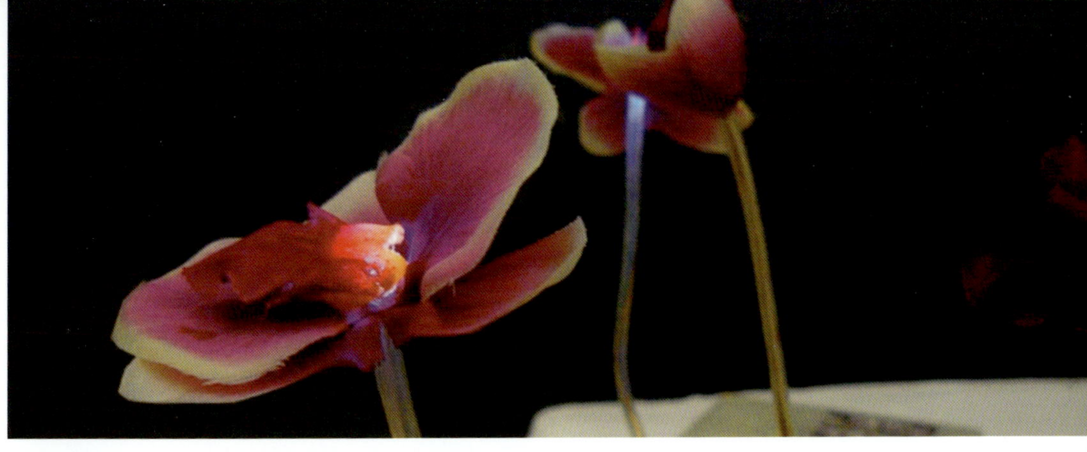

Blossom

Sajid Sadi

http://consciousanima.net/projects/blossom/

Blossom is a multi-person awareness system that connects distant friends and family, but reacts to the existing communication means by focusing on background awareness rather than direct communication, and on implicit asynchrony that breaks down notions of reply timeframes implicit in current communication technologies.

Digital communication grew out of a need for formal contact. As such, much of it is based on back-and-forth communication, setting expectations about replies and timeframes. In a shared household, however, communication is not always this explicit. There is a level of communication that comes solely from momentary shared experiences.

Blossom provides an awareness medium that does not rely on the attention- and reciprocity-demanding interfaces such as mobile phones, SMS and email. Combining touch-based input with visual and motile feedback, *Blossoms* are created as pairs that can communicate over the network, echoing the conditions of each other and forming an implicit, always-there link that physically expresses awareness, while retaining the instantaneous and long-distance capabilities that define digital communication.

SixthSense

Pranav Mistry

http://www.pranavmistry.com/projects/sixthsense/

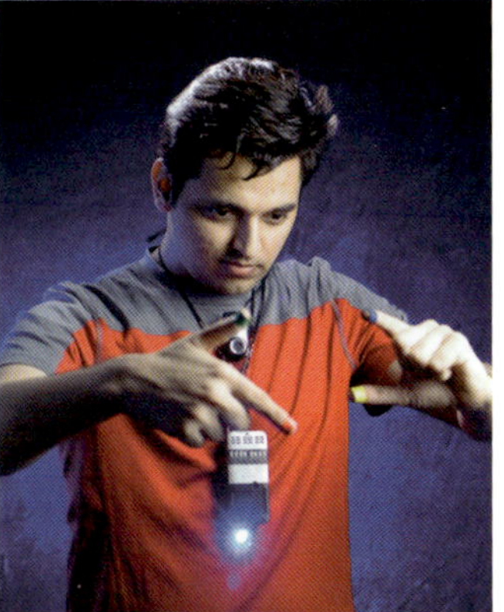

SixthSense is a wearable gestural interface that augments the physical world around us with digital information and lets us use natural hand gestures to interact with that information. By using a camera and a tiny projector mounted in a pendant-like wearable device, *SixthSense* sees what you see and visually augments any surfaces or objects we are interacting with. It projects information onto surfaces, walls and physical objects around us, and lets us interact with the projected information through natural hand gestures, arm movements, or our interaction with the object itself. *SixthSense* attempts to free information from its confines by seamlessly integrating it with reality, and thus making the entire world your computer.

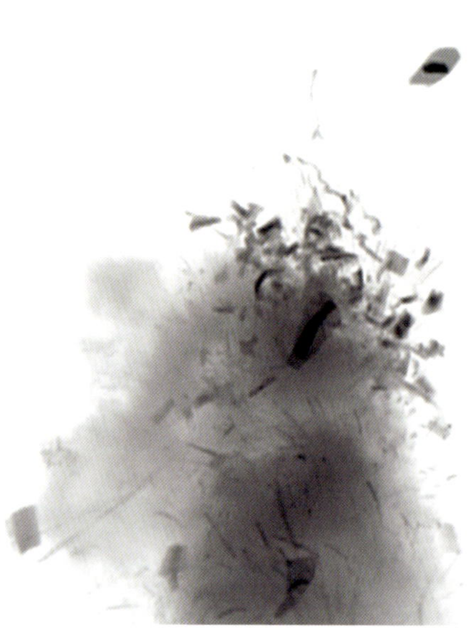

Cherry Blossoms
Alyssa Wright

Cherry Blossoms gives witness to the tragedy of war. The project starts in a backpack outfitted with a small microcontroller and a GPS unit. Recent news of bombings in Iraq are downloaded to the unit every night, and their relative location to the center of the city are superimposed onto a map of Boston. If the wearer walks into a space in Boston that correlates to a site of violence in Baghdad, the backpack detonates. A compressed cloud of confetti engulfs the scene, looking like a mixture between smoke, shrapnel and the white blossoms of a cherry tree. Each piece of confetti is inscribed with the name of a civilian who died in the war, and the circumstances of their death. With *Cherry Blossoms* human loss resonates beyond the boundary of conflict.

Sourcemap
Leonardo Bonanni, Matthew Hockenberry, David Zwarg, Hiroshi Ishii
URL: http://www.sourcemap.org/

Sourcemap is an open platform for sharing supply chain information through the web. Building on environmental impact databases, it allows business owners, designers and consumers to visualize the provenance of products together with their carbon footprint. Users can create and share the supply chains behind products, events, or even meals. The *Sourcemap* project is open-source, and actively seeking developers, contributors and companies interested in using this system to understand and optimize the way we make things.

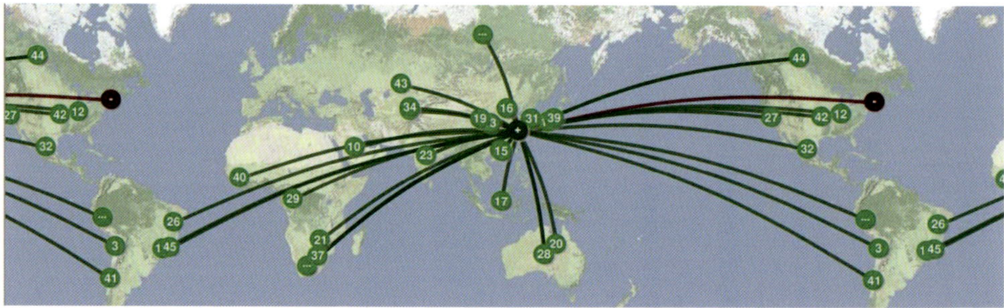

PicTouch: a Tangible Interface for Art Restoration

Leonardo Bonanni, Maurizio Seracini, Xiao Xiao, Matthew Hockenberry, Bianca Cheng Costanzo, Andrew Shum, Antony Speranza, Romain Teil, Hiroshi Ishii.
http://pictouch.org/

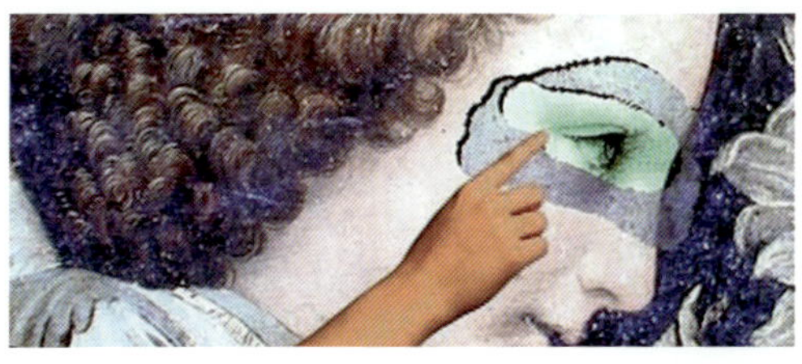

We rarely get the chance to experience a precious work of art as a restorer does: touching, repairing it, and occasionally leaving a trace. *PicTouch* is an exploration of the painting as a living and material thing, not just a static image. Using large touch-sensitive displays, it becomes possible to not only gaze at an image, but also engage directly with its canvas, stretching it, scraping away at the layers of paint, and occasionally even tearing it. *PicTouch* was inspired by the practice of art diagnosticians using medical imaging equipment to photograph paintings at invisible wavelengths of light. These infrared, ultraviolet and x-ray photographs reveal initial sketches, the order in which paint was deposited as well as varnish and subsequent changes or restoration attempts. *PicTouch* gives users intuitive access to these multiple layers through physical metaphors on a large touch display. This interface is being developed as a way to make modern diagnostic imaging of priceless artwork available to the museum going public and online through a new generation of touch-based interfaces.

g-stalt: gestural interaction, telekinesis, the hand, and cartoons

Jamie Zigelbaum, Daniel Leithinger, Alan Browning, Olivier Bau, Adam Kumpf, Kyle Buza, and Hiroshi Ishii
http://zig.media.mit.edu/Work/G-stalt

g-stalt is a whole-handed, gestural interface for media navigation inspired by the promise of technologically enabled telekinesis. Built for Oblong Industries' g-speak spatial operating environment, *g-stalt* allows users to view photographic and videographic media collaboratively and concurrently—operating the system with their hands, fingers, and gestures in three-dimensional space. Working with Oblong we have created a vocabulary of over 20 body-hand-finger configurations for *g-stalt*, which together form the initial seed of an embodied, physical language for computational interaction. In the present this grammar enables *g-stalt* users to search Flickr or rapidly navigate and play a library of Tex Avery's cartoons from MGM (1942–1955). In the future this grammar could do much, much more.

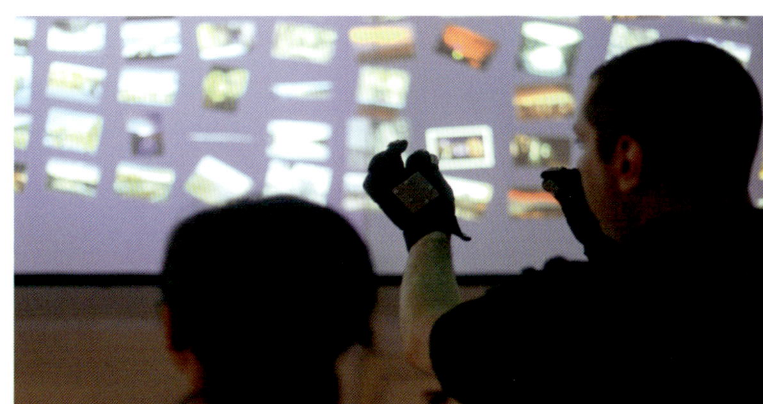

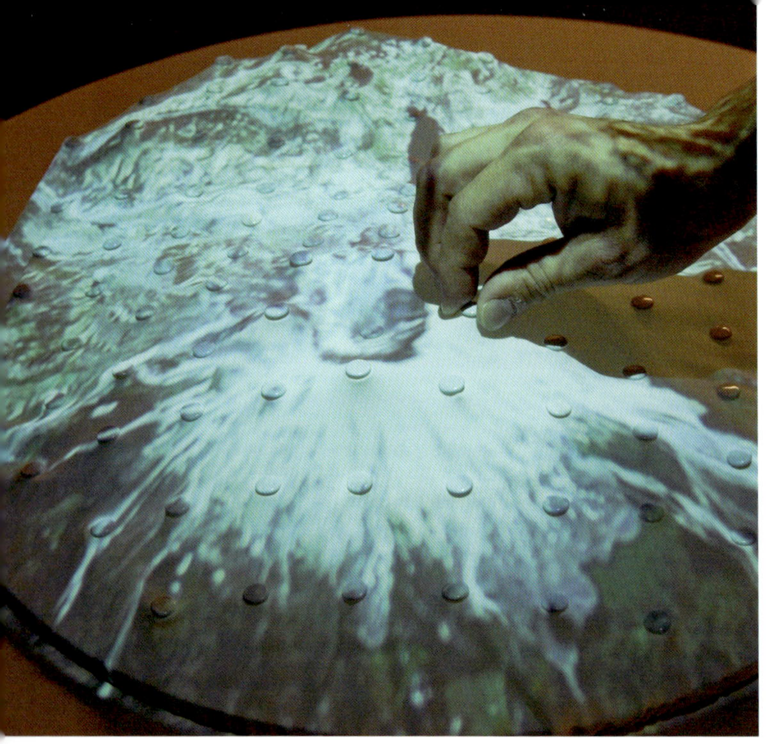

Relief
Daniel Leithinger & Adam Kumpf

Relief is an actuated table-top display, which is able to render and animate three-dimensional shapes with a malleable surface. It allows users to experience and shape digital models like geographical terrain in an intuitive manner. Therefore, *Relief* can provide a better understanding of our environmental impact by rendering time-lapse models of erosion and the effects of climate change. The tabletop surface is actuated by an array of motorized pins, which are controlled with a platform built upon open-source hardware and software tools. Each pin can be addressed individually and senses user input like pulling and pushing. The hardware configuration can be easily extended and utilized for form factors different from a tabletop display. Future versions could include expressive digital sculpting tools and music controllers.

Piezing
Amanda Parkes & Adam Kumpf
http://web.media.mit.edu/~amanda/piezing

Piezing is a garment that harnesses energy from the natural gestures of the human body in motion. Around the joints of the elbows and hips, the garment is embedded with piezoelectric material elements that generate an electric potential in response to applied mechanical stress. The electric potential is then stored as voltage in a centralized small battery and later can be discharged into a device. As a concept, *Piezing* explores a decentralized and self-reliant energy model for embedded interaction, pushing forward possibilities for mobility.

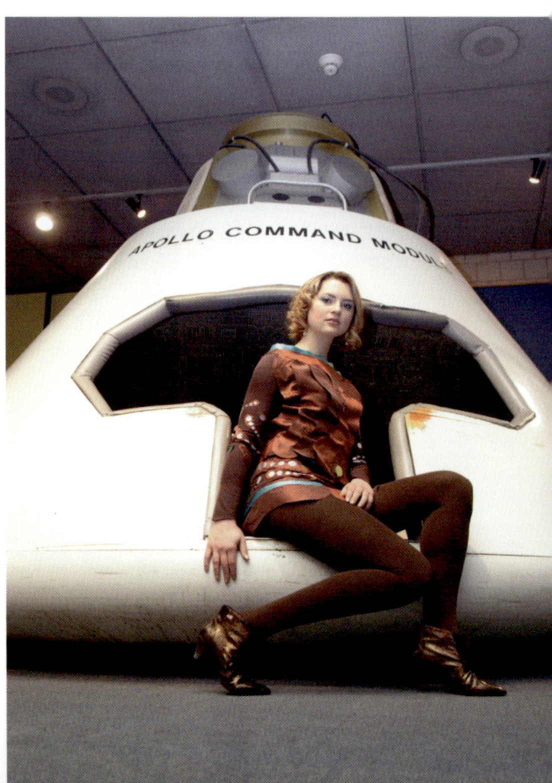

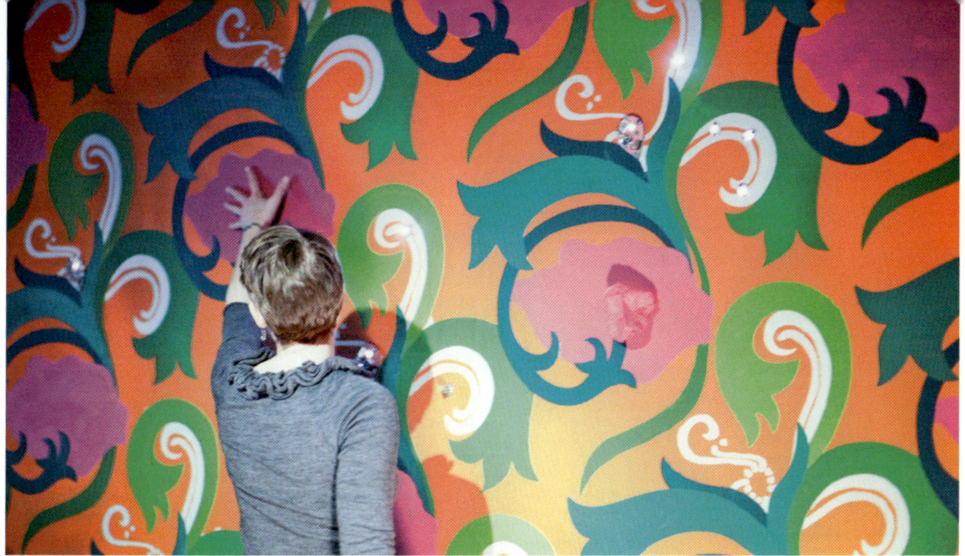

Interactive Wallpaper
Leah Buechley

This project examines the intersection of arts and crafts inspired decoration, electronics, and computation. We are investigating how a single surface (wallpaper) can be statically lovely, discretely interactive and strikingly dynamic.

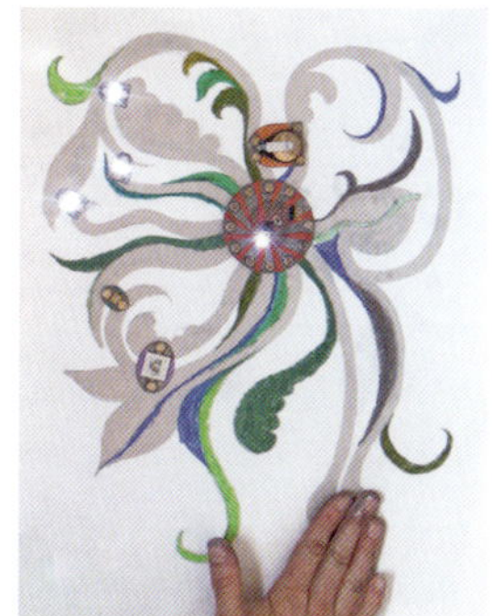

Computational Sketchbook
Leah Buechley

What interfaces might we build if we could sketch functional systems directly on paper? What will circuits look like when they are painted or drawn instead of etched or machined? This project explores the potential of paper-based computing.

LilyPad Arduino
Leah Buechley

LilyPad Arduino is a construction kit that enables people to design and build their own electronic textiles or "e-textiles". It consists of a set of sew-able electronic modules and a spool of conductive thread. E-textiles are constructed by sewing the modules to cloth with conductive thread, which provides both the physical and electrical connections between pieces.

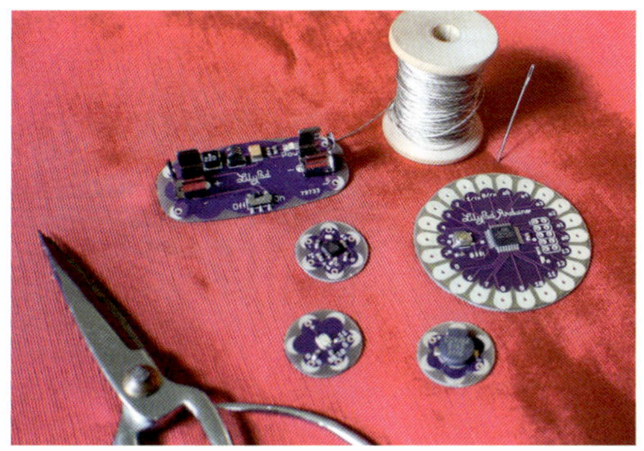

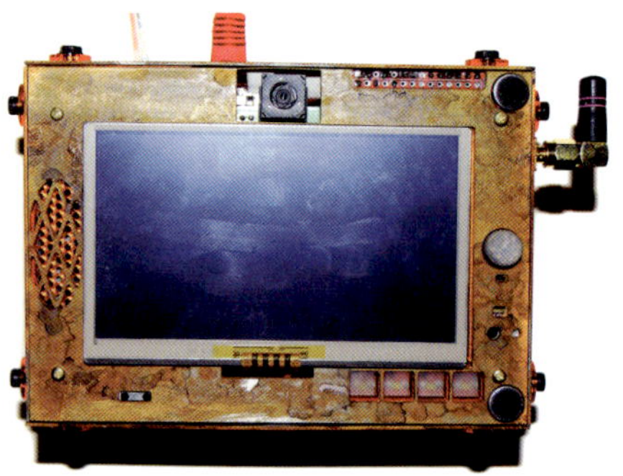

Ubiquitous Sensor Network Navigator
Alexander Reben,
Mat Laibowitz,
NanWei Gong and
Joseph Paradiso

The *Ubiquitous Sensor Network Navigator* provides a directable portal through which an observer can interact with a sensor-rich environment at the Media lab. Data is rendered intuitively, affording the observer a configurable and dynamic view into what is occurring. Sensor data is rendered at various scales of resolution (from high-level overviews to audio/video feeds and from real-time streaming to cached and temporally compressed data). In this way, visitors in Linz can be linked intimately into the professional pulse and daily life at our Laboratory.

The aural gateway integrates sound sampled throughout the Media Lab into a visual, aural and tactile experience. Real time audio data drives the experience allowing the observer to experience the overall activity of the Media Lab. Sound is streamed from 45 nodes distributed throughout the Lab and concentrated into the gateway. The observer can interact with the piece, feeling the rhythm of the Media Lab. Projected onto the surface is content gleaned from various sensors distributed throughout the Lab. The piece reflects the essence of the Media Lab as a holistic entity.

LittleBits
Ayah Bdeir
http://www.littlebits.cc

littleBits is a growing library of preassembled circuit boards, made easy by tiny magnets. All logic and circuitry is pre-engineered, so you can play with electronics without knowing electronics. Tiny magnets act as connectors and enforce polarity, so you can't put things in the wrong way. *littleBits* has a vision: to end the mysticism around engineering and electronics, to counter the black box product ideology of consumer electronics, and to fuel an explosion of creativity and innovation in artists, designer, kids and hobbyists when it comes to technology. Crave creativity? Make something! Light it, push it, turn it, twist it, bend it, buzz it, blink it, shake it!

Supported by Eyebeam Center for Art and Technology design by Luma Shihab Eldin. *www.lumaeldin.com*
Interns: Jie Qi, Axel Esquite, Youngjin Chung, Paul Rothman.
Thanks: Robert Vlacich, Spencer Russel, Smart Design

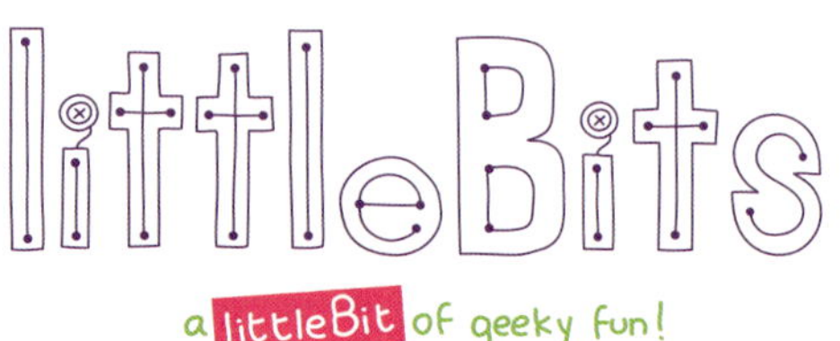

Les Années Lumière
Ayah Bdeir
http://www.ayahbdeir.com/work/installations/les-annees-lumiere/Text

Starting from the assassination of Prime Minister Hariri on February 14th 2005, till May of 2008, Lebanon underwent over 133 days of intense violence. Looking from above, each explosion was as an ephemeral but recurrent bright light across the land. *Les Années Lumière* is a bird's eye view of a little over 3 years of violence, strife and very bright lights rocking Lebanon, remembered and proportionally replayed in 45 minutes. A thin gold mesh is carved with relief representing Lebanon and tens of LEDs are distributed on the landscape controlled by a microcontroller circuit that serves as our memory of the violence. As electronics are layered and integrated in canvas, a 4th dimension of time is added to a medium that is typically static. In its title, *Les Années Lumière* asks, are the years approaching 2009 our enlightenment? Could capturing our recent history in a tangible way make our memories less painful? Could a visualization of our memories make our realities harder to replicate?

In collaboration with Rouba Khalil. *Thank you*: Axel Esquite, Eyebeam Center for Art and Technology

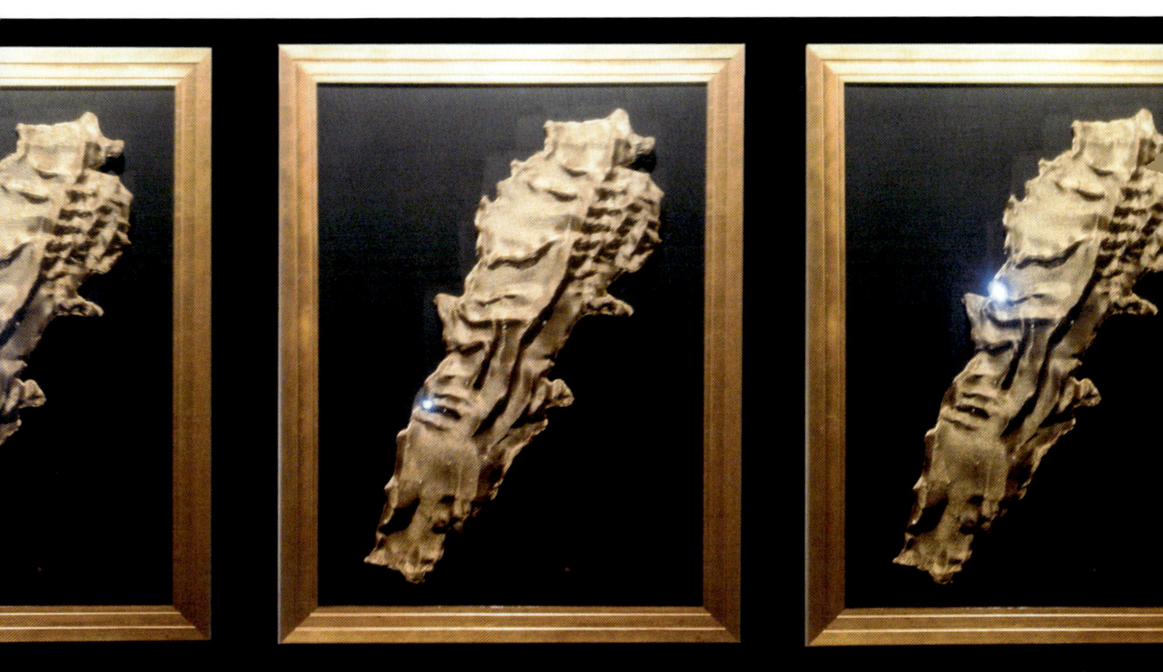

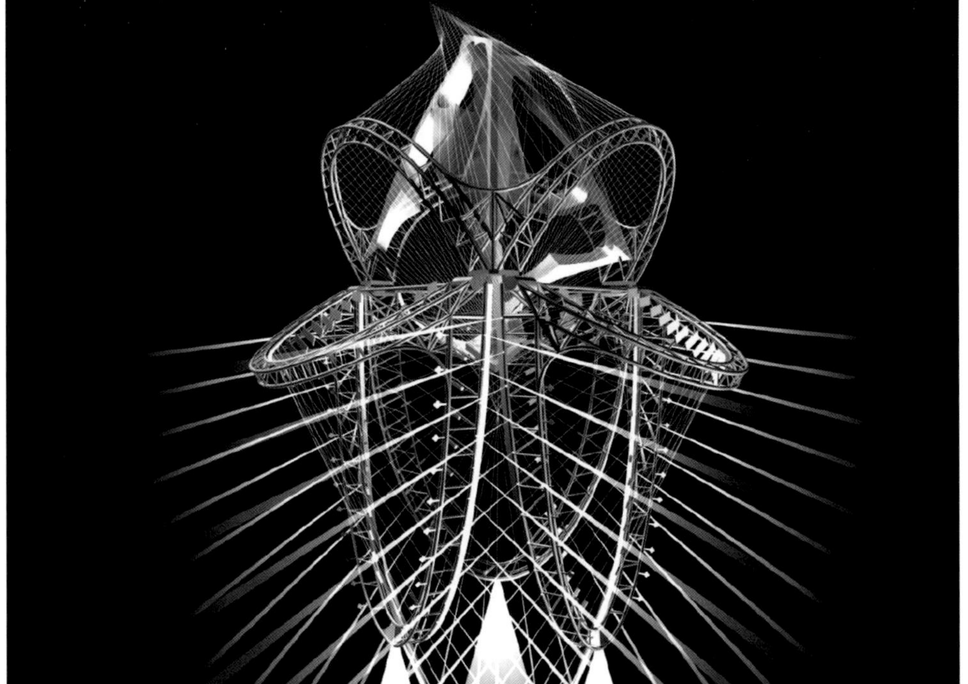

Death and the Powers

Tod Machover (composer and creative director), Robert Pinsky (librettist), Diane Paulus (director), Alex McDowell (designer), with a team from the MIT Media Lab including Peter Torpey, Elly Jessop, Andy Cavatorta, Wei Dong, Noah Feehan, Bob Hsiung, et al.
http://opera.media.mit.edu/projects/deathandthepowers/

Death and the Powers is a new opera by composer Tod Machover under development at the MIT Media Lab. It is a one-act, full evening work scored for an ensemble of specially designed Hyperinstruments, and will include a robotic, animatronic stage—the first of its kind—that will gradually "come alive" as a main character in the drama.

The original story is about Simon Powers, a rich, powerful and successful man who wants to go beyond the bounds of humanity. He is the founder of the System, a human organism material experiment that investigates the transduction of human existence into other forms. Reaching the end of his life, Powers faces the question of his legacy: "When I die, what remains? What will I leave behind? What can I control? What can I perpetuate?" As he enters the System, his family must decide whether to join him, and world leaders must decide what to do about the havoc he has left in his wake.

A new technique of Disembodied Performance is employed to translate Simon's offstage performance into an expressively animated stage, consisting of Simon's library as well as various objects including an imposing Musical Chandelier. The story is framed and complemented by a chorus of "rolling, lurching, and gliding" robots—or Operabots—that attempt to understand the meaning of death. Death and the Powers will be presented in workshop form at Harvard's A.R.T. Theater in September 2009, and the world premiere will take place at the Monte Carlo Opera in September 2010.

Under the High Patronage of Prince Albert II of Monaco, with sponsorship from Opera Futurum Ltd.

Hyperinstruments
Tod Machover, with Adam Boulanger, Mary Farbood, Gili Weinberg, Rob Aimi, Diana Young, Mike Fabio, Marc Downie, et al.
http://opera.media.mit.edu/

The Hyperinstruments Group at the MIT Media Lab was founded by Tod Machover in 1986 and has been devoted to augmenting musical expression for everyone, from high level virtuosi like Yo-Yo Ma and Prince, to the general public (as in Machover's *Brain Opera*, which received its European premiere at Ars Electronica in 1996), to children and families, and to promote health and wellness. An overview of recent Hyperinstrument work will be presented, including Music Toys (Beatbug and Shaper) from the *Toy Symphony* project (2001– 2004), a violin Hyperbow designed for Joshua Bell, and an interactive version of the Hyperscore composing software environment, which lets anyone compose sophisticated music using lines and colors. An overview video will

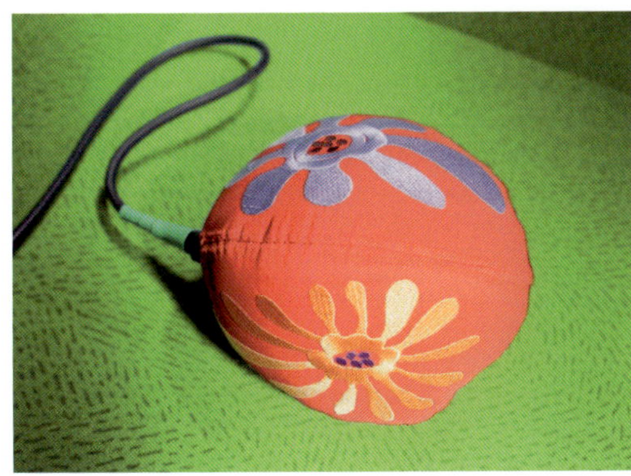

feature Hyperinstrument highlights from the past ten years with an emphasis on work in Music, Mind and Health, and a special showing will be made available of Tod Machover's 2005 *Jeux Deux* for hyperpiano, symphony orchestra featuring the Boston Pops, and interactive graphics by Marc Downie, MIT Media Lab PhD and winner of a Prix Ars Electronica in 2002.

This work was generously supported by, among others, the SEGA and CSK Corporations (Japan), the Boston Symphony Orchestra, Tewksbury State Hospital and the Massachusetts Cultural Council, and Harmony Line Inc.

Living Window
Daniel Saakes

We introduce a new material for dynamic storytelling: living windows. Our material acts as a pixel-addressable display that responds to the environment lighting. Placed in a window, it conveys rich stories based on the time of the day or the season. Our material is completely passive and can be used in a similar fashion to stain glass windows.

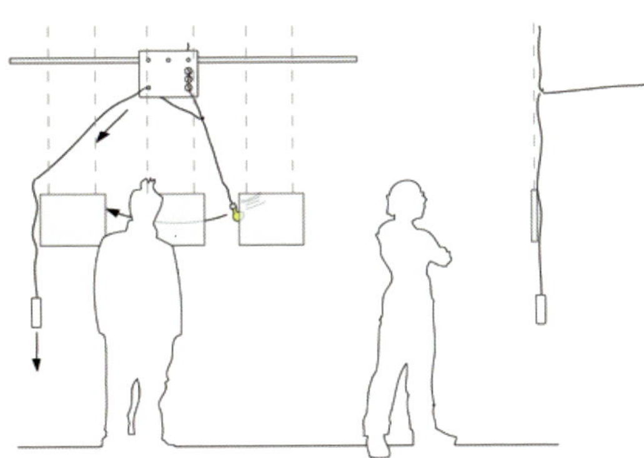

Social Garden
John Kestner
http://eco.media.mit.edu/socialgarden/

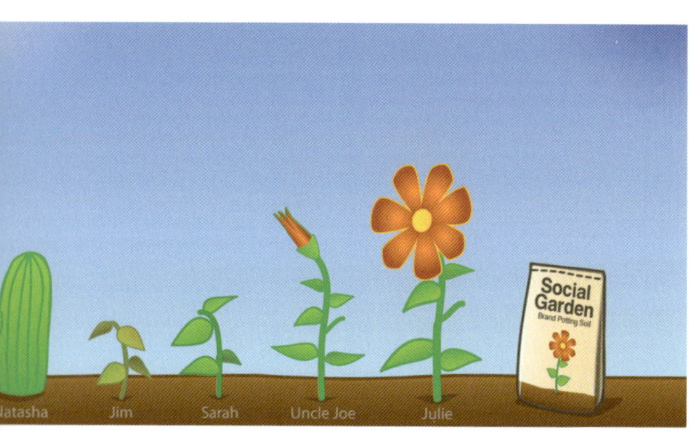

The Internet supports many great tools for communicating at a distance in order to maintain personal relationships and build social networks. However, these tools rarely help us realize which relationships are strained by lack of attention. *Social Garden* explores using virtual plants as a metaphor for relationships, encouraging us to tend to our social connections as we do our gardens. By tracking and analyzing communications through email, instant messaging, social websites, SMS, and phone, *Social Garden* proposes to give feedback on how our relationships are flourishing or wilting and organizes our social circles. We also explore the garden metaphor as a practical interface to browse and manage conversations and contacts.

Proverbial Wallets
John Kestner & Daniel Leithinger
http://eco.media.mit.edu/proverbialwallets/

We have trouble controlling our consumer impulses, and there's a gap between our decisions and the consequences. When we pull a product off the shelf, do we know our bank account balance, or whether we're over budget for the month? Our existing senses are inadequate to warn us. The *Proverbial Wallet* fosters an ambient financial sense by embodying our electronically tracked assets. We provide tactile feedback reflecting account balances, spending goals and transactions as a visceral aid to responsible decision-making.

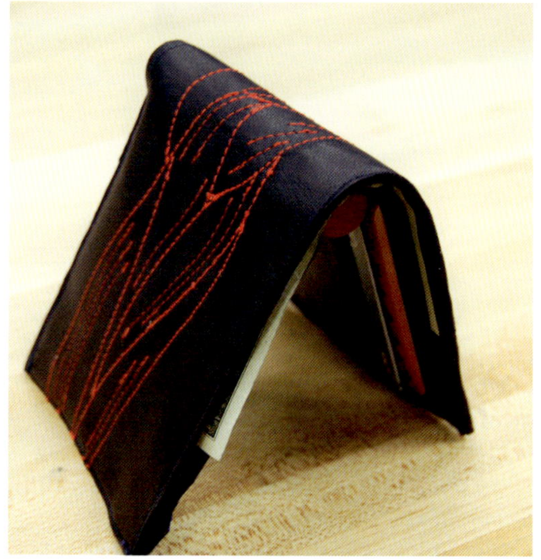

Proximeter: An ambient social navigation instrument
John Kestner
http://eco.media.mit.edu/proximeter/

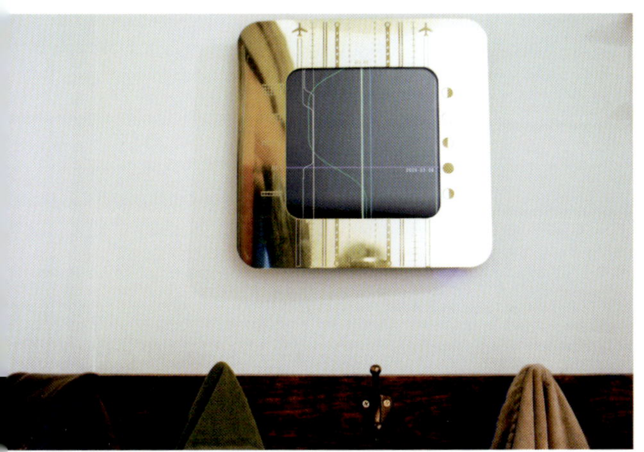

Would you know if a dear, but seldom seen, friend happened to be on the same train as you? The *Proximeter* is both an agent that tracks the past and future proximity of one's social cloud, and an instrument that charts this in an ambient display. By reading existing calendar and social network feeds of others and abstracting these into a glanceable pattern of paths, we hope to nurture within users a social proprioception and nudge them toward more face-to-face interactions when opportunities arise.

Daydar
John Kestner & Richard The

We all use systems for organizing our cluttered schedules, from the day planner to Getting Things Done. One time-honored method, if messy, is writing to-do lists. *Daydar* is a framework that makes this process social: Can you learn from the working styles of others? Can you collaboratively create an environment of healthy competition by being aware of your friends' daily accomplishments? Can this help you to find a better balance between work and play? Within this framework we are experimenting with various systems, both physical and digital, that allow you to monitor your own and others' productivity, help you to get motivated, and enable you to document and visualize the process of accomplishing whole projects.

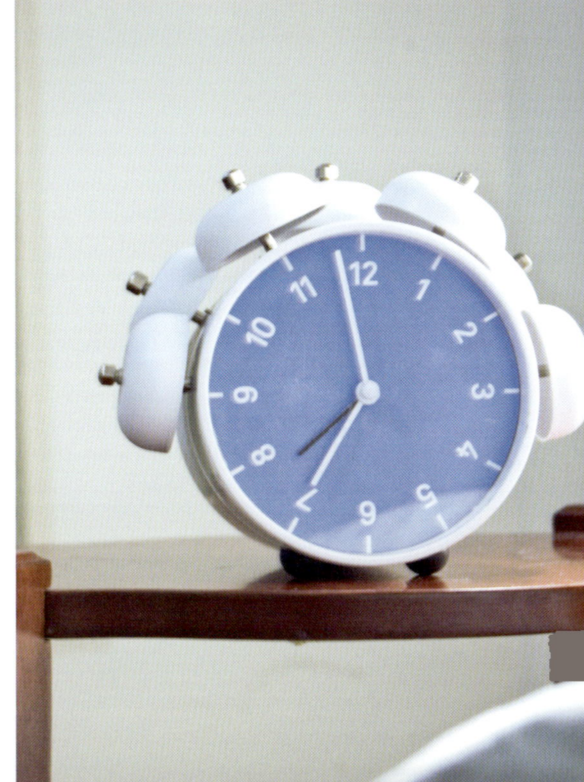

MIT Media Lab

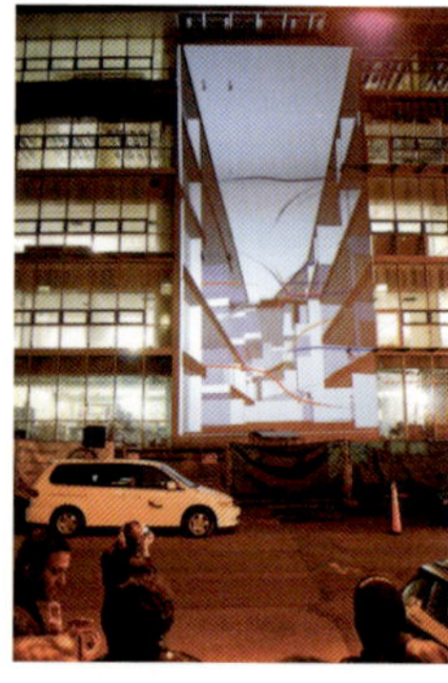

Giving Character to Characters
Richard The
http://web.media.mit.edu/~rthe/type/

In most applications using digital typography today (e.g. animation or screen display), designers rely on existing typefaces. The possibilities for altering and transforming these typefaces are exploited in many ways. What is currently not explored is another large field of typography: the dynamic, flexible and organic appearance of handwritten typography or calligraphy. This kind of typography is only brought into the digital uses such as scanning; this is because current file formats for type describe the outlines of the individual letters, not the essence/skeleton/model of a letter that we use when writing by hand. This project tries to explore the possibilities of computational and generative processes to improve and change the visual appearance of typography.

E14
Agnes Chang, Richard The, Jeffrey Warren & the Students of MAS 960

To celebrate the construction of MIT Building E14 that will be the new home of the Media Lab, *E14* is a public installation and participatory performance projected on the facade of the new building. The project seeks to capture the Media Lab community's vision for our new space and our future directions, taking into consideration the Lab's role within the Department of Architecture and Planning as well as MIT, and how the new community of E14-E15 will be the center of learning, collaboration, and innovation across all disciplines.

Cartagen
Jeffrey Warren

Cartagen is a set of tools for mapping, enabling users to view and configure live streams of geographic data in a dynamic, personally relevant way. Today's mapping software is largely based on static data sets, and neither incorporates the time dimension in its display nor provides for real-time data streams. *Cartagen* helps users to analyze and view collected and shared geographic and temporal data from multiple sources. While we live in an

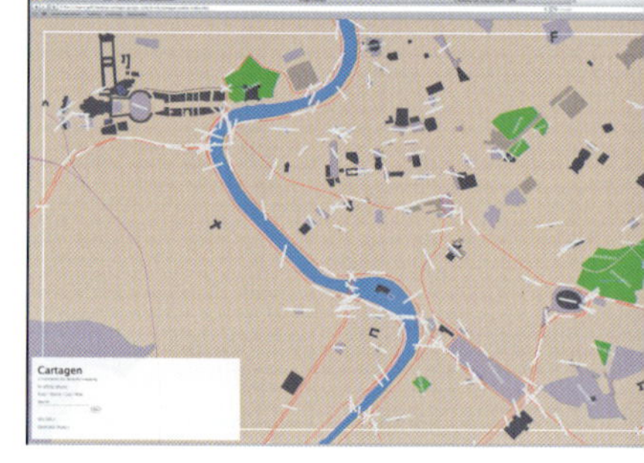

environment of real-time and temporally situated information, the mapping tools we have are not adequate for viewing, composing, or using this data. *Cartagen* uses vector-based, context-sensitive drawing methods to describe data, not merely in terms of lines and polygons, but also with adaptive use of color, movement and projection. Applications include mapping real-time air pollution, citizen reporting and disaster response.

The Loom
Richard The, Agnes Chang and Jeffrey Warren

The Loom is a participatory public installation: a digital tapestry of the virtual and real-world events in which it is situated. Visitors can "cut out" visual content from the web and collage it onto a public display wall. *The Loom* encourages collaboration among visitors, who may share a physical space or only a connection through the web. Participants' contributions will be deposited on top of one another and will accumulate over time, leaving an archaeological timeline or cyclogram of unfolding events. As the content travels to the bottom of the "fresco", it reaches the printer that continuously transfers the composition onto a large roll of paper. The printed scroll is perforated in sections and is draped across the floor so that visitors may take pieces of it home.

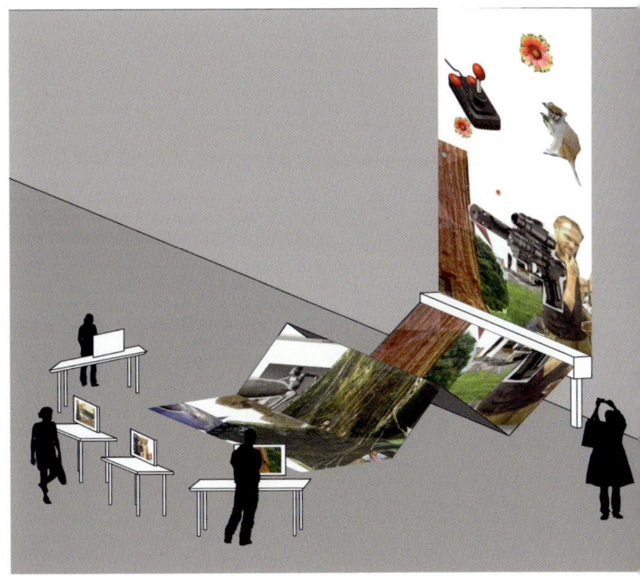

MIDE
Agnes Chang

MIDE is a programming environment that proposes a new way for artists and designers to visualize, edit and manipulate interactive software. It enables the user to define a conceptual visual representation to complement the traditional text-based representation of the users' code. The interface is designed to facilitate fluid transitions between different modes of computational representation and different levels of representational detail, with the goal of making software a more accessible and expressive medium for designers and artists.

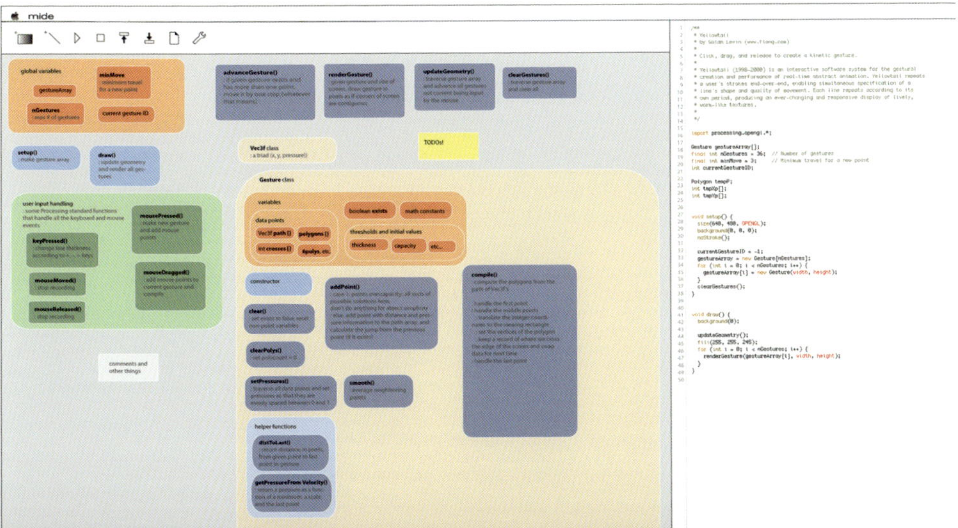

Christa Sommerer, Laurent Mignonneau, Dietmar Offenhuber,
Michaela Ortner, Varvara Guljajeva

The Royal Interface Culture Masquerade Ball

DIY Style Interaction Projects
Interface Cultures Student Projects at Ars Electronica 2009

This year's student projects from the Interface Cultures study department show a variety of interactive projects and prototypes that have been developed in the past study year. Topics circle around interactive art, audio-visual installations, wearable technology projects, gaming interfaces, information visualization and conceptual works. Weibel states in 2008: "Artists, in the age of Youtube.com, Flickr.com, MySpace.com, and Second Life, lose their monopoly on creativity. Using contemporary media everyone can be artistically creative."[1] In our department we can observe a strong movement in the direction of do-it-yourself (=DIY) style interface projects. Artists and designers here often engage in short-time collaborations and share their code and interface designs on the Internet with a peer community. We however also observe a trend towards more traditional notions of art where the idea is to create unique pieces of interactive art that convey a strong artistic and conceptual message. It is within this dichotomy of the totally open and the rather closed system that we have to see the works presented in this year's student exhibition.

For the format of the exhibition organization we have chosen to use the metaphor of DIY all the way. Students not only manage their own projects but also collaboratively organize the exhibition design, the curational direction, the flyers, posters and promotional materials. As an exhibition theme, the topic of "The Royal Interface Culture Masquerade Ball" was chosen by the students. From red carpets to Victorian-style frames, white 'theatre' masks worn around the exhibition (= the ball) by the visitors, to evening wear worn by students. This year's theme is to juxtapose modern technology with an old-style ball set-up to create a somewhat opulent atmosphere where new and old meet. The outcome of this exhibition is a learning process in itself. It should sensitize students to how complex it is to create scenarios for the presentation of interactive projects, which challenge the audience in areas such as art, scenography and interaction design. As hosts of The 1st Inaugural Royal Interface Culture Ball we invite you to experience opulent spaces, art, performance and anonymity.

**Christa Sommerer, Laurent Mignonneau, Dietmar Offenhuber,
Michaela Ortner, Varvara Guljajeva**

The Royal Interface Culture Masquerade Ball

**Do-It-Yourself-Interaktionsprojekte von Studierenden des Studiengangs
Interface Cultures bei der Ars Electronica 2009**

Die diesjährige Studentenpräsentation des Studiengangs Interface Cultures zeigt eine Auswahl im letzten Studienjahr entwickelter interaktiver Projekte und Prototypen. Diese umfassen interaktive Kunst, audiovisuelle Installationen, Wearable-Technology-Projekte, Spielinterfaces, Informationsvisualisierungen und konzeptuelle Arbeiten. Laut Peter Weibel verlieren „Künstler im Zeitalter von Youtube.com. Flickr.com, MySpace.com und Second Life ihr Kreativitätsmonopol. Mit zeitgenössischen Medien kann jeder künstlerisch kreativ sein."[1] An unserem Institut ist eine starke Tendenz zu Interfaceprojekten im Do-it-yourself-Stil zu bemerken. Die Künstler und Designer gehen oft kurzfristige Kooperationen ein und tauschen ihre Codes und Interfacedesigns über das Netz mit einer Gemeinschaft Gleichgesinnter aus. Wir beobachten allerdings zugleich einen Trend zu einer traditionelleren Kunstauffassung mit dem Ziel, einzigartige interaktive Werke mit einer starken künstlerischen und konzeptuellen Aussage zu schaffen. Die Arbeiten in der diesjährigen Studentenausstellung bewegen sich im Spannungsfeld dieser Dichotomie von total offenen und eher geschlossenen Systemen.
Der Ausstellungsgestaltung haben wir jedoch durchgehend die Do-it-yourself-Metapher zugrunde gelegt. Die Studierenden erarbeiten nicht nur ihre eigenen Projekte, sondern kümmern sich auch gemeinsam um Ausstellungsdesign, kuratorische Leitlinie, Flyer, Plakate und Werbematerial. Als Ausstellungsthema wählten die Studierenden „The Royal Interface Culture Masquerade Ball". Dieser thematische Bogen spannt sich von roten Teppichen zu viktorianischen Bilderrahmen, von weißen Theatermasken, die Besucher auf der Ausstellung (dem Ball) tragen müssen, bis zur Abendkleidung, in der die Studierenden auftreten. Mit diesem Thema wird die moderne Technik in ein altmodisches Ballambiente gestellt und eine opulente Atmosphäre für die Begegnung von Alt und Neu erzeugt. Man ist aufgefordert, sich auf eine nie endende Maskerade einzulassen und in den eigenen Wünschen zu verfangen. Der zentrale Ausstellungsraum bietet Festivalgästen einen Ort der Erholung, wo man sich an prunkvollen Tischen und auf ebensolchen Stühlen niederlassen kann und den ganzen Tag über Performances geboten bekommt. Mit dieser Ausstellung ist ein Lernprozess verbunden. Er soll den Studierenden ein Gefühl dafür vermitteln, was für ein komplexer Vorgang die Erstellung eines Szenarios für die Präsentation interaktiver Projekte ist, eines Szenarios, das sein Publikum künstlerisch, szenografisch und interaktionsgestalterisch herausfordert. Als Gastgeber des „1st Inaugural Royal Interface Culture Ball" laden wir ein, in unsere Prunkräume zu kommen und die Kunst, die Performances und die Anonymität zu genießen.

---

1 Peter Weibel, *YOU_niverse*, Ausstellungskatalog, Sevilla: Bienal de Arte Contemporaneo de Sevilla, Fundacionbiacs 2008, S. 16-26

(Aus dem Englischen von Wilfried Prantner)

WEARABLE TECHNOLOGY PROJECTS

Der Überflieger—Wearable Interfaces for Spy Pigeons
Andreas Zingerle

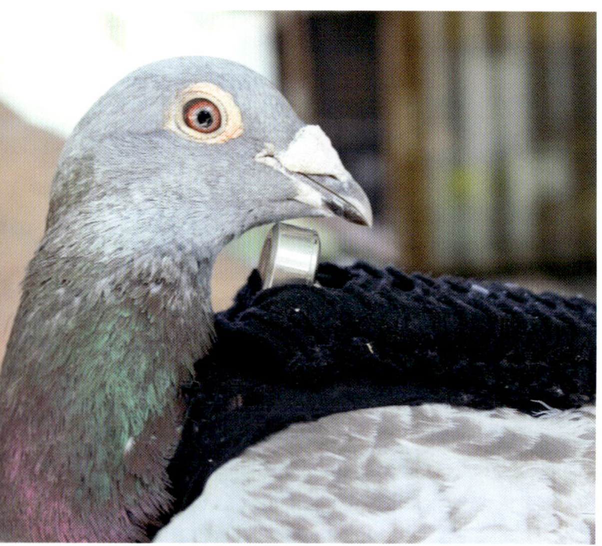

http://www.derueberflieger.com
http://www.andreaszingerle.com
Der Überflieger-Wearable Interface are wearables for spy pigeons. The project deals with the design and implementation of a wearable technology for carrier pigeons. The experimental setup allows the user to follow the flight path of a pigeon (with GPS and digital photography from its place of release back to the loft. With the project and the use of standard technology, *Der Überflieger* is a tool for people to use surveillance as a counter-performance to reflect, mirror and disorient organisations that normally have the power to observe public and private life. The documentation shows the design process and the test flights that were carried out in April 2009 in the area of Graz, Austria.

Parangonet 1.0: sonic dimension
Ricardo Nascimento

This project aims to recreate the original concept of the *Parangolé* by the Brazilian artist Hélio Oiticica. It is composed of three wearable sculptures which, through its movement in space, create and broadcast sound samples that refer to the Brazilian artistic movement called "Tropicalis" and other cultures. Each interactive garment is able to trigger and modify a different sound input. When performed together they create a sonic atmosphere that represents the cultural agglutination proposed by the tropicalists, transposing its fundamental concept, which is the mixing of cultures, to our days. A monitored dialog between the pieces and controlled by the user creates a transcultural dialog constructed between different worlds and backgrounds.

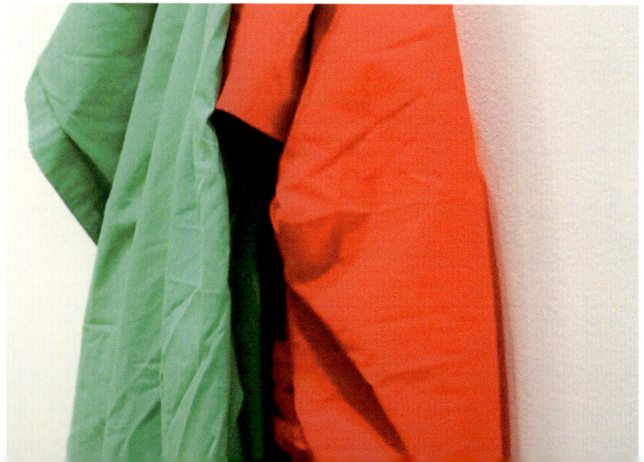

INFORMATION VISUALISATION PROJECTS

Newsshaper
Mahir Yavuz, Javier Lloret

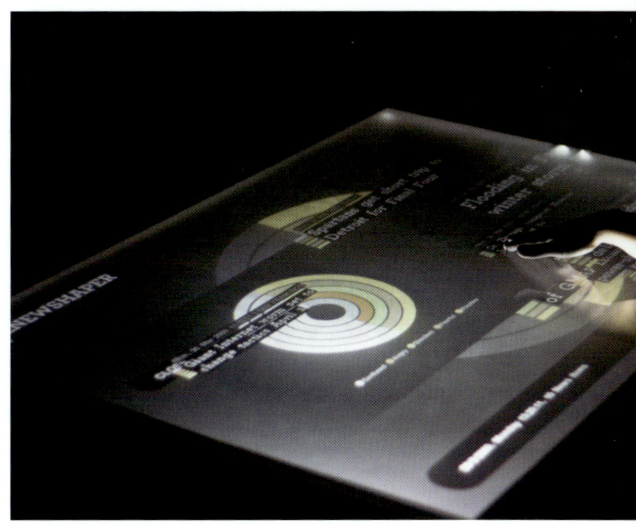

Newsshaper is a tabletop interactive system that deals with the re-contextualization of daily news items gathered from live news feeds. It allows users to create their own relational networks and 'maps' based on actual live news streamed from the Internet. Due to the dynamic nature of live data streams, the system constantly creates different content for users and due to manipulations made by the users it generates different visual results of the same content. In a more general sense, users of the *Newsshaper* system shape their own reality and perception about the daily news and share their emotional news-scape with other users. Most of the time, mass media sources deliver the daily news in a certain context. This context creates a meta-meaning which usually affects the simple meaning of the news. Thus, by tagging, by categorizing, by geo-locating, by making it popular or unpopular, mass media manipulates the perception of the daily news. *Newsshaper* allows users to break these pre-defined structures delivered by the source.

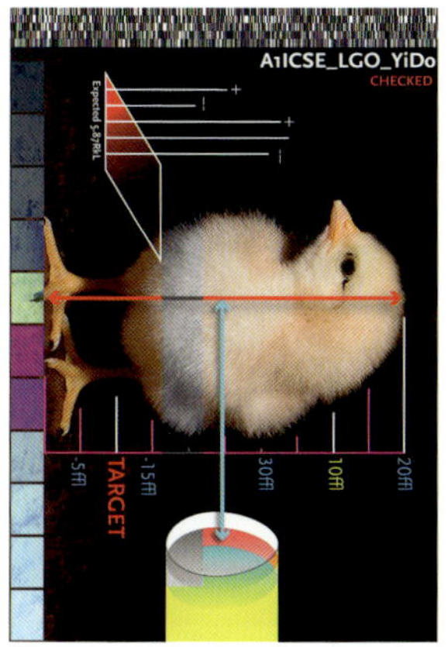

The Society of The Spectacle
Tim Devine

Incubation of a fertilised chicken egg begins on the 16th of August at 37.5 C° with a humidity of 60%. On the 3rd of September the humidity will be set to 85%. If the temperature or humidity changes too much for too long during the following three days this could be fatal to the egg. By looking at the egg you will cut off the power from the incubator.
Saturday the 5th of September 2009 marks the end of the expected gestation period for a chicken egg: a chick should hatch at some point during this day. From Sunday 6th the incubator will continue to nurture either an egg that is past gestation with no chance of life, or a baby chick.

Glific
Jayme Cochrane, Anika Hirt, Travis Kirton

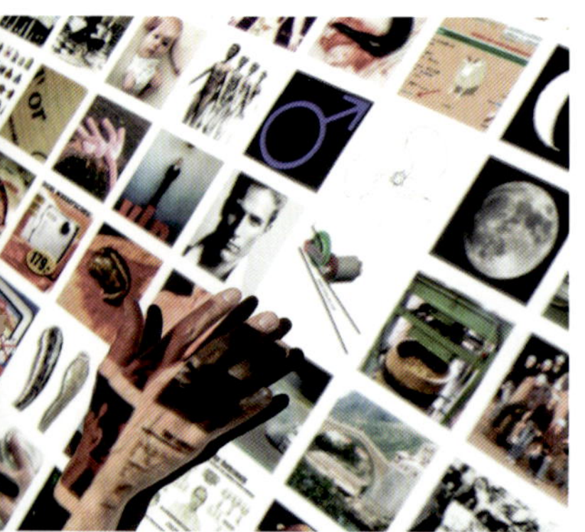

The concept of *GLIFIC* is a reversal of contemporary trends in web-based media, whereby the concept of tagging media is transformed back onto itself. Rather than tagging images, video, and content with words like Flickr, Delicious, and other social bookmarking sites, we use media (primarily images) to tag words themselves. Instead of tagging one photo with a dozen words, we seek to tag one word with a dozen images. At any given point the word AUTOMOBILE could have tens of different visual representations. Using images as tags we then rebuild narratives, news and events by replacing the words in their text.

Narratives, news and current events are translated back into a glyphic form that breaks language barriers through the re:symbolization of communication. Obama's inauguration speech, C.S. Lewis' *Alice in Wonderland*, or the continuous stream of news feeds from sources like Al Jazeera or The New York Times can be written backwards from their linguistic forms into pictographic reinterpretations.

AUDIO INSTALLATION

Couch surfing / Vergence 感應
Louis Erwin Lee, Mauro Arrighi

In Chinese, 感 means "to feel"; 應 means "to respond". Both of the characters are based on the same sign: 心 "heart". Three participants will be invited to sit on a customized couch surrounded by the spatial sound interface that generates and synthesizes real-time designed sounds according to their individual heart rate variability. Due to personal perceptual psychology and the autonomic nervous system, the outer sound field can also dynamically influence the participants' heart beat rate. After several minutes, their heartbeats might be synchronous, or chaotic. This would lead to a different, unexpected emotional and physical condition. This is similar to the way human communities are formed with different ideologies and culture.

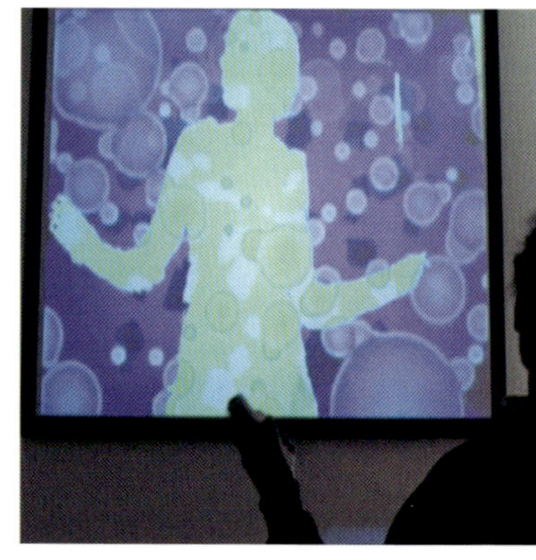

INTERACTIVE GAMES

Hello Kitty Davenport
Vintage Gaming Project
Mauro Arrighi, Irmgard Reiter,
Gregor Göttfert

The Old Interface Culture's Black Sofa becomes a new gaming interface. A second hand gaming console is connected to capacitive sensors that enable the visitors to play the game *Hello Kitty World* in a new mode. Three players sit down on the sofa. They have to practice coordination by verbal and nonverbal communication to move quickly in order to control the character's actions in the game. More visitors gather round the sofa to watch their performance and the game itself, which is displayed on a screen in front of them. The sofa interface is decorated in Hello Kitty style.

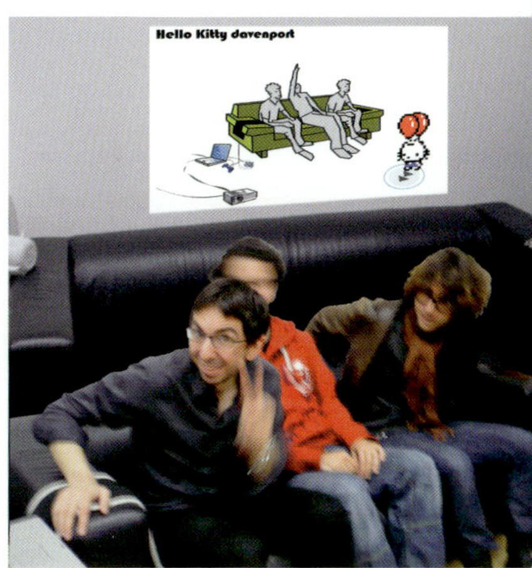

CONCEPTUAL INTERACTION

Scratch It
Jesus Cabrera Hernandez

The project aspires to question the structure of media, globalization and the individual perception of Art and Society on two sides of the world. A series of interviews and footage on the theme of Information, Media Art and Society will be recorded in Cuba, a country with an environment in which the access to the media is limited. This footage will be projected in Linz, Austria during the Ars Electronica Festival, bringing to this event the points of view on art, technology, information and society that Cuban citizens have. This is an attempt to reflect on the meaning of these terms in different societies. A screen will be made and covered with a silver rub-off surface. As people scratch part of it they uncover the projection of the Cuban footage. The metaphor of the necessity to deconstruct the information that the media transmit to us will be reflected—with the interaction of different users the big picture can be revealed. A separation between the two worlds will be made and the necessity of simple approaches to complex subjects. The idea of global human nature is countered with the answer of coming back to a simple natural interface, like scratching a surface with our hands and a coin, claiming as a metaphor to understand and deconstruct broad concepts like information art and society.

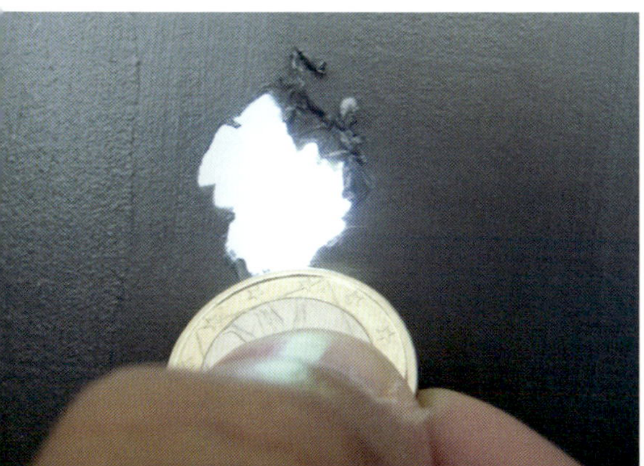

353

9.578 Files
Anika Hirt, Margit Blauhut

What is digital data and where does it go after being deleted? *9.578 Files* explores trashed and lost digital data and investigates our nascent naïveté in handling data and its storage media. By contrast it questions the possible loss of data due to digitalization and fast developing technology. Digital data from various collected media are recovered and restored. A visual memory is created out of the forgotten and discarded data that failed to be destroyed and succeeded to survive. The interaction with trashed hard drives visualizes the ease of accessing this data and pushes it back into the real world.

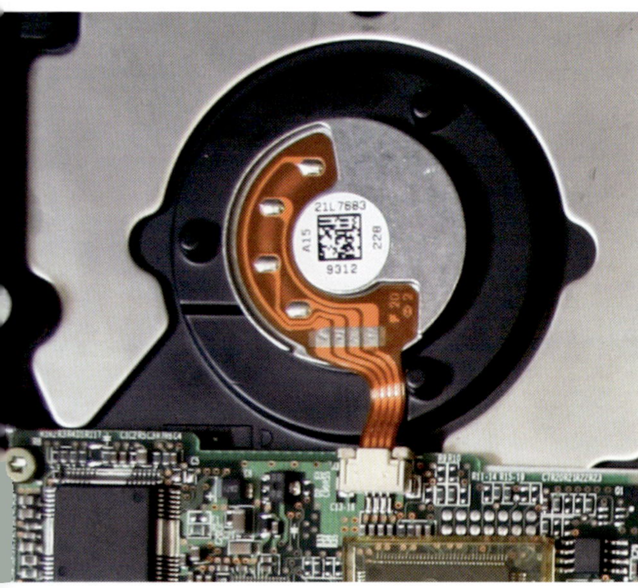

Experiment Arctic
Varvara Guljajeva, Mar Canet Sola, Andrej Boleslavsky, Kanno So

Experiment Arctic is a new media art installation that talks about global warming and its consequences. The current artwork differs from the other works in this field by its temporality. A piece of ice that is placed on the special table is allowed to melt in order to visualize the real situation that exists in the Arctic Sea. The water from the melting ice controls videos that are projected onto the top of ice and table. Visuals are about global warming, the shrinking ice in the North Pole and how they correspond to different water levels. Thus, the work aims to shake us up and raise our awareness and to experiment with a new and temporal medium like ice. Supported by the Asia-Europe Foundation.

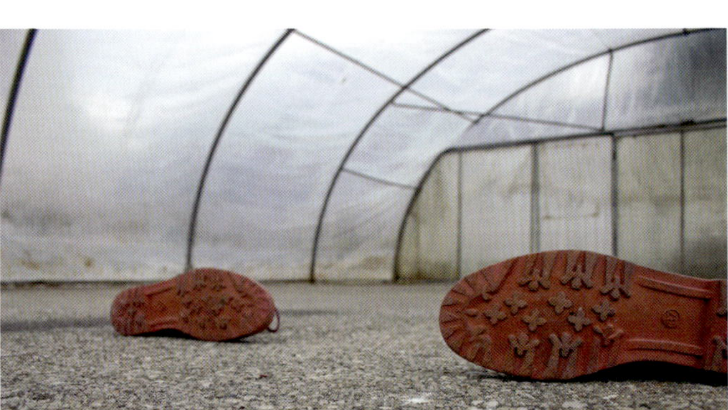

World 2020
Mar Canet, Dietmar Suoch, Timm Wilks,
Marcin Wodzyński, Marc Atanes

World 2020 is an interactive post-catastrophic landscape installation. In the year 2020 planet Earth has become a place that is almost impossible to live in, following radical climatic changes due to the effects of the continuous exploitation of resources and the high level of pollution. Several scientists have made very dramatic predictions for the next hundred years. For example, the renowned British physicist Stephen Hawking recently predicted the colonization of Mars by *2046* in order for mankind to survive. The installation *World 2020* opens a window into the future of this imaginary world. It is an immersive real-time generated scene showing where humanity just can't live anymore. Instead people live underground and the installation represents a vantage point to the Earth's surface. The audience has to wear special security goggles before they get offered a glimpse at three different scenarios of the world in *2020*. This project tries to make an impact on the public by showing a possible future scenario about our current home planet.

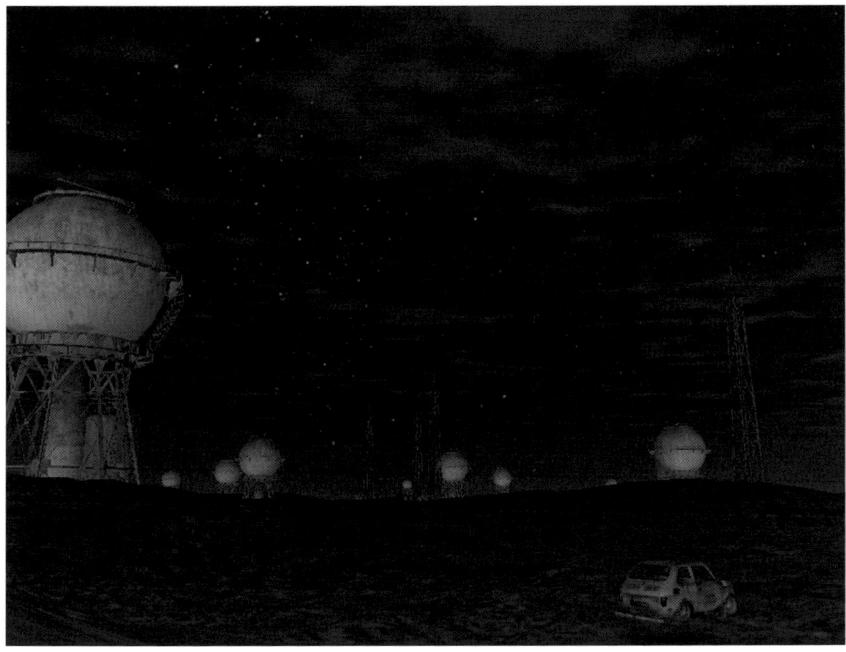

Markus Wintersberger

fhSPACE. Social media environment teaching and documentation

The St. Pölten University of Applied Sciences' Media Technology bachelor's program and Telecommunications and Media master's program will be represented at Ars Electronica this September when the international elite of media art and media technology convenes once again in Linz—this time in conjunction with the festival's 30th anniversary. A highly committed interdisciplinary team that also includes a few undergraduates from the Social Work and Media Management bachelor's program is hosting a transdisciplinary-integrative media lab September 3–8 in Linz's Brucknerhaus. Here, staffers will make their editorial decisions, edit content accordingly and forward the results to various transmission interfaces.

"Human Nature", the theme of this year's 30th anniversary festival, provides some interesting points of reference for the *fhSPACE* team (*fh* stands for *Fachhochschule*, a polytechnic college) since the retrospective look in comparison to a consideration of the way things stand today can be the basis for a very interesting and fruitful process of reflection. Over the last 30 years, media technology applications have completely pervaded the world in which we live. This has occurred so rapidly that it's actually necessary to step back, pause and intensely reflect on this phenomenon for a while. Members of this institution's student body belong to an age group that has grown up during this period; accordingly, they're completely familiar with these facts and circumstances, and capable of dealing with the complex structures of the media sphere in a positive, future-oriented way.

An all-encompassing flow of data envelops us and links us up to an information network that is updated and refreshed by the millisecond. An invisible fabric enwraps us, spinning about us its cocoon of images, signs, tones, times, spaces, thoughts and memories. The presence of this fabric is already quite apparent though, on account of its permanence, it's regarded by many as a potent threat. The cognizance of all these facts and circumstances enables us, in turn, to undertake a process of reflection on our own, to gain insights into that which has eluded our perception up to now, and to critically consider both our own standpoints and those of others.

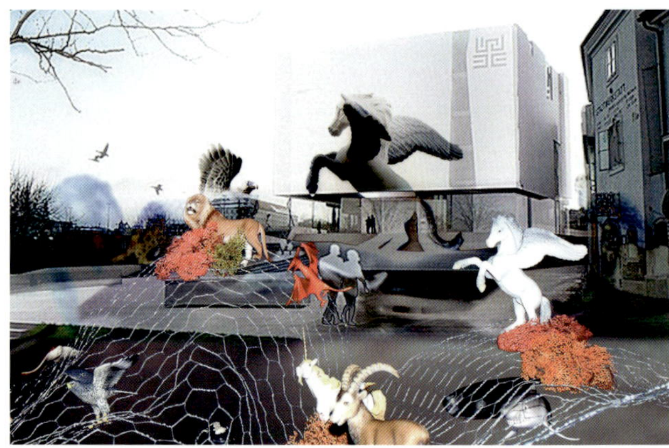

From the perspective of an interdisciplinary institution of higher education like the St. Pölten University of Applied Sciences, imbuing students with these principles is a key driving force within a program of wide-ranging academic activities, at the core of which is precisely this simultaneity—considering the past while looking forward to the future. This imagined portal of recognition in whose midst students find themselves must be

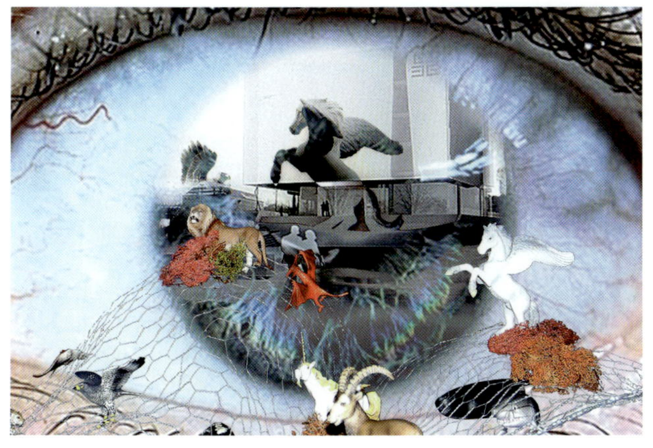

subtly supported by the faculty and administration, and responsibly translated into a form that is commensurate to the times in which we live so that its end result can be understanding within the context of our rapidly changing world. Accordingly, what's called for is an unflagging will to implement change and a corresponding readiness within structured institutions to do things in a new way in order to be able to keep pace with the constant change that characterizes modern-day reality. One of the main tasks that goes into accomplishing this is coming up with interesting pedagogical methods that are appropriate to the society that is taking shape amidst a practically holographic configuration of information.

A broad spectrum of educational and research projects developed and implemented in cooperation with extramural partners has enabled the St. Pölten University of Applied Sciences to impart a feeling for this to students, and to vividly and concretely get across to them the theoretical positions I have elaborated above.

It is precisely the integration of undergraduate teams in real production processes—as is being done in such exemplary fashion in conjunction with the 2009 Ars Electronica Festival—that creates a luxurious live presence and thereby effectuates an almost direct mediation of content—this material doesn't have to be offered; in this context, it virtually offers itself. Thus, the domain of academic instruction opens itself up to the real world; the discrete, institutional space is expanded into the public realm, and is made accessible to and comprehensible by many individuals. Learning as a process of communicating content in the public sphere thereby becomes a transparent manifestation of art in public.

Students, researchers and teachers showcase what they're capable of in an effort to thereby get across what they're trying to accomplish.

fhSPACE. Social media environment teaching and documentation
work in progress *http://www.okto.tv/fhctv*

fhSPACE TEAM
Alois Huber, Thiemo Kastel, Krzysztof Ludwinski, Hannes Raffaseder, Markus Seidl, Markus Wintersberger in collaboration with Christian Müller, Sarah Rosenwald, Alexander Kiflom, Martin Grubinger, Isabella Wagner, Thomas Tröger, Edin Karadza, Johanna Burgstaller, Kerstin Blumenstein, Andreas Wimmer, Elisabeth Schneider, Olivia Mayrzett and others.

http://www.fhstp.ac.at
http://www.campusfernsehen.at
http://www.campusradio.at
http://www.youtube.com/user/fhSPACEtv

Markus Wintersberger

fhSPACE. Social media environment teaching and documentation

Die FH St. Pölten ist mit den Studiengängen Medientechnik (Bachelor) und Telekommunikation und Medien (Master) auch diesmal wieder aktiv präsent, wenn sich im September in Linz im Rahmen der Ars Electronica, die heuer ihr 30-jähriges Jubiläum feiert, die internationale Spitze der Medienkunst und Medientechnik einfindet. Ein engagiertes, interdisziplinär agierendes Team, bei dem auch einige Studierende aus den Studiengängen Soziale Arbeit und Medienmanagement mitwirken, hat vom 3. bis 8. September ihr transdisziplinär-integratives Medienlabor im Brucknerhaus Linz eingerichtet. Von dort aus werden redaktionelle Entscheidungen getroffen, Berichte einsichtig geschnitten und auch auf diverse Sendeflächen übertragen.

Das diesjährige Festivalthema „Human Nature" in Kombination mit dem 30-jährigen Jubiläum liefert spannende Anknüpfungspunkte für das *fhSPACE*-Team, da der Blick zurück in Relation zum Blick auf das Heute Grundlage einer sehr fruchtbaren und auch spannenden Reflexion sein kann. Gerade in den letzten 30 Jahren ist eine allumfassende Durchdringung und Durchmischung unserer Lebenswelt mit medientechnologischen Anwendungen vor sich gegangen. Dies hat sich in einer derart rasanten Geschwindigkeit vollzogen, so dass es nötig ist, sich dessen auch immer wieder gewahr zu werden, innezuhalten und den Blick konzentriert diesen Phänomenen zuzuwenden. Die Studierenden selbst sind aufgrund ihrer Altersstruktur in dem konkreten Zeitfenster der letzten 30 Jahre aufgewachsen, sind mit diesen Bedingungen nahezu „evolutionär" vertraut und deshalb befähigt, mit dieser komplexen Medienweltstruktur positiv zukunftsgerichtet umzugehen.

Der uns allumfassend umgebende Datenstrom ist existent, durchwebt und vernetzt uns in jeder Millisekunde mit neuen Informationen. Ein unsichtbares Gewebe umspinnt uns, spinnt uns nahezu ein in einen Kokon aus Bildern, Zeichen, Zahlen, Tönen, Zeiten, Räumen, Gedanken und Erinnerungen. Dieses Gewebe ist einerseits bereits massiv spürbar und wird andererseits aufgrund seiner Permanenz vielerorts als starke Bedrohung empfunden. Die Bewusstheit all dieser Tatsachen befähigt uns wiederum zu eigenständiger Reflexion, Einsicht in bis jetzt uneinsichtige

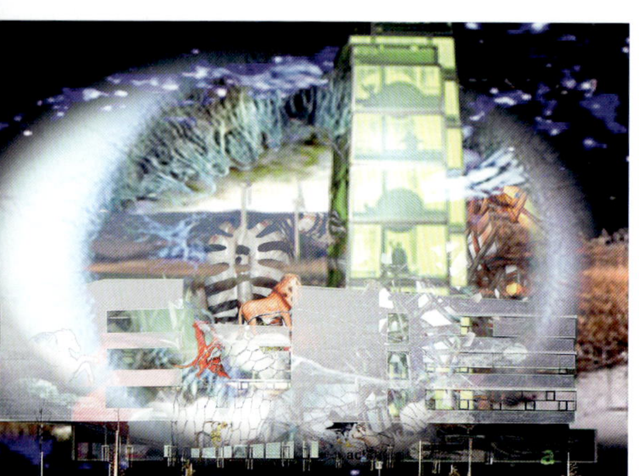

Prozesse sowie kritische Reflexion des eigenen als auch des jeweils anderen Standpunkts.

Dies zu vermitteln ist aus Sicht einer universitären und interdisziplinär agierenden Institution, wie sie die FH St. Pölten darstellt, wichtiger Antrieb und Motor innerhalb einer weiträumigen Lehr- und Lernzentrifuge, in deren Zentrum eben diese Gleichzeitigkeit eines Blicks zurück in die Vergangenheit und nach vorwärts gerichtet in die Zukunft steht. Dieses imaginierte Erkenntnisportal, in dessen Mittelpunkt die Studierenden sich befinden, muss subtil vom Lehrgebäude getragen und auch verantwortungsbewusst in eine zeitadäquate Form übersetzt werden, damit die

Verständlichkeit innerhalb der sich rasant veränderten Gegenwart gegeben bleibt. Es bedarf daher eines stetigen Veränderungswillens und einer dementsprechenden Bereitschaft zur Veränderung innerhalb strukturierter Institutionen, um sich überhaupt noch an einer aktuellen Variable von Realität zu messen. Eine der Hauptaufgaben liegt darin, daraus die richtigen und auch spannenden Vermittlungsschritte für eine in diesem nahezu holografischen Informationsbild heranwachsende Gesellschaft zu finden.

Vielfältige mit externen Partnern entwickelte und umgesetzte Projekte in Lehre und Forschung ermöglichen es der FH St. Pölten, den Studierenden ein Gefühl davon zu vermitteln und anschaulich zu machen, was ich zuvor in meinem Text als theoretische Behauptung aufzustellen versucht habe.

Gerade die Anwesenheit von Studierendenteams in realen Produktionsabläufen, wie es im Rahmen der Ars Electronica 2009 exemplarisch der Fall ist, schafft eine luxuriöse Live-Präsenz und dadurch eine nahezu direkte Vermittlung von Inhalten, die nicht mehr angeboten werden müssen, sondern sich in diesen Zusammenhängen nahezu von selbst anbieten. Der Lehrraum öffnet sich somit hin zur Realität, der geschlossene, institutionelle Raum wird in den öffentlichen Raum erweitert und für viele Personen zugänglich und einsichtig gemacht. Lernen als Vermittlungsprozess im öffentlichen Raum wird damit zu einer transparenten Erscheinung von Kunst im öffentlichen Raum.

Lehre, Forschung und Vermittlung produziert und zeigt sich.

Lehre, Forschung und Vermittlung versucht sich dadurch wieder verständlich zu machen.

fhSPACE. Social media environment teaching and documentation. Work in progress *http://www.okto.tv/fhctv*

fhSPACE TEAM
Alois Huber, Thiemo Kastel, Krzysztof Ludwinski, Hannes Raffaseder, Markus Seidl, Markus Wintersberger in Zusammenarbeit mit Christian Müller, Sarah Rosenwald, Alexander Kiflom, Martin Grubinger, Isabella Wagner, Thomas Tröger, Edin Karadza, Johanna Burgstaller, Kerstin Blumenstein, Andreas Wimmer, Elisabeth Schneider, Olivia Mayrzett u. a.
http://www.fhstp.ac.at, http://www.campusfernsehen.at, http://www.campusradio.at.
http://www.youtube.com/user/fhSPACEtv

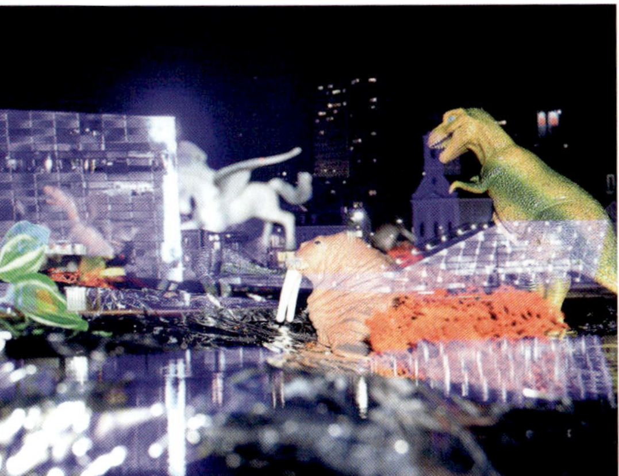
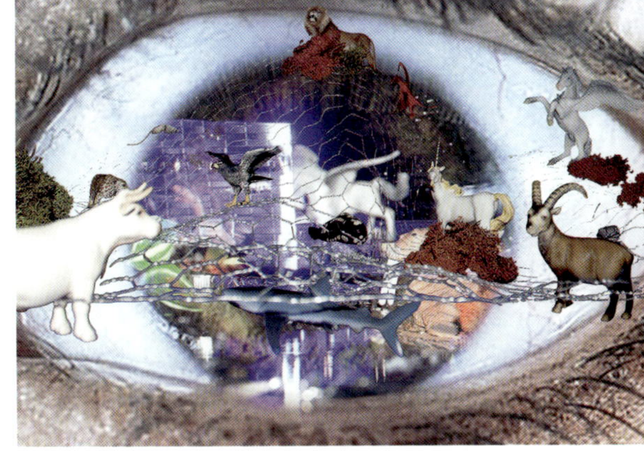

Background

There are vast fields on the boundary between Art and Society, and these fields have been created mainly by persons who are not artists in the traditional sense. Animation, Manga and Game, etc. have appeared on the social stage, become widely popular and been developed. In Japan, the boom of *Space Invaders* in 1978 and the launching of *Family Computer* in 1986 had a great influence on society. This influence can also be seen in Japanese media art works. If one of the roles of media art in our age of evolutional technology is to make a connection between technology, society and art, can we say that computer games play the same role as media art? The *Japan Media Arts Festival* in Linz, *JAPAN GAME*, focuses on an aspect of entertainment in Japanese media arts. The selected award-winning game works of the *Japan Media Arts Festival* are exhibited. All the games—a variety of Sports, Music and Adventure, etc. are playable. During the evenings, the tournaments of the games will be shown on a huge screen. We hope the audience will enjoy and focus on the artistic expression and the similarity to media art of the games.

Japan Media Arts Festival

The *Japan Media Arts Festival* has been an annual event in Tokyo since 1997 and this year the 13th festival will take place. The festival awards prizes for creative works in the fields of art, entertainment, animation and manga. Regarding the previous festival, the total number of submissions was 2,146 works and the visitors of the award-winning works exhibition reached 55,234 people. At the beginning, the contest was intended for the Japanese, but the overseas applicants have increased with each passing year and recently we have consistently received submissions from over 40 counties and regions. We can say that the *Japan Media Arts Festival*

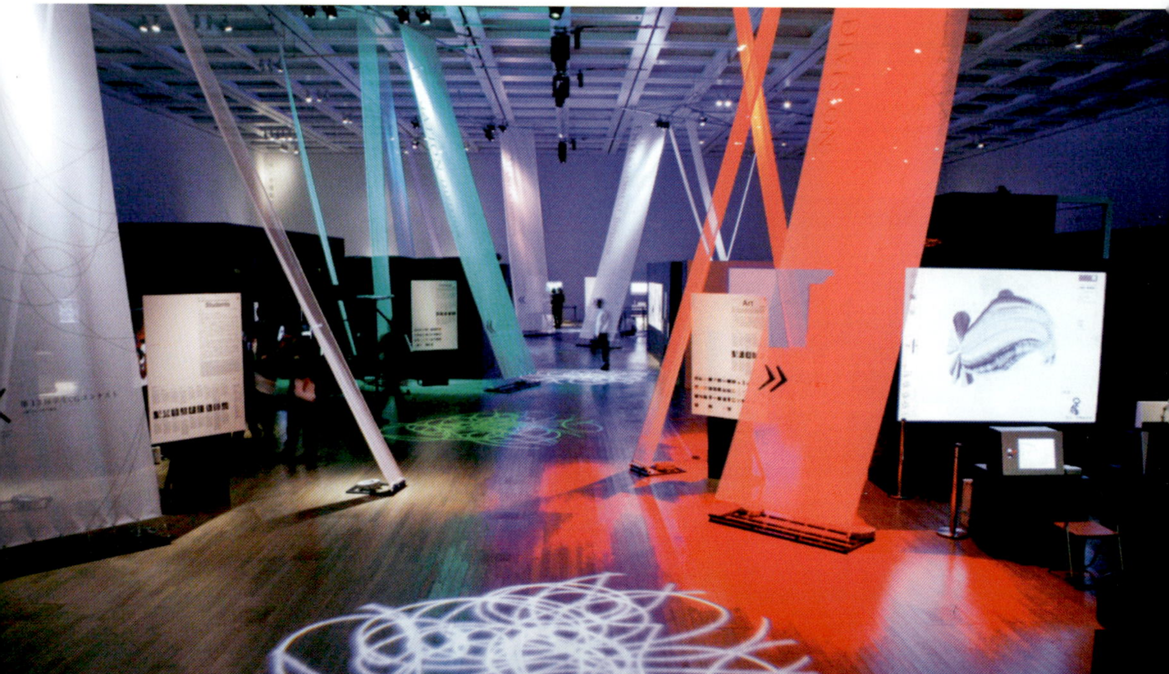

has grown into an international festival. Briefly the *Japan Media Arts Festival* has two aims. One is to designate new frames and values of culture in accordance with the changing times, without clinging on to existing cultural hierarchies. Therefore, we appreciate not only media art, but also animation, manga and entertainment works such as games.

Secondly, we help new expression and culture to take root in general and grow with the progress of digital communication technique and technology. It may be deemed that new culture is disconnected from traditional culture, but the Japan Media Arts Festival has tried to close this gap. We think that this activity helps to develop originality in a new field of culture.
Ars Electronica and the *Japan Media Arts Festival* have had a good cooperative relationship since 2003 and have maintained energetic activities in Linz and Tokyo. The *Japan Media Arts Festival* has both learned a lot from and been inspired by *Ars Electronica*.
It is a great honor to hold the exhibition of the *Japan Media Arts Festival* in Linz for the 30th memorable anniversary of *Ars Electronica*. And this is the first-time exhibition in Europe for the *Japan Media Arts Festival*.

The 13th Japan Media Arts Festival
Application Period: 16 July—25 September 2009
The 13th Award-winning Works Exhibition: 3—14 February 2010 at The National Art Center, Tokyo.

JAPAN GAME
The Mobile Ö1 Atelier at the 2009 Ars Electronica Festival
In cooperation with the Japan Media Arts Festival, Tokyo

The Mobile Ö1 Atelier has been designed especially to serve as a center of public dialog. It offers visitors the opportunity to engage in direct communication and reflection. Plus, there's a special entertainment feature this year—a presentation of Japanese media art in the field of game design.
The Mobile Ö1 Atelier set up on Linz's Hauptplatz will showcase prizewinning works from the Japan Media Arts Festival. Visitors are invited to get active and try these games out for themselves. You'll see how much contemporary media art and game design influence one another and overlap to such a great extent that it's thoroughly justifiable to call this an artform in its own right.
Radio Österreich 1 will focus on "Human Nature," the theme of this 30th Ars Electronica Festival. How are people portrayed in these game worlds? Are modes of behavior and the tasks players have to accomplish ethically acceptable? What changes are the perception and design of landscapes and architecture undergoing? How do we behave in virtual parallel worlds? Can art create completely new realities, or do we just repeatedly return to old, familiar experiential spaces?
Every evening, visitors can put their gameplaying skills to the test in tournaments conducted on a jumbo format: giant projection surfaces around the Mobile Ö1 Atelier on Linz's Main Square.

Mobile Ö1 Atelier
September 3—8, 2009, Hauptplatz Linz

Hintergrund

Weite Räume im Graubereich zwischen Kunst und Gesellschaft werden in erster Linie von Menschen geschaffen, die nicht als Künstler im herkömmlichen Sinn gelten. So sind Animation, Manga, Spiele usw. auf der gesellschaftlichen Bühne erschienen, wurden immer beliebter und entwickelten sich ständig weiter. In Japan hatten der Boom von *Space Invaders* im Jahr 1978 und das Erscheinen des Nintendo Family Computer im Jahr 1986 einen großen gesellschaftlichen Einfluss. Dies macht sich auch in den Werken der japanischen Medienkunst bemerkbar. Wenn in unserer Zeit der Entwicklungstechnologie die Medienkunst als Bindeglied zwischen Technologie, Gesellschaft und Kunst fungiert – kann man dann behaupten, Computerspiele spielen die gleiche Rolle wie die Medienkunst?

Die Ausstellung *JAPAN GAME* in Linz widmet sich dem Unterhaltungsaspekt der japanischen Medienkunst und präsentiert eine Auswahl an preisgekrönten Arbeiten aus der Kategorie Spiele. Sämtliche Spiele – sei es aus Sport, Musik, Abenteuer usw. – kann man auch tatsächlich ausprobieren. So werden in der Nacht Wettkämpfe ausgetragen und auf einem großen Bildschirm übertragen. Wir wünschen den Besuchern viel Spaß und hoffen, ihnen anhand der Vielzahl künstlerischer Ausdrucksformen die Nähe der Spiele zu medienkünstlerischen Arbeiten vor Augen führen zu können.

Japan Media Arts Festival

Das seit 1997 in Tokio stattfindende Japan Media Arts Festival geht 2009 in seine dreizehnte Runde. Im Rahmen des Festivals werden alljährlich kreative Arbeiten aus den Bereichen Kunst, Unterhaltung, Animation und Manga prämiert. Bisher wurden insgesamt 2.146 Beiträge eingereicht und 55.234 BesucherInnen gezählt. Was anfangs als rein japanischer Wettbewerb konzipiert war, entwickelte sich im Lauf der Jahre angesichts der kontinuierlich ansteigenden Zahl von Einreichungen aus aller Welt in ein internationales Festival, an dem sich bisher über 40 Länder und Regionen beteiligten.

Im Wesentlichen verfolgt das Japan Media Arts Festival zwei Ziele:

Einerseits sollen – im Einklang mit den neuesten Entwicklungen und abseits bestehender kultureller Hierarchien – neue kulturelle Rahmenbedingungen und Werte vorgegeben werden. So sind nicht nur medienkünstlerische Arbeiten, sondern auch Beiträge aus den Kategorien Animation und Manga sowie Arbeiten aus dem Unterhaltungsbereich (etwa Spiele) szum Wettbewerb zugelassen.

Andererseits fördert das Festival – angesichts der Fortschritte in der digitalen Kommunikationstechnik und -technologie – ganz allgemein die Etablierung neuer Ausdrucksformen einer neuen Kultur und ist bestrebt, die Behauptung zu widerlegen, diese neue Kultur sei von der traditionellen vollkommen losgelöst. Wir sind überzeugt, dass durch das Festival in neuen kulturellen Bereichen Originalität entstehen kann. Die Kooperation zwischen der Ars Electronica und dem Japan Media Arts Festival besteht seit 2003 und hat in Linz und Tokio zu reger künstlerischer Tätigkeit geführt. Die Ars Electronica dient dem Japan Media Arts Festival dabei als Vorbild und Inspirationsquelle.

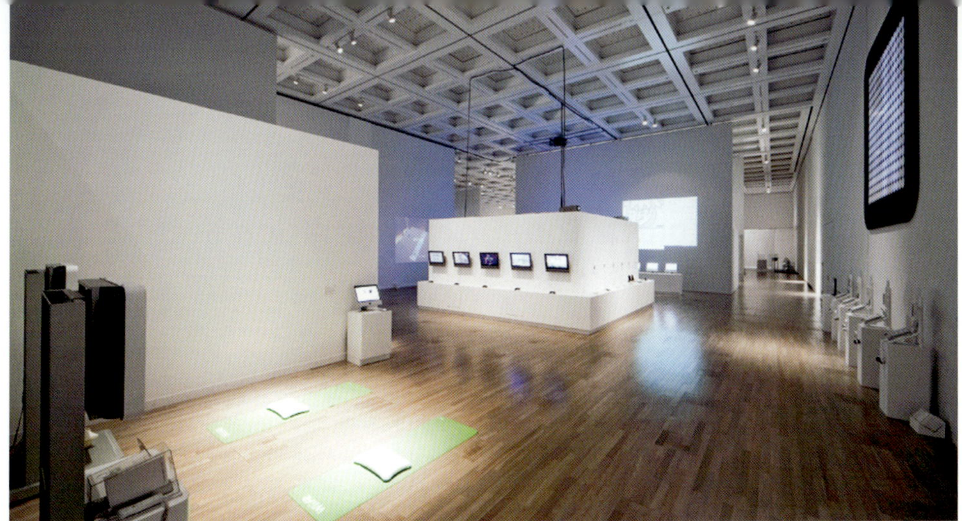

Die Einladung, anlässlich der Feierlichkeiten zum 30-jährigen Bestehen der Ars Electronica in Linz eine Ausstellung zu gestalten, ist für das Japan Media Arts *Festival* eine große Ehre. Es handelt sich dabei außerdem um die erste Ausstellung des Festivals in Europa.

(Aus dem Englischen von Susanne Steinacher)

13. Japan Media Arts Festival
Festivaldauer: 16. Juli bis 25. September 2009
Ausstellung der prämierten Beiträge zum 13. Japan Media Arts Festival: 3.–14. Februar 2010, National Art Center, Tokio.

JAPAN GAME
Das Mobile Ö1 Atelier bei der Ars Electronica 2009
in Kooperation mit dem Japan Media Arts Festival, Tokio

Das „Mobile Ö1 Atelier" versteht sich im Besonderen als Zentrum des öffentlichen Dialogs, es bietet dem Publikum die Möglichkeit zur direkten Kommunikation und Reflexion – in diesem Jahr gibt es einen besonderen „Entertainment"-Schwerpunkt, präsentiert wird japanische Medienkunst im Bereich Spiele.
Im „Mobilen Ö1 Atelier" am Linzer Hauptplatz werden preisgekrönte Arbeiten des Japan Media Arts Festivals ausgestellt und die Besucher/innen eingeladen, diese Spiele aktiv auszuprobieren. So kann erlebt werden, wie sehr sich aktuelle Medien-Kunst und Spiele-Design gegenseitig beeinflussen und so sehr überschneiden, dass durchaus von einer eigenen Kunstform gesprochen werden kann.
Zum 30. Jubiläum der Ars Electronica befasst sich Radio Österreich 1 hier mit dem Kernthema des Festivals „Human Nature": Wir werden Menschen in den neuen Spiele-Welten dargestellt? Sind die Verhaltensweisen und zu lösenden Aufgaben ethisch akzeptabel? Wie verändert sich die Wahrnehmung und Gestaltung von Landschaft und Architektur? Wie verhalten wir uns in virtuellen Parallelwelten? Kann die Kunst ganz neue Realitäten erschaffen, oder
kehren wir doch immer wieder in schon gewohnte Erfahrungsräume zurück?
Am Abend können die Besucher/innen ihr spielerisches Können in Turnieren unter Beweis stellen: Gespielt wird in ungewohnt großem Format auf riesigen Projektionsflächen beim „Mobilen Ö1 Atelier" am Hauptplatz.

Mobile Ö1 Atelier
3. bis 8. September 2009, Hauptplatz Linz

Christine Schöpf / Jürgen Hagler

Ars Electronica Computer Animation Festival 2009

They populate abstruse, bizarre and often ominous realms of the imagination, live through the most fantastic plots, turn the law of gravity on its head, and draw upon unlimited energy reserves. More and more of the 21st century's film stars aren't flesh-and-blood creatures; the source of their vitality is bits and bytes. Hollywood's new A-list includes such names as Shrek, Nemo and Wall-E; they're the bankable stars that guarantee movie studios box-office records.

Years before the first computer-animated full-length feature films hit theater screens, the computer was already making its presence felt in the field of film production. Ever since the 1980s, elaborate sets, scenes that would have involved thousands of extras, and extremely dangerous stunts have been generated by computer. In the wake of this development, special effects films became a genre receiving critical scrutiny by established film critics, whereby the basic tenor of the critique that many B-movies employed effects simply for the sake of effects was thoroughly justified. Non-commercial productions seemed to be totally outclassed in comparison to those being turned out by the major animation studios. Previously, the pioneering work of artist-scientists such as John Whitney Sr., Larry Cuba and Jane Veeder had been the driving force behind developments in the field; but at this point, the public perception came to be that Hollywood blockbusters like Terminator 2 & Co. had a lock on the leading edge. Accordingly, the art world's reaction was standoffish.

Now, a quarter century and several quantum technological leaps later, what's the current state of the art of computer animation? It's become an everyday phenomenon—in motion pictures and TV productions, action flicks and art cinema, family films like those turned out by Pixar and BlueSky Studios, commercials as well as news programming. The filmmaker's imagination is subject to virtually no limits anymore. Animation has its undisputed place at film festivals, art biennials and museums. The "short film" genre is flourishing; its aficionados can get their fill not only at lots of download portals like YouTube and MySpace but also in movie theaters and on DVD. The content spectrum—as reflected by the 500 works from all over the world submitted for prize consideration to Prix Ars Electronica 2009—is virtually unlimited. These efforts range from experimental-abstract productions, sound visualizations, short cuts and special effects all the way to classic narrative filmmaking.

The 12 programs that make up the 2009 Ars Electronica Animation Festival's lineup once again showcase the outstanding work currently being done at artists' ateliers, universities and film academies as well as in the production studios of the film and advertising industries.

Christine Schöpf, Jürgen Hagler

Ars Electronica Computer Animation Festival 2009

Sie bevölkern abstruse, bizarre und oft bedrohliche Fantasiewelten, durchleben die abenteuerlichsten Geschichten, stellen die Gesetze der Schwerkraft auf den Kopf, ihre Energie kennt keine Grenzen: Die Filmstars des 21. Jahrhunderts sind längst keine Wesen mehr aus Fleisch und Blut – ihr Lebenssaft sind Bits und Bytes. Die neuen Hollywoodgrößen heißen Shrek, Nemo oder Wall-E, und sie bringen die Kinokassen mit astronomischen Einspielergebnissen gewaltig zum Klingeln.

Schon Jahre vor den ersten abendfüllenden Computeranimationsfilmen hatte der Computer die Filmproduktion kräftig umgekrempelt: Aufwändige Bauten, Massenszenen, waghalsige Stunts etc. hielten seit den 1980er Jahren – computergeneriert – ihren Einzug ins Kino. Special-Effects-Filme wurden in der Folge zum von der etablierten Filmkritik kritisch beäugten Genre. Der Grundtenor der Kritik, B-Movies mit Effekten nur um der Effekte willen, hatte damals in etlichen Fällen durchaus Berechtigung. Nicht kommerzielle Produktionen schienen jenen aus den großen Animationsstudios gegenüber chancenlos. Hatten in früheren Jahren Künstler-Wissenschafter wie John Whitney Sr., Larry Cuba, Jane Veeder u.v.a. mit ihren bahnbrechenden Arbeiten die Entwicklung vorangetrieben, waren es jetzt in der öffentlichen Wahrnehmung Hollywood-Blockbuster wie *Terminator 2* und dessen Nachkommen. Dementsprechend reagierte die Kunstwelt darauf ablehnend.

Und wo steht die Computeranimation heute, ein Vierteljahrhundert und etliche Quantensprünge in der Technologieentwicklung später? In Film- und TV-Produktionen, egal, ob Action- oder Artfilm, Familienfilm Marke Pixar und BlueSky Studios, in Werbespots ebenso wie in Nachrichtensendungen ist sie Alltag geworden, der Fantasie der Macher sind kaum mehr Grenzen gesetzt; auf Filmfestivals hat sie ihren unbestrittenen Platz ebenso wie auf Kunstbiennalen und in Museen, das Genre Kurzfilm blüht und findet sein Publikum nicht nur auf den zahlreichen Downloadportalen wie YouTube oder MySpace, sondern auch in Kinos und auf DVD. Das inhaltliche Spektrum ist dabei – wie die 500 Einreichungen aus aller Welt zum Prix Ars Electronica 2009 zeigen – schier unbegrenzt. Es reicht von experimentell-abstrakten Produktionen, Soundvisualisierung, Short Cuts über Special Effects bis hin zum klassischen Storytelling.

Mit seinen zwölf Programmen ist das Ars Electronica Animation Festival 2009 einmal mehr Showcase für aktuelle Produktionen aus Künstlerateliers, Universitäten und Filmakademien ebenso wie aus den Produktionsstudios von Film und Werbung.

Curated by Christine Schöpf & Jürgen Hagler
Trailer Concept & Animation: Claus Helfenschneider, Alexander Piringer
Directed by: Claus Helfenschneider

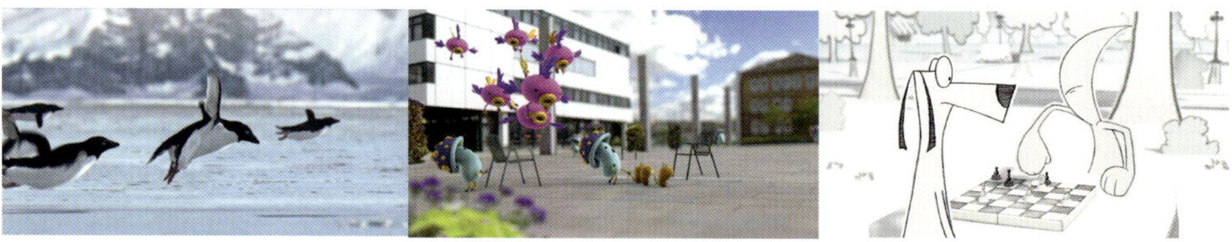

Animal Worlds

When a rookery of penguins says adios to the Arctic ice and relocates to the southern tropics, when a dispute between two rats turns into a mass brawl, when dogs bicker and cats caterwaul, then action's afoot in the animal kingdom, which once again proves: all God's creatures have feelings!

Animal Worlds

Wenn ein Pinguinschwarm dem arktischen Eis Adieu sagt und in den tropischen Süden zieht, wenn ein Streit zwischen zwei Ratten in eine handfeste Schlägerei ausartet, wenn Hunde sich zanken und Katzen kreischen, geht es in der Tierwelt rund – womit bewiesen wäre: Auch Tiere haben Gefühle.

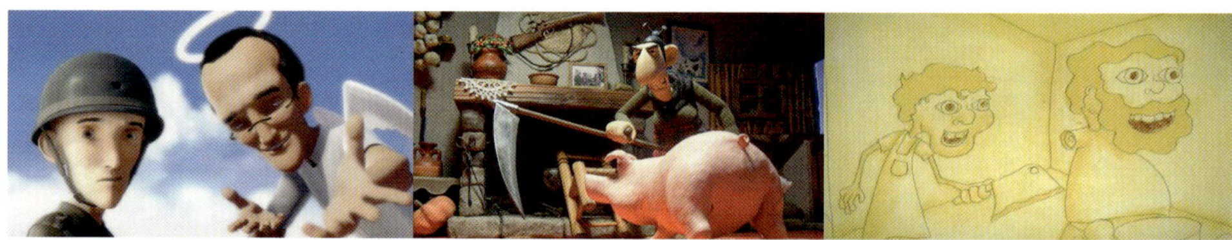

Blood & Fight

They fight: against society, with themselves, for survival. They stumble through existence on this mortal coil, wounded, at the mercy of fate, harried, hunted, persecuted. They struggle beyond the limits, to the point of bloodshed—their own and that of the others. If it's goodnight stories you seek, friend, look elsewhere!

Blood & Fight

Sie kämpfen gegen die Gesellschaft, mit sich selbst und ums Überleben. Sie irren durchs Dasein, verletzt, ihrem Schicksal ausgeliefert, gehetzt, verfolgt. Sie kämpfen bis über die Grenzen, bis Blut fließt – eigenes und das der anderen. Als Gute-Nacht-Programm ungeeignet!

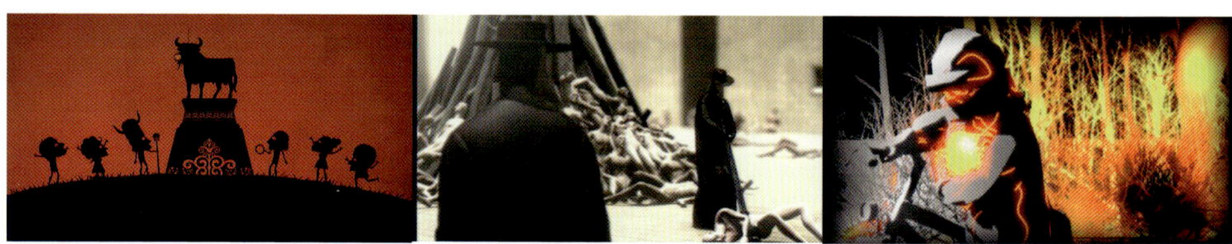

Dark Stories

Nightmares hidden behind masks awaken, twisted paths lead into the unknown, abysses yawn, apprehensions, anxieties and dark fantasies surface. Verily I say unto thee: these are no messages of good cheer. Only for strong nerves.

Dark Stories

Hinter Masken verborgene Albträume werden wahr, Irrwege führen ins Ungewisse, Abgründe öffnen sich ins Nichts, Beklemmung, Ängste, schwarze Fantasien drängen an die Oberfläche. Diese Filme erzählen wahrlich nichts Gutes und erfordern ein starkes Nervenkorsett.

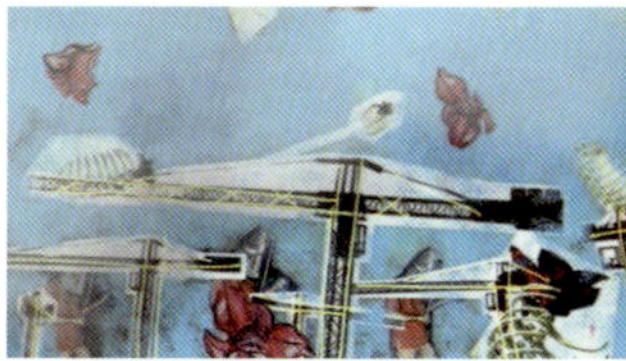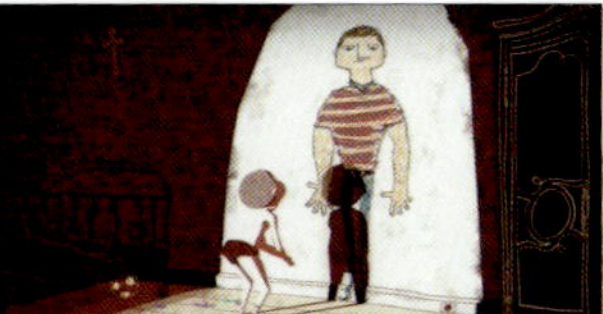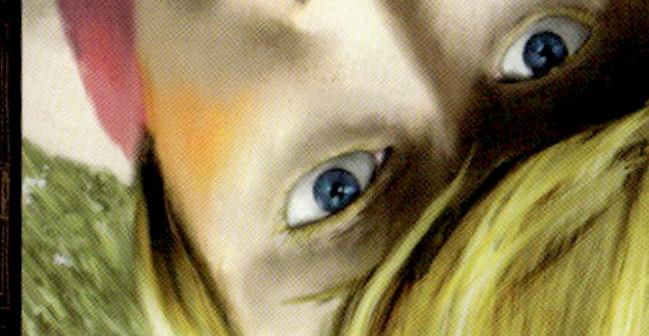

Animated Psycho

When ones internal equilibrium gets well out of whack and the sky is falling; when one feels deserted by all friends and gods alike; when one seeks shelter from the storm: mental states of emergency manifest themselves in these films in therapeutic dialogs and transforming bodies.

Animated Psycho

Wenn das innere Gleichgewicht aus den Fugen gerät und einem der Himmel auf den Kopf fällt; wenn man sich von allem und allen verlassen glaubt und Zuflucht sucht: Psychische Ausnahmezustände manifestieren sich in diesen Filmen in therapeutischen Dialogen und transformierenden Körpern.

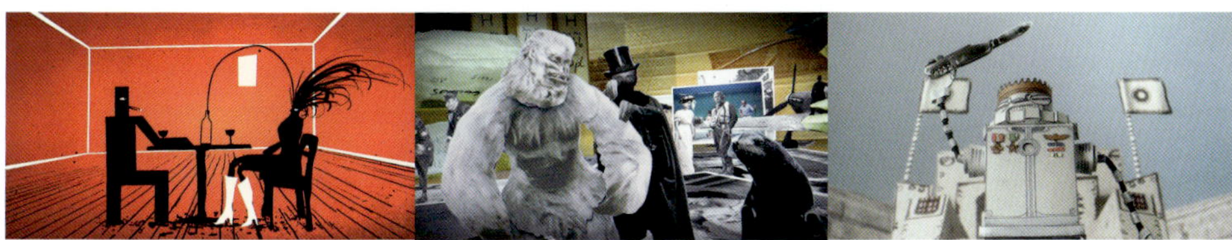

Late Night

Offbeat perspectives, subversive standpoints, spiced with trashy visuals and a dollop of sex & crime—these are the ingredients of this late-night snack. Not necessarily for diners of all ages, but by all means tasty fare for a relaxed chill-out.

Late Night

Schräge Sichtweisen, subversive Standpunkte, trashige Optik, eine Portion Sex & Crime u.v.m. sind die Zutaten für das Programm zum späten Abend. Nicht immer jugendfrei, aber allemal verträgliche Kost für einen relaxten Chill-out.

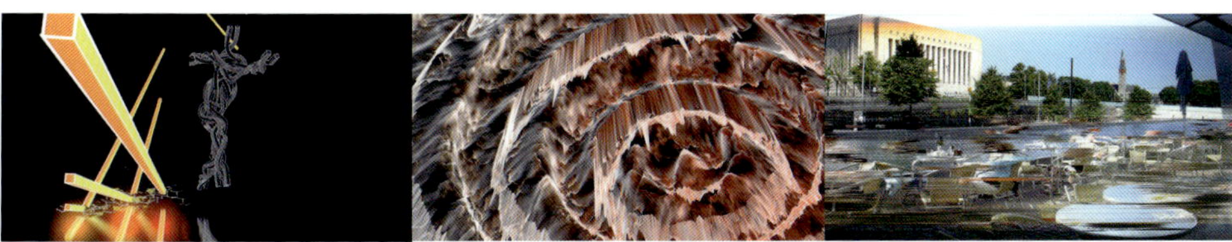

Motion Patterns

These films play with perspective and perception. Generative image design is the painting of the 21st century.

Motion Patterns

Diese Filme sind ein Spiel mit Perspektive und Wahrnehmung. Generative Bildgestaltung ist die Malerei des 21. Jahrhunderts.

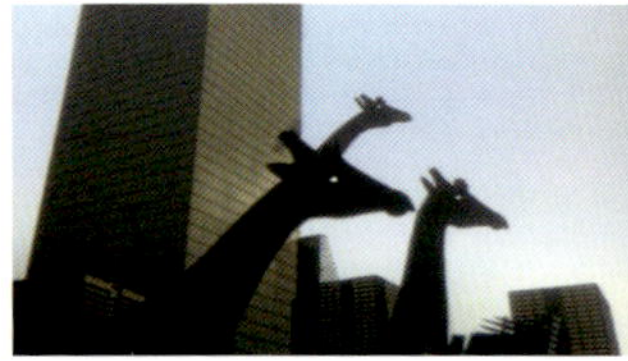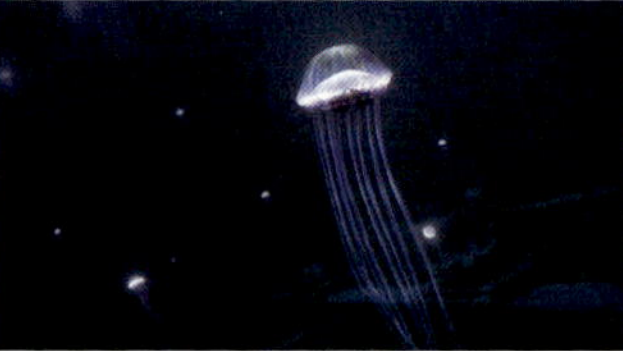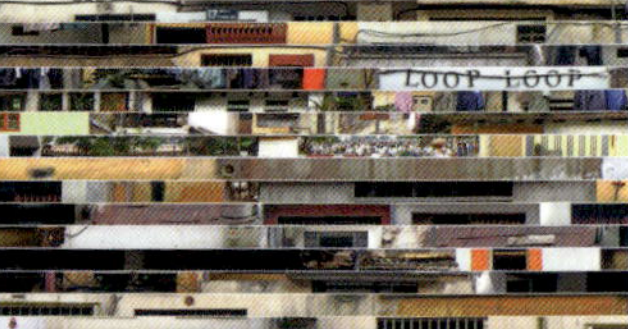

Inner & Outer Spaces

Utopian landscapes like saline deserts and alien terrains, architecture and spaces in motion emerge and reformulate themselves in continuously shifting perspectives. Space and time get a bit blurred.

Inner & Outer Spaces

Utopische Landschaften wie Salzwüsten und Alien-grounds, Architektur und Räume in Bewegung tun sich auf, formen sich in kontinuierlich wechselnden Blick-winkeln neu. Raum und Zeit verschwimmen.

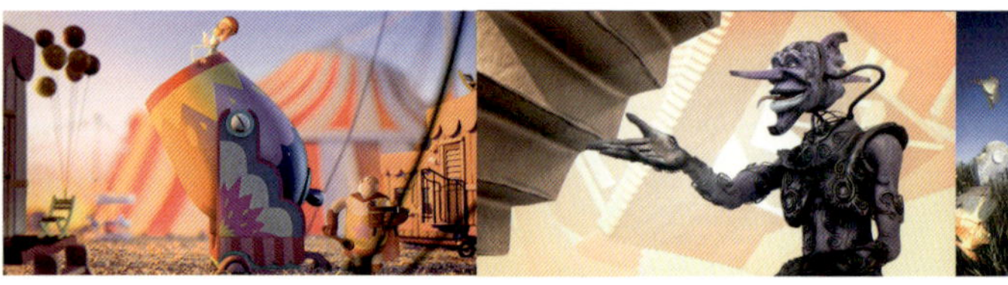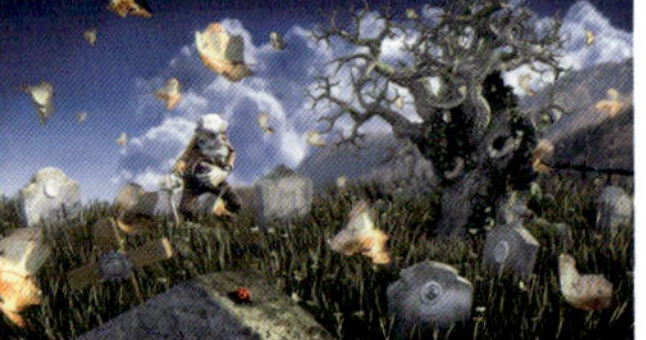

Narration

These are real-life stories. Or might have been. Or those that could only have happened in a dream. They tell of love, of the desire to flee, of protecting and helping, of deceptions and lies.

Narration

Es sind Geschichten, die das Leben schreibt oder schreiben könnte, und solche, die es nur in Träumen gibt. Sie erzählen von der Liebe, vom Wunsch zu fliegen, vom Beschützen und Helfen, von Schwindel und Lüge.

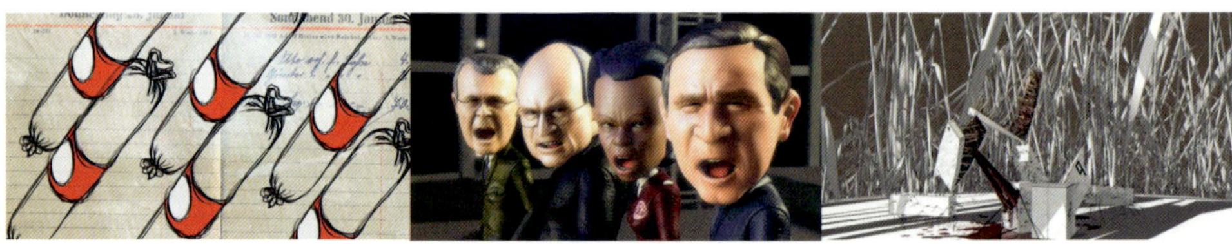

Position & Message

If you haven't already stumbled across this stuff online, here it is neatly packaged: opinions, communiqués, statements and critiques. In short, what all sorts of people have to say on a wide variety of topics.

Position & Message

Wenn Sie sie noch nicht irgendwo im Web gefunden haben – hier kommen sie im Paket: Meinungen, Bot-schaften, Statements, Kritik, kurz: Hier finden Sie, was über Gott und die Welt von Leuten so zu sagen ist.

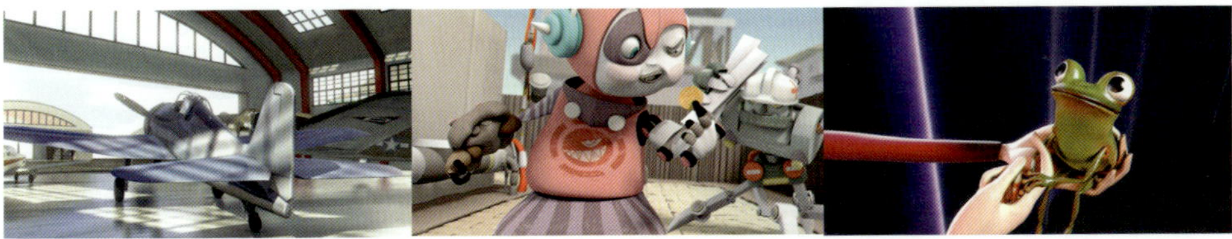

Short Cuts

Of course, it would be possible to give much more elaborate accounts of these matters, but this works too: succinct, colorful and entertaining. Just like it says, short cuts!

Short Cuts

Man könnte diese Geschichten natürlich länger und ausführlicher erzählen, aber es geht auch so: prägnant, bunt und kurzweilig – Short Cuts eben!

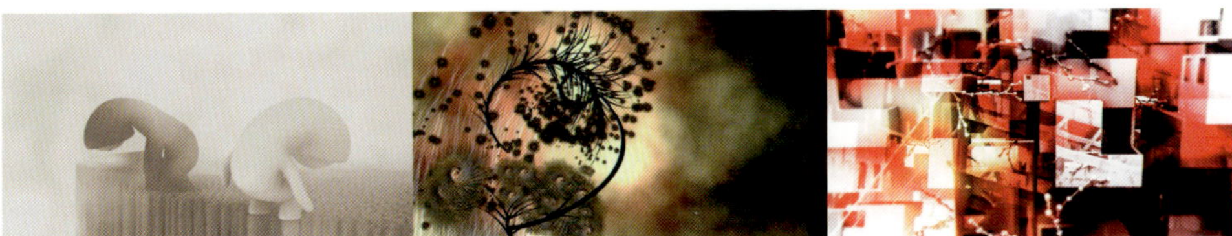

Sound & Vision

The interplay of image and sound already has a long tradition in computer animation. This program spotlights current examples of visual music: inseparable, sensual, lyrical ...

Sound & Vision

Das Zusammenspiel von Bild und Klang hat in der Computeranimation eine jahrzehntelange Tradition. Dieses Programm zeigt aktuelle Beispiele visueller Musik: unzertrennlich, sinnlich, lyrisch ...

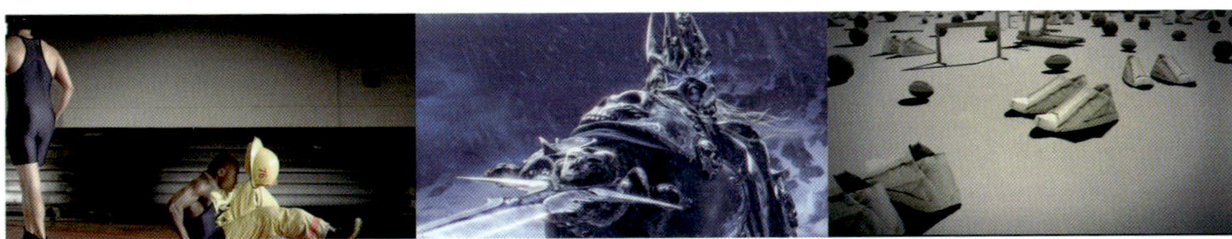

Visual Effects

What's real; what's virtual? It's increasingly difficult for observers to draw the dividing line. Considering what we encounter in films, TV shows and commercials nowadays, it seems nothing's impossible anymore.

Visual Effects

Was ist real, was virtuell? Die Grenze zu ziehen wird für den Betrachter immer schwieriger. Nichts scheint unmöglich vom dem, was uns heute in Film, TV und Werbung begegnet.

Pursuit of the Unheard
The Big Concert Evening

The quest for new possibilities of expression, to make audible in a wide array of forms what's never been heard before, can be traced back way beyond the Postindustrial Age in connection with technological development and the new approaches to creating music that have gone along with it. Ever since the dawn of music history, musical innovations have emerged, new genres have developed, previously unknown functions discovered, and the boundaries of the very concept of what constitutes music redefined. Today, we have reached a point at which this definition has been shifted so far outward that this is no longer primarily a matter of musical structure; the emphasis is now on hearing, reacting to, individually compiling and interpreting music. New spaces are being discovered, acoustic realities tested anew and boldly, creatively transformed. Sometimes the development proceeds inconspicuously; hardly noticeable, it's suddenly upon us. Sometimes, it's so obvious you can't miss it, but maybe it turns out to be no big deal after all. The artistic outcomes bring forth exciting innovation. This is an eternal cycle of the traditional and time-tested motivating new musical creativity. Fascinating creative achievements and ideas, in turn, induce the pursuit of the unheard to recommence once again, same as ever ...

The Ars Electronica Festival is celebrating its 30th anniversary in 2009. Looking back on the festival's musical history, we're immediately struck by its extraordinary diversity: early electronic rock, play-along concerts featuring home-brew instruments, the *Steel Symphony* and the *Steel Opera* ... Music is at the heart of this festival. The urge to discover new musics, to pioneer the exploration of fresh musical realms, to undertake daring tonal experiments is still undiminished.

This concert evening will be the seventh such expedition in quest of innovation. The separate concert staged in prior years to showcase current trends in digital music with performances by Prix Ars Electronica prizewinners is being integrated into the 2009 big evening concert; the result is a lineup dedicated to both the past and the present. During the first half of the evening, new technologies will share center stage with traditional genres and instruments: an "opera" performed by a tiny wireless-controlled plastic bunny, and a violin ensemble combined with 1-bit music. Audiences will then be treated to orchestral pieces by Arvo Pärt, Alan Hovhaness and Norbert Zehm visualized in ways that bring out never-before-discovered ways of seeing these sounds. The Klangpark will be filled with Bill Fontana's sound sculptures that translate the chiming of Big Ben from the Thames to the Danube in ways that are as surreal as they are impressive. No less striking is the sound of the Max Brand synthesizer, which is similar to the one presented at the 1980 festival by Robert A. Moog. This is an instrument that in 2009 would actually qualify as an object in a historical exhibit, but Elisabeth Schimana is still able to coax new sounds out of the old machine. The innovative acoustic combinations of Christian Fennesz paired with Lillevan's fascinating visualizations wrap up the pursuit of the unheard for the time being ...

(Text: Bianca Petscher)

Pursuit of the Unheard is the latest production to come out of Ars Electronica's very successful working relationship with the Bruckner Orchestra under Dennis Russell Davies and the Brucknerhaus. The aim is to try out new concepts in combining music with new forms of visual expression.
Curators: Dennis Russell Davies, Wolfgang Winkler, Heribert Schröder, Gerfried Stocker, Bianca Petscher

Programme

Antoine Schmitt, Jean-Jaques Birgé
Nabaz'mob
(Prix Ars Electronica 2009, Digital Musics, Award of Distinction)

Tristan Perich
„Active Field" for ten violins and ten-channel 1-bit music
(Prix Ars Electronica 2009, Digital Musics, Award of Distinction)
Performed by Bruckner Orchester Linz / Dennis Russell Davies

Arvo Pärt
Arbos for brass and percussion (1977/1986)
Performed by Bruckner Orchester Linz / Dennis Russell Davies

Arvo Pärt
**Concerto piccolo über B-A-C-H for trumpet, string orchestra,
harpsichord and piano (1964/1994)**
Performed by Bruckner Orchester Linz / Dennis Russell Davies
Cembalo: Maki Namekawa, *Trumpet:* Gerhard Fluch, *Visuals by* Nanook feat. System Jaquelinde

Alan Hovhaness
Lousadzak (Coming of Light) for piano and strings, op. 48
Performed by Bruckner Orchester Linz / Dennis Russell Davies
Piano: Maki Namekawa, *Visuals by* Kenneth Huff

Bill Fontana
Speeds of Time
Prix Ars Electronica 2009, Digital Musics, Golden Nica

Norbert Zehm
Symphonie "GAMES" op. 45
Performed by Bruckner Orchester Linz / Dennis Russell Davies
Synthesizer / Electronics: Norbert Zehm, *Visuals by* Roland Schrettl

Elisabeth Schimana
Höllenmaschine (composition for the Max Brand synthesizer)
Operators: Manon Liu Winter, Gregor Ladenhauf

Christian Fennesz
fennesz with lillevan visuals

Antoine Schmitt, Jean-Jaques Birgé
Nabaz'mob
(Prix Ars Electronica 2009, Digital Musics, Award of Distinction)

100 Nabaztag smart rabbits play an opera together specially composed by Antoine Schmitt and Jean-Jacques Birgé. Inviting John Cage, Steve Reich, Conlon Nancarrow and György Ligeti, this musical and choreographic score in three movements, transmitted via wi-fi, plays on the tension between the orchestral ensemble and the individual voices to create a strong and involved showpiece. This opera questions the issues of working together, organization, decision and control, which are increasingly central and difficult in our contemporary world.
Schmitt and Birgé are respectively the behavior designer and the sound designer of the Nabaztag rabbits, constructed by Violet. They have chosen to twist the industrial object into an artwork in which the choreography of the ears, the play of light and the hundred small loudspeakers hidden in the stomachs of each rabbit create a composition with three voices built on time-delay and repetition, programming and disrespect for rules.

Choreography and music: Antoine Schmitt. Jean-Jacques Birgé
With the support of Violet, after an original initiative by Guylaine Monnier (Web Flash Festival)

Tristan Perich
"Active Field" for ten violins and ten-channel 1-bit music
(Prix Ars Electronica 2009, Digital Musics, Award of Distinction)
Performed by Bruckner Orchester Linz / Dennis Russell Davies

1-Bit Music is a project by artist and composer Tristan Perich that combines his classical training in music with primitive, hand-programmed electronics that investigate the foundations of digital sound.
In 2005, Cantaloupe Music released *1-Bit Music*, custom-built electronics packaged inside a standard CD jewel case, which synthesize an album of electronic music, illustrating the struc-

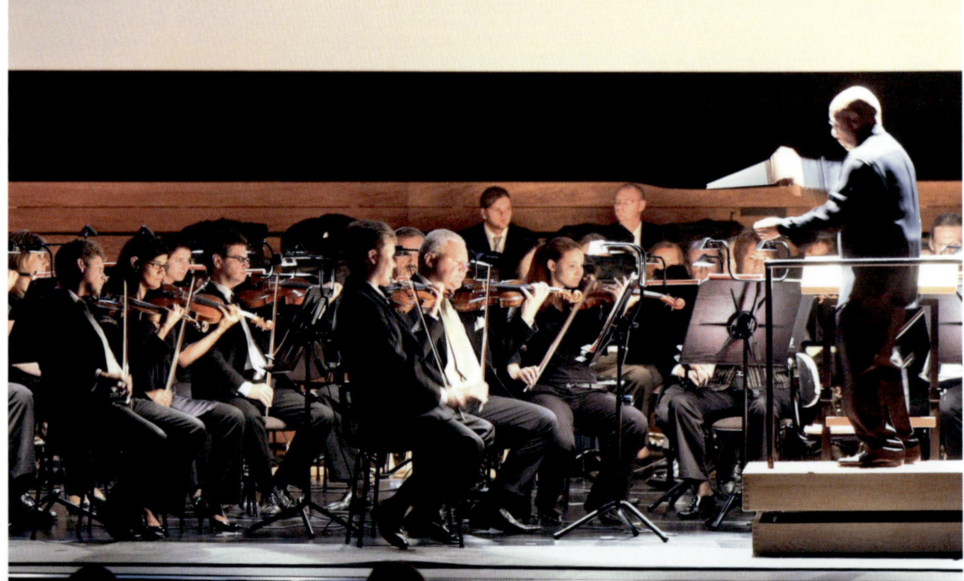

ture of the circuit and combining that transparent aesthetic with the lowest-fidelity sound. Since that release, Perich's work has shifted towards compositions for traditional classical ensemble with 1-bit audio accompaniment. The live musicians are paired with a set of speakers on stage, creating a hybrid multi-part work for acoustic and electronic sound. Connecting microchips directly to speakers, the resultant ensemble's sound is "mixed" in the air, treating the speakers as a form of acoustic instrument, approaching the concept of electronic sound as a physical phenomenon.

Arvo Pärt
Arbos for brass and percussion (1977/1986)
Performed by Bruckner Orchester Linz /
Dennis Russell Davies

**Concerto piccolo über B-A-C-H
for trumpet, string orchestra,
harpsichord and piano (1964/1994)**
Performed by Bruckner Orchester Linz /
Dennis Russell Davies
Cembalo: Maki Namekawa
Trumpet: Gerhard Fluch
Visuals by Nanook feat. System Jaquelinde

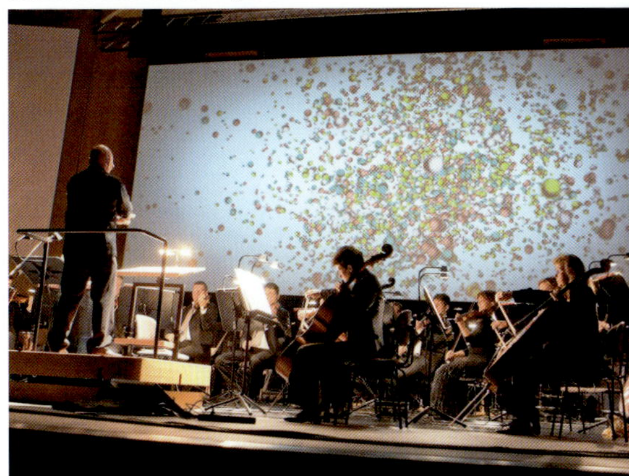
Sonorous Embodiement, 2008

Arvo Pärt is considered one of the best-known contemporary composers. Born in 1939 in Estonia, he emigrated to Vienna in 1980 and later to Berlin, where he now lives. Pärt studied composition in Tallinn. Early in his career, he worked with Western styles of musical expression (including tonal textures, aleatory music and collage technique), whereby his modernist tendencies made him a target of harsh criticism in the former Soviet Union. In the wake of a personal crisis, Pärt increasingly immersed himself in the music of the Middle Ages and the Renaissance. A subsequent reorientation accompanied by his conversion to the Russian Orthodox faith brought him to the development of his own personal style he calls Tintinnabuli (Latin: little bells). Pärt, in his own words: "I discovered that it's enough when a single sound is beautifully played. This sound, the stillness, and the act of remaining silent calm me. I work with very little material, with a voice or two. I build upon primitive material, on a triad, a particular tonal quality. The three tones of a triad have an effect like a bell."
"Arbos" and the "Concerto piccolo über B-A-C-H" were created during Pärt's early experimental phase, but both were later reworked for a different group of instruments. "Arbos" is an instrumental observation of nature, a "carpet of sound" produced by brass instruments. Pärt composed the "Concerto piccolo über B-A-C-H" in 1964 in a collage style. It was originally meant for string orchestra, oboe, cembalo and piano; he created the version for trumpet, string orchestra, cembalo and piano in 1994. He plays in four keys in the style of a Baroque suite with three movements: toccata, sarabande and ricercar.

Alan Hovhaness
Lousadzak (Coming of Light) for piano and strings, op. 48
Performed by Bruckner Orchester Linz / Dennis Russell Davies
Piano: Maki Namekawa, *Visuals by* Kenneth Huff

Alan Hovhaness (1911–2000) was born in Seattle; his father was Armenian, his mother American-born. His interest in music goes back to his childhood. He began to compose at an early age and then studied piano and composition. His creative work went through several stylistic phases. After an early period under the influence of Jean Sibelius, his style was decisively changed by his interest in meditation and mysticism, and the music of India and Armenia. He conducted numerous studies and further developed his style, which was characterized by simple, though sometimes artistically embellished melodies, more modal than tonal and featuring increasingly varied repetitions instead of thematic development. Hovhaness' work was often criticized by reviewers on account of its spare, stark plainness. From colleagues, on the other hand, he garnered praise—John Cage and jazz legend Keith Jarrett are among his admirers. *Lousadzak*, a piano concerto composed in 1944, comes across as hymnic and seems to have been influenced by Armenian folklore. Its elegant simplicity often evokes mystical and contemplative moods.

(Text: Bianca Petscher)

Bill Fontana
Speeds of Time
(Prix Ars Electronica 2009, Digital Musics, Golden Nica)

Speeds of Time is a musical deconstruction of the most famous acoustic icon and symbol of time, Big Ben. Live sensors and microphones are mounted on the clockwork mechanism and near the bells of Big Ben to generate a spatial-acoustic composition, which is placed in an historic colonnade of the New Palace Yard, directly below and within earshot of the bells. The presence of the sound sculpture in this setting interacts with the natural sound of the bells, creating a multidimensional acoustic zone. While this work was installed in Westminster, a 12-hour multi-track recording of the sound sculpture was made that makes it possible to fully recreate the real time sense of this artwork, which can be realized as an eight-channel sound installation. This recording is fully accurate to real time and, if started at precisely five seconds before 10 o'clock, it will faithfully keep time.

Norbert Zehm
Symphonie "GAMES" op. 45
Performed by Bruckner Orchester Linz / Dennis Russell Davies
Synthesizer / Electronics: Norbert Zehm, *Visuals by* Roland Schrettl

GAMES is a multimedial work for symphony orchestra, computer and synthesizers, with a video collage by Roland Schrettl.
An acoustic and visual documentation of and commentary on 30 years of computer games, this

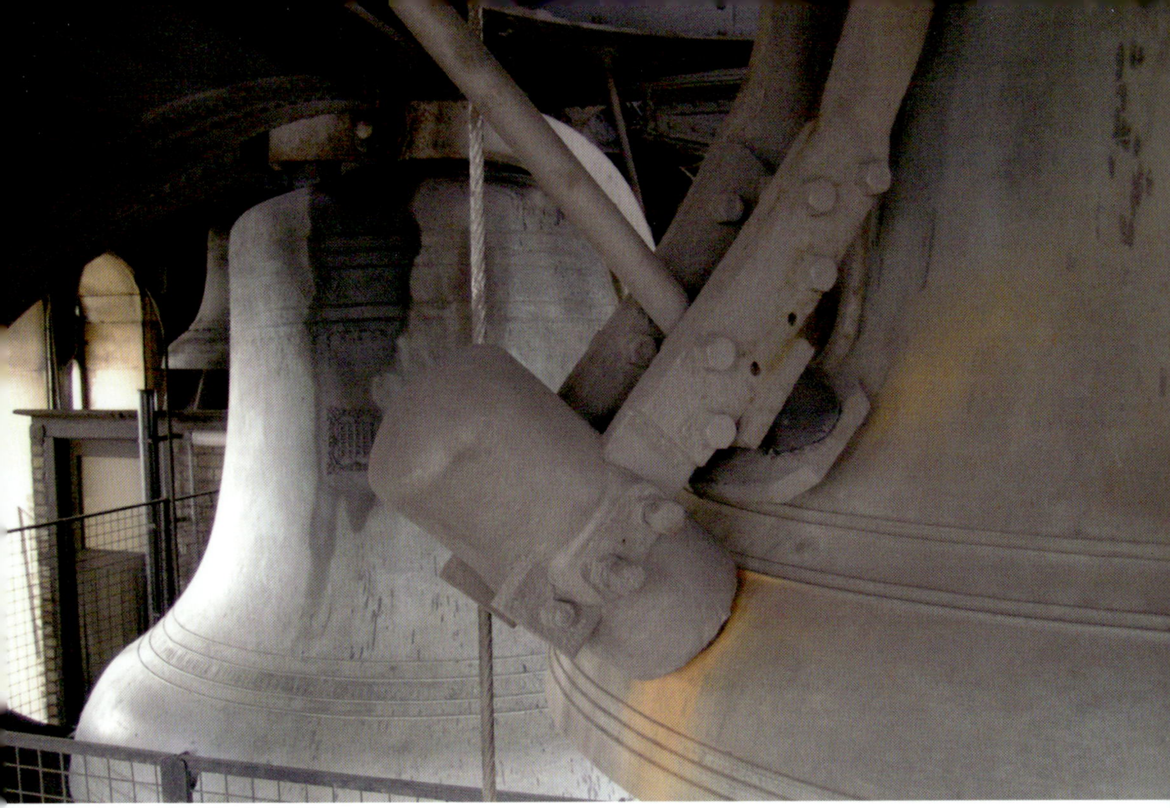

work immerses those partaking of it into the world of the cyberkids. It's a trip through time from pixel wars to virtual worlds, the saga of heroes in front of and behind the joystick.

Due to the limited technical options afforded by game consoles in computing's Stone Age, the possibilities of creating background music were correspondingly minimal. Accordingly, simple sounds or melodic riffs were very cleverly employed, using only a very few tones and noises to underscore the games' various moods and on-screen characters—from funny or sarcastic plot elements to frightening, exciting and brutal episodes.

In the computer scene, these "character sounds" attracted a cult following among computer freaks and simultaneously became signature jingles of the respective PC brands (i.e. Atari, Amiga).

We are fascinated by the use of the banality, the wittiness and the irony of this non-art—or maybe it is art after all—as building blocks for a major symphonic work.

The orchestra functions as an echo or megaphone of these computer mini-sounds and arranges entrée for us into a familiar world via new means and through the use of an innovative filter.

The composition begins with a single pixel point jumping back and forth, its movements echoed by the orchestra's sounds that develop into ever-more complex rhythmic and harmonic tonal worlds.

Le dernier cri: cellphone games (mobile gaming) closes the circle of game sound development to date. Cellphone bleeps: the simplicity of these melodies closely resemble that of the original, monotone home computer sounds from 30 years ago.

The symphony as a whole consists of five movements that span a thematic arc comprised of the various stages of computer sound development (though shedding intense light on only a selected few). The five movements: Pixels – Punktspiele; Galaxies – Vektoren; Heroes – Helden vor und hinter dem Joystick; Virtual Gaming – virtuelle Welten – eigene Welten; Mobile Gaming – Zweitwelt für unterwegs

Pursuit of the Unheard: The Big Concert Evening

Elisabeth Schimana
Infernal Machine (composition for the Max Brand synthesizer)
Operators: Manon Liu Winter, Gregor Ladenhauf

A journey inside the one-of-a-kind machine that is the legacy of composer Max Brand. This mechanical monster, the outcome of decades of development, is the distant ancestor of the Moog Synthesizer. Operated by an outstanding pianist, it snorts its sub-harmonic frequencies and spews them forth into the ether.

A trip to hell with no return ticket.

The first wiring diagrams for the Max Brand synthesizer by Bob Moog are dated 1957. Over more than 10 years, Moog, then a young engineer, built this unique apparatus on the basis of Max Brand's ideas. The sole traces left by the composer are in the interface design: two keyboards, 2 band-manuals and four foot pedals! The core components are the two frequency dividers, each with 20 sub-frequencies and an adjustable matrix of 3 blocks, each with 4 x 20 sub-harmonic modules including the first voltage-controlled modules Moog ever built (VCA, VCF, VCO).

This musical engine is the outcome of collaboration between a visionary composer and an ingenious inventor. It challenges us to take it seriously as a piece of machinery: to hammer out its mighty sounds and to summon forth its subtle vibrations.

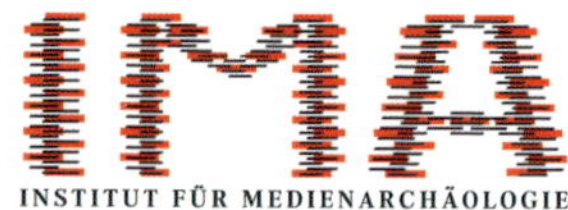

Max Brand Archive

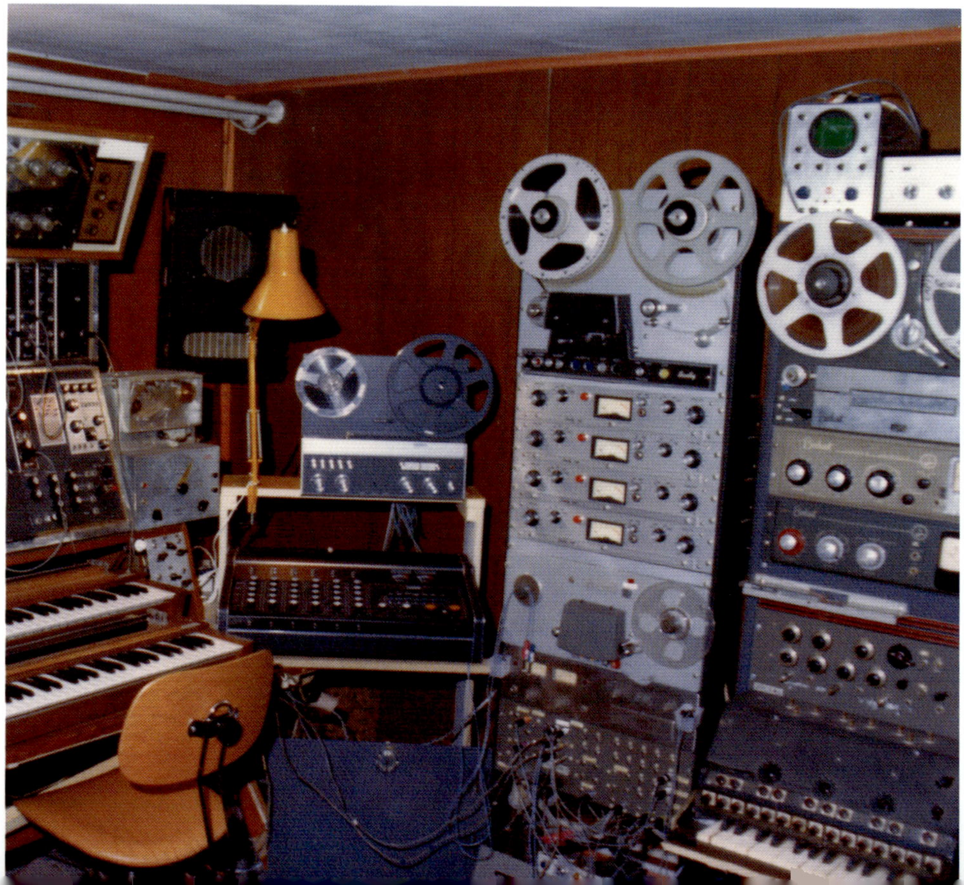

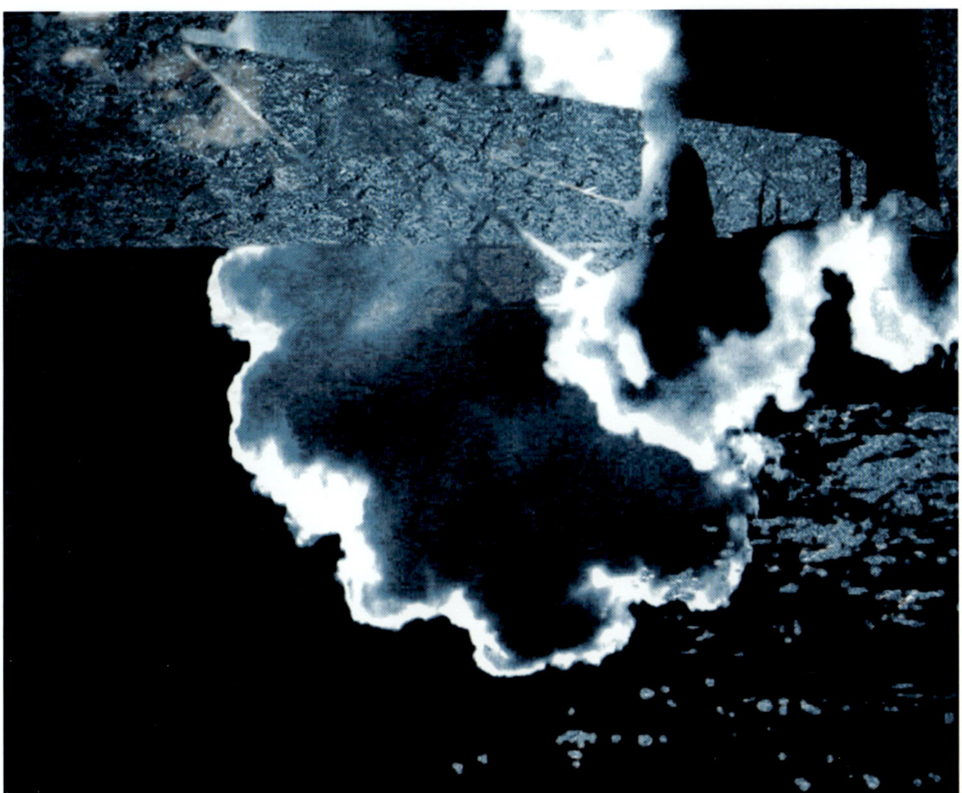

Christian Fennesz
fennesz with lillevan visuals.

Christian Fennesz uses guitar and computer to create shimmering, swirling electronic sound of enormous range and complex musicality. "Imagine the electric guitar severed from cliché and all of its physical limitations, shaping a bold new musical language." (City Newspaper, USA).
Christian Fennesz is known for his own particular musical world as well as his impeccable work in creating beautiful compositions for guitar. Somewhere between concrete music, classical and ambience sounds, he stretches musical resources and effects to create melodies and atmospheres that fuse classical and orchestral concepts with conceptual musical research and complex digital structures.
Lillevan is an animation, video and media artist. He is perhaps best known as the founding member of the visual / music group *Rechenzentrum* (1997–2008). Parallel to his work in *Rechenzentrum*, he has performed and collaborated with many artists from a wide array of genres, from opera to installation, from minimal electronic experimentalism to dance and classical music.
Lillevan and Christian Fennesz are teaming up to present new material during 2009.

Pursuit of the Unheard
Große Konzertnacht

Vom Streben nach ungehörter Musik

Das Streben nach neuen Ausdrucksmöglichkeiten, dem bisher Ungehörten, in vielfältigster Form lässt sich nicht erst im postindustriellen Zeitalter im Zusammenhang mit der technologischen Entwicklung und den damit einhergehenden Neuansätzen in der Musik verstärkt nachweisen. Vom Urbeginn der Musikgeschichte an entwickelt sich musikalisch Neues, werden neue Gattungen herausgebildet, bisher unbestimmte Funktionen entdeckt, die Grenzen des Musikbegriffs aufgelöst. Bis in die Gegenwart so weit ausgedehnt, dass es nicht mehr primär um die musikalische Struktur geht – das Hören, das Reagieren und das individuelle Zusammenführen und Interpretieren von Musik steht im Zentrum. Neue Räume werden entdeckt, akustische Realitäten neu erprobt, mutig und kreativ transformiert. Manchmal verläuft die Entwicklung unscheinbar, wird kaum bemerkt und ist plötzlich da, manchmal ist sie nicht zu überhören und am Ende vielleicht doch nicht so überzeugend. Die künstlerischen Resultate bringen spannend Neues. Ein ewig währender Kreislauf – Althergebrachtes motiviert zu neuem musikalischem Schaffen. Faszinierende neue Errungenschaften und Ideen wiederum verleiten, das Streben nach dem Ungehörten erneut fortzusetzen, wohl für immer.

Im Jahr 2009 feiert das Ars Electronica Festival sein 30-jähriges Bestehen. Blickt man musikalisch auf die Geschichte des Festivals zurück, zeigt sich eine enorme Vielfalt: frühe elektronische Rockmusik, Mach-mit-Konzerte mit selbstgebauten Instrumenten, die Stahlsinfonie und die Stahloper, … Musik ist sehr zentral vertreten, der Drang, Neues zu entdecken, ungebrochen über 30 Jahre, neue musikalische Räume wurden erobert und ungewöhnliche Experimente gewagt. Auch die in diesem Jahr schon zum siebten Mal stattfindende Konzertnacht wagt sich an Veränderungen. Gab es bisher für die aktuellen Trends in der digitalen Musik ein eigenes Konzert mit den PreisträgerInnen des Prix Ars Electronica, so werden diese 2009 integriert. Daraus entsteht ein Konzertabend, der in seinem Programm sowohl der Geschichte wie auch der Gegenwart gewidmet ist. Im ersten Teil des Abends stehen neue Technologien im Mittelpunkt – kombiniert mit traditionellen Genres und Instrumenten: eine „Opern"-Aufführung kleiner Wireless-gesteuerter Plastikhasen und ein ViolonistInnen-Ensemble kombiniert mit 1-bit music. Gefolgt von Orchesterstücken von Arvo Pärt, Alan Hovhaness und Norbert Zehm, die – visualisiert – bis dato unentdeckte Sichtweisen dieser Musik erlauben. Der Klangpark wird erfüllt mit Bill Fontanas Klangskulpturen, die Klänge des Big Ben wirken unwirklich und doch beeindruckend an der Donau. Ebenso jene des Max Brand Synthesizers, schon 1980 präsentierte Robert A. Moog einen ähnlichen Synthesizer beim Festival – 2009 eigentlich bereits ein historisches Ausstellungsobjekt –, und immer noch entlockt Elisabeth Schimana der alten Maschine neue Klänge. Mit neuen Klangkombinationen von Christian Fennesz zusammen mit faszinierenden Visualisierungen von Lillevan endet das Streben nach dem Ungehörten, vorerst …

(Text: Bianca Petscher)

Pursuit of the Unheard ist ein weiterer Schritt in der erfolgreichen Zusammenarbeit des Bruckner Orchesters Linz unter Dennis Russell Davies, dem Brucknerhaus Linz und der Ars Electronica mit dem Ziel, neue Konzepte der Verbindung von Musik und neuen visuellen Ausdrucksformen zu erproben.
Curators: Dennis Russell Davies, Wolfgang Winkler, Heribert Schröder, Gerfried Stocker, Bianca Petscher

Antoine Schmitt,
Jean-Jaques Birgé
Nabaz'mob
*(Prix Ars Electronica 2009,
Digital Musics,
Award of Distinction)*

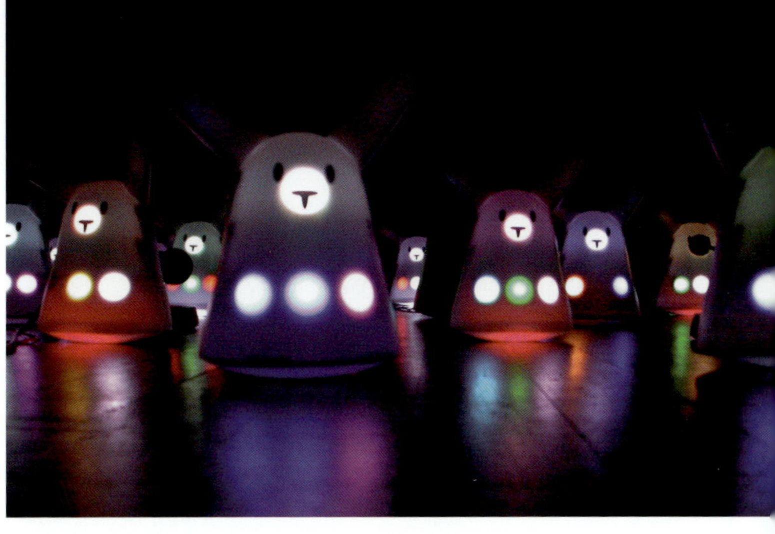

100 intelligente „Nabaztag"-
Hasen (www.nabaztag.com)
spielen gemeinsam eine
speziell von Antoine Schmitt und Jean-Jacques Birgé komponierte Oper. Diese musikalische
und choreografische Partitur lädt John Cage, Steve Reich, Conlon Nancarrow und György Ligeti
ein und wird über Wi-Fi übertragen. Sie spielt mit dem Spannungsfeld zwischen dem orchestralen Ensemble und den individuellen Stimmen, um ein starkes und engagiertes Showstück zu
produzieren. Diese Oper stellt Fragen nach Zusammenarbeit, Organisation, Entscheidung und
Steuerung, die alle in der Welt der Gegenwart immer zentraler und schwieriger werden.
Schmitt und Birgé sind jeweils Verhaltens- und Klangdesigner der von Violet konstruierten
Nabaztag-Hasen. Sie haben sich entschlossen, das Industrieobjekt in ein Kunstwerk zu verwan-
deln, bei dem die Choreografie der Ohren, das Lichtspiel und die hundert in den Bäuchen der
Hasen versteckten kleinen Lautsprecher eine Komposition mit drei Stimmen ergeben, die auf
Zeitverzögerung und Wiederholung, auf Programmierung und Missachtung von Regeln aufge-
baut ist.
Mit der Unterstützung von Violet *(www.violet.net)* nach einer Idee von Guylaine Monnier.

Tristan Perich
„Active Field" for ten violins and ten-channel 1-bit music
(Prix Ars Electronica 2009, Digital Musics, Award of Distinction)
Performed by Bruckner Orchester Linz / Dennis Russell Davies

1-Bit Music ist ein Projekt des Künstlers und Komponisten Tristan Perich, das seine klassische Musikausbildung mit primitiver, von Hand programmierter Elektronik verbindet, um die
Grundlagen des digitalen Klangs zu untersuchen.
2005 brachte Cantaloupe Music *1-Bit Music* heraus, eine eigens gebaute Elektronik verpackt
in eine Standard-CD-Hülle, die sowohl ein Album elektronischer Musik synthetisch generieren
konnte wie auch die transparente Ästhetik mit niedrigstem Lo-Fi-Klang verband.
Seit dieser Veröffentlichung hat sich Perichs Werk Richtung Kompositionen für klassisches
Ensemble mit 1-Bit-Audiobegleitung verschoben. Die Live-Musiker werden mit einem Set von
Lautsprechern auf der Bühne kombiniert, was ein hybrides mehrteiliges Werk für akustischen
und elektronischen Klang ergibt. Indem die Microchips direkt mit den Lautsprechern verbunden werden, wird der sich daraus ergebende Ensemble-Klang in der Luft „gemixt", wobei die
Lautsprecher als Sonderform eines akustischen Instruments behandelt werden, wodurch man
sich einem Konzept des elektronischen Klangs als physikalisches Phänomen annähert.

Arvo Pärt
Arbos"für 8 Blechbläser und Schlagzeug (1977/1986)
Performed by Bruckner Orchester Linz / Dennis Russell Davies

**Concerto piccolo über B-A-C-H, für Trompete, Streichorchester,
Cembalo und Klavier (1964/1994)**
Performed by Bruckner Orchester Linz / Dennis Russell Davies
Cembalo: Maki Namekawa, *Trompete:* Gerhard Fluch,
Visuals by Nanook feat. System Jaquelinde

Arvo Pärt (1935) gilt als einer der bekanntesten zeitgenössischen Komponisten. In Estland geboren emigrierte er 1980 nach Wien und später dann nach Berlin, wo er heute noch lebt. Pärt studierte Komposition in Tallinn. In seinem frühen Schaffen setzte er sich mit westlichen Stilmitteln (u. a. Klangflächen, Aleatorik, Collagentechnik) auseinander und wurde aufgrund seiner modernen Tendenzen in der ehemaligen Sowjetunion sehr kritisch betrachtet. Nach einer persönlichen Krise vertiefte sich Pärt vor allem in die mittelalterliche Musik und die Renaissancemusik. Mit einer folgenden Neuorientierung, begleitet von einer Konversion zum russisch-orthodoxen Glauben, entwickelt er seinen persönlichen Stil „Tintinnabuli" (lat. tintinnabuli: Glöckchen) – Pärt sagt selbst dazu: „Ich habe entdeckt, dass es genügt, wenn ein einziger Ton schön gespielt wird. Dieser Ton, die Stille oder das Schweigen beruhigen mich. Ich arbeite mit wenig Material, mit einer Stimme, mit zwei Stimmen. Ich baue aus primitivem Stoff, aus einem Dreiklang, einer bestimmten Tonqualität. Die drei Klänge eines Dreiklangs wirken glockenähnlich."
Arbos und das *Concerto piccolo* über B-A-C-H entstanden in der experimentelleren Frühphase, wurden beide aber später für neue Besetzungen weiterbearbeitet, *Arbos*, als instrumentale Naturbeobachtung, ein Klangteppich aus Blechbläsern. Das *Concerto piccolo* über B-A-C-H komponierte Pärt 1964 im Collagenstil, ursprünglich für Streichorchester, Oboe, Cembalo und Klavier. 1994 entstand die Version für Trompete, Streichorchester, Cembalo und Klavier. Ein Spiel mit den vier Tonarten B,A,C,H – im Stil einer barocken Suite, dreisätzig, Toccata, Sarabande und Ricercar.

(Text: Bianca Petscher)

Maki Namekawa

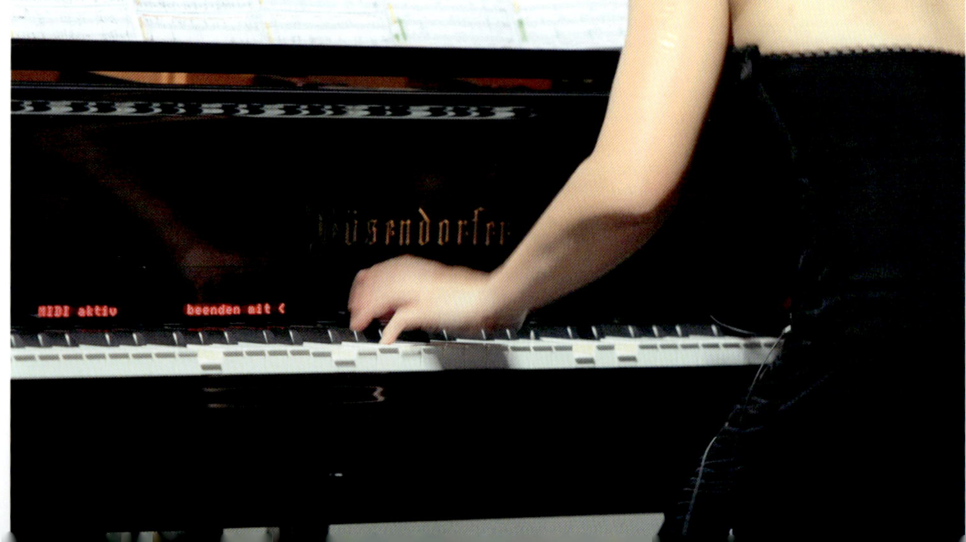

Alan Hovhaness
Lousadzak (Coming of Light), für Klavier und Streichorchester op. 48

Performed by Bruckner Orchester Linz / Dennis Russell Davies
Klavier: Maki Namekawa, *Visuals by* Kenneth Huff

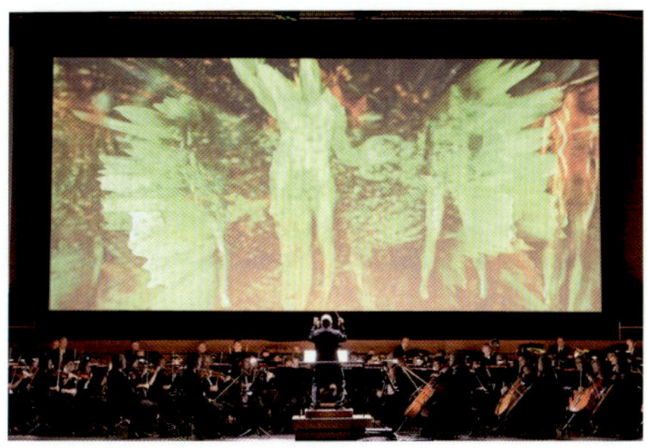

Sonorous Embodiement, 2008

Alan Hovhaness (1911-2000), geboren in Seattle als Sohn eines Armeniers und einer Amerikanerin, interessierte er sich seit seiner Kindheit für Musik, er begann schon als Kind zu komponieren, studierte dann auch Klavier und Komposition. In seinem Schaffen durchlief er mehrere stilistische Phasen. Nach einer frühen Phase, unter Einfluss von Jean Sibelius, wandelte sich sein Stil entscheidend durch sein Interesse für Meditation und Mystik und für die Musik Indiens und Armeniens. Er machte viele Studien, und entwickelte seinen Stil noch weiter – geprägt von einfacher, manchmal auch kunstvoll ausgezierter Melodik, mehr modal als tonal mit vermehrt variierenden Wiederholungen anstatt thematischer Entwicklungen. Aufgrund seiner Schlichtheit, wurde Hovhaness des Öfteren in Rezensionen kritisiert. Von Kollegen gab es andererseits aber wiederum Lob, zu seinen Befürwortern gehören u.a. John Cage und auch der Interpret Keith Jarrett. Das Klavierkonzert Lousadzak entstand im Jahr 1944, wirkt hymnisch, von armenischer Folklore beeinflusst. In seiner eleganten Einfachheit, werden oft mystische und kontemplative Stimmungen hervorgerufen.

(Text: Bianca Petscher)

Bill Fontana
Speeds of Time
(Prix Ars Electronica 2009, Digital Musics, Golden Nica)

Speeds of Time ist eine musikalische Dekonstruktion des berühmtesten akustischen Wahrzeichens und Symbols für „Zeit", des Big Ben. Live-Sensoren und Mikrofone werden auf den Uhrwerkmechanismus und nahe den Glocken von Big Ben montiert, um eine räumlich-akustische Komposition zu generieren, die dann in einer historischen Kolonnade des New Palace Yard, direkt unterhalb und in Hörweite der Glocken, platziert wird. Die Präsenz der Klangskulptur in dieser Umgebung interagiert mit dem natürlichen Klang der Glocken und erzeugt eine multidimensionale akustische Zone. Während des Zeitraums, in dem dieses Werk in Westminster installiert war, wurde eine zwölfstündige Mehrspuraufnahme der Klangskulptur angefertigt, die das Echtzeitgefühl dieses Kunstwerks nachzuempfinden erlaubt und als Acht-Kanal-Klanginstallation realisiert werden kann. Diese Aufnahme ist völlig akkurat im Bezug zur Echtzeit und braucht nur um fünf Sekunden vor zehn Uhr gestartet werden, um ganggenau und pünktlich zu sein.

Norbert Zehm:
GAMES aus Symphony No. 1 op. 45
Performed by Bruckner Orchester Linz / Dennis Russell Davies
Synthesizer / Electronics: Norbert Zehm, *Visuals by* Roland Schrettl

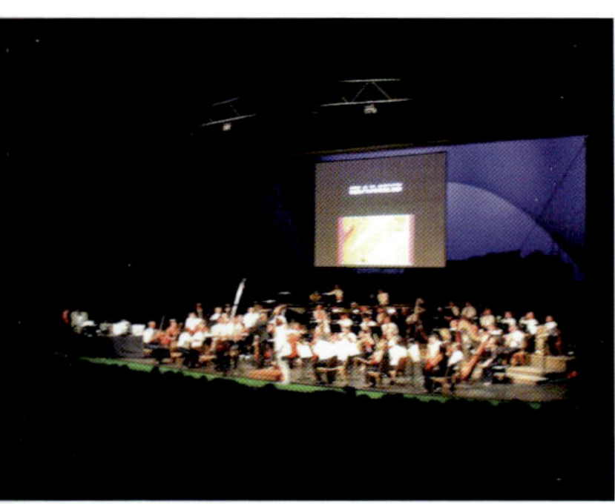

GAMES ist ein multimediales Werk für Symphonieorchester, Computer und Synthesizer, mit einer Videocollage von Roland Schrettl.

30 Jahre Computerspiele werden akustisch und visuell dokumentiert und reflektiert. Das Werk lässt den Hörer in die Welt der Cyberkids eintauchen. Durch die limitierten technischen Möglichkeiten in der Steinzeit der Computerspiele-Konsolen hatte man auch nur dementsprechend minimale Möglichkeiten, Begleitmusik zu schaffen. Solche einfachen Klang- oder Melodiezellen unterstreichen auf raffinierte Weise mit oft nur wenigen Tönen und Geräuschen die verschiedensten Stimmungen und Charaktere in den Spielen: von lustigen, sarkastischen bis hin zu furchterregenden, spannenden und brutalen Szenen.

Diese „Charaktersounds" der Computerszene wurden zu Kultsounds unter Computerfreaks und zugleich zu „Kennmelodien" der einzelnen Heimcomputermarken. („Atarisound", „Amigasound" etc.) Die Banalität, der Witz, die Ironie dieser Nicht-Kunst – oder doch Kunst? – faszinieren, um als Bausteine für ein großes symphonisches Werk verwendet zu werden.

Das Orchester fungiert hier als Echo oder Megafon dieser Computer-Minisounds und führt uns eine vertraute Welt mit neuen Mitteln und durch einen neuartigen Filter vor. Die Komposition beginnt mit einem einzigen hin und her springenden Pixelpunkt, welcher im Orchesterklang sein Echo findet, sich entwickelt bis hin zu komplexeren rhythmischen und harmonischen Klangwelten.

Der letzte Schrei: Handy-Spiele (Mobile Gaming) schließen den Kreis der bisherigen Spielesoundentwicklung. Handy-Bleep-Töne sind ja in ihrer Einfachheit den ursprünglichen monotonen Heimcomputersounds vor 30 Jahren wieder sehr ähnlich.

Die Symphonie besteht im Großen aus fünf Sätzen, die einen Bogen zwischen den verschiedenen Computerklangentwicklungen spannen, jedoch nur eine kleine Auswahl näher beleuchten. Die fünf Sätze: Pixels – Punktspiele; Galaxies – Vektoren; Heroes – Helden vor und hinter dem Joystick; Virtual Gaming – virtuelle Welten – eigene Welten; Mobile Gaming – Zweitwelt für unterwegs.

Elisabeth Schimana
Höllenmaschine (Komposition für den Max Brand Synthesizer)
OperatorInnen: Manon Liu Winter, Gregor Ladenhauf

Eine Reise ins Innere jener unikaten Maschine, die das Vermächtnis des Komponisten Max Brand und ein über Jahrzehnte entwickeltes Monster und Urahn der Moog-Synthesizer ist. Bedient von

einer erstklassigen Pianistin, schnaubt und röchelt sie ihre subharmonischen Frequenzen durch den Äther.
Eine Reise in die Hölle und nicht zurück.
Die ersten Schaltpläne für den Max Brand Synthesizer von Bob Moog sind mit dem Jahr 1957 datiert. In einem Zeitraum von mehr als zehn Jahren baut der damals

Reinhard Mayr

junge Ingenieur nach den Ideen des Komponisten Max Brand diese einzigartige Maschine. Allein in der Interfacegestaltung hinterlässt Max Brand seine Spuren: zwei Tastaturen, zwei Bandmanuale, vier Fußpedale! Herzstück sind die beiden Frequenzteiler mit je 20 Subfrequenzen und einer schaltbaren Matrix von drei Blöcken mit je 4 x 20 Subharmonischen – dazu die ersten von Moog gebauten spannungsgesteuerten Module (VCA, VCF, VCO).
Diese Maschine ist das Produkt der Zusammenarbeit eines visionären Komponisten mit einem genialen Ingenieur und fordert uns auf, sie als Maschine ernst zu nehmen und ihr ihre gewaltigen Klänge herauszuhämmern und ihre subtilen Schwingungen zu entlocken.

Christian Fennesz
Fennesz und Visuals von Lillevan

Fennesz erzeugt mit Gitarre und Computer einen schimmernden, wirbelnden elektronischen Sound von enormer Bandbreite und komplexer Musikalität. „Stellen Sie sich eine E-Gitarre jenseits des Klischees, bar sämtlicher physischer Einschränkungen vor, wie sie eine kühne neue musikalische Sprache entwickelt." (*City Newspaper*, USA)
Christian Fennesz ist für seine eigenwilligen musikalischen Welten ebenso bekannt wie für seine unvergleichlichen Gitarrenkompositionen. Seine musikalischen Ressourcen und Effekte aus dem Spannungsfeld zwischen konkreter Musik, klassischem und Ambience-Sound verwebt er in klassischen und orchestralen Entwürfen mit experimenteller Konzeptmusik und komplexen digitalen Strukturen zu Melodien und Stimmungen.
Lillevan ist Animations-, Video- und Medienkünstler und wohl am ehesten als Gründungsmitglied des Audio-Videoprojekts *Rechenzentrum* (1997-2008) ein Begriff. Neben *Rechenzentrum* arbeitet er mit zahlreichen Künstlern aus den unterschiedlichsten Genres – von Oper bis Installation, von minimal-elektronischem Experimentalismus bis hin zu Tanz und klassischer Musik – zusammen.
Lillevan und Christian Fennesz präsentieren 2009 wieder neues Material.

datamatics [ver.2.0] meets unitxt

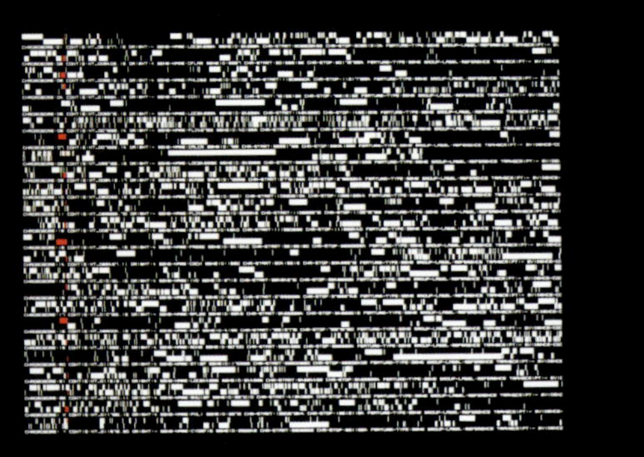

Ryoji Ikeda
datamatics [ver.2.0]

"*datamatics* showed Ikeda at the height of his artistic powers, building on his own unmistakable artistic language." (*The Wire* on Ryoji Ikeda, 2006) *datamatics* is the latest audiovisual concert in Ikeda's *datamatics* series, an art project that explores the potential to perceive the invisible multi–substance of data that permeates our world. Using pure data as a source for sound and visuals, data-matics combines abstract and mimetic presentations of matter, time and space in a powerful and breathtakingly accomplished work.The technical dynamics of the piece, such as its extremely fast frame rates and variable bit depths, continue to challenge and explore the thresholds of our perceptions.

alva noto
Unitxt Derivative Version

The title *Unitxt* could be read as "unit extended" referring to a unit of a rhythmic grid or universal text referring to a universal language, e.g. mathematics: units, constants, measurements, prefix-, SI-system of units and is represented in spoken word and by codes in sound itself.
In collaboration with derivative's touch designer software the original visuals, which are based on real-time manipulation/modulation of software-generated test patterns, has been expanded to a multi-screen set-up with a highly elaborated visual outfit to form an installation of an almost immersive quality.
This special set-up (2009) has been developed for more large scale venues and festivals of high demand. So far it has had presentations at Transmediale Berlin, followed by shows at Mutek Montréal and Sonár Barcelona.

Produced by Forma
Co–commissioned by AV Festival 06, ZeroOne San Jose & ISEA 2006
Co–produced by les Spectacles Vivants, Centre Pompidou, and YCAM
Supported by Recombinant Media Labs
Visuals support: Markus Heckmann (dervative, *http://www.touch077.com*)

forma.org.uk

datamatics [ver.2.0] meets unitxt

Ryoji Ikeda
datamatics [ver.2.0]

„*datamatics* zeigte Ikeda am Höhepunkt seiner künstlerischen Fähigkeiten, ausgehend von seiner eigenen, unverkennbaren künstlerischen Sprache." (*The Wire* über Ryoji Ikeda, 2006)
datamatics ist das neueste audiovisuelle Konzert aus Ikedas gleichnamiger Reihe. Dieses Projekt

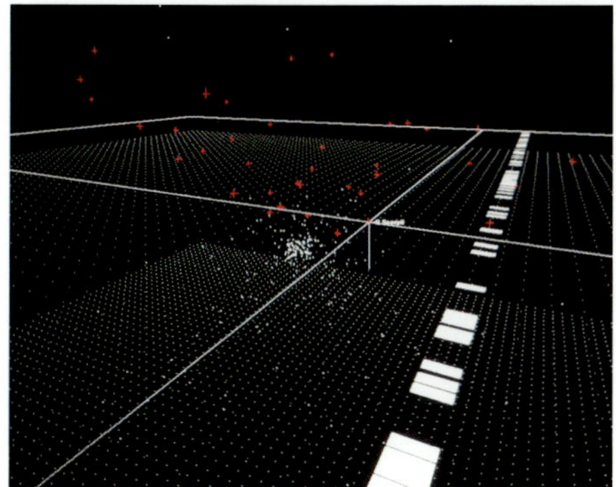

erkundet die Möglichkeiten der Wahrnehmung einer unsichtbaren Daten-Multi-Substanz, die unsere Welt durchdringt. Unter Verwendung blanker Daten als Quelle für Klang und visuelle Elemente kombiniert *datamatics* abstrakte und mimetische Präsentationen von Materie, Zeit und Raum in einer beeindruckenden und atemberaubend vollendeten Arbeit. Die technische Dynamik des Stücks, wie zum Beispiel seine äußerst schnellen Bildfolgen und unterschiedliche Bit-Tiefen, fordern immer wieder unsere Wahrnehmungsschwellen heraus und erforschen diese.

alva noto
Unitxt Derivative Version

Der Titel *Unitxt* könnte „unit extended" („erweiterte Einheit") bedeuten, was sich dann auf die Einheit eines rhythmischen Rasters oder eines universellen Textes einer universellen Sprache bezöge, z. B. jener der Mathematik: Einheiten, Konstanten, Maßeinheiten, Präfix-, SI-Einheitensystem. Diese Einheit ist Teil der gesprochenen Sprache und wird durch Codes im Klang selbst dargestellt.
In Zusammenarbeit mit der „Touch"-Designer-Software von „Derivative" wurden die ursprünglichen visuellen Elemente, die auf der Echtzeit-Manipulation/Modulation von Software-generierten Test-Mustern basieren, zu einem Multi-Screen Set-up mit einem sehr ausgefeilten visuellen Outfit erweitert. Dadurch bekam die Installation eine fast fesselnde Qualität.
Dieses spezielle Set-up (2009) entstand für sehr populäre Veranstaltungsorte und Festivals größeren Formats. Bisher war *Unitxt* bei der Transmediale Berlin zu hören, gefolgt von Shows bei den Festivals Mutek Montréal und Sonár Barcelona.

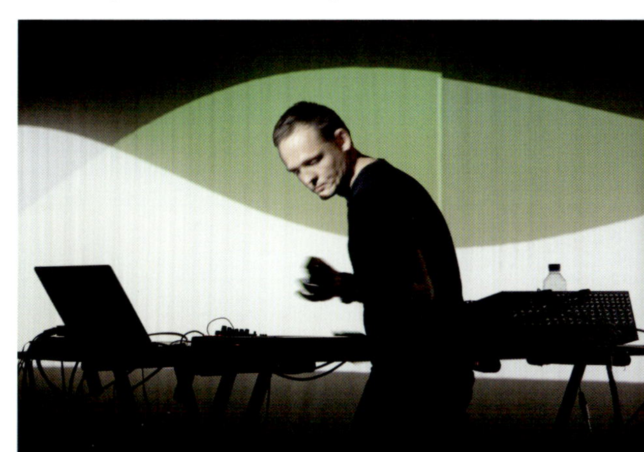

Rider Spoke

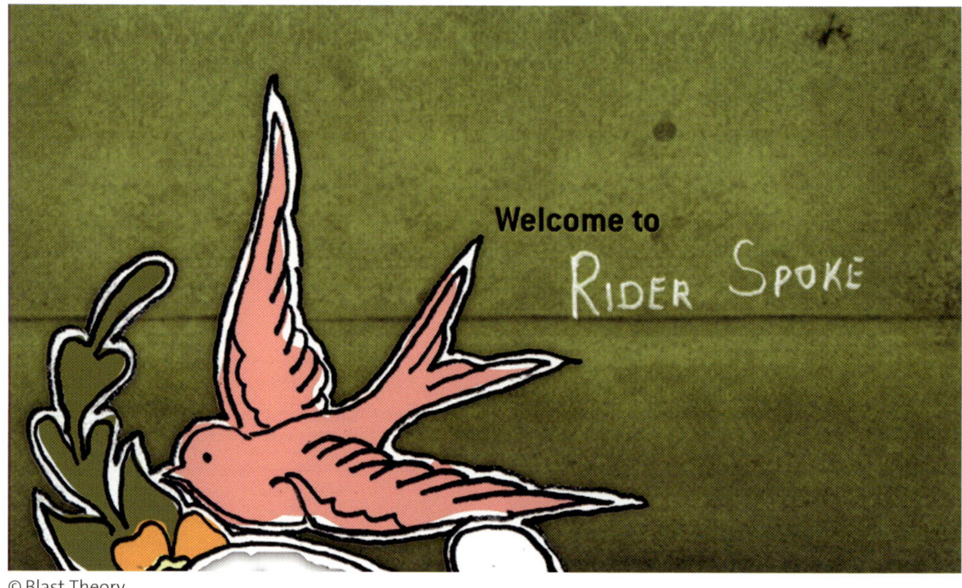

© Blast Theory

http://www.blasttheory.co.uk

Rider Spoke is a work for cyclists combining theatre with game play and state of the art technology and continues Blast Theory's enquiry into performance in the age of personal communication. *Rider Spoke* invites the audience to cycle through the streets of the city, equipped with a handheld computer. Using wi-fi technology, they search for a hiding place and record a short message there. And then they search for the hiding places of others.

The audience can take part either on their own bike or borrow one supplied by Blast Theory. Following a short introduction and a safety briefing you head out into the streets with a handheld computer (Nokia N800) mounted on the handlebars. You are given a question and invited to look for an appropriate hiding place where you will record your answer. The screen of the device acts primarily as a positioning system, using wi-fi technology to show where you are and whether there are any hiding places nearby. The interface employs imagery drawn from Mexican votive painting, sailor tattoos and heraldry: swallows flutter across the screen to show available hiding places, prefab houses indicate places where others have hidden.

Once you find a hiding place—a spot previously undiscovered by any other player—the device flashes an alert and the question. The question is one of a selection authored by Blast Theory that asks you—alone, in an out of the way spot—to reflect on your life. You then record your answer onto the device. Each hiding place combines two properties: the physical location and the electronic location as reported by the device and, for this reason, position itself is slippery and changeable. This is especially true as the University of Nottingham has designed and built a system that uses wi-fi access points to determine the position of each rider.

The other aspect of the game is to find the hiding places of others. When you find one, the device alerts you to stop and then shows you the question that that person answered and plays you their answer. The recordings that people make are only available in this context: played to a player, alone, in the place where they were recorded.

As you roll through the streets your focus is outward, looking for good places to hide, speculating about the hiding places of others, becoming completely immersed into this overlaid world as the voices of strangers draw you into a new and unknown place.

The streets may be familiar but you've given yourself up to the pleasure of being lost.

Rider Spoke continues Blast Theory's fascination with how games and new communication technologies are creating new social spaces. It poses further questions about where theatre may be sited and what form it may take. It invites the public to be co-authors of the piece and a visible manifestation of it as they cycle through the city. It locates the venue precisely in its local context and invites the audience to explore that context for its emotional and intellectual resonances.

Rider Spoke has been developed in collaboration with the Mixed Reality Lab at the University of Nottingham, Sony Net Services and the Fraunhofer Institute as part of the European research project *IPerG*(*Integrated Project on Pervasive Gaming*) and is sponsored by Trek. Blast Theory is supported by the Arts Council England South East.

A Blast Theory Production in coproduction with Nottingham University, Mixed Reality Lab. Presented by Linz09 in Cooperation with the Ars Electronica Center.

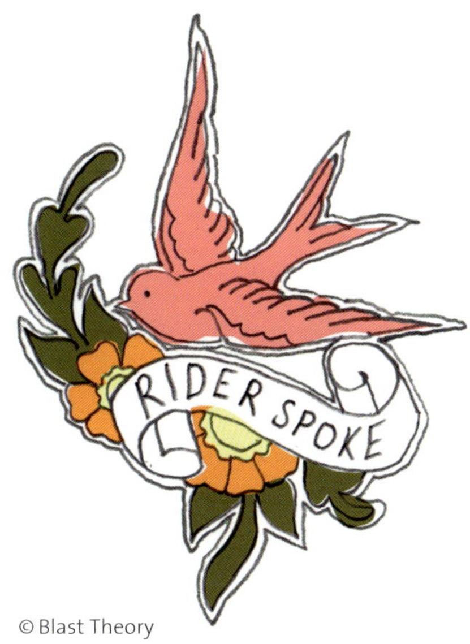

© Blast Theory

Rider Spoke

http://www.blasttheory.co.uk

Rider Spoke ist ein Projekt für Radfahrer, das Theater spielerisch mit modernster Technologie verbindet. Mit diesem Projekt wagt Blast Theory sich einmal mehr in einer Zeit der persönlichen Kommunikation in den Bereich der Performance-Kunst. *Rider Spoke* animiert die Besucher zu einer Fahrradfahrt durch die Straßen der Stadt, wobei das Fahrrad mit einem Handhelm-Computer ausgestattet ist. Per Wi-Fi suchen die Spieler nach einem Versteck, in dem sie eine kurze Nachricht aufnehmen. Dann machen sie sich auf die Suche nach den Verstecken der anderen Mitspieler.

Die Besucher können sich entweder mit dem eigenen Rad auf den Weg machen oder sich von Blast Theory ein Fahrrad ausborgen. Nach einer kurzen Einschulung und Sicherheitshinweisen geht es los: Der Handheld-Computer (Nokia N800) wird am Lenker des Fahrrads befestigt. Man erhält eine Frage und den Auftrag, nach einem geeigneten Versteck zu suchen, in dem man dann die Antwort auf die Frage aufnimmt. Der Monitor des Handhelds fungiert als Navigations-system: Über Wi-Fi wird angezeigt, wo man sich gerade befindet und ob in der Nähe Verstecke zu finden sind. Das Interface zeigt Motive aus der mexikanischen Votivmalerei, Tattoos von Matrosen und Wappen: Schwalben flattern über den Bildschirm und zeigen mögliche Verstecke an, Fertighäuser weisen auf Verstecke von anderen hin.

Sobald man ein Versteck gefunden hat – einen Ort, der von den anderen noch nicht entdeckt wurde –, blinkt eine Meldung auf, und eine aus einem von Blast Theory erstellten Pool von Fragen wird eingeblendet, die den Spieler dazu animiert, alleine an einem versteckten Ort über sein Leben nachzudenken. Die Antwort wird dann auf dem Gerät aufgezeichnet. Jedes Versteck umfasst zwei Koordinaten: den realen geografischen Standort und die auf dem Gerät angezeigte elektronische Position; eine genaue Positionsbestimmung ist daher tückisch und variabel. Dies trifft umso mehr zu, als die Universität Nottingham ein System entwickelt hat, das Wi-Fi-Access-Points zur Bestimmung des Standorts der Spieler nutzt.

Als zweite Aufgabe müssen die Spieler die Verstecke der anderen finden. Findet man ein solches, wird ein Hinweis nebst der Frage eingeblendet, die ein anderer Spieler in diesem Versteck beant-wortet hat. Die Antwort kann abgehört werden. Allerdings können die Aufzeichnungen nur am Aufnahmeort und nur von einem Spieler, der sich allein dort befindet, abgehört werden.

Während man durch die Straßen radelt, fährt man stets vorausblick-end, sucht nach möglichen guten Verstecken, spekuliert, wo die Ver-stecke der anderen sein könnten, und taucht völlig in diese Welt ein, in der man von fremden Stimmen zu neuen und unbekannten Orten geleitet wird.

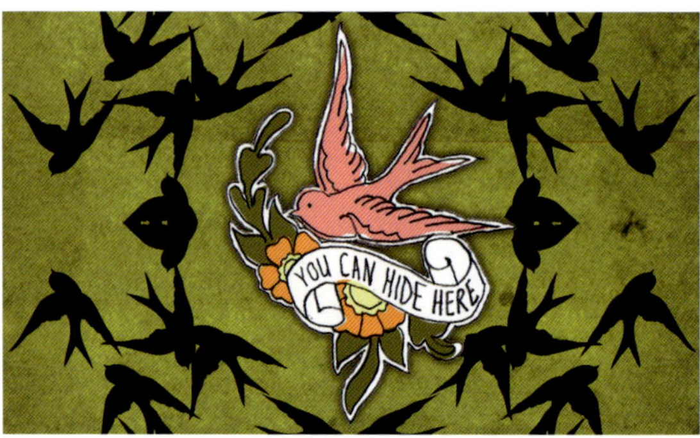

© Blast Theory

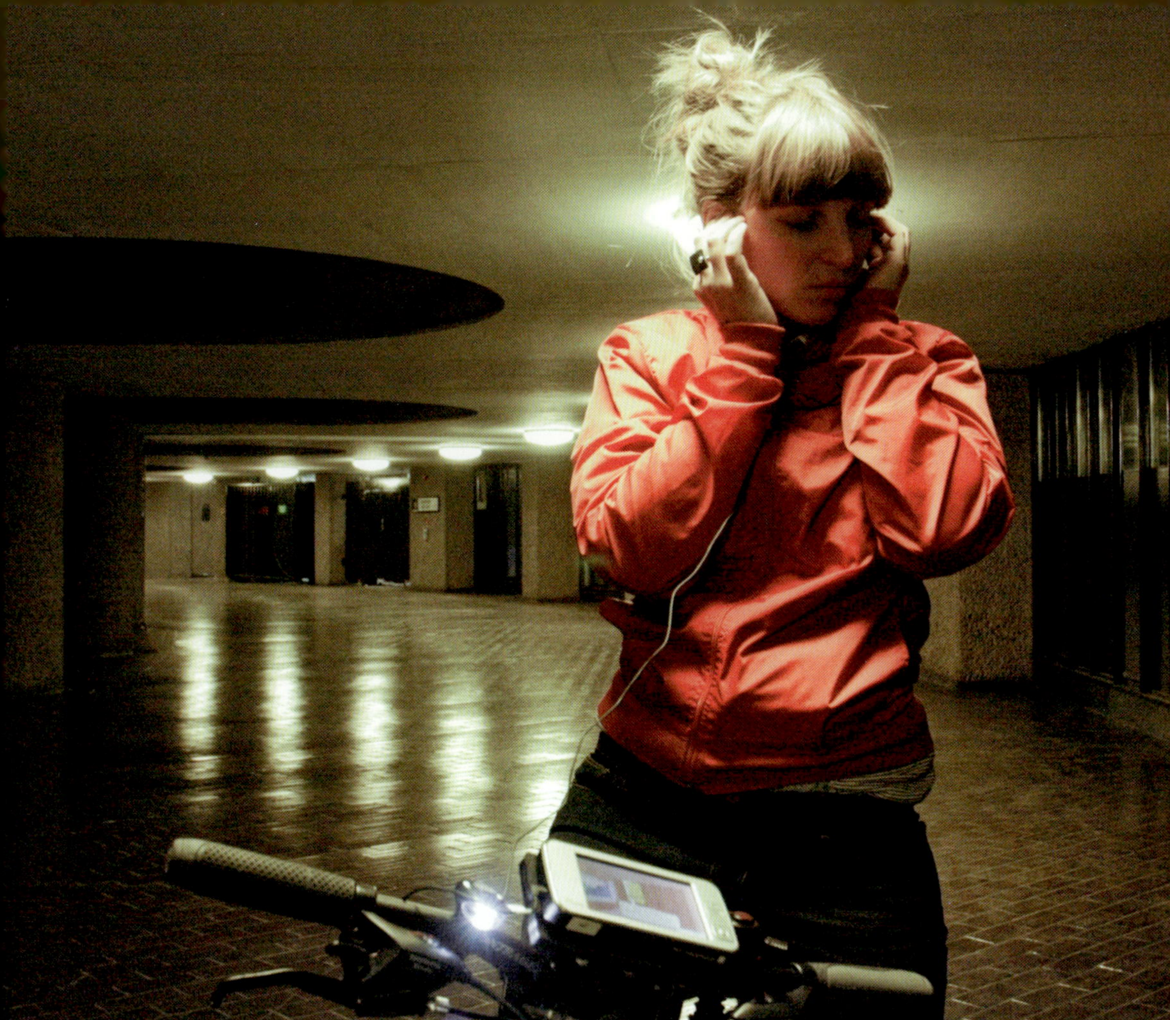

Die Straßen erscheinen vielleicht vertraut, man gibt sich jedoch dem Vergnügen hin, sich in den Straßen zu verlieren.

Mit *Rider Spoke* greifen Blast Theory einmal mehr jene Faszination auf, die Spiele und neue Kommunikationstechnologien, die neue soziale Räume zu schaffen vermögen, auf uns ausüben. Das Projekt wirft auch neue Fragen auf: Wo kann Theater angesiedelt und wie kann es gestaltet werden? Das Publikum wird zum Mitautor des Stücks und ist gleichzeitig Teil der Besetzung, die durch die Straßen der Stadt radelt. Das Geschehen ist direkt im lokalen Umfeld verortet und lädt die Spieler ein, ihre Umgebung auf ihre emotionalen und intellektuellen Resonanzen hin zu durchforsten.

Rider Spoke wurde im Rahmen des EU-Forschungsprojekts *IPerG* (*Integrated Project on Pervasive Gaming*) in Zusammenarbeit mit d*em Mixed Reality Lab an de*r Universität Nottingham, *Sony Net Services* und dem Fraunhofer-Institut umgesetzt und von *Trek* unterstützt. Blast Theory wird vom *Arts Council England South East* subventioniert.

Eine Produktion von Blast Theory in Koproduktion mit der Universität Nottingham, Mixed Reality Lab. Präsentiert von Linz09 in Kooperation mit dem Ars Electronica Center.

(Aus dem Englischen von Sonja Pöllabauer)

The Context is the Message

Exactly 10 years ago, social worker Stefan M. Seydel paid his first visit to Ars Electronica in Linz. For the occasion, he set up a special hard-coded website to which he filed daily communiqués that gave astounded accounts of his explorations. This year, to mark Ars' 30th anniversary, rebell.tv AG will be making its third trip to the Linz festival, this time with a 13-ton, 12 x 4-meter luxury "mobile communications facility". This broadcasting studio-on-wheels transports an 800-gram camera and a 3-kilo notebook in order to dispatch via wLan unedited video clips, "field correspondent" reports for rocketboom.com, announcements, links and observations to a globally-accessible bulletin board, and to get the "10 o'clock news" online each morning. "Welcome to the German-speaking part of Europe!"

Verbal interpersonal communication enables human beings to transcend our instincts and engage in intellectual exchange. Writing and literacy endow the absentee with presence. Letterpress printing solves distribution problems and delivers engineered explications of how sufficient complicatedness makes a complex world appear manageable. The computer permits us to cease having to treat the world in its actual state of incessant change as a trivial machine!

It is precisely because complexity cannot be managed by means of rules governing the reduction of information that we, calling upon our behavioral science background in the field of social work, are developing working principles that we describe with the term "The Form of Unrest". Our mission here is not to host a constantly-updated website showcasing the most relevant, hippest, coolest performing news. We're filing the observations we've made to a "viewing repository": direct, unmediated, unprocessed (TV, radio). We, amidst a state of pervasive redundancy, are network-linking that which has come to our attention in a "memorandum bin" (BLOG). We let it sit there. We wait. We sleep. Until facets occur to us and feedback strikes, and we can gain a somewhat new way of seeing what we had previously observed (print). Until topics ultimately importune upon us, issues that we can distill from the material we've amassed and then send forth on their multimedial, interactive way: *http://magazin.rebell.tv*

(Text: Tina Piazzi and Stefan M. Seydel/sms)

The Context is the Message

Vor genau zehn Jahren besuchte der Sozialarbeiter Stefan M. Seydel zum ersten Mal die Ars Electronica in Linz. Er richtete dafür eine spezielle, hardcoded programmierte Seite im Internet ein – „kein spURLoses tagebuch" – und berichtete täglich staunend von seinen Erkundungen. Zum 30-jährigen Jubiläum der Ars fährt rebell.tv AG heuer zum dritten Mal mit einem 13 Tonnen schweren, zwölf Meter langen, vier Meter breiten Luxus-„Ü-Wagen" auf. Das Unternehmen transportiert darin eine 800 Gramm schwere Kamera und ein drei Kilo schweres Notebook, um via W-Lan ungeschnittene Video-Schnipsel, Berichte als *field correspondent* von rocketboom.com, Notizen, Links, Beobachtungen im Zettelkasten und die morgendlichen „10-Uhr-Nachrichten" online zu bringen: „Welcome to the German-speaking Part of Europe!"

Die mündliche Kommunikation unter Menschen ermöglicht, weit über das Instinktive hinaus, in einen geistigen Austausch zu kommen. Die Schriftlichkeit erlaubt, das Abwesende anwesend zu halten. Der Buchdruck löst Probleme der Distribution und expliziert ingenieurhaft, wie eine komplexe Welt durch genügende Kompliziertheit bewältigbar scheint. Der Computer erlaubt uns, dass wir die Welt in ihrer tatsächlich ständigen Verändertheit nicht weiterhin als triviale Maschine behandeln müssen!

Weil Komplexität eben gerade nicht über Regeln der Reduktion von Informationen bewältigt werden kann, entwickeln wir aus dem handlungswissenschaftlichen Hintergrund der sozialen Arbeit Arbeitsprinzipien, welche wir unter dem Namen „Die Form der Unruhe" beschreiben. Es geht uns nicht darum, eine Internet-Plattform zu pflegen, welche laufend die relevantesten, hipsten, tollst performenden News präsentiert. Wir legen unsere gemachten Beobachtungen in ein „Schaulager" ab: direkt, unvermittelt, unbearbeitet (TV, Radio). Unter großer Redundanz vernetzen und verlinken wir das Beobachtete im „Zettelkasten" (Blog). Dort lassen wir es liegen. Wir warten. Wir schlafen. Bis uns Aspekte und Rückmeldungen daraus auf- und anregen und wir diese noch einmal ganz anders beobachten können (Print). Bis sich uns schließlich Themenfelder aufdrängen, welche wir aus dem zusammengetragenen Material heraus – multimedial und interaktiv – zur Darstellung bringen können: *http://magazin.rebell.tv*

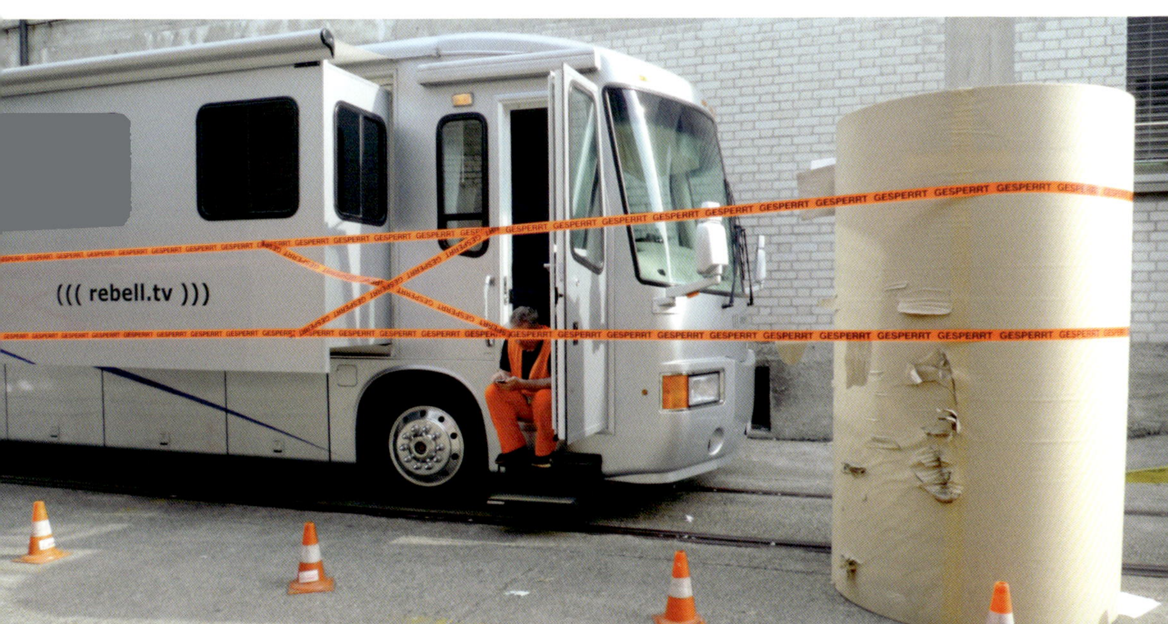

Andres Bosshard

Klanghimmel: Heavenly Sounds in the Urfahr Parish Church

Based on the fundamental concepts of Baroque *trompe-l'oeil* painting in general and particularly its cunningly stylish way of producing starkly multi-layered depth of field effects that are still capable of eliciting expressions of astonishment from modern viewers, the sound architecture designed by Andres Bosshard aims to conjure up a "sound heaven" within the local parish church in Linz's Urfahr neighborhood.

The main elements situated within the church's reverberating vault are eight resonating ceramic bodies created by David Fuchs that display extraordinary acoustic radiation qualities. The sounds emanating from the loudspeaker system are first filtered through these ceramic balls and then radiated ball-shaped into the interior space. Moreover, the spatial constellation of the eight balls forms an intentionally implemented network configuration that makes it possible to produce clear and astoundingly multi-layered tonal imagery in the church's long and quite diffused resonating space. Of particular importance are apparent tonal space movements that glide through the church's nave. Andres Bosshard spent several nights in the church before composing a tonal space choreography consisting of musical modules played live on an eight-channel stereophonic sound instrument. The sound coming directly from the balls, the reflections off the vault, interior walls and floor, and the almost inaudible sounds of the city that penetrate the church nave's walls from outside blend together with virtual sound space projections into a very fine choreophony.

(Translated from German by Mel Greenwald)

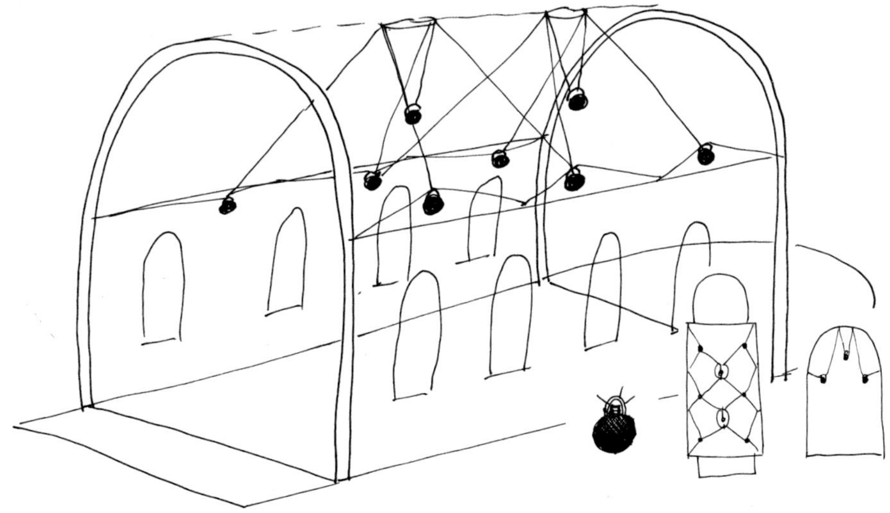

Andres Bosshard

Klanghimmel in der Pfarrkirche Urfahr

Die Grundidee barocker Illusionsmalerei aufnehmend, insbesondere deren raffinierte virtuelle Tiefenstaffelungen, die es schaffen, auch dem heutigen Auge ein ungläubiges Staunen zu entlocken, verfolgt die von Andres Bosshard entworfene Klangarchitektur, einen *Klanghimmel* in die Pfarrkirche von Urfahr zu zaubern.

Eckpfeiler des klingenden Kirchengewölbes bilden die von David Fuchs realisierten acht keramischen Klangkörper, die ganz besondere akustische Abstrahleigenschaften aufweisen. Zunächst werden durch die Keramikkugeln die Lautsprecherklänge gefiltert und danach kugelförmig in den Raum abgestrahlt. Zudem bildet die räumliche Konstellation der acht Kugeln ein bewusst gewähltes Raumgitter, das es erlaubt, im recht diffusen und langen Nachhallraum der Kirche ein klares und erstaunlich vielschichtiges Klangbild zu erzeugen. Besonders wichtig sind scheinbare Klangraumbewegungen, die das Kirchenschiff durchgleiten. Andres Bosshard verbrachte mehrere Nächte in der Kirche und komponierte auf dem achtkanaligen Raumklanginstrument aus live gespielten musikalischen Modulen eine Klangraumchoreografie. Der Direktschall der Kugeln, die Reflexionen vom Gewölbe, von den Wänden und dem Boden und die fast unhörbaren Klänge der Stadt, die durch die Mauern des Kirchenschiffs dringen, sind mit virtuellen Klangraumprojektionen zu einer sehr feinen Choreofonie verschmolzen.

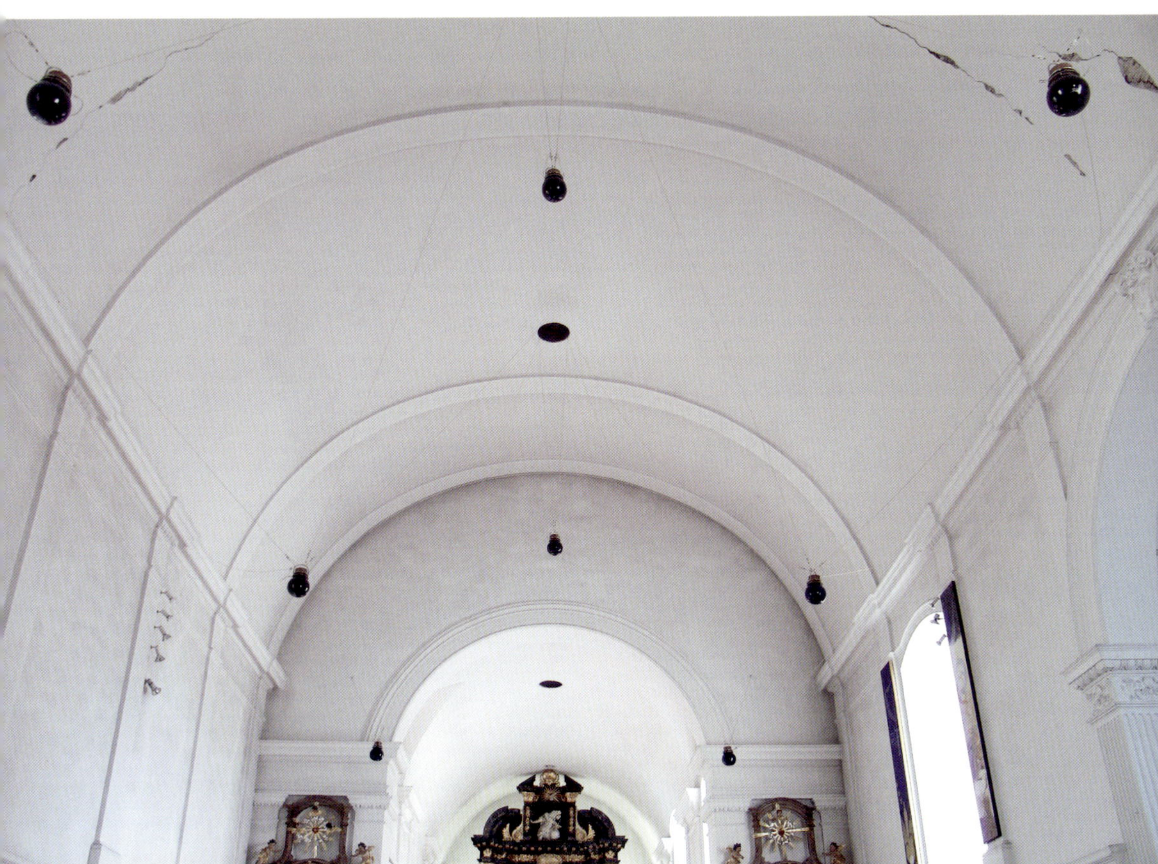

h.o + Dentsu

Buzz Bubbles

With the advancement of information technology, the environment in which we live, our actions and the ways of the market are all rapidly changing. It would seem that information search technology, such as Google's, has provided efficient means of bringing together people and information. Instead of passively receiving and sifting through a flood of information from sources such as television and advertisements, we are able to obtain only the information we seek through proactive search.

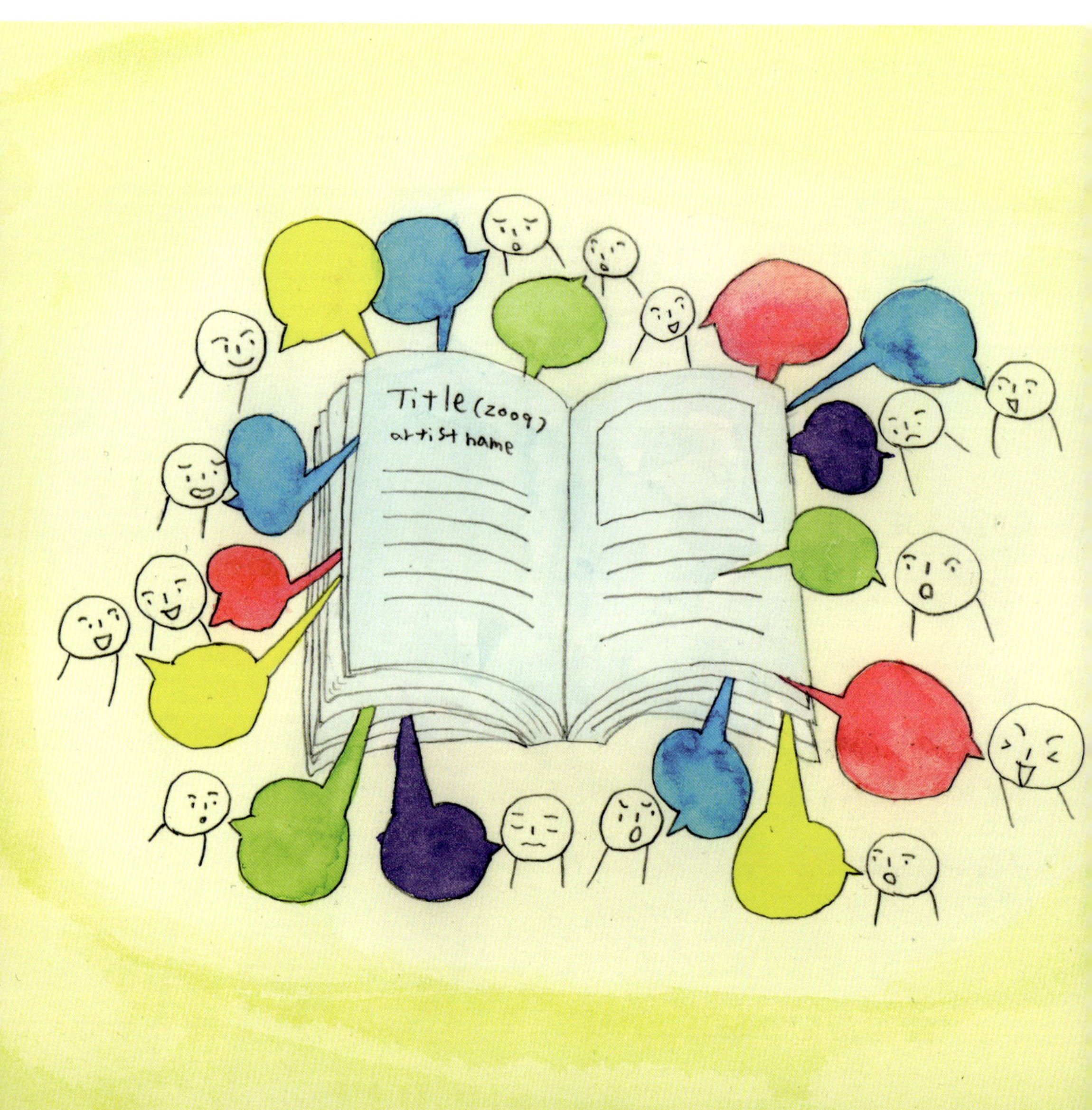

However, this seemingly efficient way of acquiring information has deprived us of opportunities to come across "unexpected encounters" with information and products. Confined in the information space of our interest, we are less likely to meet and discover new items and information previously provided by mass targeted advertising.

Therefore, in this project, targeting the 2009 Ars Electronica Festival catalog, we will create a prototype of a new advertisement system that will provoke interest in artists and works one has previously been unaware of, motivating them to pick up a catalog.

The Ars Electronica Festival catalog contains page-by-page information on participating artists, works on display, projects, conference information and scheduled performances during the festival. What would happen if we tie together this physical catalog with activity from a virtual space like the Internet?

We designed a system where "Buzz" is extracted and generated based on people's interests and activities on the Ars Electronica web site. We then map the extracted Buzz to information on the pages of the Festival catalog and convert it into physical output. At our installation site, every time there is access to the web site, Buzz is translated into output to a physical bookshop.

P.xx seems to be popular in the Asian region. (access region data)

P.xx has suddenly gained attention this week. (change in access count)

People who like P.xx seem to also access P.yy. (page movement history)

Also, based on the same system, we will print real-time designed bookmarks and paper bags to promote the sales of the festival catalog.

Through this installation, we express the social image of Ars Electronica in real time by tying together talk collected from the web with actual pages of the catalog. Visitors to the festival will be able to bring home "advertisements" generated from voices on the web. In this new bookstore, the catalog is not just a product but also a new advertisement medium. We create active physical encounters that advertisements used to provide, against today's mechanically streamlined and closed advertisement system provided by information acquisition technologies.

Google says they will digitize all books and make them searchable. In the process, books will be dismantled and the physical element of "pages" will lose its meaning. On the other hand, the way we discover information is likely to expand beyond online search into interactions with the physical world. When we look at things from both this "cloud" and "ground" viewpoint, how can we provide discovery of new products and information in a simple and straightforward manner? Ads are definitely an effective means to accomplish this. There should be an attractive method of communication that brings together people and products—unlike yesterday's ads which some consider a nuisance. In the process of pursuing this new form of advertisement, we believe we will be able to gain insight on human nature.

This project is a product of a joint project between the artist group "h.o" and the top Japanese advertising agency "Dentsu", which started in 2008. Continuing from last year's "A New Cultural Advertising Project (T-shirt project)", it is an experiment on new forms of advertising staged at the Ars Electronica festival.
h.o is: Taizo Zushi, Hideaki Ogawa, Mizuya Sato, Yuichi Tamagawa and Emiko Ogawa
Dentsu is: Naoto Oiwa, Makoto Teramoto, Yasuharu Sasaki and Tsubasa Kayasuga

Buzz Bubbles

Mit dem stetigen Fortschritt der Informationstechnologie ändern sich die Lebensumstände, das Verhalten der Menschen und die Mechanismen des Markts zunehmend schneller. Man sollte annehmen, dass Suchsysteme wie Google leistungsstarke Funktionen für eine gezielte Suche nach Informationen bieten. Wir sind nicht länger passive Empfänger, die über verschiedene Kanäle, wie Fernsehen und Werbung, von einer Flut an Informationen überrollt werden, aus denen wir die für uns relevanten Daten mühsam herausfiltern müssen, sondern wir können nun proaktiv nach für uns wesentlichen Inhalten suchen.

Diese scheinbar effiziente Form der Informationsbeschaffung verhindert jedoch, dass wir „unerwartet" auf Informationen oder Produkte stoßen, die für uns von Interesse sein könnten. Wir sind im Informationskäfig unserer Interessen gefangen: Die Wahrscheinlichkeit, dass wir Zugang zu für uns neuen Produkten oder Informationen erhalten, ist weitaus geringer als zu Zeiten der gezielten Massenwerbung.

Unser Projekt setzt beim Ars-Electronica-Katalog 2009 an. Wir entwickeln einen Prototypen einer neuen Form der Werbung, die das Interesse der Zielgruppen unserer Werbeaktion an ihnen bislang unbekannten Künstlern und Projekten wecken und sie dazu animieren soll, den Festivalkatalog zu erwerben.

Der Katalog enthält detaillierte Informationen zu den an der Ars-Electronica beteiligten Künstlern, den ausgestellten Werken und Installationen, zum Ars-Electronica-Symposium und zu diversen Aktivitäten im Festivalzeitraum. Was wäre, wenn wir den real existenten Katalog mit Aktivitäten in einem virtuellen Raum wie dem Internet verbinden?

Wir haben ein System entwickelt, das die Aktivitäten und Suchanfragen der Besucher der Ars-Electronica-Website zu einem Informationsgewirr („Buzz") verdichtet. Dieses mappen wir dann mit Informationen im gedruckten Festivalkatalog und konvertieren es in physische Produkte. Jedes Mal, wenn auf die Website zugegriffen wird, wird eine Vielfalt an Daten generiert, die als physische Artikel in einer realen Buchhandlung präsentiert werden.

P.xx scheint in Asien beliebt zu sein (regionale Zugriffsdaten)

P.xx hat diese Woche vermehrt Beachtung gefunden (Änderung der Zugriffsstatistik)

Menschen, die Interesse an P.xx zeigen, rufen anscheinend auch Informationen zu P.yy. auf (Seitenverlaufsstatistik)

Mithilfe dieses Systems werden wir auch in Echtzeit generierte Lesezeichen und Papiertaschen drucken, um den Verkauf des Katalogs anzukurbeln.

Mit dieser Installation geben wir unmittelbar Einblick in das soziale Image des Ars-Electronica-Festivals, indem wir webbasierte Informationen mit dem Festivalkatalog verknüpfen. Besucher des Festivals können „Werbeprodukte", die aus Informationsgewirr und „Stimmen" im Netz generiert wurden, mit nach Hause nehmen. In dieser neuen Buchhandlung dient der Katalog nicht nur als Verkaufsprodukt, sondern auch als Werbeträger. Wir erzeugen so jene Atmosphäre des physischen Kontakts, die früher über traditionelle Werbemittel geschaffen wurde, und kämpfen damit gegen das uniforme, enge Werbesystem an, das von modernen Suchsystemen forciert wird.

Google plant die Digitalisierung aller Bücher, um eine Volltextsuche zu ermöglichen. Bücher verlieren dabei ihre eigentliche Funktion, die einzelne „Buchseite" als zentraler physischer Bestandteil von Büchern verliert ihren Sinn. Allerdings werden sich auch unsere Suchstrategien ändern, und wir werden nicht mehr ausschließlich das Netz nach Informationen durchforsten, sondern bei unserer Suche nach Inhalten auch in direkten Kontakt mit der physischen Welt treten. Wenn wir die Welt sowohl von oben, gleichsam aus der Informationswolke des Internets, als auch von unten, aus einer bodenständigen, erdbehafteten Perspektive betrachten, wie können wir dann einfach und unkompliziert Zugang zu neuen Informationen erhalten? Werbeeinschaltungen sind hier sicher ein wichtiges Medium. Es sollte ein attraktives Informationsforum geben, das Menschen und Produkte zusammenbringt, ohne dass es als lästige Werbung empfunden wird. Wir sind überzeugt, dass wir bei unserer Suche nach neuen Werbeträgern unerwartete Einsichten in die Natur des Menschen gewinnen.

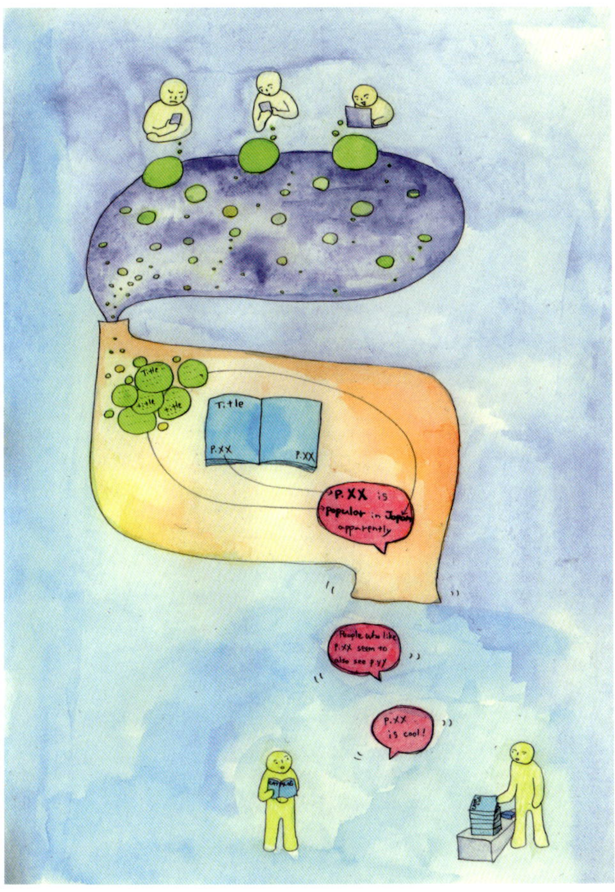

Dieses Projekt basiert auf einer Kooperation zwischen dem Künstlerkollektiv „h.o" und der renommierten japanischen Werbeagentur „Dentsu", die 2008 aufgenommen wurde. Als Nachfolgeprojekt des letztjährigen Festivalbeitrags, „A New Cultural Advertising Project (T-shirt project)", ist diese Arbeit ein Experiment mit neuen Werbeformen, die im Rahmen der Ars Electronica erprobt werden. Mitglieder von h.o sind: Taizo Zushi, Hideaki Ogawa, Mizuya Sato, Yuichi Tamagawa und Emiko Ogawa. Mitarbeiter von Dentsu sind: Naoto Oiwa, Makoto Teramoto, Yasuharu Sasaki und Tsubasa Kayasuga.

(Aus dem Englischen von Sonja Pöllabauer)

The Interior the Disco Ball

It is in the shrillest of tones and, above all, through the use of high-definition images that the arrival of a new age is being proclaimed, and these future worlds are being described with a sense of certainty that makes it seems as if good old-fashioned fortune telling had been rehabilitated and declared an exact science. Nostradamus and the Sibyls seem to have been resurrected en masse so that nothing more need be left up to the difficult task of interpretation. Equipped with diplomas, state-of-the-art technology and funding aplenty, they draw us pictures of the past, present and future of humankind—our successes and setbacks, our body and our environment, all depicted according to personal taste and the guidelines of the commissioning client. Fascinated and characteristically fatalistic, we watch as our fate is rolled out before us.

The *fabriqueee* group isn't able to summon up all that much faith in these communiqués, and thus turns its attention to a somewhat older human (self)realization machine, one that is as commonplace as it is weird, and in which certainty and deception have always gone hand in hand: the mirror.

In accordance with this approach and through the pursuit of a modular mode of working, the group's members are developing a wide range of individual projects including installations, apparatuses, sculptures and objects, works of animation and visualizations that, once set up in the *Grand Cafe zum Rothen Krebsen*, will ultimately engender a playful spatial construction that promises anything and everything except assurances and purportedly certain insights.

On the seven evenings of Ars Electronica Festival week, *fabriqueee* in cooperation with the IFEK—Institute for Expanded Art will offer the possibility of exploring *the interior the disco ball*. What's left is right; what's on top is on the bottom?

(Text: Sandra Li Lian Obwegeser vs. Joseph Reitsberger; supported by *fabriqueee*)

Das Innere der Discokugel

Laut und vor allem bildkräftig wird die Ankunft in einem neuen Zeitalter verkündet und mit einer Gewissheit von künftigen Welten gesprochen, als wäre die gute alte Wahrsagerei rehabilitiert und zugleich zur echten Wissenschaft erklärt worden. Nostradamus und die Sibyllen scheinen im Kollektiv wieder auferstanden, um nun nichts mehr der Deutung zu überlassen. Ausgestattet mit Diplomen, neuester Technologie und viel Geld zeichnen sie uns die Vergangenheit, Gegenwart und Zukunft des Menschen. Seine Erfolge, seine Rückschläge, seinen Körper, seine Umwelt, je nach Geschmack und Auftraggeber. Fasziniert und eigentümlich fatalistisch sehen wir zu, wie unser Schicksal vor uns entrollt wird.

Die Gruppe *fabriqueee* kann dem nicht so recht trauen und richtet ihre Aufmerksamkeit auf eine schon etwas ältere, so alltägliche wie unheimliche (Selbst-)Erkenntnismaschine des Menschen, bei der Gewissheit und Täuschung immer schon Hand in Hand gingen: den Spiegel.

Aus diesem Ansatz heraus entwickeln die Mitglieder der Gruppe entlang einer modularen Arbeitsweise verschiedene Einzelprojekte, die von Installationen über Apparaturen, Plastiken und Objekte bis hin zu Animationen und Visualisierungen reichen, um im *Grand Cafe zum Rothen Krebsen* letztlich ein spielerisches Raumgefüge zur erzeugen, das alles verspricht nur keine Gewissheit und vermeintlich sichere Erkenntnis.

An den sieben Abenden der Woche des Ars Electronica Festivals wird fabriqueee in Zusammenarbeit mit dem Institut für erweiterte Kunst die Möglichkeit eröffnen, „das Innere der Discokugel" zu erkunden. Was links ist ist rechts, was oben ist ist unten?

(Text: Sandra Li Lian Obwegeser vs. Joseph Reitsberger; supported by *fabriqueee*)

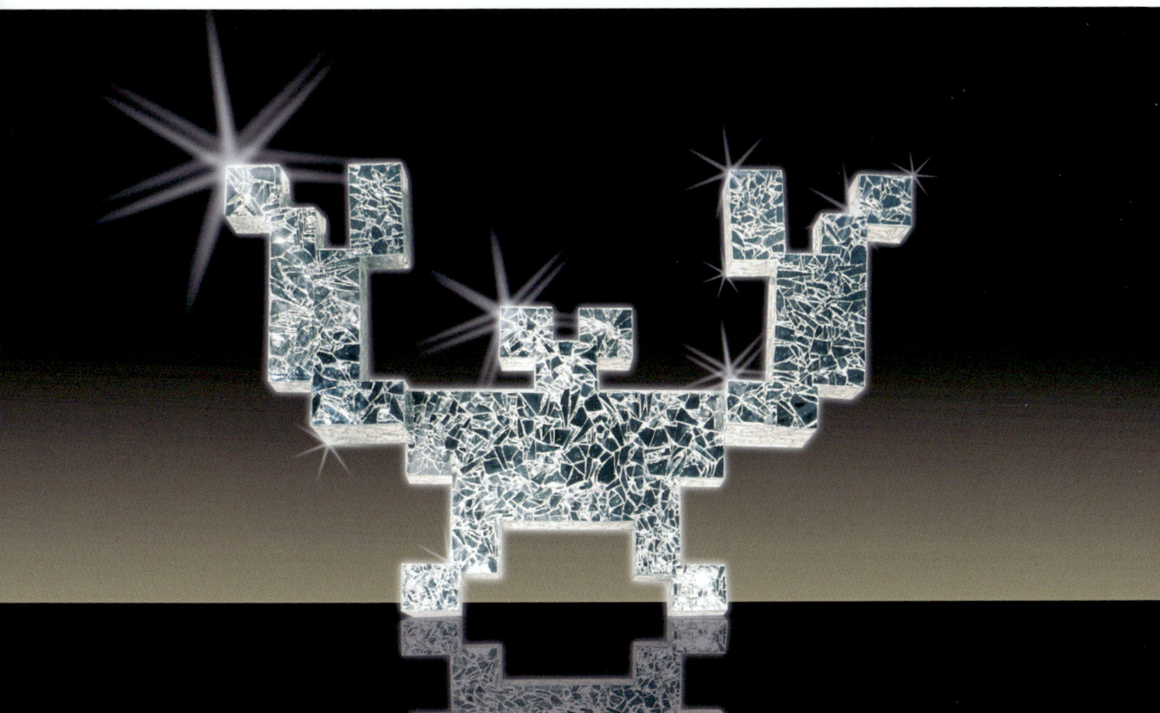

Fidel Peuegot, Karl Emilio Pircher

You May takes the public space

You May is a new furniture for the urban public space. *You May* does many things: it is a bar and a bench, conference table and quiet corner at the same time, it functions as a lounge as well as a stage or workspace. *You May* works with innovative materials, different seat heights, it plays with niches and corners. It provides communication and privacy for up to 15 persons in the same spot. The furniture itself becomes a vivid meeting point, it invites to work, discuss, eat and relax. *You May* enables the modern, mobile person to much more than just passive relaxing and therefore significantly differs from all current standard furnitures for parks and public spaces. The Vienna based design duo Karl Emilio Pircher & Fidel Peugeot provides mayors, urban planners and residents with a versatile instrument for enhancing the quality of the public space and filling it with a new lively spirit. *You May* is a cooperation between Walking-Chair Design Studio and the Danish platform LYNfabrikken. The first edition was finished during May 2009 for the Aarhus Festuge (Århus Festival Week) in Denmark and will be an exhibition part of the Ars Electronica Festival 2009 in Linz.

http://www.walking-chair.com, http://www.walking-things.com

YOU MAY Design by Walking-Chair Design Studio (Karl Emilio Pircher & Fidel Peugeot) www.walking-chair.com
Special thanks to our YOU MAY cooperation partner in Denmark: LYNfabrikken.dk & The Aarhus Festival
YOU MAY is powered by departure, wirtschaft kunst und kultur gmbh

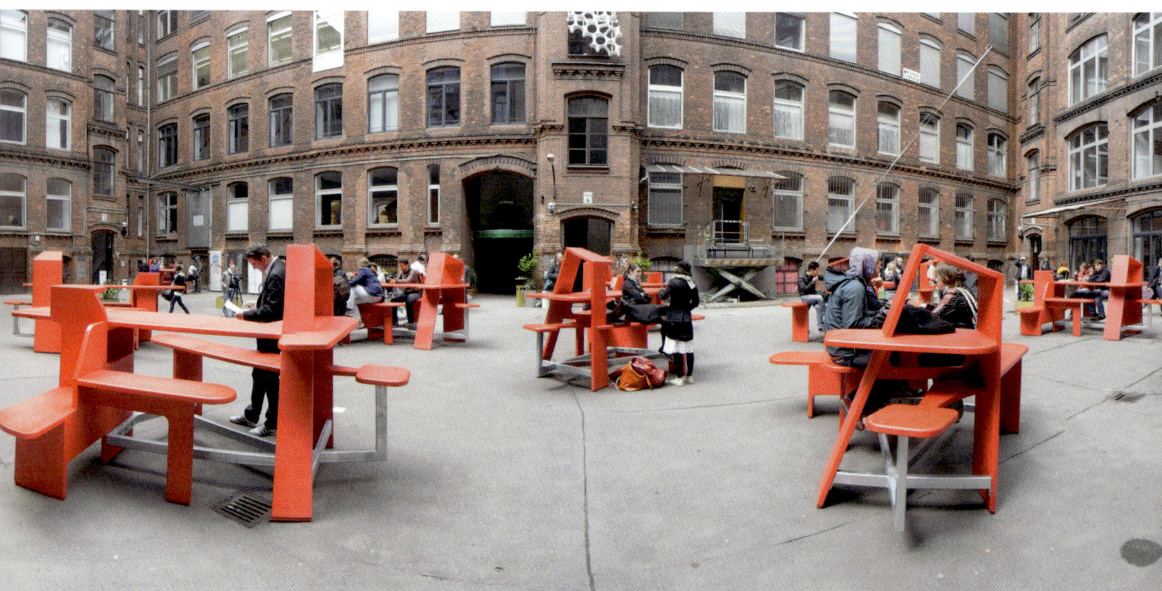

Fidel Peuegot, Karl Emilio Pircher

You May takes the public space

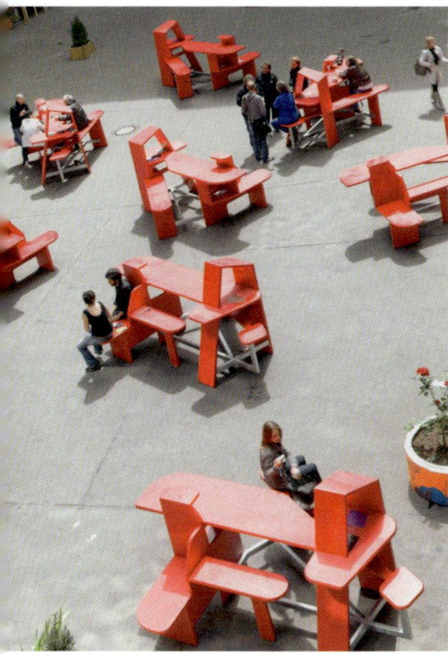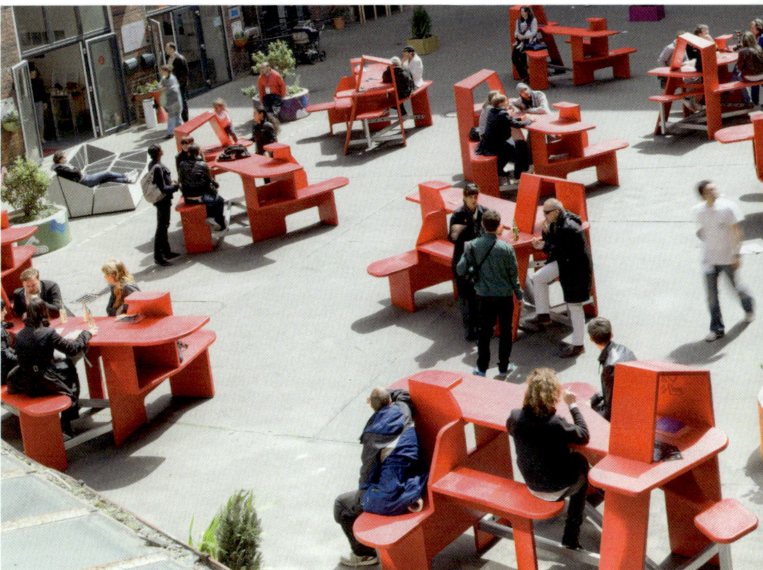

You May ist ein neuartiges Möbel für den öffentlichen urbanen Raum. *You May* kann vieles: Es ist gleichzeitig Bar und Bank, Konferenztisch und stille Ecke, es funktioniert auch als Lounge, Bühne oder Arbeitsplatz. Dabei arbeitet *You May* mit innovativen Materialien, unterschiedlichen Sitzhöhen, spielt mit Nischen und Kanten. Es schafft somit Kommunikation und Privatsphäre am selben Ort für bis zu 15 Personen. Das Möbelstück an sich wird somit zu einem lebendigen Treffpunkt, lädt ein zum Arbeiten, Besprechen, Essen und Entspannen. *You May* ermöglicht dem modernen, mobilen Menschen weit mehr als das passive Relaxen und unterscheidet sich dadurch erheblich von allen derzeitigen Standardmöblierungen für Parks und Plätze. Das Designerduo Karl Emilio Pircher & Fidel Peugeot gibt mit dieser Erfindung Bürgermeistern, Städteplanern und Einwohnern ein vielseitiges Instrument, um den öffentlichen Bereich aufzuwerten und mit einer neuen Lebendigkeit zu füllen. *You May* ist eine Kooperation von Walking-Chair Design Studio mit der dänischen Plattform LYNfabrikken, es wurde in Erstauflage im Mai 2009 für die Aarhus Festuge (Århus Festwoche) in Dänemark umgesetzt und wird am Festival Ars Electronica vom 3. bis 8. September in Linz ausgestellt.

http://www.walking-chair.com, http://www.walking-things.com

YOU MAY Design: Walking-Chair Designstudio (Karl Emilio Pircher & Fidel Peugeot) www.walking-chair.com
Besten Dank an unsere Projektpartner in Dänemark: LYNfabrikken.dk & Das Aarhus Festival
YOU MAY wird im Rahmen des Förderungsprogramms C.0901 von departure, wirtschaft kunst und kultur gmbh unterstützt.

Linz as European Capital of Culture: Three Insights

By Martin Heller

More than one half of the Capital of Culture year has passed now. The tension decreases. The head becomes free. Eventually, it is possible to speak of experiences and not only of expectations or even hopes. And of learning processes of a city like Linz that has dared to enter unknown territory with this title, its challenges and its everyday life.

Since Linz09 – this is the short form for Linz 2009 European Capital of Culture – has already had a lot of effects, in different regards. The city conveys a different feeling than one year ago. New buildings, places, festivals and other cultural initiatives are now open to the public. Clearly more guests move through the streets, other languages are to be heard, and the feeling of being host visibly lends wings to the people. Pride spreads everywhere, justifiably. The tour guide is unforgettable, who directed her group of tourists skillfully through the hustle of people during an extremely lively weekend and shouted laughingly: "It's like in Salzburg!"

Apparently, the former workers' and industrial city Linz finds its place in new dimensions. And it is Salzburg that serves as a touchstone in this context – that city which is the epitome of Austrian narcissm and seasonal place of blessing for representative sophisticated culture. But no need to be afraid: Linz definitely is not Salzburg, and it will never be. Luckily – since city identities live on their differences. Not least because Linz09 insisted on the understanding of its location between Vienna and Salzburg as a place of idiosyncratic autonomy.

This claim has much to do with the stage, which the adventure of the Capital of Culture is performed on. Linz09 has decidedly attempted to establish a state of emergency. A large percentage of all that has belonged long ago to the standard repertoire of producing, transmitting and understanding of cultural initiatives does not work here. Or it works in a different way: thus, new constraints and freedoms arise, but also necessities of explanation and justification.

In addition, Linz09 belongs to the few and particular cultural projects that a broad public claims ownership to. In this case, the population of the city itself is meant and partly also of the region or the province of Upper Austria, whose capital Linz is. Such a claim is not at all only manifested formally or on paper, but the people pronounce it openly and the media reinforce it here. The proverbial taxi driver, who feels quite indifferent to the Ars Electronica Festival or the "Brucknerfest", is suddenly attentive when it comes to the Capital of Culture, he has his opinion and will be questioned on it by curious journalists.

Why this attraction? It is certainly not based on the fact that the Capital of Culture works with public money – because this applies to the entire cultural business. Instead, other factors create this awareness: the unusual size of the project and its glamour, with high budgets and corresponding extensive media coverage, as well as the open, undefined professional concept of culture.

Therefore, from the beginning of Linz09, there has been the feeling that everything was possible for everybody. The concept and the project of the Capital of Culture lent wings to the powers of imagination of politicians and those of the tourism professionals or the independent art scene. The factual openness of the format and the corresponding leeway were understood as an invitation to think and act in accordance with the project. For many, this resulted in securing for themselves a piece of this opulent cake, which was baked there under everybody's eyes.

Many citizens of Linz have accepted this invitation. Prior to the event, this happened through an abundance of more or less spontaneous project applications, which were usable in exceptional cases. At least from the viewpoint of the directorship, which regarded itself as the artistic conscience of Linz09 and which therefore had to fulfill the difficult task to carry out more than 2.000 cancellations and to justify them. This caused a lot of discontent, even hostility, which goes without saying. At the same time, it was now essential to transform numerous more substantial ideas from the circle of project authors, artists and cultural institutions in Linz and Upper Austria into feasible projects, and to support one or the other lay author with the elaboration of his or her ideas.

Each programme of a cultural capital reflects this context in more or less distinct degree. In view of such dimensions and emotional states, lonely elitist authorship is no issue, at all. Programme development rather meant a consistent scouring, forming, connecting and processing of suggestions of the most varied origin.

Today, this is all snows of yesteryear. But the snow has left traces. All those were offended who felt called upon, but were not taken into consideration; absent understanding among the broad public that could not gain insight why such a social unrest emerged around Linz09 and why so many struggles for economic resources arose, even before the programme was started.

First insight: The public, in which the Capital of Culture was prepared, has marked the project to a high degree. Not so much its contents and its substance, but its perception and surroundings – from the first announcements via the entire preparation time until the year of the programme itself. Such a public means permanent observation, commentary in any form and it provokes uncertainty. For the simple reason that the Capital of Culture was a welcome projection space for individual needs and wishes. Thereby, culture was in each case immediately and extensively a subject. But an unpredictable one, which could be appropriated according to the respective atmosphere, by different interests. The concerns of Linz09 had therefore to be manoeuvered through an assortment of all sorts of discourses, fake struggles and real conflicts. Public attention has its price, and it binds a lot of forces.

At the latest at the beginning of the Capital of Culture year – and after an opening on New Year's Eve, when literally half of the city was on the go! – the public's response became more concrete: in the form of surprisingly lively reactions to the programme and exploding visitor numbers. Suddenly, culture meant in the former workers' city rejoicing, absorbing, consuming, with a programme that was extraordinarily dense for this middle-sized city and its surroundings. The participatory imperative, above all brought forward by the local scene, according to which cultural participation at Linz09 had to be realized primarily in the form of the own productions, was definitely off the cards now.

But it also became evident how much cultural life in Linz so far had been determined by certain standards, formats, patterns and rituals. And which surprising elements or critical projects had been missing. Or how else could many of the reactions to the Linz09-initiatives be explained? Since particularly all those offers were well received which left the well-beaten tracks and opened up experiences in previously unknown places, that had hardly been discovered so far – for instance the "Kepler Salon", a location for ongoing exchange of information to make research accessible and intelligible to the general public in a series of dialogues with the scientists themselves.

Linz as European Capital of Culture: Three Insights

Interestingly, the public also started to move now. While till now clear conditions had prevailed, and the core audience of the corresponding cultural institution was marked by more or less typical characterisations, new situations sprang into being. The new theatre venue of Linz09 for example – the "Hafenhalle09" – joined an audience that had never existed in this composition before. Apparently, the general presence of Linz09 (including special, cost-effective and tailor-made ticket offers) also prompted many people from Linz to visit established cultural institutions for the very first time. And it sometimes seduced visitors through specific themes or innovative accesses, which encouraged visiting places and making experiences that had so far hardly ever been taken into consideration.

The contribution of information and marketing channels, which Linz09 was able to open up, can hardly be underestimated in this context. Above all, a broad, diversified programme magazine published fortnightly – "Neuner" – offered previously unknown possibilities to thematise the projects of the Capital of Culture, but naturally also the dimension of culture as such. This was and still is, in view of a generally rather modest media landscape – both as regards its quality and its quantity – almost a quantum leap towards that public significance of culture which is the precondition for a lively, individual cultural life open for collective appropriation.

Second insight: Beyond the original activities as a Capital of Culture, Linz09 emphasizes the cultural mechanisms in the city and the region. It is more than obvious that a considerable percentage of the cultural audience has so far got its money's worth in cultural daily life only to a limited degree. Now, there is the chance to catch up. Up to the point where the own unchangeable cultural experience has to be claimed as legitimate demand to the single consumer. Particularly because the Capital of Culture is "owned" by everybody, suddenly everybody is asked now, at least optionally, to find a closer approach to culture in different variants – an approach that goes beyond cultural-political promises of a "culture for all". A possibly excessive demand through the Capital of Culture thus adds to the above mentioned situation – an eventual lonely overstraining of the authorities as well as of all the agents, caused by all the consequences of Linz09. The fact alone that within the framework of the Capital of Culture, the previous straightforwardness of the daily cultural programme was replaced by the constraint to take a clear selection, produced unexpected needs and demanded new competences of a city like Linz.

A European Capital of Culture receives much attention through the media – local media anyway, but also on a national and international level. In the case of Linz09, reporting started early. Amongst other matters, because the Capital of Culture programme started in the previous years already, in order to give both the city and the media the chance to get accustomed to this situation and to work towards an adequate perception.

As expected, a large percentage of this discussion was focussed on the role that Linz played as the "adopted home town of the Fuhrer" at the time of National Socialism. The exhibition "The Fuhrer's Capital of Culture," which was opened in September 2008 and attracted around 62.000 visitors until 2009, was a decisive focus. Both as regards the national and the international reception. The difficult historical burden was thus cautiously and directly addressed.

The reactions to "The Fuhrer's Capital of Culture" made obvious how much a Capital of Culture can grow out of interior and exterior entanglements. On the one hand, the exhibition provided both the city and the region with much 'food for talk', and it nourished a basic discussion on the thematisation of the past and the overcoming of past burdens. The media reports, in particular those from Germany, constituted a significant contribution in this context. The articles attributed to the city all in all an amazing degree of courage, since the city was willing to confront itself with its difficult 'legacy' even in Europe's showcase.

Only some disparaging and uninformed reports in Great Britain's tabloid papers disturbed this image by reproaching Linz of making use of Hitler for sensational marketing. This again aroused much uncertainty in Linz: Would the Capital of Culture be reduced and bound to its national socialist curse, so that its creditability would be damaged? The question was raised at the top of their voices, but not really discussed, and the answer emerged through the media's reaction in the following weeks and months. Here, increasingly the reports on an economically successful, extraordinarily convivial Capital of Culture with provincial charm, that connects decidedly contemporary culture, prevailed. These reports flattered Linz because they attributed to the city a delightfully atypical attitude in Austria, that is known for its love for the past.

We can only learn from these and other experiences. This takes into consideration the city all together, but also in particular the field of tourism. After all – and despite the global crisis the number of overnight stays has been remarkable –, these experiences give evidence of the fact that it pays off to show profile. Towns are interesting only as long as they differ from the rest. And this difference can only be used if it is not only based on single events or architectural exceptional icons. The whole city should rather be included in the process.

In the course of the Capital of Culture, Linz was successfully placed on this basis, so that through the interplay of culture, industry and nature an ideal starting point for productive, future-oriented urbaneness was created. We can build on that. Under inclusion, of course, of those cultural Linz09-projects that have left an innovative mark in the city's culture and the region: from the new Ars Electronica Center extending considerably the previous media art platform via the whole complex of the "Acoustic City" on to themes like design and architecture, which should be continued to be accommodated in a Linz-specific way in the following years.

Third insight: The sustainability of a Capital of Culture encompasses far more than is generally listed. Certainly, buildings are urbanistic improvements or the distinctive investments into the hotel infrastructure are inevitably sustainable. But there is a further, functional potential in the realm of civil society, which promises sustainable effects. The respectful combination of culture and tourism is one aspect in this regard, the depletion of blind spots of self-perception, the decided comparison of top positions with best-practice examples, or even that flexibility in the administrative and public urban environment, without which many parts of the programme could not have been realised, are further aspects. But even that emphasis of Linz09, which was from its beginning described as international, is decidedly sustainable. Because each import of ideas, formats and artistic acting which is aimed at implementations beyond mere guest performances leads to lasting effects. Since it should not be underestimated that the cultural basis of a middle-sized city necessitates ever again systematical stimuli and that renewal implies more than just constructional redevelopment, and by and large a restructuring of the personnel. In this sense, Linz09 will continue to trigger sustainability and to find passionate carriers and advocates, and not only the financial means, for ideas that have obviously proven themselves.

Linz as European Capital of Culture: Three Insights

This is the attempt to address in a first, sketch-like balance some aspects of all those elements that are invisible within the framework of Linz09. Since learning means to become first of all aware of the results to be revealed behind the facts and to draw conclusions from these. Especially if it is a form of urban development which is exclusively limited to major enterprises like the European Capital of Culture overstraining justifiably and hopefully constructively all parties involved. If Linz09 can provide some models in this context, and if these models are understood, considered and transmitted in adequate form, both in Linz and anywhere else, then all the energies, that have been invested big-heartedly and generously into this title, will have been more than worthwhile.

www.linz09.at

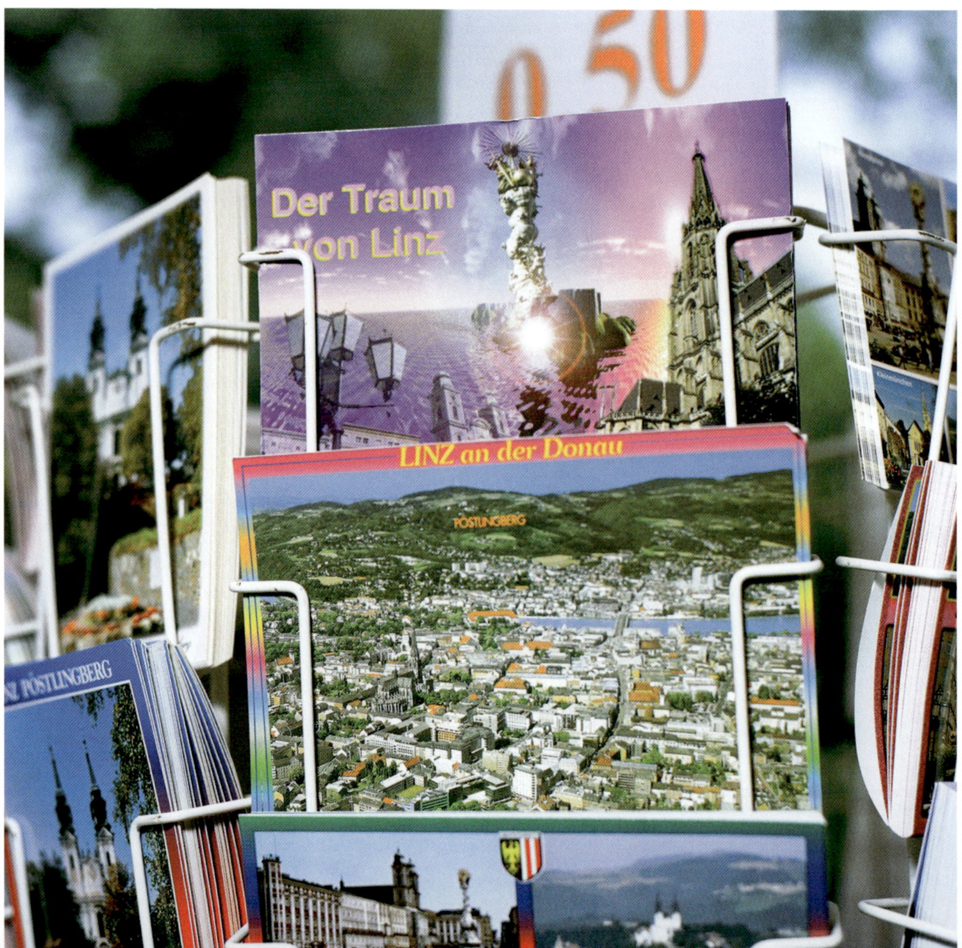

Von Martin Heller

Mehr als die Hälfte des Kulturhauptstadtjahres liegt hinter uns. Die Anspannung lässt nach. Der Kopf wird frei. Endlich lässt sich von Erfahrungen sprechen statt bloß von Erwartungen oder gar Hoffnungen. Und von den Lernprozessen einer Stadt wie Linz, die sich auf Neuland vorgewagt hat mit diesem Titel, dessen Herausforderungen und dessen Alltag.

Denn Linz09 – so die Kurzformel für Linz 2009 Kulturhauptstadt Europas – hat schon jetzt vieles bewirkt, in verschiedener Hinsicht. Die Stadt fühlt sich anders an als noch vor einem Jahr. Neue Gebäude, Plätze, Festivals und sonstige Kulturangebote lassen sich herzeigen. Deutlich mehr Gäste bewegen sich durch Straßen, andere Sprachen sind zu hören, und es wird sichtbar, wie sehr das Gefühl, Gastgeberin oder Gastgeber zu sein, viele beflügelt. Stolz macht sich breit, berechtigterweise. Unvergesslich die Fremdenführerin, die an einem äußerst belebten Wochenende ihre Touristengruppe gekonnt durch das Gewühle von Menschen steuert und dabei lachend rief: „Wie in Salzburg!"

Offenbar findet die einstige Arbeiter- und Industriestadt Linz in neue Dimensionen hinein. Ausgerechnet Salzburg liefert dazu eine Messlatte – jene Stadt, die als Inbegriff österreichischer Selbstverliebtheit und als saisonale Weihestätte repräsentativer Hochkultur gelten darf. Aber keine Angst: Linz ist nicht Salzburg und wird es auch nie sein. Glücklicherweise – denn Stadtidentitäten leben aus ihrer Differenz zueinander. Nicht zuletzt deshalb hat Linz09 darauf insistiert, im Rahmen der Kulturhauptstadt die Lage von Linz zwischen Wien und Salzburg als einen Ort eigenwilliger Autonomie zu verstehen.

Dieser Anspruch hat wesentlich mit der Bühne zu tun, auf der das Kulturhauptstadt-Abenteuer spielt und die sich als Ausnahmezustand charakterisieren lässt. Vieles, was längst eingeübt ist im Produzieren, Vermitteln oder Verstehen von kulturellen Angeboten, funktioniert hier nicht. Oder anders als gewohnt, und damit ergeben sich neue Zwänge und Freiheiten, aber auch Notwendigkeiten der Erklärung und Rechtfertigung.

Kommt dazu, dass Linz09 zu jenen wenigen und besonderen Kulturprojekten gehört, auf die eine breite Öffentlichkeit Besitzanspruch erhebt. In diesem Fall meint das die Bevölkerung der Stadt selbst und teilweise auch der Region bzw. des Bundeslandes Oberösterreich, dessen Hauptstadt Linz ist. Ein solcher Anspruch manifestiert sich keinesfalls nur formell oder auf dem Papier. Die Menschen selbst empfinden und äussern ihn unverblümt, und die Medien bestärken sie darin. Der sprichwörtliche Taxifahrer, dem das Ars Electronica Festival oder das Brucknerfest im Grunde so ziemlich egal sind, merkt bei Kulturhauptstadt auf, hat eine Meinung und wird dazu von neugierigen JournalistInnen auch gerne befragt.

Warum dieser Sog? Der Grund dafür liegt weniger in der Tatsache, dass die Kulturhauptstadt mit öffentlichen Geldern arbeitet – das gilt für den gesamten Kulturbetrieb. Andere Faktoren erzeugen dieses Bewusstsein: die ungewöhnliche Größe des Projekts zumal und sein Glanz, samt hohen Budgets und entsprechend satter Medienpräsenz, sowie der offene, nicht von vornherein auf Kunst im engeren Sinne definierte Kulturbegriff.

Es war demnach um Linz09 herum von Beginn weg ein Gefühl da, alles sei möglich, und zwar für alle. Der Begriff und die Sache der Kulturhauptstadt beflügelten die Fantasien der Politiker wie jene der Touristiker oder der Freien Szene. Die faktische Unbestimmtheit des Formats und der damit verbundene Interpretationsspielraum wurden als Einladung verstanden, mitzudenken und mitzutun. Was für viele darauf hinaus lief, sich rechtzeitig ein Stück des opulenten Kuchens zu sichern, der da unter aller Augen gebacken wurde.

Viele Linzerinnen und Linzer haben diese Einladung angenommen. Vorweg mit einer Überfülle an mehr oder weniger spontanen Einreichungen von Projektideen, die nur in Ausnahmefällen brauchbar waren. Zumindest aus der Sicht der Intendanz, die sich auftragsgemäß als künstlerisches Gewissen von Linz09 verstand und deshalb schwierige Aufgabe wahrzunehmen hatte, weit über 2.000 Absagen vorzunehmen und zu begründen. Dass damit viel Unmut, ja Feindseligkeit provoziert wurde, versteht sich von selbst. Gleichzeitig galt es, zahlreiche substantiellere Ideen aus dem Kreis freier AutorInnen, KünstlerInnen und Kultureinrichtungen in Linz und Oberösterreich in handhabbare Projekte zu transformieren sowie vereinzelte Laienautoren bei der Ausarbeitung ihrer Vorstellungen zu unterstützen.

Wohl jedes Kulturhauptstadtprogramm spiegelt diesen Kontext in mehr oder weniger ausgeprägtem Maße. Von einsam elitärer Autorenschaft kann bei derartigen Dimensionen und Gefühlslagen keine Rede sein. Programmentwicklung bedeutet vielmehr ein ständiges Durchforsten, Formen, Verbinden und Verarbeiten von Vorschlägen unterschiedlichster Herkunft.

Das alles ist, heute, Schnee von gestern. Aber der Schnee hat Spuren hinterlassen. Verletzungen bei denen, die sich berufen fühlten und nicht zum Zuge kamen; Unverständnis bei jenem breiten Publikum, dem nicht klar werden konnte, warum im Umfeld von Linz09 eine derartige soziale Unrast entstand und warum so viele Verteilkämpfe um die Kulturhauptstadt entbrannten, noch ehe das Programm zum Tragen kam.

Erste Einsicht: *Die Öffentlichkeit, in der die Kulturhauptstadt Linz vorbereitet wurde, hat das Projekt in hohem Maße geprägt. Weniger seine Inhalte und seine Substanz als seine Wahrnehmung und sein Umfeld – von den ersten Verlautbarungen über die gesamte Erarbeitungszeit bis in das Programmjahr selbst. Solche Öffentlichkeit heißt ständige Beobachtung, meint Kommentar in jeder Form und provoziert Verunsicherung. Aus dem einfachen Grund, weil die Kulturhauptstadt allen, die dazu bereit waren, eine willkommene Projektionsfläche lieferte für eigene Anliegen und Wünsche. Damit war Kultur jeweils sofort und ausgiebig ein Thema. Aber ein unberechenbares, das je nach Stimmungslage von unterschiedlichsten Interessen in Beschlag genommen werden konnte. Mit dem Resultat, dass die Kulturhauptstadt-Anliegen von Linz09 durch ein Gemenge von allen erdenklichen Diskursen, Scheingefechten und realen Auseinandersetzungen hindurch manövriert werden mussten. Öffentliche Aufmerksamkeit hat ihren Preis, und sie bindet viele Kräfte.*

Spätestens zum Beginn des Kulturhauptstadtjahres – und nach einer Eröffnung in der Silvesternacht, in der buchstäblich die halbe Stadt auf den Beinen war! – konkretisierte sich die Antwort des Publikums: in Form von überraschend lebendigen Reaktionen auf das Gebotene und explodierenden Besucherzahlen. Kultur bedeutete in der ehemaligen Arbeiterstadt nun mit einem Mal Genießen, Aufnehmen, Konsumieren, bei einem für eine Stadtregion dieser Größe außergewöhnlich dichten und reichen Programm. Der gerade vonseiten der lokalen Szene ins Feld geführte partizipatorische Imperativ, kulturelle Teilhabe an Linz09 müsse sich primär in Form von eigenen Produktionen realisieren, war je länger je gründlicher vom Tisch.

Deutlich wurde dabei aber auch, wie sehr das bisherige Linzer Kulturleben durch bestimmte Standards, Formate, Muster und Rituale charakterisiert war. Und was darin fehlte an Überraschendem, und auch an suchenden, fragenden Projekten. Anders lassen sich viele der Reaktionen auf Linz09-Angebote nicht erklären. Dass gerade das gut angenommen wurde, was die gewohnten Bahnen verliess und Erlebnisse eröffnete an bisher unbekannten, weil neuen oder noch kaum entdeckten Orten – am eindrücklichsten vielleicht im Kepler Salon, einer Art Lounge mit regelmäßigen Veranstaltungen zur Popularisierung und Befragung von Wissenschaftsthemen.

Interessanterweise wurde dabei auch das Publikum aufgemischt. Wo bisher klare Verhältnisse herrschten und sich das Stammpublikum der jeweiligen Kultureinrichtung einigermaßen schlüssig charakterisieren ließ, entstanden neue Situationen. Die neue Theaterspielstätte von Linz09 beispielsweise – die Hafenhalle09 – bringt ein Publikum zusammen, das es in dieser Form und Zusammensetzung in Linz bislang nie gegeben hat. Offenbar führt aber auch die allgemeine Präsenz von Linz09 (samt speziellen, preisgünstigen und auf die Bedürfnisse zugeschnittenen Ticket-Anbeboten) dazu, dass viele Linzerinnen und Linzer auch bereits bestehende Kultureinrichtungen erstmals besuchen. Verführt mitunter durch spezifische Themen oder innovative Zugänge, die Lust machen auf Orte und Erfahrungen, die bisher außerhalb der subjektiven Reichweite lagen.

Einen kaum zu unterschätzenden Beitrag lieferten hier die Informations- und Marketingkanäle, die sich Linz09 erschließen konnte. Vor allem ein breit gestreutes, vierzehntägig erscheinendes Programm-Magazin – „Neuner" – bot bisher nie gekannte Möglichkeiten, die Projekte der Kulturhauptstadt, aber natürlich auch die gesellschaftliche Dimension von Kultur schlechthin zu thematisieren. Das war und ist angesichts einer insgesamt sowohl quantitativ als auch qualitätiv doch eher bescheidenen Medienlandschaft fast schon ein Quantensprung bezüglich jenes öffentlichen Stellenwerts von Kultur, der doch die Voraussetzung bildet für ein lebendiges, individueller und kollektiver Aneignung gleichermaßen offen stehendes Kulturleben.

Zweite Einsicht: Linz09 macht über die eigentlichen Kulturhauptstadt-Aktivitäten hinaus vieles deutlich bezüglich der kulturellen Mechanismen in Stadt und Region. Es ist mit Händen zu greifen, wie sehr ein beträchtlicher Teil des Kulturpublikums im kulturellen Alltag bisher nur bedingt auf seine Kosten kam. Nun bietet sich die Chance, viel Versäumtes nachzuholen. Bis an jenen Punkt, an dem das eigene, unverwechselbare und durch nichts zu ersetzende kulturelle Erlebnis eingefordert werden darf als Teil der Verantwortung der einzelnen Konsumentin, des einzelnen Konsumenten. Gerade weil die Kulturhauptstadt allen gehört, sind mit einem Mal alle zumindest eingeladen, zu Kultur in unterschiedlichsten Spielformen ein Nahverhältnis zu finden, das über die kulturpolitischen Lippenbekenntnisse einer „Kultur für alle" nicht mehr abgedeckt werden kann. Zur erwähnten Unterforderung tritt demnach eine mögliche Überforderung durch die Kulturhauptstadt – eine Überforderung der herrschenden Verhältnisse wie sämtlicher Akteure durch das, was Linz09 mit sich bringt. Allein schon der Umstand, dass im Zeichen der Kulturhauptstadt die bisherige Überschaubarkeit des täglichen Kulturprogramms durch den Zwang zur dezidierten Auswahl abgelöst wurde, produziert unerwartete Nöte und fordert für eine Stadt wie Linz neue Kompetenzen.

Linz als Kulturhauptstadt Europas: Drei Einsichten

Eine Kulturhauptstadt Europas erhält viel mediale Zuwendung – lokale ohnehin, aber auch auf nationaler und internationaler Eben. Im Falle von Linz09 begann die Berichterstattung schon früh. Unter anderem deshalb, weil das Kulturhauptstadtprogramm bereits in den Jahren zuvor einsetzte, um sowohl der Stadt wie auch den Medien Gelegenheit zu geben, sich an die Besonderheiten dieser Situation zu gewöhnen und auf deren adäquate Wahrnehmung hinzuarbeiten. Erwartungsgemäß konzentrierte sich ein großer Teil dieser Auseinandersetzung auf die Rolle, die Linz als Patenstadt des Führers zur Zeit des Nationalsozialismus spielte. Die Ausstellung „Kulturhauptstadt des Führers", die im September 2008 eröffnet wurde und bis April 2009 rund 62.000 Besucherinnen und Besucher anzog, war dabei ein entscheidender Fokus, sowohl nach innen wie nach außen. Die schwierige zeitgeschichtliche Hypothek wurde damit ebenso sorgfältig wie direkt angegangen.

Die Reaktionen auf „Kulturhauptstadt des Führers" machten aber auch deutlich, wie sehr eine Kulturhauptstadt an der Verklammerung von Innen und Aussen wachsen kann. Zum einen bot die Ausstellung in der Stadt und in der Region viel Gesprächsstoff und nährte eine grundsätzliche Diskussion über die Thematisierung von Vergangenheit und deren Bewältigung. Die mediale Berichterstattung, insbesondere auch aus Deutschland, leistete dazu einen wichtigen Part, indem der Stadt insgesamt ein erstaunlicher Mut attestiert wurde, sich ihrem braunen Erbe gerade auch im Schaufenster Europas zu stellen.

Erst einige nicht nur rotzige, sondern auch unqualifizierte Berichte insbesondere in angelsächsischen Boulevardzeitungen störten dieses Bild, indem sie Linz vorwarfen, mit Hitler geschmackloses, auf Effekthascherei bedachtes Marketing zu betreiben. Dies wiederum schürte in Linz sofort Verunsicherung: Würde die Kulturhauptstadt fortan auf kreditschädigende Weise auf ihren nationalsozialistischen Fluch reduziert? Die Frage wurde lauthals gestellt, aber kaum wirklich debattiert, und die Antwort ergab sich umgehend wiederum durch den Medientenor der folgenden Wochen und Monate. Darin nämlich nahmen mehr und mehr die Berichte über eine wirtschaftlich erfolgreiche, ungewöhnlich liebenswerte, provinziellen Charme und entschieden zeitgenössische Kultur verbindende Kulturhauptstadt überhand. Die zudem Linz insofern schmeichelten, als sie der Stadt eine im vergangenheitssüchtigen Österreich erfreulich untypische Haltung zuschrieben.

Aus solchen und anderen Erfahrungen war und bleibt zu lernen. Für die Stadt insgesamt, aber auch für den Tourismus. Schließlich lässt sich daran – und an den trotz globaler Krise bislang hervorragenden Nächtigungszahlen! – demonstrieren, dass es sich lohnt, Profil zu zeigen. Städte sind dann interessant, wenn sie anders sind als andere. Und dieses Anderssein ist dann wirklich nutzbar, wenn es nicht bloß auf einzelnen Veranstaltungen oder architektonischen Ausnahme-Ikonen beruht, sondern die ganze Stadt einbezieht.

Im bisherigen Verlauf der Kulturhauptstadt ist es gelungen, Linz auf dieser Basis so zu positionieren, dass hier im Zusammenspiel von Kultur, Industrie und Natur eine ideale Ausgangsposition für produktive, zukunftssichernde Urbanität entstanden ist. Darauf lässt sich aufbauen. Unter Einschluss natürlich einer Vielzahl jener kulturellen Linz09-Projekte, die im Kulturleben von Stadt und Region innovative Akzente setzen: vom neuen, die bisherige Medienkunstplattform massiv erweiternden Ars Electronica Center über den ganzen Komplex der Hörstadt-Belange bis zu Themen wie Design und Architektur, die es weiterhin linzspezifisch zu füllen gilt.

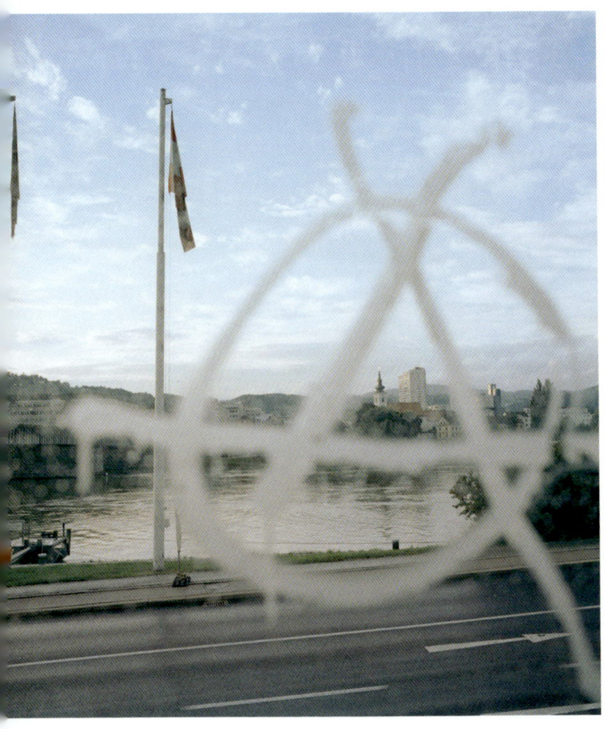

Dritte Einsicht: *Die Nachhaltigkeit einer Kulturhauptstadt umfasst weit mehr, als gemeinhin darunter aufgelistet wird. Gewiss sind gute und notwendige Bauten städtebauliche Verbesserungen oder auch die gerade für Linz so erfreulich markanten Investitionen in die Hotel-Infrastruktur sind zwangsläufig nachhaltig. Es gibt aber ein weiteres, sowohl materielles als auch zivilgesellschaftliches Potenzial an nachhaltigen Effekten. Das respektvolle Zusammengehen von Kultur und Tourismus gehört dazu, der Abbau von blinden Flecken der Selbstwahrnehmung, der dezidierte Vergleich mit Spitzenpositionen anderswo und Best-Practice-Beispielen, oder eine willkommene Beweglichkeit im administrativen und öffentlichen Stadtgefüge, ohne die viele Programmteile der Kulturhauptstadt gar nicht hätten realisiert werden können. Aber auch jener Schwerpunkt von Linz09, der von Anfang an mit Internationalisierung beschrieben wurde, ist entschieden nachhaltig. Denn jeder Import von Ideen, Formaten und künstlerischem Agieren jenseits von bloßer Gastspiel-Kultur bringt Bleibendes. Weil nicht gering geschätzt werden darf, dass die kulturelle Basis einer mittelgroßen Stadt immer wieder planmäßiger Anstöße bedarf, und dass Erneuerung mehr beinhaltet als bauliche Sanierung und hin und wieder personelle Erneuerung der Strukturen. In diesem Sinne wird Linz09 auch weiterhin bemüht sein, Nachhaltigkeit anzustoßen und für Ideen, die sich offenkundig bewährt haben, nicht bloß Finanzierungen, sondern leidenschaftliche Träger und Anwälte zu finden.*

Soweit der Versuch in einer ersten, skizzenhaften Bilanz einiges auch von dem anzusprechen, was sich innerhalb von Linz09 der Sichtbarkeit entzieht. Denn lernen heißt, sich erst einmal dessen bewusst zu werden, was an Ergebnissen freizulegen ist gerade hinter den Fakten, und daraus Schlüsse zu ziehen. Als jene Form der Stadtentwicklung, wie sie ausschließlich großen, alle Beteiligten, nochmals, mit Recht und hoffentlich konstruktiv überfordernden Vorhaben wie die Kulturhauptstadt Europas offen steht. Wenn Linz09 hier Modelle dazu liefern kann, und wenn diese Modelle sowohl in Linz selbst als auch andernorts verstanden, überdacht und in angemessener Form transportiert werden können, dann haben sich alle Energien, die viele großherzig und großzügig in diesen Titel gesteckt haben, mehr als gelohnt.

www.linz09.at

Launched in 1987 as a competition for cyberarts, the Prix Ars Electronica plays a major role in what is today the 30-year history of the Ars Electronica. With continuity over 23 years, interdisciplinarity in eight different categories, an internationality that manifested itself in 3017 submissions from 68 countries in 2009, and the expertise of 40 jury members, the Prix Ars Electronica is a seismograph for the latest innovations at the interface of art, technology and science, and thus an important barometer of trends in the digital arts. Currently, the Prix Ars Electronica includes everything from digital filmmaking, digital music, interactive art, hybrid art, community projects, [the next idea] concepts, and media art research to works by young people under nineteen.

You'll find the results of the 2009 Prix Ars Electronica and detailed descriptions of the prizewinning projects in:

CyberArts 2009
International Compendium of Prix Ars Electronica
H. Leopoldseder / C. Schöpf / G. Stocker (Eds.)
Hatje Cantz, Ostfildern-Ruit

Selected works from this year's Prix Ars Electronica will be on display in the CyberArts 2009 exhibition at the OK Offenes Kulturhaus.

In der heuer 30-jährigen Geschichte der Ars Electronica nimmt der 1987 ins Leben gerufene Prix Ars Electronica als Wettbewerb für Cyberarts einen hohen Stellenwert ein. Mit seiner Kontinuität über mittlerweile 23 Jahre, seiner Interdisziplinarität von sieben verschiedenen Kategorien, seiner Internationalität die sich 2009 in über 3.017 Einreichungen aus 68 Ländern manifestiert, und der Expertise von 40 Juroren ist der Prix Ars Electronica Seismograph für aktuelle Innovationen an der Schnittstelle von Kunst, Technologie und Wissenschaft und damit wichtiges Trendbarometer der digitalen Künste. Die aktuelle Bandbreite des Prix Ars Electronica reicht von Digital Filmmaking, Digital Musics, Interactive Art, Hybrid Art, Community-Projekten und Medienkunsttheorie bis hin zu Arbeiten der Generation u19.

Die Ergebnisses des Prix Ars Electronica und detaillierte Beschreibungen der Gewinnerprojekte finden Sie in:

Cyberarts 2009
International Compendium of Prix Ars Electronica
H. Leopoldseder / C. Schöpf / G. Stocker (Hrsg.)
Hatje Cantz, Ostfildern-Ruit

Ausgewählte Arbeiten des Prix Ars Electronica werden in der Ausstellung CyberArts 2009 im OK Offenes Kulturhaus Oberösterreich präsentiert.

Computer Animation / Film / VFX

Golden Nica

HA'Aki
Iriz Pääbo (CA) / National Film Board of Canada
http://www.nfb.ca/haaki

Awards of Distinction

Skhizein
Jeremy Clapin, Jean-François Sarazin (FR) / Dark Prince
http://www.muiye.com

The Nest That Sailed The Sky
Glenn Marshall (UK), Music by Peter Gabriel
http://www.butterfly.ie

Honorary Mentions

The Dark Knight
Dominique Vidal (FR) / BUF Compagnie
http://www.buf.com

Dix
Bif (FR) / Autour de Minuit Productions & The Mill
http://blog.autourdeminuit.com

WALL-E
Andrew Stanton (US) / Pixar Animation Studios
http://www.pixar.com

World of Warcraft: Wrath of the Lich King -
Intro Cinematic
Jeff Chamberlain, Phillip Hillenbrand (US) /
Blizzard Entertainment, Inc.
http://www.blizzard.com

Urs
Moritz Mayerhofer (DE)
http://www.urs-film.com

French Roast
Fabrice O. Joubert (FR) / Pumpkin Factory / Bibo Films
http://www.frenchroast.fr

Boris
Daniel Lundquist (AT)
http://www.uglyanimations.com

Chick
Michal Socha (PL) / Platige Image
http://www.thechickfilm.com/en/

The Spine
Chris Landreth (CA) / National Film Board of Canada
http://www.nfb.ca/thespine

This Way Up
Smith & Foulkes (UK) / Nexus Productions Ltd
http://www.thiswayupmovie.com

Audi „Unboxed"
Russell Brooke (UK), Aaron Duffy (US) / Passion Pictures,
1st Ave Machine
http://www.passion-pictures.com /
http://www.1stavemachine.com

Harmonix Rock Band II
Pete Candeland (AU) / Passion Pictures
http://www.passion-pictures.com

Digital Musics

Golden Nica

Speeds of Time versions 1 and 2
Bill Fontana (US)
http://resoundings.org/

Awards of Distinction

„Active Field" for ten violins and ten-channel 1-bit
music
Tristan Perich (US)
http://www.tristanperich.com /
http://www.1bitmusic.com

Nabaz'mob
Antoine Schmitt and Jean-Jacques Birgé (FR)
http://www.nabazmob.com

Special Mention

Max Neuhaus (US)
http://www.max-neuhaus.info

Honorary Mentions

Les arbres
Nicolas Bernier (music), urban9 (images) (CA)
http://www.urban9.com/lesarbres.php

Relative Realitäten | Relative Realities
Volkmar Klien, Thomas Grill (AT)

Waldstück
Christoph Korn (DE)
http://www.waldstueck.net

Truce: Strategies for Post-Apocalyptic Computation
Robin Meier (CH), Ali Momeni (US)
http://alimomeni.net / http://robin.meier.free.fr

Physiological Mechanics Fantasy
Lucas Fagin (AR)
http://www.myspace.com/lucasfagin

Le Tombeau de Freddie / L' Internationale
Formant Brothers (JP)
http://web.mac.com/nsakonda/

Jamming Gear
So Kanno, Kenichiro Saigo (JP)
http://kannoso.org/

Tetraktis
Manuel Rocha Iturbide (MX)
http://www.artesonoro.net

The Turbulence Sound Matrix: Signe
Steve Heimbecker (CA)
http://www3.sympatico.ca/qubeassm/TSM.html
http://www3.sympatico.ca/qubeassm/Signe.html

: am Dienstag um neun sind die Erdbeeren reif
Helmut Mittermaier (DE)
http://www.guruclub.de/mittermaier

Scherzo
Joe Diebes (US)
http://www.joediebes.com

Hybrid Art

Golden Nica

Natural History of the Enigma
Eduardo Kac (US)
with his scientific partners Neil Olszewski, Department
of Plant Biology and Neil Anderson, Department of Hor-
ticultural Science, University of Minnesota, St. Paul, MN
http://www.ekac.org

Awards of Distinction

The New York Times Special Edition
Steve Lambert (US) member of Because We Want It
http://nytimes-se.com/

EarthStar
David Haines (UK), Joyce Hinterding (AU)
http://www.sunvalleyresearch.net

Honorary Mentions

Sonolevitation
Evelina Domnitch (BY), Dmitry Gelfand (RU)
http://portablepalace.com

Common Flowers - Flower Commons
BCL / Georg Tremmel (AT), Shiho Fukuhara (JP)
http://www.common-flowers.org

Cosmic Revelation
Tim Otto Roth & KASCADE Experiment (DE)
http://www.imachination.net/cosmicrevelation/

Silent Barrage
Philip Gamblen, Guy Ben-Ary, Peter Gee, Dr. Nathan
Scott & Brett Murray in collaboration with Dr. Steve
Potter Lab (Dr. Steve Potter, Douglas Swehla & Stephen
Bobic) (AU/USA)
http://www.symbiotica.uwa.edu.au/silentbarrage

Mortal Engine
Damien Cooper, Robin Fox , Paula Levis, Gideon Obarza-
nek (AU), Frieder Weiss (DE), Ben Frost (IS) / Chunky
Move
http://chunkymove.com

Tantalum Memorial
Harwood, Wright, Yokokoji (UK)
http://www.mediashed.org/TantalumMemorial

The Kinetic Sculpture
ART+COM
http://www.artcom.de/kinetik

bios [bible]
robotlab (Matthias Gommel, Martina Haitz, Jan Zappe
(DE))
http://www.robotlab.de

ReConstitution
Eric Gunther, Justin Manor, John Rothenberg (US) /
Sosolimited
http://sosolimited.com

Corpora in Si(gh)te
Sota Ichikawa(JP), Max Rheiner (CH), Ákos Maróy (HU),
Kaoru Kobata (JP), Satoru Higa (JP), Hajime Narukawa
(JP), / doubleNegatives Architecture
http://doubleNegatives.jp / http://corpora.hu / http://
corpora.ycam.jp/

The Fragmented Orchestra
Jane Grant, John Matthias, Nick Ryan (UK)
http://www.thefragmentedorchestra.com

the idea of a tree
Thomas Traxler (AT)
http://www.mischertraxler.com

Interactive Art

Golden Nica

Nemo Observatorium
Lawrence Malstaf (BE)
http://www.fortlaan17.com/eng/artists/malstaf

Awards of Distinction

when laughter trips at the threshold of the divine
Osman Khan, Kim Beck (US)
http://www.osmankhan.com / http://www.idealcities.
com

default to public
Jens Wunderling (DE)
http://www.defaulttopublic.net / http://www.sport-
4minus.de

Red Psi Donkey
Jens Brand (DE)
http://www.jensbrand.com/

Audience
rAndom International (Stuart Wood (UK), Florian Ort-
krass , Hannes Koch (DE)) & Chris O'Shea (UK)
http://www.random-international.com / http://www.
chrisoshea.org

Perpetual Storytelling Apparatus
Benjamin Maus , Julius von Bismarck (DE)
http://www.allesblinkt.com / http://www.juliusvonbis-
marck.com

Jammer Horn
Willy Sengewald
http://www.thegreeneyl.com/jammer-horn

CONNECT – feedback-driven sculpture
Andreas Muxel (AT)
http://www.andreasmuxel.com / http://connect.andre-
asmuxel.com

Call Cutta in a box
Helgard Haug, Daniel Wetzel, Stefan Kaegi (DE)
http://www.rimini-protokoll.de/website/de/pro-
ject_2766.html

Opera Calling
!Mediengruppe Bitnik (CH) and Sven König (DE)
www.bitnik.org / www.opera-calling.com/description

Double-Taker (Snout)
Golan Levin with Lawrence Hayhurst, Steven Benders
and Fannie White (US)
http://www.flong.com/projects/snout/

Future Kiss
Lenka Klimesova (CZ)
www.myspace.com/lenyss

The Physical Value of Sound
Yuri Suzuki (JP)
http://www.yurisuzuki.com

In the Line of Sight
Daniel Sauter, Fabian Winkler (DE/US)
http://daniel-sauter.com/ / http://web.ics.purdue.
edu/~fwinkler

Watch Me!
Yasushi Noguchi, Hideyuki Ando (JP)
http://r-dimension.xsrv.jp/projects_e/watch_me/

Digital Communities

Golden Nica

HiperBarrio
http://hiperbarrio.org

Awards of Distinction

WikiLeaks
http://wikileaks.org

Piratbyrån
http://www.piratbyran.org/

Special Mention
Grass Mud Horse

Honorary Mentions

HackMeeting
www.hackmeeting.org

Pad.ma
http://pad.ma

Maneno
http://www.maneno.org/

female:pressure
http://www.femalepressure.net/

Mute
http://www.metamute.org

UbuWeb
http://ubu.com

Canchas - spontaneous soccer fields
http://www.canchas.org

feral trade
http://feraltrade.org

FLOSS Manuals
http://www.flossmanuals.net

Wikiartpedia - The Free Encyclopaedia of Art and
Network Cultures
http://www.wikiartpedia.org

Ashoka's Changemakers
http://changemakers.net

Voces Bolivianas (Bolivian Voices)
http://www.vocesbolivianas.org

Media.Art.Research Award

Media.Art.Research Award
Eye hEar: Music, Art, Film & the Culture of Synaesthesia
Simon Shaw-Miller (UK)

**Acknowledgements of a contribution to the field /
Anerkennung des Beitrags zum Wissensfeld**

Die Ordnung der Klänge
Andi Schoon (CH)

Dickson Experimental
Jan Philip Müller (DE)

[the next idea] voestalpine Art and Technology Grant

Grant

Open Sailing
Open_Sailing_Crew
www.opensailing.net

Honorary Mentions

ClimateScope
Erich Berger (AT/FI), Laura Beloff (FI), Anu Osva(FI)
http://climatescope.net

Toaster to understand today's weather
Tatsuya Narita (JP)
http://www.cutarena.com/

u19 – freestyle computing

Goldene Nica

In den Tiefen
Matej Petrek

Awards of Distinction

Having A Wonderful Time
Tarek Khalifa

Sound Machines
HLW des Schulvereins der Kreuzschwestern:

Non-Cash Prize u10

Sieben auf einen Streich
Volksschule Neußerling:
Raphael Birngruber
Laura Fischerlehner
Richard Prommer
Kerstin Füchsl
Lukas Prammer
Martin Donner
Jakob Hacklbauer

Non-Cash Prize u14

Lego Chemie
Hauptschule Dr.-Aloys-Weissenbach Telfs:

Honorary Mentions

Buddytown.AT
Daniel Stocker
http://buddytown.at/

www.daskonzept.at
Maximillian Zinner, Fabian Todt
http://www.daskonzept.at/

CityFlow - Urban Climate Simulation
Oliver Spies, Andreas Mursch-Radlgruber, Michael
Kappel, Stefan Pozar
http://www.cityflow.at/

Stop Motion Lightshow
Thomas Niedermaier

Music Robot
Johannes Masanz

IOCC - Die Polizei im Rennen gegen die Zeit
Alexander Niederklapfer, David Wurm, Magdalena
Wurm, Ehrentraud Hager
http://iocc.krmpfkrmpf-studios.com

Melt
Nana Susanne Thurner

Semantic Tag Cloud
Sinja Hemer, Jasmin Haider
http://wechselwirkungen.biz/stc/

Robot Control with Mobile Phone Motion
Leo Höckner

european II ways
Franz Fellinger

Biographies

8gg interactive(CN). As one of the earliest multi-media art groups in China, 8gg interactive consists of Jia Haiqing and Fu Yu. Their works include music, video, installation, theater, and web art. The group have successfully exhibited and performed work around the world. Their work has a clean, fresh approach that aims to be playful and fun. *http://www.8gg.com*

Eugene Ahn (US) is a New York based South Korean multimedia artist. Eugene explores the various social boundaries of the individual caused by contemporary lifestyles and the desire for connectedness through performance, interactive object making, and digital media.

Alva Noto (DE) is a stage name of sound artist Carsten Nicolai who uses art and music as complementary tools to create microscopic views of creative processes. Another alias he uses is Noto. He is a member of the music groups Signal (with Frank Bretschneider, AKA Komet and Olaf Bender, AKA Byetone) and Cyclo. (with Ryoji Ikeda).

Ars Electronica Futurelab (AT), Ars Electronica's media art R&D lab, combines the analytical and experimental aspects of a laboratory with the artistry and creativity of an atelier. The result is a space in which the tone is set by activities of transdisciplinary teams and which, depending on the demands of a particular assignment, is continually being reconfigured as a lab-atelier or atelier-lab.

ATR (Advanced Telecommunications Research Institute International, JP) was founded in March 1986 with the support of various partners from industry, academia and government, aiming to promote basic and creative research activities in telecommunications and to contribute greatly to society. We constantly pursue research and development to achieve comfortable and exciting human life in the future.

Samir Ayyad (Palestine) is a professional architect, sound artist, writer and photographer who lives and works in Gaza. He completed a training course on broadcasting and sound editing at the Islamic University in Gaza and his studies of Architecture at the Birzeit University, Palestine.

Blast Theory (UK) is renowned internationally as one of the most adventurous artists' groups using interactive media, creating groundbreaking new forms of performance and interactive art that mixes audiences across the internet, live performance and digital broadcasting. Led by Matt Adams, Ju Row Farr and Nick Tandavanitj, the group's work explores interactivity and the social and political aspects of technology.

Gabriele Blome (DE) war von 2000 bis 2007 wissenschaftliche Mitarbeiterin am Fraunhofer-Institut für Intelligente Analyse- und Informationssysteme (ehemals Fraunhofer-Institut für Medienkommunikation), Sankt Augustin. Seit November 2007 wissenschaftliche Mitarbeiterin des Ludwig Boltzmann Instituts Medien.Kunst.Forschung. mit dem Schwerpunkt »Online-Ressourcen für die wissenschaftliche Dokumentation und Archivierung von Medienkunst«.

Andres Bosshard (CH) has made public appearances as an improvisational musician and presented his projects at music & sound art festivals in Europe, America, Japan and India since 1980. In conjunction with his works of sound architecture installed in public spaces, he has collaborated with space planners and architects since 1995.

Adam Brandejs (CA) is a cross-disciplinary artist and programmer working in multiple fields and media including physical and virtual sculpture, web development, and electronics design. Adam's work has already been featured in both national and international galleries and museum displays, and his work has appeared in dozens of publications around the world.

Rebecca Bray (US). Her works reconfigure human-nature-technology relationships. She is a professor at NYU's Interactive Telecommunications Program and cofounder of the interaction agency Submersible Design. *http://rebsbray.com.*

Michael Burton (UK). As a multidisciplinary artist Michael utilises mediums including film, photography, performance, living organisms and biological systems. He leads a collaborative practice, working with organisations and individuals including with scientists, performers, choreographers, designers and architects.

Caden Enterprises (IE) is a family owned and operated business made up of husband and wife team, Chris and Janice. We want to change the way that people view adult toys and the adult industry as a whole.

Tal Chalosin (IL) co-founded Innovid *(http://www.innovid.com)*, a platform for engaging brand experiences in and around on-line video. Chalozin is head of the research and development department and is Innovid's CTO.

Alon Chitayat (IL) is a visual artist, designer, illustrator and animator producing public and private works for companies, film and television industry, as well as for galleries. Alon is the founder and CEO of „Animishmish" visual design studio *(http://www.animishmish.com)*. Alon Chitayat is also part of the collective filmmakers „O_o films".

Lila Chitayat (IL) is an architect, designer and an experimental practitioner of design through computational processes. In 2002 Lila founded LinC studio, a trans-disciplinary design environment utilizing computational patterns to produce a wide range of projects, from industrial design to space design, full-scale installations and architecture.

Dieter Daniels (DE / AT) did numerous publications, multimedia projects and exhibitions in the field of media art. 1984 co-founder of the Videonale Bonn. 1992 to 1994 director of the Video Collection at ZKM Karlsruhe. Since 1993 Professor of Art History and Media Theory at the Leipzig Academy of Visual Art (HGB). Since 2000 Co-Editor of the Online-publication *http://mediaartnet.org*. Since 2005 Daniels has been director of the Ludwig Boltzmann Institute Media.Art.Research. in Linz.

Dentsu Inc. (JP) founded in 1901, is the largest advertising company brand and the fifth largest marketing and communications organization in the world. Based in Tokyo, Dentsu has pioneered and set global standards for integrated communications through its comprehensive range of advertising and marketing services. *http://www.dentsu.com*

Stephen Downes (CA) works for the National Research Council of Canada where he has served as a Senior Research since 2001. Affiliated with the Learning and Collaborative Technologies Group, Institute for Information Technology, Downes specializes in the fields of online learning, new media, pedagogy and philosophy. Downes is perhaps best known for his daily nesletter, OLDaily.. He has published numerous articles both online and in print.

etoy.CORPORATION is art and invests all resources in the production of art beyond traditional dimensions. The aim is to take the resources, tools and legal framework of our time to create a corporate sculpture - a shareholder company registered in Zug/Switzerland that has no other purpose than cultural value. The privately held company etoy.CORPORATION SA issues etoy.SHARES (more information) to compensate its artists, investors, collectors and supporters.

Christian Fennesz (AT) is an electronic musician. A key figure in the ascent of IDM and electronica in the 1990s, Fennesz uses guitar and notebook computers to make multilayered compositions that blend melody and conventional musical instruments with harsh, irregular glitch-influenced sounds and washes of white noise.

Alois Ferscha (AT). From 1986 through 2000 he was with the Department of Applied Computer Science at the University of Vienna at the levels of assistant and associate professor. In 2000 he joined the University of Linz as full professor where he is now head of the department for Pervasive Computing and the speaker of the JKU Pervasive Computing Initiative.

Monika Fleischmann (DE) is a research artist and scientist. Since 1997 she has been Head of MARS - Exploratory Media Lab (Media Arts & Research Studies) at the GMD-Institute for Media Communication, since 2004 at Fraunhofer IAIS in Sankt Augustin, Germany. In 2008 she was appointed honorary professor for media theory and interactive media art concepts of the University of Applied Sciences in Bremen.

Pablo Flores (UR / IT), member of the International Development Research Centre (IDRC) of Canada, working on a research with DESEM Foundation about projects in 1:1 modality (one computer per child) in Latin America and the Caribbean. Universidad de la República - Proyecto Flor de Ceibo.

Flaviu Moldovan (RO) is a designer, an engineer and an artist. He does TV commercials and designs everything from websites to car rims to earn his daily bread. To compensate for the dullness of creative industry he works with electronics to make art stuff. His work is about identity and technology and how the whole world could be a better place. Sometimes he feels very much alone in his work—and sometimes he doesn't.

Gabriela Golder (AR) is a visual artist, independent curator and professor of Video and New Technologies at several universities in Argentina and abroad, she was artist in residence at the Banff Centre for the Arts, Canada; the CICV, France; the Kunsthochschule für Medien and the Schloss¹Balmoral, Germany and the Wexner Center for the Arts, United States. She received several awards like the Media Art Award from the ZKM, Germany; the first prize at Salón Nacional de Artes Visuales, Buenos Aires; the first prize at Videobrasil, Brazil; the first prize at Festival Videoformes, France and the Tokyo Video Award, in Japan.

Dietmar Hager (AT), orthopaedic trauma surgeon. He is a Fellow of the Royal Astronomical Society.

Jürgen Hagler (AT) studied art pedagogy and experimental visual design at Linz Art University. He has worked in the field of computer animation for over 10 years including stints at the Ars Electronica Futurelab and Art & Tech Institute Linz. He's also an author for the Digital Media for Artists e-learning platform, and has taught classes in 3D computer animation at Vienna's Academy of Graphic Arts and Linz Art University. He is currently head of the Animation Department at Hagenberg University of Applied Sciences.

Ursula Hentschläger (AT) started her career with a series of online interviews with media artists in 1993. Since then she has been working on theoretical and artistic projects in the fields of new media and literature. In 1999 she co-founded ZEITGENOSSEN and the intermedia platform *www.zeitgenossen.com*. Currently she is focussing on contextualising media art works from the pioneering years.

h.o (Taizo Zushi, Hideaki Ogawa, Mizuya Sato, Yuichi Tamagawa and Emiko Ogawa) is a media art group creating conceptual art works using a mixture of media combined with digital technology. „h.o" derives from the chemical symbol for water, H2O, implying h.o's interest in various forms of communication between people. *http://www. howeb.org*

Stephen Hobbs (ZA), born 1972, and Marcus Neustetter (ZA), born 1976. In addition to their solo artistic careers and their artist collective – The Trinity Session, Hobbs and Neustetter's work as an artist collaborative, fuses their interests in urban social change and virtual culture. Since 2004, their artistic practice has resulted from experimentation with the juxtaposition of hi and lo tech, dead and new media interventions.

Ryoji Ikeda (JP) focuses on the minutiae of ultrasonics, frequencies and the essential characteristics of sound itself. His work exploits sound's physical property, its causality with human perception and mathematical dianoia as music, time and space. Using computer and digital technology to the utmost limit, Ikeda has been developing particular „microscopic" methods for sound engineering and composition. Since 1995 he has been intensely active in sound art through concerts, installations and recordings.

Hiroshi Ishii (US) is a Muriel R. Cooper Professor of Media Arts and Sciences, at the MIT Media Lab. He joined the MIT Media Laboratory in October 1995, and founded the Tangible Media Group to pursue a new vision of Human Computer Interaction (HCI): „Tangible Bits." His team seeks to change the „painted bits" of GUIs to „tangible bits" by giving physical form to digital information and computation.

Werner Jauk (AT), 1953; musicologist/psychologist, scientific media-artist. Professor at the Karl Franzens University in Graz, working on „pop / music + media / art" with the focus on music as a role model for the media arts. Studies in perception, cybernetics and experimental aesthetics led him try to bridge a gap between science and arts: both follow epistemological interests working on adaptation of bodily life in dynamized and coded non-mechanistic realities and on interfaces to these virtual and mixed realities based on auditory logic and hedonistic behavior formalized in pop/music.

Daniela Kuka (DE/AT) has been a member of the technical staff at the Ars Electronica Futurelab since 2005. There, she has developed content for projects dealing with art-in-architecture, social media, interactive storytelling and information design. She has also been involved in coordinating projects designed to further regional development and, since 2007, in scientific-strategic program development.

Gregor Ladenhauf (AT) tenaciously resists compartmentalization. He has worked undogmatically but intensively on a vision of immediacy as a musician, DJ and sound designer in various constellations since 1999.

Hannes Leopoldseder(AT) has worked as a television journalist for ORF Vienna, as the managing director of ORF Upper Austria (1974-1998), and the information director of ORF Vienna (1998-2002). Honorary professor at the University for Art and Industrial Design in Linz (2009). He co-founded the Ars Electronica and Cloud of Sound in Linz (1979), and initiated the Prix Ars Electronica (1987) and the Ars Electronica Center (1996). He is also the co-editor of Ars Electronica's catalogues.

Lillevan (DE) is an animation, video and media artist. He is perhaps best known as the founding member of the visual / music group *Rechenzentrum* (1997-2008). Parallel to his work in *Rechenzentrum*, he has performed and collaborated with many artists from a wide array of genres, from opera to installation, from minimal electronic experimentalism to dance and classical music.

Lawrence Malstaf (BE) started off in theatre. He designed scenographies for choreographers and directors such as Benoît Lachambre, Meg Stuart and Kirsten Delholm. Soon he developed more into installation and performance art. Later he created larger mobile environments dealing with space and orientation, often using the visitor as a co-actor.

Isaac Mao (CN) is a software architect, entrepreneur and learning technology, social technology researcher. Isaac divides his time between research, social work, business and technology. He is now directing/advising some non-profit programs and several for-profit businesses in China. He was a Fellow at the Berkman Center for Internet & Society at Harvard Unversity.

Hye Ki Min (KR) is a multimedia artist born in Seoul, South Korea and based in New York City. Her creative practice is a multidisciplinary cross between video, sound installation and performance. Most recently, she has mixed and matched technology and music to develop two tactile interface projects that enhance people's physical senses.

Andrés Monroy-Hernández (US) is a PhD student and Bradesco Fellow at the MIT Media Lab. He is interested in understanding how the Web and mobile technologies can empower people and support collaboration, especially among youth and communities in the developing world.

Evelyn Münster (DE) has worked as a Java Web applications software developer since 2000 on various projects involving enterprise content management systems, document & knowledge management systems, social software and information visualization; since 2008, visualization researcher at the Ludwig Boltzmann Institute Media.Art. Research.

Sandra Naumann (DE) is a scholar in the field of communications and media studies. Since fall 2006, she's been involved in the conception (with Dieter Daniels) and supervision of the "Sound & Vision" research project.

Bibi Nelson, Matt Johnson, Isabel Lizardi, and Becky Pilditch are recent graduates of the Industrial Design Engineering Department at the Royal College of Art in London, UK.

Jaume Nualart (ES) works as a researcher and free software developer in public data & data visualization tools and in internet channels broadcasting projects.

Dietmar Offenhuber (AT) is a media artist with a background in architecture and is interested in spatial concepts of cognition, representation and behavior. He holds degrees from TU Vienna and the MIT Media Lab and was a founding member of the Ars Electronica Futurelab. Currently he is Professor at the Art University Linz and Key Researcher at the Ludwig Boltzmann Institute for Media Art Research.

Hyunjoo Oh (US) is a new media artist, technologist, writer and educator. She is a founding member of the digital media group, *dottedquad* and has co-directed the immersive and interactive Virtual Reality laboratory, Applied Interactives in Chicago. Her work involves Virtual Reality, data visualization, physical computing and network sound system.

Amanda Parkes (US) is a PhD candidate in the Tangible Media Group. She is a designer interested in the relationship of gesture, form, materiality, and computation in the context of hybrid physical-digital objects. Before joining the Media Lab, Amanda developed exhibits at the Exploratorium in San Francisco, freelanced internationally in multimedia design, and developed installations and programs for the Science Museum in London and the the Peggy Guggenheim Collection in Venice.

Bianca Petscher (AT) studied Musicology and German Languages at the University of Salzburg and Newcastle upon Tyne (UK). Since December 2005 she has been a member of the Prix/Festival team of the Ars Electronica and is responsible for the organization of the Prix Ars Electronica and is also in charge of the concert events during the Festival Ars Electronica.

Pierre Proske (AU) is an artist intrigued by the pervasiveness of technology in culture and its relationship to nature. His work involves exposing the unspoken relationships we have with technology to and harnessing machines into exploring new aesthetics. *http://www.digitalstar.net/*

Heimo Ranzenbacher (AT) works as a free lance author, theoretician and artist in Graz (AT). Various publications in catalogues und specialized journals; diverse addresses at symposia; diverse art projects. Since 1996, editorial work for Ars Electronica. Since 1998, Artistic Director of the media art project "Liquid Music", Judenburg (Austria). Recent projects: Exhibition concept and design "40 Jahre musikprotokoll", Graz – ORF musikprotokoll im steirischen herbst 2007; „JUniverse" - permanent installation at the planetarium Judenburg, 2008; „The Door", Graz / Judenburg 2009.

Britta Riley (US) applies a pedestrian mentality to intractable global issues, resulting in crackpot proposals for which she earnestly asks the masses to sort out the details. She calls this groundbreaking process R&D-I-Y (research and develop it yourself) and believes it will save the world.

Juliana Rotich (Kenya) is the Program Director of Ushahidi.com, an innovative non-profit web startup that creates software for mapping crises. In addition to her role at Ushahidi, she is a blogger, digital activist, technologist and environment editor for Global Voices Online.

Niklas Roy (DE) is an artist with engineering skills, a quirky sense of humor and an interest in robotics.

Teddy Ruge (UG) is the co-founder of *Project Diaspora*, an organisation aimed at connecting the African Diaspora to socially-relevant development projects in Africa. As a budding social entrepreneur, he's currently assisting several indigenous farmer organisations in Uganda move from subsistence farming to large-scale commercial farming of aloe vera and moringa.

Christoph Santner (AT) is a futurist, speaker and founder of the innovation agency TheFutureKitchen in Salzburg and Munich. As a consultant he developed innovation projects for brands like VW, BMW, O2, European Patent Office and for start-ups in the USA and Europe.

David Sasaki (US) is the Director of Rising Voices, a global citizen media outreach initiative of *Global Voices Online*. Prior to his current focus on outreach he served as *Global Voices'* Latin America Regional Editor. He transitioned into online journalism after working as a freelance web developer and English instructor in Monterrey, Mexico. He now splits his time and residence between North and Latin America and writes frequently at *Rising Voices, Global Voices*, and on his personal weblog (*http://el-oso.net/blog/*).

Elisabeth Schimana (AT) works as a no-singer, performer, composer, radio artist and artistic process manager in an electronic environment. She founded the IMA (Institute for Media Archeology) in 2005.

Marianne Schmidt (DE) studies Media Arts in Karlsruhe at the University for Arts and Design, with a focus on digital media and infoart. She works in the field of interactive performance in public space and has participated in many international exhibitions and festivals, initiating projects that experiment with communication, identity, virtual reality and data visualization. Her projects received important awards at many local and international art competitions and were presented at the documenta, European Media Art Festival, University of Cambridge or Ersta Konsthall Göteborg.

Christine Schöpf (AT) was the head of the art and science department at ORF Upper Austria (1981-2008). Since 1979, she has held a number of positions in which she has been able to contribute considerably to the development of Ars Electronica. She was responsible for conceiving and organizing the Prix Ars Electronica from 1987-2003. Together with Gerfried Stocker, she has been the artistic co-director of Ars Electronica since 1996. Honorary professor at the University for Art and Industrial Design in Linz (2009).

Roland Schrettl (AT) is a media designer, internet consultant and lecturer in e-commerce and internet at the University of Innsbruck. He has been active in the field of computer graphics, media performances, fine art digital paintings and video installations since 1985. *http://www.schrettl.eu*

Gebhard Sengmüller (AT) is an artist working in the field of media technology. Since 1992, he has been developing projects and installations focussing on the history of electronic media; creating alternative ordering systems for media content; and constructing autogenerative networks. His work has been shown extensively in Europe, the US and Japan.

Shen Shaomin (CN / AU), Live and works in Sydney, Australia and Beijng, China. He has exhibited internationally in exhibitions including the 2006 Liverpool Biennial, Mahjong at Kunstmuseum Bern, Hamburg, and Salzburg, and Dialogue at East West Gallery in Melbourne.

Noah Shibley (US) is a Seoul based new media artist, programmer, hactivist and technology concept developer. He is currently working on several scientific data visualization, Virtual Reality and social software projects.

Shahjahan Siraj (Bangladesh) is a pioneer multimedia designer and online journalist in Bangladesh. Along with professional media work, he teaches multimedia and new media at the University of Liberal Arts. Siraj is a founder of *Machizo Multimedia* and the publisher of *UnnayanNews* and UnnayanTV.

Christa Sommerer and Laurent Mignonneau (AT) are professors and heads of the master and doctoral study course »Interface Cultures« at the University of Art and Industrial Design in Linz.

Philippe Souidi (DE) is managing the CScout Trend Consultancy office in Munich.

Stadtmusik is a collaboration between the Berlin based composers Sam Auinger and Hannes Strobl with the media artist Dietmar Offenhuber. Stadtmusik deals with the perception of cities, especially the influence of acoustic phenomena. Stadtmusik analyzes the urban soundscape through sound structures triggered by urban buildings and facilities. Stadtmusik works are diagrams of these situations.

Moritz Stefaner (DE) is interested in how information visualizations and statistical methods can help to discover and organize information. He is currently a member of the scientific staff of the Interaction Design Lab and the Potsdam University of Applied Sciences and is also a freelancer in information visualization.

Gerfried Stocker (AT), born 1964. Since 1995 artistic and managing director of the Ars Electronica Center and together with Christine Schöpf artistic codirector of the Ars Electronica Festival. He has been editor of Ars Electronica catalogues since 1996.

Wolfgang Strauss (DE) is an architect, media artist and scientist.He studied and teached Architecture as assistant of Prof. Ingeborg Kuhler at the UdK Berlin. He has been head of R & D for interactive and mixed reality environments at Fraunhofer IAIS (ex IMK) - MARS Exploratory Media Lab since 1997.

Noriyuki Tanaka (JP). Since the second half of the 1980s, he has completed interactive artworks, science museum concept development and design, product development, space design, music videos, TV commercial direction, performance production, advertising, corporate identity and branding, product development, art direction of cultural programs and creative direction.

Kristen Taylor (US) is a cook, photographer, videographer, and writer unfolding the connective tissue of local food.

Team 4040 (AT) is a team of creative collaborators who come from various professional and cultural backgrounds, but who are all temporarily based in Linz. The network of 4040 extends from Austria to Portugal, Spain, Japan and Turkey. All members are graduate art students at the *Kunstuniversität Linz*: Jesus Cabrera Hernandez, Jona Hoier, Ulrike Gollner, Ebru Kurbak, Sho Kuwabara, Tiago Martins, Michael Probst, Jeldrik Schmuch, Onur Sönmez.

Daan van den Berg (NL) attempts to play with appearances and the expectations these instigate. This results in objects, furniture or products. He works as a freelancer on projects in the field of interior, architecture, visual arts and product design.

Weber & haerri (CH) is concerned with options of interaction in public space. The videoinstallation „How can the viewer be more enclosed in an art work?" by Sabine Haerri, the webcam feeds map „Campillow" by Yvonne Weber and the joint project „Moving Memories" for the Media Facade Festival Berlin 2008 are projects investigating that subject.

Manon Liu Winter (AT) focuses on the music of the 20th and 21st centuries, and works intensively on expanding the piano's sound repertoire via mechanical and electronic interventions. With programs of contemporary piano music and improvisation, she has performed as a soloist in Austria and at festivals abroad.

Markus Wintersberger (AT) studies at the University of Applied Arts in Vienna under Prof. Bernhard Leitner. Since 1995 he has been a freelance artist. Since 1996 he has held various teaching positions at Austrian universities. Intensive research and aesthetic use of media production mechanisms, both hardware and software.

Xiao Qiang (US) is the Director of China Internet Project and an adjunct professor at the Graduate School of Journalism, University of California, Berkeley. He is the Founder and Editor-in-Chief of China Digital Times, a bilingual collaborative China news website.

Norbert Zehm (AT) studierte Klavier und Komposition am Innsbrucker Konservatorium und in London an der Guildhall School of Music and Drama. Er ist als Pianist, Begleiter, Keyboardspieler und Performer in zahlreichen Festivals in ganz Europa tätig. *http://www.zehm.at*

Zhu Handong (CN), photographer, has participated in a variety of photo and modern art exhibitions, such as China-Blue Photo Show, Pingyao Photo Festival, Song Zhuang Art Festival etc. Zhu has also conducted in-depth exploration and experimentation in the areas of performance art and installation art.

Ethan Zuckerman (US) was a co-founder of Tripod.com, and later founder of Geekcorps. He currently serves as a fellow at the Berkman Center for Internet and Society. His work at the Berkman Center has included research into global media attention, and the co-founding of *Global Voices Online*. For some years he was also a contributing writer for Worldchanging.com.

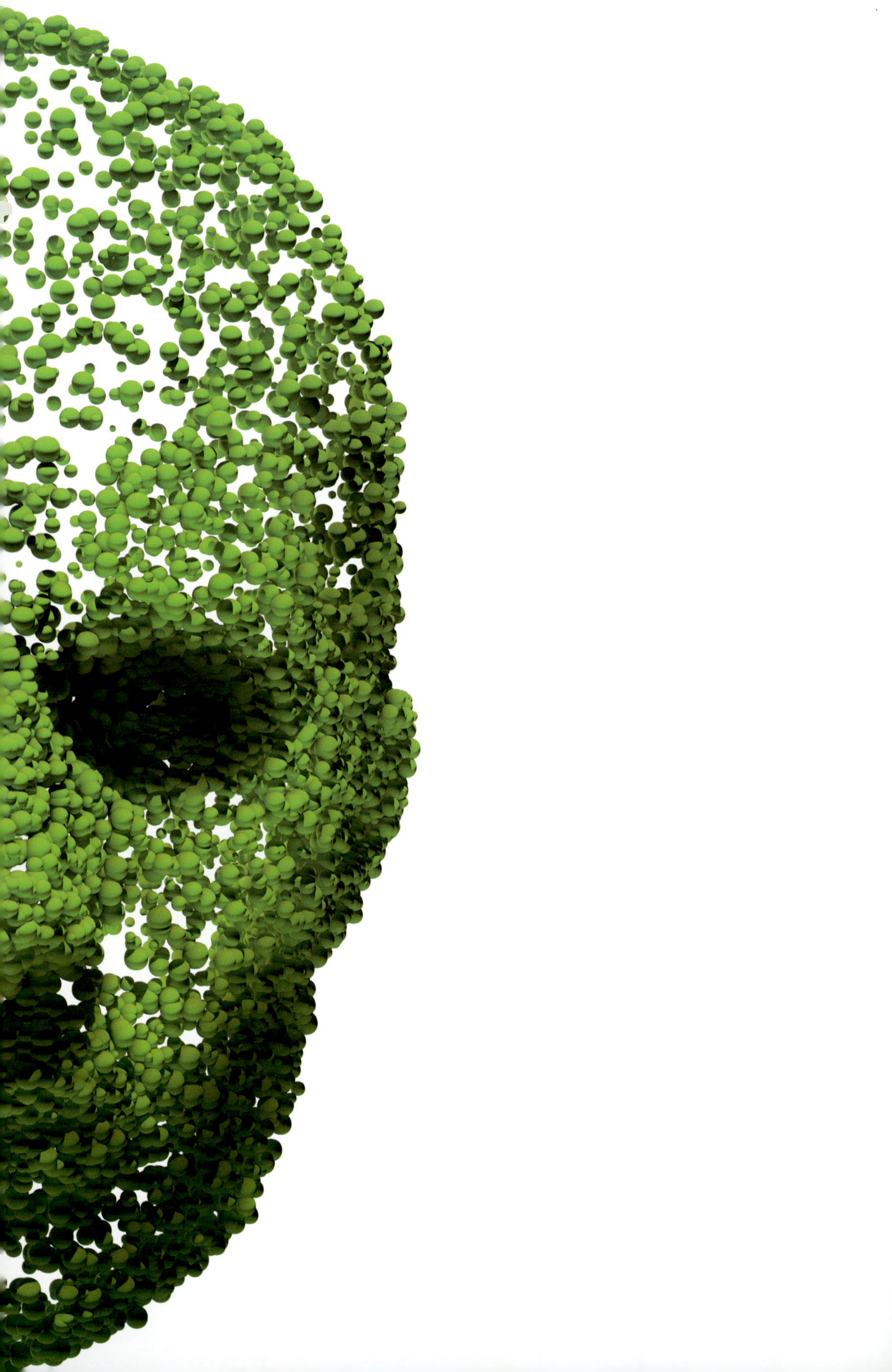

Ars Electronica Linz GmbH
is a company of the city of Linz.
Ars Electronica Linz GmbH
ist ein Unternehmen der
Stadt Linz.

Ars Electronica is supported by:
Stadt Linz
Land Oberösterreich
BMUKK
BM.W_F^a
European Commission

Organization / Veranstalter

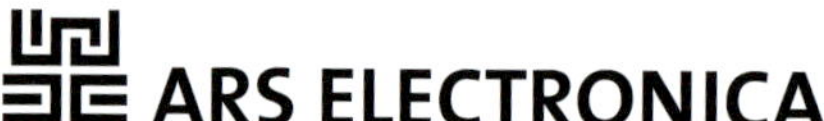

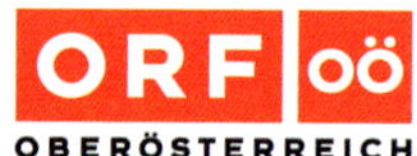

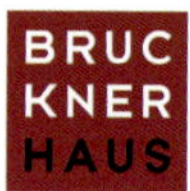

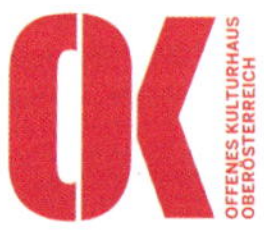

Cooperation Partners / Kooperationspartner

Kunstuniversität Linz

Lentos Kunstmuseum

Linz 09

Fachhochschule St. Pölten

Roter Krebs

Ludwig Boltzmann Institute Media.Art.Research.

Stadtwerkstatt

Japanese Media Art Festival

Ars Electronica receives support from:
Ars Electronica wird unterstützt von:

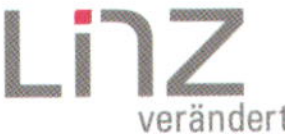 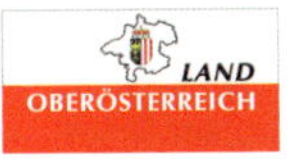 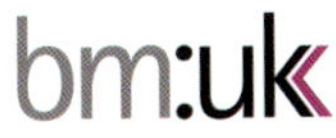 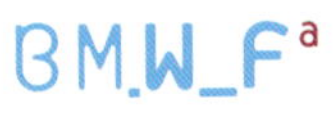 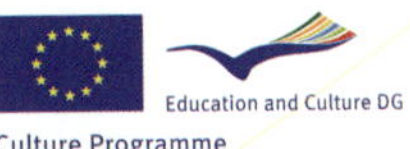

Stadt Linz — Land Oberösterreich — BMUKK — Bundesministerium für Wissenschaft und Forschung — European Commission

This work programme has been funded with support from the European Commission. This publication (communication) reflects the views only of the author, and the Commission cannot be held responsible for any use which may be made of the information contained therein.

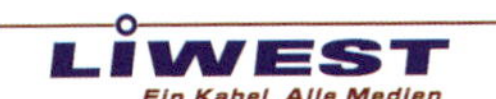 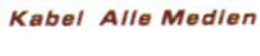 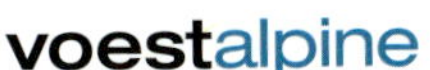 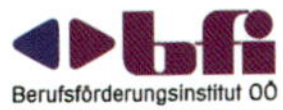

Liwest — voestalpine — bfi

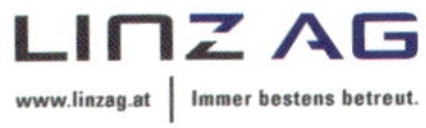 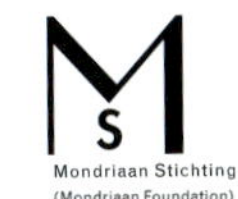 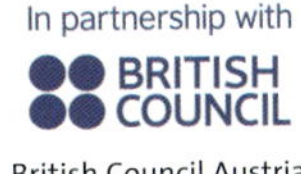

Linz AG — Mondriaan Foundation — British Council Austria

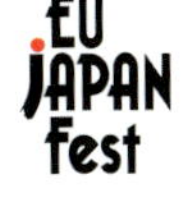  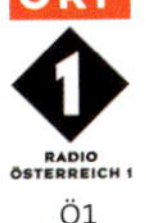 

EU-Japan Fest Japan Committee — Ö1 — FM4

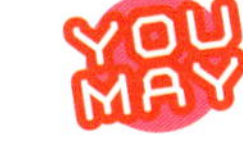 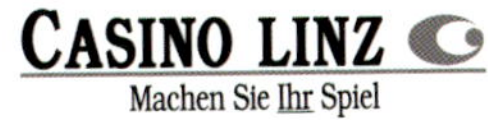

Ikea — Walking Chair (you may) — Casinos Austria

Sony DADC — Opel Günther — Messe Linz

Sony DADC — Opel Günther — Messe Linz

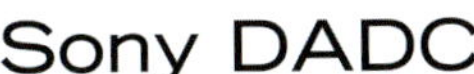 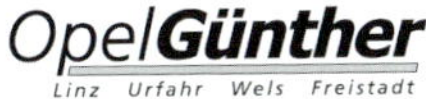 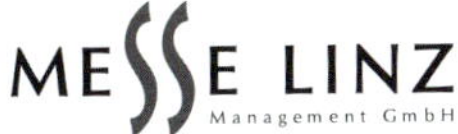

LIVA — hartl ecars — Sportgigant

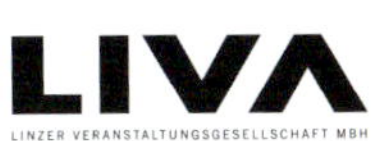 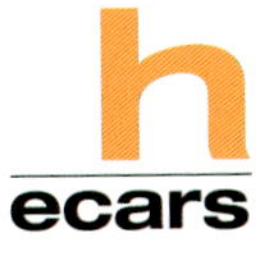

Additional Support: Triple X, KulturKontakt Austria, Microsoft Österreich

Ars Electronica 2009

Festival für Kunst, Technologie und Gesellschaft /
Festival for Art, Technology and Society

Organization
Ars Electronica Linz GmbH

Managing Directors
Gerfried Stocker, Diethard Schwarzmair
Hauptstraße 2–4, A-4040 Linz, Austria
Tel. +43.732.7272.0
Fax +43.732.7272.2
festival@aec.at

Co-organizers

ORF Oberösterreich
General Director: Helmut Obermayr

LIVA – Veranstaltungsgesellschaft m.b.H.
CEO: Wolfgang Winkler, Wolfgang Lehner

OK Offenes Kulturhaus Oberösterreich
Managing Director: Martin Sturm

Directors Ars Electronica
Gerfried Stocker / Ars Electronica
Christine Schöpf

Head of Festival
Martin Honzik

Technical Head
Karl Julian Schmidinger

Internal Organization
Cornelia Mayrhofer

Production Team
Bianca Petscher, Susi Windischbauer, Richard
Baldinger, Bernhard Böhm, Friederike Christoph,
Maria Eschlböck, Petra Fohringer, Sandra Gassner,
Gregor Göttfert, Carmen M. Lauss, Michael Lettner,
Yu-Han Chen, Dominique Hölzl, Sigrid Hofmeister-
Watanabe, Christina Langthallner, Tomislav Maric,
Emiko Ogawa, Manuela Pfaffenberger, Stefan
Proksch, Angelika Rainer, Maria Seidl, Jochen Zeirzer,
Sini Zein, Rafael Wallner, Heinz Sambs, Simon Der-
ganc, Harald Prochaska, Daniel Kiesenhofer, Gernot
Salzer, Wolfgang Ipsmiller, Klaus Redl, Rainer Redl,
Andreas Zaunmayr, Armin Pauly, Markus Dominici,
Michael Traxler, Fabian Fischer, Katrin Fartacek, Georg
Schobert, Oliver Haindl, Andreas Freudentaler, Mario
Wagner, Johannes Gangl, Johanna Goldgruber, Klaus
Eberlberger

Co-curators
80+1 – Eine Weltreise: Michael Naimark, Steve Clark,
Manuela Pfaffenberger, Ingrid Fischer-Schreiber, Isaac
Mao, David Sasaki
Cloud Intelligence Conference: Isaac Mao, David Sasaki
Campus Exhibition: Hiroshi Ishii, Amanda Parkes
Pixelspaces: Horst Hörtner, Christopher Lindinger,
Daniela Kuka, Irene Posch
Interface Cultures: Christa Sommerer, Laurent Mignon-
neau, Dietmar Offenhuber, Michaela Ortner, Varvara
Guljajeva
Pursuit of the Unheard: Dennis Russell Davies, Wolf-
gang Winkler, Heribert Schröder, Bianca Petscher
Mission Future: Christoph Santner, Philippe Souidi
Animation Festival: Christine Schöpf, Jürgen Hagler
ISWC09: Alois Ferscha, Gerfried Stocker, Kent Lyons;
Paul Lukowicz, Sabine Seymour

Prix Ars Electronica 2009

Organizer
Ars Electronica Linz GmbH

Managing Directors
Gerfried Stocker, Diethard Schwarzmair
Hauptstraße 2–4, A-4040 Linz, Austria
Tel. +43.732.7272.0
Fax +43.732.7272.2
festival@aec.at

Co-organizers

ORF Oberösterreich
General Director: Helmut Obermayr

LIVA – Veranstaltungsgesellschaft m.b.H.
CEO: Wolfgang Winkler, Wolfgang Lehner

OK Offenes Kulturhaus Oberösterreich
Managing Director: Martin Sturm

Idea: Hannes Leopoldseder
Conception: Christine Schöpf, Gerfried Stocker
Coordination: Martin Honzik, Bianca Petscher
Technical Management: Karl Julian Schmidinger
Produktionsteam / Production team: Cornelia
Mayrhofer, Susi Windischbauer, Jochen Zeirzer,
Manuel Hartmann, Ingrid Fischer-Schreiber, Mahir
Mustafa Yavuz, Irene Posch, Romana Leopoldseder,
Dominique Hölzl, Daniela Kuka, Michael Lettner,
Georg Sochurek, Gregor Göttfert,
Andreas Nimmervoll

Ars Electronica 2009
Human Nature
Festival für Kunst, Technologie und Gesellschaft
Festival for Art, Technology and Society
3.–8. September 2009 / September 3–8, 2009

Herausgeber / Editors: Hannes Leopoldseder,
Christine Schöpf, Gerfried Stocker
Redaktion / Editing: Ingrid Fischer-Schreiber
Lektorat / Copyediting: Karl Heinz Javorsky,
Catherine Lewis
Grafische Gestaltung und Produktion /
Graphic design and production: egg_design,
Evi Garsleitner *www.egg-design.at*
Schrift / Typeface: Thesis Sans
Reproduktionen / Reproductions:
Gutenberg Werbering GmbH, Linz

Druck / Printed by:
Gutenberg Werbering GmbH, Linz
Papier / Paper: BVS matt
Herstellung / Production:
Gutenberg Werbering GmbH, Linz

Erschienen im / Published by
Hatje Cantz Verlag
Zeppelinstrasse 32
73760 Ostfildern
Deutschland / Germany
Tel. +49 711 4405–200
Fax +49 711 4405–220
www.hatjecantz.com

Hatje Cantz books are available internationally at selected
bookstores. For more information about our distribution
partners please visit our homepage at *www.hatjecantz.com*.

ISBN 978-3-7757-2498-2
Printed in Austria
Umschlagabbildung / Cover illustration:
Ars Electronica Futurelab: Andreas Jalsovec, Christian Korherr